My Second Encounter with an Angel

Dialogues to Knowingness

by
Sidney Schwartz

with
Reverend Carl R. Hewitt
as Awan's Medium

My Second Encounter with an Angel
Dialogues to Knowingness
by Sidney Schwartz with Reverend Carl R. Hewitt

Copyright © 2013 Gifts of the Spirit Church, Inc.
First Edition: *Ancient Wisdom Series Vol.2*
Published in 2013.

All rights reserved. No part of this book may be reproduced, stored in a mechanical retrieval system or transmitted in any form by electronic, video, laser, mechanical, photocopying, recording means or otherwise, in part or in whole, without written consent of the publisher.

Cover Graphics by Linda Deming

ISBN# 0615775365
Printed in the U.S.A.

Dedication

As I considered my choices for this dedication, I realized this honor could only go to a group of people I have never seen. I dedicate this book to Spirit, who have diligently worked for eons to bring truth to this world. Through the use of mediums and illuminati; Spirit has tried to bring our world out of our ignorant thought patterns, into the bright light of knowingness and enlightenment. It is my hope this volume will be significant in accomplishing this goal.

I wish to express my gratitude to these invisible entities, for having confidence in me. They have guided me in so many ways: by inspiring ideas, leading me to corroborating evidence, and protecting me from harm. Their knowledge has and is recreating my life, as I evolve into new adventures. My debt to them is immeasurable. The energy of my work, in bringing their message to this world, does not begin to repay them for all they have done for me.

Acknowledgments

I have been very fortunate to be surrounded by people who supported and fostered my work as an author. I wish to acknowledge and thank them for being able to see in me what I often could not see in myself.

I first want to thank my wonderful friend and mentor, Rev. Carl Hewitt, who has been the wind at my back, and channeled much of the information contained in this book. Carl is a true spiritual brother, **selflessly giving of himself** to help and serve others. Frequently, the gift of mediumship is difficult to handle. Not only are heavy demands placed on one's time and energy, but also people continuously seek solutions to their problems. **Some mediums thrive on being the center of attention.** When these mediums lose perspective, their egos explode beyond normal boundaries, which deteriorates their mediumship. Carl has not fallen into this trap, because he does not play into people fantasies, which would place him on a pedestal. By respecting this high office, Carl remained unaffected, as he lived his "down to earth life," with his "out of this world gift." He was a most extraordinary individual. I will always be extremely grateful to Carl for all that he has done for me.

Next I extend my deep gratitude to Awan—the **A**ngel **W**ithout **A** **N**ame. Although I have never seen him, I felt his intense energy during our first conversation. His unlimited patience became evident as he

repeated his explanation of the same concept many times, until I was able to comprehend it. Awan has taught me knowledge that cannot be found anywhere else on this planet. I feel honored to be the direct recipient of Awan's teachings, and to convey the wisdom he wishes to bring to our world.

Awan explained he chose me to be his scribe, because I could interpret his teachings from two distinct points of view—Orthodox Judaism, and psychic science. My mother, Rita Schwartz, and my grandmother, Sylvia Teper instructed me in the rich traditions of my Jewish religion.

A very special thanks goes to Suzanne Kaplan-Fonsera. I recognized Suzanne's extraordinary writing talent, when she was in my sixth grade social studies class. Now as a college graduate, her skills have matured as vintage wine. After Suzanne volunteered to edit my manuscript, she masterfully rephrased my words, enabling my ideas to flow effortlessly. I greatly appreciate her enthusiasm for this extensive task, and thoroughly admire her artistry with words.

For the past thirty years, I have collected specific verses from four hundred sixty different versions of the Bible. Several of these versions are extremely rare, and are only found in major research libraries. I need to express my appreciation to two very helpful librarians, who granted me repeated access to these extremely valuable Bibles. I would like to thank Dr. Liana Lupas and the library staff at the American Bible Society of New York City. My gratitude also extends to Dr. Bill Stoneman, in charge of the Shide Library, the rare book library at Princeton University. Through their cooperation, I examined *original* editions of the earliest English Bibles, which were invaluable to my research, and the formation of my opinions.

Notes to the Readers

This book contains many dialogues I had with an Angel through Rev. Carl R. Hewitt, a trance medium. I will, however, quote two additional Spirit entities: Nathaniel and Larimer; who also spoke through Rev. Hewitt. In addition, I have also included conversations I had with Rev. Hewitt, in his *natural* state, (being himself, not in a altered-state of deep trance). These additional speakers present the reader with further insights concerning Awan's teachings. To facilitate the reading of these conversations, I have used a specific icon to label each speaker.

Symbols For Speakers

 AWAN — **A**ngel **W**ithout **A** **N**ame

 Sidney Schwartz

 Rev. Carl R. Hewitt

 Larimar Robinson

 Nathaniel

 Research, thoughts, and information that occurred after the dialogue with Awan

August 12, 2012

It will be important for the reader to know that *My Second Encounter with an Angel: Dialogues to Knowingness* was initially written during the later part of the 1990's. The manuscript of this book resided in my computer for more than a decade for several reasons:

First and foremost is that the first volume of this trilogy, *My First Encounter with an Angel* met several obstacles. It took almost one year for the publisher to edit the initial manuscript. Unfortunately, about a month after the book was finally published, the publisher went bankrupt. *My First Encounter* was never properly promoted; thus sales were quite disappointing.

More importantly, a year later in 2001, Awan's medium, Rev. Carl R. Hewitt, was diagnosed with a brain tumor. After this news, his health was like a roller coaster, of ups and downs. In 2004 Carl closed his church, *Gifts of the Spirit Church*, and moved to Charleston, South Carolina. Carl felt a strong pull to return home to the South, where he was born. He lived there for less than a year. Then his brain tumors returned, and after another operation he transitioned into the Spirit World on January 26, 2005, a few months before our next book: *Crossovers: the Origins of Homosexuality* was published. *This time the book was self-published*, but again had limited sales since promoting it would become a full time job.

Suddenly, with Carl's transition, *Gifts of the Spirit Church* passed into my care, as I assumed the role of its pastor. In 2006, I reopened the church in Connecticut, and put my full focus on developing my mediumistic skills. I took several classes the Arthur Findlay College (of Mediumship), in Stansted, England. I began also studying with several mediums in the New York metropolitan area.

In June of 2007, I retired as Middle School Teacher/Librarian, to consecrate my focus on developing my mediumship, and running *Gifts of the Spirit Church*. I continuously felt Awan's teachings pulling upon my consciousness, demanding my focus, to edit and publish the remaining books. For many years, there just never seemed to be time to accomplish this. Finally, in 2012, I felt an overwhelming sense of urgency, to finally unveil the "meat and potatoes" of Awan's teachings.

Now, as I reread this manuscript, I find my part of this story is rooted in a distant chapter of my life. I have, however, decided **the book should remain in its original timeframe;** *however*, I taken the liberty of changing Awan's references to the **20th century** to the **21st century**. Nevertheless, I also want the reader to realize, the world and my life has changed significantly since these words were embedded onto a computer disk. In those days, the internet was in its infancy; frequent trips to research libraries were required for me to corroborate Awan's teachings. **I have left all time references as they were**

originally written, in the late 1990's. However, I have updated the Bible research. When *My First Encounter* was published, I had analyzed 160 Bibles, however in late 2012, my Bible research spans 460 Bibles.

Sidney Schwartz, Rev. Carl R. Hewitt, **Angel Without A Name**

In Memoriam

Rev. Carl R. Hewitt
March 3, 1928 – January 26, 2005

Rev. Carl R. Hewitt was a visionary. He saw, and grew to understand, far beyond the "conventional box" of most people's reality. He then worked ceaselessly to share his understanding with others. The dictionary defines a **visionary** as *one whose ideas or projects are impractical, one who is given to fanciful notions with little regard for what is actually possible.* Carl was a different kind of visionary, who repeatedly made that which was deemed impossible, possible.

What was truly wonderful about Carl's life was not just his remarkable gifts, but what he chose to do with them. One would think this would have come easily to him, since he was born with the mediumistic abilities of *clairvoyance* and *clairaudience*, but it did not. At the early age of three he had a prophetic vision and innocently blurted out that his older sister, Annie, had just died. His mother, Goldie, chastised Carl for telling such "a horrific lie," only to be silenced ten minutes later when one of Carl's brothers ran into the house screaming, "Annie is dead!" During these critical childhood years, living in Shallotte, North Carolina, Carl suffered immensely because of his mediumship. On his first day of school, Spirit entranced Carl, and led him to deliver a lecture in front of the entire student body. At its conclusion, as he was leaving the stage, Spirit withdrew from him, and six-year-old Carl was bombarded with questions from the faculty such as: "Is your father a preacher?" "How do you know such big words?" and "Have you ever traveled to the Tigris and Euphrates Rivers?" Carl became frightened and cried. At recess, on the playground, older students assaulted Carl, accusing him of being "filled with the devil." **NOT one teacher** came to his rescue during this assault. This event devastated Carl.

From that day onward, Carl felt nothing but ostracism from his fundamentalist Baptist community. Local clergy worked behind the scenes to have the school nurse take Carl to Wilmington, and then to Raleigh, to have his eyes and ears examined. They were looking for an excuse to perform a lobotomy in order to silence the information that was coming through him. Even his parents, along with his brothers and sisters, would ignore Carl's questions about the invisible people he saw, and the voices no one but he heard. In so doing, they treated Carl as if he were an invisible person.

Despite these negative experiences, in July of 1954, on a scenic mountaintop overlook along the Blue Ridge parkway in northern North Carolina, Carl had yet another vision; perhaps the most important one of his life. A man dressed in a long flowing white robe told Carl that he must build a church. Carl was to pick up the gauntlet that others had carried. He was to raise the ancient standard that Saint Paul designed: "I will not have you ignorant of the Gifts of the Spirit" (1 Corinthians 12:1).

For a person whose life was a living hell because of the Gifts of the Spirit, it is truly remarkable that he dedicated his life to teaching people the truth that he himself was denied for his entire childhood and adolescence. It was a slow process for Carl to get beyond his past and to nurture the confidence needed to accomplish this mission of his vision. He slowly honed his skills as a medium, and studied for the ministry. He was ordained a minister on June 2, 1972, by the National Spiritual Alliance. Then in 1977 he took the boldest step toward fulfilling his vision: he founded his own church. Spirit then informed him that he was to name his church "The Gifts of the Spirit Church" as found in Saint Paul's statement. Next, Spirit showed Carl a vision for the Church logo, which he commissioned one of his church members to draw.

For 25 years, Rev. Carl Hewitt lived his vision. He taught the Gifts of the Spirit to everyone, not only those who crossed the threshold of his church, but also those who attended his seminars around the country. He also included those who invited him into their homes via the cable access television show. He was a tireless instrument for Spirit, constantly delivering an ever-evolving message. Carl referred to his church as a spiritual filling station. People who needed their "spiritual gas tanks" filled would attend church for a while, go out into the world, and eventually return for another dose of truth. Through weekly healing services, people were alleviated of their physical pain, and would return on Sundays to address their spiritual needs. Carl always put his

parishioners' needs above his own, giving of himself as a friend and counselor, delivering Spirit's guidance whenever it was needed.

For his entire adult life, Carl had an insatiable thirst for knowledge. He traveled, at his own expense, in search of new information to share with his parishioners. He would meet other mediums, such as Joao de Deus, a psychic surgeon in Abadiania, Brazil; Joseph Merrill in Lilly Dale, New York; and Bill English in Camp Chesterfield, Indiana. He also traveled to high-energy locations, such as the pyramids of Giza, Egypt; Chizen Itza, Mexico; Uxmal, Mexico; Tikal, Guatemala; Provence, France; and the sites of ancient oracles at Delphi and Dodona, Greece. Often, even on a trip taken for relaxation, he would discover psychically significant places. While traveling to Hawaii, he came upon several healing sanctuaries. He was also led to the location where witches were burned in Amsterdam, and to Eflatun Pinar, a ritual site in Turkey, which provided the critical piece of evidence that precipitated the book: *Crossovers, the Origins of Homosexuality*.

"I will not have you ignorant of the Gifts of the Spirit" was the driving force in Carl's life. It inspired him to make his private readings learning tools, imparting philosophy along with guidance, and greatly exceeding the scope of some mediums, who just wanted to deliver messages from "Aunt Tilly." This driving force took him to prisons and schools where he would lecture, and before TV cameras where he recorded over 70 hours of educational videos about the Gifts of the Spirit, entitled *"Making Known the Unknown."* It inspired Carl to allow the **A**ngel **W**ithout **A** **N**ame (AWAN) to use his entranced body to deliver teachings of spiritual truths. Almost without exception, these trance sessions would leave Carl totally exhausted. These sessions, along with his entire schedule of private psychic readings and weekly church services, placed heavy demands on his precious energy.

How fitting it was in February of 1996 while Carl and I were staying at a seaside resort, just outside of Corinth, Greece, that we received a dramatic message from Spirit. For in the sky over Corinth, the very city where Jesus delivered his dramatic statement through the mediumship of Saint Paul, "I will not have you ignorant of the Gifts of the Spirit" we witnessed the Gifts of the Spirit Church logo. It was as if Jesus, the originator of the message, was acknowledging that his mission, of educating people in the Gifts of the Spirit was continuing nearly 2000 years later, by another medium, who was attempting to complete the mission with as much zeal as Paul had.

Carl was an inspirational spiritual leader whose legacy is about to be discovered. I know that he will enjoy the fruits of his labor, which he struggled to achieve in this life, in a higher frequency of life.

Rev. Carl R. Hewitt walked a unique path during his life, forging new roads of consciousness, which expanded the horizons of hundreds, if not thousands, of people. Yet, his life's work was outside the parameters of most people's normalcy. Carl taught that people create their realities, and explained the techniques to alter them. All those who knew Carl, understood that he was a true visionary. Therefore, it is a true tribute that the dictionary's definition of *"**visionary**"* is too limited, and doesn't even begin to describe what Carl achieved in his life.

Countless people will miss Carl's physical presence, for many reasons. However, we must now remember Carl's teachings, and the teachings that came *through* him. For he is now living in his Spiritual body, in the Spirit World and is simply a thought away.

Rev. Carl R. Hewitt's Gravemarker

Table of Contents

Dedication — iii
Acknowledgements — v
Notes to the Readers — vii
In Memoriam — xi
Table of Contents — xvii

ONE: *Reflections — 1*
TWO: *The Power of the Invisible Soul — 5*
THREE: *Twisting the Truth — 21*
FOUR: *Moses and Passover — 35*
FIVE: *The Secrets of the Unused Brain — 57*
SIX: *Death is Not Your Best an Option — 67*
SEVEN: *Priests Invented the Devil — 83*
EIGHT: *Awan Discusses Cathedrals and Communion — 101*
NINE: *Awan Discusses Psychic Science — 123*
TEN: *— Palm Sunday and Sukkot — 133*
ELEVEN: *The Psychic Implication of the Veils — 153*
TWELVE: *Awan discusses Steeples, Holy Water, Ash Wednesday, Hell, Purgatory, and Amen — 163*
THIRTEEN: *The Altar of the Lord — 179*
FOURTEEN: *Why does God Dislike Meteorologists or "What's Clouds got to do with it?" — 193*
FIFTEEN: *The Work of the Devil — 213*
SIXTEEN: *Banishing **Fear**: the Great Satan — 227*
SEVENTEEN: *Understanding Polarity — 233*
EIGHTEEN: *Invoking the God Within — 239*
NINETEEN: *You Are God — 249*
TWENTY: *Your Passport into Forever — 263*

TWENTY-ONE: *Jesus the Christ* — 267
TWENTY-TWO: *The Circle of Life: Birth, Death, After-life* — 283
TWENTY-THREE: *Understanding Reincarnation: Repeating the Circle of Life* — 295
TWENTY-FOUR: *In My Father's House Are Many Mansions* — 315
TWENTY-FIVE: *There is Life After Death* — 323
TWENTY-SIX: *The Great Hospital* — 333
TWENTY-SEVEN: *Judgment Day* — 341
TWENTY-EIGHT: *Suicide, Abortion, and Euthanasia* — 351
TWENTY-NINE: *The War of Armageddon and 12 Days of Light* — 359

APPENDIX: *Affirmations* — 367
GLOSSARY: *of Hebrew Words* — 375
BIBLIOGRAPHY: *of Bibles Chronologically* — 377
BIBLIOGRAPHY: *of Bibles Alphabetically* — 409

About the Medium — 421
About the Author — 422
Other books by Sidney Schwartz and Rev. Carl R. Hewitt — 423

ONE

Reflections

Often I reflect on how life has taken me to places I had not anticipated. When I was a child, I spent time dream-weaving—imagining what my life would be like when I grew up. I fell in love with history in the fourth grade, and had always envisioned that I would become a high school history teacher. I was very rooted to my home, and did not ever want to leave it. I also felt very comforted by my religious beliefs. These childhood expectations extended throughout most of my adolescence and young adult life, and comprised my reality.

Today, when I reflect upon that reality, I realize just how limited and confining it was. While I am a middle school librarian, as well as a teacher of history and computers, I have become an avid traveler and love to explore new places. My childhood "dreams" never included learning about mediumship, or the expectation that psychic phenomena and mediumship would become a passion in my life. Yet, today, I cannot image my life without this knowledge. I have become an author, a far cry from the torturous struggles I endured during school-day writing assignments.

Is it any wonder that I was completely shocked when Awan enlisted me to become his scribe? I rebelliously argued I could never write a book. It took tremendous prodding, from both Awan and Carl, to convince me to remove my negative roadblocks, and seriously put my energies into writing these books. I smile as I reflect on the person I once was, for I hardly recognize him.

The more I worked at it, the easier writing became. Eventually, I learned how to put my mind into an altered, receptive state, when I sat down at my computer. Awan had promised me that those in the unseen Spirit World would assist me in my writing. I can truly say the Spirits have been at my side every step of the way. Carl has even told me that on occasion, he saw a Spirit leaning over me, putting his hands over mine, as I typed on the computer.

There are times when I sit down at the computer to write about my experiences, and the words just seem to flow. It is almost as if I hear a "dynamic small voice" in my head, reading to me, and all I have to do is type those words into the computer. Frequently, I hear words that are unfamiliar to me, although I have a vague notion of the word's meaning. Nearly every time, when I look the word up in the dictionary, I discover it is the correct word, with the precise meaning that is required. I have come to enjoy this unfolding of words.

My dialogues with Awan were made possible, though the trance mediumship of Rev. Carl R. Hewitt. Carl would quiet down his body and mind, and command his Spirit to leave his body. The Spirit of Awan would then enter Carl's body and activate the vocal cords, to conduct a conversation with me. I would tape record these sessions to capture each important word. Our dialogues seemed to take on a life of their own.

I have great respect for Rev. Carl R. Hewitt, for channeling this great body of knowledge. Trance mediumship is extremely taxing on Carl, especially since his counseling work frequently depletes his energy. Yet, he takes the time to read the drafts of my work, and clairaudiently relates any corrections that Awan dictates.

Trips to major research libraries and bookstores were also adventures. At times, it seemed that the information would fall into my hands. Very early on in my psychic education, I went to New York City to pick up a new pair of eye-glasses from my optometrist. It was a bright, frigid February afternoon, and I had a long walk to return to my parked car. I decided that I would go into a store and browse, in an attempt to escape the cold air. I suddenly noticed a bookstore, and quickly entered. After the fog evaporated from my new eye-glasses, I was in a state of shock. The bookstore that was my refuge from the cold, turned out to be **Weisers**, a psychic bookstore. I had never heard of it until that very day.

A few years later, I had learned of a new book about Daniel Dunglas Home, a famous 19th century medium. Unfortunately, because book was rather expensive, I dismissed it from my mind. About two weeks later, I suddenly couldn't get the book out of my mind. Finally, on Saturday, I was inspired to go to New York City, and visit a very large used bookstore. Much to my amazement, the book that had "haunted" my mind was sitting on the shelf, and was selling for half-price!

I had some rather unique experiences. There were times when I discovered new information, or pieced together facts, which made a very clear picture to me. I would wonder if I were the only person to understand this principle. Why would I be the one to discover this?

I felt blessed that I had met Carl, and that Awan had the confidence in me to have me become his student and scribe. As I reflected on this, I often wondered why Awan chose me. I could appreciate how my limited knowledge of Hebrew could be an asset when discussing psychic phenomena and mediumship in the Bible. However, it was not until 1998 that I came to a rather significant realization.

I attended my 30th high school reunion. I enjoyed visiting my classmates, with whom I had grown up. It was interesting to see where the paths of their lives had taken them. When I was questioned about what was going on in my life, I told them about the books I was writing. Some of my classmates were devout Christians, and were quite distressed about the path on which I was traveling. "Mediumship is the work of the devil!" was their adamant belief. We had a very animated discussion, where we exchanged ideas, but no opinions were changed.

This experience made me realize there was one crucial difference between Judaism and Christianity. The devil seemed to be a very central character to Christianity, and is a constant presence in a Christian's mind. The opposite is true for Judaism. Jews never think about the devil, and it plays no role in their religion. This realization made me understand how difficult it would be for someone raised as a Christian to have become Awan's scribe. That person would either have to eradicate deeply ingrained fears of the devil, or have never accepted this tenet of his or her faith.

As I discussed in *My First Encounter with an Angel: Revelations of Ancient Wisdom*, the conflict between the priests and the mediums began in Biblical times. The priests, who claimed to be the intermediaries between God (Spirit) and the people, received a handsome income for their services. Yet, they could not facilitate a two-way conversation between a physical person and God, which is the primary function of a psychically gifted medium. Therefore, the priests felt threatened by mediums, who could expose their lack of psychic ability, and cause the priests to lose their most valued asset—their luxurious lifestyle, gained without physical labor.

The focus of this book will be on Awan's teachings. As you will soon discover, Awan has come to the world with a great body of knowledge that he wishes to impart to as many people as possible. Many of Awan's teachings are a radical departure from the paths that religions have set down for humankind. Yet, the core of his teaching is definitely part of every one of the 12,000 religions found on the planet.

The **soul** and **brain** are the foundational principles, to understanding these teachings. In addition, Awan and I also discussed the psychic roots of many religious rituals. Throughout this book, I will attempt to bring to light as much supporting evidence as I can to substantiate most Awan's theories. This evidence, found in the Bible and other history books becomes the flying buttresses, which support the walls of Awan's Cathedral of Knowledge. The historical documentation fully upholds Awan's channeled knowledge, allowing this series of books to stand on its own.

TWO

 1. The Power of the Invisible Soul

It had been several months since I had spoken with Awan. I was brimming with anticipation as I went to Carl's office. As this deep trance session began, I watched Carl begin his now familiar procedure of going into a trance state. Carl closed his eyes, and put a blindfold over them. He then said this prayer: "Lord God of my being, unto the Father within, come forward this moment, this hour, and allow me to become the instrument between the two dimensions of life. I ask only that which is good, true and helpful pass through these lips. So be it!"

As I waited for Carl's Spirit to leave his body, my mind drifted back to the Bible verse, which described the process that I would once again witness.

> **"And the Spirit of the Lord will come upon thee, and thou shalt prophesy with them, and shalt be turned into another man."**[1]

In this case, the Spirit that would enter Carl's body would be an entity who called himself the **Angel Without A Name**. He was a powerful entity whose abounding knowledge was extremely impressive. I was slightly nervous, because I never could anticipate what information Awan would have for me. Frequently, Awan's teachings had launched "earthquakes in my soul," because so much of what he taught me was contradictory to what I had been taught as a child.

Suddenly, Carl's body went into several severe spasms. After five or six sharp jolts, his body relaxed. About a minute later, I heard the familiar tones of Awan's voice.

😇 My profound greetings to you, my scribe!

🧑 Greetings, Awan.

😇 I would like to congratulate you, my scribe, on all the hard work that you have accomplished. It is not easy for people in your dimension to change their belief systems. Since you can be rather stubborn at times, I know how difficult it was for you to reexamine life-long beliefs and to modify them. I

---

[1] 1 Samuel 10:6 [KJV].

can see by your light (aura) that you are now ready to absorb more information, but there appears to be a question that is troubling you. Let's not waste our medium's valuable energy. Please ask me your first question.

Awan, quite some time ago, you promised to teach me the information that I would need to know to ensure that when I died, that I could travel into forever safely. Please enlighten me at this time.

Yes, my scribe, I did make that promise to you, and you have finally acquired and assimilated the proper foundation of knowledge. You are now ready for this teaching.

I am so glad to hear that, Awan!

As you now understand, religions have done a great disservice to humankind. Greed motivated the clergy to disconnect the people from the ever-flowing stream of divine knowledge. As the Church slaughtered the mediums, to silence their voices, the world was plunged into centuries of dark ignorance.

Yes, Awan, I fully understand you, and agree with your assessment of religions.

Today, there are over 12,000 religions on your planet. Each one teaches their unique brand of recycled ignorance.

Awan, what do you mean by *recycled ignorance*?

Your 21st century civilization, has finally come to the realization that there is not an unlimited amount of resourses on your planet. Therefore, your governments have been educating the people to recycle—or reuse certain items. Is that not correct?

Yes, that is true, Awan.

Religions have done this for centuries. Each religion has brought its leaders together to write its laws and dogmas, that their theologians will teach their people. Once they are formulated, these dogmas are taught over and over again. Tell me my scribe, when you were younger and attended the Saturday morning Sabbath services, didn't you say the exact prayers each week?

Yes, that is true, Awan.

It was like a broken record. The same prayers and thoughts repeated over and over, for thousands of years. Don't you think that a God would tire of hearing the exact same words every week? How boring can you get?

I never thought about it that way, Awan.

Furthermore, how is a person supposed to decide in which religion to believe. I have never heard anyone say a prayer, asking which God is the true God to be worshipped. Everyone automatically prays to the same God that his or her parent worshipped. Sometimes, upon marriage a person will change his or her religion to match the spouse's religion. It is the exceptional person, who changes his or her religion, because of a compulsion to change his or her belief system.

🙂 I guess you are right, Awan.

😇 I will be teaching you a comprehensive knowingness system, my scribe. It will take you some time to absorb and utilize it. The foundation of this system rests on seven sacred keys. Jesus attempted to teach them to his disciples, and called them *the keys to the kingdom of heaven*.

> **And I will give unto thee the keys of the kingdom of heaven: and whatsoever thou shalt bind on earth shall be bound in heaven: and whatsoever thou shalt loose on earth shall be loosed in heaven.**[2]

😇 The true meaning of this statement is this. There are seven keys that unlock the sacred vaults of divine knowledge. Once a person understands these keys, he or she can use them to unlock the vaults that religions locked centuries ago. You are standing at the door, my scribe, and now I will give you these keys, one by one. You are to write these keys down, and share them with humanity.

🙂 OK Awan, I will do that.

😇 For you must understand, my scribe, this is a journey that each individual must do for him or herself. No one can open this vault for another. I cannot open the vault for you. I can only teach you these seven sacred keys, and then it is up to you, my scribe. It is your choice whether to engage this knowledge, and pick up each key and incorporate it into your life. If you choose to do so, you will be preparing your own path, your own *passport into forever*.

🙂 I don't understand, Awan. What do you mean a *passport into forever*?

😇 What must you carry with you, when you take a trip to a foreign country?

🙂 A passport, Awan.

😇 Correct, my scribe. When your soul leaves the physical body at death, and enters into my dimension, the only passport you will take is knowledge. What you think, and know, will create your reality in my dimension.

🙂 Sorry, Awan, I am still confused. I don't understand what you are trying to say.

---

[2] Matthew 16:19 [KJV].

🕊 Let me use an example. Do your remember your first trip to Camp Chesterfield, Indiana?

🧑 Yes, Awan, I remember all about it.[3]

🕊 Do you remember that my medium saw the spirit of your deceased grandmother, outside of the cafeteria, and she waited for a physical person to open the glass door, so she could walk inside.

🧑 Yes, Awan, so what is the point?

🕊 She didn't have to wait for the physical person to open the door. Her spirit body was vibrating faster than the door, and she could have walked right through it, or even the solid walls of the building. She didn't walk through them because she did not know she had the ability to walk through walls and doors without opening them.

🧑 Why didn't she know it?

🕊 She was never taught any information about her life in the Spirit World. Therefore, since she did not have the knowledge, she didn't know she could walk through solid walls and glass doors.

🧑 I think I understand.

🕊 This is what Jesus meant when he discussed the keys of the kingdom of heaven: ***whatsoever thou shalt bind on earth shall be bound in heaven***. You only take the knowledge that you learn on your plane into my kingdom. I want it to be known that death doesn't make a person a saint. When you die, you do not suddenly become a sage, with all the knowledge of the universe. In fact you only retain the knowledge that you had when you died. You are restricted by what you know. Whatever you learn on earth, will empower your destiny in my kingdom. If you only learn "fairy tales" about my kingdom, then you will live your after-life accordingly, no matter how unenlightened that existence may be.

🧑 I am beginning to understand, Awan.

🕊 After this session is over; I want you to read about the medium Mathew Manning. His experiences will give you more of an understanding of why these keys are so very important.

📖 Eventually, I read *The Strangers* written by Matthew Manning,[4] a British medium. Since Matthew was clairvoyant, he began seeing the ghost of Robert Webb, the original owner of his family's house, who died in 1733. For the last 267 years, Robert Webb had not realized that he had died. He continued to live unaware that other physical people lived on a different frequency in the same house. Before he died, Robert had much pain in his legs, which forced

---

[3] Schwartz, Sidney. *My First Encounter with an Angel: Revelations of Ancient Wisdom.* Blue Hill, ME: Medicine Bear Publishing, 1999. p. 171-192.

[4] Manning, Matthew. *The Strangers.* Gerrards Cross, Buckinghamshire: C. Smythe, 1995.

him to use two sticks as canes. For the past 267 years, he continued this painful existence, and used the walking sticks, because he did not realize that he died. Usually, a Spirit will be pain-free in the Spirit World, because the pain is limited to the physical body. However, in this case, Robert Web did not have this knowledge. Therefore, he spent 267 additional years in p a i n, simply because his ignorance kept him "**bound**" to this condition.

👼 These keys are of paramount importance. Once you possess and utilize the knowledge of these keys, you will alter your reality. If you take it far enough could even become unlimited.

🧑 I will try to learn and utilize these keys, Awan.

👼 It pleases me to hear you say that, my scribe. But rest assured this journey will not be an easy one. You have had to struggle to weigh my teachings against your teachings of the past. You have struggled to release your old views to replace them with new perspectives. You are to be congratulated for completing that struggle. But be aware my scribe, that these teachings will be far more challenging.

🧑 Well, Awan, I can certainly say that I did not enjoy all the upheaval that you created in my life, as I was living it. However, now that I look back on it, undoubtedly my life has changed for the better. Although I am not pleased to learn that I will face more storms of the soul, I trust that after I go through them, it will be well worth it.

👼 I can assure you, my scribe, that what you speak is truth.

🧑 So what is the first of these sacred keys?

👼 🗝 1. 𝔗𝔥𝔢 𝔓𝔬𝔴𝔢𝔯 𝔬𝔣 𝔱𝔥𝔢 𝔍𝔫𝔳𝔦𝔰𝔦𝔟𝔩𝔢 𝔖𝔬𝔲𝔩.

The first key is perhaps the most important. It will take us several dialogues for me to teach you what you need to know about the human soul. This is the most critical key to understand.

🧑 Where should we start?

👼 As one of your songs would say: "Let's start at the very beginning." Have you ever wondered how your universe began?

🧑 Yes, Awan, I have.

👼 Well, my scribe, it is no grand mystery. In fact, it is a very simple truth.

In the beginning, there was thought. The thought *was* the all-powerful **Source**. This **Source** has been called *God*, the *Is*, the *Divine Force*, the *Higher Power*, and numerous other names. However, currently most people address the **Source** as God, (in the singular, not plural). The **Source** was a collection of all thought, and a blending of polarities: positive and negative, good and evil, male and female. The **Source** decided that He-She needed more of an adventure. So the **Source** began to contemplate him-herself. As He-She turned within, which is a wondrous process, something spectacular happened. There was a sudden explosion of thought, which caused a magnificent light. This was the very first light ever created. This was a wonderful event that was the beginning of everything.

Today, your scientists call that explosion the *Big Bang*. It was a tremendous explosion that caused matter to come into existence. From that explosion, all the building blocks of the universe formed. All matter began traveling in all directions, away from the center of the explosion. All the planets that are in the entire universe were born from that explosion. Every star, in the billions and billions of miles of the universe, was born in that very moment. Every soul of every creature that lives in the entire universe was born at that very moment. All matter, all energy, everything was created from this one powerful explosion of thought, from the all-powerful God.

A few moments before the *Big Bang* as you understand that to be, the all-powerful God issued a command *"Make known the unknown."* It was that thought which ignited the *Big Bang*. Therefore, all matter, all souls, all energy has within itself that Divine command: *"Make known the unknown."*

Consequently, if you break this truth down to the simplest terms you will realize that the universe was created through thought. Everything that was ever created, everything that ever evolved, has used this God-energy of *thought*.

You must realize, my scribe, that God is really thought. Thought is manifested in every living and non-living creature on your entire planet, throughout the entire universe.

🙂 Awan, that is certainly a different concept of God. Are you sure about this?

😇 Yes, my scribe, be patient, and as I continue and you will learn more about the building blocks of the universe, and you will arrive at a total knowingness.

🙂 Building blocks of the universe? What do you mean?

😇 Now that you have a limited understanding that the universe, and that everything in it was created by thought, we can begin your first lesson of the "psychic realm." We will discuss the first two building blocks that are fundamental to your knowledge of psychic science. Our first dialogue will be about the *soul* and *vibration*.

Most people know they have a soul, but their knowledge about it ends with that fact. Ask a friend the following questions: *"Where is your soul located? What is it made of? What function does your soul perform in your body?"* I could almost guarantee that you would receive the unintelligent response: "I don't know," from 99% of the people you ask. For centuries, theologians and clergy have preached about the soul, claiming that they were striving to "save your soul from damnation." However, these theologians have not given the public any detailed information about the soul—the very source of life.

🙂 OK, Awan, you have peaked my curiosity. Please tell me all about the soul.

(😇) It would be my pleasure to enlighten you. Have you ever stopped and contemplated what keeps the cells of your body together? Why don't the atoms of your body bounce out into the universe? It is the soul that keeps your body as a cohesive mass. Your soul is made of energy, which is actually coagulated, manifested thought. To say it in another way, your soul, my scribe, was once a thought of the Creator of the Universe, who transformed the thought into energy. The soul is an isness. It just is.

(🧑) Awan, I don't understand that at all! What do you mean?

(😇) Well my scribe, let me start again. It may be easier for you if I will quote from your Book of Books.

> **And the Lord God formed man of the dust of the ground, and breathed into his nostrils the breath of life; and man became a living soul.**[5]

This is a very poetic rendition of a great truth. If you have a complete understanding of this passage, you will clearly realize that God created humankind with two bodies. Paul, who was canonized as a saint by the Catholic Church, also taught about the two bodies. He learned this information from the great teacher who was crucified on the cross. The man you know as Jesus came to your world to demonstrate and teach *psychic science!* Unfortunately, he did not complete his mission. When his life was cut short, Jesus had only demonstrated the *Gifts of the Spirit*. To accomplish his goal, Jesus chose Paul, a medium, and taught the **science** of the *Gifts of the Spirit* through him. Paul would hear Jesus' voice[6] through the psychic *gift of clairaudience*, and repeat the lessons to his students. It was Jesus who taught that everyone has two bodies. No prophet, not even Jesus during his lifetime, delivered that message to humanity. Therefore, we received this teaching through Saint Paul's mediumship.

> **"It is sown a physical body, it is raised a spiritual body. If there is a physical body, there is also a spiritual body."**[7]

The first body Saint Paul described was the physical body, the one that was made of "the dust of the earth." The dust is a metaphor for the physical makeup of your body. Your scientists have determined that your body is composed of water and a long list of chemicals—matter from your physical plane. Your physical body is very familiar to you, since you experience it everyday. Your physical body is the one you use in your dimension of life. You live in the Spiritual body when you enter my dimension of life. This is why Saint Paul said:

---

[5] Genesis 2:7 [KJV].

[6] Acts 9:4.

[7] 1 Corinthians 15:44 [RSV].

> **"I tell you this; my brothers: an earthly body made of flesh and blood cannot get into God's kingdom. These bodies are not the right kind to live forever."**[8]

🧑 Awan, I don't really understand.

👼 It is not that difficult, my scribe. You are born with a physical and spiritual body. When you die your spiritual body speeds up and comes to my dimension, where it will have eternal life—what Saint Paul meant when he said, *"live forever."*

🧑 How is that possible?

👼 I believe a dialogue about *vibration* will clear up your confusion. Centuries ago, all knowledge was based on superstitions. You are fortunate to be living in the your present time, which is a mental/scientific age. You have studied during your schooling that all matter is composed of atoms, and these atoms are in constant motion, traveling at different speeds. The speed of the atoms' movement determines its state of matter. For instance, a solid ice cube's molecules move very slowly. However, as an ice cube is heated the water molecules move, or vibrate, faster. This increased movement transforms the solid ice into the liquid you know as water. If you increase the water's temperature, the molecules vibrate still faster, turning the water into a gas called steam. However, the steam is invisible to the physical eyes. The increased rate of vibration, or the speed of the molecules, has changed the physical state of the molecules. However, the chemistry of each water molecule has remained unchanged. It is still comprised of one atom of hydrogen, and two atoms of oxygen. The increased rate of vibration, or the speed that the molecules move, is responsible for the physical change in the state of matter.

🧑 Yes, Awan, I learned all that in school.

👼 Exactly, my brother, however you didn't learn this. In a strange way, death is like a water molecule. When an individual dies, its Spirit body enters the Spirit World. That person's thoughts, feelings, personality and knowledge do not change. It is just in a new spiritual body, which vibrates on a higher frequency than its old physical body. But, the essence of the person has remained exactly the same, just as the chemical composition of the water molecule remained the same, when it changed its state of matter.

🧑 So you are saying that when you die, you are very much like you were on earth, but vibrating faster than you did when you were on earth.

👼 Yes, my scribe! Now you must realize that the spiritual body we have been discussing is actually your soul. Many of you have some understanding of your physical body, since you study about it in your schools. It is

---

[8] 1 Corinthians 15:50 [LIV].

unfortunate that no teacher, minister, rabbi, doctor, surgeon, or physician has ever taught you about the soul, your second body. Since it is invisible, most people are unaware that they even have a soul. Hence, it lies dormant, almost totally asleep within most people. Yet, your soul has the potential of being a "powerhouse of the universe."

Your soul is made up of a substance from a higher dimension. It is spiritual energy found in the kingdom where I reside. The Bible describes the soul as *God's breath*,[9] the force, which instills life into your body. The soul is a luminous ball of energy. It is the size of a golf ball, which lies underneath the breastbone, in the middle of your chest. When the human body was created millions of years ago, the heart, which is only a pump, was deliberately moved to the left. A cavity, or space, then remained in the middle of the chest to become the home for the soul.

As I have said so many times, your world is overrun with ignorance, which permeates everything, even your languages. You are confused about the source of love, which emanates from the soul and has nothing to do with the heart. You have words and expressions such as: *heartache, heartbreak, heartfelt, heart-free, heartless, heart-rendering, heartsick, heartsore, heart-stricken, heartstring, heart-to-heart,* and *heart-whole*. I have watched you during your winter season, and if you love someone, you send that person a Valentine card, which has an overabundance of hearts on it. Don't you realize that the heart is merely a pump, which circulates your blood? Would your boyfriend, girlfriend, husband, or wife be as happy with their "card of love" if there were a picture of a pace-maker on it? Perhaps a water or oil pump would do? Since the soul and heart reside side-by-side in your chest, it was natural for you to become confused.

It is the soul that feels love, and expresses emotions though the physical body. Emotions are the direct result of thought, and thought is energy. Therefore, all emotions emanate from the great energy-center of the body, which is the soul, not the heart.

The soul is a luminous ball of light, made up of energy. It is not a physical structure of the body, which must be made up of cells. The soul is energy. That means that when your surgeons cut the chest open to operate on the heart, they do not see the soul, because it is invisible to most human's eyes. Energy is invisible, just as the oxygen that you breathe, which keeps your body alive, is invisible to your eyes. Energy is not physical, and is *not* made up of cells.

Your scientists know that energy cannot be created or destroyed. They are partly correct in their theory. Energy was created millions of years ago, when the universe was created. Since that point in your time, energy has not been created by anyone in human form. Because the soul is energy, it continues to exist even after death comes to the physical body. At death, your soul leaves its physical body to continue its existence in my dimension of life.

The soul is an everlasting, divine light, which is the lowest frequency of light on your planet. That is the reason so very few people can see it. The light

---

[9] Genesis 2:7.

from the soul passes through the body's organs, muscles, bones, and sinew. This light travels through the body just as the energy of electricity travels through the copper wires of your house. The light of the soul radiates, or travels, through the body and creates a bubble of light around the body. This bubble looks like a hard-boiled egg standing on its end. The physical body would be the yoke — the yellow part, and the bubble of light is the white part of the egg. The light that surrounds the body, and emanates from your soul, is called the *aura* or *auric field*.

Awan, you said that the aura is the lowest frequency of light, and that is why most people cannot see it. You are confusing me. What do you mean? Is the aura less bright than the 25-watt light bulb that is illuminating this room, or are you talking about the scientific frequency of the light—the wavelength or speed that the light waves travel?

It would be the scientific frequency. It is the lowest frequency on the planet. Your eyes do not have the capacity to go into this frequency. This light is vibrating lower than your eye can detect. Do you understand so far?

Yes, I do. You said that the auric light exists at a frequency lower than the eye can detect, and yet, you also said that some people can see it. I don't understand.

My scribe, only people who have clairvoyant vision, or second sight, can see another person's aura. Clairvoyants see the aura with their "psychic eyes" (the eyes of their spiritual body), not their physical eyes. Remember, the visions, which register on the psychic eye register in a specific brain center, which is dormant in most people. The image travels from the brain center to the "psychic screen," which everyone uses to see one's dreams at night. Your eyes are not open when you dream are they?

No Awan, they are not.

Yet, you can see the pictures of your dreams. Clairvoyant vision works in the same manner. Do you understand?

Yes, Awan, now I understand.

Just before Jesus multiplied the fish and loaves he taught his disciples:

> **Do you have eyes but fail to see, and ears but fail to hear? And don't you remember?**[10]

He was not referring to the disciples' physical senses, but to their psychic perceptions. The disciples had doubts that יְהוֹשֻׁעַ בֶּן יֹסֵף (*Joshua ben Joseph*) could demonstrate the *gift of apports* and multiply the loaves and fishes.

---

[10] Mark 8:18 [NIV].

📖 Remember יְהוֹשֻׁעַ בֶּן יֹסֵף was Jesus' actual name. יְהוֹשֻׁעַ means *Joshua*, בֶּן means **son of** and יֹסֵף means *Joseph*. This is the way all Hebrew names are structured. יְהוֹשֻׁעַ בֶּן יֹסֵף means *Joshua the son of Joseph*.

👼 Jesus taught a great truth when he said:

"God is Spirit, and those who worship him must worship in Spirit and truth."[11]

🧑 I'm sorry, Awan, I don't understand that.

👼 When Jesus said, *"God is Spirit and those who worship him must worship in Spirit and truth,"* he was explaining that the soul, and Spirit that is within each of us, is made up of the universe's creative life force that we call God. This is why Jesus said:

Behold, the kingdom of God is within you.[12]

You need to realize, my scribe, that since the aura is the light of the soul, and the soul is the divine energy of God, that the aura is the light of God. Its presence around the body indicates that human beings are divine beings. This is the true meaning of this Biblical verse:

And God said, Let us make man in our image, after our likeness.[13]

Unfortunately, this verse has caused a great misunderstanding.

🧑 How is that, Awan?

👼 Theologians have used the creation story to anthropomorphize God. Instead of God making man in His image — Mankind created God in its image. *Infinite Intelligence*, which is *Divine Energy*, was transformed into an old man, with a long gray beard, dressed in a long purple flowing robe. Sometimes God is sitting on a golden, bejeweled throne, in some mysterious piece of real estate in the sky. It is of extreme importance for you to abandon the notion that God looks like a man. God is the soul and Spirit that resides equally within each human being.

🧑 It is difficult to get used to the idea that God is within, because I have always thought that God was a man in the sky.

👼 Yes, my brother, all religions have done humankind a great disservice by misleading them about the location of God. Religions have been the greatest conspiracy in the entire universe; they have deliberately concealed the truth.

---

[11] John 4:24 [NAB].

[12] Luke 17:21 [KJV].

[13] Genesis 1:26 [KJV].

🙂 Is that really true, Awan?

😇 My scribe, I realize that you cannot begin to comprehend profound depth of truth of that statement. Therefore, again, I will ask you to study the Bible and report back to me on what you learn. Research Jesus' statement that God is Spirit, and in our next dialogue we will discuss it.

🙂 OK, Awan. I will do what you ask.

😇 Good, my scribe. Now, I would like to change the subject. Would you agree that you currently have great technology on your planet?

🙂 Yes, Awan, we do have great technology.

😇 You have great aeroships that leave your planet, and go out into what you term "outer space."

🙂 Are you speaking of the space shuttle?

😇 Yes, that is what you term it. Recently your space shuttle has searched out a broken satellite and repaired it.

🙂 Yes, that is correct, Awan.

😇 Then, why can't your scientists take one of the space shuttles and have it land in heaven, my brother? Then your astronauts could go and speak with God, on his territory, as you term it.

🙂 Is that possible?

😇 My brother, it is possible, but you need not have a space shuttle. You do not have to travel through outer space to find God; you need to travel through *inner space*. God resides in the soul, which is within your chest. The distance that you need to travel is so small, because you travel there with your mind. After you have absorbed this teaching, and a few more, I will teach you how to directly communicate to the great God that is within you. For now let us leave it at that. Now, I know that since you are Jewish, you do not believe that Jesus was God.

🙂 That's right, Awan. The Jewish people regard Jesus as a prophet.

😇 That is what I want you to focus on. You must remember, in Biblical times, a *medium* was called a *prophet*. The Bible contains evidence that Jesus was considered a prophet.

🙂 Yes, Awan, I remember. The Samaritan woman called Jesus a prophet.

The woman saith unto him, Sir, I perceive that thou art a prophet.[14]

---

[14] John 4:9 [KJV].

(😇) Correct. If our dialogue occurred in Biblical times, you would refer to the man whose body I am using as a *prophet*.

(🧑) Yes, Awan, I understand that.

(😇) And you seem to be believing the information that is coming through him?

(🧑) Generally, that is true.

(😇) As time goes on, you will digest this information and accept more and more of this knowledge. So, if you can accept the words of this prophet, you should be able to accept the words of Jesus, another prophet.

(🧑) I see your point, Awan. Yes, Awan, you are right.

(😇) You must be patient with yourself. It is not easy to analyze your beliefs, and make major changes in them. People often desperately cling to the belief systems that they learned when they were children, even after they outgrow them. You can compare it to a sunrise. You start in darkness, and just before the sun appears over the horizon, the sky grows brighter and brighter. It is a gradual change. It is not the glaring change you experience when you turn on bright lights in a pitch-dark room. Changes in understanding are like sunrises; they are gradual. You cannot expect to know, understand, and accept this information all at once.

(🧑) Yes, Awan, I suppose you are right.

(😇) I want you to clearly understand, my scribe, the importance of your mission. You are living in the "End-times," meaning the end of the Age of Ignorance, *not* the end of the world, as so many people on your planet believe. It is my sincere hope that the lessons from our dialogues, that you will transcribe, will alter the future of your planet.

(🧑) How would that be possible, Awan?

(😇) If the people absorb these teachings; they will have the option of transforming their belief systems into a knowingness system.

(🧑) What on earth do you mean, Awan? What is a knowingness system?

(😇) A knowingness system means you just know, and is very different than a belief. Many people believe in concepts, which have not been proven to them. When you have knowingness no doubt exists, and no further proof is required. A knowingness connects the physical to Spirit. It means that your soul body and mind would be interconnected.

(🧑) Awan, I don't understand that!

(😇) After this session, use your dictionary and study the meaning of these words. If you just believe in a concept, you accept it based on conjecture. You have no facts to prove your belief. Knowing a concept is absolute; there is no doubt, it becomes a fact to you.

Suppose a man approached you, and told you that he had heard from his ancestors, that there were magnificently beautiful gardens on the other side of the mountain. These gardens had flowers that did not exist on your side of the mountain. You become so interested, that you decide to go to visit these gardens. It takes you three weeks to climb the rugged mountain and reach the valley on the other side. After your arduous journey, you discover there were no special gardens. The flowers on that side of the mountain were identical to your own.

It was your belief that caused you to journey across the mountain. If your inner knowingness were activated, you would have realized the man was telling you an untruth.

The knowingness that I speak of is like a baby knowing its mother. A baby does not need an introduction, a college course, or a Bible, to know the identity of his or her mother. It is an inner knowingness. Much of your life was supposed to be like this.

🧑 OK, Awan. But is it possible to know with certainty, the validity of all the information you taught about the soul, when you cannot see it for yourself? How can it become fact?

😇 When you finally absorb the information that I gave you about the soul, you will come to a realization, and will *know* that the soul is behind the breastbone. The act of knowing is very powerful, and it will awaken the soul. It is then that you will have active communication between the spiritual and physical body. When this happens your options can become limitless, as we will discuss in later dialogues.

If everyone would awaken the soul within, a great change would occur on your planet. Your planet is in an extreme state of decay, because people have been disconnected from the God within, the soul, for much too long. The earth will implode in on itself, unless people come to realize that God is within each and every person who walks your planet. This knowledge would stop these great disasters!

🧑 Awan, this is very powerful information. I certainly hope that people will be able to absorb this knowledge. I can only say that it will take me some time to digest this.

😇 I understand that, my scribe, and that is part of the process of absorbing knowledge. It is easy to build a belief system; all you have to do is accept what someone else has told you. Creating a knowingness system is more difficult, because you must add your own energy to the process, through thinking and reasoning.

🧑 I understand what you are saying, Awan.

😇 Good! I am now sensing a change in the energy, so I will withdraw from this body at this time. You, my scribe, have much to research, contemplate, and absorb. It has been a pleasure for me to bring this information through to you. My peace be with you!

🙂 My peace be with you too, Awan.

Carl inhaled sharply, and his body spasmed one time. Then he moaned softly, and stretched a bit. He softly said, "I need water." After drinking an eight-ounce glass of water, Carl looked puzzled and said, "I don't know how Awan can speak through my mouth when it is so dry." Since Carl felt so drained, he went directly to bed and slept for two and a half hours.

THREE

Twisting the Truth

God *is* a Spirit: and they that worship him must worship *him* in spirit and in truth.[15]

Following Awan's instructions, I set out to research this important verse. I must admit that I had no idea the important information I would discover by studying this small verse. For over twenty years I had collected Bible verses that pertained to the *Gifts of the Spirit*. This verse was one of them. Therefore, I began by opening my database and studying the translations I had already collected.

JOHN CHAPTER 4 VERSE 24

Abrev.	Date	Text
EWYC	1384	God is a spirit, and it behoveth them that worshipped him, for to worship in spirit and truth.
LWYC	1395	God is a spirit, and it behoveth them that worshipped him, to worship in spirit and truth.
TYND	1534	God is a spirit, and they that worship him, must worship him, in spirit and truth.
COV	1535	God is a spirit, and they that worship him, must worship in spirit and in the truth.
HOLLY	1538	{Spiritus est Deus, et eos qui adorant eum, in spiritu & ueritate oportet adorare.} God is a spirit, and they that worship him, must worship in spirit and in the truth.
TAV	1539	God is a spirit, and they that worship him, must worship him in spirit, and truth.
GRT	1540	God is a spirit, and they that worship him, must worship him in spirit, and in the truth.
MATT	1549	God is a spirit, and they that worship him, must worship him in spirit, and truth.
JUGG	1552	God is a spirit, and they that worship him, must worship him in spirit and truth.
GEN	1560	God is a Spirit, and they that worship him, must worship him in spirit and truth.
BISH	1568	God is a spirit, and they that worship him, must worship him in spirit, and in truth.
RHEIM	1582	God is a Spirit, and those that adore him, must adore in spirit and veritie.
KJV	1611	God is a Spirit, and they that worship him, must worship him in spirit, and in truth.
HAAK	1657	God is a Spirit: and they that worship him must worship him in spirit and in truth.
MACE	1729	God is a spirit, and they that worship him must worship him in spirit and in truth.

---

[15] John 4:24 [KJV].

SIMON	1730	God is a Spirit; accordingly they that worship him, must worship him in spirit and in truth.
WHIS	1745	God is a Spirit: and they that worship him, must worship him in spirit and in truth.
CHAL	1750	God is a spirit, and they that adore him, must adore him in spirit and in truth.
WESL	1755	God is a spirit, and they that worship him, must worship him in spirit and in truth.
PUR	1764	God is a Spirit; and those who worship him, must worship him with the Spirit and the Truth.
WYNNE	1764	'God is a Spirit, and they that worship Him must worship in spirit and in truth.'
HAR	1768	God is a pure and perfect mind—and those, who offer him their religious homage, ought to address him with virtuous sincerity and rectitude of heart.
WORS	1770	God is a Spirit, and they that worship Him must worship in spirit and truth.
CLEM	1790	"God is a Spirit: and those, who adore him, must adore him in spirit and in truth."
RAY	1799	God is a Spirit; and they that worship him must worship him in spirit and in truth.
THOM	1808	God is Spirit; and they who worship him ought to worship in spirit and truth.
BELS	1809	God is a spirit: and the worshippers of him out to worship him in spirit and in truth.
WAKE	1820	God is a spirit: and his worshippers must worship him in spirit and in truth.
BOTR	1824	"God is a Spirit: and they that worship him must worship him in spirit and in truth."
WEBR	1841	God is a Spirit: and they that worship him must worship him in spirit and in truth.
CONE	1850	God is a spirit: and they that worship him must worship him in spirit and in truth.
MURD	1851	For God is a Spirit; and they that worship him, should worship in spirit and in truth.
SAWY	1858	God is a Spirit, and those that worship him must worship in spirit and in truth.
KEN	1862	God is a Spirit, and they who worship Him, must worship Him in spirit and in truth.
YNG	1863	God is a Spirit, and those worshipping Him, in spirit and truth it behoveth to worship.'
ABU	1866	God is spirit; and they that worship him, must worship him in spirit and in truth.
SMITH	1867	For unto such hath God promised his Spirit. And they that worship him, must worship him in spirit and in truth.
HARM	1870	Not Translated.
ALF	1875	God is a Spirit, and they that worship him, must worship him in spirit, and in truth.
JUSMI	1876	God is a Spirit: and they worshipping him must worship in spirit and truth.
ERV	1885	God is a Spirit: and they that worship him must worship in spirit and truth.
CAMB	1889	God is a Spirit: and they that worship him must worship in spirit and in truth.
SHAR	1892	God is spirit, And they that worship him must worship in spirit and in truth.'
ROTH	1897	God is spirit; And they that worship him In spirit and truth must needs worship.
YLT	1898	God [is] a Spirit, and those worshipping Him, in spirit and truth it doth behoove to worship.'
GRANT	1899	God is a Sprit; and those that worship him must worship him in spirit and in truth.
GDBEY	1900	Not Translated.
ASV	1901	God is a Spirit: and they that worship him must worship in spirit and truth.
CENT	1901	God is a Spirit: and they that worship him must worship him in spirit and in truth.
WEY	1903	God is Spirit; and those who worship Him must bring Him true spiritual worship."
TCNT	1904	"God is Spirit; and those who worship him must worship spiritually and truly."
HORNN	1911	A spirit is God; and for those who will worship him it is right for them to worship him in spirit and in truth.
MORD	1912	God is Spirit: and they that worship him must worship in spirit and in truth.
PAN	1914	God is Spirit: and who worship him must worship in spirit and in truth.
DARBY	1920	God [is] a spirit, and they who worship him must worship [him] in spirit and in truth.
FENT	1922	God is Spirit; and those worshipping Him must worship in spirit and in truth."

MOFF	1922	"God is Spirit, and his worshippers must worship him in Spirit and in reality."
RIVER	1923	"God is spirit, and those who worship him must worship in spirit and in truth."
OVER	1925	God is Spirit; and those who worship Him, must worship Him in spirit and in truth."
LAMSA	1933	For God is Spirit; and those who worship him must worship him in spirit and in truth.
WADE	1934	"God is Spirit; and those who worship Him must render to Him worship that is Spiritual and Real."
GREB	1937	God is a spirit and those who worship Him must therefore be under the guidance of a spirit of God and of the divine truth when they come to do Him homage."
SPEN	1937	"God is spirit; and His worshipers must worship in spirit and truth."
SMGO	1939	God is spirit, and his worshipers must worship him in spirit and in sincerity."
DIAG	1942	"God is Spirit: and those worshipping him must worship in Spirit and Truth."
KNOX	1944	God is a spirit, and those who worship him must worship him in spirit and in truth.
MODL	1945	God is a Spirit and His worshipers must worship Him in spirit and in truth.
SWANN	1947	God is a spirit and they who worship him must worship in spirit and truth.
LETCH	1948	God is a Spirit; and those that worship him must worship him in spirit and in truth.
DART	1950	Not Translated.
OGD	1950	God is Spirit: then let his worshippers give him worship in the true way of the spirit.
WILL	1950	"God is a spiritual Being, and his worshipers must worship Him in spirit, and reality."
RSV	1952	"God is spirit, and those who worship him must worship in spirit and truth."
KLLI	1954	"God is Spirit, and his worshipers must worship in spirit and in truth."
WEST	1958	God is a spirit, and those who worship him must worship in spirit and truth.
NASB	1960	"God is spirit; and those who worship Him must worship in spirit and truth."
EXPN	1961	God as to His nature is spirit, and for those who are worshipping, it is necessary in the nature of the case to be worshipping in a spiritual sphere, and in the sphere of truth.
NOLI	1961	God is a spirit, and his worshippers must worship him in spirit and in truth."
NWT	1961	"God is a Spirit, and those worshipping him must worship with spirit and truth."
MKJV	1962	God is a spirit, and they who worship Him must worship in spirit and in truth.
NORL	1962	"God is a Spirit, and those who worship Him must do so in spirit and in truth."
AMP	1965	God is a Spirit (a spiritual Being) and those who worship Him must worship Him in spirit and in truth (reality).
CONF	1965	God is spirit, and they who worship him must worship in spirit and in truth."
ANCR	1966	"God is Spirit, and those who worship Him must worship in Spirit and truth."
JER	1966	"God is spirit, and those who worship must worship in spirit and truth."
BARC	1968	'God is a spiritual being, and his worshippers must offer him a truly spiritual worship.'
NAB	1970	God is Spirit, and those who worship must worship in Spirit and truth.
ABBR	1971	"Soon true worshippers will worship God who is spirit, in spirit and in truth."
LIV	1971	For God is Spirit, and we must have his help to worship as we should.
BYIN	1972	"God is a spirit, and those who worship must worship in spirit and truth."
PHIL	1972	"God is Spirit, and those who worship him can only worship in spirit and in reality."
WMF	1975	"God is a Spirit and it follows naturally that to worship God properly it must be done in Spirit, with no phony overtones," concluded Jesus.
BECK	1976	God is a spirit, and those who worship Him must worship in spirit and in truth."
NEB	1976	'God is spirit, and those who worship him must worship in spirit and in truth.'
TEV	1976	God is Spirit, and only by the power of his Spirit can people worship him as he really is.

NIV	1978	"God is spirit, and his worshipers must worship in spirit and in truth."
WORR	1980	"God is a Spirit; and those who worship Him must worship in spirit and truth."
NKJV	1982	"God is Spirit, and those who worship Him must worship in spirit and truth."
RDB	1982	"God is spirit, and those who worship him must worship in spirit and truth."
CLNT	1983	"God is spirit, and those who are worshipping Him must be worshipping in spirit and truth."
NLFB	1983	God is Spirit. Those who worship Him must worship Him in spirit and in truth."
NJER	1985	God is spirit, and those who worship must worship in spirit and truth.
ORIG	1985	Not Translated.
EB	1987	God is spirit. Those who worship God must worship in spirit and truth."
ETR	1987	God is spirit. So the people that worship God must worship in spirit and truth.
WBC	1987	God is Spirit, and those who worship him must worship in the Spirit and in the truth."
MCORD	1988	God is spirit, and those who worship him must worship in spirit and truth.
MONT	1988	"God is spirit, and those who worship him must worship him in spirit and in truth."
GNC	1989	"God is spirit, and those worshipping him must worship in a spiritual manner and in accordance with the truth."
REB	1989	'God is spirit, and those who worship him must worship in spirit and in truth.'
NRSV	1990	"God is spirit, and those who worship him must worship in spirit and truth."
NCV	1991	God is spirit, and those who worship him must worship in spirit and truth."
REC	1991	God is Spirit, and those who worship Him must worship in spirit and truthfulness.
UNVAR	1991	"God is spirit, and His worshipers must worship in spirit and truth."
FUNK	1993	"God is not tied to place, and those who worship God must worship him as he truly is, without regard to place."
GLT	1993	God [is] a spirit, and the ones worshipping Him must worship in spirit and truth.
MESS	1993	God is sheer being itself—Spirit. Those who worship him must do it out of their very being, their spirits, their true selves, in adoration."
BBC	1994	"You gotta worship the Almighty in a truly righteous fashion, in the spirit and in the truth."
COMP	1994	"God is not tied to place, and those who worship God must worship him as he truly is, without regard to place."
KJ21	1994	"God is a Spirit, and they that worship Him must worship Him in spirit and in truth."
CCB	1995	"God is spirit and those who worship God must worship in spirit and truth."
CEV	1995	God is Spirit, and those who worship God must be led by the Spirit to worship him according to the truth.
GODWD	1995	"God is a spirit. Those who worship him must worship in spirit and truth."
INCL	1995	"God is spirit, and those who worship God must worship in spirit and truth."
NIrV	1995	"God is spirit. His worshipers must worship in spirit and in truth."
LATT	1996	God is a Spirit, and they that worship him, must worship him in spirit, and in truth.
NLT	1996	For God is Spirit, so those who worship him must worship in spirit and in truth."
WEB	1997	"God is a Spirit, and those who worship him must worship in spirit and truth."
CJB	1998	God is a Spirit, and they that worship him, must worship him in spirit, and in truth.

As I studied this information, my eyes froze on the notes that I had taken many years before, but which I had forgotten. **HOLLY** was an early parallel edition of the Latin and English New Testament, with Johan Hollybushe as its translator. I remembered while typing the English translation of John 4:24, that my eyes had just drifted to the Latin. I remembered thinking that it was curious that the English was a twisted form of the Latin. Hollybushe' New

Testament stated the Latin as: *Spirit was God,* yet in English, as in 397 of the 399 versions of the New Testament, it read *God is Spirit.* I remember noticing that discrepancy, but never pursued it any further.

Here are the only two English versions, which kept the word order of the original Greek and Latin New Testaments.

A spirit is God; and for those who will worship him it is right for them to worship him in spirit and truth.[16]

For The Spirit is God, and it is fitting that those who worship him worship in The Spirit and in The Truth[17]

Now, years later, as Awan suggested that religions conspired to hide the truth from the people, I became more curious about this example of "Scripture twisting." Were there any implications of switching the word order in this verse?

My first step in exploring this topic would be to confirm that the Latin translation was correct. **HOLLY** was in Schide Library—the rare book library of Princeton University. I did not have the time to travel back to Princeton, to re-examine this verse. However, I went on the internet and found a site that had the (Latin) Vulgate Bible available to study.

Spiritus est Deus et eos qui adorant eum in spiritu et veritate oportet adorare.[18]

Again, this confirmed the fact that in Latin the phrase is: *Spirit is God.*

Next, I wondered about the wording of the original Greek. I do not read nor understand Greek, however, I did have an interlinear Greek-English New Testament. John 4:24 looked like this:

πνευμα ο θεοσ	και	τουσ	προσκυνουντασ
Spirit [is] God	and	the [ones]	worshipping

εν	πνευματι	και	αληθεια	δει	προσκυνει [19]
in	spirit	and	truth	it behoves	to worship

Even without any knowledge of the Greek language, I again recognized the manipulation of words. The second word θεοσ clearly resembled the

---

[16] John 4:24 [HORNS-1911].

[17] John 4:24 [OANT-2009].

[18] http://diderot.uchicago.edu/Bibles/VULGATE.form.html.

[19] Marshall, Alfred, Rev. D. Litt. *The Interlinear Greek-English New Testament: The Nestle Greek Text with a Literal English Translation.* Grand Rapids, MI: Zondervan Publishing House, 1958. p. 371.

Latin *Deus*, which means *God*. Therefore, the original Greek had to read, *Spirit is God*.

Does the word order make any difference? My mind raced back to when I had studied algebra. In math there is the commutative law.

> **"An operation obeys the cummutative property if the order of the two numbers involved doesn't matter. The commutative property for addition states that a+b=b+a for all a and b."**[20]

This mathematical law means that it doesn't matter if you say 3+4 or 4+3; they both will equal 7. If we were dealing with mathematics, both phrases *God is Spirit*, and *Spirit is God* would have identical value (meaning).

However, the English language does not follow the principles of mathematics. English has its own rules of grammar. The phrases *God is Spirit*, and *Spirit is God* are examples of *subject complements*—specifically a *predicate nominative*.

> **A *predicate nominative* is one kind of subject complement. It is a noun or pronoun that explains or identifies the subject of the sentence. Predicate nominatives follow linking verbs.**
>
> **Example Seaweed is *algae*. [*Algae* is a predicate nominative following the linking verb "is." It identifies the subject, seaweed.]**[21]
>
> **The subject of a sentence is the part about which something is being said.**[22]

Therefore, the subject is the topic of discussion. The focus or emphasis belongs to the subject of the sentence. In the phrase *God is Spirit*, we are talking about *God*. Conversely, *Spirit* is the main focus of the phrase *Spirit is God*.

To some this may be "Much Ado about Nothing." There seems to be so little difference between these two phrases. However, it is my contention, based on discussions with Awan, that these phrases are the result of the Church's attempts to keep the truth hidden from humanity.

---

[20] Downing, Douglas, Ph. D. *Dictionary of Mathematics Terms: 2nd edition.* Hauppauge, NY: Barron's Educational Series, Inc., 1995. p. 48-9.

[21] Warriner, John E. *English Composition and Grammar: Benchmark Edition.* San Diego, CA: Harcourt Brace Jovanovich, Publishers, 1988. p. 267-8.

[22] Warriner, John E. *English Composition and Grammar: Benchmark Edition.* San Diego, CA: Harcourt Brace Jovanovich, Publishers, 1988.p. 184.

My curiosity had been peaked about this verse. I decided to expand my exploration into Bibles in languages other than English, in order to see how this verse is stated. Would other languages follow the sentence structure of the original Greek and Latin New Testaments, which said *Spirit is God*, or would the word order be twisted, as in English, to read *God is Spirit*?

I discovered that my "hunch" was correct. In all the languages that I could read and had access to, the phrase read: *God is Spirit*.

I was extremely fortunate to discover several extremely comprehensive websites [http://bibledatabase.net and http://www.biblegateway.com/], which provides easy searching for a particular verse in many versions of the English Bible, as well as in other languages. The following is information from the languages that I could understand:

JOHN CHAPTER 4 VERSE 24

| KJV | God is a Spirit: and they that worship him must worship him in spirit and in truth. (KJV) |

Greek

1991 Byzantine Majority Text	πνευμα ο θεοσ και τουσ προσκυνουντασ αυτον εν πνευματι και αληθεια δει προσκυνειν (Byz)
1991 Byzantine Majority Text Transliterated	pneuma o theos kai tous proskynountas auton en pneumati kai aletheia dei proskynein (ByzX)
Nestle-Aland 26th/27th Ed.	πνευμα ο θεοσ και τουσ προσκυνουντασ αυτον εν πνευματι και αληθει α δει προσκυνειν (NA26)
Nestle-Aland 26th/27th Ed. Transliterated	pneuma o theos kai tous proskynountas auton en pneumati kai aletheia dei proskynein (NA26X)
Nestle-Aland 27th Ed. UBS 4th Ed. with diacritics	pneàma ‹ qeÒj, kaˆ to†j proskunoàntaj aÙtÕn ™n pneÚmati kaˆ ¢lhqe…v de‹ proskune‹n. (N27U4)
1894 Scrivner Textus Receptus	πνευμα ο θεοσ και τουσ προσκυνουντασ αυτον εν πνευματι και αληθει α δει προσκυνειν (Scrivner)
1894 Scrivner Textus Receptus Transliterated	pneuma o theos kai tous proskynountas auton en pneumati kai aletheia dei proskynein (ScrivnerX)
1550 Stephanus Textus Receptus	πνευμα ο θεοσ και τουσ προσκυνουντασ αυτον εν πνευματι και αληθει α δει προσκυνειν (Stephanus)
1550 Stephanus Textus Receptus Transliterated	pneuma o theos kai tous proskynountas auton en pneumati kai aletheia dei proskynein (StephanusX)
Tischendorf's 8th Ed. GNT	πνευμα ο ψεοσ και τουσ προσκυνουντασ ενπνευματι και αληψεια προ σκυνειν δει (Tisch)
Tischendorf's 8th GNT Transliterated	pneuma o pseos kai tous proskynountas enpneumati kai alepseia proskynein dei (TischX)

1881 Westcott-Hort GNT	πνευμα ο θεοσ και τουσ προσκυνουντασ αυτον εν πνευματι και αληθεια δει προσκυνειν (WH)
1881 Westcott-Hort GNT Transliterated	pneuma o theos kai tous proskynountas auton en pneumati kai aletheia dei proskynein (WHX)
Westcott-Hort with NA27U4 variants	πνευμα ο θεοσ και τουσ προσκυνουντασ αυτον εν πνευματι και αληθεια δει προσκυνειν (WHNU)
Westcott-Hort with NA27U4 variants Transliterated	pneuma o theos kai tous proskynountas auton en pneumati kai aletheia dei proskynein (WHNUX)

Latin

Jerome's Latin Vulgate 405 AD	Spiritus est Deus et eos qui adorant eum in spiritu et veritate oportet adorare (Vulgate)

Italian

Italian La Nouva Diodati (LND)	Dio è Spirito, e quelli che lo adorano devono adorarlo in spirito e verità". (ItaLND)
Italian La Sacra Bibbia Nuova Riveduta	Dio è Spirito; e quelli che l' adorano, bisogna che l' adorino in spirito e verità». (ItaNRV)

Spanish

Spanish La Biblia de Las Americas (LBA)	Dios es espíritu, y los que le adoran deben adorarle en espíritu y en verdad. (SpaLBA)
Spanish Reina-Valera Actualizada (RVA)	Dios es espíritu; y es necesario que los que le adoran, le adoren en espíritu y en verdad. (SpaRVA)
Spanish Reina-Valera (RV)	Dios es Espíritu; y los que le adoran, en espíritu y en verdad es necesario que adoren. (SpaRV)
Spanish Sagradas Escrituras	Dios es Espíritu; y los que le adoran, en Espíritu y en verdad es necesario que adoren. (SpaSEV)
Spanish Valera	Dios es Esp'edritu; y los que le adoran, en esp\'edritu y en verdad es necesario que adoren. (SpaVNT)

Portuguese

Portuguese A Biblia Sagrada Traduzida em Portugues	Deus é Espírito, e importa que os que o adoram o adorem em espírito e em verdade. (PorBRP)

Filipino

Filipino Nga Cebuano	Ang Dios espiritu, ug ang mga magasimba kaniya kinahanglan managsimba diha sa espiritu ug sa kamatuoran." (PhiCeb)

French

French Louis Segond Version (LSG)	Dieu est Esprit, et il faut que ceux qui l'adorent l'adorent en esprit et en vérité. (FreLSG)
French Darby's	Dieu est esprit, et il faut que ceux qui l'adorent, l'adorent en esprit et en

Version	vérité. (FreDrb)
French Nouvelle Edition de Geneve	Dieu est Esprit, et il faut que ceux qui l'adorent l'adorent en esprit et en vé (FreNEG)

German

German Luther Version	Gott ist Geist, und die ihn anbeten, die müssen ihn im Geist und in der Wahrheit anbeten. (GerLut)
German Schlachter Version	Gott ist Geist, und die ihn anbeten, müssen ihn im Geist und in der Wahrheit anbeten. (GerSch)
German Bengel Version	Ein Geist (ist) Gott; und die ihn anbeten, müssen in Geist und Wahrheit anbeten. (GerBen)
German Elberfelder Version	Gott ist ein Geist, und die ihn anbeten, müssen in Geist und Wahrheit anbeten. (GerElb)

Dutch

Dutch Leidse Vertaling (LEI)	God is geest, en zij die aanbidden moeten in geest en waarheid aanbidden. (DutLEI)
Dutch Lutherse Vertaling (LU)	God is Geest, en wie hem aanbidden, moeten hem in Geest en in waarheid aanbidden. (DutLU)
Dutch Statemvertaling (SVV)	God is een Geest, en die Hem aanbidden, moeten Hem aanbidden in geest en waarheid. (DutSVV)

Danish

Danish Bible	Gud er Ånd, og de, som tilbede ham, bør tilbede i Ånd og Sandhed." (Dan)

Norsk

Norsk Bible	Gud er ånd, og de som tilbeder ham, bør tilbede i ånd og sannhet. (Norsk)

Melanesian

Melanesian Pidgin Bible	God em i Spirit. Na ol man i lotu long em, ol i mas lotu long strong bilong Holi Spirit na long pasin i tru." (Mel)

Hebrew

Orthodox Jewish Brit Chadasha	"Hashem is Ruach (Spirit) and it is necessary for the ones worshiping him to worship in the Ruach Hakodesh and Emes." [Yechezkel 36:26-27; 37:14] (ORTHJBC)

Indonesian

Indonesian Bahasa Indonesia Sehari-hari	Sebab Allah itu Roh, dan hanya dengan kuasa Roh Allah orang-orang dapat menyembah Bapa sebagaimana Ia ada." (IndBIS)
Indonesian Terjemahan Baru	Allah itu Roh dan barangsiapa menyembah Dia, harus menyembah-Nya dalam roh dan kebenaran." (IndTB)

What is so fascinating is that the original Greek always uses the phrase *Spirit is God,* as does the Latin Vulgate. Only the **German Bengel Version** keeps the original meaning of the Greek in tact by saying *"Ein Geist (ist)*

Gott (one Spirit is God)." Yet, in all the other languages the Bibles say: *God is Spirit*. It made me wonder why the Romance languages (Italian, Spanish, Portuguese, and French) had reversed the word order, since these languages were based on the Latin. Notice that the words are all quite similar.

Language/Bible Version	God	Spirit
Jerome's 405 AD Latin Vulgate	Deus	Spiritus
Italian La Nouva Diodati (LND)	Dio	Spirito
Italian La Sacra Bibbia Nuova Riveduta	Dio	Spirito
Spanish La Biblia de Las Americas (LBA)	Dios	espíritu
Spanish Reina-Valera Actualizada (RVA)	Dios	espíritu
Spanish Reina-Valera (RV)	Dios	Espíritu
Spanish Sagradas Escrituras	Dios	Espíritu
Spanish Valera	Dios	Esp\'edritu
Portuguese A Biblia Sagrada Traduzida em Portugues	Deus	Espírito
French Louis Segond Version (LSG)	Dieu	Esprit
French Darby's Version	Dieu	esprit
French Nouvelle Edition de Geneve	Dieu	Esprit

The same held true in the German languages, which would include English, German, Dutch, and Norwegian. We can easily see that each of these verses has God as the subject of the sentence.

Language/Bible Version	God	Spirit
German Luther Version	Gott	Geist
German Schlachter Version	Gott	Geist
German Bengel Version	Gott;	Geist
German Elberfelder Version	Gott	Geist
Dutch Leidse Vertaling (LEI)	God	geest
Dutch Lutherse Vertaling (LU)	God	Geest
Dutch Statemvertaling (SVV)	God	Geest
Danish Bible	Gud	Ånd og
Norsk Bible	Gud	ånd og

The Hebrew *Hashem*, is an unique word to refer to the name of God, outside of prayer. רוּחַ (*rûach*) is the Hebrew word for *wind, breath mind, Sprit*.[23] It is interesting to see the Indonesian Bible uses Islamic imagery. *Allah* is the Islamic name for God, and *Roh* is clearly related to the Hebrew word רוּחַ (*rûach*) for Spirit. Arabic and Hebrew, from the Semitic family of languages, are quite similar.

---

[23] Harris, R. Laird, ed. *Theological Wordbook of the Old Testament Vol. 2*. Chicago: Moody Press, 1980. p. 836.

My Second Encounter With An Angel

Language/Bible Version	God	Spirit
Orthodox Jewish Brit Chadasha	Hashem	Ruach
Indonesian Bahasa Indonesia Sehari-hari	Allah	Roh
Indonesian Terjemahan Baru	Allah	Roh

After I finished this research, I remained puzzled. It seemed odd to me that the Bible translators should all (with one exception) decide to substitute the subject for the subject complement in all of these Bibles. I pondered this for a few days, but I could not understand how, or why, this had happened.

I decided to give Carl a call, and asked him if I could have an appointment with Awan to report my findings, and ask his opinion as to why this had occurred. Carl agreed to meet with me the following Saturday morning. However, he could not guarantee that I would talk with Awan. Carl explained that humans have no way to summon a Spirit. If I thought about speaking with Awan, I could draw his attention to me, and he could choose to meet with me. However, it was Awan's decision.

Early Saturday morning I arrived in Carl's office. He made his usual preparations to go into a deep trance state. After saying his prayer, he seemed to drift off; he even snored several times. Suddenly, his body shuddered, and about ten seconds later I heard the familiar sound of Awan's voice.

(😇) My profound greetings to you, my scribe!

(🧑) Greetings, Awan.

(😇) How may I serve you today, my scribe?

(🧑) Awan, I have completed the research that you requested. I studied the phrase *God is Spirit* in the English Bibles, as well as Bibles in many other languages.

(😇) And what have you discovered?

(🧑) The original Greek clearly states, ***Spirit is God***. The Latin Vulgate agrees. However, there are only two English Bibles and one German Version that says ***Spirit is God***. All the rest of the Bibles have switched the word order. I feel that the two phrases, ***God is Spirit*** and ***Spirit is God***, are very different from each other. Why did translators in so many languages twist this verse around?

(😇) Congratulations, my scribe, that is an excellent question! Before I answer your question, let me explain something else, which occurred before the time that the Bibles were translated into all the different languages.

(🧑) OK, Awan. Explain away!

(😇) During our last dialogue, I told you that religions have been the greatest conspiracy in the entire universe. The leaders of religions deliberately wanted the people to believe that God was outside of each human being, and placed God up in the sky, instead of within each person's chest.

Originally, people did not want to accept that God was outside of them. Therefore, the leaders of religions came up with a way to divert people's attention outward, rather than inward. They came up with the "original set of training wheels."

What on earth are you talking about, Awan?

A good choice of words, my scribe! This thought did not come from my dimension, but from yours. The priests created the idea that Gods were made of stone, clay or marble. You could make a statue of God, and worship the statue, an image you could easily see with your physical eyes. This was how the priests trained people to ignore the God within. Priests used statues, or idols, to break people's habits of turning within to communicate with God.

I found this interesting fact that confirms Awan's claim.

A vast population of statues inhabits the churches; in Chartes [a cathedral in France] they number about 1,800.[24]

Now I understand your analogy to training wheels!

It was very important for religions to make people believe that God was outside of themselves. For that was the only way to control the people's minds, and coerce them into supporting the priesthood. Think about this my scribe. If you close your eyes, and go within, your closet of prayer, as Jesus taught, can anyone really interfere with that communication?

Well, only if someone shouted, and brought you out of the meditative state.

Yes, that is true. Do you need a priest, minister, rabbi, or Bible to establish communication with the God within? Do you need to be in a temple, synagogue, church, or cathedral to communicate with God?

No, Awan, you do not.

That was the point! Eventually, people forgot that God was within, despite the fact that Jesus taught this very fact.[25] The Catholic Church continued to grow for many centuries, until most Europeans were under its control.

Then, after the invention of the printing press, people became hungry for knowledge, and the wealthier class learned to read. It was then there developed a great demand for reading the Bible. Up until that point in time, the Church totally controlled the Bible, which *remained in Latin*. Most people, however, wanted to read the Bible in their own *everyday* language. Slowly these translations were made, despite the fact that many of the

---

[24] McGeoch Angus. *Cathedrals: A Hundred Jewels of European Architecture.* Munich, Germany: I. P. Verlagsgesellschaft, 1998. p. 12.

[25] Luke 17:21.

translators were going against Church teachings, for which they could pay with their lives.

👤 Yes, Awan, I remember reading that the Church was so angry with John Wyclif, who was the first person to translate the Bible into English, that they exhumed his dead body, and burned it.[26]

📖 I later found additional information about this topic.

> **The crowd flocked to Wyclif's "true preachers." The listeners, for the first time head the Bible in their own language and they were overjoyed.... The established Church, of course, could not tolerate this kind of threat to its authority.... Archbishop Arundel, in 1408 prepared a Constitution, which the Provincial Council at Oxford adopted it declared in part:**
>
> **The Holy Scripture is not to be translated in to vulgar tongue [everyday language], nor a translation to be expounded, until it shall have been duly examined, under pain of excommunication and the stigma of heresy.[27]**

👼 You must realize, my scribe, people were very much aware of the fact that Spirits existed. The people who practiced the "pagan" religions held special séances at the end of October. The energy is quite high to communicate between the two dimensions at that particular time of the year. This is the real origin of your holiday of Halloween, a celebration of a time when Spirits and people could communicate. The Church wanted to entice the pagans into their religion, so they incorporated All Soul's Day, the day after Halloween, when people were supposed to communicate with the deceased relatives. People even understood that they had a Spirit within themselves.

This is why it became so important for the Church to deal with the verse that you researched. If all the Bibles read, *Spirit is God*, then people would begin to understand that the Spirit within each person is God. Then they could communicate, or pray to the God within, and bring about many changes in their lives. By forcing the translators to say, *God is Spirit*, instead of, *Spirit is God*, they were able to conceal this truth for another 500 years. It is my hope, my scribe, that this book will again bring this truth to light.

👤 I am beginning to understand. The Church wanted people to pray to a non-existent God out in the sky somewhere, in order to keep people from finding the true God within.

---

[26] Kerr, Johnn Stevens. *Ancient Texts Alive Today: the Story of the English Bible.* NY: American Bible Society, 1999. p. 39.

[27] Kerr, Johnn Stevens. *Ancient Texts Alive Today: the Story of the English Bible.* NY: American Bible Society, 1999. p. 38-39.

(😇) That is the exact truth. It is important for people to understand, that when they turn within they no longer visualize an old man as God. Instead, they should visualize the luminous ball of light that dwells in the middle of their chest as God.

(🙂) Awan, you said that you could communicate with the God within, to bring changes into your life. How is that accomplished?

(😇) My scribe, I am most eager to teach that to you. However, you are not quite ready. There are a few more concepts that you first need to comprehend. Soon, I will be able to share that information with you.

(🙂) I look forward to that, Awan.

(😇) I am sensing a change in the energy, and must soon withdraw from this medium's body. I am most pleased with our dialogue today. You are well on your way to creating a knowingness system.

(🙂) Thank you, Awan.

(😇) My peace be with you, my scribe.

(🙂) Peace be with you too, Awan.

Within three seconds, Carl suddenly breathed so sharply, it sounded like a loud snort. Then he began coughing. He looked exhausted and weak, as if he had been doing hard physical labor for many hours. He was so groggy, that I had to hold his glass of water to his lips. After he took a few sips, he stretched and yawned. I assisted Carl to his bed, so he could take a long nap. After his four hours of sleep, Carl still was tired for the rest of the day.

FOUR

Moses and Passover

The next time I had the opportunity to speak with Awan was late in April. Carl prepared himself to go into trance, in his usual fashion, by closing his eyes, and saying the prayer. For some reason, it appeared that Awan was having difficulty entering Carl's body. There were no spasms, however. For nearly five minutes, Awan was silent. I was very surprised by the topic of our conversation.

(😇) My greetings to you, my scribe.

(😊) Greetings, Awan.

(😇) I was with you recently, as you were with your mother celebrating Passover. I watched as you read your book, before and after the holiday meal.

(😊) Yes, Awan, the Passover service is called the *Seder* and the book I was reading aloud is called the *Haggadah*.

(😇) Yes, I watched you recite your *Haggadah*, and I was shocked as I listened to your words.

(😊) Why is that, Awan?

(😇) Before I respond, please tell me what is your purpose for reading the *Haggadah*?

(😊) Jews gather to celebrate the *Seder*, which commemorates when the ancient Hebrews were freed from slavery in Egypt. We read the *Haggadah*, which retells the story of liberation. We are supposed to think that we personally were liberated from the bondage of slavery in Egypt. We are not supposed to think that it only happened to our ancestors, thousands of years ago.

(😇) I understand. However, it seems that much of what is discussed in your *Haggadah* has nothing to do with your deliverance from slavery. If you don't mind, my scribe, let's make Moses the subject of our dialogue today. I know that you have read your Book of Books, and know the story of Moses' early life.[28] Shortly after his birth, Moses was placed in a basket, and put onto the Nile River. He was rescued by the Egyptian Princess and grew up as a member of the royal court.

---

[28] Exodus 1 - 2.

🧑 Yes, Awan that is correct.

👤 After Moses left Egypt, he became a shepherd in the land of Midian. The job of a shepherd required him to spend much time by himself, tending his flock. During this time alone, Moses developed his psychic abilities. He did this by learning to meditate, quieting his mind and body, and letting his thoughts go deep within him. He then brought his entire focus to his soul, in the middle of his chest. Slowly he opened communication with his God-within, the soul within his body. Eventually, Moses' brain began to open, and he became clairaudient and clairvoyant. One day Moses came upon a wondrous sight; a bush in flames, yet there was no smoke, and the fire did not destroy the bush.

📖 For the sake of clarity, I will quote the Bible. This is the original **DOU** (Catholic Douay Bible) of 1609. It was the first translation of the Latin Vulgate into English. (This edition of the Douay is quite interesting, for it continuously uses the phrase **"our Lord"** instead of **"the Lord,"** in the Old Testament. Were the Catholics implying that Moses was speaking to **Jesus** instead of **Jehovah**? In 1750 the **CHAL** (Challoner Revision) replaced **"our Lord"** with **"the Lord."**)

> **And Moses fed the sheep of Jethro his father in law the priest of Midian: and having driven the flock to the inner parts of the desert, he came to the mountain of God, Horeb. And our Lord appeared to him in a flame of fire out of the midst of a bush: and he saw that the bush was on fire, and was not burnt. Moses therefore said: I will go, and see this great vision, why the bush is not burnt. And our Lord seeing that he went forward to see, he called him out of the midst of the bush, and said: Moses, Moses. Who answered: Here I am. But he said: Approach not hither, loose of thy shoe from thy feet: for the place, wherein thou standest, is holy ground.**[29]

👤 Moses was having a clairvoyant vision when he saw the burning bush. There was a physical bush, however the flames that Moses saw were actually *Spirit Lights*. To explain *Spirit Lights* in the simplest terms, the flames were sparkling psychic energy. The image of the bush illuminated by a fire-like substance was registering in the clairvoyant center, instead of the visual center, of Moses' brain. Moses was seeing, what would appear to be a burning fire, but the flames would not be hot. You should remember that these flames were created from the Spirit side of life; therefore, they would be vibrating on a much too high a vibration to burn the physical wood of the bush.

It is significant that your Book of Books says: *"When the Lord saw that he went forward to see...."* This phrase indicates this was Moses' first clairvoyant

---

[29] Exodus 3:1-5 [DOU].

experience. The Spirit was not certain that the vision being projected was on the correct frequency that Moses could see. Remember, my scribe, each medium has his or her own unique frequency, as does each of your radio stations. When Moses stepped forward, and said, *"Here I am,"* the Spirit Control realized that the image was projected on the correct frequency, because Moses saw Spirit's vision, and heard Spirit's words.

Awan, what is a *Spirit Control*?

A *Spirit Control* is a Spirit who is assigned to protect a medium. Let us talk about the medium that I am using at the moment. His Spirit Control is a Tuscarora Native American, named Chief Lone Eagle. Before I am able to enter this medium's body to speak with you, I must first receive Lone Eagle's permission. If the medium's body is too tired, Lone Eagle will refuse my request. Also, if a negative entity from lower levels of the Spirit World wanted to speak through this medium, Lone Eagle would block access to the medium. We sometimes call the *Spirit Control* a *doorkeeper*, since he or she acts as a security guard for the medium.

Remember, my scribe, when your Book of Books uses the word *God*, or *the Lord*, it really refers to a *Spirit*. In Biblical times, when a physical person spoke to a spiritual being, they addressed that being as *the Lord*, as a sign of respect. It is of extreme importance, my scribe, that the people of your planet break their habit of thinking that God is an old man sitting on a throne in some piece of real estate in the sky.

I still have trouble with that, Awan. I was taught there is only one God.

That is still true, my scribe. There is only one God, which is divine energy. A piece of that divine energy is in every flower, tree, animal, and human being. This is why Jesus said, "God is Spirit."[30] Your Spirit, or soul is comprised of the same substance (energy) as God. As I will soon teach you, in detail, that originally each human was a God, until the brain was shut down, and the *Age of Ignorance* commenced. In your present time, we say in this dimension, that every human is a God in the embryo. You all have the potential to become God, but you have quite a ways to go to achieve Godhood. Jesus again tried to teach you this when he said:

"Is it not written in your Law, I said, Ye are gods?"[31]

I am beginning to understand.

Later during the dialogue at *the burning bush*, the Spirit and Moses get into an intense argument. God wants Moses to be his messenger. Moses refuses, claiming not to be a good speaker. Some Bibles say that Moses had a *speech impediment.*

---

[30] John 4:24.

[31] John 10:34 [KJV].

📖 After this session, I found the verses Awan had mentioned. It appears Bible translators kept altering the words that described Moses' speech problem.

EXODUS CHAPTER 4 VERSE 10

LIV	1971	But Moses pleaded, O Lord, I'm just not a good speaker. I never have been, and I'm not now, even after you have spoken to me, for I have a **speech impediment.**[32]
BYIN	1972	clumsy mouth and tongue.
GEDD	1792	difficult utterance, and a faltering tongue.
YESC	2010	dull of mouth, and dull of tongue, I.
LTOG	2006	frail-sounded and delay-tongued I-be.
CPDV	2008	greater impediment and slowness of tongue.
ARATN	1987	halting of mouth, halting of speech am I.
VW	2009	heavy mouth and a dull tongue.
ARTB	2008	heavy mouth, and a heavy tongue.
WBC	1987	heavy of lip and thick of tongue.
STONE	1996	heavy of mouth and heavy of speech.
HAAK	1657	heavy of mouth and heavy of tongue.
ETHO	1862	heavy of speech and of a deep tongue.
ARATO	1987	heavy of speech and unintelligible of expression
ARAON	1990	heavy speech and indistinct articulation.
ALTER	2004	heavy-mouthed and heavy-tongued.
CCB	1995	I cannot find words to express what I want to say.
NCV	1991	I cannot speak well. I speak slowly and can't find the best words.
NIrV	1996	I don't speak very well at all.
LIVT	1981	I find it difficult to speak and find the right language.
ICB	1986	I speak slowly and can't find the best words.
EEBT	2003	I speak slowly and I speak with difficulty.'
CB	2010	I speak slowly, with a slow tongue.
INCP	2007	I speak slowly and with a wooden tongue.
GODWD	1995	I speak slowly, and I become tongue-tied easily.
MESS	2002	I stutter and stammer.
ISV	1998	I talk too slowly and I have a speech impediment.
AEB	2001	I'm a poor speaker and I talk slowly.
NLT	1996	I'm clumsy with words.
TAV	1539	impediment of speech, and am slow tongued.
BBC	1993	Look, God, I dont speak so hot. I stutter.
KNOX	1944	more faltering, more tongue-tied than ever.
NWYC	2010	more hindered, and of slower tongue.
DOU	1609	more impediment and slowness of tongue.

---

[32] The following Bibles also use the word *impediment*: **TAV, DOU, CHAN, CLEM, KEN, WEST.**

EWYC	1384	more latsum and of more slow tongue.
LWYC	1395	more lettid and slower tongue.
ABBR	1971	Moses said, But I am not a public speaker.
BECK	1976	my speech is slow, and my tongue is awkward.
WMF	1975	my tongue sticks to the roof of my mouth.
CJB	1998	My words come slowly, my tongue moves slowly.
EB	1987	not a good speaker. I speak slowly and can't find the best words.
TEV	1976	poor speaker, slow and hesitant.
TPB	2000	slow and hesitant in speaking.
NEB	1976	slow and hesitant of speech.
BOTR	1824	slow and impeded utterance
CEV	1995	slow at speaking, and I can never think of what to say.
EPBL	1994	slow heavy of speech mouth, and of a slow heavy tongue.
NLFV	1986	slow in talking and it is difficult for me to speak.
CEB	2011	slow mouth and a thick tongue.
GRT	1540	slow mouthed and slow tongued.
FENT	1922	slow of mouth and heavy of tongue.
YNG	1863	slow of mouth and slow of tongue
BAS	1944	slow of speech and have an awkward tongue.
KJV	1611	slow of speech and of a slow tongue.
MODL	1945	slow of speech and of an awkward tongue.
KENT	1921	slow of speech and slow in expressing my ideas.
NEUV	2011	slow of speech, and of a stammering tongue.
RAY	1799	slow of speech and utterance.
OJB	2002	slow of speech, and of a slow lashon.
WEBR	1841	slow of speech, and of a slow tongue.
MOFF	1922	slow of speech, I have not command of words.
JER	1966	slow speaker and not able to speak well.
SCH	2005	speech defect.
ETHJ	1862	staggering mouth and staggering speech.
THOM	1808	stammering voice and a faltering tongue.
LAMSA	1933	stutterer and slow of speech.
KEN	1860	suffer impediment and am slow of tongue.
OGD	1950	talking is hard for me, and I am slow of tongue.
ARATJ	1987	tongue-tied and I speak with difficulty.
ABDNT	2002	tongue-tied and slow of speech.
BREN	1844	weak in speech and slow-tongued.
OTFTS	2008	weak voice, and am slow of tongue.
WETC	2001	You know that I speak slowly and don't use the best words.
CLEAR	2000	You know that my words don't flow smoothly when I speak.

74 Differing Translations

There are four of these translations that are quite interesting. The first would be **OJB**'s translation *"slow of speech, and of a slow lashon.'* Since this is a Jewish translation it is absolutely remarkable that suddenly the translators are unable to translate the Hebrew word לָשׁוֹן (*lashon*) into the English word *tongue*! **INCP**'s phrase: *"I speak slowly and with a wooden tongue"* is quite fascinating, since I know of no one who has a wooden tongue. Obviously the translators were not interested in an accurate translation of the original Hebrew words. I am not sure if either **WBC**'s phrase: *"heavy of lip and thick of tongue,"* or **WMF**'s *"my tongue sticks to the roof of my mouth"* would be a cause for a speech impediment.

👼 There was a reason why your Book of Books says Moses had a *speech impediment*. Didn't you study Hebrew when you were a child?

🧑 Yes, Awan, but that was a long time ago.

👼 Do you remember how you would translate the word *tongue* into Hebrew?

🧑 If I remember correctly, the Hebrew word was לָשׁוֹן (*lashon*).

👼 Yes, that is correct. You might not remember, however, that the Hebrew word לָשׁוֹן (*lashon*) has two meanings. One is *tongue* and the other is *language*.

🧑 Now that you mention it, I remember that is true.

👼 Look it up in your reference books, and you will discover that I am right.

📖 I did look it up after the session. Again Awan was correct. It was interesting that **LIVT** is the *only* one of the 234 Old Testaments that used the word *language*.

Most Bible translators used the wrong meaning, when they used *tongue* in their translations, instead of *language*. We know this because the concept that Moses had a speech impediment is totally discredited by Moses' description found in Acts 7:22 of the New Testament.

ACTS CHAPTER 7 VERSE 22

KJV	1611	And Moses was learned in all the wisdom of the Egyptians, and was mighty in words and in deeds.
WMF	1975	a great and knowledgeable warrior.
CLEAR	2000	a great leader in words and actions.
BECK	1976	a great man in what he said and did.
TEV	1976	a great man in words and deeds.
NASB	1960	a man of power in words and deeds.
WILL	1950	a mighty man in speech and action
FPV	2002	a power to be reckoned with in the politics of Egypt.
CPV	1969	a powerful man in both what he said and did.
NLFV	1986	a powerful man in words and in the things he did.
TVB	2012	a powerful man-both as an intellectual and as a leader.

NEB	1976	a powerful speaker and a man of action.
MODL	1945	ability in speech and in deeds.
BARC	1968	able both in speech and in action.
ACC	2008	Able in words and [in] works [of] him
AUV	1994	accomplished speaker and an effective leader.
EPBT	1994	capable in words and in works.
ABDNT	2002	consistent in his words and also his deeds.
NASC	2000	dynamic in his words and actions.
KLLI	1954	effective in word and deed.
MURD	1851	eminent in his words, and also in his deeds.
HAR	1768	eminently distinguished for his genius and his achievements.
MAEV	2001	enabled in words and works.
SWHI	2012	established in his words as well as his deeds.
EPSNT	1849	excellent in words (and) also in deeds.
GABV	2009	excellent speaker and quite enterprising.
PHIL	1972	excellent speaker but a man of action as well.
HEIN	1863	existing in his words and deeds.
GREB	1937	forceful in word and deed.
HAMM	1845	great abilities above other men, both for speaking and also for managery of business
OGD	1950	great in his words and works.
MACE	1729	great influence by his counsels and actions.
ISV	1999	great man in speech and action.
GODWD	1995	great man in what he said and did.
GNC	1989	great power in both word and deed.
CB	2010	great power of speech and action.
RENNT	1985	great speaker and worker.
WWENT	1969	He knew how to talk and could do great things.
SNT	2007	his words and actions were powerful.
MESS	2002	impressive as a thinker and an athlete.
OJB	2002	in dvarim (words) and pe'ulot (deeds) he was given ko'ach (strength).
BLB	2006	learned the Egyptian language and culture.
AMP	1965	mighty (powerful) in his speech and deeds.
EPBL	1994	mighty able in words and in deeds works.
AV7	2008	mighty in words and deeds.
THOM	1808	mighty in council and in actions.
LORA	1826	mighty in his speeches and actions.
RHEIM	1582	mighty in his words and in his deeds.
EWYC	1384	mighty in his words and works.
ANT	1956	mighty in speech and action.
WAKE	1820	mighty in words and actions.
UTV	2001	mighty in words and in business.
LIV	1971	mighty prince and orator.
EEBT	2003	Moses said and did some very powerful things.
WEY	1903	possessed great influence through his eloquence and his achievements.
REC	1991	powerful in his words and works.

JER	1966	power both in his speech and his actions.
JMNT	2006	powerful and able in his words, thoughts, ideas and verbal expression – as well as in his acts and works.
SCAR	1798	powerful both in words and actions.
WETC	2001	powerful in all he said and did.
DIKSN	1833	powerful in eloquence and in action.
SINAI	1993	powerful in his reasonings/ words and works.
FENT	1922	powerful in his speech and actions.
CVSS	1944	powerful in his words and works.
NIV	1978	powerful in speech and action.
INCP	2007	powerful in speech and deeds.
ETR	1987	powerful in the things he said and did.
PENN	1836	powerful in words and in deeds.
CTNT	2005	powerful in words and in his actions.
PUR	1764	powerful in Words and Works.
NARY	1718	powerful in words, and in his deeds.
ICB	1986	powerful man in the things he said and did.
TPB	2000	powerful mentally and physically.
NIrV	1996	powerful speaker and a man of action.
LDNT	1999	powerful speaker and a man of outstanding accomplishments.
FBV	2010	powerful speaker and leader.
CEB	2011	powerful words and deeds.
LATT	1996	powerful, in words and actions.
APNT	2009	prepared in his words and also in his actions.
HRV	2001	prepared in his words and also in his deeds.
ARNC	1996	prepared in words and also in works.
TCNT	1904	proved his ability both by his words and actions.
BALL	1902	showed ability in his words and deeds.
WADE	1934	showed capacity alike in speech and action.
ANCR	1967	skilled in planning and doing.
CCNT	1977	spoke and acted with power.
HORNN	1898	strong in his words and his works.
SMGO	1939	strong in speech and action.
RIVER	1923	strong in words and in deeds.
CEV	1995	strong man and a powerful speaker.
MOFF	1922	strong man in speech and action.
ANDJ	1984	very powerful speaker and learned how to do many things well.
GAN	2004	very talented.
KNOX	1944	vigorous, too, in speech and in act.
LAMSA	1933	well versed in his words and also in his deeds.

94 Differing Translations

The most surprising translation is **BLB**'s *"learned the Egyptian language and culture,"* which totally supports the argument that Moses did not speak Hebrew. In 94 translations have some enlightening descriptions of Moses:

warrior [WMV], *leader* [CLEAR], *politician* [FPV], *intellectual* [TVB], *prince and orator* [LIV]. Moses' speaking ability is described as: *great* [TEV], *power in words* [NASB], *mighty man in speech* [WILL], *powerful man in words* [NLFV], *dynamic in his words* [NASC], *eminent in his words* [MURD], *excellent speaker* [GABV], *mighty in speech* [ANT], *powerful in eloquence* [DIKSN]. If these descriptions were accurate, why would Moses claim he could not speak well?

Bible translators deliberately mistranslated Exodus 4:10 to conceal an important fact. Moses was not complaining to the Spirit that he could not speak well. Moses didn't have the *language*—he did not know how to speak Hebrew! Remember, since Moses grew up in the Egyptian court, his native language was Egyptian. He did not speak Hebrew, the language of the slaves.

That would mean that Moses was speaking Egyptian to the Spirit/God.

Precisely! If Moses' Spirit Control (God) spoke Egyptian, he would have to be Egyptian. The Hebrews would not want to pray to an Egyptian God, they would want to pray to a Hebrew God. Therefore, the Bible translators did some "Scripture-twisting." By merely using an alternative meaning, *tongue*, instead of *language*, for the Hebrew word לָשׁוֹן (*lashon*), they managed to conceal the ethnic origin of the Spirit. It was much easier for theologians to keep the members of their congregations under their control, if they asked fewer questions.

I am beginning to see your point.

A few months later, I came upon this quote, which corroborates Awan's statement. This information comes through the medium Ursula Roberts. Using the *gift of clairaudience*, she communicated with Tek-Sek, an Egyptian scribe, who was a very close friend of Moses. Here is how Tek-Sek reports the same Biblical conversation:

> **"But the Lord said [to Moses], go to Pharaoh and tell him that I wish you to lead forth this people, and surely will I also lead you in the wilderness. Then said I: but the people will not listen to me. I have not the *tongue with which to speak the Israelite words*, for I was raised in the court of Egypt.**
>
> **Aaron shall speak. He speaks the tongue of the people. You will have the words for Pharaoh, for you are of Egypt. My Spirit will be upon you both until this thing be done."[33]**

I also found further evidence proving that the Spirit who spoke with Moses had Egyptian ancestry.

---

[33] Roberts, Ursula. *I Knew Moses*. London: Psychic Press Ltd., 1973. p. 98.

> **It is claimed by some writers that the Lord Jehovah of the Hebrews was the spirit of an Egyptian priest and King of Salem.... Jehovah was the Spirit of an Egyptian...**[34]
>
> **He is referred to in the "Egyptian Book of the Dead," as Gehokah, and existed long before Moses.**[35]

As their dialogue continues, the Spirit tries to convince Moses to become his medium. Spirit would tell Moses clairaudiently what to say, and Moses would repeat what he was hearing to the Pharaoh or the Hebrews.

Here is the Bible passage:

> **The Lord said to him, "Who gave man his mouth? Who makes him deaf or mute? Who gives him sight or makes him blind? Is it not I, the Lord? Now go; I will help you speak and will teach you what to say." But Moses said, "O Lord, please send someone else to do it."**[36]

Again, my scribe, so many people on your planet have been mislead by their religious leaders. According to your religion, who was this God? Was it the same entity who created the universe, the animals, men and women, and caused the great flood?

According to the Bible the answer would be, "Yes."

If that is the case, my scribe, why would God need Moses to be his messenger to Pharaoh? God appeared to Moses[37] and Abraham[38]. Therefore, God, himself should be able to appear to Pharaoh, and demand the Hebrews' freedom. Why would God need a middleman? Why not simply "do the job" himself? Why didn't God create a booming voice that would have been heard throughout the land of Egypt? If God created the planets, the universe, and a forty-day flood, then couldn't he create a wondrous spectacle that would have scared the robe off of Pharaoh? To placate this mighty God, Pharaoh would have instantly freed the Hebrews. So, why did this omnipotent God try to coerce Moses to become his spokesperson? Why would the creator of the universe need a measly little human to be his messenger?

I never thought about this. I can't answer your questions.

---

[34] E. W., Rev. *All the Spiritualism of the Christian Bible: and the Scripture Directly Opposing It*. Detroit, MI: (Self-publshed), 1922. p. 14-15.

[35] Hull, Moses. *Encyclopedia of Biblical Spiritualism. Vol. 1*. Cassadaga, FL: National Spiritualist Association of Churches, 1962. p. 155.

[36] Exodus 4:11-13 [NIV].

[37] Exodus 3:2-6.

[38] Genesis 26:24.

(😇) There is a reason you cannot answer my questions, my scribe. It was *not* the Almighty God who created the universe, who spoke to Moses from the burning bush. The Spirit person speaking to Moses was another Moses, who lived in my dimension. Yes, the Moses on this side was an enlightened entity, but not as enlightened, or advanced as the entity who created the universe. When you read in your Book of Books, about the conversation that took place at the burning bush,[39] you will come to realize that it was Moses speaking to his ***Spirit Control***.

Let me describe to you the belief held by most Christians and Jews. God Almighty is an ancient old man, who sits on his bejeweled golden throne, with a marvelous golden crown, on a cloud somewhere. He was extremely talented and creative, and enjoyed impersonating a film director. One day he snaps his fingers, and yells "Lights, action, cameras!" This caused a big bang, and the universe began. Suddenly, lights, planets, oceans, land, animals, plants, and humans were all created. You have to admit, my scribe, this would be an extremely powerful entity. Yet, this omnipotent, omnipresent God, who had the power to create the universe, needs Moses to speak for him?

Moses complains that he is not up for the job, for he has abandonment issues, and problems with self-confidence and self-esteem. This powerful God becomes angry, yet he submits to (an insignificant human) Moses' demands. He compromises and allows Aaron to assist Moses when speaking with pharaoh and the Hebrews.

Use your brain, my scribe. If this were Almighty God, the creator of the universe, he truly would be all-powerful. All he would have to do was reach out and touch Moses on his lips (similar to the depiction on the ceiling of the Vatican's Sistine Chapel, of God touching Adam). Instantaneously, Moses' speech impediment would be healed. He would have been energized, his self-esteem would be operating 1000%, and Moses would have charged out of Midian on an express camel to Egypt.

(🙂) Awan, aren't you being a bit irreverent?

(😇) My scribe, I need to wake people up, and make them think. I will use whatever tools are at my disposal. Unfortunately, I am not the omnipotent God. I cannot create a booming voice to be heard all over the world. I cannot make all the alarm clocks and bell towers ring to make people use what few brain cells they have. Humanity has been so programmed to think only in one particular way, that when some enlightened entity comes along and presents a logical argument that is constructed along another path of thinking, it shocks many people. However, it also causes people to think in other directions, even if it is only for a brief moment. Again, my scribe, I am here to wage war on fear, ignorance, and superstition. I want every person who reads this book to engage his or her brain, to think, and ask him or herself this question. Why is only 10% of my brain working? Is the other 90% stuffing, so

---

[39] Exodus 3:2-4:17.

my brain will not rattle around in my skull? A little shock value or irreverence, as you might term it, can go a long way to accomplish this goal.

🧑 I guess I understand your point.

😇 If the entity who spoke with Moses were God Almighty, as you have been led to believe, then why didn't God Almighty, with his omnipotent power, make the changes in Moses, to enable him to speak perfectly, so that he could talk directly to the people, instead of instructing Moses to use Aaron as his spokesperson? If he was the creator of all, why didn't he create Moses perfectly, since he planned Moses' destiny to be an instrument of the Spirit?

Now think about this, my scribe, isn't it unusual that a mortal man would win an argument with the creator of the universe? Moses was to get his wish of not to become the primary spokesman, when God agreed to let Aaron be Moses' spokesman. The Creator of the Universe could have struck Moses dead for defying him, just as he killed all the people by drowning them during the flood in Noah's time. Why would an omnipotent God tolerate an impudent argument from a mere human, that he had created?

📖 The Bible reads:

> **Then the Lord's anger burned against Moses and he said, "What about your brother, Aaron the Levite? I know he can speak well. He is already on his way to meet you, and his heart will be glad when he sees you. You shall speak to him and put words in his mouth; I will help both of you speak and will teach you what to do."**[40]

😇 Spirit was desperate to convince Moses to be the medium. As you are well aware, my scribe, not everyone is blessed with the *Gifts of the Spirit*. The Pharaoh was not psychically gifted; he did not have clairvoyant vision. So the Spirit could not appear to Pharaoh, as he appeared to Moses.

The Spirit entity speaking to Moses was also unable to materialize and speak directly to Pharaoh. To be able to materialize, a Spirit entity would need to extract ectoplasm from the physical body of a medium. Materialization can only take place under certain conditions. The conditions at the Egyptian court would have been far too negative for a Spirit materialization to take place. Therefore, both materialization, and direct voice (Spirit directly speaking to humans) were out of the question. Consequently, the *gift of clairaudience* was the only method the Spirit could use to get his message to Pharaoh. Clairaudience requires a medium.

🧑 It sure makes sense to me.

---

[40] Exodus 4:14-15 [NIV].

🧝 Now my scribe, you have heard my medium teach the people who attend his church services, that the knowledge of psychic science enhances one's understanding of the Bible.

👤 Yes, Awan, he often says that.

🧝 I would love to know how the Jews and Christians who believe that Moses is speaking with God Almighty explain the next verse of your book of books, in which Moses is called God?

📖 This is the verse Awan is discussing:

EXODUS CHAPTER 4 VERSE 16

GRT	1540	And he shall be thy spokesman unto the people: he also shall be thy mouth and **thou shalt be his God**.
CCB	1995	Aaron will speak for you as a prophet speaks for his god.
KENT	1921	act as your spokesman to the people.
SMGO	1939	act the part of God to him.
ARTB	2008	are as God to him.
NIV	1978	as if you were God to him.
HAAK	1657	be a God to him
ARATO	1987	be a leader for him.
HRB	2009	be a Mighty One (Elohim) for him.
BATE	1773	be Aleim to him;
LIV	1971	be as God to him, telling him what to say.
JER	1966	be as the God inspiring him.
UTV	2001	be Elohim to him.
ANCR	1999	be for him as Deity.
ARATN	1987	be for him as one seeking instruction from before the Lord.
BREN	1844	be for him in things pertaining to God.
ALTER	2004	be for him like a god.
TYND	1530	be his God.
LIVT	1981	be his guide.
STONE	1996	be his leader.
HTETT	2009	be his leader.
KNOX	1944	be his representative with God.
ARATJ	1987	be his teacher (who) seeks instruction from before the Lord.
SWHI	2012	be like an Elohim to him.
TEV	1976	be like God, telling him what to say.
NEB	1976	be the god he speaks for.
AEB	2001	be the things of God to him.
ETHO	1862	be thy interpreter.
RAY	1799	be thy speaker to the people.
GLAZ	1935	be to him as a chief.
SSBE	1981	be to him as Elohim.

GEN60	1560	be to him as God.
THOM	1808	be to him as the Oracle of God.
NIBEV	2008	be to him as Yahweh.
JPS1	1917	be to him in God's stead.
FENT	1922	be to him in place of Divine Messengers.
HSTV	2003	be to him in place of the Gods.
STERN	1933	be to him instead of chief.
HLYNB	1963	be to him instead of Elohim.
BISH	1568	be to him instead of God.
CEKJV	2004	be to him instead of the mighty one.
YS	2010	be to him instead of YAHWEH.
KEN	1860	be to him on the part of God.
APB	2007	be to him the things for God.
NETS	2007	be to him the things pertaining to God.
HIRS	1989	be unto him as a Lord.
JB2000	2000	be unto him as God.
GRANT	1899	be unto him instead of God.
BELL	1818	be with him before God.
CPDV	2008	be with him in those things that pertain to God.
ETR	1987	be your official speaker.
FRIED	2003	become a god for him!
ROSN	1977	become to him as Elohim.
ROTH	1897	become to him as God.
EPBT	1994	become to him in the stead of Elohim:
MESS	2002	decide what comes out of it.
BYIN	1972	have you for God.
OTFTS	2008	help him with regard to the things of God.
NWT	1961	serve as God to him.
ARAON	1990	serve him as a teacher.
MOFF	1922	shall inspire him.
CB	2010	stand in relation to him as I stand to you.
MODL	1945	take the part of God.
YNG	1863	thou art to him for God.
ISV	1998	to act in the role of God for him.
ETHJ	1862	unto him the principal, seeking instruction from before the Lord.
TANK	1985	with you playing the role of God to him.
CLEAR	2000	you can tell him what I want said.
EEBT	2003	You will be like God to him. You will tell Aaron what to say.
ICB	1986	You will tell him what God says. And he will speak for you

69 Differing Translations

My Second Encounter With An Angel

(👼) People who believe this conversation is between Moses and God Almighty have a major problem on their hands. How can a mortal man be a God? What powers could one man possess that would make him a God to another? Later, in your Book of Books, one of The Ten Commandments states:

Thou shalt have no other gods before me.[41]

Wasn't "the Lord" elevating Moses to be Aaron's God? Would not Aaron be violating this commandment? My scribe, can you see how this verse becomes impossible to understand, without knowledge of psychic science?

(🧑) I understand your point, Awan. Now please explain the verse with your psychic knowledge.

(👼) It is most simple my scribe. The Spirit was making an analogy. First, let us clearly understand what was to happen. The Spirit Moses would clairaudiently speak to the medium Moses, who would repeat the words to his brother, Aaron, who would repeat them to the Pharaoh, or the Hebrew people.

(🧑) I clearly understand that, Awan.

(👼) Did Moses know which words were correct words to say to Pharaoh?

(🧑) No, Moses heard the Spirit's words, and repeated them to Aaron.

(👼) And your Book of Books calls that Spirit, *God* or *the Lord*.

(🧑) Yes, Awan.

(👼) Did Aaron know which words were correct words to say to Pharaoh?

---

[41] Exodus 20:3 [KJV].

👤 No, Aaron would hear Moses' words, and repeat them Pharaoh. Oh, now I understand. Moses would be Aaron's God because Moses was acting as the source of the information that Aaron would repeat.

😇 Precisely, my scribe. This analogy rests on a clear understanding of mediumship. In Biblical language the prophet delivers the words of God. In psychic language the medium delivers the words of the Spirit. The words are interchangeable when you understand psychic science. Those ignorant of the *Gifts of the Spirit* become stuck in a theological quagmire.

👤 I clearly understand that now.

😇 Now, let us return to your holiday of Passover. As I listened to you recite your *Haggadah*, don't you find it rather strange that the story of Moses' encounter with God at the burning bush is conspicuously absent from the *Haggadah*? Would the Hebrews had gained their freedom from the Egyptians without this conversation?

👤 It is my opinion that they would not have.

📖 There is irony in the fact the *Haggadah* ignores the protagonist of the Jewish exodus, while the Bible applauds the prophet who led the disgruntled Hebrews, acknowledging his mediumship.

> **And there arose not a prophet since in Israel like unto Moses, whom the Lord knew face to face, In all the signs and the wonders, which the Lord sent him to do in the land of Egypt to Pharaoh, and to all his servants, and to all his land, and in all that mighty hand, and in all the great terror which Moses shewed in the sight of all Israel.[42]**

😇 As you read the *Hagaddah*, I heard you mention many Biblical people. Do you remember who they were?

👤 Well, since most of the *Seder* is recited in Hebrew, I do not understand everything that is said.

😇 I was very surprised by the list which included the following: Abraham, Isaac, Jacob, Esau, Laban, David, Jesse, Aaron, Abimelech, Elijah, Daniel, Haman, and Esther. Did you notice anyone in particular that was *not* mentioned?

📖 After this dialogue, I reread the English translation of the *Hagaddah*. Throughout the *Haggadah*, much of the Hebrews' history is told. Many people—rabbis, Jewish heroes, and even enemies, are mentioned (see chart). I found that Moses' name is only mentioned once during the *Seder*, and in an indirect reference!

---

[42] Deuteronomy 34:10-12 [KJV].

"And Israel saw the strong hand which the Eternal had shown against Egypt, and the people revered the Eternal and believed in the Eternal and His servant Moses."[43]

Jewish Heroes[44]	
Name	**Number of times in Haggadah**
Jacob	9
Abraham	8
Joseph	3
David	3
Laban	3
Isaac	3
Daniel	2
Aaron	2
Esther	1
Ahasuerus	1
Jesse	1
Elijah	1
Moses	1
Esau	1
Nahor	1
Terah	1
Joshua	1
Enemies	
Pharaoh	8
Haman	2
King Belshazzar	1
Sisra	1
Og king of Bashan	1
Shion, king of Amorites	1
Rabbis	
Eliezer	3
Akiba	2
Gamliel	1
Jose	1
Ben Zoma	1
Tarfon	1
Elazar	1
Joshua	1

---

[43] Goldberg, Nathan, Rabbi. *Passover Haggadah: A New English Translation and Instructions for the Seder*. NY: Ktav Publishing House, Inc. 1966. p. 18.

[44] Goldberg, Nathan, Rabbi. *Passover Haggadah: A New English Translation and Instructions for the Seder*. NY: Ktav Publishing House, Inc. 1966.

Awan's complaint is still valid. Moses was the central character who facilitated the Hebrew's exodus. Yet, this is the only mention of Moses' name during the entire retelling of the exodus.

🧑 Now that you mention it, Moses' name was hardly mentioned.

😇 What is your opinion of that?

🧑 It seems very strange to me. Moses was essential to the liberation of the Hebrews. He was the medium who heard Spirit's voice. After the Hebrew's liberation, he delivered God's instructions to the people. Yet, they mention Haman, who was an enemy of the Jews. Both Haman and Esther had nothing to do with the holiday of Passover, but were the central characters to the celebration of Purim, another Jewish holiday.

😇 I was totally shocked that the writers of your *Haggadah* chose to omit Moses from their story. Your people would still be in Egypt if it hadn't been for Moses. Why do you think the writers did that?

🧑 I really don't know.

😇 I am surprised my scribe, I thought you would have picked up on it by now. I can tell you the answer. Do you want an accurate answer, or the one the rabbis would tell you?

🧑 Actually, I would like to know both.

😇 Your rabbis would say that the reason Moses is omitted from the *Haggadah* is that the Jews did not want to create another savior.

📖 After this dialogue, I found corroborating evidence for this statement.

> **... the Rabbis who put together the traditional Haggadah were careful not to include Moses in the retelling. They did not want people to worship him.**[45]

🧑 I don't understand.

😇 Your *Haggadah* was written after Jesus came to the world. Many Jews thought that Jesus was הַמָשִׁיחַ *Ha-maw-shee'-akh* (the *Messiah*) who would save them from Roman domination. These Jews veered away from Judaism, and became the first Christians. The Rabbis didn't want another savior to cause another group to splinter away from Judaism. Therefore, they wrote that God, himself, was the savior of the Jewish people. They banished Moses from the *Haggadah*'s account of the Exodus, by totally ommitting his name. As a result, you hardly mention Moses' name during your celebration of the *Seder*.

---

[45] Goldin, Barbara Diamond. *The Passover Journey: a Seder Companion.* NY: Viking, 1994. p. 34.

📖 Later, I discovered Awan was again accurate with his historical facts. The *Haggadah* was written after Jesus had lived.

> **It is evident, then that at the time of the completion of the Mishnah (200 C. E.) the Haggadah already had a fairly fixed form.**[46] [C. E. is the Jewish equivalent of A. D.]

📖 I found it fascinating, however, that the *Haggadah* mentions most of the characters involved with the holiday of Purim (Esther, Ahasuerus, and Haman). It is so ironic that the rabbis were hesitant to honor Moses at the *Seder*, but have no qualms about considering Queen Esther as a "savior for her people," when celebrating the holiday of Purim. Was the reason for a lack of concern the fact that Esther was a woman, or that **she did not have any of the** *Gifts of the Spirit*?

📖 I decided to reread the *Haggadah* to see the exact wording of the passage Awan had discussed.

> **And the Eternal brought us from Egypt: not by means of an angel, nor by means of a Seraph, nor by means of a messenger; but the most Holy [God].**[47]

📖 A few months later, I also discovered a similar quote in the Bible:

> **And the Lord brought us forth out of Egypt with a mighty hand, and with an outstretched arm, and with great terribleness, and with signs, and with wonders.**[48]

📖 Both these quotes make it very clear that God was responsible for the liberation of the Hebrews. When it reads: *"nor by means of a messenger,"* (which is another term for a ***prophet***) it implicitly states that Moses had nothing to do with the Hebrews redemption from Egypt. God is getting all the credit. Yet, it was Moses who suffered years of aggravation and grief, as the Hebrews bitterly complained to him, about food and water.[49] Frequently, they said they would have been better off as slaves in Egypt, rather than wandering in the desert.[50]

👤 So what is the accurate reason?

---

[46] "Haggadah, Passover" *The Universal Jewish Encyclopedia*. Landman, Isaac., ed. Vol. 5. NY: Universal Jewish Encyclopedia Co., 1941.

[47] *Passover Haggadah: DeLuxe Edition*. General Foods Corporation, 1965. p. 17.

[48] Deuteronomy 26:8 [KJV].

[49] Exodus 17:3.

[50] Exodus 16:3.

(👤) The real reason has to do with the conflict between the priests and the prophets.[51] The *Haggadah* ignores the mediumship of Moses, (the role prophet played in the exodus story) while emphasizing Aaron and the priesthood. Aaron's name is mentioned several times in the *Haggadah*, as well as the priests and the Temple in Jerusalem.

📖 I found the passages to which Awan referred.

> **Passover offering which our fathers ate in the *Temple* days, what was the reason for it?[52]**

> **Eternal our God, have mercy on Israel Your people, on Jerusalem your city and Zion the dwelling place of Your glory on the royal house of David Your anointed, and on *the great and holy Temple* called by Your Name.[53]**

(👤) Do you remember as you read your *Haggadah* the prayers asking God to restore his holy Temple in Jerusalem? Do you remember that Aaron's name was mention three or four times in your *Haggadah*?

📖 These were the prayers Awan mentioned.

> **May it be thy will, O Eternal, our God, and the God of our ancestors, speedily to rebuild thy holy temple in our days, and grant us our share in thy Law.[54]**

The lyrics of אַדִּיר הוּא *a-deer hu*, an upbeat concluding hymn of the *Seder* declares the Jewish longing for the restoration of the Temple in Jerusalem. It was at this temple that the priests had the central role in Judaism, and ate the sacrificial meat of the animals that were offered to God.[55]

> **God is Mighty! May He soon rebuild His Temple. Speedily, speedily, in our days soon.[56]**

---

[51] A full discussion of the "Conflict between the Priests and Mediums" can be found in: Schwartz, Sidney. *My First Encounter with an Angel: Revelations of Ancient Wisdom*. Blue Hill, ME: Medicine Bear Publishing, 1999. p. 145-170.

[52] Goldberg, Nathan, Rabbi. *Passover Haggadah: A New English Translation and Instructions for the Seder*. NY: Ktav Publishing House, Inc. 1966. p. 21.

[53] Goldberg, Nathan, Rabbi. *Passover Haggadah: A New English Translation and Instructions for the Seder*. NY: Ktav Publishing House, Inc. 1966. p. 29.

[54] *Passover Haggadah: DeLuxe Edition*. General Foods Corporation, 1965. p. 57.

[55] Leviticus 6: 15-16.

[56] Goldberg, Nathan, Rabbi. *Passover Haggadah: A New English Translation and Instructions for the Seder*. NY:

My Second Encounter With An Angel

To shift the focus away from the mediumship of Moses, the *Haggadah* repeatedly emphasizes that God was responsible for the Exodus. This quote from the *Haggadah* says:

Then Adonai [God] took us out of Mitzrayim [Egypt] Not by an angel. Nor by a seraph. Nor by a messenger. Rather, the Holy One Himself.

Yes, I do remember that.

Did you not find it curious that your *Haggadah* is totally silent about the mediumship of Moses? They do not even mention Moses' name, yet they yearn for Aaron and the temple, where the daily sacrifices kept the priesthood fed with the best of foods?

It did not occur to me.

Do you remember how you felt when the Passover meal was completed?

Yes, Awan, I was stuffed. I usually don't eat that much at one meal.

The priests had a Passover meal three times a day. There was so much food that they continually gorged themselves on free food. No wonder the priests who wrote your *Haggadah* have you long for the restoration of the temple. With a new temple, the priesthood would revive their system of daily sacrifices, and their unlimited supply of free food. Perhaps now you can understand why your *Haggadah* is silent about Moses' mediumship?

Now I understand your point.

If mediumship were so irrelevant, then why did God need the help of the prophet, Moses, as recorded in chapters 3-4 of the Bible's book of Exodus? Why did God insist that Moses tell Pharaoh to release the Hebrew slaves? If mediumship were unnecessary, why didn't God just create a booming voice, and deliver the message to Pharaoh Himself? If God is the all-powerful creator of the universe, why didn't he touch Moses on the mouth and heal his stammering? Why did God concede to Moses, and allow Aaron to speak for Moses? The entity speaking from the burning bush was not the all-powerful creator of the universe; but rather was a highly evolved Spirit. Therefore, the "God"/Spirit required a prophet/medium to be his spokesperson.

Not only did Moses have to deliver God's / Spirit's message, but he had to lead the people out of Egypt. Moses was the one in communication with Spirit. Throughout their 40-year journey the Hebrews complained about their food, water, and living conditions. Moses had all the aggravation in dealing with their complaints.[57] Moses' reward for his endless dedication in serving as the bridge between the two dimensions; is being totally ignored during the

---

Ktav Publishing House, Inc. 1966. p. 44.

[57] Exodus 17:2-4.

annual retelling of the Passover story. From my point of view, there would have been no Exodus without Moses, the prophet/medium.

There is now a shift in the energy, so I must leave you at this time. It has been my pleasure to dialogue with you this fine day, my scribe. My peace be with you.

Thank you so much, Awan, this conversation has been most enlightening. Peace be with you, too.

As Awan vacated, Carl's body shook, a bit stronger than usual. Carl did not move for quite some time. Eventually he opened his eyes, and I handed him a glass of water, which he eagerly drank. Carl's energy was so depleted, that he did not get up from his chair for at least ten minutes. He then went directly to bed, and took a three- hour nap.

FIVE

2. The Secrets of the Unused Brain

This trance session also took place in Carl's office. Carl sat in his chair, with the lights dimmed. He closed his eyes, and said his prayer. His breathing became rhythmic and he began to snore. There was a short, loud intake of breath, and two sudden jolts in his body. Fifteen seconds later, Awan began to speak.

My profound greetings to you, my scribe.

Greetings, Awan.

I can tell from your auric field that you are beginning to absorb what I taught you about the soul.

I have been working at it, Awan.

2. The Secrets of the Unused Brain.

You are now ready for to learn the second important key. However, first, I need to clear up a misunderstanding that you have. The scientists of your world are as rigid and dogmatic as your theologians. If scientists cannot see, measure, touch, or sense something—it does not exist. Hence, they will not believe anything that does not comply with the rules they have created.

Your scientists have misled you about the way you view the brain. They have not intentionally lied to you. They have not told you the truth because they literally cannot *see* the truth. Scientists taught you that the brain is responsible for thought and maintaining the functioning of the body. This is not the case. Thoughts are energy, therefore, thoughts comes from the great invisible energy center of your body—*your soul*. Unless a person has clairvoyant vision; the soul is not visible. Since none of your scientists have second sight, they cannot see the soul. The soul, *not* the brain, stores a person's memories. The brain is simply a complex receiver.

Let us make a comparison with the picture box you term *television*. On this very day that we are speaking, some people have placed what you term a dish on their house. This dish is a receiver of electronic waves. Thousands of miles away, pictures created in a television studio are converted into signals that are beamed into outer space. A satellite captures these waves and bounces them back to your planet. That dish captures the signals that originated thousands of miles away, and sends them to your television where they are converted, as we spoke of before, so that you can see them.

In the beginning, the Spirit of God [deep thought] hovered over the entire universe. There came a time in its evolution that it turned in on itself, as I explained previously, contemplated itself, and caused a great explosion, which your scientists term *"the big bang."* Thought was the driving force of the universe's creation. Thought is eternally surrounding you. Every invention that a human has ever, or will ever, create was originally a thought that was *first* conceived in my dimension.

There is a *river of thought*. It contains all the thoughts and wisdom of the entire universe. It lies very close to all of you, yet so very few of you expand your consciousness to access it. A few exceptional people, who were considered geniuses, Albert Einstein, and Thomas Edison, expanded their consciousness, and received information from the *river of thought*. Because the *river of thought* is invisible, most of you are unaware of it. The brain was designed to receive information from the *river of thought*. It is the soul, however, where thought is processed and recorded for all time.

Awan, I don't understand. Where exactly is this *river of thought*?

If you could place your hands on either side of your head, and move them approximately thirteen inches away from your head, you would find the *river of thought*. Everything that ever was, and ever will be is in the *river of thought*. Since thought is energy, it can never be destroyed. In your present time, most people living on your planet were not taught to expand their mind or consciousness to tap into this *river of thought*. Your religions have taught you there are devils, demons and darkness in the unseen side of life. This has programmed fear into the cells of your body, mind and soul. This fear prevents you from reaching out into the *river of thought*.

Two thousand years ago, when Jesus was on your planet, he taught:

"Ask, and it shall be given you: seek, and ye shall find: knock, and it shall be opened unto you."[58]

When you have a thought or a question, your soul picks it up and it goes out into the light field around your body. Your body is a transmitter, and it transmits the thought that you are contemplating. Your soul is the core of the transmitter. Your soul picks up your thought, and transmits it out into your auric light. If your aura touches the *river of thought*, the thought is transmited and eventually, or sometimes instantly, you will receive an answer. In other words, you receive the answer for the question you were asking. The soul is the transmitter while the brain is the receiver.

I think I am beginning to understand.

Good! It is also important for you to understand this next concept. The *energy* behind the thoughts and words causes the soul to pick up, record, and store these thoughts. The energy of the thought combines with the energy of the soul. Therefore, the soul is like a combination of video recorder and

---

[58] Matthew 7:7 [KJV].

computer. It continually records all events of a person's life, and the interactions with other people. Yet, like a computer, it also has programmable memory. It is the soul's memory that often causes you problems in your physical life. If a parent chastises a child, or if other children taunt a child, these negative experiences are recorded in the child's soul. The person will often be reacting to this event throughout his or her entire life. Often if someone undergoes a very traumatic experience, it is vividly recorded in the soul.

You must remember that the soul is the *modus operandi* of the body. The soul's energy is what animates the body. It is what keeps the physical body alive. Many people confuse the characteristics of the soul with the brain's characteristics. It is the soul, not the brain, that is responsible for keeping the body functioning, your heart beating, and your lungs breathing, even while you sleep. Think about this. Since the soul is energy, it needs no rest, and can keep working while the body sleeps and repairs itself. Have you ever been mentally tired?

Yes, I tend to get silly, and then I just want to totally collapse.

So if you are mentally tired, doesn't that mean your brain is tired and needs to rest? The brain is a physical structure of the body, made up of cells. It requires rest just as the muscles of your body do. How could your brain, a physical part of your body, remain vigilant, keeping your body functioning without rest for 80, 90, or 100+ years? You can't stay awake for 100+ years without sleep. Since the soul is energy, it needs no rest. The soul controls all the metabolic functions of the body. It keeps the heart beating, and your body breathing even while you are asleep.

It is difficult for me to believe that the soul controls the body, rather than the brain. Does the soul control all our automatic processes, such as breathing, digesting, and eliminating?

That is correct. Let's discuss the body's natural elimination process. After the stomach has digested all the food, it goes into the intestines. After the intestines absorbed all the nutrients from the food, a message is sent to the soul. The soul informs the brain, and then it would be what you term, "a call of nature." You would have to go and eliminate, or as you say in your terms "go to the bathroom." It is controlled by the soul.

The scientists think that the brain is responsible for signaling elimination. You just said that the soul has to trigger the brain, therefore, how could the brain be responsible for controlling elimination?

When I just used the word brain; I was referring to the entire electrical system of the body. I was not referring to the top of your head where all the gray matter is. Your brain is the receiver of thoughts. Thought comes into your light field, or aura that is around the body.

Most of you listen to your wave-box (radio), as you travel in your auto-machines. If someone removes the antenna from your auto-machine, you are no longer able to hear your radio-waves. The antenna acts as the receiver that picks up the waves of which you are so fond. Your aura, or light field is similar to that antenna. When your aura expands, it becomes the antenna that picks up thoughts from the *river of thought*, and it feeds them to the brain. So the brain is the receiver of thought, just as your radio is the receiver of the radio-signals from the antenna.

I want you to clearly understand, my scribe, for centuries the people who are living on your planet have been steeped in ignorance. I am well aware that your civilization considers itself very advanced and highly intelligent. However, 21st century people would seem quite backward compared to the ancient people who once lived on your planet.

Why is that?

The people who are living on your planet, today, are only using 10% of their brain capacity. The most brilliant, intelligent people on your planet only use 33% of their brain. In all humans at least 2/3 of the brain is shut down. It is not dead but is dormant. It was put to sleep, centuries ago, and genetically it has remained asleep through the centuries.

What do you mean? I don't understand what you are saying.

There was a time, eons ago, when all people used 100% of their brain capacity. These people utilized the *Gifts of the Spirit*. It was as natural to them as breathing. It was not something unique or foreign to these ancient people, as it is for you today. You must realize if you used 100% of your brain, you could ulitize all the *Gifts of the Spirit*, and you would have abilities to do things that are currently unimaginable to you.

Let me give you an example. You are working with limited brain capacity. Even though you have been to university, and received a good education, you are still limited as to what you can do. Despite your education, less than 1/3 of your brain is working. Visualize for a moment, if your entire brain were operating, you would not see things in a limited fashion. You would see things unlimited. You could see into the past and future, and would know all things. The 2/3 of the brain that is shut down was intended for processing the *Gifts of the Spirit*. Do you understand?

That is not clear to me, Awan. Please explain it further.

All right. Let us talk about your eyesight. Please explain to me how that works?

Well, light is reflected from an object and it goes into the eyes. This light is focused through the eye's lens and the image falls on the retina. That image is converted to electrical signals, which travel through the optic nerve to the brain. Once it arrives in the brain its signals are interpreted, so you process and understand what you are seeing.

Basically, that is correct. Now what part in the brain receives these signals?

Awan, I really don't know.

(😇) The visual center is situated in the cuneus of the occipital lobe.

(🧑) Where is that?

(😇) It is in the back of your head. However, what is important is that you understand that electrical impulses from the eye travel along the optic nerve to a very specific center of the brain, which is in charge of interpreting what you see.

(🧑) Yes, that is correct, Awan.

(😇) The same is true for your sense of hearing, tasting, smelling, and feeling. They all go to the specific center for that particular sense.

(🧑) Yes, I understand that.

(😇) The specific brain centers which process the *Gifts of the Spirit* are located in the 2/3 of the brain that is dormant in most people. Let us talk about the *gift of clairaudience*, the ability to hear Spirits' voices. Put your hands behind your ears and feel the bumps where the bone protrudes. The center for clairaudience resides in your brain underneath that protrusion. Each gift has a specific center of the brain, just as there are specific centers for your other senses. All those centers for the *Gifts of the Spirit* are located in the 2/3 of the brain that is asleep.

(🧑) I am beginning to understand. Since those centers are asleep, and not functioning, people are not clairaudient, or clairvoyant.

(😇) That is correct. Now in ancient times, all people were clairvoyant, since 100% of their brains were functioning. They could see the aura's light, the light of God, emanating from each person's soul. They understood that their souls were energy, the same energy that is God. Since everyone had God within them, everyone was equal.

They were people who respected and cared for each other, and were not competitive, warring people. No human would ever think of lifting his or her hand to harm another, because every human could see the light of God around everyone else. How could one God hurt another God? Therefore, these ancient people treated everyone equally. They did not think that men were superior to women, or that people with one skin tone had more rights than another. They understood that God was within everyone, and that everyone was completely equal.

These people were very brilliant because one hundred percent of their brains were actively functioning. According to your history books, people back in ancient times were savages. How could a savage person with the intelligence equivalent to some of your animals, create the pyramid at Giza? How could savages build their ancient cities, where stones were cut and placed in such a way that you cannot even slip a piece of papyrus between them? How could a savage cut rock at an acute angle, and make such intricately carved stones to place into their temples that you find at Chichen Itza, Uxmal, and other Mayan sites? Your present day scientists and scholars do not understand how this was accomplished, nor can they provide you with the technology to duplicate these ancient structures.

Your soul/Spirit is divine, ever-lasting energy, which means it is immortal. It matters not if you live your life as a saint or sinner, your soul will live on after you die. It has to because the Soul is energy—and this energy is the essence of God. As a person communicates with his or her God, their aura or light field expands. When it expands far enough it touches the *river of thought*. It is then this person has access to all the knowledge in the universe.

Now you should understand, my scribe, what made these ancient people so advanced. The ancients built the pyramids to remind all the people of the future that God was within and your soul is immortal.

How did pyramids accomplish that? I don't understand.

You need to do some research to discover the meaning of the word, *pyramid*. You will learn that it means, *fire in the middle*.

After this trance was over, I found a definition of the word pyramid. Our English word *pyramid* comes from the Greek word *pyro*, which means *fire or heat*. The Greek word *mesos* means *at or near the middle. Pyramid means fire in the middle*.[59]

If you look at a diagram of the great pyramid at Giza, you will discover that 1/3 from the top capstone, or 2/3 up from the base is the King's Chamber. Now if you **sit** in lotus fashion with your legs crossed, you would be in a triangular shape. Measure 1/3 from the top of your head, or 2/3 from the floor and you would be at the center of the chest, the location of the soul. Even the pyramids built on your side of the globe, in what you term the Yucatan Peninsula, were built for the same reason. There are openings about 1/3 down from the top. These great civilizations wanted to speak to all the people who would live on the planet, and remind them of where God is located. God is within; it is your soul located 1/3 down your body, behind the breast bone, in the middle of your chest. (See diagram on p. 322).

Awan, I always wondered how the pyramids were built.

The ancient people built the pyramids by using thought. They employed a tool, very similar to your laser light to cut the stones, into straight-sided blocks. It was as easy as you would cut butter with a hot knife. Next, they moved those stones, with their minds.

Awan, that sounds preposterous! How could people move a block of stone that weighed tons with their minds?

Through mental concentration, the ancients made the molecules of the stones move faster. Once these molecules moved at a certain speed, the molecules of the stones were no longer affected by gravity. Therefore, the stones levitated into the air, then these blocks of stone would be like large

---

[59] Akins, W. R. *The Secret Power of the Pyramids.* NY: Franklin Watts, 1980. p. 53.

blocks of Styrofoam. The ancients simply maneuvered these stones with their minds, deliberately positioning each one.

🧑 This is very difficult to believe.

😇 I do not understand why you feel that way my scribe. Tell me, if you held the glass of water that is sitting on my medium's desk, and turned it upside down what would happen?

🧑 The water would spill all over the desk.

😇 Why?

🧑 The gravitational pull of the earth would pull the water droplets towards the earth, and the water would land on the desk.

😇 Precisely, my scribe. Now what would happen, if I asked you take the water in that glass, and pour it into a pot, heat the pot on the stove?

🧑 The water would get hot.

😇 And wouldn't the water turn into steam?

🧑 Yes, Awan.

😇 And could you take that steam, and pour it over this desk?

🧑 No Awan, that is impossible.

😇 Correct, my scribe. The ancient people could levitate stone as easily as you can boil water. It is even the same process. As you heat the water, the molecules began to move faster. At a certain point, the molecules are moving so fast that they are not longer affected by the gravitational pull of the earth. You say that it "has changed its state, and has become a gas called steam." Nevertheless, gravity no longer affects these molecules.

📖 One day, months after this session, I found this quotation, which confirmed that the Egyptians could levitate objects.

> **The Hermetic books themselves are not specifically magic books, though they do contain a section detailing how the ancient Egyptians were able to make spirits move the statues of their gods.**[60]

😇 Cough, cough.

🧑 Would you like some water?

😇 It will be necessary, because the medium is not yet prepared for the energy that we are using. [*Awan drinks some water. Pause.*] I am going to pull away and let someone else use the instrument. The body is starting to sweat, as you would term it, because it was not totally prepared for the energy that

---

[60] Cohen, Daniel. *Dealing with the Devil*. NY: Dodd, Mead & Company, 1979. p. 23.

is being used.

🙂 OK

🙂 Well, a jolly good evening to you.

🙂 Good evening, Nathaniel.

Nathaniel is a Spirit who often spoke through Carl when he was in trance. He lived his last life in Great Britain, and therefore the greeting of "A jolly good evening" was always said in a thick British accent. The accent was not used during the rest of the conversation. Nathaniel's flamboyant personality always made for colorful conversations.

🙂 It is always a pleasure that I am able to touch back with you. I did not think that I would be able to step in, and take over "center stage," with such a great and powerful teacher who was coming through.

🙂 Would you like some more water, Nathaniel?

🙂 I think that the instrument is all right at the moment. We are not sure that the body can take the energy that is going to be necessary.

🙂 Is there anything that I can do to help?

🙂 No, there is nothing that you can do. The body is being gradually attuned to a higher vibration. As you probably realize, it takes more energy to adjust the medium's body to those higher levels of consciousness. The medium's physical body has to be revved up as you might term it, to make the link with this entity of such a high level. I have, through the years, been able to adjust to this body quite well. But if you would compare the energy that I use—let's see how you would figure it out? In your electricity, you use 120 volts, then I would be operating on that voltage. And this other entity would be operating on triple that amount, if you can figure that out. So the body is not always able to maintain such a high frequency. It is not always good for the heart.

🙂 Does that mean that you have to raise the energy within the body so that it is operating on a different level than that of his normal state of consciousness?

🙂 That is correct. The human body can withstand quite a bit, but there comes a time when it throws the body into jeopardy or danger, as you know it to be. There have been mediums in your past, whose Spirit Controls did not monitor the energy well enough. As a result the medium slipped out of the body and did not return. In other words, the medium died. We do not want this to happen to this instrument.

🙂 I certainly agree with you, Nathaniel!

🙂 I am deeply sorry to inform you, that we will have to terminate this session. We are unable to satisfactorily stabilize the body. Therefore, we need to leave this body immediately. Do not be concerned; this will in no way endanger the medium. I bid you farewell at this time.

🙂 Good bye, Nathaniel.

Carl's body severely spasmed several times. Again he began coughing. I assisted him in drinking some water. Carl looked quite pale; it was very obvious that his energy was utterly depleted. I assisted him to his bed, and he slept for the next five hours.

The next day Carl and I discussed Nathaniel's appearance. Carl told me that for years, Nathaniel has been present when he went into trance. It is usually Nathaniel who "takes the body over," while other Spirit doctors and chemists, monitor the energies required to maintain Carl's body. Apparently, the Spirit people were extremely busy, making numerous adjustments, because at the time it was no longer able to sustain the increased vibrational rate of Awan's lowered frequency.

As I witnessed these sessions, it was so easy to forget that so many other Spirit people are extremely busy at many tasks to make this communication possible. I personally do not see them, and it is easy to forget that they are present. This session taught me just how fragile and involved this communication is.

SIX

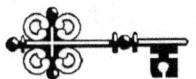 ## 3. Death is Not Your Best Option

About three weeks later, Awan again had me summoned to Carl's office. He was very anxious to finish our dialogue about the brain. I was apprehensive this time, more so about Carl's well-being, than wondering if the information would be difficult for me to handle. Following the usual procedure, Carl said his prayer, and proceeded to go into a deep trance state. This time there seemed to be a rather smooth transition as Carl's Spirit left his body, and Awan entered.

😇 My profound greetings to you, my scribe.

🙂 Greetings, Awan!

😇 I want to assure you that today conditions are optimal. We should not have a problem with the body as we did during the last session.

🙂 I am very glad to hear that, Awan.

😇 As you should remember, since the ancient people's brains were working at full capacity, their civilizations were totally peaceful. They lived in perfect harmony with all people. They also did not suffer from disease and their bodies never died.

🙂 Wait a minute Awan! I can understand how you say that these ancient people could levitate stones that weighed tons with their minds, but how could they be free from disease? What do you mean they did not die? Everyone dies eventually!

😇 What makes you so sure about that?

🙂 Because everyone, and everything, dies.

😇 Death is an unnatural state. You were never meant to die. Why do you think you must die?

🙂 I don't know, that is the way it is.

😇 Correct, that is the way it is, because no human living on your planet is using 100% of his or her brain. Today, when a baby is born its thymus gland is rather large, the size of a ripe peach. When the child reaches puberty, the thymus gland begins to release death hormones in the body, and it begins to slowly shrink. This is when the aging process begins. By the time you are 25 it dwindles to the size of a grape. It is the size of a pea when you are 50, and totally disappears when you are 75 years old.

When you reach a point of total knowingness, and your brain opens, and functions at 100%, specific changes begin in the physical body. Your thymus gland activates, and starts producing protein. This would cause the cells of your body to reverse themselves, and you would grow younger rather than older. Protein would begin replacing the acid in the body. No germ, bacteria, virus, or any type of disease can live in an environment that is protein based. Germs require an acid base to survive. Your body also reverses itself, and you would continue to grow younger until the body returns to the way it was when you were 23 years old.

Women who had passed the prime of life, past the point of their season of blood, would return into their season of blood, and they could bear children again. In Biblical times some people who you would consider very elderly, were still fertile and bore children. The Bible says Abraham fathered a child at the age of 100, and his wife, Sarah, gave birth at the age of 90. In your time, women do not give birth at the age of 90 because their brains are not functioning at 100% capacity. How do you account for that?

After the trance session, I found the Bible verse Awan had mentioned.

> **Then Abraham fell upon his face, and laughed, and said in his heart, Shall a child be born unto him that is an hundred years old? and shall Sarah, that is ninety years old bear?[61]**

I just assumed that one of their years was actually a month, or perhaps their calendars were different.

You are correct, they had different calendars in those days, but that does not account for what happened to Abraham and Sarah. They both used 100% brain capacity. The human body was designed to live forever. When the brain is 100% operational, the pineal gland remains a constant size. The thymus gland is the body's natural fountain of youth, in charge of keeping the body young and in full repair. It constantly rejuvenates cells, which arrests the aging processes at about 23 years of age. This would explain why your Bible describes people who lived for almost one thousand years. After this session, study the beginning chapters of your Book of Books. You will find a long list of people who lived very long lives.

 After the session I found the following verses in the Bible.

> **All the days of Seth were nine hundred and twelve years: and he died.[62]**

---

[61] Genesis 17:17 [KJV].

> **All the days of Enosh were nine hundred and five years: and he died.**[63]
>
> **All the days of Enoch were three hundred sixty and five years.**[64]
>
> **And all the days of Methuselah were nine hundred sixty and nine years: and he died.**[65]
>
> **And all the days of Lamech were seven hundred seventy and seven years: and he died.**[66]
>
> **And Noah was over five hundred years old: and Noah begat Shem, Ham, and Japheth.**[67]

😇 I want you to understand, my scribe, your Bible is inaccurate. These people **did not die**. In those days, a person lived for as long as he or she desired. Then the person would ascend, taking both the physical and spiritual bodies to my dimension. Since the other people no longer saw the person's physical body, the writers of the Bible claimed the person died.

 Awan, what do you mean? How could people not die? What is ascending?

😇 ✠⚷ 3. 𝔇𝔢𝔞𝔱𝔥 𝔍𝔰 𝔑𝔬𝔱 𝔜𝔬𝔲𝔯 𝔅𝔢𝔰𝔱 𝔒𝔭𝔱𝔦𝔬𝔫.

When you ascend, you leave your dimension, and take your physical body with you. You do not leave it behind, as you do when you die. When you wish to ascend, you simply speed up the molecules of your body. The molecules move at an increasing speed. At a certain point, the gravitational pull has no effect on molecules of the body. The body will levitate, just as the stones of the pyramid. Eventually, these molecules move faster than the speed of light. Just before they cross the line from visible to invisible, (the speed of light) there is a great explosion of light. It is similar to the sonic boom that occurs when one of your airplanes travels faster than the speed of sound. After the explosion of light, the molecules are now vibrating in a higher dimension, and are no longer visible to the people on your planet. This is ascension, when you travel to my dimension, and you have the molecules of your physical body with you. Your body is now vibrating at levels where it is visible to the people here in my dimension.

 This is fascinating.

---

[62] Genesis 5:8 [KJV].

[63] Genesis 5:11 [KJV].

[64] Genesis 5:23 [KJV].

[65] Genesis 5:27 [KJV].

[66] Genesis 5:31 [KJV].

[67] Genesis 5:32 [KJV].

🕊️ Your Book of Books names three people who ascended into my dimension. They were Enoch, Elijah, and Jesus. However, Methuselah, Abraham and Sarah and many others also ascended. Your religions have changed a great deal in that Book of Books of yours. They do not want you to know the truth.

📖 After the session I read about Enoch in the Bible. I had not remembered that name during my discussion with Awan. It surprised me to find this interesting verse.

> **When he [Enoch] was 365, and in constant touch with God, he disappeared, for God took him!**[68]

The phrase *"constant touch with God"* would indicate that Enoch was in constant communication with his God within. According to Awan, the knowledge that God is within can lead to the brain functioning at 100%, which would empower his ascension. The phrase *"he disappeared, for God took him,"* would describe the fact that physical person could not see Enoch's physical body, because he ascended and took it with him to a higher dimension.

👤 Awan, the Bible doesn't say Elijah ascended; it says that Elijah went to heaven in a *chariot of fire*.[69]

🕊️ Think about this, my scribe. When Elisha, Elijah's student, witnessed Elijah's ascension, he had a difficult time explaining it to other people. Elisha watched Elijah speed up the vibrational rate of his body. During this process, the earth lost its gravitational effect on Elijah's body, causing him to float up in the air. Then, Elijah's body became transparent. At a certain point, as Elijah's transparent body was floating in the air, there was a explosion of light. It was then the molecules of Elijah's body were no longer visible to Elisha. Elijah entered my dimension with both his spiritual and physical bodies, at the moment of the explosion.

Elisha was in a predicament. How could he explain what he witnessed to anyone else on your earth plane? Who would be able to understand it? Therefore, Elisha used images and terminology that other Biblical people could understand. Elisha said that Elijah left this world on a flaming chariot, because a chariot was the mode of transportation of his day. The chariot was burning, because that was the only way Elisha could describe the great explosion of light. Yet, your Book of Books states:

> **"He [Elisha] took up also the mantle of Elijah that *fell from him*, and went back, and stood by the bank of Jordan."**[70]

---

[68] Genesis 5:24 [LIV].

[69] 2 Kings 2:9-13.

[70] 2 Kings 2:13 [KJV].

My Second Encounter With An Angel

🧑 If Elijah were taken up in a chariot of fire, with horses of fire, then Elijah's body would have been burned. How could Elijah's mantle not burn along with the body? Do you think Elijah's mantle was made of asbestos? Did they have inflammable fabrics in Biblical times? The answer is no. Elijah made the molecules of his body vibrate faster. He did not alter the speed of the molecules of his mantle. Therefore, the mantle remained behind after Elijah ascended.

👼 That really makes sense. Now please explain Jesus' ascension to me.

😇 Jesus wanted to prove to the people on earth that death is an illusion. He wanted to prove that the soul lives on, after the transition you term *death*. That is one of the main reasons he came back to your dimension. Jesus was the last person to have 100% of his brain functioning. This enabled him to demonstrate **all** the *Gifts of the Spirit*. After his crucifixion, Jesus' body was placed in the tomb, and a big heavy stone was rolled in front of the tomb. They packed the same type of mud used to make bricks around the stone. The sun's heat baked the mud tightly sealing the tomb.[71]

A few days later, Jesus' soul returned and entered the tomb, because it vibrated on a higher frequency than the molecules of the tomb. Therefore, Jesus' molecules easily moved between the rocky tomb's molecules. Once inside the tomb, Jesus' Spirit reentered his physical body. Then Jesus accelerated the molecules of his physical body, to the point that it went into light, which caused a great explosion. The explosion was so great that it broke the seal, and pushed the stone away from the tomb, leaving the entrance to the tomb open.[72] Later, when people went inside the tomb they did not find Jesus' body, because Jesus had taken it into my dimension.

👼 So that would mean that when Jesus wanted people to see him, he would simply lower his frequency until he was visible to other people.

😇 That is exactly correct.

👼 This is certainly fascinating,

😇 Do you realize, my scribe, just how much Elijah and Jesus had in common? They both performed the *gift of apports*, and multiplied food.[73] They both brought dead people back to life.[74] They both ascended to my dimension.[75] So please explain to me why the Jews call Elijah a *prophet* and the Christians call Jesus a *God*? Why don't Christians call Elijah a God, too? Why haven't the Cardinals of the Catholic Church canonized Elijah as a *Christ*? They cannot use Elijah's religion as an excuse since **both Elijah and Jesus were Jewish.** Why are there no churches with this sign above the door?

---

[71] Matthew 27:66, Mark 15:46.

[72] Mark 16:4, Luke 24:2, John 20:1.

[73] Elijah—1 Kings 17:10-16. Jesus—Matthew 14:15-21.

[74] Elijah—1 Kings 17:17-24. Jesus—John 11:40-44.

[75] Elijah—2 Kings 2:9-12. Jesus—Acts 1:9-10.

✝ First Church of Elijah Christ ✡

👤 That is a good question, Awan.

👼 So many people live their entire lives without analyzing their beliefs. After the brain was shut down, and hardly anyone utilized the *Gifts of the Spirit*, the lines of communication between my dimension and yours were severed. Today, only a limited amount of information travels between our dimensions, which usually occurs during your dream state. It is only then that we can impress our thoughts, through pictures, upon your subconscious minds. However, most people can't interpret their dreams, so many of our messages are lost.

Eventually, my scribe, you will have acquired enough knowledge, that I will teach you how to "go within" and communicate to your "God within." You will learn how to reprogram the information stored in your soul. At that point, you can choose to command your soul to fully open your brain. If you can accomplish that you would have the ability to perform the *Gifts of the Spirit* and ascend. Once your brain is 100% operational, you do not have to die, you can reprogram that script from your soul. This is what the prophet Ezekiel was trying to teach.

📖 After this dialogue, I found this verse:

> **For I have no pleasure in the death of him that dieth, saith the Lord GOD: wherefore turn *yourselves*, and live ye.**[76]

It seems very logical to me that the phrase ***turn yourselves*** could easily mean ***turning within***, as Awan described.

👼 Now my scribe, since we have been talking about so many of the *Gifts of the Spirit*, and ascension, let me tell you about the schools of ancient wisdom As I said before, in ancient times all the people used 100% of their brain. All around your planet, there were schools of ancient wisdom, when people's brains were totally operational.

👤 Awan, if these people used all of their brains, why did they need schools?

👼 That is a good question, my scribe. Since the ancients used 100% of the brain, they could demonstrate the *Gifts of the Spirit*. However, you must realize that a totally functioning brain just provides the capacity for these gifts. You still must develop the skills to use them. It is similar to your great artists. Do you think that Rembrandt, Monet, Renoir, Michelangelo, Titian or

---

[76] Ezekiel 18:32 [KJV].

Van Gogh painted masterpieces the very first time they dipped their brush into paint?

🧑 No Awan. I guess I see your point.

😇 People would go to these ancient schools of wisdom to learn how to use the *Gifts of the Spirit*, just as young artists who have abundant talent, go to art school to refine their painting skills and abilities.

🧑 Where were these schools located?

😇 Actually they were all over the planet. However, there are still remnants of them in certain locations. The pyramids at Giza, Chitza Itza, Uxmal, Copan, Tikal, are where a few of these ancient schools were located.

🧑 Could you describe their classes?

😇 These schools were places where the students, who were called initiates, dedicated themselves to spiritual development. They lived at the school for seven years.

🧑 That is a long time! What did they learn?

😇 They had to master quieting the physical body, and using their spiritual body.

🧑 I don't understand.

😇 Another way to explain it is these initiates learned to ignore the "everyday" part of the brain, and rely on another sections of the brain, which received information from my dimension.

🧑 That sounds difficult.

😇 Not really, my scribe, it just takes focus and discipline. Hundreds of initiates learned to be in an altered state of consciousness, meaning their physical bodies were shut down. They then operated through their spiritual body, which became very active. Often, the initiate was blindfolded, so no light would play on the eyelids, which would draw his or her consciousness away from the inner God. Each student had to pass seven tests to graduate from the school.

🧑 Could you describe these tests?

😇 In Chitza Itza and Uxmal, there was one test where the initiates had to walk up steps of the pyramid to the top, and then back down, while being blindfolded. No one was allowed to speak. Students knew if they were going too fast, because they would suddenly enter the auric field of the person ahead of them. This would tell them to slow down.

Sometimes, an initiate would loose his or her focus and stumble. That person would usually roll down the steps of the pyramid, and die. Archaeologists have found many human remains at these ancient schools, and claimed this was evidence of human sacrifices. Sometimes, certain ceremonies were conducted over these dead bodies. However, my scribe, I want to make it perfectly clear that these people lost their lives because they did not pass the test. They were not sacrificed.

😇 That is very interesting. What were some of the other tests?

👼 There were many pedestals at these schools. The initiates were taught how to levitate, by increasing the speed of the molecules of their physical bodies, so that gravity would no longer keep them on the ground. The initiate had to sit on the ground and levitate and sit on top of the pedestal. This is the origin of the expression "Don't put me on a pedestal," which is supposed to mean "don't make me a god." For you see, my scribe, when you mastered all seven tests you truly were a God.

😇 That is fascinating.

👼 The seventh test was ascension. The initiates had to speed up the body, faster than when they levitated. Once the molecules were traveling at the speed of light, there was an explosion of light and these people left your dimension and came into mine, taking the physical body with them.

😇 Awan, who were the teachers of these ancient schools of wisdom?

👼 The great teachers who taught at these schools, all came from the higher levels of my dimension. These great masters would lower their frequency and materialized to teach the initiates. After the lesson was finished, they would increase their frequency, dematerialize, and return to my dimension.

The students had no idea where this teacher came from or what the teacher looked like, since during most of the lesson the initiates were blindfolded. I hope you realize, my scribe, these teachers came from a higher dimension, not up in the sky; but from an existence which exists on a higher frequency of vibration.

😇 Yes, I understand that. Awan, I have a question. What caused the brain to shut down? Why do 21st century humans only use 10% to 33% of their brains, when the ancient people used 100%?

👼 It was religions that shut down the brain.

😇 Religions! How could it be religions? What religions?

👼 Religions.

😇 Which ones? Judaism and Catholicism were not yet created.

👼 The ancient people, using 100% of their brains, saw a time was approaching where religions would cause ignorance to be rampant upon the entire planet. Therefore, these enlightened people decided to ascend from your world before ignorance would occur. However, they built time-capsules, before they left, for future generations. That is why there are pyramids around your planet. The pyramids were designed to remind future generations that *God was within*.

My Second Encounter With An Angel

Eventually, there came a time when jealously set in, and certain people thought that they were better than the rest. These people, that we would term *tyrants*, decided that it would be grand if they could dominate and control other people. The first stage of the tyrants' plan of domination was to preach that God was not inside of every human, but outside of the body. The tyrants claimed that the God within did **not** exist. The God who is doing all the good things is out in another dimension. They did not use the word dimension, but they pointed to the sky. These tyrants preached there was only one way to communicate with the God living in the sky. Then they argued they were the **only** ones who knew the secret method. To talk to God you needed one of these tyrants and must obey the rules they created. Later, these tyrants became known as priests.

As people's brains began to shut down, they no longer had total knowingness. This caused them to loose their independence. When they no longer could go within to find the answers they sought, they had no choice but get their answers from the priests, who claimed they could communicate with the God living in the sky. This God had all the answers. Therefore, people became dependent upon their priests. Every time they had a question, they would seek out a priest for the answer.

The majority of the people were happy with their lives before the priests started these religions. It would only be natural that many of the people would rebel against the priests who were changing the system. The priests labeled people who rebelled against them as *evil*.

The second stage of the priests' plan was to create *fear*. This powerful emotion would help them gain control over the people. Subsequently, the priests taught that the invisible God was not alone in the sky. There were other invisible beings, called demons and devils, who were extremely powerful and evil. The priests very slowly convinced the people if they used the *Gifts of the Spirit*, they were actually worshipping and honoring these evil beings. Naturally, all the people who rebelled against the priests were worshippers of the devil. Despite all these ploys, groups of people continued to reject the priests and their newly created religions.

The final stage of the priests' plan was to create a crutch, something tangible that would convince people that God was outside of the body. Therefore, priests forced the people to bow down and worship statues and idols. This shifted the people's focus away from the souls in their bodies, and out to these statues. In this way they trained the people to believe that God was outside of them.

📖 After this conversation, I discovered information, which corroborated Awan's statements.

The legions of statues in and outside of the cathedrals were staggering. Statues frame the covered entrance to the cathedral, which is capped by a pointed arch.[77]

---

[77] Perdrizet, Marie-Pierre. *The Cathedral Builders*. Brookfield, CT: Millbrook Press, 1992. p. 6.

> **Outside the cathedral, a whole population of stone figures decorate its facades and entranceways. The cathedral of Nôtre Dame in Paris has 1,200 such statues. At Reims, you can count as many as 3,000 of them.[78]**

(😇) It was a very slow process, to get the people to abandon their old ways. Eventually, the priests convinced the people that the *Gifts of the Spirit* was the work of some evil entity. As the people became afraid and stopped utilizing the *Gifts of the Spirit*, different chambers of the brain slowly stopped functioning. Inactivity allows the brain center go to sleep; I believe the proper term is *atrophy*. This state of atrophy was genetically passed from one generation to the next.

A few years back, you injured two of your fingers and needed an operation to have them fixed.

(👤) Yes, Awan, my hand was in a cast for about seven weeks.

(😇) And what happened after the cast was removed. Could you move your fingers?

(👤) No. They were very stiff, I had to do all sorts of exercises to make them move again.

(😇) That is correct. The same principle applies to the brain. When the people ceased using the *Gifts of the Spirit*, their brain centers shut down or atrophied, just as the muscles in your fingers did when you stopped using them.

(👤) That makes sense.

(😇) 🗝 4. 𝔓𝔯𝔦𝔢𝔰𝔱𝔰 𝔍𝔫𝔳𝔢𝔫𝔱𝔢𝔡 𝔱𝔥𝔢 𝔇𝔢𝔳𝔦𝔩.

It was a very slow process, of several thousands of years, before the priests were actually able to shut down the entire 2/3 of the human brain that controlled the *Gifts of the Spirit*. It was then that human beings became very ignorant, because they were completely disconnected from the God within, and from the *river of thought*. Even though in your present time, you think you are extremely intelligent, only the slowest 1/3 of the brain is working in humans all over the planet.

The priests succeeded in shutting the brain down by placing fear in the minds of the people, making them believe God was outside of their bodies, and the *Gifts of the Spirit* was the work of the devil. Those tyrants became the priests of your religions. It was the goal of religions to make people subservient to the priests' wishes, and in this way the priests could live off the masses of people. You are already aware of this fact.

---

[78] Perdrizet, Marie-Pierre. *The Cathedral Builders*. Brookfield, CT: Millbrook Press, 1992. p. 36.

🧑 Yes, Awan, I understand how the priests made the people support them. So you are saying that there is no devil, and the priests created the devil to put fear in the minds of the people.

😇 Yes, the priests created the devil in order to create fear in the minds of the people. Many of the great civilizations whose people had their brains totally functioning, the ones who built the pyramids, saw that an *Age of Ignorance* was descending on your planet. They did not wish to participate in any part of it, so these great people ascended, to live on other planets in your universe. There will be a time when they will return.

Have you ever wondered why God spoke to the people in Biblical times, but does not speak to people today?

🧑 Yes, Awan, I have often thought about it. I even remember, as a child, asking that question to my Sunday school teacher.

😇 After the priests succeeded in making the people believe that there was a devil, the people were afraid of the *Gifts of the Spirit*, which was labeled the Devil's work. This broke the communication link between the Sprit World and your dimension. People would not listen to the voices coming from my world.

On your planet today, you have communication that depends on waves—you term *radio*. You also have the ability to jam these waves so the people will not hear them through their radios.

🧑 That's right Awan. The medium often speaks of when he was a boy, living in North Carolina, he was able to hear the radio broadcasts coming from Cuba. Today no Americans can hear Cuban radio stations, because our government jams the signals.

😇 That is correct. The Church was successful in jamming our communication. When people believe the voices of my dimension are the voices of devils and demons, the fear blocks their ability to hear us. It acts as a jamming mechanism, so a person will not hear our voices, despite the fact they have the *gift of clairaudience.*

I am feeling a shift in the energy, so I must quickly withdraw. Before I go, I ask you do some thinking and explore in your libraries, and see how much of this information about theologians' creation of the devil, you can find. Do not become frustrated when you discover that you will not find much of it, because the priests have done a good job in covering their tracks. Have you heard of the Library of Alexandria?

🧑 Of course I have.

😇 This Library of Alexandria held all the scrolls of ancient wisdom, collected from many ancient civilizations. These were the records of people who did marvelous feats because their brains were 100% operational. These civilizations recorded invaluable information, gleaned from the *river of thought.*

When Christianity became the official religion of Rome, the priests wanted everyone to convert to their new religion. They also wanted to control all knowledge, so they rewrote the laws and history, to make them fit their belief system. The people who refused to accept these new doctrines were destroyed and killed.

The priests fanned out all over the world, searching for books that contradicted their new religion. They burned any that they found. It was on the priests' orders that the great Library of Alexandria, Egypt was deliberately burned in order to destroy all the tablets and scrolls. To replace these lost scrolls, the priest distributed copies of a new book, the **Holy Bible**, which corroborated their new teachings.

The energy is diminished. I must leave you at this time. My peace be with you.

Thank you Awan.

As Awan withdrew Carl's body trembled. A soft moan escaped his lips, as Carl slowly regained consciousness. Carl drank his water quickly, shook his head, and complained that he hated going into trance, since it usually left him exhausted. Carl left his office and went to take a nap.

A few days later, I did some research about the Library of Alexandria. I discovered that this library had 400,000 scrolls in its collection.[79] I also came across this description of the city of Alexandria. It indicates that Alexandria was a great intellectual center. Since Christianity wanted to control people minds, and how they thought, is it any wonder that they destroyed the city, with its great library, that stored so much knowledge?

> **Two thousand years ago the Egyptian city of Alexandria was one of the greatest cities in the world. Rome may have been the center of power, but Alexandria was the intellectual center. Here Egyptians, Romans, Greeks, Jews, Persians, and people from dozens of other cultures met to trade goods and ideas. At that time Alexandria had a university, an observatory, and the finest libraries in the world. It was a home for philosophers and magicians, during the first centuries of the Christian era there were often little difference between the two.**[80]

---

[79] Avi-Yonah, *Ancient Scrolls. Minneapolis*, MI: Lerner Publications Company. 1973. p. 30.

[80] Cohen, Daniel. *Dealing with the Devil*. NY: Dodd, Mead & Company, 1979. p. 21.

School of Ancient Wisdom at Chichen Itza

This famous pyramid has staircases on all four sides. The picture on the right was taken from the top of the pyramid. The campus of this ancient school was quite large and included an observatory, where students studied the heavens. Notice all the pedestals for leviation in front of the second pyramid. Thee are 1000 pedestals at this site.

This ring at **Uxmal** was another of the tests for the students. Again the Students were to levitate, but this time they must make their body pass through thei rign. The picture on the right is a photoshoped image simulating this test. A famous 19th century medium, Daniel Dunglas Home, performed an identical feat, when he levitated out of a second story window and reentered the room though another window.

The School of Ancient Wisdom at Uxmal, Mexico

The massive size of the Uxmal pyramid was overwhelming. Yet, it "hidden message" is visible: the window placed on third of the way down, indicates the location of the soul in the human body. All the buildings of this ancient school were amazing with their intercalate decorative carvings.

These pedestals were one of the tests for the initiates, who had to levitate and sit on top of the pedestal. Again the picture on the right was photoshopped.

My Second Encounter With An Angel 81

The Arch at Labná

The pyramid at Uxmal

Uxmal   Uxmal   Kabah

Intricate carvings indicate that the Mayan had advance technology. Notice the stone chair in the center picture, which mediums used and eventually became the origin of the cathedra in cathedrals. (See chapter 12.)

SEVEN

4. Priests Invented the Devil

As Carl and I were proofreading this chapter, Awan instructed Carl that he wanted to insert this message. This time, Awan clairaudiently dictated these words to Carl who repeated them to me, and I typed them into the computer.

 My sisters, and brothers. The chapter that you are about to read may disturb those of you, who are entrenched in religious belief systems. I have returned to this planet, to present truths through my medium and scribe. I cannot change history just so it coincides with your preconceived man-made doctrines. I ask that you read this chapter, and this entire book with an open mind, then weigh and judge the information for yourself. Do not go running helter-skelter, from pillar to post, looking for someone outside of you to tell you whether or not this information is correct. Have that conversation between your mind and your soul to determine the answer yourself. As I have mentioned many times in these books, all of you are dealing with recycled ignorance. You would have to go back many centuries to find the inception of the doctrines that you learned from your clergyman. From my perspective, when the councils of theologians created these inaccurate dogmas, it was based on ignorant conjectures, not knowledge from my dimension. Therefore, as these doctrines were taught from generation to generation, people learned recycled ignorance. These doctrines kept people enslaved to churches. These religious dogmas will not serve you well, during the turbulent times that will soon occur on your planet.

* * * * *

Awan's new assignment to research the origin of the devil was quite a challenge. It was like putting a thousand piece jig-saw-puzzle together. I was very intrigued when I found pieces of the puzzle that corroborated Awan's theory: the priests had created the devil. I began my research by examining the Old Testament, and the beliefs of the Hebrews. All of the neighboring nations surrounding the Hebrew's homeland were polytheistic, meaning they believed in **many** gods. However, the Hebrews were monotheistic; they believed there was only **one** God. This belief is clearly evident in their most sacred prayer:

$$\text{שְׁמַע יִשְׂרָאֵל יְיָ אֱלֹהֵינוּ יְיָ אֶחָד}$$

Hear, O Israel: the Lord our God, the Lord is One.[81]

If evil existed in the world, God, Himself, created it; because there was not another God to blame. There is much evidence in the Bible, which states that God created evil. If the devil existed when Adam and Eve lived in the Garden of Eden, as many Christians believe, then why are the following verses in the Bible? Why didn't the Devil send evil upon human beings instead of God?

> **I form the light, and create darkness: I make peace, and *create evil*: I the Lord do all these things.**[82]

It seemed that 20th century Christian Bible translators become apprehensive with the idea of God having an evil side. The Christians preached from their pulpits about how the Devil would send evil upon you. If God sent evil into the world, these theologians might lose credibility with the congregations. Could this be the reason that the word **evil** is missing from the following translations?

> **I form the light and create darkness, I make weal and *create woe*, I am the Lord who do all these things.**[83]

> **The One forming light and creating darkness, Causing well-being and *creating calamity*: I am the Lord who does all these.**[84]

In the book of Genesis, we learn that God created a tree of knowledge of *good* and *evil*. It would be impossible to understand *good* without understanding *evil*. The contrast is needed to differentiate the two polarities.

> **And out of the ground made the Lord God to grow every tree that is pleasant to the sight, and good for food; the tree of life also in the midst of the garden, and *the tree of knowledge of good and evil*.**[85]

---

[81] *Service of the Synagogue: Day of Atonement* NY: Hebrew Publishing Co., (no date). p. 18.

[82] Isaiah 45:7 [KJV].

[83] Isaiah 45:7 [RSV].

[84] Isaiah 45:7 [NASB].

[85] Genesis 2:9 [KJV].

Remember that Awan taught that God was energy. The next time you look at a battery that you put in your flashlight or remote control, notice that there are two poles to the battery. One side is labeled positive, the other negative. Electricity, which is energy, has both a positive and a negative side to it. The ancient Hebrews understood that God also had a positive and negative side to Him. Awan keeps teaching us that God is within, and that the soul is energy. He taught that the soul is an isness, which doesn't know right from wrong. That would mean that the soul contains **both** positive and negative energy, [good and evil if you wish to use those terms]. That is why the soul does not care what you do. Everything that you do is for the experience of it, whether it be positive or negative. If you had only positive experiences, you would be lacking. You would eventually not know that your experiences were good, unless you had the negative ones as a basis of comparison.

These next six verses again show that God controlled evil, and that God, not the Devil, dispensed evil unto the people. Again notice how the **NASB** nervously avoids the word *evil*. Do they not want to raise questions in the minds of the Christian readers that God is controlling evil, and not the Devil?

> **Therefore it shall come to pass, that as all good things are come upon you, which the Lord your God promised you;** *so shall the Lord bring upon you all evil things*, **until he have destroyed you from off this good land which the Lord your God that given you. [KJV]**[86]

> **And it shall come about that just as all the good words which the Lord your God spoke to you have come upon you,** *so the Lord will bring upon you all the threats*, **until He has destroyed you from off this good land which the Lord your God has given you. [NASB]**[87]

> **For, behold, I will bring** *evil* **upon all flesh, saith the Lord. [KJV]**[88]

> **I am going to bring** *disaster* **on all flesh,' declares the Lord. [NASB]**[89]

> **Therefore thus saith the Lord, Behold, I will bring** *evil* **upon them, which they shall not be able to escape; and though they shall cry unto me, I will not hearken unto them. [KJV]**[90]

---

[86] Joshua 23:15 [KJV].

[87] Joshua 23:15 [NASB].

[88] Jeremiah 45:5 [KJV].

[89] Jeremiah 45:5 [NASB].

[90] Jeremiah 11:11 [KJV].

> Therefore thus says the Lord, "Behold I am bringing *disaster* on them which they will not be able to escape; though they will cry to Me, yet I will not listen to them. [NASB][91]

These next verses are interesting. The Bible explains that Saul became a prophet, as he went into trance. That verse read:

> And the Spirit of the Lord will come upon thee, and thou shalt prophesy with them, and shalt be turned into another man.[92]

We must remember Awan's teaching, that the word **Lord** was used to show respect for an invisible entity from the Spirit World. It was customary for a person of a lower socio-economic class to address a member of the aristocracy as *my lord*. Also there are many levels of the Spirit World, some levels of enlightened beings, and some that would be termed ignorant, or malicious beings. In the following verses, we discover that Saul did not understand the techniques of mediumship very well. For an enlightened being, *the Spirit of the Lord*, left Saul and a lower level Spirit, an *evil Spirit from the Lord*, became associated with Saul.

> But the Spirit of the Lord departed from Saul, and an evil spirit from the Lord troubled him. [KJV][93]

> Now the Spirit of the Lord departed from Saul, and an evil spirit from the Lord terrorized him. [NASB][94]

We have seen the evidence from the Bible that God controlled both good and evil. There is no mention of Satan, or a Devil. Now let's look at something that will become very interesting, and indeed curious. In the Ten Commandments, one of the most important communications that God delivered to the Hebrews, especially since he did it with his own voice (through trumpet mediumship),[95] God states:

> Thou shalt have no other gods before me.[96]

---

[91] Jeremiah 11:11 [NASB].

[92] 1 Samuel 10:6 [KJV].

[93] 1 Samuel 16:14 [KJV].

[94] 1 Samuel 16:14 [NASB].

[95] Schwartz, Sidney. *My First Encounter with an Angel: Revelations of Ancient Wisdom*. Blue Hill, ME. Medicine Bear Publishing, 1999. p. 171-177.

[96] Exodus 20:3 [KJV].

My Second Encounter With An Angel

Thou shalt not bow down thyself to them, nor serve them; for I the Lord thy God am a jealous God.[97]

Most people believe that the Almighty God, who created of the whole univrse, and good and evil, issued these commandments. If this were true, then who would this God envy in the universe? What could Asherah, Astarte, Baal, Moloch, or any other god do that would be more powerful than the creator of the universe? If God had to power to create evil, then he also had to have the power to destroy evil.

And God saw that the wickedness of man was great in the earth, and that every imagination of the thoughts of his heart was only evil continually. And it repented the Lord that he had made man on the earth, and it grieved him at his heart. And the Lord said, I will destroy man whom I have created from the face of the earth.[98]

God caused the great flood, and drowned all the wicked people. This proves that God did have the power to destroy wickedness and wicked people. Therefore, if God were jealous of the god of Moab, or Asherah, a Canaanite gods, or all the other neighboring gods, why would not God be jealous of Satan? If there really were a devil, who controlled evil, wouldn't God be jealous of that devil? The devil would be threatening God's territory by usurping God's power over evil. Why would God not destroy his competitor, the Devil, who was wickedness personified? God had already destroyed almost all the wicked people on the earth with the great flood. He also, according to the Bible, destroyed the wicked people of Sodom.

But the men of Sodom were wicked and sinners before the Lord exceedingly.[99]

Then the Lord rained upon Sodom and upon Gomorrah *brimstone and fire from the Lord out of heaven;* And he overthrew those cities, and all the plain, and all the inhabitants of the cities, and that wish grew upon the ground.[100]

This last verse totally tarnished my "silvery vision" of heaven. I thought heaven was a wonderful place where God and all his saints had their beautiful homes. I did not realize that Heaven had a low rent district, where they kept the fire and brimstone, to rain down upon all those sinful people, from the wrong side of the tracks. It was my understanding that all the fire

---

[97] Exodus 20:5 [KJV].

[98] Genesis 6:5-7 [KJV].

[99] Genesis 13:13 [KJV].

[100] Genesis 19:24-25 [KJV].

and brimstone was in hell, with the Devil stoking the fires. Did some ancient Biblical writer mix up his metaphors?

Getting back to the original point: if God were a jealous God, and discussed the fact that no one should worship a foreign god, why didn't he specifically state that you should not worship Satan, because he is a devil? Why didn't he mention the devil at all? The very first mention of the devil in the Old Testament occurs in 1 Chronicles 21:1 (the 14th book of the Bible). The second appearance of the devil occurs in the book of Job (the 19th book of the Bible).[101]

Charles Bradlaugh, in his essay, *A Few Words about the Devil* continues this thought.

> **The Old Testament speaks a little of the Devils, sometimes of Satan, but never of "The Devil," and it seems almost too much, in Matthew, to usher him in, in the temptation scene, without introduction, and as if he were an old acquaintance. I do not remember reading, in the Old Testament, anything about the lake of brimstone and fire; this feature of faith was reserved for the warmth of Christian love to inspire; the Pentateuch [the first five books of the Bible] makes no reference to it. Zechariah, in a vision, saw "Joshua, the High-Priest, standing before the angel of the Lord, and Satan standing at his right hand to resist him."[102] Why the Devil wanted to resist Joshua is not clear; but as Joshua's garments is in a very filthy state, it may be that he was preaching to the Priest the virtues of cleanliness. It is often said that cleanliness if next to godliness; I honestly confess that I should prefer a clean sinner to a dirty saint. Jesus said that one of the twelve disciples was a Devil,[103] but I am not prepared to say whether he meant the unfaithful and cowardly Peter, to whom he entrusted the keys of Heaven, or Judas who sold him for money, just as would nearly any bishop of the present day. The bishops preach that it is as difficult for a rich man to get into Heaven as for a camel to go through the eye of a needle; yet they enrich themselves, and their families, as greedily and carelessly as if they, at any rate never expected to smell brimstone as a consequence.[104]**

---

[101] Job 1:6, 7, 8, 9, 12.

[102] Zechariah 3:1.

[103] John 6:70.

[104] Bradlaugh, Charles. *A Few Words about the Devil: and other Biographical Sketches and Essays.* NY: Charles P. Somerby, 1875. p. 9.

There is one indisputable fact concerning the origin of the devil; God had very little to say to about his powerful enemy. When one studies the Old Testament, one discovers that God continuously communicated to humanity through his mediums (prophets). Read the Bible, and you will discover that the Lord spoke with Adam, Eve, Cain, Noah, Abraham, Hagar, Isaac, Jacob, Joseph, Moses, Joshua, Samuel, Elijah, Elisha, Nathan, Shemaiah, Ahijah, Micaiah, Huldah, Job, Isaiah, Jeremiah, Ezekiel, Daniel, Hosea, Joel, Amos, Obadiah, Jonah, Micah, Nahum, Habakkuk, Zephaniah, Haggai, Zechariah, and Malachi. This is a long list of prophets (mediums) who lived over several centuries. One would think that God would tell at least one of these people about the devil, if such a dangerous, evil entity really existed. Yet, God was silent. He never warned the Hebrews, his chosen people,[105] about the evil devil. Since the Bible says it was *"the Lord"* speaking to this long list of people, it becomes easy to believe that there is only one entity speaking to each of these holy men and women of the Bible. Awan contradicts this notion, when he taught *"the Lord"* was a term of respect, therefore it was many different Spirit people speaking to all these clairaudient people.

> **"The silence of the Scriptures concerning these evil demons (which are pretended to be the managers of the oracles) have not only left us at liberty to believe nothing of them, but it obliges us to believe the contrary; for can it be possible that the Scriptures should not have instructed the Jews and Christians in a thing which it so extremely important for them to know, (and which they could never have found out by their natural reason) ... So if the oracles had been delivered by evil demons, God would have made it known to us to have prevented us from believing that He Himself delivered them or that there was something divine in false religions."[106]**

What Bernard De Borhem Di Foneneile was saying is that a true and loving God would have warned his people of the danger of demons or devils. Think about this, and reason it out for yourself! Since God was concerned for the physical welfare of thousands of Egyptians, God warned the Pharaoh of a drought, by enabling Joseph to interpret the Pharaoh's dream, and made sure that Pharaoh understood the message.[107] This saved thousands of lives. God literally spoke the Ten Commandments directly to the Hebrews because He was concerned with the Hebrews physical lives, and wanted them to live together morally.[108] God instructed Samuel to anoint Saul as king, simply because the Hebrews wanted a king.[109] God was concerned about the

---

[105] Deuteronomy 14:2.

[106] Di Foneneile, Bernard De Borhem *"History of Oracles and the Cheats of the Pagan Priests"* London, 1688.

[107] Genesis 41:14-40.

[108] Exodus 20:1-17.

[109] 1 Samuel 9:16.

physical welfare of a single woman when God enabled Elijah to multiply flour and oil for her, so she would not go hungry.[110] Through several of the prophets, God warned the Hebrews that if they continued to disobey his commands they would be exiled to Babylon.[111]

In all of these examples, God was concerned with the physical welfare of His people. Isn't it logical that God would also be concerned with the spiritual welfare of His people? If Satan, devils and demons really existed, God in his infinite wisdom, having great love and concern for his people, would surely have warned his people, of the spiritual dangers of listening to demons, through his mediums or prophets. God would have told Moses, Samuel, Elijah, Elisha, Jeremiah, Isaiah, or anyone from the long list of people who he directly spoke to, how dangerous the Devil is. God did not discuss a devil with any of these mediums.

It is the author's opinion that God had a perfect opportunity to inform the Hebrews about Satan when he was delivering the Ten Commandments. The lines of communication were opened, and the Hebrews heard God's own voice discussing murder, adultery, and honoring thy father and mother. Why didn't God issue an Eleventh Commandment?

"Thou shalt be exceedingly fearful of the evil Satan who is out to capture your eternal soul, and roast it in the fires of hell."

Since God was silent on the subject of the devil, it would indicate that devils and demons did **NOT** exist. Therefore, as Awan stated: *it was man who created devils and demons, not God.*

Now it is time to get very specific, and discover where we find the word שָׂטָן (*Satan*) in the original Hebrew Bible. *The Englishman's Hebrew and Chaldee Concordance of the Old Testament* is a book that translates Hebrew words into English, and also lists exact locations in the Hebrew text of the Bible. By using this book, we find the word שָׂטָן (*Satan*) occurs twenty times in the Old Testament. However, there are two distinct meanings for the Hebrew word שָׂטָן (*Satan*). The first meaning for שָׂטָן (*Satan*) is *adversary*. Nine of the twenty-four times שָׂטָן (*Satan*) occurs in the Bible, שָׂטָן (*Satan*) means *adversary*.[112] The remaining fifteen times שָׂטָן (*Satan*) is used as the name for the Devil. Let me list the Biblical verses that contain the word שָׂטָן (*Satan*).

---

[110] 1 Kings 17:7-16.

[111] Jeremiah 13:15-27, Isaiah 3:1-26.

[112] *The Englishman's Hebrew and Chaldee Concordance of the Old Testament. Vol. 2.* London: Walton and Maberrly, 1866. p. 1205.

> 1 Chronicles 21:1
> Job 1:6, 7, 8, 9, 12,
> Job 2:1, 2, 3, 4, 6, 7
> Psalms 109:6
> Zechariah 3:1, 2[113]

So it comes down to the fact that שָׂטָן (*Satan*) is used in only four books of the Bible, and all of those books were later writings. We do not find the word שָׂטָן (*Satan*) in any of the books before *1 Chronicles*, meaning that God never mentioned שָׂטָן (*Satan*) to Adam, Eve, Cain, Noah, Abraham, Hagar, Isaac, Jacob, Joseph, Moses, Joshua, Samuel, Elijah, or Elisha.

For those readers who would say, that the devil has many names let us look under the name of הֵילֵל (*Lucifer*). There is only one place that הֵילֵל (*Lucifer*) is used in the Bible.[114]

> **How art thou fallen from heaven, *O Lucifer*, son of the morning! how art thou cut down to the ground, which didst weaken the nations!**[115]

Many versions of the Bible do not choose to translate הֵילֵל as *Lucifer*.

> **How you have fallen from heaven, *O morning star*, son of the dawn! You have been cast down to the earth, you who once laid low the nations.**[116]

None of the Spirits who spoke with the following prophets/mediums: Adam, Eve, Cain, Noah, Abraham, Hagar, Isaac, Jacob, Joseph, Moses, Joshua, Samuel, Elijah, Elisha, Nathan, Shemaiah, Ahijah, Micaiah, Huldah, Isaiah, Jeremiah, Ezekiel, Daniel, Hosea, Joel, Amos, Obadiah, Jonah, Micah, Nahum, Habakkuk, Zephaniah, Haggai, or Malachi mentioned the Devil, because no such being existed. As late as 200 years before the Babylonian captivity, the prophet Amos reaffirms that God is responsible for evil:

> **Shall there be evil in a city and the Lord hath not done it?**[117]

---

[113] *The Englishman's Hebrew and Chaldee Concordance of the Old Testament. Vol. 2.* London: Walton and Maberrly, 1866. p. 1205.

[114] *The Englishman's Hebrew and Chaldee Concordance of the Old Testament. Vol. 1.* London: Walton and Maberrly, 1866. p. 362.

[115] Isaiah 14:12 [KJV].

[116] Isaiah 14:12 [NIV].

[117] Amos 3:6 [KJV].

Jeffrey Burton Russell points out in his book entitled, "The Devil: Perceptions of Evil from Antiquity to Primitive Christianity" that:

> **In pre-exilic Hebrew religion Yahweh made all that was in heaven and earth, both of good and of evil. The Devil did not exist. The Hebrew concept of the Devil developed gradually, arising from certain tensions within the concept of Yahweh.**[118]

What Russell is stating is important. The concept of the Devil developed gradually. It happened after Nebuchadnezzar, the king of Babylonia, captured Jerusalem, and burned Solomon's Holy Temple in 586 B. C.[119] Then the Hebrews were enslaved by the Babylonians, and were forced to walk from Jerusalem, five hundred miles east to Babylon. It was in Babylon that the Hebrew religion would change drastically. Before the Babylonian captivity, the Hebrews worshipped God by offering an animal for sacrifice at the Temple in Jerusalem. With the destruction of the temple, sacrifices were no longer possible. It was in Babylon that Judaism underwent radical changes in order to insure their religion would not die in a foreign country.

> **The destruction of Jerusalem and the Temple and the accompanying breaking up of the nation produced a most profound impression upon the religious development of Israel.**[120]

> **Ezekiel exercised probably a more profound influence upon the later developments of Judaism than any other man.**[121]

> **On Sabbaths and on holy days, the small exiled Jewish community would gather in his home to worship God as best they could in that foreign land, and perhaps, to hear Ezekiel read the law and interpret it.** *He was, in truth, the founder of the first synagogue.*[122]

---

[118] Russell, Jeffrey Burton. *The Devil: Perceptions of Evil from Antiquity to Primitive Christianity.* NY: New American Library, 1977. p. 174.

[119] Peters, John Punnett. *The Religion of the Hebrews: Handbooks on the History of Religions:* Cambridge, MA: Harvard University Press, 1932. p. 285.

[120] Peters, John Punnett. *The Religion of the Hebrews: Handbooks on the History of Religions:* Cambridge, MA: Harvard University Press, 1932. p. 308.

[121] Peters, John Punnett. *The Religion of the Hebrews: Handbooks on the History of Religions:* Cambridge, MA: Harvard University Press, 1932. p. 291.

[122] Cohen, Mortimer J. *Pathways Through the Bible.* Philadelphia. Jewish Publication Society of America. 1946. p. 399.

My Second Encounter With An Angel

> Contemporary with Ezekiel in the Babylonian exile and in close touch with him, at least so far as thought was concerned, were certain priests who seemed to have devoted themselves to a codification and explanation of the holiness laws of the Jews.[123]

Russell describes the writing of the Old Testament.

> The Old Testament was compiled over a long period from about 900 B. C. to about 100 B. C. Most of its books were written down in the present form during and after the period of the Babylonian Captivity (586-538) and show traces of Canaanite, Babylonian, Iranian, and Hellenistic influence.[124]

During their captivity, the Hebrews reformulated their religion, by transcribing their oral traditions and history. To state it in a much clearer way, it was the time that they *wrote the first copies of the Bible*. While they were living in this foreign land, they interacted with people from different cultures, who worshipped other gods. It is unclear as to the number of foreign rituals and beliefs Judaism absorbed.

> It is a commonly accepted opinion that only after the Babylonian captivity did the Hebrews have any clear and precise ideas regarding *demons*. Finding themselves, during that period, in continuous if not intimate contact with Mazdeism, the Hebrews had opportunity to learn certain of its teachings, and in part, to adopt them; and among these doctrines, that concerning the origin of evil must have found easy access to their minds....[125]

It was during their captivity in Babylon that the Hebrews came in contact with followers of Zoroastrianism, the religion of the ancient Persians.

> ...Zoroastrianism, Zoroastrianism was basically a dualistic religion, that is, it held that the cosmos was ruled by two principles, one good, the other evil.[126]

---

[123] Peters, John Punnett. *The Religion of the Hebrews: Handbooks on the History of Religions:* Cambridge, MA: Harvard University Press, 1932. p. 295.

[124] Russell, Jeffrey Burton. *The Devil: Perceptions of Evil from Antiquity to Primitive Christianity.* NY: New American Library, 1977. p. 175.

[125] Graf, Arturo. *The Story of the Devil.* NY: The Macmillan Company, 1931. p. 10-11.

[126] Cohen, Daniel. *Dealing with the Devil.* NY: Dodd, Mead & Company, 1979. p. 74.

> One of the oldest religions in the world to believe in the devil is Zoroastrianism. Also called Mazdaism, Zoroastrianism was founded by the Persian prophet Zarathushtra around 1200 B. C. Once the most popular religion of Persia (modern Iran)....[127]
>
> Zoroaster is the name the ancient Greeks gave the prophet Zarathushtra. Zarathushtra means "golden splendor."[128]
>
> Zoroaster held dualistic beliefs, meaning there were two equally powerful gods, a good god and an evil god that were competing to win over the souls of human beings.[129]
>
> Zarathushtra believed in two separate spirits or principles, one evil and one good. These spirits originated from a single source called Zuvran, which is beyond good and evil. This view is different from the ancient Hebrew belief that good and evil are inseparable and that evil is simply the dark side of one all-powerful God. Because of this dualism, Zoroastrianism was the first religion with a truly independent devil. Zoroastrians called the evil being Ahriman.[130]

The Zoroastrian idea of two gods, one good and one evil, was appealing to the Hebrews. This would enable God to be totally good. However, the idea of dualism posed a problem for the Hebrews because they believed in only **one** God. So the idea of Satan, a fallen angel, was inserted into the Bible, but it took centuries for the concept to be accepted. By that time the Hebrews had finished writing the Bible. In was not until the time of Jesus that the Hebrews accepted the notion of demons and devils, although it *never* became a central theme in Judaism.

> After about 200 B. C. many Jewish thinkers moved toward a strongly dualistic position—that is, of seeing the world caught in a struggle between two nearly equal rivals, one good, one evil.[131]

---

[127] Schouweiler, Thomas. *The Devil: Opposing Viewpoints*. San Diego, CA Greenhaven Press, 1992. p. 24.

[128] Carus, Paul. *The History Of The Devil and the Idea of Evil: From the Earliest Time to the Present Day*. NY: Land's End Press, 1969. p. 50.

[129] Holt, Olga. *Exorcism*. NY: Franklin Watts, 1978. p. 11.

[130] Schouweiler, Thomas. *The Devil: Opposing Viewpoints*. San Diego, CA Greenhaven Press, 1992. p. 26.

[131] Cohen, Daniel. *Dealing with the Devil*. NY: Dodd, Mead & Company, 1979. p. 81.

> Not surprisingly, the Devil in the New Testament is a far more prominent, powerful and well-defined figure than the Devil of the Old Testament.[132]

The writers of the New Testament were seeing devils and demons everywhere. Anything that was unpleasant, or anything that they did not understand, was considered "the work of the devil."

> As they went out, behold, they brought to him a dumb man possessed with a devil. And when the devil was cast out, the dumb spake, and the multitudes marveled, saying, It was never so seen in Israel. But the Pharisees said, He casteth out devils through the prince of devils.[133]

KJV represents nearly half the Bibles that claim that the dumb man was possessed with a devil. **NAB** represents the other half that says dumb man was possessed with a demon. This indicates the mindset of the first century apostles. When the New Testament was written, medicine and psychology were unknown sciences.

> The ancients believed that most sickness were caused by evil as spirits. In Egypt sickness itself was considered to be a demon. If a person was ill, it was because he was possessed by a demon.[134]

Early Christians believed that the devil existed, and it became part of their popular culture. It is very similar to people who are afraid of Friday the 13th, black cats, or avoid walking under a ladder. Most people are aware of all these superstitions, yet not many people still believe in them. Yet at one point in human history, most people did believe in these superstitions.

> The early Christians believed that the world was indeed in the grip of the Evil One, and that the final battle between good and evil, between Christ and the Devil, was nearly at hand.[135]

> Once Christianity was the official religion of the Roman Empire, it became the dominant religion of the people living in the cities throughout the empire. But the people living in rural areas still practiced their polytheistic religions. The Romans called the rural people pagans.

---

[132] Cohen, Daniel. *Dealing with the Devil*. NY: Dodd, Mead & Company, 1979. p. 82.
[133] Matthew 9:32-34 [KJV].
[134] Holt, Olga. *Exorcism*. NY: Franklin Watts, 1978. p. 9.
[135] Cohen, Daniel. *Dealing with the Devil*. NY: Dodd, Mead & Company, 1979. p. 82.

> A 'paganus' in Latin was either a country peasant or, in the language of the army, a civilian.[136]

When the *urban Christian Romans* set out to spread their new religion to the *rural pagans*, the interaction of the two groups caused some changes in Christianity; just as Judaism changed with its interaction with Zoroastrianism.

> Many anthropologists believe that the common image of Satan is the result of the merger of two traditions. One is ancient Hebrew theology, the basis for later Christian and Muslim thoughts. The other tradition developed in the pagan religions that flourished in Europe before the introduction of Christianity.[137]
>
> Between the years 400 and 600, Christian missionaries from Rome, the new capital of Christianity, brought their religion to the pagans of Europe, who were still worshipping earth gods and fertility gods in the tradition of Pan. The missionaries spread throughout the continent, rapidly converting pagan Europe to Christianity. In the process, most elements of the pagan religions were repressed or extinguished.[138]
>
> But although the Christians wiped out the pagan religions, elements of those religions were incorporated into Christianity. For example, to make the new religions more acceptable, Christians moved the dates of their holy days to concur with certain pagan festivals. Christmas, the anniversary of Christ's birth was moved to the day of the pagan Mithras Sun Feast, the midwinter celebration of the god of light and truth. The Christian holy days became intertwined with several pagan traditions. For example, the pagan springtime Ostara festival of fertility, growth, and the resurrection of life became Easter, which celebrates the resurrection of Jesus.[139]
>
> The mixing of the two culture affected the way the devil was seen as well Christian missionaries went to great lengths to

---

[136] McManners, John. *The Oxford Illustrated History of Chrisitanity*. Oxford: Oxford Univ. Press, 1990. p. 61.

[137] Schouweiler, Thomas. *The Devil: Opposing Viewpoints*. San Diego, CA Greenhaven Press, 1992. p. 12-14.

[138] Schouweiler, Thomas. *The Devil: Opposing Viewpoints*. San Diego, CA Greenhaven Press, 1992. p. 21-22.

[139] Schouweiler, Thomas. *The Devil: Opposing Viewpoints*. San Diego, CA Greenhaven Press, 1992. p. 22-23.

> vilify the old pagan pantheon of gods. They insisted there is only one God. Some pagan gods, however, would not die. One was Pan. He was especially threatening to Christians because he represented sensuality, materialism, and a strong connection to life on earth, values that are contrary to Christian doctrine. Christians therefore tended to identify Pan as a corrupting or evil being. Eventually his image became associated with that of the devil they knew, who Pan somewhat resembled.[140]

When I began to analyze what Awan had said to me, and what I read in all these books, I realized that Awan was correct. Awan stated that the priests created the Devil to place fear in the people's minds. The devil never existed. I could see from this research that nowhere in the Bible does God issues a warning concerning the Devil. Not even in the Ten Commandments, when God himself is speaking directly to the Hebrews (through trumpet mediumship).

I believe this one piece of evidence is most powerful to prove that the devil is not some evil spiritual force. The devil, as was confirmed through research, was introduced into Judaism during the Hebrew's captivity in Babylon. As Christianity was forming, the mythology about the devil was absorbed slowly, to a small degree, into Judaism. However, this mythology was more pronounced in Christianity, and grew further as pagan folklore was incorporated into Christian devil mythology.

From my understanding of Awan discussions, there are many Spirit entities on the lowest levels of the Spirit World, who would be very negative, or evil, if you wish to use that term. These negative Spirits exist; however, there is no all-evil entity, known as Satan or the devil, who resides in the Spirit World.

Throughout history, theologians used the devil as a puppet. By dangling the threat of this evil being in front of the people, priests terrorized illiterate people into believing anything that the Church wanted them to believe. The devil does **NOT** exist, but the myths of the devil's existence are very real, and had a profound effect on the history of this planet.

* * * *

Rev. Hewitt frequently shared much of Awan's teachings during his Sunday lectures at *Gifts of the Spirit Church*. One theme that was often stressed was how the priests created the devil.

About three months after I had finished this chapter, Nancy, one of the church-members, came up to me with an excited look on her face.

"Sid, you will never believe what I have just found in this book. This says exactly what Awan has been saying, but in more detail."

---

[140] Schouweiler, Thomas. *The Devil: Opposing Viewpoints*. San Diego, CA Greenhaven Press, 1992. p. 23.

I quickly read the passage she was showing me. "I can't believe it, Nancy," I said, "This really is amazing!"

I will close this chapter with this last piece of evidence, which thoroughly substantiates Awan's premise.

> **Osiris, according to the Egyptians, was murdered by a brother called Set. Set became fanatically jealous of his brother Osiris on account of the great love of the people for Osiris, which ended in Set murdering him. About ten thousand years after the time of Thoth, the vile, unscrupulous Egyptian priesthood, to bring fear and dread into the hearts of the people and so enslave them for their priestly purposes, turned Set into the devil of today. Before a devil was invented by the Egyptians, a devil was unknown.**[141]

---

[141] Churchwsard, James, Col. *The Children of Mu*. Albuqueque, NM: Be Books, 1992. p. 159.

Salon-de-Provence–the Home of Nostradamus

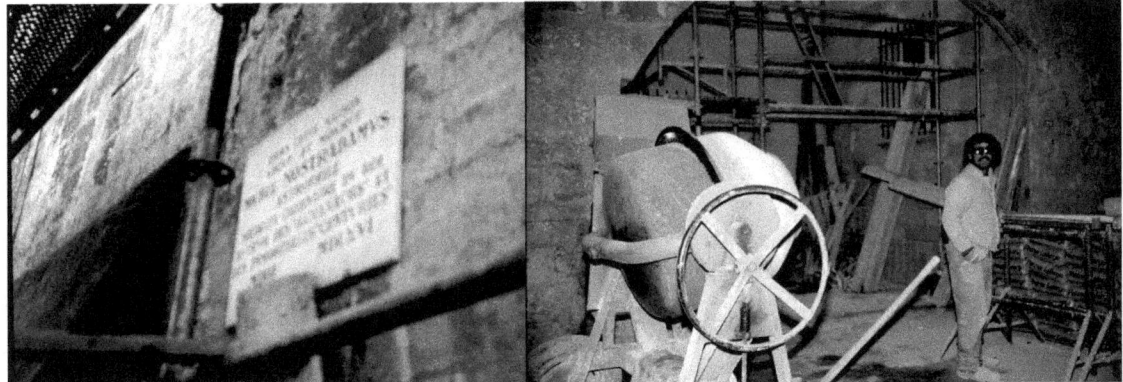

In February 1992, Carl and I took a trip to Spain and France, and we drove to Salon-de-Provence, the home of Nostradamus. We visited the house in which he lived, but unfortunately, it was being restored and was under construction.

We then decided to visit Collégiale Saint-Laurent, the church where Nostradamus was buried. I walked to the side of the building to photograph the church (picture to the left). When I returned Carl asked me with a very annoyed tone, "Where were you?" I replied I was just on the other side of the building. Carl continued, "You will not believe what happened! As I approached the doors to the church, they flew open. I examined the doorway; there is no electric eye. Spirit people opened the door for me!"

Carl Hewitt standing in front of the tomb of Michel de Nostredamus

The memorial plaque of Michel de Nostredamus

EIGHT

Awan Discusses Cathedrals and Communion

Recently, I had traveled to Paris, France, and decided to visit Nôtre Dame, one of the world's most famous cathedrals. As I was walking down the aisle of this magnificent cathedral, this thought suddenly swept across my mind. This most famous building, the cathedral of Nôtre Dame, was a monument of recycled ignorance. It high, arched ceiling vaults were supposed to reach upwards to God. Yet, I found myself thinking of the tons of stones bearing downward upon its foundation. Cathedrals were not reaching up to God; instead they were heavy weights bearing down on people, entrapping their minds. As I gazed at the beauty of the famous rose stained-glass windows, and the many magnificent statues contained within the cathedral, I felt a calm quietness encompass me. It was different than other cathedrals I had visited, in which I felt a heavy oppression, and a deep foreboding negativity. It was only after the dialogue that is contained in this chapter, that I realized how accurate these thought were.

* * * *

This dialogue took place in Carl's darkened office. After reciting his usual prayer, Carl closed his eyes. Awan seemed to overtake Carl's body effortlessly, since Carl's body did not spasm.

😇 My greetings to you, my scribe.

🧑 Greetings, Awan.

😇 I see that you have been busy in your libraries. Please tell me what you have concluded.

🧑 I understand your point, that the priests created the devil. If there really were a devil, then some Spirit person would have told Abraham or Moses, or Samuel, or another medium, to warn the people. Moses received hundreds of instructions, specifying how the people were to conduct their lives. He also gave the world one of the earliest law codes, the Ten Commandments. It would only be logical that Spirit would have warned Moses, if the devil existed. I am sure Spirit would want the people to know about such a devious entity! The fact that information of the devil's existence did not come through any of the early patriarchs or prophets indicates no devil existed. Therefore, the conception of the devil occurred after the time of Moses, Samuel, Elijah and Elisha.

Precisely. The religions on your planet have been able to shut down the brains of the people, to the point where the people believe anything their theologians tell them. You have done much traveling, and have been to many places. Have you gone to those grand monuments to superstitions; I believe that you term them *cathedrals*?

Yes, Awan, I have been to several famous European and American cathedrals.

The priests did many things to entice people into their religion. They built enormous buildings, that you term cathedrals. The Bishops told their congregations that the higher the building, the closer to heaven they would be. This would make it much easier for God to hear their prayers. If you worshipped in a building that was equivalent to what you would term a skyscraper, you would be much closer to the feet of God, living in a piece of real-estate in the sky. God was getting older every year; he might be getting hard of hearing. There would be great advantages to praying in a cathedral that was closer to God's ears. You can travel the world over, and you will discover that wherever you go, the Catholic Church is the tallest building in every town. It was all part of the priests' elaborate plans to enslave people to their dogmas.

This is a substantiating statement I found.

> **All through Europe, in villages, towns, and large bustling cities, the spires of cathedrals built in the Middle Ages rise majestically to the skies. In small towns, the cathedral is the longest, widest, and tallest of all the buildings by far.**[142]
>
> **Bishops and townspeople competed to build the largest and the most beautiful cathedral. The tallest medieval cathedral spire was at Strasbourg in France. Almost 490 feet high (as high as a 45-story building today), it remained the tallest building in Europe for hundreds of years, until the Eiffel Tower was built in Paris during the 19th century using newly invented cast iron.**[143]

---

[142] Perdrizet, Marie-Pierre. *The Cathedral Builders*. Brookfield, CT: Millbrook Press, 1992. p. 6.

[143] Macdonald, Fiona. *A Medieval Cathedral*. NY: P. Bedrick Books, 1991. p. 28.

👤 Of course there was no truth in the priests' explanation. The priests had no regard for the welfare of their people. They did not care, what kind of hardship it was for the people to donate extravagant sums of money in order to build these monuments to their own egos. Nor did they care how many people lost their lives while working on building these tall and elaborate buildings.

📖 These statements were corroborated by other sources.

> **The construction of a cathedral required first and foremost a very substantial financial investment in order to obtain the enormous site and meet other initial expenses.[144]**

> **It was the bishop who, out of his own funds and the revenues of his diocese, provided the money necessary for the execution of his project. A whole category of bishops appeared who were very concerned about the profitability of their properties.[145]**

> **The money to build cathedrals came mostly from gifts—of land, farms, houses and jewels, and gold and silver coins. People believed that by giving to the Church, they would help to win forgiveness for their sins.[146]**

📖 These next quotes demonstrate how priests' egos were involved with building cathedrals. The "ends would justify the means," no matter what the human cost.

> **When bishop Bernard de Castanet came to Albi in 1277 the Inquisition was raging with particular ferocity in the Languedoc, one of the richest and most flourishing regions in Europe. The bishop was himself head of the Inquisition in southern France and at the same time deputy Inquisitor General for the whole country. On the very day of his arrival in a city tyrannized by persecution and murder, he and his chapter [a group of clergymen who controlled the money.[147]] decided to build a new cathedral, which later came to be known as the Cathedral of Hate.[148]**

---

[144] Icher, François. *Building the Great Cathedrals*. NY: Harry N. Abrams, 1998. p. 40.

[145] Icher, François. *Building the Great Cathedrals*. NY: Harry N. Abrams, 1998. p. 40.

[146] Macdonald, Fiona. *A Medieval Cathedral*. NY: P. Bedrick Books, 1991. p. 6.

[147] Macaulay, David. *Cathedral*. Boston: Houghton Mifflin, 1973. p. 7.

[148] McGeoch Angus. *Cathedrals: A Hundred Jewels of European Architecture*. Munich, Germany: I. P. Verlagsgesellschaft, 1998. p. 20.

> Or, a bishop may have seen a wonderful cathedral in a neighboring town and, backed by the church and the bourgeoisie, collected the funds to replace his old cathedral with a new, more beautiful one.[149]
>
> According to a legend recorded in the 19th century, the devastating fire, which destroyed the Early Gothic cathedral of Reims in 1210, was started by the bishop himself. This was the only way he could commission the building of a new cathedral that would surpass all other churches.[150]
>
> A new cathedral was an attractive idea for yet another reason. At the time the people of nearby Amiens, Beauvais, and Rouen were building new cathedrals. The people of Chutreaux did not wish to be outdone, on earth or especially in heaven.[151]

📖 This last quote shows how well the clergy had indoctrinated their followers. Christians felt the deeds they did during their physical life would be replicated in their after-life. This belief is demonstrated in the following Bible verse:

> And I will give to thee the keys of the kingdom of the heavens; and whatsoever thou mayest *bind upon the earth* shall *be bound in the heavens*; and whatsoever thou mayest *loose on the earth* shall be *loosed in the heavens*.[152]

While it is true that you earn your place in the Spirit World according to your actions, it does not mean you will have a xerox copy of your physical life in the Spirit World. The people of Chutreaux would not find a magnificent cathedral awaiting them in the Spirit World.

😇 Now my scribe, explain to me why cathedrals have those horribly ugly creatures on them?

🧑 Do you mean gargoyles?

---

[149] Perdrizet, Marie-Pierre. *The Cathedral Builders*. Brookfield, CT: Millbrook Press, 1992. p. 18.

[150] McGeoch Angus. *Cathedrals: a Hundred Jewels of European Architecture*. Munich, Germany: I. P. Verlagsgesellschaft, 1998. p. 48.

[151] Macaulay, David. *Cathedral*. Boston: Houghton Mifflin, 1973. p. 5.

[152] Mathew 16:19 [KJV].

(😇) Yes that is what I mean. Do you realize that those wondrous pieces of stone have fantastic power in them?

(🧑) They do?

(😇) According to the theologians who had them placed on those buildings, they were supposed to protect the people inside the cathedral. These gargoyles, as you term them, would keep evil spirits, demons, and devils out of the building. They were what you might term "medieval burglar alarms," to protect the people from devils.

(🧑) Really, I didn't know that.

(📖) However, I later found substantiating evidence:

> **They [gargoyles] served as protectors. It is a common belief, through many cultures, that in order to keep away 'evil' spirits one must utilize something frightening. Hence, the grotesque nature of these carvings. This idea is similar to some Halloween practices of donning costumes of spooks or ghouls in order to keep out the spirits that roam more readily on All Hollow's Eve. Grotesques were also an educational device. For the illiterate vulgate [common people], this was useful. Through the use of art, Church doctrine could be taught. Some gargoyles when shown eating or snatching a naked human are in actuality demons devouring or carrying off human souls. The terrors of Hell were a common subject for artwork. There existed grotesques with large grins, toothful smiles and protruding tongues.**[153]

(😇) I know that this will be outside of your 21st century experience, but I want you to realize, my scribe, that the average person living in the Middle Ages was very ignorant; he or she could not read or write. Books in those days had to be written by hand, because the printing press had not yet been invented. Only the most-wealthy aristocrats, and the clergy, could afford books.

When a person went into a cathedral, it became a "living textbook" to teach the people their religion. It could be compared to a child's "picture book." The pictures help the illiterate child learn and follow the story. Until very recent times, Catholic Church services were said in Latin. The average person did not understand that language. So to convey the stories of their religion, cathedrals became necessary. Statues were placed all around, to divert people's attention away from the God within, to a God without. Bible stories were told in picture form, in colorful stained glass windows. The Church's crucial message that "Jesus died for the sins of people of all times," was clearly illustrated in picture form in the "stations of the cross." Gargoyles were deliberately designed as scary, and horrifying as possible. These images

---

[153] http://web.lemoyne.edu/museums/begieral/cult.html [Le Moyne College, Syracuse, NY].

were created to scare Hell *into* people's consciousness. All this was done to marry Christian ideology to illiterate people, who could not understand the Latin words being spoken by the priests.

📖 A few months later, as I was doing some research, I came upon a passage that amazed me. The author's words were almost identical to Awan's.

> **Not least of all, the cathedral was a teacher for those who knew how to receive its instruction. Like a gigantic book, the cathedral tells the story of medieval people—how they spent their lives, what they knew about the world, what their religious beliefs and traditions were, and how they felt about God.[154]**
>
> **The cathedral builders recreated almost all of this knowledge on stained glass and in stone for everyone to see.[155]**

During my February vacation in 1992, Carl and I traveled to Europe. We rented a car, and drove from Madrid to Barcelona. Then making an impromptu decision, we drove across southern France, and visited Nostradamus' house in the city Salon-de-Provence. On our return trip, we stopped in Narbonne. As usual, the tallest building in this small city was the cathedral. Carl informed me that Spirit wanted us to visit it.

My impression of this cathedral is rather vague. Its interior was elaborately decorated. However, what made an indelible impression upon Carl and me was a particular archway. It had an unusual engraved decoration of an alternating pattern: a baby's head and a skeleton. This pattern was repeated many times.

Carl immediately told me, what he was clairaudiently hearing. This arch was created to teach the people that the road to hell is paved with the souls of unbaptized babies. This must have been a century's old teaching, because evidence of it existed during the life of Joan of Arc (1412-1431).

> **At Lagny, she was called to the church in which a baby, who had not stirred for three days, had been laid before an image of the Virgin. Other young girls of the town were praying there for the baby's life; and when Joan came, he yawned, changed colour and recovered sufficiently to be baptised before dying. He could then be buried in hallowed ground, a privilege not permitted to the stillborn.[156]**

---

[154] Perdrizet, Marie-Pierre. *The Cathedral Builders*. Brookfield, CT: Millbrook Press, 1992. p. 38-39.

[155] Perdrizet, Marie-Pierre. *The Cathedral Builders*. Brookfield, CT: Millbrook Press, 1992. p. 40.

[156] Warner, Marina. *Joan of Arc: The Image of Femlae Heroism*. NY: Alfred A. Knopf, 1981. p. 91.

📖 I found proof that priests used art as a method to teach religious doctrine to their followers. The text of the Catholic, Vulgate Bible was in Latin. Catholic priests said the mass in Latin until Vatican II, which took place from 1962-1965.[157]

> **To make religious ceremonies more meaningful, sweeping liturgical reforms were initiated. The use of national languages or the vernacular was approved on a broad scale for liturgical celebrations.[158]**

The only people who spoke, or understood, Latin were the priests. Yet, ironically, the word **Vulgate** means:

> **... the speech of the common people and especially of uneducated people.[159]**

📖 Awan's claim that priests incorporated artwork (statues, paintings, gargoyles, stained glass) to teach their theology of "heaven and hell," just as children can understand stories by looking at picture books, could also be substantiated.

> **In the time when illiteracy was an almost universal condition and belief in a literal, waiting Inferno prevailed, the purpose of most cathedral sculpture was not to decorate but didactic. It was intended, in short, to scare the hell out of its beholders, and there is every reason to believe it did a credible job, presenting the horrors of damnation in living color....[160]**

👼 Furthermore, my scribe, since the priest spoke a mysterious foreign language [Latin]; it implied that God would only speak Latin. Therefore, the average person required the priest as his or her translator to talk with God. This placed the priests exactly where they wanted to be, as the intermediaries between the God in heaven, and the people on earth. Therefore, their role was indispensable, thus allowing them to extort whatever they wanted from the people.

🧑 I certainly see your point, Awan.

---

[157] The Encyclopedia Americana. International Edition. Vol. 27. Danbury, CT: Grolier, 1986. p. 911.

[158] The Encyclopedia Americana. International Edition. Vol. 27. Danbury, CT: Grolier, 1986. p. 912.

[159] *Merriam-Webster's Collegiate Dictionary—10th edition.* Springfield, MA: Merriam-Webster, Inc., 1997. p. 1326.

[160] Jacobs, Jay. *The Horizon Book of Great Cathedrals.* NY: American Heritage Publishing Co., 1968. p. 48.

(👼) Returning to the subject of gargoyles, I want you to reason this out, my scribe. How could a piece of stone do what their God couldn't do? Not even Jesus could keep devils and demons away, how did the people expect a cold piece of stone to protect them from devils?

(🧑) What do you mean? It says in the Bible, that Jesus healed people by casting out demons and devils.[161]

(👼) Yes, but you must realize that in those days, people believed devils and demons caused illness. The priests taught that all illness, and every type of pain that occurred in the human body, was the work of the devil, not of God. The priests would say to a person "Your pain is because you do not believe in our God, who lives in heaven. You believe in another, which is "the Evil One," (which later on became the devil). As long as you do not believe in our God, you will have these pains in your body. Your family is not faithful to our God. Therefore, the devil has caused your illness, because of your disbelief in our God." These pains were real medical problems such as a ruptured appendix, or a gall bladder attack. The priests had no medical knowledge, but they understood the power of fear, which they used to dominate the minds of the people. This was driven home, in every aspect. What started out as illnesses of the body: an open sore that would not heal, a broken limb, a stroke—was caused by the devil. For millenniums, the priests all over your world have focused their preaching on the devil.

📖 I later discovered confirmation of these statements.

> **The ancients believed that most sicknesses were caused by evil spirits. In Egypt sickness itself was considered to be a demon. If a person was ill, it was because he was possessed by a demon.**[162]

(👼) However, your Book of Books describes an incident where Jesus couldn't keep devils and demons away at his last *séance*.

(🧑) Pardon me, last *séance*? Jesus conducted a séance?

(👼) Yes, you understand that Jesus was a medium, just as the man whose body I am using is a medium.

(🧑) Yes, Awan, I understand that.

(👼) And you know that when spiritual guidance comes through a medium, it is termed a *séance*. What we are doing right now is a séance.

(🧑) Yes, but the Bible doesn't mention the last séance, it describes the *last supper*.

---

[161] Matthew 9:27-34.
[162] Holt, Olga. *Exorcism*. NY: Franklin Watts, 1978. p. 9.

My Second Encounter With An Angel

(😇) That is what I am talking about. You have had the experience that after attending a séance the medium is often tired and hungry. Many mediums prefer not to eat a heavy meal before they do their mediumistic work. Therefore, after the conclusion of the séance the medium is often famished. You have been to séances where you sat down to eat a meal after the conclusion of a séance with my dimension.

(🧑) Yes, that is true.

(😇) That is what happened in Jesus' time. Jesus and his twelve students went to the upper-room, which was actually their séance room. Remember our discussion about the cabinet.[163]

(🧑) Oh yes, I understand. The Old Testament talks of a *roof chamber*,[164] which was the cabinet, or séance room. It was often built on the roof or high on the building, to avoid the negative vibrations of the people on the ground level.

(😇) Correct. Jesus' upper room had three wooden bars to slide to across the door. I believe that these would be termed *door jams*. These door jams were made of solid oak, so this door could be locked and the room would be impenetrable. Now if this were just a room in which to dine, why would they need maximum security?

(🧑) I understand what you are saying. Séance rooms always have locks on them. If a séance is interrupted, it can be very dangerous, even fatal, for the medium.

(😇) Precisely. Just as my medium is in a trance state, and I am speaking with you this very moment, Jesus went into trance during that last séance. Jesus' Spirit teachers: Elijah and Moses, took turns using Jesus' voice box, just as you have witnessed two Spirits taking turns using this medium.[165] Elijah and Moses gave final instructions to the disciples (students) on what they were to do after Jesus' death. Remember on the Mount of Transfiguration,[166] Moses and Elijah had already instructed Jesus, on the preparations he was to make before his crucifixion. For Jesus to accomplish his mission, the disciples also had to carry out certain tasks after Jesus' death.

(🧑) That makes sense.

(😇) After they finished the séance, they sat down to celebrate the Passover feast.

(🧑) You mean they had a *Seder*, just like the ones that I attend?

---

[163] See Schwartz, Sidney. *My First Encounter with an Angel: Revelations of Ancient Wisdom.* Blue Hill, ME: Medicine Bear Publishing, 1999. p. 119-140.
[164] 1 Kings 17:19, 2 Kings 1:2, 2 Kings 4:10 [SON], 2 Kings 23:11 [COV], 2 Kings 23:12 [NIV].
[165] See chapter 5.
[166] Luke 9:28-36 [KJV].

(👼) Well, your *Seder* has been changed since Jesus' time, however some of the rituals are the same. They did eat Matzo and they did dip food into salt water.

(👤) I see.

(👼) After I leave this man's body, go into your Book of Books and find the verses of what happened to Judas after Jesus handed him some food that was dipped in the salt water.

(📖) I later found the verses Awan was discussing.

> **Jesus answered, He it is, to whom I shall give a sop, when I have dipped it. And when he had dipped the sop, he gave it to Judas Iscariot, the son of Simon. And after the sop, *Satan* entered into him. Then said Jesus unto him, That thou doest, do quickly.**[167]

(📖) I consulted a dictionary to learn the precise meaning of the word **sop**.

> **SOP anything soaked or dipped in liquid to be eaten.**[168]

(📖) Now, this verse was making sense to me. The Last Supper was a *Seder*. It is customary to dip several vegetables in the salt water (that represented tears of slavery) before eating them. Apparently, this custom was practiced 2000 years ago, as evident by this verse.

(👼) You will see one of the changes that theologians made in that text. The theologians set up a confrontation between Jesus and Satan, to put fear in the minds of the people. The Bible tells us that Satan entered into Judas, and caused Judas to betray Jesus. If you believe this story, then you must have much of your brain shut down, or you are totally blinded by the Christian dogmas.

(👤) Why do you say that, Awan?

(👼) Now, reason this out, my scribe. Many Christians believe Jesus was God incarnate, which gave Jesus all kinds of miraculous abilities. (You understand those miracles as demonstrations of the *Gifts of the Spirit*.) There are several instances recorded in your Book of Books where Jesus touched people. A woman touched Jesus' hem and was healed.[169] Jesus healed blind men by laying on of the hands.[170] During Jesus' arrest, the servant of the high priest

---

[167] John 13:26-27 [KJV].

[168] Skeat, Walter W. Rev. *An Etymological Dictionary of the English Language*. Oxford: Claredon Press, 1882. p. 574.

[169] Matthew 9:20-22 [KJV].

[170] Matthew 9:28-30 [KJV].

had his ear cut off; Jesus reattached the ear by touching it.[171] So the energy that ran though Jesus' body was very powerful, because his brain was operating at 100%, therefore, he could heal people.

🙂 I understand that, Awan. What is the point that you are trying to make?

👼 The point is this, my brother. Theologians claimed that Jesus was God. Jesus, himself, handed Judas a piece of bread that he had dipped into the salt water. The Bible says that Satan entered Judas right after Judas ate the sop. If a person believes this Bible verse, he or she should question the rite of *communion*. If food from *Jesus' own hand* could **NOT** keep Satan out of a Judas, then how could the bread from a mere priest's hand repel Satan? Furthermore, how effective would a stone gargoyle be in keeping the devil out of a cathedral?

🙂 Oh, I am beginning to see your point.

👼 Consult some books in your libraries, and discover the meaning of *communion*.

📖 I found the following information in a Catholic Bible:

Communion—The act of receiving the Eucharist.[172]

The Eucharist is the sacrament, which nourishes and keeps strong the soul's supernatural life.[173]

📖 In other sources I discovered that the Catholic mass, especially the communion service, was supposed to help a person ward off the devil.

The ancient Egyptians wore bells as amulets, and their descendants, the early Copts, followed their example, and used them to drive away evil spirits during the celebration of the Eucharist.[174]

COMMUNION CHALICE/WINE c1000 This is the holy drink against one full of elfin tricks and for all temptations of the devil.[175]

---

[171] Luke 22:51 [KJV].

[172] O'Connel, John P. Monsignor, editor. *The Holy Bible with the Confratery Text*. Found in the section entitled *A Practical Dictionary of Biblical and General Catholic Information*. Chicago, IL: The Catholic Press, Inc., 1965. p. 54.

[173] O'Connel, John P. Monsignor, editor. *The Holy Bible with the Confratery Text*. "The Holy Eucharist" found in the section entitled *The Seven Sacraments*. Chicago, IL: The Catholic Press, Inc., 1965. p. 268.

[174] Budge, E. A Wallis, Sir. *Amulets and Superstitions*. London: Oxford University Press, 1930. p. 215.

[175] Opie, Iona and Tatem, Moira, editors. *A Dictionary of Superstitions*. Oxford: Oxford University Press, 1989. p. 93.

> **The rites of the Church, if faithfully administered proved effective means of opposing the Devil. Attendance at Mass enabled men and women to resist temptation, if the worshipper made full use of the opportunity.**[176]

📖 It would appear that Awan was telling the truth when he said that the devil was created to put fear in the minds of the people. This kept them coming back to the Church in attempts to receive protection. While in Church, people put money into the collection plates. Apparently, according to Church teachings, the devil was everywhere.

> **The Church warned men that devils could insinuate themselves into herbs and that those who picked such herbs were immediately possessed by evil spirits. The faithful were enjoined to say long prayers and to make the sign of the Cross when they gathered herbs, and patients who took herbs as medicine were bidden to sing the sixteenth Psalm as a protection against any devils who might be lurking in the draught.**[177]

> **Stonehenge was the work of the Devil.** [178]

👼 You understand the soul is divine energy.

🧑 Yes, Awan.

👼 If energy cannot be created or destroyed, how could a Eucharist, which is simply a holy cracker increase energy? Your physical body derives its energy from the digestion of food—that is true. However, physical food does not nourish the spiritual body. If your motor-car went dead, because there was no energy in its battery, would you start putting crackers into the battery?

🧑 But you can charge the car's battery, and make it run again.

👼 This is true, you can charge your spiritual body too. The spiritual body gets it energy from the knowledge it receives. If a clairvoyant were here watching this dialogue, he or she would see the aura around your body expand. The light from your soul is radiating further away from your body, because the soul has this knowledge stored in is memory banks. As you hear my words, the soul is reactivating these cells, which expands your auric field. You are feeding your soul, if you wish to use that term. But as of yet, you have not eaten any crackers, with or without cheese!

---

[176] Edwards, W. *A Mediaeval Scrap-Heap.* London: Rivingtons, 1930. p. 141.

[177] Edwards, W. *A Mediaeval Scrap-Heap.* London: Rivingtons, 1930. p. 134.

[178] Edwards, W. *A Mediaeval Scrap-Heap.* London: Rivingtons, 1930. p. 130.

👤 No Awan, I haven't eaten any crackers today. Although you say my aura is expanding, I do not feel that it is larger.

😇 I beg your pardon, my brother, please describe to me how you feel after one of our sessions.

👤 I usually feel very high, and quite charged up, and have an uplifting feeling.

😇 That is because your aura has expanded. No, my brother, since you do not have clairvoyant vision, you cannot see the light around the body, so you cannot directly see this change in your aura. You can feel it, however, through your emotions as you have just described.

👤 That is very interesting, Awan.

😇 If you had a time machine, and could travel back before Christianity was created, when people who wanted to commune with God, or to say it in another way, commune with Spirit, sought out a person with the *Gifts of the Spirit*. That gifted person would go into an altered trance state, just as this man did at the beginning of our session. This allows me to take over the voice box of this body, and use it to speak with you. The identical phenomena happened centuries ago.

You must remember that the Catholic Church was trying to wean the people from believing that God was within. Originally, there were thousands of people who did not accept this new religion. Since most of them lived in rural areas, these non-believers of Christianity were called *Pagans*. Many of the Pagan religions practiced the *Gifts of the Spirit*. Many pagans knew and communicated with the God within.

📖 This statement corroborates Awan's claim.

> **By the fourth century, 'Pagan'... was being used non-polemically to describe anyone who worshipped the spirit of a given locality or *pagus*.**[179]

📖 From this statement we understand that these people were worshipping Spirit, just as Jesus had described when he said: **"God is spirit, and those who worship him must worship in spirit and truth."**[180]

😇 The Catholic Church declared war on the Pagans. Catholic Priests gave the Pagans a choice; convert to Christianity, or be slaughtered. The priests wanted every person alive to worship the God they created. This God looked like a man, and lived in heaven, in a mythical piece of real-estate in the sky. These theologians placed all the statues of their holy family, and saints, around their churches to help divert the worshipper's focus away from the

---

[179] Jones, Prudeence and Pennick, Nigel. *History of Pagan Europe*. NY: Barnes & Noble Books, 1999. p. 1.
[180] John 4:24 [RSV].

soul in their chest, and out to these statues. These statues were what you might term the "ancient training wheels," that you now have for your bicycles. After the people believed that God was without, instead of within, they had to harmonize the two opposite concepts. After all, they did not remove this quote from the Bible:

Behold, the kingdom of God is within you.[181]

The theologians needed a way for God to be outside of the body and inside too. So to put God back into the physical body, they developed the communion service. The priest started giving the people crackers, as you would term it, or bread, and wine which was to symbolize, the body and the blood of God. The priests put the cracker on the people's tongues, and as the people would eat the bread, they were putting the God into their body, at least temporarily. This is how the theologians could have a God within, and still keep God up in the sky. This is the true story of how, and why the Catholic Church created communion.

🙂 Achoo! [I sneezed].

😇 May the Lord God of your being come forward and release the natural antihistamines in your body to calm your nasal irritations.

🙂 Thank you, Awan. Why didn't you simply say, "God bless you"?

😇 Why should I? Do you use that phrase?

🙂 Yes, Awan, I do.

😇 And what other of the Pope's decrees do you obey?

🙂 What do you mean, Awan?

😇 Do you understand why you use the expression, "God bless you"?

🙂 No, Awan, to be truthful I don't.

😇 There are millions of robots, like yourself, who keep spouting forth archaic utterances. They sound like parrots with only a three-word vocabulary. Yet, they do not have the slightest inkling of what these words mean. It astonishes me that it has never occurred to people alive today to question the meaning of this expression. People on your planet are about 2 degrees more intelligent than they were 1,700 years ago. Some people in my dimension are not even that generous.

Your expression: "God bless you" goes back to what you term *The Middle Ages*. Medieval people believed that when you sneezed, a devil was trying to enter your body. Pope Gregory I declared that everyone should bless a person who sneezes, to prevent the devil from entering that person's body. Now you know the origin of your custom.

---

[181] Luke 17:21 [KJV].

👤 That is interesting.

👼 So do you think that it is necessary for me to stop a devil from flying up your nose?

👤 No Awan, I think the words you used would be much more effective.

👼 Go to your library and look it up for yourself, and you will discover that I speak the truth.

📖 I later discovered this quote at the library.

> **Some people even believed that sneezing indicated an intrusion into the body of foreign objects or beings, such as evil spirits in various guises as ghosts, fairies, gnomes or demons which jumped out when the act of sneezing took place. Hence there was danger to others when someone sneezed in their presence, because the evil occupants expelled might become tenants of the body of another individual. Spirit were supposed to travel from person to person.[182]**
>
> **Pope Gregory decreed that people should say a special prayer or wish for the person who sneezed. This is why people began saying God bless you after a person sneezed.[183]**

📖 I recently discovered similar beliefs existed in 1887 concerning yawning.

> **When yawning make the sign of the cross instantly over the mouth, or the evil spirit will make a rush down and take up his abode in you.[184]**

👼 I am sorry if I insulted your ego, when I discussed the low intelligence level of the people living in your dimension. Please do not be offended. However, you must realize that 2/3 of your brain is dormant. How could you possibly be highly intelligent using so little brain capacity? The people of your planet are all so complacent with their world. They are so ignorant that they cannot even realize their own ignorance. If your race is so intelligent, why haven't I heard one single human pray to their God, asking for their brain open, which would provide total knowingness? I have never heard that prayer once in all the billion of prayers I have heard, in search of the ears of a non-existent God.

---

[182] Lys, Claudia de. *A Treasury of American Superstitions*. NY: Philosophical Library, 1948. p. 305.

[183] Lys, Claudia de. *A Treasury of American Superstitions*. NY: Philosophical Library, 1948. p. 306.

[184] Opie, Iona and Tatem, Moira, editors. *A Dictionary of Superstitions*. Oxford: Oxford University Press, 1989. p. 454.

🙂 That was intriguing, Awan. I understand what you mean.

👤 You must realize, it was the goal of the Catholic Church to place fear in the minds of the people. The primary tools to accomplish this goal were demons and devils. As soon as people opened their eyes in the morning, their very first thought was how to protect themselves from the devil's eternal hell fires. This was a very successful ploy for the Church. They had the people brainwashed to believe exactly what they said. The Church taught the people these evil beings were everywhere. They were in the air, in the flowers, and in the trees. Therefore, the Church controlled all knowledge.

📖 Again I found proof that medieval people would not even question anything their priests told them.

> **Christians began to pray in front of these relics so that the saints would ask God to cure them. People thousands of them, traveled from distant regions and even from other counties to witness these relics first-hand.... All cathedrals had relics. Whether they were authentic or not was not a question medieval people asked themselves.**[185]

🙂 Is that why the Church persecuted Galileo, when he said that the earth revolved around the sun?

👤 That is correct. Galileo was going against the current teachings of the Church, which was against all new learning. Before what you term *the Renaissance*, the Church did not want anyone to learn to read, because then people might learn something that contradicted Church doctrine. However, the Church developed a back-up plan. If someone went against Church doctrine, that person was in league with the devil, and was burned at the stake. Any new invention might erode the Church's power; therefore, the devil must have inspired it. Even popes were accused of doing the devil's work. When you are in your library, see if you cannot find the proof of this as well.

📖 While doing some research in a college library, I discovered these quotes:

> **Gerbert, who became Pope Sylvester II, and died in 1003, was one of the greatest scientists of the times. He was a skilled mathematician and was reputed to have introduced the Arabic numeration into Europe.... Although the Pope's personal conduct was exemplary, men could not forgive him for his mathematics, and the orator who pronounced his**

---

[185] Perdrizet, Marie-Pierre. *The Cathedral Builders*. Brookfield, CT: Millbrook Press, 1992. p. 42.

funeral sermon declared that "He paid homage to the Devil and came to a bad end."[186]

Legend says the first printed book caused its seller's arrest, when folk accustomed to books hand-copied by scribes denounced multiple identical copies as the Devil's work![187]

The next stronghold of the devil was in Germany; the former method of sawing lumber was to put a log upon a scaffolding, and one man take his position under the log and another on top; one pulled the saw down and the other pulled it up. The thought occurred to one man that a little mountain stream near by could be utilized to turn a flutter-wheel, a crank could be fixed to the wheel, a shaft to the crank and a saw to the shaft, and thus a great amount of manual labor could be saved. He went to work and built his mill and was put to death for it.[188]

God had said: "In the seat of thy face shalt thou eat bread;" but this was a labor saving machine; man did not half sweat sitting with his arms folded and watching water saw his lumber. This invention if not rebuked, would be followed by other laborsaving inventions, and thus God Almighty's curse would be thwarted. The man who invented it did it by the aid of the devil and was put to death.[189]

As a boy, I was often warned by the ministers that the devil was in the abolition movement. God and the Bible in favor of slavery; the devil was trying to overthrow God's precious law, by repealing the clause which says, "Cursed be Canaan," etc.

Every church in Christendom denounced the abolitionists, and said slavery was a divine institution, until Infidels and heretics carried it on to success. I have in my possession to-day books containing the resolutions passed by all the

---

[186] Edwards, W. *A Mediaeval Scrap-Heap*. London: Rivingtons, 1930. p. 135.

[187] O'Neill Richard. *The Middle Ages*. Godalming, England: Colour Library Books Ltd., 1992. p. 86.

[188] Hull, Moses. *All About Devils; or, An Inquiry as to Whether Modern Spiritualism and other Great Reforms Emanate from His Satanic Majesty and his Subordinates in the Kingdom of Darkness*. 5th ed. Whitewater, WI: M. Hull, 1902. p. 39.

[189] Hull, Moses. *All About Devils; or, An Inquiry as to Whether Modern Spiritualism and Other Great Reforms Emanate from His Satanic Majesty and his Subordinates in the Kingdom of Darkness*. 5th ed. Whitewater, WI: M. Hull, 1902. p. 40.

> **leading churches in favor of the divinity of slavery and against fire-eating infidel abolitionists.**[190]

📖 When Carl read this chapter, he told me the following story. During the 1930's, one of his sisters-in-law adamantly refused to install electricity in her house, because as with other technological advances, electricity was the work of the Devil!

👼 Whenever the Church felt threatened that it might lose its stronghold over the people; priests would play their "devil card."

📖 I recently visited the Women's Rights National Historical Park, in Seneca Falls, New York. There is an excellent museum that documents the struggle women had in order to obtain their right to vote, and to inherit property. They had a huge obstacle to conquer because the Bible proscribed a subservient role to women.[191] One of the exhibits on display in the Women's Rights museum was entitled, "The Woman's Bible." It states:

> **In 1895, Elizabeth Cady Stanton published *The Woman's Bible*, a series of commentaries on Biblical passages about women.... *The Woman's Bible* outraged not only the clergy, who proscribed condemned it as the work of the Devil....**[192]

👼 Now my scribe, it saddens me to inform you that I am a bit disappointed in you.

🧑 I am sorry Awan, what have I done?

👼 You did a very wicked thing this morning, my scribe?

🧑 Awan, I cannot imagine what you are talking about?

👼 I am referring to the wicked deed you did at breakfast.

🧑 Wicked deed? Awan, I didn't do anything wicked at breakfast.

👼 Unfortunately, you did my scribe, you worshipped a false god at breakfast?

🧑 Awan, is everything all right with you and the medium? You are not making any sense. This is unlike you.

👼 Well my scribe, when you sat down to eat your eggs, didn't you drink a cup of coffee?

---

[190] Hull, Moses. *All About Devils; or, An inquiry as to whether modern Spiritualism and Other Great Reforms Emanate from His Satanic Majesty and his Subordinates in the Kingdom of Darkness.* 5th ed. Whitewater, WI: M. Hull, 1902. p. 46-47.

[191] 1 Corinthians 14:34-35, Ephesians 5:24, 1 Timothy 2:12.

[192] Museum Exhibit: *The Woman's Bible.* Seneca Falls, NY: Women's Rights National Historical Park.

🧑 Yes, Awan I did. What is so wicked about having a cup of coffee?

👼 Coffee is the drink of the devil! By drinking coffee you are worshipping the evil god!

🧑 Awan, you must be joking.

👼 No, my scribe, I am serious. At one time coffee was considered to be the devil's drink. However, one of the Popes decided to try a cup of coffee, and he liked it. He used his infallible spiritual powers, and baptized coffee. Through this ritual, he saved the beans, and converted coffee into a "Christian drink."

🧑 Awan, it sounds to me like you are drinking wine, instead of chock full of nuts—the heavenly coffee!

👼 Once again, my scribe, go to your libraries and you will discover that I am speaking the truth.

📖 A few days later, I researched coffee, and again discovered the accuracy Awan's history.

> **When coffee was first seen in Italy, some clerics suggested that it should be excommunicated because it must be the devil's work. The pope, Clement VIII (1592-1605), decided to see for himself, and he enjoyed the cup so much the declared instead that "coffee should be baptized to make true Christian drink."[193]**

📖 In my next conversation with Awan, we continued discussing this topic.

👼 Well my scribe, what did you discover in your library?

🧑 Once again, Awan, you spoke the truth. Pope Clement VIII baptized coffee, converting it to a Christian drink.

👼 Now my scribe, I want you to reason this out. Why do Catholics baptize their newborn babies?

🧑 The way I understand it — to wash away original sin.

👼 Do you know what would happen if a baby should die without receiving baptism?

🧑 I believe, according to Catholic doctrine, the soul of that baby would go directly to hell.

---

[193] Thorn, Jon. *The Coffee Companion: The Connoisseur's Guide to the World's Best Brews*. Philadelphia, PA: Running Press, 1995. p. 14-15.

(👼) That is exactly what Catholics believe. A priest must baptize each baby to have its soul saved from the devil. So my question to you is why is it **NOT** necessary for the coffee growers to bring all their coffee beans to the priests? Why aren't the priests at the factories where coffee is roasted, baptizing each coffee bean, to eradicate the devil from the bean? If Pope Clement VIII could baptize a few coffee beans and it would perpetually rescue all the coffee beans from the devil, why didn't he do the same for the souls of babies?

(🧑) That is a good question, Awan!

(👼) For over 1,700 years, the Church has taught its followers not to ask any questions. When a man or woman was bold enough to think for him or herself and ask a priest a question, the priest would respond, "It is a mystery of the Church." This is why so many people are ignorant of the true history of the Church, in ritual and deed. Perhaps now, my scribe, you understand how foolish all this talk about a Devil really is.

(🧑) Why do so many people still believe all of this mythology about devils? Don't they have any common sense?

(👼) Common sense comes from the *river of thought*; where all knowledge of the universe is stored. Remember the *river of thought* is very close to you. Visualize a river, and see the shoreline, the outer edge, closest to the bank of the river. Common sense is along the shoreline of the *river of thought*. It is the closest edge of the river to you. As one concentrates and communicates with the God within, one's auric field expands. When it expands beyond thirteen inches, it touches the *river of thought*. When you allow your mind to expand, you can draw on information from the *river of thought*. As your aura expands, it first goes though the edges of common sense, and when it expands further, you access the knowledge of the universe.

(🧑) That is very interesting.

(👼) Religious leaders do not want you to realize that God is within. If you do not communicate with the God within, then you will not tap into the *river of thought*, thereby discovering the fallacy of religious dogmas. For once the stranglehold of religious dogma is broken, people will leave their churches, synagogues, and temples. Many people in high levels of large religious institutions know that God is within, but conceal this knowledge from the people. To protect their steady flow of money into their churches, theologians teach that my dimension is an extremely dangerous place. It is filled with devils and demons, whose goal is to kidnap your soul, and fuel the fires of hell. These carefully crafted myths were designed to scare people from expanding their minds, from reaching out and discovering the truth. The fear of the devil has shut down the people's ability to access the *river of thought*. What is so sad, my scribe is that the devil is just a myth.

(🧑) Awan, my grandmother often used common sense, yet she was very religious. What caused that?

(👼) Judaism is not a restricting religion. It allows a person to expand his or her mind and thoughts, and to think for him or herself. Judaism does not make the people believe one interpretation of the Bible. On the contrary, the opposite is true. The Jewish people love to debate the hidden meaning of Bible verses. If ten men were debating the nuances of a verse, they would arrive at ten different conclusions. Judaism allows the people to spread out in thought, so they reach out into the *river of thought*.

Many Christian religions and the Catholic Church do not allow their followers that freedom. These Churches have one very specific way to interpret the Book of Books. You must accept that one specific interpretation. This causes many Christians to shut their minds down, because they cannot reason anything outside of the book. If it is not in the Bible, it doesn't exist. That is how closed-minded they have become.

📖 I later found this Bible verse, which corroborates Awan's statement.

> **But you must understand that this is of the highest importance: no prophecy of scripture can be interpreted by a single human mind.**[194]

(👼) In the years to come, people will approach you and say: "I never imagined I would be interested in psychic science." These people will have broadened their thinking, and begin exploring new avenues of thought. This is something that another person cannot force them to do. The person must have the desire within him or herself. Each person is responsible for his or her own thought processes. The *river of thought* is the same distance from each person. It is not closer to one person, and a further from another. You know certain people who are rather limited in their thinking. Yet, they have a fantastic education, but it is all book knowledge. They can't go beyond that. You have professors on your plane who are highly educated according to your standards. These brilliant professors cannot figure out a simple tasks using common sense. If it is not written in a book, these professors do not know the first thing about accomplish these tasks.

🙂 I understand you completely, Awan, I know some people who would fit that description perfectly.

(👼) Jesus came to the world to teach humanity that life continues after the transition of death. He wanted the people to know that God was within, not out in some heavenly palace. He also wanted people to know their potential, after witnessing what he could do with 100% of his brain working. This is the true meaning in the verse:

> **"Truly, truly, I say to you, he who believes in Me, *the works that I do shall he do also, and great works than these shall he do; because I go to the Father.*"**[195]

---

[194] 2 Peter 1:19 [PHIL].

The *works* Jesus mentioned were the ***Gifts of the Spirit***. Throughout his life Jesus communicated with my dimension, specifically to the Spirits of Moses and Elijah. Your religions want you to believe that he was communicating with "his Father." For further proof, go into Book of Books and read the story entitled the Mount of Transfiguration. Jesus arranged this séance to allow his advanced students to witness this special phenomenon. Now I ask you, aren't you able to relate what Moses and Jesus did, to what you, yourself, have witnessed in séance rooms?

Jesus was a great medium. The word medium began being used within the last one hundred and fifty years of your counting. Before that time Jesus would have been called a ***prophet***, ***oracle***, ***seer***, or ***man of God***.

You must remember one thing, when you are dealing with the unseen side of life, or psychic phenomena. There are people on your planet who are unscrupulous, and are willing to "pull the wool over the people's eyes" to make money by faking such a divine experience as a séance. You must remember that fact! You cannot trust that all psychic phenomena is genuine, but that does not mean that all psychic phenomena is fake, either. You need to be aware of this before you can trust a particular medium.

The energy is beginning to diminish, and I must withdraw from this body. It has been a pleasure to talk with you today, my scribe.

Thank you Awan, this dialogue has been most enlightening.

It amazed me how the process of entering and leaving the trance state was exactly the same, yet always different. Carl's body quaked as Awan withdrew. Upon regaining his consciousness, Carl drank two glasses of water. Yet, today, Carl's energy level was high, and he did not need to take a nap.

---

[195] John 14:12 [NASB].

NINE

Awan Discusses Psychic Science

Carl prepared for this trance session in the usual fashion. He said the prayer then closed his eyes, as if he were going to sleep. His breathing became slow and deliberate. Suddenly his body jolted as if he had been shocked by electricity. It spasmed four times. Still these spasms were not as severe as in other sessions. About a minute later, Awan began to speak.

My greetings to you, my scribe!

Greetings, Awan.

You have reached a new beginning point in your search for knowledge, my scribe.

I have, Awan? I don't understand.

As we have discussed many times, religions have altered the entire course of the history of your planet. When religions created their devils and demons, they succeeded in placing fear in the minds of humankind, which closed down the brain. This meant that people no longer sought the God-within, and the lines of communication between our two dimensions were severed.

Yes, Awan. I now understand all of that.

Yes, my scribe, but you probably do not realize that almost every religion was created as a result of a psychic event.

Really, Awan. I did not know that!

As I told you in our very first dialogue, almost every time someone in my dimension spoke to a human, a new religion was formed. Think about it my scribe. How did Judaism begin?

The first Hebrew was Abraham, who followed God's instructions to move from Ur to the Land of Canaan.

You said, "Followed God's instructions."

Yes, Awan.

(👼) That means he heard the voice of God, which indicates that Abraham was *clairaudient*.

(🧑) Oh, I see your point. All religions began though the psychic *gift of clairaudience*. Jesus heard Spirit voices; so did Mohammed, who began the religion of Islam; Martin Luther, who founded Lutheranism; and Joseph Smith, who began the (Mormon) Church of Jesus Christ of Latter-Day Saints.

(👼) And your list would go on for a long time, my scribe. However, I must correct you, *clairvoyance* was also involved. Many of the people you just mentioned also saw visions, in addition to hearing the voices from my dimension. I want you to completely understand that all religions began with the seeds of psychic science. You will find vestiges of psychic science in all religions. You are interested in history, are you not, my scribe?

(🧑) Yes, Awan, I was a history major in college.

(👼) In future dialogues, we will be exploring the psychic origins of religious rituals, and holidays. I think you will discover it enlightening. You will come to understand that religions absorbed psychic techniques into their belief systems, yet they outlawed the practice of psychic science. When one comes to understand the truth behind these religious rituals, and holidays, on can strip away the religious dogma, and begin to practice the *Gifts of the Sprit*, the way the Ancients did, when they built the pyramids.

(🧑) This sounds intriguing, Awan. Where do we begin?

(👼) We need to begin with an important concept. Many people have not understood that psychic (soul) phenomena are really a science.

(🧑) Yes, I remember that the word *psychic* really means *soul* and *mind*.

(👼) That's correct. As in most sciences, there are certain rules, or laws that must be followed. On a very simple basis, you cannot expect water to freeze unless you cool it below 32° Fahrenheit. You cannot expect water to evaporate unless you heat it above 212° Fahrenheit. The people now living on your planet understand that. Psychic science works in the same manner. Certain rules or laws must be followed before a psychic event, or the *Gifts of the Spirit*, can occur. Now, it is time for me to explain two of these basic laws.

The *Gifts of the Spirit* can only be carried out when psychic energy is flowing. Think about this. You have a certain amount of electrical energy within your body. Why can't you hold a light bulb in your hand and make it light up? You need more than electricity and a light bulb to produce light from a light bulb. You also need copper wires for the electricity to flow to create a circuit, as you term it. You must put the light bulb in the lamp, which has copper wires attached. Then you plug the lamp into the socket, and turn on the switch. Only then will the bulb give off light. You have no problem understanding that. Your scientists understand all this information, and do not expect you to light a bulb by holding it in your hand.

Psychic science is like trying to light that bulb, when you cannot see it or the lamp, or the socket. The energy required to link the two dimensions is invisible to your eyes. You must take our word for it. There is no way to prove the laws of psychic science to you. This is what was so frustrating for so many mediums over the past one hundred and fifty years, as they tried to prove to scientists that psychic phenomena actually exists. The scientists demand physical, tangible proof to substantiate that psychic science is a real science. The scientists also want mediums to produce the phenomena on demand, regardless of the circumstances. This does not work with psychic science, since there are many variables, and all of which must be met before the phenomena can occur. This was not always possible under the conditions the scientists demanded.

Now, for the first law: ***Thoughts are things***, or to say it another way ***Thoughts are energy***. Much of psychic phenomena, or the ***Gifts of the Spirit***, as you term it, is produced by energy, which is influenced by thought. For certain types of phenomena, the thoughts of the Spirit person and the medium make the phenomena happen. For other types of phenomena, thoughts can influence whether or not the phenomena can take place. Tell me my scribe, if you had a little toy car made out of iron, and you placed a magnet three inches away from the front end of the car, what do you think would happen?

🧑 The car would move forward towards the magnet.

😇 Why?

🧑 Because the magnetic pull would cause the car to move forward.

😇 That is exactly right. Now, can you see this magnetic energy or pull, as you term it?

🧑 No, it is invisible.

😇 So, an invisible energy, or pull as you term it, influences the car and makes it go forward.

🧑 Yes.

😇 Some types of psychic phenomena work this way. The energy we use would cause the car to be pulled forward. Let us say that we had a magnet trying to pull the car forward for a certain type of phenomena. And let us say that there is a person who does not believe the validity of psychic phenomena. They are skeptical, to the point that they are extremely negative. They also have a mental pull, remember that thoughts are energy. It may be equivalent to four magnets, placed at the rear of the car. So we are pulling forward with the strength of one magnet, and the negative person is pulling on the back of the car with the strength of four magnets. Do you think the car will move forward?

🧑 No, it would probably move backward.

(👼) Yes. And all this is happening before your eyes, yet the magnetic pull is invisible to your eyes. You must remember, my scribe, the laws of psychic science have never changed. What was true in Biblical times is still true today. Negative thought energy blocks psychic phenomena from taking place. When this session is over, be certain that you look in your Book of Books for the passage where Jesus said that he was not honored in his own hometown. Notice that it says that he could not perform any miracles that day.

📖 After the trance session I found the verses Awan referred to:

> **But, Jesus said to them, "A prophet is not without honor except in his home town, and in his own household." And He did not do many miracles there because of their unbelief.**[196]

(👼) The negative thought energy emanating from the people of Nazareth, who attended the meeting, was so overpowering that Jesus could not override it with his own positive energy. Despite the fact that Jesus was the most powerful medium that ever lived, because 100% of his brain was working, he still was unable to perform any miracles (a religious word usually describing a psychic event). This is how powerful negative thought energy is; it can prohibit psychic phenomena from happening. Psychic science cannot be conducted in the midst of total negative energy.

Now I want you to ponder this, my scribe. If Jesus were God himself, as millions of Christians believe, then Jesus could have performed miracles twenty-four hours a day, for years at a time. God would have unlimited energy. Think of all the energy that was needed to create the universe. Healing someone, or multiplying a little food is child's play compared to creating a universe. So why couldn't Jesus perform those miracles that day in Nazareth? How could the negative thoughts of the citizens of Nazareth cancel out the omnipresent, omnipotent creator of the universe?

This very small verse proves that Jesus was **NOT** God, but a wonderful medium, just as the man whose body that I am using is a wonderful medium. Now, do not misunderstand me. I am not suggesting that this medium is as advanced, or as psychically gifted, as Jesus. Although Jesus was the greatest medium who ever lived, he still was confined to the limitations that all mediums have. He had to follow the laws of psychic science.

🧑 This is fascinating!

(👼) You must remember that the laws of psychic science have not changed since the beginnings of time. The phenomena and the way it its carried out, is the same today as it was in the time of King Tut, Moses or Jesus. Psychic science has never changed, just like the laws that govern magnetic pull have not changed.

---

[196] Matthew 13:57-58 [NASB].

🧑 I understand, Awan.

👼 Good, my scribe. Now, the second law of psychic science is **light can effect psychic phenomena**. Just as thought is energy, so is light. You have on your planet an instrument called a **light meter**.

🧑 Yes Awan, I have one, I use it when I take pictures. It measures the amount of light that is present.

👼 Yes, my scribe, light travels on waves; frequency is involved.

🧑 Wait a minute, Awan. Are you saying that the frequency of light disturbs or interferes with the frequencies emanating from your dimension?

👼 That is precisely correct, my scribe. Often, if light is present, psychic phenomena cannot occur. It takes much less energy for us to work in the dark, than it does to work in daylight, because the light waves interfere with the waves we create. However, it also depends on the medium. You have what you term batteries, is that correct?

🧑 Yes, they store energy.

👼 And batteries come in different sizes?

🧑 Yes, some are 1.5 volts and some are 9 volts.

👼 And what do those sizes mean?

🧑 They are measurements of the amount energy the battery contains.

👼 Correct. Mediums are similar to batteries. Not all mediums can conduct the same amount of psychic energy. Some mediums may conduct 3 volts, while another 9 or 18 volts. It should become obvious that the 3 volts medium could never work in daylight, while the 18 volts medium could. It has to do with the medium, and the Spirits working with him or her. That is why some mediums can work in daylight, but most prefer to work in darkness. Working in the dark is much easier, since it requires less energy, and is less draining on the medium's energy resources.

This is why you are sitting in a dimly lit room. If this room was brightly lit, it would make it much more difficult for this medium to allow me access to his body, to speak with you.

🧑 I think I understand.

👼 People who are skeptical of psychic science claim that mediums work in the dark to make it easier for them to fake the phenomena. The darkness enables them to hide their tricks, or, what you might term, slight of hand. This is not the case. Unfortunately, there are some people who do fake mediumship, it happens much too frequently. However, genuine mediums need darkness, not to fake it, but to have enough energy to carry out their work.

Let me tell you a story that you might be familiar with. It has to do with a story in the Bible that is usually entitled "the wedding at Cana." It really was the first psychic feat that Jesus performed, and it was at his sister's wedding.

What I have just said might upset many of your Bible readers. When I said that Jesus had a sister, I meant that. As I have previously stated, your Book of Books has been changed. Jesus' family history was changed because the Church did not want the public to know that he had a sister and two brothers. Jesus was the only one of the family who had the *Gifts of the Spirit*, which enabled him to change the water, into wine.

📖 Later I read the Bible story of "the wedding at Cana," in John 2:1-11. I found a surprise in verse 12; since I had no idea that the Bible said that Jesus had brothers.

> **After this he went down to Capernaum, with his mother and his brothers and his disciples; and there they stayed for a few days.**[197]

📖 I was even more surprised when **UNVAR** indicated that Jesus also had sisters.

> **Afterwards he went down to Capharnaum, and so did his mother, his brothers and *sisters*, and his students, and they stayed there a few days.**[198]

📖 I was further surprised while reading **CONF**, a Catholic Bible, to find this quotation.

> **I confess to Almighty God, to Blessed Mary ever Virgin...**[199]

📖 I found it confusing that Mary could continue to be a virgin, after the Bible admits the Jesus had at least two brothers. Were all of Mary's children conceived through Immaculate Conception? If this is the case, then the **trinity** should have been Jesus, Brother #1 and Brother #2.

👼 The Bible story of "the wedding at Cana," will illustrate that mediumship requires darkness. The Bible does not discuss eighteen years of Jesus' life, when Jesus was 13-29 years old. It was during that time that Jesus studied at various mystery schools, which were advanced schools for mediums. Jesus studied with the Essenes, in Israel; and then traveled to other mystery schools throughout Asia, as far away as India and Tibet.

---

[197] John 2:12 [RSV].

[198] John 2:12 [UNVAR].

[199] O'Connel, John P. Monsignor, editor. The Holy Bible with the Confratery Text. *The Holy Eucharist* found in the section entitled *The Seven Sacraments*. Chicago, IL: The Catholic Press, Inc., 1965. p. 268.

My Second Encounter With An Angel

Moses was Jesus' Spirit Control, just as Chief Lone Eagle is the control for the man whose body I am using. Moses frequently spoke with Jesus clairaudiently.

🧑 Moses was speaking to Jesus!?

😇 Yes, my scribe. It was Moses who informed Jesus that his sister was getting married, and the exact date of the wedding. He told Jesus to leave India on that very day, so that Jesus would be Cana in time for the wedding. Jesus arrived in the nick of time, to save the day, when he performed his first so-called "miracle," by turning the water into wine.

Jesus' reputation had spread far and wide; he was a powerful prophet and medium. Therefore, many uninvited people decided to attend the wedding, hoping that Jesus would return for this joyous occasion. They wanted to meet this home-town celebrity, when he returned for the wedding. When Mary saw how many uninvited guests had arrived for the wedding, she became quite agitated. Mary was a very kind and loving woman. How could she refuse anyone hoping to see her famous son's entry into her house? But the problem remained: how could she possibly be a good hostess, and provide food and drink for all these guests? She definitely did not have enough wine for all these people. Mary was pacing the kitchen floor, trying to figure out what she could do. Suddenly, the back door to their house opened, and Jesus stepped into the kitchen.

Immediately Jesus saw from his mother's face that something was wrong. Jesus said, "Blessed mother, on a day like this you should be joyful, yet you look so upset. What is the matter?"

"Oh, Jesus," Mary cried, "I only have seven jars of wine. All these uninvited guests have come, hoping to see you. I do not have enough wine for even one sip for each person. What am I going to do?"

Jesus replied, "Mother, I want you to stop worrying. Have your servants borrow as many jars as they can from the neighbors. Make sure each jar has a cover on it. Then have them fill all the jars with water. Now give these instructions your servants, and stop worrying."

The worried expression remained upon Mary's face. She thought her son was suffering from sunstroke, or that he was crazy. Nevertheless, she had nothing to lose, so she told the servants to borrow covered jars from the neighbors, and fill them with water. The servants scurried throughout the neighborhood, and within an hour's time the kitchen was full of covered jars of water.

"Arrange these jars in rows so that I can walk between them," Jesus instructed the servants.

Once the jars were lined up as soldiers, Jesus said to the servants, "Please leave the kitchen, and close the door behind you. I will call for you when I need you."

Once he was alone, Jesus went to work. Jesus walked over to the first covered jar. He held his hands over it, closed his eyes, and began to concentrate. He then focused on, what you might term, the little movie screen, in the middle of his forehead. It is the same screen on which you watch your dreams on while you sleep. He visualized the pot filled with water, and then he saw the jar filled with sweet, rose-colored wine. He saw this as clearly as you see the pictures on your television sets.

Through the power of his *thought*, the water molecules transformed themselves into wine molecules. Because Jesus had all the *Gifts of the Spirit*, and was such a powerful medium, he could change that jar of water into wine in about a minute. He then continued until all the jars contained wine. When he had finished, Jesus went and fetched the servants. He told one of them to call his mother back into the kitchen. Mary came into the kitchen, still looking very worried.

"Look mother, all these jars have wine in them." Jesus said.

"Jesus, I don't have time for your jokes." Mary said, in a sharp tone.

Jesus opened one of the jars, grabbed a cup, and filled it with the soft rose-colored liquid. "Here, mother, taste this and tell me what you think," he said.

With an absolutely astonished look on her face, Mary took the rose-colored liquid and slowly drank the whole cup. This rose-colored liquid tasted sweet as honey, and the alcohol content was quite obvious. Immediately, Mary's expression changed. She had a broad smile on her face. She hugged her son, and said, "Oh Jesus, how ever did you do this?"

"I doubt that you could understand, mother," Jesus responded.

"No matter," Mary said, then she took her cup and dipped in into the wine jar again. Her demeanor started to change; the worried expression left her face as she began to "mellow out."

👤 Awan, I don't understand. Jesus changed the water into wine in the kitchen. Wasn't it daylight when this happened?

😇 Yes it happened in daylight. But, Jesus needed to have each pot covered. The water molecules were in complete darkness since the water was in opaque, baked clay jars. Jesus could not have changed the molecules of water into wine in transparent glass containers. Not even Jesus could defy the laws of psychic science.

👤 I understand your point.

😇 Before the Christian age, people would go to speak to those in my realm, whom the Bible terms as God. They traveled to a gifted medium, who would sit inside a tent, cabinet, or even a cave. It was always a small, confined, dark place that facilitated communication with people residing in the Spirit World.

The Book of Books mentions several instances when a family would build a room on the top, or roof, of their house. It was not really a room, as you know rooms to be. The average Bible reader would think the family built a guest bedroom for Elisha.[200]

📖 Here is the verse to which Awan made reference:

---

[200] 2 Kings 4:9-10.

Let us make a small roof chamber with walls, and put there for him a bed, a table, a chair, and a lamp, so that whenever he comes to us, he can go in there."[201]

🧘 It is true that the room was furnished as a guest bedroom, but this room was a medium's cabinet, a small darkened room where a **man or woman of God** could communicate with the unseen side of life. These small rooms were curtained, to produce darkness during the day, and were high in elevation to avoid the negative thought vibrations of the everyday people. A medium frequently goes into trance while he or she is lying down. Therefore, a bed could be quite useful in a cabinet. It is as simple as that.

The energy is beginning to diminish, and I must leave this body. I leave you with my peace.

🧑 Thank you, Awan.

Five seconds after Awan's final words, Carl inhaled sharply, and his body quaked. Carl was groggy, as a person would be awakening from a deep sleep. I handed Carl a glass of water, which he eagerly drank. The exhaustion was clearly evident on Carl's face, and he went directly to bed.

---

[201] 2 Kings 4:10 [RSV].

TEN

Palm Sunday and Sukkot

On a bright, refreshing April morning, I received a phone call from Carl. Once again, Awan was summoning me for another lesson. Early the next Saturday morning, I was sitting in Carl's darkened office. Carl leaned back into his chair, closed his eyes, and recited his prayer. After a few minutes, Carl's body spasmed. Then, the tones of Awan's now familiar voice filled the room.

😇 My profound greetings to you, my scribe.

🧑 Greetings, Awan.

😇 I wished to speak to you, my scribe, because of what I have witnessed very recently on your planet.

🧑 What is that, Awan?

😇 I have been watching millions of Christians and Jews carrying out their rituals. They do everything that their priests, ministers, and rabbis instruct them to do. They feel that they are carrying out the rites that God wishes them to do. Unfortunately, they have been so mislead for so many centuries, that they do not have the slightest notion their beloved rituals really have deep psychic meanings, which predates their religions.

🧑 This sounds very interesting, Awan! Could you be more specific? What rituals are you discussing?

😇 I will begin by discussing **Palm Sunday**. I watch so many Christians buy their palms, and carry them into their churches. Yet, they have no idea why they do this.

🧑 Isn't it to commemorate when Jesus made his grand entrance into Jerusalem, about a week before he died?

😇 Yes, that is the reason, my scribe. However, do you understand why they used **Palms**? Why not leaves from other trees? There were many different types of trees that grew in the countryside in those days.

🧑 I have no idea, Awan. Why did they use palms?

(👼) It all goes back, my scribe, to your lessons about psychic energy. Do you remember why the mediums sat under certain trees?

(🧑) Of course, Awan. The trees acted as an antenna that helped the medium draw enough psychic energy needed to communicate with those in your dimension.

(👼) Very good, my scribe, it greatly pleases me that you remembered the information that we discuss. Do you remember why mediums sat in cabinets, or in a hollow of a tree using a sheepskin to cover the opening?

(🧑) It was to enable ectoplasm to be withdrawn from their bodies.

(👼) That is sometimes correct. What would be another reason?

(🧑) To help the Spirit people use the vocal cords of the mediums. Psychic energy works best in the dark.

(👼) That is correct. Now when a medium goes into a meditative state in a cabinet, the vibration of his or her body begins to rise. His or her frequency increases, as the Spirit lowers its frequency so that the two meet in the middle. This enables the communication. It is not easy for the medium to stay at this higher vibration. In effect, the medium's body becomes charged with energy. More energy is needed in the body to maintain the communication. Do you understand so far?

(🧑) Well Awan, no, I do not.

(👼) Well, let me put it another way. Are familiar with what you term a light bulb?

(🧑) Yes, Awan, of course.

(👼) Let us suppose that a medium is a 25 watt bulb in his or her normal everyday life. It is now time for the medium to become an instrument of the Spirit. The medium sits in a cabinet and meditates. Now the medium transforms him/herself into a 100-watt bulb. That bulb is brighter is it not?

(🧑) Yes, Awan, it is brighter.

(👼) Does the 100-watt bulb require more energy than a 25 watt bulb?

(🧑) Yes, Awan. Oh, I get it now.

(👼) So our medium is now operating at 100 watts instead of 25. A sudden jolt, or loss of concentration would cause the medium's wattage to decrease. If it fell too low, there wouldn't be enough energy remaining to keep the light bulb lit— so communication would be interrupted. Do you understand?

(🧑) Yes, Awan, I now understand. Oh, that is why mediumship is so tiring for the medium's body! All that additional energy is required for the communication with your dimension. And a good portion of it comes from the energy reserves of the medium.

🪽 Yes, my scribe, now you are thinking! In ancient times, people had a keen understanding of how this energy worked. The people who assisted the mediums protected them as a precious treasure. The medium was their only link to my dimension. Often, they would carry the medium in what you term a *sedan chair*, not allowing the medium to walk when he or she was about to become the instrument of the Spirit.

👤 Why is that, Awan?

🪽 If the medium were barefoot, much of the psychic energy would be drained from the medium's body. Your 100-watt medium could easily become a 75-watt medium, and that may be too low to be in communication with my dimension.

👤 That is interesting, Awan.

🪽 Now we come back to what happened in Jerusalem nearly 2000 years ago, when Jesus entered the city. The people understood that Jesus was a prophet. They understood that he was in communication with people in my dimension. Therefore, they greeted him with palm branches. The leaves of a palm tree have special qualities. They act in the same fashion as the insulation around your electrical wires. The people came and waved the palm branches. Then they placed them on the ground, like a grand green carpet. This would allow Jesus to walk, and not lose any of his precious psychic energy.

👤 That is fascinating, Awan.

🪽 Have you ever wondered where your expression "rolling out the red carpet" came from?

👤 I have to admit; I never thought about it.

🪽 The origin comes from the time when palm leaves were placed on the ground, as a carpet, so the medium could walk to wherever he or she needed to deliver his or her message from my dimension. A bride walking on a white carpet to the altar also comes from this ancient custom. The Catholic Church no longer have their parishioners place the palms on the ground, but the tradition of bringing palms for the medium/prophet is still commemorated, although not understood.

👤 It is too bad that more people do not understand the psychic truth of the rituals they perform.

🪽 Yes, my scribe, I agree, and perhaps the books of my teachings, which you are so diligently working on, will help. However, make no mistake about it, the Christians are not the only ones who do not understand their rituals. The Jews also have many traditions steeped in psychic truths that hardly anyone presently remembers.

👤 Could you be more specific, Awan?

🪽 Let's continue talking about those palm branches, my scribe. Do you know when the Jews use palm branches?

🙂 Yes, Awan, they use them during the holiday of *Sukkot.*

😇 Please tell me what you know of that holiday, and why are the palms used.

🙂 *Sukkot* is a holiday that commemorates the Hebrews wandering in the dessert for forty years. We are supposed to live in a סֻכָּה (*sukkah*) small hut, for a week. We eat our meals in this סֻכָּה (*sukkah*)/hut, and sleep there. Then, we are supposed to bring a לוּלָב (*lulav*)—a collection of palm branches, myrtle, willow leaves, and an etrog, which looks like a big lemon, into the סֻכָּה (*sukkah*)/hut. As we say a special prayer, we shake the leaves in the six directions around us.

😇 Why, my scribe?

🙂 To be truthful, I do not know the reason, but I know it is done.

😇 If you were to read about this holiday, you would discover that you shake the לוּלָב (*lulav*) in six directions to dramatize that God is everywhere. However, that is not the true meaning behind your holiday. Again you, yourself are unaware of the psychic truth behind this ritual. What else are you supposed to do with leaves of palm trees?

🙂 That is all I know, Awan.

😇 Yes, my scribe I can understand that because of where you live. Tell me, what do you put on the roof of your סֻכָּה (*sukkah*) hut?

🙂 It is a tradition to put corn stalks on the top, and tie fruits and vegetables to commemorate the harvest. Part of the holiday is supposed to be a Thanksgiving for an abundant harvest.

😇 That is true for your part of the world. However, originally, in the land of Israel, they did not use corn stalks they used ***palm leaves*** instead. It was imperative for the Hebrews to use the palm leaves.

🙂 Why, Awan?

😇 You are missing the whole point of this holiday, my scribe. Do you remember how you first learned about psychic phenomena?

🙂 Of course, Awan, I met this medium for a reading, and eventually, he invited me to attend his psychic development classes.

😇 And what was the point of these classes?

🙂 People wanted to learn to become mediumistic, and communicate with those living in your dimension.

😇 Yes my scribe, you are correct. The Jewish holiday of *Sukkot* was designed to be the one time during the year when everyone attended psychic development classes. You must remember, my scribe, that the harvest had just been completed. It was too soon to plant the next crop. Therefore, people had some "leisure" time to pursue spiritual development. People lived for a week, in what you call a סֻכָּה (*sukkah*)/hut, which is nothing in the world but a *cabinet*.

Yes, Awan, I have noticed that they look very similar.

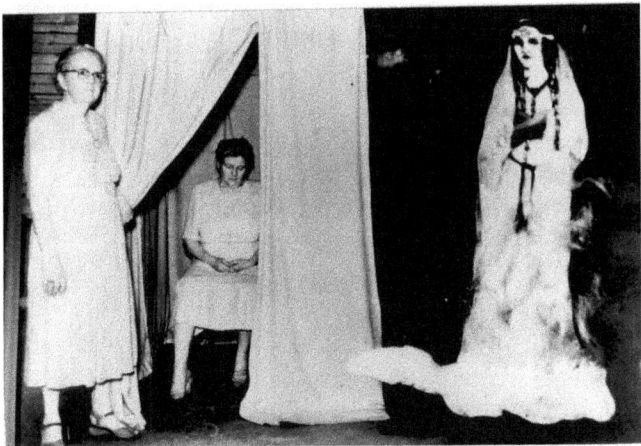

This picture was taken with infra-red film, during a materialization séance, in 1953. The woman sitting In the cabinet (hut/tent/סֻכָּה *sukkah*) was the medium, Ethel Post-Parrish. The white cloudy substance being withdrawn from her body is called ectoplasm. The Spirit of Silver Belle molded the ectoplasm (pillar of cloud) and animated it, to speak with the people in attendance. The same phenomena occurred in the Meeting Tent (Exodus 33:7-11) and on the Mount of Transfiguration (Luke 9:28-32).

This is a picture of a סֻכָּה (*sukkah*), which was in the display window of a Judaica store. Notice that the medium's cabinet and this sukkah are nearly identical. It is the author's contention that the sukkah served as a place for psychic development to occur.

People were supposed to spend as much time as possible in this cabinet. The roof was made of palm branches, to act as insulation. It helped retain the psychic energy that would build in the cabinet. People would bring in the palm and myrtle branches and shake them all around themselves. These trees have psychic energy within them. You are supposed to shake them in the six directions around you to energize the סֻכָּה (*sukkah*)/hut, and to help you attune with my dimension.

Do you remember when Spirit materialized spoke to Moses in the meeting tent?

Yes, Awan, it is discussed in Exodus 33:11.

Now the Lord talked with Moses, as a man talketh with his friend. At times, he [Moses] returned to the camp; but the

young man, his attendant, Joshua the son of Nun, never departed from the *council-tent*.[202]

(😇) Some Bibles referred to the *Meeting Tent* as the *Council-Tent*. Do you remember the Hebrew name for that tent?

(🧑) Yes, Awan it was called אֹהֶל מוֹעֵד (*o-hel mo-aid*).

(😇) Correct my scribe, and do you remember what is the literal translation of אֹהֶל מוֹעֵד (*o-hel mo-aid*)?

(🧑) Yes, Awan, אֹהֶל מוֹעֵד (*o-hel mo-aid*) means the *Tent of the Appointed Time*. Spirit would meet for a séance at regular intervals of time. It would be similar to people having a weekly appointment with their doctor or therapist.

(😇) Correct, my scribe. You remember that a cabinet was required for a Spirit to materialize?

(🧑) Yes, Awan. Spirit would withdraw ectoplasm, a condensation of the medium's life force energy. It has a smoky appearance, which is why the Bible describes it as a "*pillar of cloud*." Then Spirit sculpts the ectoplasm to resemble a body, and animates it. It would be similar to a person slipping into a wet suit. The Spirit slips on this physical ectoplasm, which molds to its spiritual body. Then Spirit creates a voice box out of the ectoplasm, so when the materialized Spirit speaks, physical people will hear their words with their physical ears, and see the body of the Spirit with their physical eyes. This is why Moses could speak to Spirit *face to face*.

(😇) The same process occurred on the Mount of Transfiguration. Jesus took his three most advanced students to witness the materialization of Moses and Elijah. This is why the Bible says that Peter asked if the disciples should build a tabernacle (or tent). He was asking if Jesus needed a cabinet. If you look hard enough, my scribe, you will discover that actually Peter asked if he should build a סֻכָּה (*sukkah*).

(📖) The verse Awan referred to is:

And it came to pass, as they departed from him, Peter said unto Jesus, Master, it is good for us to be here; and let us make three tabernacles, one for thee, and one for Moses, and one for Elias: not knowing what he said.[203]

Here are the 27 different ways this verse is translated:

---

[202] Exodus 33:11 [GEDD].
[203] Luke 9:33 [KJV].

LUKE CHAPTER 9 VERSE 33

KJV	1611	And it came to pass, as they departed from him, Peter said unto Jesus, Master, it is good for us to be here; and let us make **three tabernacles**, one for thee, and one for Moses, and one for Elias: not knowing what he said.
EWYC	1384	tabernacles
MACE	1729	apartments
WESL	1755	tents
THOM	1808	booths
LING	1836	huts
PRYSE	1916	dwelling-places
FENT	1922	dwellings
LAMSA	1933	shelters
KNOX	1944	arbors
ANT	1956	bowers
NORL	1962	shrines
AMP	1965	booths or huts
CPV	1969	chapels
WWENT	1969	places
ABBR	1971	churches
NTEE	1974	brush arbors
WMF	1975	historical markers
NLFV	1986	altars
GNC	1989	places of shelter
SINAI	1993	tents/tabernacles
NCS	1994	sacred tents
OJBC	1997	sukkot
BECKN	2001	temporary shelters
IEB	2001	holy tents
MESS	2002	memorials
DASV	2010	memorial shelters
TVB	2012	structures

27 Differing Translations

📖 As Awan predicted, I recently found a sixteen variation of this verse. It was highly significant. The **OJBC** reads:

> **And it came about, just as they departed from Rebbe Melech HaMoshiach, [Jesus] Kefa [Peter] said, "Adoni, [Lord] it is good for us to be here; let us make shalosh [three] *sukkot*, [*sukkot* is the plural form of *sukkah*] one for you and one for Moshe Rabbeinu [Moses] and one for Eliyahu HaNavi**

[Elijah the prophet]." (Kefa did not know what he was saying.)²⁰⁴

> In late August, 2004, as I was driving home from Charleston, South Carolina, after spending the summer at Carl's home; I noticed a billboard advertising a Bible warehouse. It was along I 95 in northern North Carolina. I decided to take a break from driving and stop and see if they had any new editions of the Bible. There were no unusal Bibles, however, I was completely shocked, when I discovered a children's book that was for sale, entitled "Who Is Jesus?"
>
> In this book there is a picture from a hand-painted manuscript (404 fol 3r) that is housed in the Armenian Cathedral and Museum in Julfa Isfahan, Iran. [*Who is Jesus?: Son of God, Son of Man*. Green Forest, AR: Master Books/New Leaf Press, 2000. p. 26.] This manuscript contains a picture of Jesus on the Mount of Transfiguration. What makes this picture unique from the other hundreds of pictures of this scene is that *Jesus is standing in a (cabinet) black box!* To my knowledge, this is the only picture, which accurately portrays that the *gift of materialization* was performed on the Mount of Transfiguration.
>
> The manuscript's illustrator would have to had knowledge of mediumship, for there is no other explanation for depicting Jesus in a black box, with Moses and Elijah standing on either side.

📖 Here is definitive proof, that a סֻכָּה (*sukkah*) is equivalent to a cabinet, which is a place where **séances** were conducted.

👤 Do you remember, my scribe, that when Solomon built the First Temple in Jerusalem, that he built the דְּבִיר (*debir*), the *Holy of Holies*, which was actually a cabinet?

👤 Yes, Awan, I remember it was discussed in 1 Kings 6:16.

👤 There is one Bible that had a very accurate description of the true purpose of the דְּבִיר (*debir*). It was a place to go to study with Spirit teachers.

📖 After the session, I reread the specific verse:

> **He also built twenty cubits broad at the back of the House as a verandah, of cedar, from the floor to the height of the walls. He built it for himself, as a Lecture Hall to discuss Philosophy with Philosophers.²⁰⁵**

Awan was correct when he said that **FENT** was the only Bible, which referred to the cabinet in this manner.

---

²⁰⁴ Luke 9:33 [OJBC].
²⁰⁵ 1 Kings 6:16 [FENT].

1 KINGS CHAPTER 6 VERSE 16

KJV	1611	And he built twenty cubits on the sides of the house, both the floor, and the walls with boards of Cedar: he even built them for it within, even for **the Oracle**, even for the most holy place.
WBC	1985	adytum
TAV	1539	choir and place most holy.
THOM	1808	dabir-the Holy of Holies.
EWYC	1384	heavenly answering place
LAMSA	1933	Holy of Holies.
BERK	1969	house an inner room
EPBT	1994	house for the pulpit
ARATJ	1987	house of atonements
OGD	1950	inmost room
LWYC	1395	inner house of God's answering place
DOU	1609	inner house of the oracle to be Sanctum Sanctorum
GEDD	1792	inner oracle
VTB	2012	inner place
KENT	1921	inner room
RNV	2007	inner sacred place
RSV	1952	inner sanctuary
MOFF	1922	inner shrine
RDB	1982	innermost part of the house
NWT	1961	innermost room
FENT	1922	Lecture Hall to discuss Philosophy with Philosophers.
LIV	1971	Most Holy Place
ARTB	2008	nave
GEN60	1560	oracle
THB	2003	oracular sanctuary
STONE	1996	Partition to be the Holy of Holies.
SHAR	1892	Place of the Oracle
TYND	1537	quere and place most holy
UTV	2001	Sacred Place.
WELL	1861	sanctuary, even for the most holy place.
GRT	1540	secret place of the temple, even in the most holy.
ROTH	1897	shrine, even for the holy of holies.
ISR	1998	Speaking Place, as the Most Set-apart Place.
RVIC	2004	Word

33 Differing Translations

The סֻכָּה (*sukkah*)/hut was a family's personal דְּבִיר (*debir*). It was a place to hear and study the *living word of Spirit*.

📖 One day as I was surfing the internet, I came across the website entitled: "Review Answers—Sukah, Daf 28, which provided further evidence that the סֻכָּה (*sukkah*) was a cabinet. I had no idea what **Daf** meant, but fortunately it was explained.

> "Dafyomi," or a "page (Daf) a day (Yomi)," refers to the system of Talmud study founded in 1927 by Rabbi Meir Shapiro, one of the foremost leaders of world Jewry. Although Jews have always studied the Talmud, Rabbi Shapiro's goal was to unite Jews all over the world by having them study the same page of Talmud each day, ... with his system of a page a day, would take seven years (2,711 pages).[206]

📖 The next quote is part of **Dafyomi** from **Maseches Sukah**:

> One is obligated to eat, drink and sleep in the Sukah — and to perform all one's other occupations there too e.g. walking around (which one would normally have done in the house) and *learning*.[207]

📖 This supports Awan's claim that סֻכָּה (*sukkah*)/hut and the דְּבִיר (*debir*), were like mini lecture halls to learn wisdom from Spirit.

👤 Awan, I just had a thought. Is shaking the a לוּלָב (*lulav*) similar to when the wise women of pagan religions (witches) would draw a circle in the ground, in order to have a charged area to perform their ceremonies?

👼 Yes, my scribe. You have already seen how certain psychic practices were carried out by many different cultures around the world. Psychic science does not change from country to country, culture to culture, or even during differing time periods. As you have heard my medium say repeatedly, "The laws of psychic science have never changed. What was true in Biblical times is still true today." By drawing a circle, the practitioners of Wicca [witches] were energizing their own personal space, which would allow them to raise their vibration. One day you will discover evidence of this.

📖 In the course of my research, I discovered a photograph of a group of witches from Salem, Massachusetts.[208] Along the bottom of the picture there was a blue band of energy, which resembled a felled tree. Eastman Kodak claimed this blue energy band was "static electricity." Ms. Cabot, one of the witches, claimed:

---

[206] http://www.dafyomi.co.il/central.htm.

[207] http://dafyomi.co.il/sukah/reviewa/su-ra-028.htm#a11.

[208] "Massachusetts' North Shore: Harboring Old Ways." *National Geographic Magazine.* April 1979. p. 585.

> "... that electricity is actually in the room. It forms the perimeter where our magic circle was. No question about it."[209]

📖 At times psychic energy can be captured on film. This photograph offers proof that the energy created in a magic circle, or energy fields, such as those created by shaking a לוּלָב (*lulav*), actually exist!

👤 As we have already discussed my scribe, the Jewish people have had a long tradition of being psychic/prophetic/mediumistic people. Your Bible chronicles the history of Hebrew prophets/mediums from cover to cover. To ensure that the Jews would always have prophets in their midst, they developed this holiday, which is nothing more than an annual psychic development class. It was to last for seven days. It was hoped that by being in this psychically energized environment, mediums would develop. From time to time this would happen.

👤 This is fascinating.

👤 Now, my scribe, tell me what אֻשְׁפִּיזִין (*ushpizin*) are?

👤 Awan, I feel like I am back at school, and this whole conversation is my final exam. I have never heard of the word אֻשְׁפִּיזִין (*ushpizin*).

👤 It is part of your holiday of *Sukkot*.

👤 Unfortunately, Awan, my family never built a סֻכָּה (*sukkah*)/hut. The only time I was in one was when I went to the synagogue to celebrate the holiday. Most synagogues build a סֻכָּה (*sukkah*)/hut.

👤 I think you will be very surprised to learn that the אֻשְׁפִּיזִין (*ushpizin*) are visitors you are supposed to invite into your סֻכָּה (*sukkah*)/hut. Most of your books call these visitors—*unseen guests*. I think you would easily recognize them as Spirit people.

👤 What?! Jews invite Spirit people to the סֻכָּה (*sukkah*)/hut?

👤 My dear scribe, how can you possibly have a psychic development class unless people from my dimension come and attempt to communicate with you? Of course, Spirit people are there. Perhaps now your interest will be peaked to do some research into your holiday. The energy is beginning to fluctuate, so I must leave you at this time. Go to your library, do your research, and in our next conversation, we will begin at this point. My peace be with you.

👤 Thank you, Awan. My peace be with you, too.

---

[209] "Massachusetts' North Shore: Harboring Old Ways." *National Geographic Magazine.* April 1979. p. 585.

📖 The very next day, I went to the library and began researching the holiday *Sukkot*. I discovered that Awan had described the holiday very accurately. However, I was most interested in learning about the אֻשְׁפִּיזִין (*ushpizin*). I found it extremely ironic that I was about to learn more information about a Jewish holiday from a Spirit person, than from any rabbi, or religious teacher I had ever encountered.

📖 It turns out that the אֻשְׁפִּיזִין (*ushpizin*) were famous people.

> The [physical] people you invite will eat the food prepared for the אֻשְׁפִּיזִין (*ushpizin*) — invisible guests "who see but who are not seen." The אֻשְׁפִּיזִין (*ushpizin*) are the seven patriarchs and seven matriarchs, who are invited into the sukkah. Each night one patriarch and one matriarch are specifically welcomed, but extra food is not set out unless real people are invited.[210]

📖 Here is the prayer which invites the אֻשְׁפִּיזִין (**ushpizin**) into the *sukkah* / סֻכָּה / hut.

> May it be Your will, Lord my God, and God of my ancestors, to cause the *Shekhinah* [Divine Presence] to dwell in our midst. Spread over us Your shelter of peace by virtue of our fulfillment of the mitzvah of *Sukkah*. Surround us with the light of Your Holy Glory. May it spread over our heads as an eagle that stirs in its nest....[211]

> I invite the illustrious guests to my table: Abraham, Isaac, Jacob, Joseph, Moses, Aaron, and David. Sarah, Rebecca, Rachel, Leah, Miriam, Hannah, and Deborah.[212]

> On the first night say: Abraham, you are welcome to join us; welcome, too, are all the illustrious guests: Isaac, Jacob, Joseph, Moses, Aaron, and David. Sarah, you are welcome to join us; welcome, too, are all the illustrious guests: Rebecca, Rachel, Leah, Miriam, Hannah, and Deborah.[213]

📖 The reason for inviting the אֻשְׁפִּיזִין (*ushpizin*) into the סֻכָּה (*sukkah*) is as follows:

---

[210] Drucker, Malka. *Sukkot: A Time To Rejoice*. NY: Holiday House, 1982. p. 30.
[211] Drucker, Malka. *Sukkot: A Time To Rejoice*. NY: Holiday House, 1982. p. 30.
[212] Drucker, Malka. *Sukkot: A Time To Rejoice*. NY: Holiday House, 1982. p. 31.
[213] Drucker, Malka. *Sukkot: A Time To Rejoice*. NY: Holiday House, 1982. p. 31.

My Second Encounter With An Angel

The invisible guests are invited into the sukkah because they were wanderers and because of their importance in Jewish history.[214]

📖 Of course, there was no evidence in the books that I read confirming the psychic information that Awan had told me. However, it made perfect sense to me. I eagerly awaited my next conversation with Awan, which took place about a week after I had done this research.

😇 Greetings, my scribe. Tell me, what have you learned about your holiday of *Sukkot*?

🙂 Greetings Awan, I have learned much. I really was shocked to discover that the Jews invite so many Spirit people into the סֻכָּה (*sukkah*)/hut.

😇 And did you discover what is written in your סֻכָּה (*sukkah*)/hut?

🙂 You are supposed to put up a sign that reads: בָּרוּךְ הַבָּא meaning *"Blessed be he who comes"* or *"Welcome."*[215]

😇 Yes, my scribe, I must say, that I was a bit surprised as I watched you in your library—you did not put all the pieces of the puzzle together.

🙂 What do you mean, Awan?

😇 Do you remember when you traveled to Lily Dale, and attended a message service in the auditorium there?

🙂 Yes, Awan, I remember.

😇 Do you remember what people would say when a Spirit would come to talk with them?

🙂 Yes, Awan, they said, "You are welcome." Oh my God, it is the same thing! בָּרוּךְ הַבָּא means *You are welcome!*

😇 Precisely! Now, my scribe, do you realize the implication of all of this?

🙂 What do you mean, Awan?

😇 Even for the Jewish people who do not accept the psychic truth of their rituals and holidays, the fact that they invite all the dead patriarchs and matriarchs into their סֻכָּה (*sukkah*)/hut proves that the most orthodox Jews would have to believe in life after death.

🙂 Awan, you are correct. The Jewish people do not discuss the after life very much. It is not a central theme to Judaism as it is in Christianity.

---

[214] Drucker, Malka. *Sukkot: A Time To Rejoice*. NY: Holiday House, 1982. p. 32.

[215] Drucker, Malka. *Sukkot: A Time To Rejoice*. NY: Holiday House, 1982. p. 61.

(👤) Yet, on a certain level, they would have to accept communication between the two dimensions, otherwise this ritual would not exists. Now, my scribe, please tell me what you know about the Jewish holiday of *Shemini Atzeret*.

(👤) Quite frankly, Awan, I know nothing about it.

(👤) I know, my scribe, neither do your rabbis. Centuries ago, it was decided to add another day to the holiday of *Sukkot*. It was hoped that the additional time would lead to the development of more mediums.

📖 A few days after this conversation, I returned once again to the library to corroborate what Awan said about *Shemini Atzeret*. This is what I found:

> **Shemini Atzeret is really the mystery holiday of the Jewish year. No one can say precisely what it means, and even those who know find it hard to explain its importance....**[216]
>
> **The clue to *Shemini Atzeret* is the word "atzeret,' which means "*tarry*" in Hebrew. The holiday is an extra day added to *Sukkot* for no other reason than to lengthen the joy of it. Everyone wants the joy of the season to tarry, or stay so *Shemini Atzeret* is a way of saying "Stay a day longer."**[217]

The irony of that phrase, "stay a day longer," caused the hair on the back of my neck to stand. The people enjoyed their time communicating with Spirit so much that they wanted Spirit to stay a day longer and lengthened the holiday. I certainly understood that feeling. Often at the end of a psychic development class, I felt so spiritually charged and energized, I felt as though I could fly. I also wanted the class to be longer, I didn't want to go home. So many pieces of this puzzle were fitting together and making so much sense!

(👤) Now, my scribe, please explain what is *Yiskor*?

(👤) *Yiskor* is a special religious service, prayers that you say, after your parents, siblings, or children have passed over into your dimension. Those prayers are said four times a year.

(👤) Yes, my scribe, and one of those times is *Shemini Atzeret*. You see, my scribe, *Yiskor* is "the final exam" of your psychic development class. If you successfully developed as a medium, you would hear messages from your deceased parents or relatives during the *Yiskor* ceremony. This was all very well planned centuries ago. However, as Judaism abandoned its psychic/prophetic/mediumistic heritage, its people no longer understood the significance of their psychically rich holiday, סֻכָּה *Sukkot*.

---

[216] Drucker, Malka. *Sukkot: A Time To Rejoice*. NY: Holiday House, 1982. p. 36.

[217] Drucker, Malka. *Sukkot: A Time To Rejoice*. NY: Holiday House, 1982. p. 37.

🧑 That truly is sad, Awan.

😇 It is much more than sad, my scribe, it is tragic. Do you remember the conversation that you had with the man who knew my medium?

🧑 Are you referring to Larimar? (See chapter 25)

😇 Yes, that is the entity to which I refer.

🧑 Yes, Awan, I really learned much from that conversation. It amazed me the that his soul was able to arrive on the 5th level of the Spirit World, instead of the 3rd, simply because of a short conversation he had during the last hour of his life.

😇 Yes, my scribe, that is the point. Much valuable information can be transmitted from my dimension to yours, which would greatly help the evolution of not only your people; but everyone on the entire planet. It is my hope that the body of information that I am transmitting to you will be an example of what is possible when people of your realm can dialogue with people in my realm.

🧑 Now, I understand, we could have been more spiritually advanced if this link had not been severed.

😇 I am feeling a change in the energy, so I will leave you at this time. My peace be with you my scribe.

🧑 Peace to you, Awan.

Carl's body remained still for about a minute, and suddenly he coughed. After drinking a full glass of water, Carl seemed to have more energy than usual. However, he was still tired and napped for an hour.

* * * *

📖 There were two more quotes from *Maseches Sukah* of the *Dafyomi,* which had interesting psychic implications.

> **According to Rebbi Eliezer, one is not permitted to go from one *Sukah* to another—irrespective of whether it was to eat in the one on one day, and in the other, in the next (or even if both were on the same day) or it was to eat in one and sleep in the other.**[218]

📖 What struck me about this quote was how it agreed with the laws of psychic science. Once a group of people forms a "circle," for psychic development, a process begins where the group members blend their vibrations. It is a coming together that occurs on a subconscious level. Once

---

[218] http://dafyomi.co.il/sukah/reviewa/su-ra-027.htm # 5 (a).

the blending is achieved, it greatly enhances communication with the World of Spirit. If a brand new person were allowed to enter the circle, it would disrupt the existing blend of energy, and would set back the groups development, for a while.

📖 When Rebbi Eliezer prohibited people from traveling from one סֻכָּה (*sukkah*)/hut (one development circle) to another, it was because the existing psychic energy would be disrupted.

📖 The next Dafyomi quote supports other evidence in the Bible.

> ...the Tana always speaks of the *Sukah* as being higher than the house, because they used to build their Sukos on the rooftops).[219]

📖 This fact reminded me of how the סֻכָּה (*sukkah*)/hut and cabinet were similar in nature. The Bible clearly discusses that the prophets Elijah and Elisha both had their cabinets in the upper portion of a house. Compare how the Hebrew word for cabinet אֲלִיָּה (*al-ee-yaw'*) was translated in these two verses.

1 KINGS CHAPTER 17 VERSE 19

KJV	1611	And he said unto her, Give me thy son. And he took him out of her bosom, and carried him up into a **loft** where he abode, and laid him on his own bed.
OJB	2002	aliyyah (upper room)
LIVT	1994	attic
ABBR	1971	bedroom
COV	1535	chamber
LIV	1971	guest room
TYND	1537	loft
EPBL	1994	loft an upper room
NWT	1961	roof chamber
GEDD	1792	roof-room
SWHI	2012	rooftop chamber
KNOX	1944	room
NLFV	1986	room on the second floor
CJB	1998	room upstairs
NWYC	2010	solarium
LWYC	1395	soler
EWYC	1384	sowping place
DOU	1609	upper chamber

---

[219] http://www.dafyomi.co.il/sukah/reviewa/su-ra-028.htm. # 11 (a).

HAAK	1657	upper room
STONE	1996	upper story
BAPT	1912	upper-chamber
ARTB	2008	upper-room dwelling
JBPR	1980	upstairs chamber
GODWD	1995	upstairs room

23 Differing Translations

📖   Here we discover that Hebrew word, אֱלִיָּה (*al-ee-yaw'*) was an upper room on the roof, just as the סֻכָּה (*sukkah*)/hut. They both contained a bed, as we discover in the next verse, which describes Elisha's אֱלִיָּה (*al-ee-yaw'*) upper chamber or medium's cabinet.

2 KINGS CHAPTER 4 VERSE 10

KJV	1611	Let us make **a little chamber**, I pray thee, on the wall; and let us set for him there **a bed**, and a table, and a stool, and a candlestick: and it shall be, when he cometh to us, that he shall turn in thither.
POLA	2003	bijou booth, I pray thee, on the wall
TYND	1537	chamber with a little wall
ABBR	1971	extra room
PUR	1764	little Chamber at the Wall
GRT	1540	little chamber I pray thee, with walls
COV	1535	little chamber of boordes
TFFR	1986	little chamber on the roof
BELL	1818	little chamber on the wall
EPBL	1994	little chamber upper room, I pray beseech thee, on the wall
DOU	1609	little chamber
SMGO	1939	little enclosed roof chamber
THB	2003	little loft, please, on the wall
NWT	1961	little roof chamber on the wall
LIV	1971	little room for him on the roof
VTB	2012	little room for him—just a simple setting
KNOX	1944	little room for his use
UTV	2001	little room I ask you, on the wall
NAB	1970	little room on the roof
BECK	1976	little room on the roof with walls
NLFV	1986	little room on the second floor
OGD	1950	little room on the wall
LWYC	1395	little soler
EWYC	1384	little soupynge place
HIRS	1989	little upper apartment by the wall
HAAK	1657	little upper chamber of a wall

BYIN	1972	little upper room on the wall
JUSMI	1876	little wall chamber
GURGO	1877	little wall-upper-chamber
GLT	1993	little walled roof room
SWHI	2012	little walled rooftop chamber
WELL	1861	little walled upper-chamber
YESC	2010	roof chamber side small
OJB	2002	small aliyyat kir (walled upper room)
LIVT	1994	small attic
AMP	1965	small chamber on the [housetop]
RDB	1982	small chamber on the roof
GEDD	1792	small chamber over the wall
LXEB	2010	small enclosed room [upstairs]
TANK	1985	small enclosed upper chamber
MOFF	1922	small guest-chamber for him
SEPZ	1970	small place
NET	1999	small private upper room
ANCR	1988	small roof chamber by the wall
RSV	1952	small roof chamber with walls
NIrV	1996	small room for him on the roof
GUTN	2002	small room in the attic
CEV	1995	small room on the flat roof our house
JER	1966	small room on the roof
WMF	1975	small room on the wall
THOM	1808	small room up stairs
HSTV	2003	small room, on the wall
DARBY	1920	small upper chamber with walls
CCB	1995	small upper room for him
NKJV	1982	small upper room on the wall
BAPT	1912	small upper-chamber on the wall
ARTB	2008	small upper-room over the wall
JBPR	1980	small walled upper chamber
STONE	1996	small walled attic
ASEPT	2009	upper chamber, a little place
BREN	1844	upper chamber, a small place
APB	2007	upper room a small
MODL	1945	upstairs guest chamber

62 Differing Translations

📖 It is interesting to discover how אֱלִיָּה (*al-ee-yaw'*) is translated very differently in these two verses. These chambers were actually cabinets. They were placed on the roof so the medium could escape the negative thoughts of people. The סֻכָּה (*sukkah*)/hut is supposed to be on the rooftop, because it also was to serve as a site to communicate with the Spirit World.

📖 I discovered another ironic fact as I studied the word אֲלִיָּה (*al-ee-yaw'*). I used an internet site entitled the *Blue Letter Bible*,²²⁰ to look up the meaning of אֲלִיָּה (*al-ee-yaw'*). This site lists where each Hebrew word is used in the **KJV** Bible. The word אֲלִיָּה (*al-ee-yaw'*) appears 20 times in **KJV**,²²¹ and is translated as:

> *chamber* **12 times**, *parlor* **4 times**, *going up* **2 times** and *loft* **1 time.**

📖 When my eyes focused on the words: ***going up***, I felt intense chills go up my spine. I quickly studied אֲלִיָּה (*al-ee-yaw'*) and slowly pronounced it. I had heard that word thousands of times, during synagogue services. אֲלִיָּה (*al-ee-yaw'*) or (*Aleah*) is the name of the honor of being called up before the Torah, to say the blessings over it. The irony was overwhelming. In modern day Judaism, the only way to talk with God, is having an אֲלִיָּה (*al-ee-yaw', Aleah*). After receiting the paryer over the Torah, often an addition prayer is said, asking God to heal a sick person.

📖 I had once again proved a theory I had discovered several years before. You only have to scratch the surface of religious rituals very lightly, for it to bleed psychic science. Someone long ago had taken the word אֲלִיָּה (*al-ee-yaw', Aleah*), the cabinet (*inner-room*) where a medium communicated with Spirit, and used the identical word for their substitute for mediumship—being called up to the Torah. The lifeless scroll replaced the living word of God. In other words, when you were called before the Torah, Judaism's most precious honor, it was supposed to be the equivalent of being in a cabinet, and talking directly to God.

📖 Now my curiosity peaked. I searched my database of Bible verses for the term *inner-room*. I found 1 Kings 22:25 in some Bibles contained the phrase *inner-room*. **KJV** translated it using a different phrase:

> **And Micaiah said, Behold, thou shalt see in that day, when thou shalt go into an *inner chamber* to hide thyself.²²²**

📖 When I looked up 1 Kings 22:25 in the *Blue Letter Bible* I discovered that this time the Hebrew word for *inner chamber/room* was חֶדֶר (*kheh'-der*).²²³ I immediately recognized that word, because in the Yiddish language a חֶדֶר (*kheh'-der*) was the word for ***classroom***, or ***Hebrew School***. This reaffirmed

---

²²⁰ http://www.blueletterbible.org/index.cfm
²²¹ Strong's Number 05944.
²²² 1 Kings 22:25 [KJV].
²²³ Strong's Number 02315.

that the cabinet was supposed to be a place of learning, or as **FENT** had said a *lecture hall*.[224]

📖 It occurred to me that what William Shakespeare said, was so fitting in this instance. "What's in a name? That which we call a rose by any other name would smell as sweet." It does not matter what Hebrew word we use, סֻכָּה (*sukkah*)/*hut*, דְּבִיר (*debir*)/*Holy of Holies*, אֱלִיָּה (*al-ee-yaw'*)/*a little chamber*, or חֶדֶר (*kheh'-der*)/ *inner chamber—classroom,* it is all the same. These various terms for a medium's cabinet were the location people went to seek the *living word of Spirit* — the most sacred place for divine communication.

---

[224] 1 Kings 6:16 [FENT].

ELEVEN

The Psychic Implications of Veils

When I arrived at Carl's office for this dialogue, Carl told me Awan had clairaudiently given him special instructions. After Carl took out his portable tape recorder, he said we would have this dialogue outside, in the woods, behind his house. Awan instructed Carl to sit leaning against an oak tree, and put a towel over his head, before going into trance. So with tape recorder, towel, and a water bottle in hand, we went to the woods. We found a big oak tree for Carl to lean against. He then placed the towel over his head, so that it covered his entire face, and draped down to the center of his chest. Carl then complained that this was a bit stifling, however, making the best of it, he said he was ready to begin. Carl recited his traditional prayer, and within three minutes, I heard the sounds of Awan's voice. This time Carl's body did not spasm as Awan's soul exchanged places with Carl's.

👼 My profound greetings, my scribe!

🧑 Greetings, Awan

👼 I am sure that you are wondering why I decided to change our usual procedure today. Therefore, I will answer your question before you ask it. In ancient times, mediumship always took place outside, in natural settings. The forest provides an excellent setting for this work because there are fewer people, and therefore fewer negative thoughts to impede the communication from my dimension. All the animals such as deer, raccoons, rabbits, and squirrels that inhabit this place, all live their lives in the positive frequency, which enhances Spirit communication. The trees, especially oak trees, also provide excellent antennas, to bring in our frequencies. However, I know by now that you understand this.

🧑 Yes, Awan I do.

👼 The instrument followed my instructions, and put a towel over his head, without understanding the reason behind it. Therefore, my scribe, when my medium comes out of this trance, I want you to teach him this information. As you know, he is unable to hear what we discuss, because his soul is outside of his body, and vibrating on a frequency much too high to listen to our discussion.

Do you remember what a cabinet is?

🧑 Yes, Awan, it was a small enclosed space needed to improve communication with your realm, and to build up ectoplasm for materialization mediumship.

👼 That is correct. You also are aware that my medium is not a materialization medium?

🧑 Yes, I know, the medium is a mental medium, whose gifts include clairvoyance, clairaudience, trance, and healing.

👼 Most people are familiar with working in a cabinet, although, they do not know the term. I want you to understand, my scribe, when you watch illusionists or magicians perform much of their "magic" when an object is underneath a cloth, to create "dark conditions." That cloth creates a miniature cabinet. It is much easier for us to manipulate energy in darkness. This is the reason we asked the medium to wear this towel. It is creating the same effect as a cabinet, creating darkness around his vocal cords. When the instrument puts the cloth (veil) over his head, it makes it easier for us to utilize his body in a trance state, and we use less of his energy than if he had not worn it.

🧑 That is very interesting, Awan.

👼 The custom of wearing a cloth over one's head is really quite ancient. Centuries ago, before religions eliminated the gifted people, it was mostly women who had the *Gifts of the Spirit*. Women tend to be more sensitive to our dimension than men. Before women went into a meditative state, to become the instrument of the Spirit, they would use something to cover up their heads. They did this for two reasons: to build up psychic energy, and to help keep light off their closed eyelids. The darkness facilitated going within, and entering a trance state.

Prior to the start of Christianity, women wore a shawl around their shoulders. When they felt the presence of a Spirit entity, they would cover their head, and go into trance. After a few minutes, a different voice would come through the fabric.

🧑 Now I understand, Awan. I just watched this medium follow the same procedure!

👼 Exactly, my scribe, that is why I wanted my medium to have this session in the woods, with his face covered with a veil. When the Catholic Church began, they passed a law that women had to wear a hat in Church. The hat was to cover up the top of the head, not the entire face and vocal chords. The priests claimed if a woman wore a hat it would keep the spirits out, and prevent spirits from entering her body. Wearing a hat on the top of the head is different than having a cloth draped over the face and vocal cords. The Catholic priests did not want to take any chance in having their secret revealed. If a woman slipped into a trance state, a Spirit like myself could use her vocal cords to address the whole congregation. We in the Spirit World would eagerly reveal the falsehoods taught by the Church. This is why the

Church mandated that women must wear hats in church, and were not allowed to speak in their holy building.

📖 I found where the theologians inserted these ideas into Bible.

> **The women must not be allowed to speak. They must keep quiet and listen, as the Law of Moses teaches. If there is something they want to know, they can ask their husbands when they get home. It is *disgraceful* for women to speak in church.**[225]

📖 Here are the different terms the Bible translators created to describe why women should be silent in the churches.

1 CORINTHIANS CHAPTER 14 VERSE 35

KJV	1611	And if they will learn any thing, let them ask their husbands at home: for it is **a shame** for women to speak in the Church.
TYND	1534	**a shame** for women to speak in the congregation.
COV	1535	**becommeth not** women to speak in the congregation.
HOLLY	1538	**uncomly** unto a woman to speak in the congregation.
CONF	1965	**unseemly** for a woman to speak in church.
SWANN	1947	**cause of shame** to a woman to speak in church.
NORL	1962	**disgrace** for women to speak in the church.
WEY	1903	**disgraceful** for a married woman to speak at a church assembly.
BYIN	1972	**disgraceful** for a woman to speak in meeting.
WADE	1934	**disgraceful** for women to speak in Church.
LETCH	1948	**disgraceful** for women to speak in the church.
GNC	1989	**disgraceful thing** that a woman should make her voice heard in a meeting of the congregation.
WAKE	1820	**dishonourable** for a woman to speak in a congregation.
JER	1966	**does not seem right** for a woman to raise her voice at meetings.
EWYC	1384	**foul thing** to women for to speak in church.
MESS	1993	God's book of the law guides our manners and customs here. Wives have not license to use the time of worship for unwarranted speaking. Do you—both woman and men—imagine that you're a sacred oracle determining what's right and wrong? Do you think everything revolves around you?
HAR	1768	**highly indecent** for a woman to deliver public discourse in a Christian assembly.
ABBR	1971	If they want to know something, let them ask their husbands at home.
MODL	1945	**improper** for a woman to speak in church.
WESL	1755	**indecent** for a woman to speak in the assembly.
DIAG	1942	**indecent thing** for a Woman to speak in the Assembly.

---

[225] 1 Corinthians 14:34-35 [CEV].

WORS	1770	**not become** women to speak in a public assembly.
KLLI	1954	**not proper** for a woman to speak at a service.
KNOX	1944	**not seemly.**
WMF	1975	**shame** for a woman to speak in the church.
CCB	1995	**shameful** for a woman to speak in Church.
OVER	1925	**shameful** for women to speak in the congregation.
SPEN	1937	**shocking** for a woman to speak in church.
NEB	1976	**shocking thing** that a woman should address the congregation.
TCNT	1904	**unbecoming** for a married woman to speak at a meeting of the Church.

30 Differing Translations

📖 Furthermore, the Church also stripped women of any status in the community. They were to have no power or authority over a man.

> **In my opinion it is right for a woman not to be a teacher, or to have rule over a man, but to be quiet.**[226]

📖 The Church then specifically mandated that men were not to wear a veil, or cover their heads. It is fascinating that the early Christians were converted Jews. According to Jewish custom a man is always supposed to have his head covered, but that rule does not apply to women. Christian doctrine is in direct opposition to Judaism.

> **A man who wears a veil when praying or prophesying dishonors his Head; but a woman who prays or prophesies with her head uncovered dishonors her Head, for it is exactly the same as if she had her hair cut short.**[227]

📖 These verses clearly state that men are not to cover their heads during prayer or while prophesying. It is interesting to note that this verse tells us that women were allowed to prophesy. Perhaps this was done through sign language, since they were not allowed to speak in the Church! This next quote is more specific.

> **Every man praying or prophesying, having *anything down over his head* shames his Head.**[228]

📖 Women, on the other hand, had to cover their heads; some Bibles describe that covering as a veil.

---

[226] 1 Timothy 2:12 [OGD].

[227] 1 Corinthians 11:4-5 [WEY].

[228] 1 Corinthians 11:4 [GLT].

> **If a woman will not wear a veil, let her also cut off her hair. But since it is a dishonor to a woman to have her hair cut off or her head shaved, let her wear a veil.**[229]

📖 While the Bible indicates that women's heads are to be veiled, is not specified. If it did not cover the throat and vocal cords, then there would be no enhancement to psychic communication. The Church officials would constantly monitor the length of a woman's veil.

👤 It is not important for the enhancement of trance communication to cover the back of the head. King Tut's head-dress could be turned around to help condense the psychic energy, making better conditions for the *gift of trance* to occur.

👤 I later found further information about this.

> **Especially characteristic was the striped linen headcloth, the *khat*, which was bound round the brow and was then folded to hang down on each side of the face to the shoulders. The material was tied at the rear and hung down in a tail. This was a royal head-dress, which has been made familiar by the gold mask of Tutankhamun.**[230]

👤 The Greek Patriarch's headdress, the Arab *kaffiyeh*, and turbans, all served the same purpose. They could be easily worn, rolled up on top of the head, but then could be unrolled, dropped down over the face and used as a veil during psychic communication.

Jewish women would drape their face with a cloth when lighting their Sabbath candles. This, too, is the same custom, which has its roots in psychic science. Theoretically, the women would channel information from the Spirit World, as they lit the candles to mark the beginning of the Sabbath.

👤 That is very interesting, Awan. Wait a minute, Awan, I remember when I attended an orthodox synagogue, the men would take their טַלִּית *tallis*/prayer shawls and put them over their heads when they said certain prayers. However, they did not cover their faces and vocal cords. Does this custom have roots in psychic science? Were they trying to create a cabinet?

👤 The men would cover their heads to form a cabinet. It was a way to build up psychic energy, to increase the communication with God.

👤 That must be true, they always did this when they said the silent prayers, ones that were said individually instead of prayers that were simultaneously said by the whole congregation.

---

[229] 1 Corinthians 11:6 [WEY].
[230] Yarwood, Doreen. *The Encyclopaedia of World Costume*. London: B. T. Batsford, 1978. p. 141-142.

(😇) That is correct.

(🧑) It was also done when the כֹּהֵן (kôhen)/*priest* blessed the people during the New Year's service. The priest would cover his head with his טַלִּת *tallis*/prayer shawl.

(😇) This all goes back to the ancient customs, when the priests were gifted mediums. They covered their heads with their prayer shawls to increase psychic energy. Once the energy built up, they could project this energy to all the people of Israel. They called this *"blessing the people."* The custom is still practiced today, however, I must admit to you that hardly any energy is transmitted. The priests of today are **NOT** gifted mediums.

You must remember, my scribe, the laws of psychic science have never changed. There was a time when gifted people traveled from place to place. In that time period gifted people were known as *wizards* instead of *prophets* or *mediums*. You have seen many pictures of wizards, who always wore long capes, which served as their cabinets, and a trumpet on their head, as a hat. It made traveling much easier. However, whenever they needed to, they simple took their trumpet put it in front of them, and completely covered their body in their cape. They would then go into trance, and a Spirit could speak through the trumpet. That was how mediumship was conducted during that part of your history.

(🧑) That is very interesting.

(😇) Now, my scribe, there is a description in the Bible, where Moses used a veil. The priests who had control of your "sacred texts" altered this story. Moses used the veil, when he became the instrument of the Spirit, and allowed Spirit to speak through him, to explain the rules to the people. However, when you read your Bible, you will discover that it says the opposite.

(🧑) After this dialogue, I found the verses describing Moses using a veil.

> **When Moses finished speaking to them, he put a veil over his face. But whenever he entered the LORD's presence to speak with him, he removed the veil until he came out. And when he came out and told the Israelites what he had been commanded, they saw that his face was radiant. Then Moses would put the veil back over his face until he went in to speak with the LORD.**[231]

(😇) There was a reason why this verse was altered. The writers reversed the way Moses used the veil, so that the readers of the Bible would not try to become clairaudient or clairvoyant. At this point, I wish to ask you a question, my scribe.

---

[231] Exodus 34:33-35 [NIV].

🙂 OK, Awan. What is your question?

👼 I was with you recently when you went to the synagogue to celebrate the Bar-mitzvah of your neighbor. I noticed that you were curious why the Rabbi and many of his congregation covered their eyes when they said the שְׁמַע (Shema) prayer.

🙂 I asked the Rabbi about that.

👼 I know you did. I inspired you to do so. Do you remember the Rabbi's answer?

🙂 Yes, he said that they covered their eyes to say the שְׁמַע (Shema—Judaism's most holy prayer), to be reminded that you cannot look at the face of God and live.

👼 You did not realize the full implication of the Rabbi's answer, when he told it to you. Therefore, I will explain it a bit further. When you live in the physical body, you are living in a lowest frequency of vibration. At death, when the spiritual body leaves the physical body, the spirit body increases its rate of vibration. Therefore, it is not possible for a physical being to see the face of Spirit, with the physical senses. It is only the spiritual body that can see the face of God.

Long ago, theologians inserted into your Book of Books: "you cannot see the face of God and live." The motivation was to make people afraid to attempt to see Spirit. To state it very simply, religions were trying to make people afraid to participate in psychic development, and become clairvoyant (having second sight). This is was part of the massive cover-up that religions have created. By placing fear of clairvoyance in the minds of the people, no one would even attempt to see the face of God, which is Spirit. This is why Christian religions created their unseen demons and devils. It was all done to keep people disconnected from the World of Spirit, and the information of your past present and future.

There are several passages in the Bible, which claim that it is dangerous to see the face of God. One is when Jacob wrestled with an angel, another when Moses asked to see God's glory.

📖 Here are the verses Awan mentioned:

> **Jacob named the spot Peniel (God's-face), saying, "I have seen God face to face, and yet I am alive!"[232]**
>
> **Then Moses said, "Now show me your glory." And the LORD said, "I will cause all my goodness to pass in front of you, and I will proclaim my name, the LORD, in your presence. I will have mercy on whom I will have mercy, and I will have compassion on whom I will have compassion.**

---

[232] Genesis 32:30 [MOFF].

> **But," he said, "you cannot see my face, for no-one may see me and live."**[233]

(👼) When the Rabbi answered your question, he was really saying, we cover our eyes to remind ourselves not to try to become clairvoyant, and see, or communicate with Spirit people.

(🧑) You were right, Awan, I totally missed the point.

(👼) There is one more topic I would like to discuss with you today.

(🧑) OK, Awan, what is it?

(👼) I noticed that when you were in the synagogue, you had some thoughts while the men were taking the Torah scrolls out of the ark.

(🧑) Yes, Awan, I did. The ark where the Torah scrolls are kept reminded me of a medium's cabinet. They look quite similar; both are small areas with curtains in front of them.

(👼) What else did you think about at that time?

(🧑) I thought about a verse in the Coverdale Bible.

> **And whosoever would *ask any question* at the Lord went out unto the Tabernacle of Witness.**[234]

(👼) What did that verse mean to you?

(🧑) The people in Moses' day had the opportunity to go out to the *Tabernacle of Witness*, which many Bibles called *the Meeting Tent*, to talk *directly* to God. It was a *two-way conversation*. The person would ask a question and God would answer it, speaking through a medium, who was entranced in the cabinet.

(👼) You are correct with your description.

(🧑) The people were hearing the *living* word of God.

(👼) Correct. Do you also remember the other verse in your Book of Books that discusses this two-way conversation, between God and the ordinary person?

(🧑) Yes, Awan. It is in the first book of Samuel

---

[233] Exodus 33:18-20 [NIV].
[234] Exodus 33:7 [COV].

> **At that time a prophet was called a seer, and so whenever someone wanted to ask God a question, he would say, "Let's go to the seer."[235]**

😇 That is correct. These verses clearly demonstrate that the ancient Hebrews totally understood that they must go to a *seer* or *prophet*, to seek the *living word of God* (ask God a question). There have been many other terms for the person having the *Gifts of the Spirit*, such as *mantis, shaman, soothsayer, oracle, sorcerer, wizard, witch, manus, man in white clothing, man/woman of God, psychic, medium, instrument, diviner of a ghost, and person with a familiar spirit.*

Today you use the word *medium* instead of the word *prophet* or *seer*. When the priests sought to eliminate their competition, and turn the people away from mediumship, they replaced the living word of God (the words from the medium's mouth) with the words of the Bible (a lifeless, inanimate book). The priests kept the people's reverence for the living word, but directed it towards the inanimate Torah scrolls.

🧑 Is that why during the synagogue service, when some Jewish men have a processional and carry the Torah scrolls through the congregation, the people kiss the Torah?

😇 Yes, it shows their reverence for the *word of God*. Christians also believe that the Bible, the *word of God*, can protect them. Many Christians will not sleep without the Bible under their pillow, or by their bed. If they are afraid, they hold the Bible as the knights of old held their shield. That mere book is supposed to protect them from evil devils and demons, which do not exist in the first place. The Bible became the policeman for the people. All the man-made laws were written into it to keep the people in-line, doing exactly what the priests wanted.

🧑 Is that really true?

📖 I later found conformation of Awan's statements.

> **Simply leaving a Bible open is said to keep evil spirits away and it was once quite common for busy mothers to leave their babies unattended but for the company of an open Bible left in the cradle. Sleeping with a Bible under the pillow is said to aid peaceful sleep and also to promote the wisdom and intellectual development of young children.[236]**

😇 Yes, my scribe. Originally when the people heard the living word of God coming through a medium, they always obeyed. They did this out of respect for the Spirit who was speaking. Practical experience also taught them it was

---

[235] 1 Samuel 9:9 [TEV].

[236] Pickering, David. *Dictionary of Superstitions*. London: Cassell, 1995. p. 31.

wise to follow the advice an entity, who could see into the past, present and future. The priests capitalized on this precedence when they condemned mediumship as the work of the devil, and created the Holy Bible, which contained their laws. It amazes me that with all the people who study the Bible, no one ever asks their priest, minister, or rabbi, to hear the word of God through the lips of a prophet, just as your ancestors did during Moses' and Samuel's lifetimes.

There is a shift in the energy, so I must now vacate this body. It has been a pleasure to talk with you again, my scribe. My peace be with you.

👤 Peace to you too, Awan. Thank you for the dialogue.

Carl's body gave three jolts, as Awan withdrew. After drinking the entire contents of the water bottle, I explained to Carl why Awan wanted him to wear the veil. Then I recapped Awan's teaching for the day. It was then I noticed that Carl seemed to have more energy after this trance session than usual. We gathered our possessions, and walked back to the house. Carl felt strong enough that he did not need to take a nap to regain his energy.

TWELVE

Awan discusses Steeples, Holy Water, Ash Wednesday, Hell, Purgatory, and Amen

It had been a few months since my last conversation with Awan. I was curious about Awan's topic for today. Carl began to prepare himself to go into trance. He closed his eyes, and said his prayer. In about three minutes, Awan began to speak. Awan's entrance into Carl's body was effortless.

My profound greetings to you.

Greetings, Awan.

I have watched you doing your research. I can see from your light that you have gained much understanding of the battles people endowed with the *Gifts of the Spirit*, have been fighting for centuries. Each person who has picked up the torch of knowledge has carried it, to illuminate a path for all humanity. You are the one who is now holding this torch. It is my fervent wish that you carry it for a very long distance. There still is much ground to cover, to help humanity understand how deeply religions have cheated them from their God-given destiny.

I hope that I will live up to your expectations.

I am sure that you will give it your best effort. Now, there are a few matters I wish to discuss with you today. I think it is time for you to understand the psychic roots of some of your religious rituals.

OK, Awan, that sounds very interesting.

Before Christianity began, everyone knew about the gifted people. They were known by many names, such as *prophet, seer, mantis, shaman, soothsayer, oracle, sorcerer, wizard, witch, manus, man in white clothing, man/woman of God, psychic, diviner of a ghost, and person with a familiar spirit, medium, instrument*. When a person wished to commune with a Spirit being [remember Jesus said God is Spirit,[237] and ancient people referred to the invisible Spirit people as *The Lord*, as a sign of respect,] he or she would

---

[237] John 4:24 [CONF].

journey to a special place. Often, it was a small cave with a covering such as a blanket over the opening. A person seeking advice would sit outside, in silence. People took turns entering the dark and damp cave. Once inside, the person would sit for his or her conference with Spirit, who was speaking through the person known as the *prophet*. People became very accustomed to this type of dialogue with people of my dimension.

📖 I later discovered the people of Crete worshipped their goddess in a cave near Knossos.[238] This quote also substantiates Awan's claim that people used to go to caves to speak with the invisible entities, often called gods.

> **The practice of consecrating mountain caves to the god is undoubtedly a heritage of the time when temples were not yet constructed.[239]**

😇 Then the new religion of Christianity formed. The Christians' new God was the great teacher who was executed on the cross. The priests of this new religion wanted the people to gather in large buildings to commune with God, instead of the tents or caves. At first, the people refused to gather inside these buildings, because they did not resemble the original tent, cave, or cabinet.

The priests needed a strategy that would entice people into the brand new assembly halls. To make the people feel more comfortable, the priests decided to incorporate the ancient psychic practices into their new buildings. Therefore, they built a cubicle, as you term it, and put it on the roof of the large building. Then they went out and preached to the people, proclaiming: "We have invented a method for all of you to commune with God, rather than one person at a time. We have taken your sacred building, the cabinet, and put it up on the roof of our new Church. Now you can all gather in the big hall, underneath of the cabinet, to commune with God." This is the reason your churches have steeples.

📖 I later found this corroborating evidence.

> **The Church spent centuries prohibiting displays of reverence that involved nature. Worship should take place indoors away from the natural elements. Christians destroyed outdoor temples and built churches with roofs in their stead.[240]**

🙂 Wow, that is fascinating. Why did they put the cones on top of the steeples?

---

[238] Jones, Prudence and Nigel Pennick, *A History of Pagan Europe*. NY: Routledge, 1995. p. 7.

[239] Cumont, Franz. *The Mysteries of Mithra*. NY: Dover Publications, Inc., 1956. [Reprint of The Open Court Publishing Company edition of 1903]. p. 30.

[240] Ellerbe, Helen. *The Dark Side of Christian History*. San Rafael, CA: Morningstar Books, 1995. p. 142.

My Second Encounter With An Angel

(👼) As you have witnessed, my scribe, the trumpet was often associated with the cabinet.[241] It was usually placed outside the cabinet, where the person seeking advice would see and hear it, after forming a voice box of ectoplasm from the medium's body. Spirit would pick up the trumpet, and a voice would speak through the trumpet. At first, the people would not accept the new churches, even though the cabinet was sitting atop of the building. They mistrusted the new churches because they could not figure out how they could hear the voice of Spirit (God) through the trumpet, when they could not see it from down on the ground. Therefore, the priests decided to place the trumpet on the top of the cabinet. This way the people could see both the trumpet, and the cabinet, from the ground. Then the priests began to preach, "We will have a medium climb up and sit inside of the cabinet on the roof. The voice of God will then speak through the trumpet, and all of you will hear that voice because you will sit underneath the trumpet." Sadly, the gullible people believed the priests. They began to gather into the building, which became the Church. Once the people were inside the Church, the priests would not allow them to leave unless they made an offering of coins or gold. That was the beginning of tithing, donating a certain percentage of your income to the Church.

🙂 That sure makes sense, Awan.

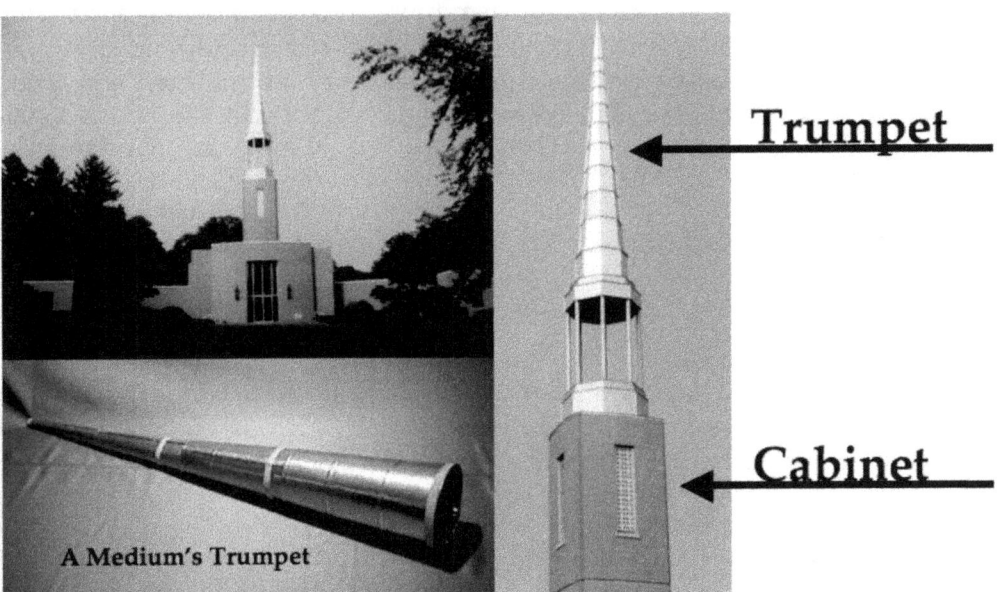

A Medium's Trumpet

(👼) It took many years for the priests to gather and convert all the people into their religious fold. It was a slow process to convince the people to abandon their mediums, who had guided them from inside a cave, tent, or cabinet. Therefore, for many years the priests faked mediumship. Simultaneously, the priests forbade mediumship outside of their churches. Anyone caught

---

[241] Schwartz, Sidney. *My First Encounter with an Angel: Revelationsof Ancient Wisdom*. Blue Hill, ME. Medicine Bear Publishing, 1999. p. 171-192.

demonstrating the *Gifts of the Spirit* in a little house, cabinet, or cave was slaughtered. Many gifted mediums were butchered as animals. Some mediums fled for their lives, and lived as hermits in caves. These were the original hermits. You will find in your books that the word *hermit* is a term for a holy person who would leave civilization turning his or her back on everything. These people were hiding to protect their lives. The priests offered a great bounty to anyone who killed a medium, and brought his or her head back to the high priest. This is the extreme that priests went to try to eliminate anyone who had the *Gifts of the Spirit*.

From the very beginning of the priests controlling the church, they were preaching and teaching fear. By keeping fear in the minds of the people, they would be enslaved them to the newly created dogmas. The people would be afraid to think for themselves, and would follow all the priests' instructions. The priests were very cruel people. It did not matter if the priest spoke the truth or told a lie, if you didn't agree with what the priests said, they would abuse, torture, or even kill you.

The priests dressed in magnificent robes, resembling royalty. That was the image of the leader. It was all part of their plan to attract more people into their churches.

Why did the Catholic Church create Holy Water?

As you know, long before Catholicism there were people who used 100% of their brain. These people would take a vessel of water and hold it in their hands. The energy from their souls would travel through their left arms, into their hands, though the vessel of water, into their right hands and arms, and return to the soul. This created a circuit, as you would know it, energizing the molecules of the water, and turning the water into healing water. After the person energized the water, he or she would drink it. The energy from the water invigorated the physical body. The Catholic Church used this idea, changing the name from *healing water* to *holy water*. However, a priest is the only person allowed to use holy water.

Do the priests do anything to the water to make it holy?

No, they simply take it from wherever they can find water. It can be a stream, lake, rainwater, or right from the faucets you have today. They just call it holy water. Some people were so ignorant that they thought that even priest's urine could be holy water. The priests would do anything to lock a person's mind, and prevent them from independent thinking. They kept filling their minds with fear, until the people accepted the new religion, and became frightened of my dimension. They manipulated guilt, and the things that took place inside confessional booths were a disgrace.

What do you mean?

There continued to be many people suspicious of the new churches, because they were not convinced that trumpet mediumship would occur in the new church steeples. Nor did these people, who were familiar with psychic science, think that Spirit wanted to speak to a large number of people, rather than a single individual.

The priests did everything possible to entice the people into their churches. To convince more people that priests were the links to the other dimension, instead of the mediums, the priests created the confessional booth. It replicated the individual session a person had with a medium. A person would sit on one side of the confessional booth, with the priest on the other side. A screen separated them, as the curtain or sheepskin had at the medium's cabinet. The person would then have a one to one conversation with the priest, who was supposedly in communication with God.

The priests would sit in the cabinet, that they called the confessional booth, and they would imitate what the genuine oracles used to do. The priests claimed that they were channeling God's words and thoughts. Unfortunately, the priests were not psychically gifted, and were only faking mediumship. That is the reason the priests brought the cabinet into the new church building.

🙂 It is difficult to believe that people believed all the fallacies the priests told them.

😇 It was unfortunate that the people were so gullible. After they gathered into these churches, the priests needed a way to keep them returning week after week. So they next invented a grand money-making scheme.

🙂 What was that, Awan?

😇 They invented something so scary; it made everyone on your planet fearful of it. The priests invented Hell.

🙂 Invented Hell??? Are you saying that there is no such place as Hell?

😇 That is correct.

🙂 For centuries, millions of people have believed that hell existed. The clergy constantly preached about it from their pulpits. How could millions of people believe in something that doesn't exist?

😇 That is a good question, one which requires a rather lengthy answer. You are familiar with what you would term *the Holy City*?

🙂 Do you mean Jerusalem?

😇 Yes, that is precisely it. During Biblical times, on the outskirts of the great religious city of Jerusalem, there was a refuse garden; to put it in more familiar terms—the city dump. It was on a barren hill, with no trees or bushes around. It looked like a large pit, about 500 feet across. Everyone in the city, who tried to keep their place clean, would dispose of the items they no longer needed at this dump. At one point, there was so much debris that someone set fire to it. Since people were constantly bringing new rubbish, the embers would never grow low. The soaring flames of fire were constantly flickering. Check the records of your people, my scribe, you will discover that this place was called גֵיהִנוֹם (*Gehenim*).

There were many classes of people living in Jerusalem; some rich people, and many poor people. When someone of the wealthier class died, a grand funeral was held. The person was either buried, or placed in a sarcophagus, depending on what the custom was at that time. The poor person, however, could not afford a burial plot nor a sarcophagus. The poor person had only one option. He or she would take the body of his or her loved one, to

גֵּיהִנּוֹם (*Gehenim*), the city dump. The body was thrown into the dump, and was burned.

As the world evolved, there came a time when the people thought that burning a body at the city dump was not the most elegant way to handle their dead. So they decided to gather some wood, and build a casket, and make it look more glamorous. After all, throwing a person in a dump was rather crude. Even today, in some places on your planet, they cremate bodies. In other places, they cover the body with butter or olive oil, and use certain types of wood to create the fire. I say, it doesn't matter how it is burned, you are just discarding the worn-out physical body.

Over time, mythology grew around גֵּיהִנּוֹם (*Gehenim*). You must remember that people were not as educated in those days as they are in your time. People were always trying to explain the unknown. When people went to גֵּיהִנּוֹם (*Gehenim*) they would see many bodies that were disposed of during the night. There were always skeletons visible in גֵּיהִנּוֹם (*Gehenim*), because they had not yet finished burning. Every skeleton looked identical. This gave the priests an idea. The priests began saying that the person burned there would always be on fire, since the fire itself never went completely out. Therefore, souls of these people would always remain in that pit, and would burn for eternity; that was the penalty for being sinful, or disobeying Church rules. The priests created this myth to frighten the people, and keep control over their lives.

📖 Several years after this conversation, I came upon evidence, which supports this concept of גֵּיהִנּוֹם (*Gehenim*).

> **In early Christian teaching, after the final judgment, the wicked will be condemned to a hell of fire called *gehenna*, a Greek word derived form the Hebrew *Gehinnom* and referring to the desolate Valley of Hinnom, south of Jerusalem, where trash fires burned incessantly and where ancient human sacrifices had been offered to Canaanite gods.**[242]

👤 Who created it? Was it the Jewish priests or the Catholic priests?

😇 It was the Catholic priests.

📖 Again evidence validates this claim. Before Christianity, ***Sheol*** not Hell exists in Jewish thought.

> [In] the ancient Hebrew texts of Genesis...all the dead—*both righteous and wicked*—were dispatched to a gloomy underworld realm called *sheol* ....[243]

---

[242] Shelter, Jeffery L. *"Hell Hath No Fury." U. S. News & World Report.* Vol. 128. No. 4. Jan. 31, 2000. p. 46.

[243] Shelter, Jeffery L. *"Hell Hath No Fury." U. S. News & World Report.* Vol. 128. No. 4. Jan. 31, 2000. p. 46.

📖 This concept of an underworld assembly of good and righteous was changed after Christianity came into existence.

> **By second century B. C., when the Hebrew Scriptures were translated in Greek, *hades* replaced *sheol* in the "Greek Bible, and the two concepts became firmly melded into popular thinking.**[244]

📖 Eventually the distinction between these words and concepts were melded into the concept of hell, an eternal place of torment for wicked souls.

> **...In English bibles, which frequently translate all three terms—*sheol, hades* and *gehenna*—simply as "hell."**[245]

👼 Hell was created to frighten the young children, especially the disobedient ones, who rebelled against Church teachings. Often the young ones grew up thinking there really was a גֵיהִנּוֹם (*Gehenim*)/Hell. The priests created Hell to put fear in the minds of the people. Once the people were fearful, they would eagerly follow all the instructions of the priests to escape this terrible, eternal punishment. Then the priests had them "eating out of the palms of their hands." They trained the people to bring them as much money as possible, which financed their very extravagant lifestyles. They could afford the finest of clothes, the best of food, the best cars. Since they claimed to be Jesus' messengers on earth, no one was allowed to question any of their actions. This provided the priests with the freedom to be sexual with men or women. They could even molest their children without anyone complaining. Now you understand, my scribe, how far a little fear can go; and it has lasted for seventeen centuries.

📖 I later discovered this quotation, which proved that not only children believed in Hell. In 'The Bible of the Poor' a section of Fiona Macdonald's book: *A Medieval Cathedral*, François Villon, a 15th century French poet, describes his mother's feelings as she walked through her local church.

> 'I am a woman, poor and old,
> Quit ignorant, I cannot read.
> They showed me, in my village church
> A painted Paradise with harps
> And Hell where the damned souls are boiled.
> One give me joy, the other frightens me....'[246]

---

[244] Shelter, Jeffery L. *"Hell Hath No Fury." U. S. News & World Report.* Vol. 128. No. 4. Jan. 31, 2000. p. 46.

[245] Shelter, Jeffery L. *"Hell Hath No Fury." U. S. News & World Report.* Vol. 128. No. 4. Jan. 31, 2000. p. 46.

[246] Macdonald, Fiona. *A Medieval Cathedral.* NY: P. Bedrick Books, 1991. p. 26.

😇 You must remember, my scribe, the people were extremely ignorant. They could not read or write their own language, so how could they possibly understand the Church service, which was recited in Latin. The people had no idea what the Priests were saying during the masses. Therefore, the Church incorporated techniques to teach the people in non-verbal ways. This is why stain-glass windows, and gargoyles were included in cathedrals and churches. It was like having "picture books for children." The people would learn the Bible stories from the pictures in the windows. They could see the scary images of hell, by looking at the devilish, scary gargoyles. This was all the priests' plan to reinforce their concepts of God, heaven and hell, in the people's minds.

📖 Here is a quote that again corroborates Awan's statement.

> **Until the later Middle Ages, most ordinary people could not read or understand the words of church services, which were in Latin, The only ways they had of learning about Christianity were listening to sermons or by looking at the scenes from saint's lives and Bible stories shown in wall paintings, status and stained glass.**[247]

😇 Now that we have discussed how the Catholic theologians created Hell, you should also know they created *Purgatory*.

🙂 Awan, being Jewish, I do not know what *Purgatory* is.

😇 You are probably much better off. Before I explain it, you must understand that no such place exists.

🙂 OK, Awan, I understand that.

😇 *Purgatory* was supposed to be a holding pen, a state in-between earth and heaven. It was not supposed to be a pleasant place, however, it was a great money-maker for the Church.

🙂 What do you mean?

😇 I am referring to the period of time when the Catholic priests were selling indulgences to the people. As a matter of fact, my scribe, do you know how most of the saints gained their sainthood?

🙂 No, Awan, I assume they lived an admirable life, free from sin.

😇 Actually, my scribe, the families of the saint purchased the title of sainthood for a very high price!

📖 A few weeks later I found this quotation, which corroborated Awan's statement. Apparently the Church used to practice *simony*, the act of auctioning off Church jobs to the highest bidder. The Pope, who would win the prize of best fund-raiser by selling church positions, was Boniface IX. This pope is described as:

---

[247] Macdonald, Fiona. *A Medieval Cathedral*. NY: P. Bedrick Books, 1991. p. 26.

> ...a murderer and probably the greatest simoniac in history. He sold every living [church position] to the highest bidder with the result that Germany and France swarmed with Italian clerics on the make.... No one, it was said, ever made more money out of the canonization of a saint.[248]

📖 Apparently, Awan was correct when he said you could buy yourself the office of sainthood.

👤 Most of the people of the time of what you term the Middle Ages, could not read and write. Only the wealthiest classes and the clergy received an education. The poor wretched people could not read or write. Consequently, they believed their priests' description of the horrific place called *Purgatory*. They used their last pence, or shekel to buy an indulgence, which was to liberate their family members from purgatory. All of the money from the sale of indulgences went to finance the construction of what you know as the Vatican [more specifically, St. Peter's Basilica]. This information is not something new, but it has been concealed by the lies that were given to the poor ignorant people grasping for something to believe in.

Also the theologians were constantly looking for new sources of money to finance the construction of their very expensive cathedrals. Indulgences went a long way in providing a new source of money.

📖 After the trance session, I found this information, which substantiates these statements.

> Money to pay for a cathedral comes from a number of sources. Added to the steadily growing revenues of the chapter and its dependencies are the profits from indulgences, which are the bishop's monopoly. Many an avaricious baron has made peace with God by a handsome gift to a cathedral building fund. Deathbed bequests are an especially fruitful source.[249]

> As they lay dying, lord and merchants willed their earthly goods to the cathedral. They did this because they were religious and also because they wanted the protection of the Virgin Mary or a saint so that they might enter paradise.... The priests had told them over and over that making a profit was not worthy of a Christian.[250]

---

[248] De Rosa, Peter. *Vicars of Christ*. NY: Crown Publishing, 1988. p. 92.

[249] Gies, Francis and Joseph. *Daily Life in Medieval Times: A Vivid, Detailed Account of Birth, Marrriage and Death; Food, Clothing and Housing; Love and Labor in the Middle Ages.* NY: Black Dog & Leventhal Publishers, 1990. p. 303.

[250] Perdrizet, Marie-Pierre. *The Cathedral Builders*. Brookfield, CT: Millbrook Press, 1992. p. 15.

> Popes Honorius III and Urban IV granted *indulgences* to those people who would finance the building of the cathedrals in Reims, Clermont-Ferrand, Bourges, and Narbonne. Collections were organized throughout the entire kingdom from those among the faithful who wanted to obtain forgiveness for sins they had committed or would yet commit.[251]

📖 I then researched the date that St. Peter's Basilica was rebuilt.

> The restoration [of St. Peter's Basilica] continued until 1506, when Pope Julius II decided to rebuild the church completely. He demolished the original church, and only the tomb and a few details of the earlier structure remain.[252]

📖 I would soon discover that the timeframe Awan was describing was accurate.

🙂 Could you go back into time, and describe how the priests sold indulgences?

😇 In those days, each village would have what you would term a town-square. The church would usually be on the square.

📖 This statement confirms Awan's words.

> Religious ceremonies began in the cathedral and rippled out into the square in front of the cathedral....[253]

😇 The church bells were the only direct method of communicating with the townspeople. The bells were rung in a certain pattern that notified the people of a town meeting. All the people left their homes and came to the square, because it was there that they received news dealing with their church or their government. Another pattern of bells announced the beginning of a Church service. The town-square was also the gathering place for the people when they had free time from their labor. It was the meeting place for all occasions.

📖 Historians again verifies Awan's claims.

> Its [the cathedral's] bells warned the citizens of fire or danger and called their merchants together to discuss the affairs of the town. Every Sunday the bells rang to alert the

---

[251] Icher, François. *Building the Great Cathedrals*. NY: Harry N. Abrams, 1998. p. 46.

[252] "St. Peter's Basilica." *The World Book Multimedia Encyclopedia:* Macintosh Version 3.2, Chicago, IL: World Book Inc., 1996.

[253] Perdrizet, Marie-Pierre. *The Cathedral Builders*. Brookfield, CT: Millbrook Press, 1992. p. 47.

> townspeople and the people who worked in the surrounding field that it was time to stop their work or play and hurry to the cathedral to hear the bishop say Mass.[254]

🕊️ Once the people gathered, after being summoned by the church bells in the steeple, the priest would stand up high on the steps of the church. Then he announced that there was a special visiting priest, who wished to speak to them. The local parish priest would signal for the other priest to make his appearance. The visiting priest came forth, along with some men carrying what you would term as chests.

📖 Again we can find historical documentation, which corroborates Awan's claims.

> Collection boxes or chests set up all around the city, not only in churches, provided another means of soliciting donations.... Of course, things were different when the urban and rural populations were pressured too intensely.[255]

🕊️ These chests would have been about four feet long, 2½ feet wide, and 2½ feet high. The tops of these chests were almost dome-like, and in many cases decorated with real gold ornamentation. Inside, these chests were lined with a material that would be similar to velvet, in your time. This material was woven with gold threads in it. These chests were designed in a way that bars of wood were put through locks, so two or four men would carry the chests. It would depend on the weight of the contents whether two, or four men, would be needed. In any case, these men came marching in, carrying chests, put them down, and opened them. The parish priest would have a list of all the people who had died, and hand it to the visiting priest. The local church kept close records of who was living, and who had died.

👤 Yes, Awan, that was my impression.

🕊️ Then the parish priest gave the visiting priest the list of people who had recently died. In a very solemn voice, the visiting priest would read aloud all the names of those who had died. Of course, these names were relatives of those who had gathered in the square. The visiting priests would tell the people, "I can hear the voices of your dead relatives. They are crying out, 'Help me! Help me!' It is so horrible, they are screaming in agonizing pain, suffering tremendously, in the stopover known as Purgatory."

The priests claimed that the souls of these people were trapped in Purgatory. They could not advance any further into heaven, because Purgatory was the stopover between earth and heaven. There was only one way to have the souls of these departed relatives released from Purgatory and enter heaven. Their relatives, the ones standing in the square, had to put money into the chests. Unless the people paid the Church an ample amount

---

[254] Perdrizet, Marie-Pierre. *The Cathedral Builders*. Brookfield, CT: Millbrook Press, 1992. p. 8.
[255] Icher, François. *Building the Great Cathedrals*. NY: Harry N. Abrams, 1998. p. 44.

of money, the soul of their relatives would remain in purgatory, suffering a great deal, for all of eternity.

This was what you would term "a scam." Purgatory does not exist. The people being as naive and innocent as they were, believed everything a priest would tell them. They would put their hard-earned money into the chests.

🙂 Would the people have brought their money with them or would they have to race home to get it?

😇 Often when the bells rang, the people understood to bring money with them. There was a certain signal or pattern of ringing the church bells that would mean come to the town square and bring some money with you.

🙂 I understand.

😇 Consequently, the people would throw their coins into these elaborate chests. If a family threw enough money into the chests, then the priest would tell the family that their relative had been released from Purgatory, and had gone into heaven. The people believed that the priests could hear the voices of the dead. However, the priests would never utter those words until a certain amount of money was placed into the chest.

🙂 When was this system of selling indulgences created?

😇 It was created in the beginning of what you would term the *Inquisition*; when priests were determined to convert everyone to their religion.

📖 Some research proved Awan' statements were 100% correct. The Spanish Inquisition began in 1478.[256] Pope Sixtus IV created the system of selling indulgences for the dead between 1471 and 1481. Sixtus IV became Pope in 1471, and died in 1481,[257] which is around the time of the start of the Spanish Inquisition. Sixtus IV was a very ingenious pope, creating innovative money-making methods for the church. The Church sold indulgences prior to 1506, when the construction of the new St. Peter's Basilica began.

> **Sixtus was the first pope to license the brothels of Rome; they brought him in thirty thousand ducats a year. He also gained considerably from a tax imposed on priests who kept a mistress.[258]**
>
> **It was in the area of indulgences that Sixtus showed a touch of genius. He was the first pontiff to decide that they could be applied *to the dead*. ... Souls in torment for their misdemeanors could be released by his [Sixtus] word, provided their pious relatives dipped into their pockets.... Simple folk were led to believe that the pope, or those who came to their village and sold the pope's pardon, guaranteed their dead would go to heaven on the wings of**

---

[256] Bachrach, Deborah. *The Inquisition*. World History Series. San Diego, CA: Lucent Books, 1995. p. 50.

[257] De Rosa, Peter. *Vicars of Christ*. NY: Crown Publishing, 1988. p. 452.

[258] De Rosa, Peter. *Vicars of Christ*. NY: Crown Publishing, 1988. p. 101.

indulgences.[259]

🧝 As you have recently learned, the priests and the prophets were always opposing each other. For centuries, the priests had done everything in their power to silence the mediums, by destroying their physical bodies. In this manner, the medium would be unable to reveal to the people how they had been misled.

🧑 Yes, Awan I understand that now.

🧝 In the early days of Christianity, the priests employed two methods to execute mediums. The first was to drive a wooden stake through the medium's heart. The second was to tie the medium to a stake, and burn him or her alive. Burning at the stake was more popular, because it created a grand spectacle for the people. The priests made it mandatory for every person in the town to gather in the town square to watch the executions. The priests knew that a person forced to watch such an agonizing death, would not attempt to become a medium. A special day and time, Tuesdays at 10:00 a.m., was set aside to burn mediums.

Many people would come with their robes on, and hoods over their faces. These were the followers and students of the medium who was being burned at the stake. Late Tuesday nights, under the cloak of darkness, many followers would come, still wearing their robes, to gather some of the ashes from the outer perimeters of the fire, where their teacher had been burned. They would take these ashes and press them in the middle of their forehead, where their third eye, or psychic eye, was. The students were hoping that these ashes would open their psychic eyes, and give them clairvoyant vision. They then would become a medium and carry on their teacher's work. Do you understand?

🧑 Yes, I do.

🧝 The idea that the remains of a deceased medium's body has special psychic powers is quite ancient. You will find evidence of this concept in your Book of Books. After this session, read about Elisha's death.

📖 I later found the verse that Awan wanted me to read.

> **And it came to pass, as they were burying a man, that behold, they spied a band of men; and they cast the man into the sepulchre of Elisha: and when the man was let down, and touched the bones of Elisha, he revived, and stood up on his feet.**[260]

🧝 This practice of students putting their medium's ashes on the middle of their forehead continued for some time. The priests began noticing on Wednesday mornings, many people at the market place, and around the

---

[259] De Rosa, Peter. *Vicars of Christ*. NY: Crown Publishing, 1988. p. 101.
[260] 2 Kings 13:21 [KJV].

town, with a soiled spot in the middle of their forehead. These priests did not understand the significance of the spot of ashes. The priests were always creating new methods to keep the people happy. Their main goal was to maintain high attendance at Church services, which ensured large sums of money in the collection plates. Therefore, the priests decided they would set aside a certain day in the year to distribute the ashes. It was always a Wednesday morning, and this is the origin of Ash Wednesday.

🧑 That is an interesting story, Awan.

😇 Some of the martyred medium's students were highly distraught over their teacher's execution. They would reach in closer to the stake, and take two handfuls of ashes, and rub them over their entire face and arms. It was then that an interesting discovery was made. The dirt from their arms and faces disappeared. What had happened was that by reaching closer to the stake, the ashes had mixed with the dissolved fat from the burned medium's body. The liquid fat, combined with the ashes, formed soap. Soap was discovered because mediums were burned at the stake.

🧑 I had never known that, Awan.

😇 The gifted people were burned at the stake for a very long time. It was done to silence them.

🧑 What a horrible death these people suffered, and their only crime was providing guidance and enlightenment from the World of Spirit.

😇 Yes, that is true, my scribe. I am sensing a change in the energy. Therefore, I will give you only one more piece of information at this time.

🧑 What is that, Awan?

😇 Why do you say *Amen* at the end of a prayer?

🧑 Gee, Awan, I have no idea.

😇 The reason goes back to a great teacher, similar to Jesus, but who lived 563 years prior to him. His name was Buddha Amen and was a small man, in the frame of the body. When he would come out on the balcony to speak with the people in the courtyard, he needed to stand on a tall stone to make him look taller. When he finished his sermon he would step back down from the block of stone. The crowds could no longer see him, so they began to chant his name. Amen! Amen! Amen! Eventually, it became customary to say his name, *Amen*, after his speeches. This custom began to travel to different cultures, and eventually was attached to the end of prayers. Amen began to mean: *it is finished*, or *it is ended*. For the last 2000 years, people say *Amen* at the end of their prayers, yet no one has ever questioned the reason why.

People on your planet are constantly saying expressions without knowing their meanings. Yet, the energy of these words affects their lives. It is time that you wake up and say what you mean, and mean what you say.

I must quickly withdraw from this body. Before I leave, I want you to study the story of Abraham in your Book of Books. Read the story of when he created an altar, in the original Hebrew. We will dialogue about it during our next session. My peace be with you.

Thank you, Awan. I will study that story soon. Peace be with you, too.

Awan withdrew. Carl's body went into severe spasms, after the second one he began coughing. I helped him drink some water. This session came to an abrupt halt. Carl seemed extremely tired, and went right to bed.

* * * * *

An article in the January 31, 2000 edition of *U. S. News & World Report* announced that the Catholic Church had changed its concept of Hell, from a physical place to a state of mind.

> ...In Civilta Catolica, an influential Jesuit magazine with close ties to the Vatican. Hell, the magazine declared, "is not a 'place' but a 'state,' a person's 'state of being,' in which a person suffers from the deprivation of God."[261]
>
> A few days later, Pope John Paul II told an audience at the Vatican that "rather than a place, hell indicates the state of those who freely and definitively separate themselves from God." To describe this Godforsaken condition, the pontiff said, the Bible 'used a symbolical language" that "figuratively portrays in a 'pool of fire' those who exclude themselves from the book of life...."[262]
>
> The pope's more conservative critics complained that by dousing hell's flames, the pontiff had undermined a historic Biblical doctrine and surrendered a potent theological weapon in the church's struggle against evil.[263]

According to Awan, it also destroyed the best money making feature it had ever created. What is more fascinating is this new declaration restored hell back to what it had been centuries ago. The Council of Constantinople in 553 rejected Origen's view that hell was a temporary place for the soul to under remedial reformation.[264]

---

[261] Shelter, Jeffery L. *"Hell Hath No Fury."* U. S. News & World Report. Vol. 128. No. 4. Jan. 31, 2000. p. 45.

[262] Shelter, Jeffery L. *"Hell Hath No Fury."* U. S. News & World Report. Vol. 128. No. 4. Jan. 31, 2000. p. 45.

[263] Shelter, Jeffery L. *"Hell Hath No Fury."* U. S. News & World Report. Vol. 128. No. 4. Jan. 31, 2000. p. 45.

[264] Shelter, Jeffery L. *"Hell Hath No Fury."* U. S. News & World Report. Vol. 128. No. 4. Jan. 31, 2000. p. 47.

THIRTEEN

The Altar of the Lord

A week passed before I had the time to study the Bible, by reading the story of Abraham, as Awan had asked me to do. I consulted my *NIV Interlinear Hebrew-English Old Testament*,[265] which translates each Hebrew word into English. One day, Abraham (clairaudiently) hears the voice of God asking him to pack up his possessions and migrate to a land that would be revealed to him.

> **The LORD had said to Abram, "Leave your country, your people and your father's household and go to the land I will show you.**[266]

Abraham listened to this invisible voice, and began his journey, which would be about 500 miles long. He walked in whatever direction his Spirit voices directed.

> **Abram traveled through the land as far as the site of the great tree of Moreh at Shechem. At that time the Canaanites were in the land.**[267] **The Lord appeared to Abram and said, "To your offspring I will give this land." So he built an** *altar* **there to the Lord,** *who had appeared to him.*[268]

This **appeared** to be a rather uncomplicated verse, where Abraham had a clairvoyant vision of his Spirit Control. I would eventually learn this was not the case. However, initially, my eyes seemed to freeze on one specific Hebrew word מִזְבֵּחַ (*mizbêach*), the Hebrew word for *altar*. When I looked up the word מִזְבֵּחַ (*mizbêach*)/*altar* in *The Englishman's Hebrew and Chaldee Concordance of the Old Testament* I discovered that מִזְבֵּחַ (*mizbêach*)/*altar* is

---

[265] Kohlenberger, John R., III. *The NIV Interlinear Hebrew-English Old Testament*. Vol. 1. Grand Rapids, MI: Zondervan, 1979. p. 27.
[266] Genesis 12:1 [NIV].
[267] Genesis 12:6 [NIV].
[268] Genesis 12:7 [NIV].

used in the Hebrew Bible approximately four hundred times.²⁶⁹ Then I continued reading the story of Abraham in the Bible I discovered this verse:

> **And where he had first built an altar. There Abram called on the name of the Lord.²⁷⁰**

There seemed to be a connection between an *altar* and *calling on the name of the Lord*, a poetic phrase to describe a dialogue between Abraham and his Spirit Control. As I pondered this for a while I suddenly thought of another Biblical story. I quickly leafed through the Bible to Genesis 28:11-22 the story of Jacob's dream. I took interest in what Jacob did after he awoke from this dream.

> **And Jacob rose up early in the morning, and took the stone that he had put for his pillows, and set it up for a pillar, and poured oil upon the top of it. And he called the name of that Place Beth-el....²⁷¹**
> **And this stone, which I have set for a pillar shall be God's house...²⁷²**

After studying my reference books, I discovered that both Genesis 28:18 and Genesis 28:22 contained the Hebrew word מַצֵּבָה (*matstsêbâh*), which has the meaning of *pillar & images*.²⁷³ Jacob had named the מַצֵּבָה (*matstsêbâh*)/*pillar* בֵּית אֵל *Beth-el*, which literally translates as *house of God*. So Jacob created a pillar because of the communication between himself and God. There seemed to be a psychic connection between these two Hebrew words מִזְבֵּחַ(*mizbêach*)/*altar*, and מַצֵּבָה(*matstsêbâh*)/*pillar*. What I found interesting is that מַצֵּבָה /*matstsêbâh*/ *pillar* is also the Hebrew word for a *tombstone*. I wondered where מַצֵּבָה (*matstsêbâh*)/*pillar, images* was used in the Bible. So using *The Englishman's Hebrew and Chaldee Concordance of the Old Testament* I read the story where Jacob makes a covenant, or agreement, with Laban.²⁷⁴

> **So Jacob took a stone and set it up as a pillar.²⁷⁵**

---

[269] *The Englishman's Hebrew and Chaldee Concordance of the Old Testament Vol. 1.* London: Walton and Maberrly, 1866. p. 681.
[270] Genesis 13:4 [NIV].
[271] Genesis 28:18-19 [KJV].
[272] Genesis 28:22. [KJV].
[273] *The Englishman's Hebrew and Chaldee Concordance of the Old Testament Vol. 1.* London: Walton and Maberrly, 1866. p. 752.
[274] Genesis 31:43-55.
[275] Genesis 31:45 [NKJV].

My Second Encounter With An Angel

What could be the connection between these two Hebrew words מַצֵּבָה (*mizbêach*)/*altar* and מִזְבֵּחַ (*matstsêbâh*)/*pillar*? They both were made of stone. They have a similar sound, but the fact was since these Hebrew words had different consonants there was no linguistic link between the Hebrew words מִזְבֵּחַ (*mizbêach*)/*altar* and מַצֵּבָה (*matstsêbâh*)/*pillar*. Then I decided that I would ask Awan about these two Hebrew words in our next dialogue.

About three weeks later, Carl agreed to go into trance. After covering his eyes, and saying the prayer, Carl went into the silence. The transition of Carl leaving his body and Awan slipping in was extremely smooth this time.

(👼) My greetings to you, my scribe.

(🧑) Greetings, Awan.

(👼) I have observed you in your hovel, as you were busy doing your homework.

(🧑) Yes Awan, I read the about Abraham in Bible, as you asked me to do.

(👼) And what did you learn?

(🧑) I learned that Abraham went to a place called Shechem.

(👼) Let me interrupt you, my brother, to ask you a question. Why did Abraham end his traveling at Shechem?

(🧑) I don't know why Awan, the Bible doesn't say.

(👼) No, perhaps the version you read did not say, but others versions do provide information to answer my question. Abraham traveled to Shechem because it was a great center for mediumship, with an accumulation of psychic energy present.

(🧑) It was? Why do you say that?

(👼) There were special oak trees in Shechem, which contained a great deal of psychic energy. These trees acted as giant antennas that would pick up and amplify the signals from my dimension. **It was very common for mediums to be associated with oak trees.** They would often sit in a hollow of an oak tree with a sheepskin covering the opening; as it acted as a cabinet that also enhanced communication with my dimension.

After this session, read some other versions of the Bible, and notice the different names some Bibles use for the *oak tree* in Shechem. I also want you to read about Joan of Arc, because **she lived near a special beech tree.**

Rev. Carl R. Hewitt sitting in a hollow of a Sequoia Tree.

(📖) This quote was taken from the transcripts of Joan of Arc's trial.

> **Joan: Quite close to the town of Domremy [her home town] there is a tree called the Ladies' Tree, and others call it the Fairies' Tree, near which is a spring of water; and I have heard tell that those who are sick and have the fever drink the water of this spring and ask for its waters to recover their health I have witnessed this myself but I do not know if it cures them or not. It is a big tree called beech....[276]**

* * * * *

What follows is a chart of the unique Bible translations of this verse.

GENESIS CHAPTER 12 VERSE 6

KJV	1611	And Abram passed through the land unto the place of Shechem, unto the **plain** of Moreh. And the Canaanite *was* then in the land.
FENT	1922	Alon-Moreh
OJB	2002	Elon Moreh
KJV	1611	plain of Moreh
WETC	2001	the big tree at Moreh
ETR	1987	the big trees at Moreh
ABDNT	2002	the Chestnut of Moreh
JUSMI	1876	the erect oak tree
CPDV	2008	the famous steep valley
CLEAR	2000	the giant oak of Moreh
MITCH	1996	the great oak of Moreh
ICB	1986	the great tree of Moreh
BREN	1844	the high oak
TEV	1976	the holy place at Shechem
NIrV	1996	the large tree of Moreh
THOM	1808	the lofty Oak
EPBT	1994	the mighty oak of Moreh
KEN	1860	the noble vale
LIV	1971	the oak at Moreh
COV	1535	the Oak Grove of More
BATE	1773	the Oak of Moreh
LAMSA	1933	the oak of Mamre
TYND	1537	the oak of More
TPB	2000	the Oak of Oracles
AMP	1965	the oak or terebinth tree of Moreh
BBC	1993	the oak tree at Moreh
GODWD	1995	the oak tree belonging to Moreh
NET	1999	the oak tree of Moreh

---

[276] Pernoud, Régine. *Joan of Arc: By Hersel and Her Witnesses.* NY: Stein and Day/Publishers, 1966. p. 21-22.

HAAK	1657	the Oak-bush Mereh
PUR	1764	the Oaks of Moreh
EPBL	1994	the plain mighty oak of Moreh
GEN60	1560	the plain of Moreh
ARATN	1987	the Plain of the Vision
ARATJ	1987	the plain that had been pointed out
ETHJ	1862	the plain which had been shown
CEV	1995	the sacred tree of Moreh
MOFF	1922	the shrine of Shechem
ROTH	1897	the Teacher's Terebinth
SOLA	1884	the terebinth grove of Moreh
JPS1	1917	the terebinth of Moreh
ALTER	2004	the Terebinth of the Oracle
MODL	1945	the terebinth tree of Moreh
GEDD	1792	the turpentine-tree of Moreh
KNOX	1944	the Valley of Clear Seeing
SEPZ	1970	to the high oak
CGV	2007	to the oak of Moreh
AEB	2001	where there was a tall tree
FENT	1922	Alon-Moreh
OJB	2002	Elon Moreh
WETC	2001	the big tree at Moreh
ETR	1987	the big trees at Moreh
ABDNT	2002	the Chestnut of Moreh
JUSMI	1876	the erect oak tree
CPDV	2008	the famous steep valley
CLEAR	2000	the giant oak of Moreh
MITCH	1996	the great oak of Moreh
ICB	1986	the great tree of Moreh
BREN	1844	the high oak
TEV	1976	the holy place at Shechem
NIrV	1996	the large tree of Moreh
THOM	1808	the lofty Oak
EPBT	1994	the mighty oak of Moreh
KEN	1860	the noble vale
LIV	1971	the oak at Moreh
COV	1535	the Oak Grove of More
BATE	1773	the Oak of Moreh
LAMSA	1933	the oak of Mamre
TYND	1537	the oak of More
TPB	2000	the Oak of Oracles
AMP	1965	the oak or terebinth tree of Moreh
BBC	1993	the oak tree at Moreh
GODWD	1995	the oak tree belonging to Moreh
NET	1999	the oak tree of Moreh
HAAK	1657	the Oak-bush Mereh

PUR	1764	the Oaks of Moreh
EPBL	1994	the plain mighty oak of Moreh
GEN60	1560	the plain of Moreh
ARATN	1987	the Plain of the Vision
ARATJ	1987	the plain that had been pointed out
ETHJ	1862	the plain which had been shown
CEV	1995	the sacred tree of Moreh
MOFF	1922	the shrine of Shechem
ROTH	1897	the Teacher's Terebinth
SOLA	1884	the terebinth grove of Moreh
JPS1	1917	the terebinth of Moreh
ALTER	2004	the Terebinth of the Oracle
MODL	1945	the terebinth tree of Moreh
GEDD	1792	the turpentine-tree of Moreh
KNOX	1944	the Valley of Clear Seeing
AEB	2001	where there was a tall tree

43 Differing Translations

Of all the translations, **ARATN** with its phrase: *Plain of the Vision*, and **KNOX** with its phrase: *Valley of Clear Seeing* provide the most psychic information. Clearly Abraham traveled to Moreh because it was famous for its psychic energy, which facilitated Spirit communication in the form of Clairvoyance—seeing spirit and visions. **MOFF** uses the phrase: *the oracular oak*, which clearly indicates the psychic nature of that particular tree. The true nature of mediumship is revealed in **ROTH**'s phrase: *Teacher's Terebinth*. The higher purpose of mediumship is to gain guidance and knowledge from the other dimension, as I was receiving from Awan, a very powerful teacher. Yet it was **FENT** that intrigued me the most, since its phrase: אֵלוֹן מוֹרֶה *Alon-Moreh* was NOT translated from the Hebrew language, where אֵלוֹן (*Alon*) means *tree* and מוֹרֶה *Moreh* means *teacher*. Why didn't translate **FENT** it? We can find a clue in the next quotations.

> The Israelites, like many peoples in the ancient world, believed that certain places were holy. These were usually associated with aged trees, mountains, or man-made markers such as standing stones or altars.[277]
>
> When Abraham entered the land of Canaan, the Lord first appeared to him at a traditional Canaanite shrine at Shechem—a sacred tree called the oak of Moreh, meaning the oak of the soothsayer.[278]

---

[277] *ABC's of the Bible: Intriguing Questions and Answers About the Greatest Book Ever Written*. Pleasantville, NY: The Reader's Digest Association, Inc., 1991. p. 54.

[278] *ABC's of the Bible: Intriguing Questions and Answers About the Greatest Book Ever Written*. Pleasantville,

This sacred location אֵלוֹן מוֹרֶה *Alon-Moreh* would be the location of several other Bible stories. Charles John Ellicott in his book entitled *Elliot's Commentary on the Whole Bible: A Verse by Verse Explanation* explains:

> **The plain of Moreh. Heb. The oak of Moreh. It was here that Jacob buried the strange gods brought by his household from Haran (chapt. xxxv: 4)**[279]

Ellicott is referring to this Bible verse (Genesis 35:4):

> **And they gave unto Jacob all the strange gods, which were in their hand, and all their earrings which were in their ears; and Jacob hid them under the oak which was by Shechem.**[280]

745 years after Abraham arrived at אֵלוֹן מוֹרֶה *Alon-Moreh* in Shechem, we read of the same location in Judges 9:37. After almost seven and a half centuries the name had changed, and was now called the *Elon-Meonenim*.

> **And Gaal spoke again and said: 'See, there come people down by the middle of the land, and one company cometh by the way of Elon-meonenim.'**[281]

Charles John Ellicott in his book entitled *Elliot's Commentary on the Whole Bible: A Verse by Verse Explanation* confirms that אֵלוֹן מוֹרֶה *Alon-Moreh* is the identical location as אֵלוֹן מְעוֹנְנִים *Elon-maonenium*.

> **By the plain of Meonenim – Rather the way to the Enchanters' Terebinth (Septuagint Bible: "of the oak of those that look away;" Vulgate Bible: "which looks towards the oak;" ... Hence, though the terebinth is nowhere else mentioned by this particular name, it is at least a probable conjecture that it may be the ancient tree under which Jacob's family had buried their idolatrous amulets (Genesis xxxv, 4).**[282]

NY: The Reader's Digest Association, Inc., 1991. p. 54.

[279] Ellicott, Charles John. *Elliot's Commentary on the Whole Bible: A Verse by Verse Explanation*. Vol.1. Grand Rapids, MI: Zondervan Publishing Company, 1981. p. 58.

[280] Genesis 35:4 [KJV].

[281] Judges 9:37 [JPS1].

[282] Ellicott, Charles John. *Elliot's Commentary on the Whole Bible: A Verse by Verse Explanation*. Vol.1. Grand Rapids, MI: Zondervan Publishing Company, 1981. p. 225.

Because Elliot refers to Genesis 35:4 (the verse where Jacob buried the strange god) in his discussion of אֵלוֹן מוֹרֶה *Alon-Moreh* in his commentary of Genesis 12:6, and then refers to the identical verse in his commentary אֵלוֹן מְעוֹנְנִים *Elon-maonenium* found in Judges 9:37; we have to conclude that this is the identical location!

Once again there is a long vocabulary list of English translations for the Hebrew name אֵלוֹן מְעוֹנְנִים *Elon-maonenium*.

JUDGES CHAPTER 9 VERSE 37

KJV	1611	And Gaal spake again, and said, See there come people down by the middle of the land, and another company come along by **the plain of Meonenim**.
		CHARMERS
TYND	1537	the charmer's oak
GRT	1540	the plain of the charmers
		CONJUERERS
ROTH	1897	the Conjurers' Terebinth
		DIVINERS
BATE	1773	the oak of divination
RSV	1952	the Diviners' Oak
NKJV	1982	the diviners' Terebinth Tree
ARATJ	1987	the plain of the diviners
ISV	1998	the diviner's oak tree
NET	1999	the oak tree of the diviners
AB	2005	the way of Diviners' Terebinth Tree
RNV	2007	the diviners' great tree
		FORTUNE-TELLERS
MODL	1945	the fortune-tellers' oak
BECK	1976	the Fortune-tellers' Tree
TEV	1976	the oak tree of the fortunetellers
VW	2009	the plain by way of the fortunetellers
		MAGICIANS
GURGO	1877	the Magician's Tree
ETR	1987	the Magicians' Oak
		SOOTHSAYERS
PUR	1764	the Oak of the Soothsayers
NIV	1978	the soothsayers' tree
REB	1989	the Soothsayers' Terebinth
YESC	2010	the plain of the ones soothsaying
		SORCERERS
MKJV	1962	the Sorcerers' Oak

THB	2003	the Oak of the Sorcerers
		PSYCHIC PRACTIONERS
COV	1535	the witch Oak
MOSES	1884	the Oak of the Cloud-observers
MOFF	1922	the road from Augur's Oak
OGD	1950	the oak-tree of the Seers
NLFV	1986	the oak tree of those who tell the future
CEV	1995	the tree where people talk with the spirits of the dead
MESS	2002	the Oracle Oak
EEBT	2003	the prophet's tree
CGV	2007	the Psychics' Oak
NETS	2007	the direction of Watchers' Oak
		MEONENIM
GEN60	1560	the plain of Meonenim
HAAK	1657	the Oak Meonenim [or even plain of the Star-gazers Soothsayers Jugglers]
BOTR	1824	the turpentine-tree of Meonenim
LEES	1856	the grove of Me'onenim
YNG	1863	the oak of Meonenim
HAUPT	1898	the Meonenim Tree
EPBL	1994	the plain mighty oak of Meonenim
EPBT	1994	the mighty oak of Meonenim
NSB	2003	the big tree of Meonenim (big tree of magic)
		OAK TREE
EWYC	1384	that beholdith the oak
DOU	1609	the way that looketh to the oak
KNOX	1944	the oak-tree
CPDV	2008	the way that looks towards the oak
		אֵלוֹן מְעוֹנְנִים **UNTRANSLATED HEBREW**
THOM	1808	the way of Elon-maonenium
BREN	1844	the way of Helon Maonenim
FENT	1922	the road of Alan-Maonim
SMGO	1939	the direction of Elon-meonenim
TPB	2000	the road of Elon-meonenim
AEB	2001	the road from Helon-MaOnenim
OJB	2002	the Elon Me'onenim
		MOUNTAIN
ASEPT	2009	the way of mount Meonenim

54 Differing Translations

This long list of terms brings to our attention that this oak tree in Shechem was a very special and sacred location. It was a site of concentrated psychic energy, where people would consult psychic/mediumistic practitioners, using many modalities of communicating with the Spirit World.

Is it any wonder that after a 500-mile journey, Abraham ended up at this unique location of concentrated psychic energy!

* * * * *

(😇) Now, you must understand that much of the psychic truth has been translated out of the Bible. Yet fortunately much psychic truth remains, if one is adequately educated in psychic science to recognize it. Now that you understand about the oak trees, please continue telling me what else you learned about Abraham.

(🧑) Once at Shechem, Abraham set up an altar to communicate with his Spirit Control. The Hebrew word for *altar* is מִזְבֵּחַ (*mizbêach*). Afterwards, I read the story of Jacob's dream. Jacob communicated with his Spirit Control, and then he set up a pillar, which is מַצֵּבָה (*matstsêbâh*)/*pillar, images.* There seems to be some sort of psychic connection between these two Hebrew words מִזְבֵּחַ (*mizbêach*)/*altar* and מַצֵּבָה (*matstsêbâh*)/*pillar.* Could you please enlighten me as to the psychic meaning between these two words?

(😇) You would have to go far back into time when communication between my dimension and yours was an everyday occurrence. People understood at that time that for communication to happen, the oracles, prophets or mediums, needed to be grounded. This is a term that you understand in your present time because of your electricity.

(🧑) Yes, Awan, I understand.

(📖) My knowledge about science is far less than my knowledge of history. I had heard of the term *grounded*, but in fact I did not really understand it. However, I knew that there were plenty of people living in the physical plane that could explain this principle of electricity. So I told Awan that I understood this concept, not wanting to waste valuable psychic energy to learn information that I could easily find on this plane of existence.

(📖) A day or two after this session, I began talking to Carl about what Awan had said. I asked Carl what exactly *grounding* meant. Carl explained to me that the radio came out in 1927. Apparently, the signals were very weak, compared to today's standards. In order to get the radio to work, you had to drive a steel pipe into ground. Then you wrapped a wire around the pipe, and attached the other end to the radio. Once you did this, you could clearly hear the radio signals. If you did not "ground" the radio you did not get any kind of sound at all; the radio was just dead. After World War II the radio systems changed, and radios no longer needed to be grounded. So it seemed that by grounding the radio, the radio reception increased, or the circuit was completed.

(😇) The medium would sit down, and lean against a big rock that had its base deep within the ground. The grounded stone grounded the medium and improved the medium's connection with the Spirit World.

In your present time, before you were born, they developed what you know as the radio. It was very crude in the beginning stages. Over the years, they kept working on this system, and engineers developed it, improving it along the way. In your present time, you have a different set of sounds come out of each of your speakers [stereo] that amplify the radio frequencies. In other words, the system of radio communication was refined and improved from the initial stages.

Yes, Awan, I understand that.

From time to time, Spirit people would discover new ways to improve communication with your dimension. Then Spirits would explain the new techniques to their clairaudient mediums. When the mediums followed these new instructions, there was an improvement in the communication between the two dimensions.

Originally, the prophet would ground him or herself by leaning against the big stone, enabling grounded communication to take place. Then it was discovered on my side of life that a cabinet would improve communication. Therefore, a Spirit instructed that a large piece of cloth, or skins, be placed over the stone as the prophet leaned against the stone. This was the original cabinet, an enclosure covering the medium. In some areas where the weather changed rapidly, they decided to cover this rock, which was fashioned to look like a chair, with a large cloth, or skins, whatever was available. Now this stone was inside of what looked like a tent. They realized that the communication with my dimension was much stronger. This was the beginning of cabinet.

I never knew that.

When your ancestor, Abraham wanted to communicate with his Spirit Control, he gathered some rocks together, and sat leaning against them. Then he covered himself, and the rocks, with cloth and communicated with his Spirit Control.

But the Bible says that he built an altar to the Lord. Didn't he sacrifice an animal?

Your thinking is based upon the Bible translators' misinterpretations. I will see that the correct information will come into your hands, and you will discover that altars and pillars were exactly alike during Abraham's time; and those words would have been used interchangeably.

About a month after this discussion I came across this passage, as I was doing some research in a library.

> **Numerous altars have been uncovered among the ruins of the ancient Near East. The most typical kind was composed of a pile of rough stones.[283]**

---

[283] *ABC's of the Bible: Intriguing Questions and Answers About the Greatest Book Ever Written*. Pleasantville, NY: The Reader's Digest Association, Inc., 1991. p. 61.

📖 Awan was apparently correct once again. It was easy to figure out that מַצֵּבָה (*matstsêbâh*)/pillar was a pile of stones, but this quote proved that מִזְבֵּחַ (*mizbêach*)/altar was **also** pile of stones.

🧑 So if Jacob built a מַצֵּבָה (*matstsêbâh*)/*pillar*, which is a pile of stones why did he call it, *the house of God*. How could a pile of stones be a house?

👼 What kind of houses existed in the days of your ancestor, Jacob?

🧑 I suppose that Jacob lived in a tent.

👼 Yes, my brother, Jacob lived in a tent. And what was that tent made of?

🧑 I suppose cloth, or skins. Oh, I see what you are saying. When Jacob communicated with Spirit he sat by the pile of stones, leaned against it and was covered by the cloth of a tent. Therefore, he created a cabinet, but he was in the same kind of tent that he himself lived in. So he could simply think of it as God's tent, or house, because God would come to talk with him when he sat by the pillar, and was covered by the tent-cloth.

👼 Very good, my friend, I am glad to see that you are beginning to think and reason some of these things out for yourself. As time progressed, people began to realize that leaning up against a pile of stones was not too comfortable. So, for the comfort of the medium, they fashioned chairs made out of stone. The ancient custom of having a special stone chair for a prophet, inside the crude cabinets, set the precedent for having a special chair for specific people. This is the origin of a king's throne, reserved only for the leader of a country.

🧑 Yes, Awan, Recently I visited the National Cathedral in Washington D. C. The guide explained there is one specific feature that differentiates a Church from a cathedral. Only a cathedral has a *cathedra*, which is a special chair, on a raised platform, reserved only for the bishop. Can this custom be traced back to ancient mediums?

🧑 Months after this conversation took place I found a further definition of the word *cathedra*.

> **The word 'cathedral' comes from the Latin word *cathedra*, meaning a chair or throne, because it was from their chairs in these building that the early bishops taught Christianity.[284]**

👼 That is correct. As time proceeded, people discovered that they did not need a stone, or a stone chair, as long as the medium was in a small enclosure, such as a tent or a cabinet. This is why Moses set up a tent where he spoke to

---

[284] Watson, Percy. *Building the Medieval Cathedrals*. Minneapolis, MN: Lerner Publications Company, 1976. p. 4.

My Second Encounter With An Angel

God, face to face.[285] The medium would wear a loose fitting robe, sit barefoot on the earth inside the tent, and still be grounded. The earth is a good conductor of psychic energy. As time progressed, these cabinets were modernized.

🙍 That is very interesting. Awan, I am curious about something. Today the Hebrew word מַצֵּבָה (*matstsêbâh*)/*pillar* means **tombstone**. Is there any psychic significance to tombstones?

👼 As far as your tombstones are concerned, they would come under another category. You have to go back to ancestor worship to understand the origins of this custom. Go back to when many people were ignorant. Let's assume that the matriarch of a family, the great-great-grandmother, died. Shortly after her death, her Spirit materialized in her house, and spoke with the most sensitive person of the family, who could pick up on her vibration.

🙍 OK, I understand that, Awan.

👼 The family notified their priest that their dead great-great-grandmother had visited their home, and gave them information about their future. In those days, people always sought the answers to their questions from the priests. The priests would say, that this was very bad, and that the family member must go and lay a heavy stone on his or her great-great-grandmother's grave, to hold her Spirit down, and keep it inside the grave. The family obediently followed their priest's instructions. *Originally, they did not put the person's name on the stone.* Over the years, large fields became covered with stones, covering the graves of many different people. It then became difficult for a certain family member to remember exactly where a particular relative was buried. This gave the priests the idea, they would take a large portion of land and sell small plots, for as much gold as they could get. Then they would sell the people a stone, with a person's name engraved on it, so they would always know where their dead ancestor was buried. This was turned into a massive business.

📖 I later found this quote, which implies that Christians created cemeteries.

> **It should be stressed that, unlike the Romans, the Christians would integrate the cult and the memory of the dead within the walls of the city by establishing the cemetery in an enclosed space; this element became an important part of the complex of buildings that was arranged around the cathedral.[286]**

👼 In the beginning, the stone was supposed to hold the Spirit down, into the ground. This is totally ridiculous and impossible. When the body dies and is buried, the Spirit is no longer in the body. The Spirit has already left the

---

[285] Exodus 33:7-11.

[286] Icher, François. *Building the Great Cathedrals.* NY: Harry N. Abrams, 1998. p. 16.

physical body, and entered into my dimension. It leaves at the last heartbeat then *immediately* enters my plane of existence.

🧑 Awan, I find this fascinating. Today there is a Jewish custom called an unveiling. One year after a person dies, there is a ceremony held at the person's graveside. A cloth is placed over their tombstone. Family members gather and say prayers. Then the tombstone is uncovered.

😇 This ceremony is a remembrance of when the altar-stones were covered, and the medium spoke from underneath the cloth. In a forgotten way, the Jewish people are still carrying out ancient traditions. You do not expect your loved one to talk though the covered-up tombstone, yet you carry out rituals that were performed for a psychic reason centuries ago.

🧑 As long as we are discussing the psychic meaning behind certain religious customs and rituals, can you tell me if there is any psychic significance in why Jewish men wear tephillin (phylacteries) when they pray? [*Tephillin are two boxes with hand-written Bible quotations inside. Each box is attached to leather straps. One is placed on the forehead, and the other under the arm to be near the heart.*]

😇 They thought that perhaps these small boxes with scrolls would do the same thing as getting inside a cabinet. Underneath the arm, there is a gland. When there is a disease in the body, that gland swells to stop the poison from traveling to other parts of the body. It is like a safety valve. The Jewish men thought that if they placed a box with a handwritten prayer inside of it under the arm, and one on the forehead, that they would be able to become connected to my dimension. In your terms, you might describe it as being plugged in. However, this idea doesn't work.

There is a change in the energy; I will withdraw at this time. My peace be with you.

🧑 Thank you Awan, my peace be with you, too.

Awan effortlessly withdrew from Carl's body, which did not shudder. Carl awoke from his trance very thirsty, but was not groggy at all. After five minutes, Carl's energy was fine, and he continued his daily activities, without needing a nap.

FOURTEEN

Why does God Dislike Meteorologists or "What's Clouds got to do with it?"

This chapter is the result of over a decade of periodic research. After all those years, suddenly and finally, the light came on, and I finally understood, what Awan had tried to teach me. In the last chapter the discussion focused on altars being cabinets. I have to admit, I can be very stubborn at times. And despite the fact that I had never been able to disprove any of Awan's statements; I just could not accept the idea that Abraham built a cabinet when the Bible states that he built an altar.

As with so much of my Biblical research, the solution to the problem is found by studying the original Hebrew text of the Old Testament. There is significant psychic information embedded in the Hebrew words that never gets translated into English. This is also true for this topic.

I will begin this discussion at what will appear to be a rather odd place. In Deuteronomy 18: 10-12 "God" gives his disapproval of a long list of psychic practices:

> [10] There shall not be found among you any one that maketh his son or his daughter to pass through the fire, or that useth divination, or *an observer of times*, or an enchanter, or a witch.
> [11] Or a charmer, or a consulter with familiar spirits, or a wizard, or a necromancer.
> [12] For all that do these things are an abomination unto the LORD: and because of these abominations the LORD thy God doth drive them out from before thee.[287]

The 234 versions of the Old Testament that I have studied has provided a long vocabulary list of words describing these psychic practices which God prohibited. It was truly amazing how several Hebrew words can be translated so differently.

---

[287] Deuteronomy 18:10-12 [KJV].

DEUTERONOMY CHAPTER 18 VERSE 10

KJV	1611	There shall not be found among you any one that maketh his son or his daughter to pass through the fire, or that useth divination, or **an observer of times**, or an enchanter, or a witch.
		AUGURY
ETHJ	1862	and auguries
ERV	1885	one that practiseth augury
		BIRDS/FOWLS
LWYC	1395	and [to] chittering of birds
COV	1535	or that regardeth the fowls crying
TAV	1539	or that regardeth the flight of fowls
GRT	1540	or a regardeth of flying of fowls
GEN60	1560	or a marker of the flying of fowls
HAAK	1657	or that giveth heed to the cry of birds
GFT	1999	or a chooser out of days or that regards the flying (flaying) of souls
NETS	2007	one who practices **ornithomacy**
		CHARMER
NAB	1970	charmer
		CLOUDGAZER
EPBT	1994	a cloudgazer
		CLOUDS
BATE	1773	one that consulteth the clouds
BELL	1818	revealing discoverers by a cloud
BOTR	1824	or an observer of the clouds
YLT	1898	an observer of clouds
EPBL	1994	or an observer of times a cloudgazer
		CONJURER
UTV	2001	or a conjurer
		ENCHANTMENTS
FENT	1922	and enchantments
LAMSA	1933	or is an enchanter
FISCH	1997	or an enchanter
KJHN	1999	or an enchanter
		FORTUNE/FORTUNETELLING
SCH	2005	or tell fortunes
APB	2007	or one prognosticating and foretelling
		MAGIC
HLYNB	1963	nor anyone who practices magic
EB	1987	Don't let anyone use magic

CEV	1995	And don't try to use any kind of magic
NIrV	1996	Don't use magic to try to explain the meaning of warnings in the sky or of any other signs.

MISCELLANEOUS

TYND	1537	or a maker of dismal days
LIV	1971	or be a serpent charmer
NLFV	1986	or tells the meaning of special things
GUTN	2002	divines (on the basis of strange occurrences)

OMENS

THOM	1808	or consulteth omens
BREN	1844	who deals with omens
KEN	1860	or observeth dreams and omens
JUSMI	1876	and taking omens
KNOX	1944	or keep watch for dream-revelations and omens
MODL	1945	observing omens
NASB	1960	or one who interprets omens
NWT	1961	or anyone who looks for omens
TEV	1976	or look for omens
NIV	1978	interprets omens
LIVT	1981	who divines by omens
ARATN	1987	or those who observe omens
STONE	1996	one who reads omens
NLT	1996	or allow them to interpret omens
WBC	2001	an omen reader
AEB	2001	looking for omens
OJB	2002	a m'nachesh (one who interprets omens)
CPDV	2008	nor one who observes dreams or omens
OTFTS	2008	or omens
ASEPT	2009	or that dealeth with omens

SIGNS

OGD	1950	or a reader of signs
BYIN	1972	or believes in signs
BECK	1976	one who can tell good or bad luck by signs
ICB	1986	No one should try to explain the meaning of signs
NCV	1991	or try to explain the meaning of signs
CLEAR	2000	interpreting signs
CEB	2011	is a sign reader

HIDDEN/SECRET ARTS

ROTH	1897	hidden arts
GRANT	1899	or that useth secret arts

SATAN

EWYC	1384	nor be there keeper of devils
EEBT	2003	You must not become a servant of Satan and obey him

		SORCERER
GEDD	1792	or a sorcerer
BAPT	1912	a sorcerer
MOFF	1922	no sorcerer
JER	1966	or sorcerer
RDB	1982	sorcerer
FOX	1995	a hidden-sorcerer
CCB	1995	who is a sorcerer
WEB	1997	one who practices sorcery
MESS	2002	sorcery
INCP	2007	who practices … sorcery
VW	2009	or sorcery
		SPELLS
CONF	1965	or caster of spells
THB	2003	or one who determines oracles by whispering spells
		SOOTHSAYER
PUR	1764	Soothsayer
		TIMES
KJV	1611	or an observer of times
RAY	1799	or superstitiously regard times, (as lucky, or not so)
LEES	1856	one who is an observer of times
WELL	1859	is an observer of times
ETHO	1862	observing times
JBPR	2004	a diviner of [auspicious] times

83 Differing Translations

I was really unclear on the distinction between these words, and what their accurate meanings were, so I decided to look up the dictionary definition for them.

Term	Dictionary Definition
Augury[288]	[1.] Art or practice of foretelling event by auspices or omens; divination.
[Augur][289]	[2.] One reputed to foretell events by omens; a soothsayer; a diviner; a prophet.
Charmer[290]	[a] one who used the power of enchantment; a magician; an enchanter [b] one who subdues, overcomes, etc., as if by magic power

---

[288] *Webster's New Int'l Dictionary: Unabridged, 2nd Ed.* Springfield, MA: G. & C. Merriam Co., 1947. p. 181.

[289] *Webster's New Int'l Dictionary: Unabridged, 2nd Ed.* Springfield, MA: G. & C. Merriam Co., 1947. p. 181.

[290] *Webster's New Int'l Dictionary: Unabridged, 2nd Ed.* Springfield, MA: G. & C. Merriam Co., 1947. p. 453.

[charm][291]	[1.] A blended or confused noise of voices or notes of birds...
	[1.] To affect by or as by a charm or magic; subdue or control, summon, etc., by incantation or magical influence; spell...
Cloudgazer [also known as nephelomancy]	A study of clouds and their various formations, as a means of divining future events. [292]
	In Nephelomancy prognostication were made by omens interpreted from the color, direction it moves, position in the sky and shape of a cloud or cloud formations.[293]
Conjurer[294]	One who practices magic arts; one who pretends to act by the aid of supernatural power; ... magician. Juggler.
Divination[295]	[1.] The act or practice of foreseeing or foretelling future events or discovering hidden knowledge often accompanied by rites in which the unseen powers are assumed to co-operate.
Enchanter[296]	One who enchants; a sorcerer or magician; also one who delights as by an enchantment.
Enchant[297]	[1.] To act on by charms or sorcery; to get control of by magic, or to endow with magic; esp., to lay under a spell.
Consulter with familiar spirits[298]	consulter with familiar spirit a supernatural spirit or demon supposed to attend on or serve a person.
Foreteller[299]	One that foretells
Foretell[300]	To predict; to tell before occurrence; to prophecy...
Fortune teller[301]	One who professes to tell future events in the life of another.
Magic[302]	[1.] The art, or body of arts, which claims or is believed to be able to compel a deity or supernatural power to do or refrain from doing some act or to change temporarily the order of natural events, or which claims or is believed to produce effects by the assistance of supernatural beings, as angels demons, or departed spirits, or by a mastery of secret forces of nature.
Necromancer[303]	One who practices necromancy
Necromancy[304]	The art of, or device for, revealing the future by pretended communication with the spirits of the dead; hence, magic in general; conjuration; enchantment.

---

[291] *Webster's New Int'l Dictionary: Unabridged, 2nd Ed.* Springfield, MA: G. & C. Merriam Co., 1947. p. 453.

[292] "Nephelomancy - Encyclopedia." Nephelomancy - Encyclopedia. Encyclo Online Encyclopedia, n.d. Web. 01 Oct. 2012. <http://www.encyclo.co.uk/define/nephelomancy>.

[293] "Nephelomancy - Nephelomancy, Divination by Clouds - Occultopedia, the Occult and Unexplained Encyclopedia." Nephelomancy - Nephelomancy, Divination by Clouds - Occultopedia, the Occult and Unexplained Encyclopedia. The Occult and Unexplained Encyclopedia, n.d. Web. 02 Oct. 2012. <http://www.occultopedia.com/n/nephelomancy.htm>.

[294] *Webster's New Int'l Dictionary: Unabridged, 2nd Ed.* Springfield, MA: G. & C. Merriam Co., 1947. p. 565.

[295] *Webster's New Int'l Dictionary: Unabridged, 2nd Ed.* Springfield, MA: G. & C. Merriam Co., 1947. p. 760.

[296] *Webster's New Int'l Dictionary: Unabridged, 2nd Ed.* Springfield, MA: G. & C. Merriam Co., 1947. p. 842.

[297] *Webster's New Int'l Dictionary: Unabridged, 2nd Ed.* Springfield, MA: G. & C. Merriam Co., 1947. p. 842.

[298] *Random House Unabridged Dictionary. 2d Ed.* New York: Random House, 1993. p. 696.

[299] *Webster's New Int'l Dictionary: Unabridged, 2nd Ed.* Springfield, MA: G. & C. Merriam Co., 1947. p. 990.

[300] *Webster's New Int'l Dictionary: Unabridged, 2nd Ed.* Springfield, MA: G. & C. Merriam Co., 1947. p. 990.

[301] *Webster's New Int'l Dictionary: Unabridged, 2nd Ed.* Springfield, MA: G. & C. Merriam Co., 1947. p. 995.

[302] *Webster's New Int'l Dictionary: Unabridged, 2nd Ed.* Springfield, MA: G. & C. Merriam Co., 1947. p. 1479.

[303] *Webster's New Int'l Dictionary: Unabridged, 2nd Ed.* Springfield, MA: G. & C. Merriam Co., 1947. p. 1635.

Observer of times[305]	To cloud over, act covertly, practice magic, to auger from the appearance of clouds; using the clouds for supernatural information and wisdom. Horoscopes, astrology, zodiac; using the stars and the moon for wisdom.
Omen[306]	An occurrence or phenomenon supposed to portend, or show the character of, some future event; a foretoken; also an augury or prognostic; foreboding; presage.
Ornithomacy[307]	Divination by observation of birds, their flight, etc.
Soothsayer[308]	[1.] A speaker of truth. [2.] One who foretells events; a prognosticator
Sorcerer[309]	One who practices sorcery; a magician; wizard.
Sorcery[310]	The use of power gained from the assistance or control of evil spirits, esp. for divining; divination by black magic; necromancy; witchcraft.
Witch[311]	[1.] One who practices the black art; or magic; one regarded as possessing supernatural or magical power by compact with an evil spirit esp. with the Devil; a sorcerer or sorceress; — now applied chiefly or only to women.
Wizard[312]	[1.] A wise man; a sage. [2.] One devoted to the black art; a magician; sorcerer.

Until I had completed this chart, I did not realized how this list of words, is really like a plate of spaghetti. Each word (strand of spaghetti), and its meaning is so intertwined with all the others, that without understanding all the words; one cannot really understand any of them. I had assumed this long list of words was due to inaccurate translation, however, I now understand that is not the case.

Two of the words I will need to focus on are: *Sorcerer/Sorcery* and *Cloudgazer/Nephelomancy,* for these words will become the key to unlocking a new understanding about Abraham's mediumship. *According to the definition a **sorcerer** gains knowledge through an evil spirit.* At least this definition acknowledges the practitioners' ability to communicate with someone in the other dimension. That fact is missing from the definition of a *Cloudgazer,* who only interprets the movement and shape of clouds.

The central theme of our entire list of psychic practitioners found in Deuteronomy 18:10 is that all these people accessed information from a person living in another dimension. Since the psychically ungifted person

---

[304] *Webster's New Int'l Dictionary: Unabridged, 2ⁿᵈ Ed.* Springfield, MA: G. & C. Merriam Co., 1947. p. 1635.

[305] "Exposing the Occult." Exposing the Occult. World Overcomers Outreach Ministries Church, n.d. Web. 01 Oct. 2012. <http://www.exposeoccult.com/index.php?option=com_content>.

[306] *Webster's New Int'l Dictionary: Unabridged, 2ⁿᵈ Ed.* Springfield, MA: G. & C. Merriam Co., 1947. p. 1700.

[307] *Webster's New Int'l Dictionary: Unabridged, 2ⁿᵈ Ed.* Springfield, MA: G. & C. Merriam Co., 1947. p. 1722.

[308] *Webster's New Int'l Dictionary: Unabridged, 2ⁿᵈ Ed.* Springfield, MA: G. & C. Merriam Co., 1947. p. 2399.

[309] *Webster's New Int'l Dictionary: Unabridged, 2ⁿᵈ Ed.* Springfield, MA: G. & C. Merriam Co., 1947. p. 2400.

[310] *Webster's New Int'l Dictionary: Unabridged, 2ⁿᵈ Ed.* Springfield, MA: G. & C. Merriam Co., 1947. p. 2400.

[311] *Webster's New Int'l Dictionary: Unabridged, 2ⁿᵈ Ed.* Springfield, MA: G. & C. Merriam Co., 1947. p. 2939.

[312] *Webster's New Int'l Dictionary: Unabridged, 2ⁿᵈ Ed.* Springfield, MA: G. & C. Merriam Co., 1947. p. 2942.

could not see or hear the invisible Spirit person, the conclusion was drawn that this information came through supernatural powers. Therefore, it had to come from some evil source, and must be banned.

However, this is only one perspective. I believe all these practices were banned because the information was being gained from sources other than the priests. It was the priests who claimed to be the intermediary between God and the people. They had set up a system of sacrifice for people to atone their sins. A person brought an animal to the priest to sacrifice;[313] the priest burnt the offering to God,[314] and then took the barbequed meat off the altar and sat down and ate a delicious meal.[315] Any communication, which bypassed this process, meant less meat for dinner! Therefore, all unauthorized communication with God, or Spirit was banned.

Through this understanding, when I read Deuteronomy 18:10-12 today, I understand that it was not **God** who dictated these prohibitions, but the **Priests**, who wanted to ban all mediumship. Robert Elliott Friedman explains in his book entitled: *The Bible with Sources Revealed: A New View into the Five Books of Moses*[316] that much of the Pentateuch was written by the priests.

Rev. Harold B. Hunting, in his book entitled: *The Story of Our Bible: How it Grew to be What it is* concurs that many of the laws made by priests (and not by God) were included in the Bible.

> **The earliest Bible of the Hebrews, that is, the earliest writings, which were regarded as divinely inspired and sacred, were written laws and legal decisions of the priests. Half-civilized nations always put their laws under the direct sanction of the Gods, in order that evil-doers may be restrained by fear of supernatural vengeance. ...Deuteronomy was combined with earlier laws and also with an elaborate system of later priestly regulations.**[317]

The priests wrote the "Laws from God" to protect their system of free food. This not only included a ban on people, who utilized these psychic practices, but demanded their execution.

Thou shalt not suffer a witch to live.[318]

---

[313] Leviticus 4:27 [NKJV] [P].

[314] Leviticus 4:24 [NKJV] [P].

[315] Leviticus 6:26 [NASB] [P].

[316] Friedman, Richard Elliott. *The Bible with Sources Revealed: A New View into the Five Books of Moses.* San Francisco: HarperSanFrancisco, 2003.

[317] Hunting, Harold B. *The Story of Our Bible: How it Grew to be What it is.* NY: C. Scribner's Sons, 1915. p. 219.

[318] Exodus 22:18 [KJV].

> Besides a Man or Woman when there is in them a familiar spirit, or who is a Sorcerer, shall be quite put to death: they shall stone them with Stones, their Blood being chargeable on themselves.[319]

The concept that the priests invented the system of sacrifices for an endless supply of free food was well known, even in Biblical times. Several Biblical prophets/mediums confronted the priesthood telling them that they were not carrying out God's/Spirit's wishes.

Isaiah told the priests that God did not want animal sacrifices.

> What are all these sacrifices for? Do you think I need burnt offerings of sheep and other fatted animals to hear your prayers? I'm tired of all your ritual sacrifices that have no meaning. Do you think I delight in all this blood?[320]

Jeremiah not only told the priests that God did not want animal sacrifices, but he wanted ALL the people to **obey the words of the prophets/mediums.**

> [21] This is what the LORD of Heaven's Armies, the God of Israel, says: "Take your burnt offerings and your other sacrifices and eat them yourselves! [22] When I led your ancestors out of Egypt, it was not burnt offerings and sacrifices I wanted from them. [23] This is what I told them: 'Obey me, and I will be your God, and you will be my people. Do everything as I say, and all will be well!'
> [24] "But my people would not listen to me. They kept doing whatever they wanted, following the stubborn desires of their evil hearts. They went backward instead of forward. [25] From the day your ancestors left Egypt until now, I have continued to send my servants, the prophets—day in and day out. [26] But my people have not listened to me or even tried to hear. They have been stubborn and sinful—even worse than their ancestors.
> [27] "Tell them all this, but do not expect them to listen. Shout out your warnings, but do not expect them to respond. [28] Say to them, 'This is the nation whose people will not obey the LORD their God and who refuse to be taught. Truth has vanished from among them; it is no longer heard on their lips.[321]

---

[319] Leviticus 20:27 [PUR].

[320] Isaiah 1:11 [CLEAR].

[321] Jeremiah 7:21-28 [NLT].

Hosea told the priests that they were not teaching people spiritual truths, but only interested in the free food when they ate the sin offerings brought by the people.

> ⁶ My people are being destroyed
>   because they don't know me.
> Since you priests refuse to know me,
>   I refuse to recognize you as my priests.
> Since you have forgotten the laws of your God,
>   I will forget to bless your children.
> ⁷ The more priests there are,
>   the more they sin against me.
> They have exchanged the glory of God
>   for the shame of idols.
> ⁸ "When the people bring their sin offerings, the priests get fed.
>   So the priests are glad when the people sin!
> ⁹ 'And what the priests do, the people also do.'
>   So now I will punish both priests and people
>   for their wicked deeds.
> ¹⁰ They will eat and still be hungry.
>   They will play the prostitute and gain nothing from it,
> for they have deserted the LORD
> ¹¹   to worship other gods.
> "Wine has robbed my people
>   of their understanding.
> ¹² They ask a piece of wood for advice!
>   They think a stick can tell them the future!
> Longing after idols
>   has made them foolish.
> They have played the prostitute,
>   serving other gods and deserting their God.[322]

Hosea repeats the same message in Hosea 6:6.

> **For I desired mercy and not sacrifice; and the knowledge of God more than burnt offerings.[323]**

Amos tells the priests that God is not interested in feasts or animal sacrifices, but wants people to live righteous lives.

---

[322] Hosea 4:6-12 [NLT].

[323] Hosea 6:6 [LAMSA].

> ²¹ "I hate, I despise your religious festivals;
>   your assemblies are a stench to me.
> ²² Even though you bring me burnt offerings and grain offerings,
>   I will not accept them.
> Though you bring choice fellowship offerings,
>   I will have no regard for them.
> ²³ Away with the noise of your songs!
>   I will not listen to the music of your harps.
> ²⁴ But let justice roll on like a river,
>   righteousness like a never-failing stream!³²⁴

Micah accuses the priests of being corrupt and not fulfilling God's expectations.

> **Her leaders judge for reward. Her priests give rulings for a price. Her prophets divine for money. Yet they rely on God, saying, "God is surely in our midst. No harm will come our way."³²⁵**

Yet, the priests would not relinquish their control over the people and the system of sacrifices continued until the destruction of the second temple in the year 70 C. E.³²⁶

Now let us focus on the topic of this chapter: why does God disapprove of Cloud gazers? Did he consider the science of meteorology evil? No, not at all. The answer again lies with understanding the original Hebrew words.

But first, we must discuss a few points of Hebrew grammar. Hebrew words are composed of three constants root. Words that share these consonants are considered linguistically linked into a family of words. It is the vowels the dots and dashes above and beneath the constants, which changes the meanings of words. However, the vowels are not always written down. In fact, in the Torah scrolls, the hand written first Five Books of Moses, used in synagogue worship, **the vowels are NEVER written down**. Therefore, over time certain words have been traditionally used in a specific verse.

---

³²⁴ Amos 5:21-24 [NIV].

³²⁵ Micah 3:11 [LIVT].

³²⁶ Alpher, Joseph, ed. *Encyclopedia of Jewish History: Events and Eras of the Jewish People*. NY: Facts on File Publications, 1986. p. 51.

When reading Deuteronomy 18:10 in *The NIV Interlinear Hebrew-English Old Testament* I discovered NIV translated the Hebrew word מְעוֹנֵן *meaw-nan'* as *practicing sorcery*.327

The root word for מְעוֹנֵן *meaw-nan'* is עָנַן *aw-nan'*, which is also the root for the word מְעוֹנְנִים *menomenim*, the second name of the oak tree in Shechem to which Abraham migrated.

As listed in the Bible chart Judges 9:37 of the last chapter, the many translations of the word מְעוֹנְנִים *menomenim* clearly indicate a various psychic practices that occurred at this location. The list included: *Augur's, Charmers, Cloud-observers, Conjurers', Diviners', Fortune-tellers', Magicians', Oracle, people talk with the spirits of the dead, prophet's, Psychics', Seers, Soothsayers, Watchers', Witch.* This extensive list enhances our understanding that this very special oak tree in Shechem was a place of concentrated psychic energy.

There is another Hebrew word, that shares the same root letters as עָנַן *aw-nan'/sorcerer* but has different vowels. The word עָנָן *aw-nawn'* is translated as *cloud*.

In Genesis 9:14 Noah sees the cloud הֶעָנָן *heh-aw-nawn'*.

14 And it shall come to pass, when I bring a cloud over the earth, that the bow shall be seen in the cloud,328

And here is the answer to our question. The root letters for the words עָנַן *aw-nan'/sorcerer* and עָנָן *aw-nawn'/cloud* are ענן. They are intertwined to the point that they become inseparable. James Strong in his book entitled: *The New Strong's Complete Dictionary of Bible Words* assigns Hebrew words their own identification number, and refers to a word by its number. This source clearly shows the intertwined linguistic link between עָנַן *aw-nan'/sorcerer* and עָנָן *aw-nawn'/cloud*.

> 6049. עָנַן *aw-nan'*; a primitive root; to cover; use only as a denominative (derived from a noun) from 6051, to cloud over; figuratively to act covertly, i. e. practise magic:— x bring, enchanter, Meonemin, observe (r of) times, soothsayer, sorcerer.329
>
> 6051. עָנָן *aw-nawn'*; from 6049; a cloud (as covering the sky), i. e. the nimbus or thunder-cloud:— cloud(y).330

---

327 Kohlenberger, John R., III. *The NIV Interlinear Hebrew-English Old Testament. Vol. 1.* Grand Rapids, MI: Zondervan, 1979. p. 536.

328 Genesis 9:14 [ASV].

329 Strong, James. *The New Strong's Complete Dictionary of Bible Words.* Nashville, TN: Thomas Nelson Pub., 1996. p. 479.

330 Strong, James. *The New Strong's Complete Dictionary of Bible Words.* Nashville, TN: Thomas Nelson Pub., 1996. p. 479.

Furthermore, עָנָן *aw-nawn'*/*cloud* is the Hebrew root for the הֶעָנָן word *heh-aw-nawn'* translated as *cloud* in the phrase *pillar of cloud* in Exodus 33:9. In Exodus 33:7-11 we find a description of where Moses spoke to God "face to face as a man speaks with a friend." By reading the description closely we discover that inside this closed meeting tent (which acted as a cabinet) a *pillar of cloud* appeared, and God spoke to Moses employing this cloudy pillar.

The gift of materialization is the appearance of "temporary ectoplasmic forms in various stages of solidity and completeness."[331]

> **Ectoplasm [is] a subtle living matter present in the physical body, primarily invisible but capable of assuming vaporous liquid or solid states and property. It is extruded usually in the dark from the pores and the various orifices of the body....**[332]

Under the right conditions, Spirit is able to withdraw the ectoplasm from the cells of the medium's body and utilize a type of life force energy that emanates from the ectoplasm. Ectoplasm is highly sensitive to light, and therefore, most materializations occur in a completely dark room. However, under very special conditions, which Spirit determines, ectoplasm may be produced in daylight, but this is very rare

Ectoplasm is made up of **Life Force Energy**. Spirit withdraws it from the medium's body, and concentrates it. Spirit then condensates it and then ectoplasm becomes visible.

This process is very similar to the formation of snowflakes. When water evaporates over oceans, lakes, and rivers water vapor rises into the air and can gather into clouds. When the temperature is low enough, around -10 C (14 F), water vapor in clouds condenses and freezes onto a tiny water droplet, which attaches onto dust particles, or pollen that is in the air. As more of these droplets attach the snowflake becomes heavier, and at a certain point, will fall to the earth.[333]

After the ectoplasm is extracted out of the cells of the medium's body, Spirit mixes other spiritual chemicals and energy with it. After this process is completed, this ethedralized ectoplasm has been made sensitive to thought. Then Spirit People can sculpt the ectoplasm through thought energy into the body of a person, who had died and now living in the Spirit World. If there is not sufficient energy, Spirit will materialize only part of the body, such as a hand.

---

[331] Blundson, Norman. *A Popular Dictionary of Spiritualism*. NY: The Citadel Press, 1962. p. 128.

[332] Blundson, Norman. *A Popular Dictionary of Spiritualism*. NY: The Citadel Press, 1962. p. 69.

[333] "A Snow Crystal Primer." A Snow Crystal Primer. Snowcrystals.com, n.d. Web. 11 Oct. 2012. <http://www.its.caltech.edu/~atomic/snowcrystals/primer/primer.htm>.

Now this is the key fact of our Biblical discussion: ectoplasm is a substance that resembles a cloud! A Bible translator who was also educated in psychic science would translate the Hebrew word הֶעָנָן *heh-aw-nawn'* as *ectoplasm!*

Now with this understanding we can read of a materialization séance recorded in Exodus 33:7-11.

> **7 Moses used to take a tent and set it up far outside the camp. He called it the "tent of meeting." Anyone who wanted to ask the Lord a question would go to the tent of meeting that was outside the camp.**[334]

The *tent of meeting* was a special tent, which acted as the cabinet for this séance. The fact that *people could ask a question of the Lord* implies that they would receive a direct answer. Since the Spirit would be incased in ectoplasm, which is partially comprised of physical matter, the sounds generated from ectoplasmic voice box that would be created, would vibrate in the range of human hearing. Therefore, psychically ungifted people, who were not clairaudient, would be able to hear what the Spirit had to say. This is confirmed in verse 11, when the Bible says: *"Thus the LORD used to speak to Moses face to face, as a man speaks to his friend."*

> **8 Whenever Moses went out to the tent, all the people rose up, and every man stood at his tent door, and looked after Moses, until he had gone into the tent.
> 9 When Moses entered the tent, the *pillar of cloud* would descend and stand at the door of the tent, and the LORD would speak with Moses.**[335]

The pillar of cloud was ectoplasm. The Hebrew word in this verse is הֶעָנָן *he-aw-nawn'*, is the word translated as *cloud*.

> **10 And when all the people saw the *pillar of cloud* standing at the door of the tent, all the people would rise up and worship, every man at his tent door.
> 11 Thus the LORD used to speak to Moses face to face, as a man speaks to his friend. When Moses turned again into the camp, his servant Joshua the son of Nun, a young man, *did not depart from the tent.***[336]

Materialization is the most physically taxing gift of the Spirit. The ectoplasm withdrawn from the mediums' body is partially comprised of the

---

[334] Exodus 33:7 [NIrV].

[335] Exodus 33:8-9 [RSV].

[336] Exodus 33:10-11 [RSV].

medium's energy. When the séance is finished, *the ectoplasm returns into the medium's body*. However, some of the ectoplasm is used up during the séance, therefore the medium is exhausted after the séance. Notice that in verse 11, Joshua, who was the materialization medium, was too tired to leave the tent of meeting. Further, proof that this was a materialization séance.

The laws of psychic science have never changed. What was true in Biblical time can still happen today, if the conditions are right. In 1953, a materialization séance was photographed with infa-red film. I am including the` wondrous pictures of this rare phenomenon.

Silver Belle was a Native American princes and the Spirit Control of the materialization medium Ethel Post Parrish. When Silver Belle materialized at a séance, she spoke to the attendees, just as Moses and Elijah spoke to Jesus, Peter, James and John on the Mount of Transfiguration.

A second materialization séancet that is recorded in the Bible is the story of the Mount of Transfiguration. Jesus took his most advanced students, Peter, James and John to an isolated mountaintop to escape any negative energy.

The fact that the Bible described Jesus as having **clothes that were white and glistering** indicates that ectoplasm, which is luminescent, was being withdrawn from Jesus.

> **[29]And as he prayed, the fashion of his countenance was altered, and his raiment *was* white *and* glistering.[337]**

Moses and Elijah were described as *appearing in glory* meaning that they both materialized in a *pillar of cloud/ectoplasm*.

> **[31]who, appearing in glory, were speaking of His departure, which He was about to accomplish at Jerusalem.[338]**

We have already discussed that after Moses and Elijah had materialized, and gave Jesus instructions about his death, Peter asked Jesus if he should build three *tabernacles/tents/huts/sukkots/cabinets*. Peter understood that a cabinet was needed for materialization, despite the fact that the Bible claims that he did not know what he was talking about.

> **And it came about, as these were parting from Him, Peter said to Jesus, "Master, it is good for us to be here; and let us make three tabernacles: one for You, and one for Moses, and one for Elijah"— not realizing what he was saying.[339]**

---

[337] Luke 9:29 [KJV].

[338] Luke 9:31 [NASB].

[339] Luke 9:33 [NASB].

So now I will employ the technique of Bible translators, who interchange words at will, regardless of whether or not it is psychically accurate. I must ask two provocative questions. ***Did God use sorcery to speak to Moses?*** Most observant Jews and Christians would be a horrified by such blasphemous question. The word הֶעָנָן *heh-aw-nawn'*/*cloud* is in this Bible story it is linguistically linked to the word עָנַן *aw-nan'*/*sorcerer*?

Ths second provocative question is: ***Was Jesus a sorcerer when he discussed his future, with Moses and Elijah on the Mount of Transfiguration?*** The story of the Transfiguration is a second Biblical record of a Materialization séance.

Since Moses and Elijah discussed Jesus' future, Jesus was being an ***observer of times*** ("using the clouds for supernatural information and wisdom"), which again is a translation of the Hebrew word עָנַן *aw-nan'*/*sorcerer*. Deuteronomy 18:10-12 banned necromancy meaning communication with the dead. Yet Jesus was getting advice from Moses who had been dead for 1482 years and Elijah who had been dead for 928 years.[340] Jesus directly disobeyed this Hebrew law!

The answer to both these provocative questions is a loud and resounding *NO*! However, one must understand psychic science, and the gift of materialization to come to that conclusion.

Now let's return to the original question posed in this chapter: ***Does God dislike Meteorologists?*** A fundamentalist who accepts the "literal" words of the Bible could come to the conclusion. However, psychic science provides us the understanding that when a meteorologist ***observes clouds***, it does not contradict the Biblical prohibition of Deuteronomy 18:10, since he is not utilizing any ***gift of the Spirit***.

Abraham followed the instructions of Spirit which led him to אֵלוֹן מוֹרֶה *Alon-Moreh* a psychically charged oak tree in Shechem. Genesis 12:7 reads:

> ⁷**The LORD *appeared* to Abram and said, "To your offspring I will give this land." So he built an altar there to the LORD, who had appeared to him.**[341]

The question now arises, how did the Lord appear to Abraham. I decided to look at the original Hebrew word that is translated *appeared*. Using the *NIV Interlinear Hebrew-English Old Testament*, I discovered that the Hebrew

---

[340] Sprague, E. W. Rev. *All the Spiritualism of the Christian Bible and the Scripture Directly Opposing It.* Detroit, MI: (self published), 1922. p. 249.

[341] Genesis 12:7 [NIV].

Silver Belle Materialization Séance 1953
Ethel Post-Parrish, Medium — Jack Edwards, Infrared Photographer

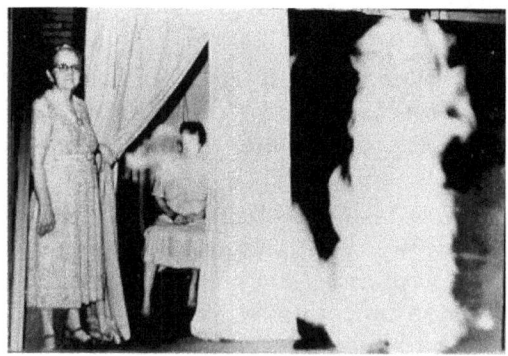

1. The white, smoky ectoplasm is being drawn from medium, sitting inside of the cabinet.

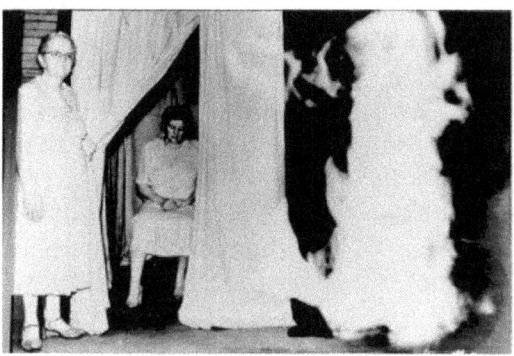

2. The Pillar of Cloud coming from the medium's body forms from the ground upwards.

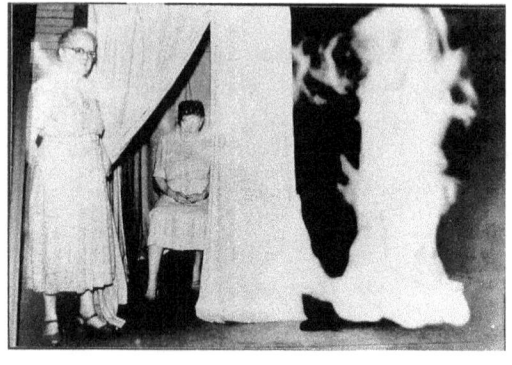

3. This type of phenomena is how Moses spoke to God face to face in Exodus 33:7-11.

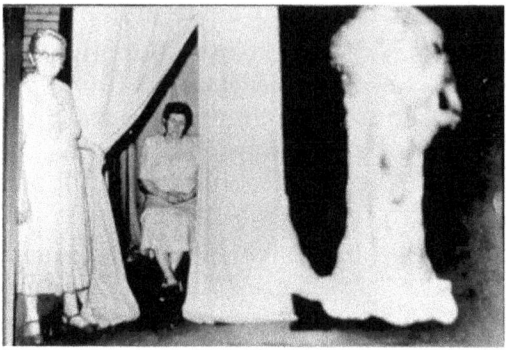

4. More of Silver Belle's features are formed in the column of ectoplasm.

5. The fully formed Silver Belle is now speaking to the people attending the séance.

6. Silver Belle blesses everyone, as her ectoplasmic form breaks up, retracting into the medium's body, Not all returns, the medium will be exhausted.

word וַיֵּרָא *va-yaar-aw/appeared* was used in the opening phrase of this verse: The LORD *appeared* to Abram and said.³⁴² I then discovered that the root word for וַיֵּרָא *va-yaar-aw/appeared* is רָאָה*raw-aw'*, which has the Strong number of 7200.

The New Strong's Complete Dictionary of Bible Words states:

> **7200. רָאָה râ'âh, raw-aw'; a primitive root; to see, ... *appear*, approve, behold, ... have experience, gaze, take heed, ... look ... meet, ... perceive, ... see (-r, ...), shew (self), ... spy, stare, ... view, *visions*.**
>
> **7202. רָאֶה rấ'eh, raw-eh'; from 7200; seeing, i.e. experiencing:— see.**
>
> **7203. רֹאֶה rô'eh, ro-eh' active participle of 7200; a *seer* (as often rendered); but also (abstract) *a vision*:— vision.**
>
> **7204. רֹאֵה rô'êh, ro-ay' for 7203; *prophet*; Roëh, an Israelite:— Haroeh [including the article].**

Once again we have a plate of spaghetti, Hebrew words so linguistically intertwined, that we need to look at all of them to understand the meaning of one. Now that we have examined the Hebrew words, we realize that Abraham did not just see the Lord in Genesis 12:7. Abraham did more than act as a prophet, seer, or having visions when he saw the Lord/Spirit near the oak tree in Shechem.

Since אֵלוֹן מוֹרֶה *Alon-Moreh* the *special oak tree at Moreh* is associated with the Hebrew word עָנָן *aw-nawn'/cloud*, we can conclude that Abraham did not see the Lord clairvoyantly. Instead we can conclude that Abraham saw the Lord through the *gift of materialization*, where the Lord appeared in a *pillar of cloud* or *ectoplasm*. Abraham even did what Peter suggested; Abraham built an altar that Awan explained was a *cabinet*. With all the pieces of the puzzle connected a clear picture emerges, and it is one of a *materialized Spirit* speaking with Abraham.

One further point must be made that deals with the story of three visitors who visit Abraham in Genesis chapter 18.

> **¹The LORD *appeared* to Abraham by the *oaks of Mamre*, as he sat at the entrance of his *tent* in the heat of the day.**

---

342 Kohlenberger, John R., III. *The NIV Interlinear Hebrew-English Old Testament. Vol. 1.* Grand Rapids, MI: Zondervan, 1979. p. 27.

> **²He *looked* up and saw three men standing near him. When he saw them, he ran from the tent entrance to meet them, and bowed down to the ground.**[343]

These two verses again have the same Hebrew word וַיַּרְא *va-yaar-aw /appeared,* which tells us that once again Abraham saw these visitors, though mediumistic gifts. The Lord and the three visitors were *materialized Spirits.* Abraham sat by אֵלוֹן מוֹרֶה *Alon-Moreh* the psychically charged oak tree of Mamre, at the door of his tent, which acted as the cabinet for this materialization.

---

[343] Genesis 18:1-2 [NRSV].

Materialization Séances

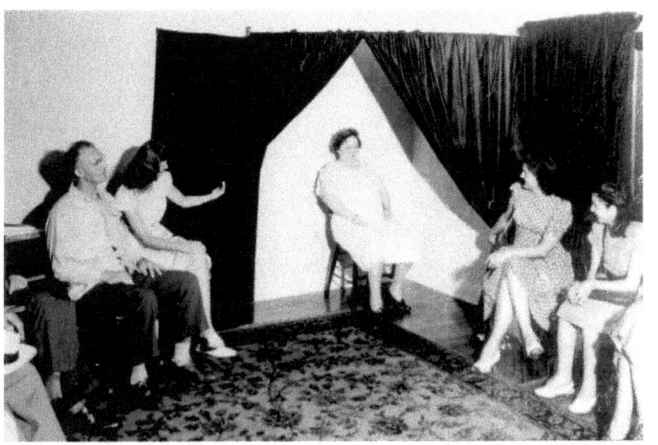

This picture shows a group of people sitting with a materialization medium, inside of a cabinet. A group such as this one sits to provide energy for the medium. A group like this can sit for years before any phenomena takes place.

This picture shows a medium, who is developed enough to produce ectoplasm, which is coming out of her mouth. When enough ectoplasm is produced a fully materialized form of a Spirit will manifest.

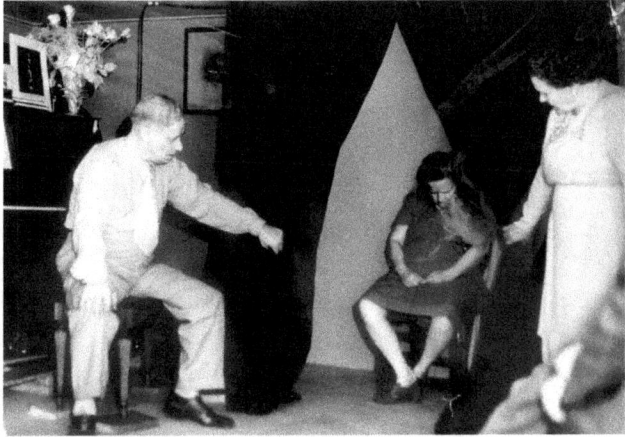

This picture shows a fully materialized spirit, made of ectoplasm, who would be able to speak to the ungifted sitters at the séance. Materializtion is one of the several types of physical mediumship. Materializtion is the most demanding and depleting to the medium's energy.

FIFTEEN

The Work of the Devil

Rev. Carl Hewitt was born endowed with the *Gifts of the Spirit*. Although his parents were devout Baptists, their church disavowed Saint Paul's decree, and they were not educated in the *Gifts of the Spirit*.[344] Hence, Carl's parents did not understand his mediumistic abilities. Living in the midst of the "Bible belt" would become a tremendous burden for a psychically gifted child, because Fundamentalist Christians consider mediumship to be "the work of the devil."

This is a conversation I had with Carl, about his own experiences.

I would like you explain how the concept of the devil has affected your life?

I grew up attending the Baptist Church. I clearly remember the preachers lecturing more about the devil than about God. Even as a child, I could not believe in a devil. According to the Bible, God created the universe, earth and everything on it. This would mean that God was all-powerful. If the devil were a fallen angel, how could he be a competitor to the omnipotent creator of the universe? A loving God would want to protect the people he created, as a parent protects his children. If the devil were such a threat to humanity, wouldn't God destroy him, as he destroyed the wicked people in the flood during Noah's lifetime? Somehow nothing about the devil made any sense to me, therefore, I never believed any of it.

Tell me about your childhood experiences.

I was the 11th child of the family. My family's house was large, at the very end of the peninsula, called Monogram, which protrudes into the Shallotte River. There were two small towns, along Route 17, equal distance from our house, in the southeast corner of North Carolina. Many people traveling from New York to Florida, in those days would travel Route 17, the coastal highway.

My father married twice. His first wife, and oldest son died on the same day, during the flu epidemic of 1918. Because the flu had been so contagious, no one came to help my father bury the dead. Therefore, my father had to

---

[344] 1 Corinthians 12:1-11.

build the coffins, and dig the graves for his wife and child, while being in the throes of despair and grief.

Since he was left alone with eight children to raise; it did not take long before my father married my mother.

🙂 I guess that is understandable.

🙂 They had three more children. I was his last child, and was conceived in July 1927. I had always had many questions about my childhood, but no one would ever answer them. These mysteries plagued me. In 1983, the day after I conducted my mother's funeral, my oldest half-sister, Madie, invited me out to lunch, which was very unusual for her. As we approached the restaurant, Madie insisted that I keep driving. I asked her, "Where do you want to go?"

She replied that she wanted to drive to the end of the peninsula, to the "old-Homestead" the house where she and all my other brothers and sisters had been born. This surprised me, because no one would ever answer my question: "Why I had not been born in the Homestead like my other 10 brothers and sisters?"

When we arrived at the location of our old Homestead, everything looked totally different. Instead of the isolated, natural setting that I remembered as a child, we were staring at a cluster of modern-luxury homes. It no longer had any resemblance to the area I remembered as a child.

The Homestead was situated on a bluff, overlooking the Shallotte and little Shallotte rivers. Holden Beach and the inlet were to the left. I vividly remember the abundant seafood: fish, oysters, crabs and clams that I caught in the Shallotte River, just a few steps away from our homestead. Across the Shallotte River, from the Homestead, there had been the "Old Native American burial grounds" Someone had taken a bulldozer, and desecrated these holy grounds. Today, luxury houses sit on those sacred grounds, which deeply saddened me.

As we looked at the modern view of our ancestral home, Madie confided in me. My parents had made all their children take an oath never to reveal any of this information to me, until they had both died. Since my father had died in 1964, my sister could no longer carry the burden of these secrets.

Then she revealed my long-secret personal history, which included events that happened before I was born and in my early childhood. "Strange occurrences" began happening at the Homestead, from the night of my conception. As my sister relayed this information to me, I clearly understood that she was describing advanced (physical) psychic phenomena. Since my sister had no knowledge of psychic science, there was no way that I could explain to her what she had witnessed fifty years before. So I listen carefully, and was grateful that she was finally sharing this vital information with me.

Two years before my conception, my father had purchased a phonograph. It was an early model that had to be cranked up and played wax cylinders. These phonographs had a giant horn on them that amplified the sound. In the evening, after long hours of working on the farm, the family would gather in the living room and listen to the phonograph. You must remember, that this was an expensive item in those days; and was the family's only source of entertainment.

From what my sister told me, the first strange event that happened occurred at noon-time, a few days after my conception. My family was gathering to eat their noon-day meal, which was the main meal of the day.

As Daddy walked through the living room, a voice spoke to him from the horn of the phonograph. This totally startled my father, because no one had cranked it up. Furthermore, he heard words, which were not recorded on any of the wax cylinders. Naturally, this frightened my father.

👤 I wonder what the voice said?

👤 I am not sure.

📖 After this discussion, I had an opportunity to ask Awan if he knew what had been said. Awan told me that he was the one who spoke through the phonograph, because the horn was very similar to a medium's trumpet. Awan had told Carl's father, that the child that was just conceived would be a boy, who would be a valuable instrument of the Spirit (medium), who would help bring a new truth to the world. Unfortunately, Awan admitted, he was unaware that Carl's father was so steeped in Baptist theology, and would consider such a psychic event, "the work of the Devil." The spirit people were unaware of the hardship that was being created for Carl, their future medium.

👤 My father was a staunch Baptist, who read the Bible daily. Whenever something happened that could not be explained, the Baptists claimed that it was "the work of the Devil." My father became so frightened by this voice that he took the phonograph and hid it up in a crawl space in the attic. He simply left it there. He never took it out, or used it again. He was thoroughly convinced the Devil used the phonograph to speak to him, that he "removed" it to protect his the family.

Still, my father was not at peace. Therefore, he simply packed up all the family's belongings, boarded up the house, and he forced my mother, and my brothers and sisters, to move out of the house. They moved to a dilapidated house about ten miles away.

When his family questioned the move, he would not respond all. He would not even say, "I don't know." It was his belief, as well as many other Baptists that even mentioning the Devil by name would be an invitation into his family's lives. My father thought he was running away from the Devil, and a change of location would protect his family.

Once the family had settled into their "new" home, the unusual phenomena again reoccurred. Immediately, lights appeared on the wall. When a member of my family touched the wall where the light was, the wall was warm despite the fact it was during the winter. My father would awaken in the morning he would find words written on the wall. These words were never in English, and were in "foreign tongues" to use an expression that my father used. No one was curious enough to search out a schoolteacher or college professor to get these messages translated into English. Since it was during the depression, no one could afford to take photographs of these words to get them translated.

📖 This reminded me of Matthew Manning, another medium I had read about.[345] He had the *gift of automatic writing*. When he was an adolescent, Spirit people would write messages to him on the walls.[346] This also reminds me of the famous "Writing on the Walls" story in the Bible. Spirit created a hand out of ectoplasm, and wrote a message to King Belshazzar.

> **Suddenly a human hand was seen writing on the plaster wall of the palace. The hand was just behind the lampstand, and the king could see it writing. He was so frightened that his face turned pale, his knees started shaking, and his legs became weak.**[347]

📖 Since the message was in Hebrew and not in Persian, Daniel was called upon to interpret it.

👤 Now my father became convinced that the devil was chasing him. He again packed up the family's belongings and moved. He provided no reason to his family—he just kept on moving. The phenomena did not stop. During the nine months of gestation, while my body was developing in my mother's womb, my family moved eight times. The last home my family moved into, was owned by a man named Hall—hence they called it the Hall House. It was there that I was born.

I came into this world, on March 3, 1928, at 12:05 a. m. My sister said that two white birds kept pecking on the glass, trying to get through the window. It is highly unusual that birds should be awake at midnight, attempting to gain entry into a house!

👤 What kinds of birds were they?

👤 Awan has told me that they were doves. Then after daybreak, another bird tried to get into the house. This time it was a big bird with many colored

---

[345] Manning, Matthew. *The Link*. NY: Holt, Rinehart and Winston, 1975.

[346] Manning, Matthew. *The Strangers*. Gerrards Cross, Buckinghamshire: C. Smythe, 1995.

[347] Daniel 5: 5-6 [CEV].

feathers on it. No one knew what type of bird it was, because they had never seen one like it.

My father wanted to move again, however, my mother had lost so much weight, and was so exhausted, that she put her foot down and refused to move. She said, "I am staying right here. I don't care what happens!"

🧑 What happened next?

🧑 I was not quite four months old, when the next strange event happened. It was a hazy, June afternoon, without a cloud in the sky, and not a bit of breeze. It was extremely hot and muggy summer's day. We were still living at the Hall House. Like all southern houses in those days, there was a large porch in front of the house, and it had a swing on it, as well as a few rocking chairs. As I understand it, it was the 16th or 17th of June. My mother was sitting in one of the rocking chairs, and I was nursing on her left breast, as she rocked. Madie was swinging in the swing sitting opposite of my mother. She was only ten years younger than Mama, and they were very close. Mama had become very thin, and quite silent. Apparently, she was having a difficult time understanding all the strange events that had occurred since she had conceived me. She was also exhausted after my father insisted that the family move practically once a month. So as she was rocking in her chair, thinking, she finally broke her silence and asked this question. "I wish to God, I knew why so many strange things have been happening to this family, ever since I conceived this child?"

At the split second that Mama had finished asking this question, there was a thunderous explosion, and a bolt of lightning struck a tree, almost directly in front of my mother. The lightning split that tree, right in the middle. It was a small tree, about 5 or 6 inches in diameter. Then the lightning continued through the tree and hit my mother in the middle of her forehead. Actually, it touched the frontal lobe, which is called in psychic terms, "the third eye,"—the screen on which we see our dreams.

My mother's body jolted violently, lunging forward, and I was shot from my mother's arm into the air, like a cannon ball. Fortunately, Madie reacted quickly and caught me, so I was unharmed. Mama lay unconscious on the floor of the porch.

Meanwhile, my father was doing some carpentry work, behind the house. My brothers and sisters were having fun on the swings my father had made by tying ropes onto this very large tree behind the house. They all came running to discover what had caused this loud explosion.

My father yelled to my brother, "Go and fetch the doctor." Then he picked up my mother off the porch floor, and took her into the house and laid her on the couch. He discovered that her pulse was extremely weak, so he took a towel, and was massaging her with cold water, attempting to get her heart to beat stronger.

All this time, Madie was holding me. I was content as could be. I had not even cried during all this.

When the doctor arrived, he examined Mama. The doctor said that my father had given my mother the proper treatment.

Madie then asked, "Doctor, do you want to examine the baby?"

The doctor responded, "There is no reason to examine the baby—the baby is dead."

Madie, said, "What is the matter with you, doctor? The baby is not dead. This is the baby."

The doctor responded, "Well, everyone must be confused in all the commotion. That is not the baby."

Madie got quite angry with the doctor. "This is the baby that Mama was rocking."

The doctor said to Madie, "Come over here." He pulled the sheet that was covering mama, to reveal her breasts. "Look at this burn on the nipple of the left breast. That can't be the baby, because the baby's mouth would also be burned."

"Well, doctor," Madie exclaimed, "This is the only baby around here. I cannot explain why Carl does not have a burn mark on his mouth."

🙂 That is quite a story, what do you make of it?

🙂 Awan has since told me that all this was done to try to show my parents, that I would become an instrument of the Spirit. However, they never could understand all the phenomena that happened around me.

My mother and father knew that at times, I spoke about topics that were far beyond the capability of a young child. They would wonder how I knew this information. I would use words that only adults would know. When I was three years old, a visitor came to the house. I heard a voice, which told me information about the visitor. I simply blurted out what I had just heard, not realizing that there might be consequences to the words I was uttering. Sometimes, when this happened, people would run out of the house as fast as they could. Others would tell my parents, "How does that youngin' know this information?" My father could not give an answer, and therefore would remain silent. He was afraid to mention to anyone that he thought the Devil was after him.

I was about four years old, (because I remember that all my other brothers and sisters were at school) when a man driving an old pickup truck came to our house, selling fish. My father talked with anyone who came by. Living at the extreme end of the peninsula, we did not get that many visitors.

This man had put some old washtubs filled with ice in the back of the truck. Daddy picked me up, and the man pulled back the canvas that covered the tubs. I saw many different types of fish, being chilled on the ice. Daddy had to pick me up, because I was too small to see that high.

As Daddy was putting me down, I heard a voice say to me, "Ask how many jars of white lighting are under those fish." I didn't give it one bit of thought, and I tugged on the stranger's pants leg. "Hey mister," I said, "How many jars of white lightning do you have under those fish?"

A shocked expression came over the stranger's face. Without saying a word, he jumped into his truck, and drove away in lightning speed. My father was angry with me, and ran around trying to catch me, but he was not successful.

Approximately three hours later, one of my father's friends came to our house. He said to my father, "Did a stranger come by here today, trying to sell you fish?"

Daddy said, "Yes he did."

"Did you hear that he is now in jail. Underneath the fish he had jars of white lightening."

My father looked at me, with amazement in his eyes. Now as I look back on those days, it surprised me that my father did not compare what was happening to me with what had happened in the Bible. Samuel told Saul that that his father's donkeys had returned home.[348] Samuel told Saul that he would meet three men going to Bethel. It happened just as Samuel said.[349] Spirit told Elijah that a widow would provide for him.[350] Spirit told Elisha that the price of flour would drastically drop the next day. This prophecy came true the next day.[351] Jesus told the Samaritan woman that she was living with a man who was not her husband.[352]

It did not occur to my father to expand his thinking beyond the dogmas that he was taught, to make these comparisons. He believed the church's teaching that all the miraculous events only happened in Biblical times. Today, I have come to know that this is incorrect. The psychic events that occurred in Biblical times can still happen to day, in the presence of a genuine medium.

One day when I was eight years old, I saw my sister, Annie dying. She lived only four miles from where we were staying. I was very upset, and began crying. I ran to my mama, and put my arms around her. "Annie's gonna die!" I said. My mama was outraged at what I just said. She immediately began spanking me, while she said in a rather sharp tone of voice, "How dare you say such a terrible thing!" This only made me cry some more.

About twenty minutes later, one of my half-brothers came running into the house. He was hysterical. He said, "Annie is dead!"

My mother turned her head slowly in my direction, with her mouth wide open. She had the most puzzled look on her face, trying to figure out how I could possibly have known of my half-sister's death.

Your family had no idea that you could tell the future because of your mediumistic abilities? If your parents were so devout, how did they reconcile that so many people in the Bible "talked to God," and *heard* his response? How could they ignore that Paul wanted Christians educated in the *Gifts of*

---

[348] 1 Samuel 9:20

[349] 1 Samuel 10:3,9.

[350] 1 Kings 17:9.

[351] 2 King 7:1,16.

[352] John 4: 16-18.

the Spirit, and describes how séances should be conducted (Chapters 12 and 14 of 1 Corinthians)?

🙎 My family followed the belief system created by the Baptists. The *Gifts of the Spirit* were ignored, and even shunned, despite direct statements to the contrary.[353] The Baptists certainly believed in the Devil. I think they believed in the Devil more than they believed in God. Anything that could not be explained was the "work of the Devil." When someone died, or got into an accident, it suddenly became the will of God. I didn't accept that idea either.

🙎 How did the Devil affect your father's life, which in turn affected your life as a child?

🙎 The concept of the devil greatly affected my father's life. Never once had any member of my family mentioned the word *Devil*. Yet, my sister admitted my father thought that the Devil was chasing him, because of the psychic phenomena that happened, even from the time I was conceived. Their belief system was if you mentioned the word Devil, it was like inviting the devil into your life. Therefore, he never said the word, and just told his family that they were moving, without providing an explanation. However, Daddy didn't think I had anything to do with this.

📖 I discovered the practice of not saying the word **Devil** went back to 1678.

Devil, 'Taboo word' c. 1678... Talk of the devil, and he'll either come or send.[354]

🙎 Awan told me that he has gone to visit other universes. and all the parts of our universe. I would think that it would cover a very big area. Awan has said that the entities living in the rest of the universe have no Devil, and do not know of such a being. Doesn't that prove that man created the Devil? The beings in rest of the universe know that God is within. Therefore, they all get along, and love each other. There is no hate, crime, or war. It is only on earth, that we think that God lives outside ourselves, somewhere in an elite piece of real estate in the sky.

🙎 Please tell us some other psychic experiences that you had as a child?

🙎 When I was four years old, I was sitting in a Baptist Church, next to my father. Daddy gave me three pennies, which was worth something in those days, to put in the basket. This man, someone who had walked into town with a Bible under his arm, got up and read a passage of the Bible. Then he began hammering away about the Devil. He proclaimed that it was a sin to go out fishing, or cook a meal on Sunday. It was then that I heard a Spirit voice that was as clear as that preacher's. I had heard Spirit voices all of my

---

[353] 1 Thessalonians 5:16-22.

[354] Opie, Iona and Tatem, Moira, editors. *A Dictionary of Superstitions.* Oxford: Oxford University Press, 1989. p. 118.

life. The voice said to me, "What that preacher is saying is not right." So I began tugging on my father's shirtsleeve, and said, "Daddy, what that man is saying is not right." I was only repeating what the voice had told me.

Wasn't that similar to what you presently do when you give a psychic reading?

Yes, I suppose it is.

Tell me what happened to you when you went to school.

I began school in a huge country school, which housed all the grades from 1st to 12th grade. We did not have kindergarten in those days. I began my schooling in first grade. My classroom happened to be near the auditorium.

Three Spirits came and got me, and I immediately entered a deep trance state.

Apparently, we walked over to the auditorium, and I walked onto the stage. I lectured all the high school students and teachers, who were sitting in the auditorium, waiting for the principal to address them. In those days, because there were no public address systems in the schools, students periodically assembled in the auditorium to hear announcements, etc.

So, I had taken the stage and lectured all these students, on my very first day of school! Can you picture a little boy lecturing a packed auditorium, without a P. A. system? Yet, everyone heard his voice very clearly? When I stepped off the stage, I came out of the trance, and faced all the teachers, rapidly firing questions at me. "Is your father a preacher?" "Have you lived on the shores of the Tigris and Euphrates Rivers?" "Where did you learn such words?" These questions were coming at me at lightning speed, and I had no idea what these teachers were talking about! Today, I understand that my Spirit, and consciousness, had left my body. Someone else had addressed those people. I had no knowledge of what had been said, and did not even realize that I had left my body. The Spirits that were working with me had not yet taught me about the *Gifts of the Spirit*. Therefore, I was in as much ignorance as everyone else in that auditorium. I became overwhelmed, and began to cry.

Two or three days later, a woman dressed in Wedgwood blue uniform came to my came to my classroom. She was the county nurse and told my teacher that I was to accompany her. She came over to me and took me by the hand, and led me out of the classroom.

She did not utter a word to me. She did not tell me where we were going, or why I was being taken from school. She simply led me out of the school into the back seat of a car. I stood up in the back seat of the car. I was kind of excited, because this was a treat for me. Remember, this was during the Great Depression. We were too poor to own a car. Yet, it bothered me, that I had to idea were I was going.

The nurse drove to Wilmington, North Carolina, which was thirty-five miles from my home. We went to the top floor of a six-story building, to a doctor's office. The doctor put me into this big chair that was opposite a window. I was amazed at the view from the window. I remember studying the Cape Fear River, and the forests beyond that. I had never been in such a high building, and everything looked so different. I had never been higher than the top of an apple tree.

I remember the doctor examined my eyes; he then put some drops in them, which blurred my vision. Then he examined my ears. Yet, neither the nurse nor the doctor explained to me why I was having this examination.

It was much later in life that I realized they were examining me to try to determine why I could hear voices and see people who were invisible to everyone else. All these devout Baptists were convinced that it was the Devil who was communicating to me. It is my belief that if they had found some physical evidence of why I had these psychic abilities, they would have locked me away, for the rest of my life, in an insane asylum, as was done to so many mediums in those days.

The doctor did not find anything wrong with my eyes or ears. So the nurse took me home to my family. I was thoroughly surprised, when the same nurse returned to my classroom, a few days later. It as early in the morning, and again she took me for a car ride. This time we traveled to Raleigh-Durham, which was a five-hour drive from Shallotte.

During this whole trip, the nurse never said a word to me. She did not even tell me where we were going. I remember that she stopped at a roadside stand, and bought me a hotdog and a Pepsi Cola on the way to Raleigh, and again on the return trip. Again this was a treat for me, because in those days a hotdog and a Pepsi would cost 10¢, which was a lot of money during the depression.

Our final destination was Duke University. Again a doctor, who has some kind of affiliation with the university, examined my eyes and ears. Apparently, this doctor did not find anything wrong, although he never told me the results of the examination, or even why I was being tested.

Again we return home. Everyone in the community shunned me. I was an outcast, because the whole community thought I was possessed by the Devil, and even talking to me would be inviting the devil into their lives. It was terrifying and frustrating when adults would never talk to me. This was difficult to endure.

In those days, many preachers walked around with a Bible under their arms. Spirit explained to me that many of them had never studied theology. Most were unemployed, and would make a buck or two preaching to a group of people. Even ex-convicts upon their release from prison, would buy a Bible, and traveled around. In those days people were so gullible that they thought anyone who carried a Bible, was a preacher.

My father would invite these traveling preachers to stay with us. He had a particular goal in mind. I had to sleep in the same bed with these preachers, because my father thought that by doing so, the Devil would leave me.

I would often crawl under the bed, because so many of these preachers, to be quite blunt, stank! One of these preachers must have eaten beans that day, and spent the entire night expelling flatulence! The whole room was filled with his foul-odor.

My father dragged me from one church to another, where they were going to pray over me to get the Devil out of me. I really didn't understand what was going on. I never believed there was a Devil.

🙂 You certainly had a difficult childhood.

🙂 I had one friend, whose name was **Dixie Hewitt**. I am not sure if she was related to me or not. We understood each other, because she too was a medium. She also heard voices, and saw visions that most people could not detect. These gifts became such a burden to her that one-day she walked into the woods with her daddy's shotgun, and she took her own life.

I had reached the breaking point when I was fourteen years old and decided that I had to leave home. As I was walking home that day, my mother was working in the garden. She looked up at me and instantly knew what I was about to tell her. She said, "Son, I know you feel you must go, and I will not try to stop you, but please keep in touch."

As I made my way into the world, I would stop in every building that had a steeple on it. I asked the priest, minister, or preacher if they could explain to me why I heard voices and saw visions. Most of these members of the clergy, treated me worse than a dog, and many threw me bodily out of their churches. It was many years later until I finally found someone who understood mediumship and could explain it to me.

It was so very liberating for me, when I found someone who was also a medium. I no longer felt that I was a "freak of nature." I then began to read every book I could find on the subject. Eventually, I learned how to manage my gifts, and began to carry out the instructions that the Spirit people wished me to do.

🙂 I thank you for sharing this information with me. Perhaps your experiences will allow people to see how the belief in the Devil has impeded mediumship, and shut off communication between the two dimensions of life.

🙂 Yes, Awan has explained to me that eventually, people will begin to accept this work. Children will be encouraged to develop their natural psychic abilities. For when abilities are nurtured and encouraged, instead of being suppressed, the *Gifts of the Spirit* blossom. Once communication between the two dimensions becomes an everyday occurrence, our world will once again have enlightened and brilliant civilizations. Then the people used the *Gifts of the Spirit* to build the pyramids, will return to our planet.

Carl's Parents
Alvie and Goldie Hewett

Carl Hewitt
At age 6

Carl Hewitt (left)
At age 11

At age 11

Carl Hewitt
At age 14

At age 19

At age 22

Carl Hewitt
At age 33

At age 56

My Second Encounter With An Angel

Carl delivering a Spirit message

Carl lecturing at Lilly Dale

Carl's Ordination
June 2, 1974

Carl and a statue of Chief Lone Eagle

A TV interview in Charleston, SC

Carl lecturing at Gifts of the Spirit Church, which he founded.

Carl in his reading room

This photograph was taken at Psychic Pathways, a one-day healing symposium, sponsored by Rev. Carl Hewitt, on October 29, 1977. Marian Butler, a medium, was speaking at the podium. Meanwhile, on the left, Dennis Fare, the president of the National Federation of Spiritual Healing in Shortacres England, was in a state of meditation preparing, himself to be the next speaker. The picture captured a circular bubble that is the spirit energy, which was about to entrance Mr. Dare. A clairvoyant would have seen this energy, but was not visible to those without this psychic gift.

Rev. Hewitt performed this wedding, at the insistence of the bride, because he did not "feel good" about the marriage. During the ceremony, Rev. Hewitt felt "a bit strange." When the photographer developed the pictures, he was furious, because he thought the pictures were ruined. Spirit had surrounded the bride to protect her. Unfortunately, these predictions were accurate, and the marriage was soon annulled. I have altered the faces of the bridal party to protect their identity.

SIXTEEN

 **5. Banishing *Fear*—the Great Satan!**

Carl dimmed the lights, and sat in the chair behind his desk. After he put on a pair of blindfolds, he said his prayer. After about two minutes, his body spasmed four times. It was almost a minute later that I heard Awan's voice.

Greetings, my scribe!

Greetings, Awan. It is so good to be talking with you again.

This next step in your learning might well be the most simple, however it may turn out to be the most difficult to achieve. You must conquer שָׂטָן Satan.

Satan? I don't understand, Awan. You have told me time and again there is no Satan.

That is correct my Scribe, there is no all-powerful evil entity named Satan.

So what are you talking about?

Tell me my scribe, do you remember the true meaning of שָׂטָן (*Satan*)?

Yes, Awan. In the Hebrew language the word שָׂטָן (*Satan*) means *adversary* or *enemy*.

Exactly right, my scribe. And what is the true adversary or enemy, to humankind?

I don't know, Awan.

Humankind has one true adversary, which paralyzes most people into stagnation. It causes people to fail to reach their full potential. It limits humankind's thoughts, dreams, and desires. When people cannot even think or dream of new and exciting adventures, it becomes impossible for people to live to their potential.

You are losing me, Awan. I do not understand what you are trying to say.

 **5. Banishing Fear – the Great Satan.**

The Great Satan, for humankind is a simple four-letter word: **FEAR!**

Fear? Fear is Satan?

Yes my scribe, Fear is Satan; the most devastating enemy to humankind that was ever created.

Awan, I still don't understand.

You should, my scribe. You certainly have not conquered your fears. Tell me, when I first asked you to become my scribe, and to write my teachings down into a book, did you do so eagerly?

No, Awan, I thought you were crazy at the time.

And why was that?

I thought that I could not become a writer.

And why was that?

I had never done much writing, and I was afraid that I couldn't write well enough.

Did you hear what you just said? *You were afraid you could not write well enough*. You are accurately describing your feelings at the time. It took much convincing on my part, and the part of my medium, for you to finally consent to give it a try. Is that not true?

Yes, Awan. I needed constant prodding.

Yes, you needed to conquer your fear of writing. Then, once you finished writing your first book, describe what happened to you.

I had a very difficult time finding a publisher.

And why was that?

I was afraid to send it to a publisher. I thought that it was not good enough, or that the publishers would not believe the information contained in the book.

It took further prodding from my medium and I to again bolster your confidence, and proceed to get the manuscript published. What would have happened if we did not keep after you to conquer this fear?

I guess the book might never be published.

Are you beginning to see how powerful fear is? It was your destiny to become my scribe. Before you were born, you, my medium and I all agreed that we would do this project. Your fears could have easily sabotaged the plan. It could have robbed you of achieving your destiny.

👤 But it didn't.

😇 Correct my scribe, it didn't. But how many other opportunities occurred in your life that you just let slip away, because your fears did not let you sail out into uncharted waters?

👤 I don't know, Awan.

😇 I do know my scribe, there were many. I am not trying to make you feel badly, but in your earlier life, you have to admit, you were a far different person than you are today.

👤 That is true, Awan.

😇 You were riddled with fears. In our dimension of life, we sometimes refer to the great Satan, **FEAR**, as a *virus*!

👤 A *virus*?

😇 Yes, my scribe. When a human being comes down with a virus, it robs them of all their energy. The person usually lingers in a bed for many days, trying to rebuild their strength. Fear is just like a virus. It causes men and women to linger in stagnant patterns. Religions have taught you to fear the unknown. That fear robs you of opportunity. You said yourself that you had never done much writing, so you were afraid you would not be good enough. That was your thought, as you described it.

👤 Yes, Awan.

😇 You did not say to me, "Awan, I have never done much writing, this will be a new and challenging endeavor. Let me give it a try." That would have been a statement from one who is not infected with the virus of **FEAR**. Fear robs humankind of opportunities for growth and enlightenment.

👤 I am beginning to understand, Awan.

😇 Again my scribe, in your youth you were riddled with fear. You were afraid of saying the wrong thing to people, you were afraid to talk to new people. You were afraid to try new experiences. Your most relaxed moments were when you were totally alone.

👤 That is true, Awan.

😇 You were one of the masses, my scribe, riddled with insecurities and doubts, which are just fancy words for fear. You, and the people who will read this book, need to realize that you must change your ways, by establishing new patterns. You must recognize that fear is simply a ghost of ideas that were placed into your mind by other people. You are the only one that can live your life my scribe.

👤 What do you mean by that, Awan?

😇 When it is time for you to lay aside your physical body, and come into my kingdom, can anyone else to do that for you?

🧑 No, Awan, of course not!

😇 Then why would you let the wishes and desires of others outweigh your own wishes and desires? Why would you believe someone else's idea that you can or cannot achieve a certain goal? Why would you accept someone else's fear into your own consciousness?

🧑 I am beginning to understand what you are saying.

😇 You must recognize that fear was placed into the minds of humankind to prevent people from seeking wisdom from my dimension. The longer you feed energy to your fears, the longer you will be fulfilling the wishes of those ancient theologians who have long since died and left your plane. Recognize your fears. Look them in the eye, speak to them, and tell them to dissipate. As it said in the Book of Books, you need to rebuke Satan and put him behind you. When you place your fears behind you, you are then free to explore the unknown, and to venture forth. You will make known the unknown. You need to accomplish this, my scribe.

🧑 I will try, Awan.

😇 Unfortunately, my scribe, trying is not good enough. That response indicates that you are not truly committing to this venture. This is a very black and white issue, as you term it. Either you have fears, or you don't. While having less fear is beneficial, it is not enough for you to take this first key, put it in the keyhole, and turn it. What will you find once you open the door of this vault of knowledge?

🧑 I don't know, Awan.

😇 Precisely, and if fear is involved with engaging the unknown, the key will not unlock that door, and you will never gain the knowledge you are seeking.

🧑 I am beginning to understand why you said that this would be difficult.

😇 Yes, my scribe, it is difficult, but you must remember that it is very far from impossible, just as far from impossible as it was for you to have your book published. In my dimension, all things are possible. You just have to focus in on your desires to make them happen in your life. However, fear is a stumbling block to this process.

🧑 OK, Awan.

😇 The energy is beginning to diminish, and I must soon withdraw from my medium. Let me just say to you, my scribe, that you are just about ready to receive an immensely important teaching. It will allow you to address your remaining fears, and you will learn how to banish them from your life. I have just one more lesson before I can teach it to you. So be patient, my scribe. You are doing well in acquiring this ancient wisdom. It has been a pleasure to speak with you today, my scribe, and I trust I have left you much to think about.

🙍 You certainly have, Awan.

😇 Contemplate well, my scribe. My peace be with you.

🙍 My peace be with you too, Awan.

Carl's body convulsed three times, then relaxed. About thirty seconds later, he began to cough. I quickly gave him a glass of water, but he was so weak that I had to hold it for him. A look of exhaustion was clearly evident on his face. Carl took a three-hour nap.

SEVENTEEN

Understanding Polarity

It was nearly a month before I had my next opportunity to speak with Awan. When the day finally arrived, Carl complained that he did not sleep well the night before. I thought that might make it difficult for him to go into trance. Carl began his preparations for going into trance by closing his eyes, and saying his prayer. I was surprised, however, because the transition seemed to be very smooth, and very rapid.

My profound greetings, to you my scribe!

Greetings, Awan.

The message that I wish to share with you today, is an important one, which will enhance your spiritual growth, if you choose to accept it. However, I must warn you that it will be a radical departure from your regular thinking patterns. There is no point in my insisting that you believe, and accept, what I am about to tell you. I do ask that you take the time to ponder it. If it seems at all plausible to you then I would advise you to begin incorporating it into your daily life. If you choose to reject this message, that is your choice, and that is acceptable, too. The choice is yours.

This sounds like it is going to be very important information.

Yes, it is, my scribe. People in your dimension have lived for countless centuries under the dark cloud of ignorance. For thousands of years your religious institutions have taught you many beliefs, which you hold as sacred truths, and no one was ever allowed to contradict them. Your thinking and behavior patterns were based on these beliefs. This message is an attempt to alter the way that you think. What I am referring to can be termed *polarity*.

Since you were a child, you were taught that certain deeds are good and others are bad. Have you ever contemplated who decided which deeds were good and which were bad? Have you ever realized that another society or culture could label an action good, while your own culture would label it bad. Which of these opposite views would be right and which one wrong? That, in itself, is a polarity.

Awan, I do not understand what you are trying to say.

Let's discuss some specific examples. The Judeo-Christian tradition views suicide as sinful—a deed going against God. Yet, during World War II, Japanese pilots performed suicide missions. The Japanese viewed these suicidal acts as heroic, instead of bad, sinful, or shameful. Your own society considers it a crime to commit murder, yet people consider it good to kill the murderer. When the execution takes place isn't the executioner murdering the murderer? Shouldn't the executioner then be killed since he murdered the murderer? Isn't it a crime, or sinful, too?

Another example is even more basic. Women, and even some of the men, in your culture today, starve themselves to maintain a certain "correct" body image. These people feel that if they put on a few more pounds they will no longer be attractive. Their whole self-worth is based on what number comes up on their scale. Who decided that 110 pounds is good, and 124 is bad, for a particular height? If you could enter a time machine and go back 100-150 years, you would discover the opposite. People, who had more weight on them, even to the point of being portly, were considered attractive and were sought after.

If I were to ask you to hold your arms out, flap them, and begin to fly, you would tell me that I was crazy. Everyone knows that humans can't fly, not without a machine. What I am explaining to you may appear to be as illogical as that. Simply put, all actions provide life-experience, and therefore should not be labeled as good or bad. It was the religious leaders who assigned the label good or bad on certain actions. As I suggested in the examples I just gave, sometimes what is good in one case is bad in another.

Well Awan, I understand what you are saying, but I don't see your point.

Let me become more specific, and return to our discussion of the soul. The soul is an *isness,* meaning it just is. The soul knows not right from wrong. One of the main functions of the soul is to record all the experiences a person has. To express this more precisely, all the emotions (thought energy) of your experiences are absorbed into your soul, which is a ball of energy.

To put it the easiest way I can: the soul is just like electricity, your energy source. Electricity is also an isness. You cannot claim that electric current is good or bad. Some people in your dimension have good applications for electricity. They heat their homes, and cook their food with this energy source. Others have bad applications, like using electricity in a chair to kill people. Yet, the energy itself is not concerned about how it will be used. It just exists, and flows though the copper wires as it is supposed to. The electricity does not think, "Oh no, I will not go through this wire to power up that electric chair—murder is forbidden in the Ten Commandments. It is a grave sin. I will not flow." That does not happen. The electricity just flows through the wires and will boil water as easily as it will "fry a person." That is the expression that some people use?

Yes, Awan. Some people use that expression.

🕊 The same principle applies to the soul, it is energy, like electricity. The soul just exists, in a neutral state. It is neither: bad or good, positive or negative, right or wrong.

Your soul does not get trapped in your polar thinking of good and bad. You spend so much energy in good vs. evil, on vs. off, fat vs. thin, rich vs. poor, black vs. white. You are constantly making judgments and categorizing events, people, and things into one group, of which you approve, or another that you disapprove. However, your soul does not do this. It allows. It lets you be. It lets you experience, either end of the spectrum. It is your choice to do something good, or do something bad. Either way it is an experience. That is what the soul seeks. It wants to gather as much knowledge, and as many experiences, as it can, regardless of how it fits into someone's polar view.

I have heard many people on your planet get so very upset with people in their lives, whether it is their children, friends, parents or spouses. They judge their actions, calling them good or bad. Of course if the actions are good, everything is fine. However, if the person considers the actions as bad, then there is a problem. The judgment is: you are ruining your life, you are making a mistake, you are committing a sin, or you are abandoning your religion. The real truth is that the action is neither bad nor good, because the soul gains experience, from every action.

The experience provides knowledge. After a baby burns his or her finger on a hot stove, he or she owns the experience of "hot." It is no longer a theory, or conjecture. The child has learned that hot can be painful, and most likely will decide not to put his or her finger on the hot stove again. Although this is a simple example, all of life's experiences work in the same manner. We acquire experiences for the knowledge they bring to us. However, if we do not learn the lesson of that experience, we tend to repeat the same experience over and over again until we finally assimilate the knowledge.

I have taught you that God created the universe through the power of thought. God, which is not a person, but is actually energy, replicated itself. Your soul residing in your body is a small piece of that divine energy. Like all energy, your soul contains both the positive and negative polarities. Let me restate that so you understand. God contains evil as well as good. All energy does. God is not 100% good, nor 100% evil. God is a mixture of polarities, and so is your soul.

Your religions have convinced people they can commit whatever sin, or crime they please. Forgiveness is easily obtainable by simply walking into a Church, sitting down in a little cubicle, and asking the priest for God's forgiveness. All will be forgiven by saying a certain number of prayers, prescribed by the priest. This is **NOT** the case. It simply doesn't work that way. There is no one on your planet, who has the power to do that. Every person has to forgive his or her own self, for any wrongs that he or she committed, after they have sought forgivness from the person they have wronged.

When a person finds the source that is within, that person will discover that the soul within does not judge. It does not acknowledge the polarity that currently exists on your plane of existence. The soul within your body being an isness, it is neutral, without polarity. Therefore, the soul is not able to judge you, because that judgment would have to be either positive or negative. Your soul allows you to do everything that you want to do because you do it for the experience of it. Soul is both positive and negative since it is energy.

🧑 I don't know, Awan, I understand what you are saying; yet I am confused.

😇 I know that this is a difficult concept for you to understand, partly because you lack the intellectual capacity to understand it. Please do not be insulted by that statement, but reason this out. Let's say a certain concept requires 15 ounces of brain power to understand. If your brain worked at 33% it would be equivalent to 5 ounces. How could you possibly understand a 15 ounce idea, with a brain capacity of 5 ounces? It is impossible.

In my dimension, we communicate through telepathy. We exchange thoughts not words; therefore, we are not limited by language. I can think a picture, or an idea, and another angel can easily understand my thoughtform, as we term it. When people in my plane of existence communicate with people on your planet, we are forced to use language. Simply put, sometimes we lack the words to describe certain thoughts. Other times you could not understand the concepts because your brains are so limited.

🧑 Awan, this is so difficult to accept, because I have been taught about being good, and praying to have my sins forgiven for all of my life. How do you expect all the Jews and Christians to accept this teaching about the soul?

😇 If there were only one truth, why are there 12,000 religions or belief systems? For example, if the Southern Baptists thoelogy were true, does that mean the other 11,999 beliefs systems are false? Wouldn't the whole entire world want to be Southern Baptists? Why aren't you a Christian?

🧑 I am not a Christian because I believe that Jesus was a great teacher, and medium. I do not believe he was a God or savior of the world. Awan, do you accept Jesus as your own personal savior?

😇 My answer would depend on your definition the word *savior*. What is Jesus supposed to save me from? Fundamentalist Christians believe that unless you accept Jesus as your personal savior, you will not get into heaven.

How would it be possible for Moses to enter heaven 1482 years[355] before Jesus came to unlock the gates of heaven? You are Jewish, my scribe. Moses, Elijah and Jesus were your distant cousins. Your Book of Books explains that Moses died,[356] and Elijah ascended into my dimension (on a fiery chariot).[357] Let's discuss Moses, since he experienced a "normal" death, as his everlasting

---

[355] Sprague, E. W. Rev. *All the Spiritualism of the Christian Bible and the Scripture Directly Opposing It.* Detroit, MI: (self published), 1992. p. 249.

[356] Deuteronomy 34:5-6.

[357] 2 Kings 2:11-12.

soul permanently left his body and entered my kingdom. Where did he go for 1482 years before his conversation with Jesus, on the Mount of Transfiguration?[358] He was not in purgatory, or suspended animation, as Catholics would believe. Those imaginary places were created to make Catholics fear death. Moses was living, breathing, and having his being in my dimension of life. Christians might have a difficult time accepting that a Jewish soul can enter heaven. However, I assure you, my scribe, Moses' spirit body (soul) lives with me in heaven, although I do not choose to use that term.

The only people Jesus saved were the ones who understood his teachings. For Jesus said in your Book of Books, *"even if you do not believe in me as man, believe in the works that I do."*[359] You are aware there are mediums throughout your world that demonstrate the *Gifts of the Spirit*. It is their *works* that you could compare with Jesus; it is all the same type of work. Jesus never taught a religion, he simply taught the people how they could communicate with other dimensions by looking within themselves and they would find the Kingdom of God.

Returning to answer your original question—Jesus of Nazareth may have saved me because he has served as an example of how to live my life. Let me make a bold statement here: it is the teachings of *Gifts of the Spirit* that will save a person from ignorance, fear and superstition. Therefore, knowledge of *Gifts of the Spirit* becomes the savior of people. For when people understand and utilize these gifts, then they will be doing the *works* Jesus performed. For Jesus stated very clearly:

> **Verily, verily, I say unto you, he that believeth on me, the *works* that I do, shall he do also, and greater works than these shall he do.**[360]

To countless generations his life was an example of how a person who had 100% brain capacity could demonstrate all the *Gifts of the Spirit*. He showed love and compassion for all human beings. He did not judge people (he only told the adulteress not to sin anymore,[361] and he did not chastise the Samaritan woman for living in sin.)[362] He lived his life according to the highest philosophies, and would not compromise those philosophies for any reason. Therefore, Jesus served as a powerful example that all people can live their lives according to his standard of Christhood; this can save humanity from living totally in ignorant chaos, and save eons of time in evolution.

Do not be confused, my scribe, by my last statement. *Christ* is an ancient title, coming from the Greek word *Christos*. It's meaning is identical to the

---

[358] Luke 9:28-33.
[359] John 14:11.
[360] John 14:12 [KJV].
[361] John 8:11.
[362] John 4:17-18.

Hebrew word מָשִׁיחַ (*Messiah*) and means *"anointed one."*[363] Do not become bogged down with outdated theology just because I use the word **Christ**. When I say **Christ**, I am referring to a man/God or woman/God realized. To say it the simplest way I can, to become a Christ, you must come to the realization that your Soul is God. Then you must begin communication with that God. Once that link is established, you can reopen your brain to 100% capacity, and then you become a Christ.

Many Christians believe that Jesus died for the sins of the world. With his death, he abolished everyone's sins. Christians go out and commit every type of sin imaginable from Monday through Saturday. Then they flock to their churches on Sunday morning, and pray to Jesus to forgive them, and all their sins are washed away. They then wake up bright and early on Monday morning, and begin sinning all over again. It doesn't matter how sinful they live their lives, as long as they ask Jesus to forgive them before they die, they will be saved from the fires of hell, and reap the sweet rewards of heaven.

Do I personally feel that Jesus will erase all my sins? No, I do not. I do not believe that he has the power to do that. I have become the "master of my own ship;" therefore, I must create my own destiny. I cannot look for someone outside of myself to do that for me. However, knowing that the greatest perfection is possible allows me to also attempt to walk in Jesus' path, and obtain perfection. In that way, Jesus has saved me; however, it is totally different concept than most Christians believe.

If all the people throughout your world followed the teachings of Jesus, and understood and knew that God is within, then no one on your planet would do any harm, to another human being. They would know they would be harming a fellow God. This is the reason Jesus taught his students (disciples) to love thy neighbor as thyself,[364] and love the Lord God of your being with all your heart, soul, and mind.[365]

I am beginning to sense a disturbance in the energy, and I must leave this body. It has been a pleasure to talk with you again, my scribe. Ponder these words carefully; allow your soul, which will recognize my teachings as true, to influence your mind. It may take some time for this to happen. Be patient with yourself, my scribe. My peace be with you.

Thank you Awan, I will try to follow your advice. My peace be with you too.

It surprised me that Carl came out of trance very easily this time. After drinking some water, he seemed to recapture his energy. He did not even need to take a nap.

---

[363] McBrien, Richard P., ed. *The HarperCollins Encyclpedia of Catholicism*. NY: HarperCollins, 1995. p. 308-309.

[364] Matthew 22:39.

[365] Matthew 22:37.

EIGHTEEN

 6. Invoking the God Within

The process of Carl entering the trance state was becoming like a ritual. He closed his eyes, said his prayer, and his breathing became deep and rhythmic. Within two and a half minutes, Awan was speaking to me.

😇 My profound greetings to you, my scribe!

🧑 Greetings, Awan.

😇 My scribe, I can see in your auric field, that you are disturbed. Apparently you have reached a stumbling block in transforming the information that we have been discussing into a knowingness. How may I assist you, my brother, to dissolve this impasse?

🧑 Awan, some of what you have taught me is so difficult to accept, because throughout my life, I have been told to be good, and to pray for forgiveness for all my sins. How do you expect Jews and Christians to accept this teaching about the soul, where good and bad do not matter?

😇 My scribe, it is very simple. Once you awaken the Lord God that lives within you, and begin to communicate with your soul, the powerhouse of the universe, you come into a knowingness. Your communication will expand your light, which will touch the river of thought, and you will simply know within you what is true.

Now my scribe, would you be interested in learning how to communicate with your God?

🧑 Yes, Awan, I would.

😇 It is really a very ancient teaching. Ancient people not only understood that God was within, they prayed to their soul—their Lord God that lived within their bodies. There is no benefit in sending prayers out to a God in the sky, as religions have taught you to do, because no one is there. You must remember, my scribe, that God is within.

Unfortunately, there came a time that tyrants succeeded in placing fear in the minds of humankind, which shut down the brain. These tyrants taught the people that God lived in heaven, not within. Centuries later, Jesus came to this planet to teach humankind the true location of God. Jesus told you, *"Behold, the kingdom of God is within you."*[366] But, theologians have ignored that great teaching because they desire to keep their control over the people.

Awan, some Bibles translate that verse differently. One reads: *Jesus said, "The kingdom of God is in the midst of you."*[367] Another translation is: *Jesus said, "For, you must know, the kingdom of God is among you."*[368] Do you think that the theologians retranslated this verse in an attempt to obscure the truth?

That is correct, my scribe. Today, because of the false teaching of religions, most people, all over your planet, are looking for God outside of themselves. Whenever people on your planet wish to communicate to God, they send their thoughts in the wrong direction. They send their prayers out to some imaginary being, God sitting on a magnificent golden throne, in some heaven found in the sky or outer space. The people, who believed this myth, have been misled. This is the reason that most people have been disconnected from God. Everywhere on your planet, at this very moment that I am speaking to you, there is chaos your world. Young people do not believe anything anymore, because they feel in that their parents, and ancestors have lied and mislead them. This is why they think nothing of killing each other, or their own parents.

Jesus said:

> **"Believest thou not that I am in the Father, and the Father in me? The words that I speak unto you, I speak not of myself: but the Father that dwelleth in me, he doth the works.**[369]

Jesus knew how to communicate with his great God, the soul that was within him, that he called **Father**. He did not send his prayers and thoughts outward to a God in an imaginary heaven. He directed his prayers inward. That all-powerful God helped him with his life's work. In your present time, all humans have within them an equivalent amount of God that Jesus had. However, your God, your soul is invisible to you because most of you do not have clairvoyant vision.

In a test laboratory, a researcher will accidentally mix several ingredients together and form a new *polymer*. It will be clear as glass. When a person looks through the clear substance, towards another human being, he or she will see the auric field of the other person. Your scientists will claim they accidentally discovered this substance. I want you to know, my scribe, this will be no accident. Spirit people, in this dimension, have been working on this formula for quite some time. As I have stated before, your scientists will

---

[366] Luke 17:21 [KJV].

[367] Luke 17:21 [RSV].

[368] Luke 17:21 [JER].

[369] John 14:10 [KJV].

not believe anything they cannot see and test. This new substance will provide the scientist indisputable proof that the aura, the God-light of the soul, surrounds every human being.

👤 This is fascinating. Why aren't more people aware of this information?

😇 That has a lot to do with your scientists. If scientists do not know the answer, they will create one, whether it is true or not. They rarely admit that they do not have an answer. Think about this, your so-called advanced scientists are just now discovering that the brains of males and females are not identical. They are discovering there are different amounts of specific chemicals present in a male brain vs. a female brain. They are also discovering that the size of different portions of the brain is different depending on the gender of the person. What do you think causes all that?

👤 Isn't it resulting from genetics, the information carried on the genes?

😇 That is partly true, but the soul is greatly involved too. The soul is the *modus operandi* of the entire body, meaning it controls the body. All the knowledge, and all our experiences during our entire lifetimes are recorded in the soul. Most of the child's traits have a lot to do with the previous life. When the soul chooses to reincarnate, it enters the baby's body in the womb to come back into the physical world. It is the soul that commands how the fetus should develop. Everything about your body from the color your eyes, hair, personality, skin tones, muscles, bones, and everything is recorded in the soul.

Let me discuss your life for a moment. You once lived a life where you were always hungry, because of a great lack of food. Your body was wracked with diseases, because of malnutrition. You did not live long, and eventually, died of starvation. Since the soul controls the body and its thought process, it holds in memory what happened to you in other lifetimes. If the body cannot get food, the soul remembers that experience of starvation. When you reincarnated, in this present life, you have a tendency to eat far more than you need at one time. You feel there is no tomorrow, so you eat everything today. This is what you have been doing.

👤 Is that why I was allergic to all solid food when I was born? I couldn't eat much; I carried it over from another life?

😇 That is correct. You did not have those foods in the other life. It was not recorded in your soul. When you tried the food, it would not be digested in the proper way, therefore, your body would reject it. Your body was not programmed for such foods. It was a slow process; for your soul had to be reprogrammed again.

👤 That's astounding! Too bad people do not understand all of this information.

😇 For instance, let's say in one of your lifetimes, you were brought up on goat's milk. You drank goat's milk your entire life. You died of old age. When you decide to reincarnate into another body, you would find yourself drawn to goats, regardless to where you travel. You would have the desire to try goat's milk. When you tried it, you would find yourself liking it a great deal. The memory of that experience is recorded in the soul.

🙂 Awan, why did you decide to discuss goat's milk?

😇 Because this is one the experiences that you had in your present life.

🙂 Yes. That is very true.

😇 You had lived many lifetimes, when your world was enduring tremendous famines and droughts. There were many lifetimes that you were hungry, day in and day out.

🙂 So what should I do?

😇 You must learn to communicate directly to your God-within, your soul. You need to reprogram your soul, so you eat the proper amount of food?

🙂 And how do I do that?

😇 You simply turn within yourself, go within your *closet of prayer*, and deprogram your soul then reprogram it. Jesus taught about the closet of prayer:

> **"But thou, when thou prayest, enter into thy closet, and when thou hast shut thy door, pray to thy Father which is in secret; and thy Father which seeth in secret shall reward thee openly.**[370]

If Jesus were teaching this lesson, in your present day, he wouldn't use the word *closet*. Instead, he would have used the term *auric field*, which is the light around your body that emanates from your soul. Your soul is a great, all-powerful God, and it lives within your own body, behind the breastbone, in the middle of your chest. It is your soul that leaves the physical body at death, carrying all the knowledge that you have obtained during your life. Reason it out, my scribe, when the physical body dies, both the heart and brain dies along with it. You would arrive in my dimension, utterly ignorant, without knowing a single fact, if your memory were stored in the brain. Not only are all your memories stored in your soul, just as information stored on the hard drive of your computer, but there is a blueprint of the appearance of your physical body. So if you should have the rare opportunity, to use a medium to communicate back to your loved ones still living on earth, you can project that image to the medium, who describes it to your loved ones, and they will recognize you.

Unfortunately, the powerful God within remains dormant and asleep. It is not dead, but is waiting for you to find it, and awaken its great power. You must turn your consciousness or absolute focus inward toward your soul and

---

[370] Matthew 6:6 [KJV].

aura. Do not think of any religious images; block out all outside dogma. Then you can wake up this sleeping God, when you address it properly.

When it comes to praying to God, do not look outside of yourself at some vision that was created by others. You need to focus on the soul within yourself, and the light it produces. Go within yourself, focus on the middle of your chest, under your breastbone, where the soul resides, and address your soul, that is your God in these words: **Lord God of my being.** Your soul is *the God of your being*. It is an isness that is eternal *energy*, and will live forever. Your soul produces the aura, the light that surround the physical. The aura is *the Lord of your being.* It cannot be destroyed, or torn from your physical body, its temple. The phrase *Lord God of my being*, addresses the soul, and the aura, light the soul produces. You need to address the light, in order to reach its source—the soul.

Your ancestors, in Biblical times understood all these terms. Study your Book of Books to see what the widow told Elijah, and what the prophet Micaiah had to say. Then you will discover these people understood these terms.

📖 The next day I found the verses Awan had mentioned.

> **"As *the Lord, your God*, lives," she answered, "I have nothing baked; there is only a handful of flour in my jar and a little oil in my jug. Just now I was collecting a couple of sticks to go in and prepare something for myself and my son; when we have eaten it, we shall die."**[371]

📖 Because the woman had second sight or clairvoyance, she could see the light around Elijah's body. She understood this light was the **Lord God** of Elijah's being. To say it another way, the light was radiating from Elijah's soul, within his chest. She understood that the soul is divine energy. The soul is God. Because the ancient people knew that God had given life, as was stated in Genesis; therefore, she understood that she was seeing Elijah's God. If she did not have this understanding, then she would have said **"As the Lord, OUR God, lives."**

> **And Micaiah said, As the Lord liveth, even what *my* God saith that will I speak.**[372]

📖 Again why didn't Micaiah said, **As the Lord liveth, even what OUR God saith.** Wasn't this the God of all the people? This demonstrates that Micaiah understood that God was within himself, just as God is within every human.

---

[371] 1 Kings 17:12 [NAB].
[372] 2 Chronicles 18:13 [KJV].

(🕊️) When you address the **Lord God of your being,** you are communicating with both your soul, and its auric field. Remember how important the aura is in accessing the *river of thought*, and communicating with entities of my dimension. For when entities such as myself see the expanded light, we are drawn to it. It is then, that we will communicate with you.

👤 That makes a lot of sense, Awan.

(🕊️) 🔑 6. Invoking the God Within.

Find yourself a quiet relaxing place where you can be at peace. Sit down in a darkened room, and close your eyes. It is even better if you put blindfolds on, to prevent any light from penetrating your eyelids. Put yourself in the state of meditation, and focus on yourself. Put your focus, or your complete concentration on the soul, lying under the breastbone, in the center of the chest. Now expand your focus to the aura, the light produced by the soul. Next, visualize your aura, as an egg shaped bubble of light that surrounds your body. Picture it as a bubble of violet-blue light surrounding your body. Do not allow your mind to go wander, or visualize anything but your auric field. Focus in on what you are doing because this links you up with your *God within*. When you can clearly see yourself sitting in a bubble of violet-blue light in your mind's eye, then say these words with forcefulness, passion, and energy:

> **Lord God of my being**
> **Unto the father/mother within** (use the appropriate gender)
> **Come forward this moment this hour...**

You must remember that thoughts or words are things; they have their own energy. The words that you are using are energizing or empowering the source. When you say *"Lord God of my being unto the father within come forward this moment this hour,"* the auric light expands around your body. Your auric field is now larger than it was before. Your God is waking up, because your soul has heard your words and is following your command. You are the captain of your ship (your body) and the soul will follow your instructions that you are ready to give it.

> **Bring forth the Christ that is within me.**

Remember the word *Christ* is an ancient word. It means God/man realized or God/woman realized. Let me explain it another way. When you realize that God is your soul, living in the middle of your chest, you can begin communicating with it and it will awaken. Then you can command your soul to reopen your brain to 100% capacity. When this finally happens, you become a Christ.

Now the next instructions would be for what you need in your life. In your case you should say:

> Erase my desire for foods that are harmful to my body.
> Replace it with the desire for healthful foods for my body.
> Allow me to desire only the amount of food that my body requires.
> So Be It!

When the soul hears the words "*So Be It!*" it records these words, and will now remember this instruction forever. It is like pressing the **Return** or **Enter button** on your computer. You have just reprogrammed your soul. You must work on this, since it will take quite some time to reverse the process. Remember, your soul has been dormant for many years. Everyone's soul on your planet has been asleep since the beginnings of religions. Religious leaders taught that God is outside of you; out on a piece of real estate in the sky. This is not at all true. So you must work at the process daily, to awaken the soul, and have it come forward. It would be likened to one who is in a very deep sleep. You would have to call the person over and over again, to wake the person up. Eventually, you will find the desire for the proper foods would come through, and you would not find yourself eating foods, especially sweets, which are not good for you.

Thank you Awan I will begin using this immediately.

Good! Now, let me make one thing very clear to you, which is extremely important! When you wish to erase a memory, or desire, from the soul you need to replace it with something else, something that you wish to empower. You can modify the affirmation I just gave you to reprogram your soul any way that you wish. Remember the soul is like the software of a computer. When you are born into this world, your soul is already programmed. It has all the events and emotions of your past lives. As you live your present life, your soul adds more information to the program.

You use a computer don't you?

 Yes.

Please explain how they work.

The information that you type into the computer is changed into a number. For instance if you type the letter A, the computer converts the A into the number 65 in binary code. Now the number 65 is a group of eight 0's and 1's. Next the computer takes eight memory chambers, and places one of the 0's and 1's in each chamber. Those individual memory chambers are called *bits*.

Yes. The soul works similar to your computer. It has bits or memory chambers too, only they are not physical, they are within the energy of the soul. When you load a new program in the computer, the computer will react differently. It will do different tasks. By using this affirmation, you are putting a new program in the soul, and changing the information already recorded in the soul. After time the soul will follow the new instructions. You can change your entire outlook on life, develop self-esteem, and erase the bad memories that you have during this lifetime, as long as you replace it with something, such as love for all humankind.

🙂 This is very powerful information.

😇 Indeed it is.

🙂 Awan, you said before that when we are born into this world, our soul carries the memory of our past lives. Is our karma (where you have to pay for the bad things that you did in previous lifetime) stored there too?

😇 You pay your karmic debts through remorse. Then what you do is ask the Lord God of your being to remove that experience from your soul, which is the recording data-bank as you would term it. Therefore, when it is erased, it will not bother you anymore. Have you ever had an experience where you did something and you couldn't get beyond it, it was always hounding, or haunting you?

🙂 Yes.

😇 You must go to the source of it. It would be like a tape or CD that keeps playing the same song over and over and over again. You would go into your own closet of prayer, which you have to do within your own consciousness. The closet of prayers is your own cocoon of light, your auric field, that is around your body. So you go into that state of meditation, turning within, and then ask that the ***Lord God of your being, to remove that experience from your soul. Remove it this moment this day, and forever more. And replace it with love for humanity.*** Keep doing this. One day you will notice that it will no longer affect you at all. It is erased. As long as you can recall it and feel it, and experience it, you still have it. Continue to do this, and the day will come that it doesn't bother you anymore. After a while you will say, I haven't thought about that in a long time. That means it is being erased. Continue to do say the affirmation, and eventually it will be erased from your life.

🙂 Is there an affirmation to heal disease?

😇 This is a general prayer to heal your body. Please feel free to adjust it when you are suffering from a specific condition or ailment.

> **Lord God of my being**
> **Unto the father/mother within**
> **Come forward this moment this hour.**
> **Bring forth the Christ that is within me.**
> **Release the enzymes from my brain**
> **Into my bloodstream**
> **That my body, your Temple be Healed.**
> **So Be It!**

When you say: *"release the enzymes from my brain into my bloodstream that my body your temple be healed"* the soul will immediately go into action. It sends a message, which activates the brain, and releases the enzymes into the bloodstream. This is how the body carries out its natural healing. The healing enzymes race through the bloodstream and find the organ of the body that is not functioning normally. The enzymes gather around that organ to repair it. However, it won't work this way, unless you understand the basics, and put your absolute focus on your soul as you say the affirmation. This information becomes the key, to unlock the door that separates you from the powerhouse of the universe, the God within you.

At this time, the energy is dwindling; I will soon need to leave this body. But before I do, realize that what I have taught you today, is the same information that Jesus taught his disciples in the upper room. It was this very subject, that upset the priesthood so very much. For if you understand where God is, then you no longer need the priests and their man-made ideology, which is only a guise for a massive business; one that keeps them living in a lavish lifestyle. It was for this reason, those priests in those days plotted to destroy Jesus to silence this very teaching.

I will see to it that a Christian teaching will cross your path that will prove to you that many Christians still do not want people to understand the truth about the eternal soul that is your God.

I must vacate this body now. Study this lesson carefully. Use it, and it will change your life! My most profound peace be with you.

Peace be with you too, Awan. Thank you so much for this powerful lesson.

About five seconds later, Carl's body went into spasms. He moaned softly, and complained that his mouth is very dry. I picked up the glass of water, and assisted him in drinking it. This most powerful session was over. Carl was totally exhausted, took a nap, which lasted for three hours.

* * * *

About a year later, as I was on a trip to Nevada, when a magazine rack of pamphlets suddenly caught my eye. I decided to take one. The publication was entitled: *The Sign of the Times,* Vol. 121 No. 11. It contained an article by Russell Holt entitled: *By the Book.* It was a question and answer column, which, in this issue, discussed reincarnation. The author did not think reincarnation was a valid philosophy. I was not surprised at that. However, what utterly shocked me was the author did **not** believe in an immortal soul:

> **"The Bible is clear that human beings do not possess an immortal soul."**[373]

---

[373] "By the Book." Holt, Russell. *The Sign of the Times,* Vol. 121. No. 11. p. 21.

I was under the impression that all Christians believed in an after-life in heaven. However, Mr. Holt uses three Bible verses to back up his theory.

> **And the LORD God formed man *of* the dust of the ground, and breathed into his nostrils the breath of life; and man became a living soul.**[374]   **Genesis 2:7**

Genesis 2:7 states that God created the souls. This concept is in total agreement with Awan's explnation, when he discussed how souls were created during the "Big Bang" in the second chapter of this book. However, the imagery is different.

> **Behold, all souls are mine; as the soul of the father, so also the soul of the son is mine: the soul that sinneth, it shall die.**[375]   **Ezekiel 18:4**

Ezekiel 18:4 states that souls belong to God, while Awan states that the soul is part of God energy. Souls cannot die; however, souls can become so lost from their source thus becoming "dead in Spirit, "(which will be discussed in later in this book).

> **Who only hath immortality, dwelling in the light which no man can approach unto; whom no man hath seen, nor can see: to whom *be* honour and power everlasting. Amen.**[376]   **1 Timothy 6:16**

If 1 Timothy 6:16 were correct and Jesus alone was immortal. How was it possible for Moses, who had died 1482 years, and Elijah who had died 928 years before, to talk with Jesus on the Mount of Transfiguration?[377]

It appears that Mr. Holt does not understand 1 Corinthians 15: 40, 44-49, when Paul discusses that after the physical body dies the spiritual body, or soul goes on to live in the Spirit World. Most people call that life the after-life. The soul lives on, irrespective of your religious philosophy. However, it is the knowledge that you gather in this life that will determine the quality of your after-life; whether you will sleep for eternity, as those who are dead in Spirit, or continue your path of evolution.

---

[374] Genesis 2:7 [KJV].

[375] Ezekiel 18:4 [KJV].

[376] 1 Timothy 6:16 [KJV].

[377] Luke 9:28-33.

NINETEEN

 7. You Are God

It was a beautiful summer day, that Carl suggested that we hold this trance session in the woods behind his house. After gathering his blindfolds, water bottle, a towel and sleeping blanket, we went out into the woods and found a big oak tree. Carl leaned the sleeping bag against the tree, and sat upon it with his back leaning against the tree. He put on his blindfolds. He then placed the towel over his head so that it completely covered his head and neck. Carl recited his customary prayer, and was silent for about three minutes. It seemed that the energy of the oak tree, enabled Awan to enter effortlessly into Carl's body.

😇 My profound greetings to you my scribe!

🙂 Greetings, Awan.

😇 Today, I wish to dialogue about a topic, that I am sure you will find difficult to accept. Therefore, I need you to keep your skepticism in check, and allow your mind to follow my words. I need you to look at the whole picture, instead of becoming bogged down in the small detail.

🙂 OK. Awan, I will do my best.

😇 Excellent, my scribe. I am using this man's body to speak with you, to enlighten you, my scribe. Then you are to write down your experiences, and impart my words to all the people willing to hear my message. It is my sincere hope that my teachings will help educate the masses, and help create a new atmosphere for the dawn of the *Age of Knowledge*.

🙂 Yes, Awan. I understand that is your desire.

😇 I have tried my best to have you learn the secrets of the soul. For once you accept the fact that the soul in your body is made up of divine energy, identical God's energy, then you can realize that God is within.

🙂 Yes, Awan, I think I finally understand that.

👼 I cannot stress too much, my scribe, that you must burn away the image that God is an old man sitting on an bejeweled throne, in an imaginary piece of real estate in the sky. That concept has to be completely erased from your mind. You need to **KNOW** that God is your soul, and resides in the middle of your chest.

🧑 Why is that so important, Awan?

👼 As I have taught you my scribe, the soul is the *modus operandi* of the entire body. If you wish to open your brain, have total knowingness, access the *Gifts of the Spirit,* and live without disease forever, you have to awaken your soul. Think of it this way my scribe. I have often seen you watch your picture box.

🧑 You mean the television?

👼 Yes, that is what you term it. I have watched you use a small box that you hold in your hand to go from one frequency to another.

🧑 Do you mean the remote control that changes the channel?

👼 Yes that is what you term it. Now tell me my scribe, what would happen if instead of pointing your remote control at your picture box, you pointed it in the opposite direction. Would the channel change?

🧑 No, Awan, it wouldn't.

👼 Why not? You pushed the button didn't you. Why shouldn't it work?

🧑 When I push the button, the remote control sends some sort of signal to the television, which changes the channel. If I point the remote away from the television, the signal goes in the wrong direction, and will have no effect the television.

👼 Correct, my scribe. Now you can easily understand this concept. When you send your prayers and thoughts into outer space, towards an old man wearing a beard and crown, your thoughts, like the signal from the remote just travels in space for eternity. It will have no effect, because there is no God in outer space to receive your thoughts/prayers/signals. Your God is within, just as Jesus tried to teach you 2000 years ago.

For, behold, the kingdom of God is within you.[378]

Once again, my scribe, I need to remind you that ***Thoughts are things.*** Thoughts are made up of energy. It is this thought energy, when directed to the God within, your soul, will activate and awaken it.

Let's compare the religions on your planet to your telephone system, as it was one hundred years ago. In those days, when you wanted to communicate with your neighbor who lived at the other end of town, you walked over to

---

[378] Luke 17:21 [KJV].

your telephone and cranked the handle. This sent a signal to an operator, at another location. You had to tell to the operator who you wished to speak with, and she physically moved some wires, to make the connections for the sound waves (energy) to travel from your phone to the phone belonging to the person with whom you wished to speak

Your religions want to act like the telephone operator between you and God. They have placed statues around their churches to make you believe that you send your prayers outward to a saint or god up in the sky somewhere. Think about this, my scribe, when your astronauts are traveling in outer space, do they send their prayers further upward, or downward, back toward earth? Where is the exact location of the piece of real estate in the sky, where the all-powerful God sits on his golden bejeweled throne?

Have you ever wondered why the statues in churches are often seen crying, or bleeding? Do you think these are tears of joy? No, my scribe, the Spirit people cause these statues to cry because Spirit is so saddened that so many millions of humans, who are being deceived by their religious leaders. They feel sorry for the people on this planet because they have all been mislead as to where God is. If you want to find God, look in a mirror; for the all-powerful God is the soul in your chest.

And while I am speaking of misconceptions: if you think that a special stone or crystal has power in it, then you should probably grow another head, because the brain that you have is working at 0%.

You have infinite power within yourself; it is the soul, located under your breastbone, right in the middle of your chest. If you would only activate it, by directing your focus, sending your thoughts, prayers, and affirmations to the middle of your chest, where the God within you resides, your soul will *eventually* hear them and act upon them. I said *eventually* because for most of your physical life, you have ignored your soul, and have not communicated with it. You have pressed the button on your remote, ten thousand times, but you were pointing it in the wrong direction. Therefore, since you have ignored your soul, it has gone asleep. Let me restate it in another way so you could understand. If you stayed home waiting for a phone call, and no one called for forty-five years, you would become bored waiting, and would go and do something else. You would not sit by the phone for 45 years. Therefore, when it finally rings, it might take you several minutes to run from where you are to answer it.

You must be patient with your soul, for it will be surprised when you finally remember to talk to it. It will take a bit of time for it to awaken, but once it does, it will follow your commands. Do you understand?

🧑 Yes, Awan, it all makes sense to me now.

😇 Very good, my scribe. Now, the next step, then my brother, is to realize that you *are* God.

🧑 What!?

(👤) It is unfortunate, my scribe, that the millions of Christians living on this planet totally ignore the teachings of the person they consider their God. Jesus clearly stated:

> **Jesus answered them, Is it not written in your Law, I said, Ye are gods?**[379]

(👤) ⚜ 7. You are God.

You are God. You have all the power of a God, except you have ignored the mighty God within you for all of your life. Countless billions of people have prayed to an illusionary man in the sky, as your religions have taught you to do. It is truly ironic and sad. Priests, who controlled your religions, were supposed to help you unite with God, instead they have kept you isolated from God. It was priests who put fear into your minds. They have harnessed your thoughts, so that you will only think in patterns that they want you to think, and will not think freely. The more that they can limit your thought, the more they protect their lifestyle. However, humanity is paying a very high price to keep the priests satisfied. You have abandoned the powerful God within, which could manifest all your dreams and desires into reality.

Jesus said, "to find the kingdom of God to look within."[380] Think about that powerful truth. What happens when you look within? You sit in a meditative state, and you focus on your soul. You focus or constrict your entire consciousness onto your soul in the center of your chest. You then begin a conversation, communing with your soul, and can now command it to do whatever you desire. Don't you realize that you are using thought energy—divine energy to manifest your desired change into your life?

You are Gods, because you have the ability and God-power to manifest your desires. The all-powerful God, the Source, or Infinite Energy manifested this wondrous universe. Most people would say He created the Universe. You also have the ability to create. This is why you are a God.

Jesus used this identical thought energy, when he turned the water into wine, and performed all the other psychic feats that Christians call miracles. Every human has this God-given ability, lying dormant in his or her chest. All you have to do is harness this thought energy by sending your thoughts and prayers inward to your soul. Once your soul awaken you can manifest your desires into your life. It is then that you will use your birthright that the all-powerful God gave to humanity.

I have returned to your planet to wage war on ignorance, fear, and superstition. However, my greater mission is to reveal to you that **YOU ARE GOD**. Every human is a God. The color of a person's skin, creeds, beliefs, or

---

[379] John 10:34 [KJV].
[380] Luke 17:21.

race does not matter. All humans who live, breathe, and have their beings in your physical world are Gods.

I understand that it is difficult for you to believe that you are a God. The moment you try to think of yourself as a God, immediately your mind brings up your fears, insecurities, and your past, of which you are ashamed. You feel helpless; therefore, you cannot believe in your divinity. It is a travesty that your religions have taught you to think this way. You should never feel less than your glorious potential, which is your Godhood, because if you do, you immediately dismiss your powerful divinity.

You cannot accept that you are divine, because you have been the witness of your own cruelty, gossip, malicious, abandonment ruthlessness, lies and unjust act, especially the most grievous act of all, of **not** loving who you are. To redefine God you must remove him from that mysterious piece of real estate in the sky, or outer space, and out of your religions, churches and the "Holy Bible." The most difficult task you can face, is to reorient your thinking 180°, and to begin to love yourself, and feel you are worthy to be a God. Knowing that you have the potential to regain your Godhood, will give you hope, and a powerful reason to love yourself.

When you know you are God, you realize that you are connected to everything outside of yourself. Everyone has a spark of the divine, which is one's soul. Every human is a God. Therefore, if you decide to declare "war" on another person, you are actually waging war on yourself. If you judge another person, you have not harmed that person, you have harmed yourself, because every word you say, and thought you have is energy. Since you created that energy on your frequency, it travels out into the universe, collects more of the same negative energy and returns back unto you, not the person you sent it to. The energy is traveling on your frequency; therefore, it has your address on it, and cannot go to anyone else. If you blame and hate the world for all of your misfortunes, then you will suffer a miserable life, and usually you will come down with a serious disease. This happened to you because of your negative thoughts. You created the disease yourself.

When you love life, and all those around you; you actually love yourself. Remember that Jesus taught:

But I say unto you which hear, Love your enemies, do good to them which hate you.[381]

He wanted people to realize that it is your perception that makes someone your enemy. The day that you change your thinking and begin emanating loving thoughts instead of hateful ones, is the day you will stop suffering. You will then find love where only hatred had existed. You will no longer want to hate anyone, because you do not want to be hated. This is why Jesus taught:

Thou shalt love thy neighbor as thyself.[382]

---

[381] Luke 6:27 [KJV].

You automatically evolve with wisdom and understanding, as you become a divine being. For you will realize that everything that you think, say and do, will come back to you one hundred fold. This is why I have taught you: "thoughts are things."

You need to reorganize your thinking, and bring your existence to come into harmony with this teaching. Your entire destiny is held in your hands in that single moment, that you decide to change. Do you look at yourself with hate, or will you love yourself?

A God is one who manifests his or her own destiny. It is also divine to allow others their truths. You do not need to go out and save the world. You need to conquer your own thoughts and emotions. You need to allow people to evolve at their own paces. When you bring this concept into your own consciousness, it will provide understanding. Can you understand another person's anger towards you does not belong to you. You need not absorb it or return that anger. That anger is part of the other person's journey. This was the true meaning behind Jesus' teaching:

> **If anyone strikes you on the cheek, offer the other also; and from anyone who takes away your coat do not withhold even your shirt.**[383]

If you believe that everyone dislikes you it is because you dislike yourself. Everyone is a mirror of your own self-perception.

Once you realize that you are a God, even a God in the embryo, then you will no longer do anything to hurt yourself again. However, it is an arduous task to you change yourself, and to keep yourself from falling back into your habitual patterns.

The worse thing you have ever done is not to love yourself. The second worst thing is to believe people who tell you that you are a sinner. You are not a sinner. Men and women are not evil in their souls. No human is born in sin, original or otherwise. Don't you realize the soul is holy energy? It is beautiful not evil.

You cannot accept that you are a God, because religions have programmed you to believe that God is perfect, and human being are imperfect. Theologians used every method they could think of to reinforce this idea. They even made the members of their congregations sing about their imperfection.

What do you mean by that, Awan?

After this session look up the words to the religious hymn entitled: *Amazing Grace*.

---

[382] Matthew 22:39 [KJV].

[383] Luke 6:29 [NRSV].

📖 I followed Awan's instructions and once again Awan was correct. I discovered that Virginia Harmony wrote *Amazing Grace* in 1831.[384]

> **"Amazing Grace! how sweet the sound,**
> **That saved a wretch like me!**
> **I once was lost, but now am found,**
> **Was blind, but now, I see."**[385]

😇 Never believe anyone, I do not care what title that person may possess, who tries to separate you from the love of God. You don't need to be saved. What do you need saving from—**Life**? You just need to wake up and consider yourself beautiful, and to love every fiber of your being.

Your brain is a New Testament that the divine lives in you. Your brain testifies to you that there is more to you than you ever have known. You soul contains the same testimony. From this day forward, to become God, love and adore the temple within, and live righteously from the soul's point of view. You need to conquer your alter ego, and your personality, which often wants to put your needs and wants ahead of others. Jesus was conquering his alter ego when he spent 40 days alone in the wilderness.

> **And the Spirit immediately drove him out into the wilderness. He was in the wilderness forty days, tempted by Satan; and he was with the wild beasts; and the angels waited on him.**[386]

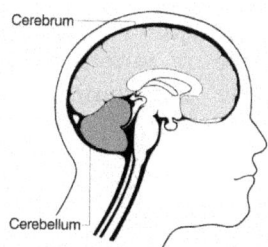

Jesus was not confronting Satan, an all-powerful evil being, who had horns on his head. Jesus was confronting the negative aspects of his own personality, which you term alter ego. You must remember that Jesus' brain was fully operational. The 2/3 of the brain that allowed him to manifest the *Gifts of the Spirit* is actually what Jesus termed "the Kingdom of God." You know that part of the brain as the lower *cerebellum*, and it connects your mind to the divine consciousness, and the *river of thought*. The *cerebrum* is the section of the brain where your ego, alter ego and personality reside. Therefore, Jesus was actually deciding which part of his brain would rule his life, the divine or the human part. This is actually what I have been describing to you during this dialogue.

---

[384] Methodist Church, Inc. The Methodist Hymnal: Official Hymnal of the Methodist Church. Nashville: Methodist Publishing House, 1966. p. 92.

[385] Methodist Church, Inc. The Methodist Hymnal: Official Hymnal of the Methodist Church. Nashville: Methodist Publishing House, 1966. p. 92.

[386] Mark 1:12-13 [NRSV].

👤 Awan, I am doing my best, but wow, this is difficult. How can I possibly be God?

😇 My scribe, you have the potential to be a God, however, you are not, at this moment, because your God is still asleep. You have not awakened him yet. In the moment that Spirit created the universe, through His intense power of thought, He imprinted a special thought into all the souls he created: **"Make known the unknown."** This was humanity's charge; to use your 21st century terminology, this was your *mission statement*.

👤 I certainly have heard about mission statements. Everyone is busy creating them.

😇 Humanity's mission statement is *to make known the unknown*. However, centuries ago, religious leaders made people extremely fearful of the unknown. Churches taught that the dark, unknown is filled with devils and demons, out to capture your soul and put it in a pit of eternal fire. Yet, even your Book of Books contradicts that teaching. Read where Spirit gave Moses The Ten Commandments, and you will discover that God was in the darkness.

👤 After the session, I found the verse Awan described:

> **And the people stood afar off, and Moses drew near unto the thick darkness where God *was*.**[387]

😇 The reason you feel you are not a God is because you have given all your power away. You essentially gave away power to people, or social institutions, that you feel have authority. You allow these groups whether it is your church, or your parents, or even your peers to intercede, and manipulate your thinking. Think back my scribe, to your very own childhood.

👤 It was not my favorite time of my life, Awan.

😇 And why was that my scribe?

👤 Many children picked on me because of my weight; they called me names.

😇 You still carry that hurt with you, despite the fact it occurred so many decades ago. You also are having difficulty accepting my teachings, because when you were a child you were taught an ideology. Much of what I say counters that teaching. You have come a long way, my scribe, but you still have further to go.

👤 I believe you are correct, Awan.

---

[387] Exodus 20:21[KJV].

(👼) You need to understand, my scribe, that you truly are the master of your destiny. What you think — will come to pass—it will manifest. It has to because you are a God.

(🧑) OK, Awan. You said I would have difficulty with this and I am. Please explain this to me in another way; I do not understand what you are trying to teach me.

(👼) Let me use this example. Let us say Doris has an alcoholic father. When he drinks he becomes very abusive to her, and belittles and ridicules her. She becomes what you term a victim. She is very unhappy because of what her father tells her. Doris' soul recorded all these experiences. Doris grows up and becomes an adult. She learned from authority figures, subconsciously, that the unknown is terrifying. She meets and marries Ted, her "prince charming." Ted is a perfect husband. Well, Ted does have this one quality, which is not very endearing. Ted has a short temper, and when he becomes angry, he belittles Doris. Ted blames Doris for everything that goes wrong. Eventually, Ted becomes an alcoholic.

Doris has just recreated her childhood. She finds herself in the same predicament that she was when she was a child.

(🧑) You know, Awan, I have heard of this quite often. How does this happen?

(👼) As I said before, my scribe, ***thoughts are things***. Despite the fact that Doris was unhappy with her father, these thought patterns were imprinted in her soul. Doris subconsciously recreated this same situation. If Doris had dealt with her father, realized the psychological dynamics, and resolved it, she would have gained knowledge from this experience. That knowledge would have been recorded in Doris' soul. However, throughout her life, Doris, kept pondering why her father had treated her so badly. She became entrenched in her past, and the more she thought of it, the more these thoughts drew another man into her life, who fell into the same pattern.

(🧑) So you are telling me that if Doris had totally resolved the issue, she would no longer dwelled on it and would not have recreated it.

(👼) That is precisely correct, my scribe. People need to resolve their "issues" they carry around from their past. They need to abolish victimization, jealousy, envy, hatred, and malice. These are all aspects, which degrades the spiritual self that is your soul. To say it another way: These issues strip your God of its power! You need to realize that your past is held together by your own mind.

Now answer this question: Where do you record thoughts, my scribe?

(🧑) In the soul, Awan.

(👼) Correct! So reason this out. When you generate a thought with your brain, it is recorded in the soul. Your soul is a ball of light. Therefore, can make a comparison. Your thoughts are like your photographic slides. Your soul is the slide projector. Your thought, therefore, is beamed out into your auric field, the light that emanates from the soul.

👤 So a clairvoyant could see those thoughts because they are in the aura.

😇 That is correct, my scribe. Now I want you to realize that your auric field is magnetic. Therefore, when Doris kept contemplating how her father mistreated her, those thoughts kept being transmitted into her auric field. It magnetized or attracted a husband, who was identical to her father. Ted subconsciously knew that Doris would be compatible. To say it another way, Ted's soul could read Doris' aura, and this is what attracted Ted to Doris. This is a demonstration of one of the universal laws: **Like attracts Like**.

Doris never understood that she saw herself as a victim. Therefore, she could not understand why Ted turned out to be like her father. To avoid recreating your past, you must take responsibility for your actions. Experiences are neither good or bad, you have them to glean their knowledge. However, if you blame another person for the experience, you remain in that focus, and never look deeper for the knowledge of the experience.

You must take responsibility for the event. Say to yourself: "I created this experience to gain knowledge of _____. I do not blame my parents, nor my 1st grade classmates, nor my teacher, nor my minister, priest, or rabbi. I cannot tell you why, or when I got the idea to create it, and bring this even into my life, but I have. Otherwise the experience would not have occurred.

As you begin thinking in this manner, you will eradicate the *victim's excuse*—there is no other person to blame. People have a difficult time in doing this because most humans are afraid to confront their own choices. This state of fear empowers people to blame another person, allowing them to focus their energy away from their own actions. Being a victim keeps the past alive, and prevents you from gaining knowledge from the experience. Victimization robs you of your own energy, and continues to enslave your God. Therefore, your God is compelled to recreate the identical situation, in hopes that you will finally break your pattern. Perhaps during the second time, you will resolve the issue, gain knowledge from the experience, and move on. Unfortunately, very few manage to do this, forcing the soul to recreate and recycle the problem multiple times.

👤 Why can't people deal with it the first time, Awan?

😇 It is not easy for a person to take responsibility for what has happened in his or her life. Taking responsibility is the bravest of spiritual endeavors. It is called the **Dark Night of the Soul**, where suffering energy returns to its creator—which is you!

I want you to understand this, my scribe. To take responsibility you have to rid yourself of your excuse of victimization. You have to realize that you had this experience to gain knowledge from it. Then as you relive the painful experience, the energy that you term emotion goes through your emotional body. The emotion causes many physiological changes, your mood changes, your heart beats faster, the speed of your breathing changes, you may even cry—which is extremely healthy for your soul. This emotional energy is returning, as you resolve the issue, and you begin to gain the knowledge from the experience. This is something that you have to do for yourself; no one else can do it for you.

Very few people have the spiritual strength to do this. Most people get scared and run. It is quite simple. Unless the divine God within, located in the middle of your chest, is awake; it can never create the marvelous. Unless it has been defined within you, the unknown cannot be made known.

There is a simple way to stop being a victim. You need to sit down on a daily basis, go into your closet of prayer, as I taught you, and remove your victimization from your soul. You close your eyes, put on a blindfold, and you focus on (visualize) your soul, in the middle of your chest. Then you see yourself sitting in a bubble of light, which is your auric field. Then you say these words aloud and with passion:

> **Lord God of my being**
> **Unto the Father/Mother within**
> **Come forward this moment, this hour**
> **And bring forth the Christ from within me.**
> **Go into the memory bank of my soul,**
> **And erase for evermore**
> **All memories of my victimization,**
> **And replace those memories**
> **With love for all humankind.**
> **So Be It!**

You need to do this on a daily basis. Then one day, you suddenly will realize, that your victimization no longer bothers your. It no longer exists. It is then you can terminate saying this affirmation.

This is powerful information, Awan.

Indeed it is my scribe. The energy is still stable, so we can continue to dialogue. There is one more concept I wish to discuss with you. I want you to extend your arms straight out from your body, as if you were being put on a cross.

OK, Awan, I have my arms stretched out.

What would you estimate is the distance from your left fingertips to the right.

OK Awan. I would say it is about five feet.

That is the size of the auric field of an open minded person, who learns to communicate with his or her soul. The aura of a closed-minded person is so close to his or her body, that it is barely perceptible. It appears as if the light is almost totally out. People with such a small dim aura are *dead in Spirit*.

I have heard that term, but never understood it.

(😇) Now, your auric field is not static. There is movement of energy within the aura. If a person is open-minded and radiates love, that positive energy flows through the aura, and touches the *river of thought*. That love goes out into the universe, magnetizes more love to it, and eventually returns to its Mother/Father creator, reenters that person's aura, bringing in more love, and the love feeds the body. The physical body can easily absorb this loving energy.

However, if the person has negative thoughts of jealously, hatred, or malice the same process happens. That negative energy goes out into the *river of thought*, increases, and returns to its owner. Then the physical body absorbs a grand dose of negative energy, which can cause diseases, especially cancer.

(🙂) That is fascinating, Awan.

(😇) Think of it this way, my scribe. If you place a live plant on your windowsill, and give it water from your faucet, every other day, the plant will thrive. The light energy it receives, combines with the water molecules. Photosynthesis takes place, allowing the leaves to grow and expand. This is a positive situation.

Having negative thoughts is like putting rubbing alcohol in water, before you water the plant. The plant has no way to filter out toxins, so the plant becomes overwhelmed and dies.

I have seen many people on your planet, whose whole life is focused on money instead of love. Often the negative emotion of greed is intertwined with thoughts of money. People are so determined to collect and hold onto their money that thoughts about money remain within the auric field. The thought goes out into edge of auric field; then it goes back and feeds the body. It is similar to stone thrown in the middle of a pond. It causes waves that go out to the outer perimeter which then return back towards the center of the pond.

If one's primary focus is on money, the person's bank account may grow, but his or her body suffers from this lack of positive energy. The body cannot continue to function properly without positive energy. Eventually the body weakens and disease manifests. This is what Jesus meant when he talked of two masters.

(🙂) I found the verse Awan referred to after the deep trance session.

> "No-one can serve two masters. Either he will hate the one and love the other, or he will be devoted to the one and despise the other. You cannot serve both God and Money."[388]

---

[388] Matthew 6:24 [NIV].

(👼) I am sensing a change in the energy, so I will have to leave you at this time. I hope you will take some time to think about thoughts! It is extremely important. My profound peace be with you.

(🧑) Thank you for this wonderful information, Awan. My peace be with you too.

Carl sat quietly for 30 seconds, and suddenly he moaned softly. I need some water, he said, with a parched sounding voice. Carl drank all the water in the small bottle. Because he felt groggy, we sat and discussed the information that Awan had discussed. After about 15 minutes we went back to his house, and Carl took a short nap.

TWENTY

Your Passport into Forever

A few days later, Carl phoned me and said, "Awan wishes to speak with you again, can you be in my office at 10 o'clock, Saturday morning." At the appointed time, Carl and I sat in Carl's darkened office. Carl placed the blindfold over his eyes, said his prayer, and quieted himself. Slowly he slipped into trance. This time, Awan slipped into Carl's body without causing it to jolt.

My profound greetings to you, my scribe!

Greetings, Awan.

I have asked you here today, to tie up some loose ends, as you would term it. We have been dialoguing for nearly a year about the keys. I felt that it was important for you to digest each one in your own time. Now that we have thoroughly discussed each one, I think it is important that we review them, so you can understand the grand picture these keys present.

OK, Awan, I am ready.

Let's review each key. It is important that you be able to explain them in your own words. It is then that you have incorporated this knowledge into your own consciousness. It is the first important step in creating a knowingness system.

Now, please tell me about: 1. The Secrets of the Soul.

The soul is divine, eternal energy, located behind the breastbone in the middle of the chest. It is the soul, which has all our memories that we take into the Spirit World. It is also the soul, which runs the entire body, and maintains our health.

That is very good, my scribe, however, you omitted some very important information. The Soul is like a computer; not only does it keeps the body functioning, and records all your emotions and actions; it can be programmed to carry out a person's wishes and desires. People have confused the heart with the soul. The heart is just a pump, and has no connections with human emotions.

The soul is the child of the Spirit, and is each human's omnipotent God. That is the reason that Jesus taught:

For, behold, the kingdom of God is within you.[389]

The most empowering concept that I can teach you is to communicate with your soul, because once it reawakens, it can make you as unlimited as you can possibly become. All you have to do is to think unlimited and you will become unlimited.

Now, explain: 2. 𝔗𝔥𝔢 𝔖𝔢𝔠𝔯𝔢𝔱𝔰 𝔬𝔣 𝔱𝔥𝔢 𝔅𝔯𝔞𝔦𝔫.

At one time, the human brain functioned at 100% capacity. People could utilize all the *Gifts of the Spirit*. No one aged, or had any disease, because all the brain functioned. People had fantastic, peaceful civilizations. Everyone realized that all humans were Gods.

That was a wondrous time, my scribe. Fortunately, the world will reenter into that vibration once again.

Now explain: 3. 𝔜𝔬𝔲 𝔚𝔢𝔯𝔢 𝔑𝔢𝔳𝔢𝔯 𝔐𝔢𝔞𝔫𝔱 𝔗𝔬 𝔇𝔦𝔢.

When the brain works at 100% of it capacity, humans have the ability to ascend. Instead of dying, they can speed up the molecules of their bodies and enter into the Spirit World with their physical body.

There are fantastic advantages of taking your body with you, my scribe. You can travel the entire universe in an instant, and visit the dimension where ascended masters reside.

Now explain: 4. 𝔗𝔥𝔢𝔯𝔢 𝔍𝔰 𝔑𝔬 𝔇𝔢𝔳𝔦𝔩.

A small group of people, that you called tyrants, decided they wished to dominate the masses. They began to teach an evil being, called the devil, enabled the *Gifts of the Spirit*. This seed of fear, once implanted in the human mind, began to grow. Slowly people became afraid of their psychic gifts, and stopped using them. Then parts of the brain, responsible for demonstrating these gifts began to atrophy. Since the brain no longer worked at 100% capacity, disease, and death became common. These tyrants, who eventually became priests, became the leaders of society. They assumed political and theological controlled over the people, enslaving them to their man-made dogmas.

The devil became the most important aspect of many religions. This grand scheme became the great money-maker for religions.

---

[389] Luke 17:21 [KJV].

Please explain: 🔑 5. **Fear is the Great Satan.**

👤 It was fear, which shut the brain down, millenniums ago. Fear is like a grand virus, which prohibits us from reaching our potentials. We are constantly battling our fears, which are our true *adversaries*, the literal meaning of the word *Satan*. Once we learn to give up our fears, we can begin our transformation to becoming unlimited.

😇 Fear has polluted the human mind, just as humans have polluted the rivers and oceans. It is just as difficult to return the brain to its unpolluted state, as a river.

Please explain: 🔑 6. **Communicate with your Soul.**

👤 Religions have taught us that God is an old man sitting on a bejeweled throne up in the sky somewhere. People think they must send their prayers outward and upward for God to hear them. This is a horrific mistake. All prayers should be directed to your own soul, in the middle of your chest. Your soul is your God.

😇 This key is probably the most important. You need not go to a church or temple to communicate with God. Your God is with you always (omnipresent), because He or She resides in you. There is a God residing within every human being. You need to follow Jesus' instructions: "go into your closet of prayer," to communicate with God. Do you remember what your closet of prayer is?

👤 Yes, Awan, it is closing your eyes, and seeing yourself sitting in a bubble of light, your own auric field, that emanates from your own soul.

😇 That is correct. While this key is the easiest for you to do, yet it is the most difficult to accomplish. I will explain why after we review the final key.

Now, please explain: 🔑 7. **You are God.**

👤 Humans have the potential to be God. It takes time to awaken the God within, because we have spent almost a lifetime ignoring it. Once it is awakened, it can reopen the brain and eventually it can function at 100% capacity. It is then that immortality can be achieved, disease conquered, and one can utilize all of the *Gifts of the Spirit*.

😇 You will become an unlimited God once that is achieved, my scribe.

👤 It sounds so easy, yet it is not.

😇 That is the point of this dialogue, my scribe. To awaken the sleeping God within, you must have a knowingness. This is why these keys are so important. Without knowing the truth of these seven statements, you cannot awaken your sleeping God.

🙂 That is what I do not understand. I just explained these keys, Awan, but my God has not awaken yet.

😇 Yes, my scribe, because you still do not have a knowingness. Reciting the keys is just substituting one belief system for another. When I say you must have knowingness, I am referring to a particular state of mind, where you no longer have doubt about the validity of the keys. It is not a maybe or a probability. Your rock-solid knowledge will exist in an emotionless state, which will transcend all time and space. It is then in this special state of knowingness, when you address your God, it will begin to respond.

🙂 So your thinking will effect if you can awaken your God?

😇 That is precisely correct. Your thoughts are extremely important, my scribe. Once you awaken your God, you can manifest any thought you have. It is then, my scribe, that it becomes important that you control your thoughts so you will not manifest any negative conditions into your life.

🙂 I understand, Awan.

😇 When you finally enter a state of knowingness, you become indestructible. It is then that you "validate, or stamp, your passport into forever." These keys merge into knowledge, which is indestructible, because it is recorded into your soul. It is then you will know how to travel to the higher levels of the Spirit World, and beyond.

🙂 I can now understand why these keys are so essential.

😇 I hope that the readers of this book will also be able to understand. I am sensing a change in the energy so I must leave this body. It has once again, been a pleasure to speak with you this day. I can see from your auric field, that you have finally synthesized the keys. Once you conquer the remnants of your doubt, you will forge this information into a knowingness system. For this I am quite pleased. My profound peace be with you, my scribe.

🙂 My peace be with you too, Awan.

Carl sat still for a few moments, and then softly moaned. "I need some water," he said in a soft pleading voice. I assisted him as he drank the entire glass. "I feel so washed out, why do these trance sessions deplete me so much?"

After assisting Carl, to his bedroom, he slept for 3 hours. Despite his long nap, he still lacked energy for the rest of the day.

TWENTY-ONE

Jesus the Christ

This session took place about two weeks later. Again it was a warm summer's day. Carl and I decided to repeat our outdoor procedure. We sat in the same spot, under the shade of a large oak tree. After Carl blindfolded his eyes, and veiled his face, he said his prayer. It only took 2 minutes for Awan to begin to speak. Again, Awan smoothly entered Carl's body.

😇 My profound greetings to you, my scribe!

🧑 Greetings, Awan.

😇 Today, I wish to dialogue about the great teacher who walked your planet 2000 years ago. His name was יְהוֹשֻׁעַ בֶּן יֹסֵף (*Joshua ben Joseph*), yet you know him by the name Jesus.

🧑 OK, Awan. I am ready to learn.

😇 Let me start by giving you some background information. There is a special level in the World of Spirit, known as **the Great White Brotherhood**. It has twelve ranges of frequencies, where the most enlightened beings of the universe reside. We are, what some of you might term, great masters since we have mastered most of the knowledge of the universe. It has been our custom, for centuries of your time, for one of us return to your planet every 500-700 years as a teacher, and way-shower, in an attempt to enlighten your dark ignorant world.

Our efforts have always failed, yet small accomplishments were made on each attempt. We have come to teach your world the path towards truth, but in your ignorance, you have polluted our teachings and have turned us into "Savior-Gods." Osiris, Abraham, Krishna, Buddha, Jesus, and Mohammed were just a few of these grand illuminati, grand enlightened entities, who attempted to alter the course of history, and evolution of your planet.

All of these illuminati were functioning with 100% brain capacity, meaning that they were all mediumistic. These great teachers needed to be in constant communication with people in my dimension, so that the teaching could constantly be refined to meet the needs of the people. You must understand, the amount of ignorance on your planet varied according to the culture, and which religion controlled that culture. Each teacher was trying to purify belief systems into a knowingness system, in the same manner that I am working through this medium with you, my scribe.

I want you to clearly understand that people who are psychic are on the fringe edge of being the gifted ones. There is a vast difference between being psychic, and being a medium. It is only the mediums, who have the capacity to be a clear communication link between the two worlds. Some psychics had been mediums in other lives, but lost their true gifts because they absorbed the teachings of religions.

👤 Awan, this is all very fascinating. Tell me are you a member of the Great White Brotherhood?

😇 Yes, my scribe. I am one of the twelve, however, I am not about to reveal any more of my identity to you.

👤 I understand, Awan.

😇 Approximately 2000 years ago, Jesus met with our council, and informed us that he wished to return to your planet. He felt that people had advanced to the point where they could again learn ancient truths.

Our council had a great debate on the issue; we all felt that it could not be accomplished. We carefully studied conditions on your planet. Remember, my scribe, we are not in a heaven or located in outer space, therefore, we do not look down through the clouds. We are on higher level of vibration, therefore, we lowered our frequency to study your planet. What we found was utter chaos, especially in what you term the Middle-East. That area was overrun by many religions, all ruled by money-hungry priests. Each religion thought it was correct, and was antagonistic towards the others. There is even evidence of this remaining in your Book of Books, when the woman at the well was surprised that Jesus spoke to her. The Jews and Samaritans were antagonistic towards each other, just as the Jews and Arabs are today.

📖 I found the verse Awan discussed.

> **The Samaritan woman said to him, "You are a Jew and I am a Samaritan woman. How can you ask me for a drink?" (For Jews do not associate with Samaritans.)**[390]

😇 After careful deliberation, the council told Jesus that he could not bring enlightenment to your world. It was still too ignorant, and entrenched in its religions, to relearn ancient wisdom. However, Jesus was adamant. He said, "I can no longer watch people living in ignorance, I must attempt to show humanity the truth." His idealism and sense of adventure were burning bright. He convinced us to allow him to try.

Jesus did not wish to work with humanity as a Spirit, ghost or apparition, who would require the use of a medium. Therefore, since he needed a body,

---

[390] John 4:9 [NIV].

he would have to be born in the normal fashion. However, this posed a problem, because in those days no humans were born with 100% of their brain operational. Therefore, Jesus created a unique method of coming into your world.

Jesus, along with the rest of our council, had been closely watching a female member of the Essenes for quite some time. The Essenes were an enlightened group of people, which I consider an ancient school of wisdom. The Essenes clearly knew that God was within, and they practiced the *Gifts of the Spirit* on a daily basis. Many of the Essenes became pure instruments of the Spirit.

There was a 13 year-old Essene girl named Mary, who was extremely pure in Spirit. When she came into her first season of blood, Jesus lowered himself seven levels of vibration and implanted himself in the egg in her womb. He reprogrammed the existing DNA in order to create a body whose brain would be totally operational. Therefore, Jesus was born endowed with all the *Gifts of the Spirit*. Jesus did this alone; no copulation was involved in his conception.

Awan, are you really saying the doctrine of *Immaculate Conception* is true? That can't be possible!

Think about this, my scribe. To change the water into wine at the wedding at Cana, Jesus altered the chemistry of the water molecules, by rearranging electrons. This formed the other chemicals required to make a molecule of wine.[391] Since he had the knowledge, and ability, to accomplish this amazing feat, why couldn't he reprogram the genes of the DNA molecules inside Mary's womb?

Yes, my scribe, *Immaculate Conception* did occur. Jesus implanted himself in the womb of a virgin. Not only did this fulfill a prophecy, but it was the only method Jesus could use to come into your world with a fully operational brain. In those days, there were no two people on the planet whose genetics could produce a child with 100% brain capacity. Therefore, there was no other choice.

Awan referred to Isaiah's prophecy:

Therefore the Lord himself shall give you a sign; Behold, a virgin shall conceive, and bear a son, and shall call his name Immanuel.[392]

Jesus adjusted his vibration to match the vibration of Mary's body. He implanted himself in the womb without intercourse. The rest of the brotherhood stayed around Mary's aura (energy field) to help mold the baby's body. Once Jesus' soul entered the baby's body, the brotherhood remained nearby, in their aeroship, high in sky. The magi, Zoroastrian priests

---

[391] John 2:6-9.
[392] Isaiah 7:14 [KJV].

from Persia, who studied astrology, mistook our aeoship to be a star. Therefore, they traveled eastward, towards this "star," which became known as *"the Star of Bethlehem."*

👤 In a way, that makes sense, Awan.

👼 Because of his brain, the environment of his body was protein based, and Jesus was never sick during his life. This should also help to explain his extraordinary gifts. Go to your library and find a book entitled: *The Aquarian Gospel*. It is about Jesus' life, and was transmitted from another entity in my realm to a medium in your world. Read of the extraordinary dream Jesus had when he was only seven years old.

📖 Here is the passage:

Dream of No Death

"The home of Joseph was on Marmion Way in Nazareth; here Mary taught her son the Lessons of Elihu and Salome. And Jesus greatly loved the Vedic Hymns and the Avesta; but more than all he loved to read the Psalms of David and the pungent words of Solomon."

"The Jewish books of prophecy were his delight; and when he reached his seventh year he needed not the books to read, for he had fixed in memory every word."

"Joachim and his wife, grandparents of child Jesus, made a feast in honour of the child, and all their near of kin were guests. And Jesus stood before the guests and said, I had a dream, and in my dream I stood before a sea, upon a sandy beach. The waves upon the sea were high, a storm was raging on the deep."

"Some one above gave me a wand. I took the wand and touched the sand, and every grain of sand became a living thing; the beach was all a mass of beauty and of song. I touched the waters at my feet, and they were changed to trees, and flowers and singing birds, and everything was praising God."

"And some one spoke, I did not see the one who spoke, I heard the voice, which said, THERE IS NO DEATH. Grandmother Anna loved the child; she laid her hand on Jesus' head and said, I saw you stand beside the sea; I saw you touch the sand and waves; I saw them turn to living things and then I knew the meaning of the dream. The sea of life rolls high; the storms are great. The multitudes of men are idle, listless, waiting like dead sand upon the beach.

Your wand is truth. With this you touch the multitudes, and every man becomes a messenger of holy light and life. You touch the waves upon the sea; their turmoils cease; the very winds become a song of praise. There is no death, because the wand of truth can change the dryest bones to living things, and bring the loveliest flowers from stagnant ponds and turn the most discordant notes to harmony and praise."[393]

Jesus, at the age of six, started teaching anyone who would listen. However, your Bible records his first teaching at the age of twelve, when he and his parents had traveled to the Temple in Jerusalem. Jesus was more interested in teaching the elders because the people's education was in the elder's hands. The elders were amazed at the knowledge Jesus taught.

One particular elder knew of the secret Essene school, on a dessert oasis, a two-day's walk from Jerusalem. When he heard Jesus teach, he realized that Jesus would greatly benefit from attending that school. Yet, this scribe was afraid to mention it to Jesus, and break his vow never to reveal the school's existence.

It was only after Jesus' parents returned to the temple looking for their missing son, that this elder made his decision. He followed Jesus and his parents out of the temple, down the street a ways, and away from the others elders. Then this elder took Mary and Joseph off to the side, and spoke with them without Jesus being able to hear their discussion.

He explained how Jesus could advance his knowledge by studying mediumship at the Essene's school. He could not receive that kind of education at his home in Nazareth. Mary and Joseph released the boy to the elder, who later accompanied Jesus to the Essenes' school. Within a matter of a few weeks, Jesus was the best student at the school.

After four months, Jesus talked with the Essene masters, and informed them that Spirit had been urging him to leave the school, and go out into the world to teach the *Gifts of the Spirit*. The Essenes cautioned him that world was not ready to accept the *Gifts of the Spirit*; these teachings would contradict the deeply entrenched dogmas and creeds of most religions. Jesus' teachings would threaten religious leaders' incomes, who would strike out in retaliation. Jesus would endanger his own life if he taught his truth. Jesus said he was willing to take that chance, and quietly he bid farewell to his teachers.

---

[393] Levi. *The Aquarian Gospel of Jesus the Christ: The Philosophic and Practical Basis of the Religion of the Aquarian Age of the World.* Chapter 16 Verses 1-14. Santa Monica, CA: De Vorss & Co., Publishers, 1975. p. 50.

Within three days, he met his cousin, John, who was also traveling through the countryside, baptizing people. Many people thought John was a religious fanatic. Although they were cousins, the two were very opposite from each other. Jesus was on his way to India, to study at the great schools in that country. Jesus and John traveled together for a while, but John lost interest and returned to Israel. Jesus continued his journey to India, always listening to the voice of Moses, his connection to the Spirit World. You would now use the term *Spirit Control*.

😇) Now, my scribe, there is another misconception in your Bible that I wish bring to light. It has to do with Jesus being tempted by the Devil.

🙂 Awan, that is a good point. If there is no Devil, how did this passage get into the Bible?

📖 Here is the Bible verses being discussed.

> Then Jesus was led up by the Spirit into the wilderness to be tempted by the devil. He fasted forty days and forty nights, and afterwards he was famished. The tempter came and said to him, "If you are the Son of God, command these stones to become loaves of bread."
>
> But he answered, "It is written, 'One does not live by bread alone, but by every word that comes from the mouth of God.'"
>
> Then the devil took him to the holy city and placed him on the pinnacle of the temple, saying to him, "If you are the Son of God, throw yourself down; for it is written, 'He will command his angels concerning you,' and 'On their hands they will bear you up, so that you will not dash your foot against a stone.'"
>
> Jesus said to him, "Again it is written, 'Do not put the Lord your God to the test.'" Again, the devil took him to a very high mountain and showed him all the kingdoms of the world and their splendor; and he said to him, "All these I will give you, if you will fall down and worship me."
>
> Jesus said to him, "Away with you, Satan! for it is written, 'Worship the Lord your God, and serve only him.'" Then the devil left him, and suddenly angels came and waited on him. [394]

😇) You realize by now, my scribe, how much of the Bible has been edited by theologians who incorporated their own theology into the Holy text. This event in Jesus' life was very different from the description recirded in the Bible.

---

[394] Matthew 4:1-11 [NRSV].

🧑 Really, Awan. Please tell me the real story.

😇 Jesus was as human as all the other people who lived on the earth plane, 2000 years ago. It was Jesus' brain, which made him unique. Since it was 100% operational, he could demonstrate all the **Gifts of the Spirit**, and communicate with my realm.

🧑 Yes, Awan, I understand that.

😇 Jesus voluntarily decided to go out into the desert to fast for forty days and nights.

🧑 Why Awan, what was he trying to accomplish?

😇 Jesus was trying to maintain his spiritual balance. His alter ego, that the Bible calls *the devil*, was tempting him.

🧑 Awan, you are losing me, what are you trying to say?

😇 Tell me something, my scribe. Haven't you met many mediums since you have become acquainted with this work?

🧑 Yes, that is true, Awan.

😇 And did you think all these mediums were of equal status?

🧑 No Awan, I felt some were better than others.

😇 And what, in your opinion, caused some mediums to be poorer than others?

🧑 I might not be correct with this assumption, Awan; however, I felt that some mediums had such a high opinion of themselves that it affected their work. These mediums were more concerned about being "a star" than an instrument of the Spirit. Their egos were so large, that there was hardly room for the spirit to work through him or her. They did not approach mediumship with humility.

😇 Yes, my scribe, this is precisely correct. Jesus did not want to fall into that trap. He knew that he was going to be the best prophet (medium) that **ever** lived! Yet, he needed to keep his ego in check. However, at times he did have thoughts emanating from his alter ego, which wanted to feed his ego, and make him a "Super-Star." I believe you even have a story entitled "Jesus Christ Superstar."

🧑 Yes, Awan, that was a play and a movie.

😇 Jesus was concerned that his alter ego would try to convince him that he was a "superstar." If that had happened, his mediumship would have deteriorated. Jesus, knew the prophecy:

The meek shall inherit the earth.[395]

He certainly was not seeking "stardom," as you would understand it. So he went out into the desert to confront this human temptation of allowing the alter ego to run rampant. Jesus achieved balance while he was in the desert, and was no longer bothered by the problem.

So why did the translators change this from alter ego to the devil?

Very simple, my scribe. The devil was being cast as the opponent to God. It would make for much better reading, and would also provide people with hope. If Jesus could conquer the devil, than perhaps, if you followed all of the Church's dogmas and rules, you too could "Rebuke Satan."

I now understand what you mean.

Good, my scribe, I would now like to focus this dialogue on another famous story of the New Testament—The Mount of Transfiguration.

OK, Awan, please enlighten me.

Moses was Jesus' Spirit Control (the Spirit who controls which Spirit may speak or demonstrate through Jesus) and Elijah was a Spirit teacher (and taught Jesus spiritual lessons). This is the reason Moses and Elijah appeared to Jesus and his disciples on the Mount of Transfiguration.[396] I want you to think carefully about what I am about to explain.

Jesus was teaching the *Gifts of the Spirit* to his disciples. Yet, only three of his students, Peter, James, and John, reached a point of beginning to understand the laws of psychic science. Read in the Scriptures of when Jesus was holding a healing service, and demonstrated the *gift of apports* (making food materialize out of nowhere).[397] Jesus demonstrated the *Gifts of the Spirit* in a natural setting, in the foothills of the mountains. He did not go to the marketplace, stand on a rock, and plead with passersbys for money to build a magnificent temple. He did not plead for food, and new sandals, so that he could keep his ministry in business. Jesus taught the people because he loved them, and wanted to teach them, through his demonstrations of the *Gifts of the Spirit* (psychic phenomena). He also wanted the people to know that the soul is immortal, and continues to live in the Spirit World after the death of the physical body.

Jesus clairaudiently heard Moses' instructions: he was to select his most advanced students, leave the crowds with their negative thought vibrations, and climb up into the mountains where the energy was clear. Jesus went through the crowds, and found Peter, James, and John healing the sick, doing their works as he taught them to do. Jesus whispered to each of them to

---

[395] Psalms 37:11.
[396] Luke 9:28-31.
[397] Luke 9:10-15.

follow him, without saying a word to anyone. The uninvited students showed how upset they were through their body language.

The three students followed silently behind Jesus. After a long steady uphill hike, they were very tired and short of breath. Jesus motioned to his students to sit down in a particular clearing. They sat down without saying a word.

Suddenly, the disciples began to experience something that was very difficult for them to express in words. They were totally unaware that they were about to witness the greatest séance that the world had ever known. Peter, James and John could hardly believe their eyes, as two gleaming pillars of cloud started to form on either side of Jesus. These pillars of cloud started building from the ground upwards, and grew to be almost six feet tall. Then it was as if two sets of invisible hands were sculpting statues of two great prophets out of a cloud-like material, called ectoplasm.

An immense amount of psychic energy is needed to form one pillar of cloud, let alone two. When the process was complete, the two ectoplasmic men, Moses and Elijah, began conversing with Jesus! As the students watched this drama unfold, in this rather remote mountainous area, they actually thought they had to be dreaming. How could this possibly be real? Moses had been dead for 1,482 years and Elijah for 928 years.[398] Yet, they had materialized right before their eyes, and were talking with their teacher. Incredibly, they were *very much alive!*

As their doubt began fading, a grand realization permeated their souls— all that Jesus had taught them was true! They now had tangible proof! Can you imagine the joy and exultation these three disciples felt as they witnessed this most fantastic séance, between three of Judaism's most famous leaders? This event would forever change their lives. Gone would be all doubt that life continues after the change known as death. Here these two long-dead prophets were talking to the disciple's Master, Jesus. There had always been a shadow of doubt in the minds of Peter, James, and John, whether or not Jesus was really in communication with these two prophets on a daily basis. For Jesus had often told them he clairaudiently heard Moses' and Elijah's voices. Now Peter, James and John, had absolute proof that Jesus had told them the truth!

However, the thrill of the moment faded when the disciples heard the content of the conversation. Moses and Elijah were describing the events that were about to take place; Jesus would be arrested, scorned and crucified. The two Spirit entities also reminded Jesus that he could raise the vibration of his spiritual body, so he could escape feeling much of the physical pain his body would have to endure.

Moses and Elijah arranged this séance so Jesus' three students could witness the *gift of materialization*. Jesus had taught all his students about the *Gifts of the Spirit*. His students had learned their lessons well, which is why

---

[398] Sprague, E. W. Rev. *All the Spiritualism of the Christian Bible and the Scripture Directly Opposing It.* Detroit, MI: (self-published), 1992. p. 249.

Peter suggested building a tabernacle, (which some Bible translate as tent,)[399] which you would call a cabinet, in your present time. Peter understood that in most cases a cabinet is needed for the *gift of materialization* to take place.[400]

It was appropriate that Elijah and Moses were Jesus' Spirit teachers. For Jesus demonstrated all of the *Gifts of the Spirit*. He was the only Biblical prophet to do so. On the other hand, Moses and Elijah had also demonstrated many of the *Gifts of the Spirit* when they lived on your earth plane. Moses was clairaudient and clairvoyant when he heard, and saw his Spirit teacher at the Burning Bush.[401] Moses demonstrated dowsing when he struck the rock and water gushed forth.[402] Moses attended a materialization séance, where his student, Joshua, was this medium. This allowed Moses to speak "*... to God face to face as a man speaks with his friend.*"[403] This was what Moses was doing at the present moment, when he was speaking with Jesus. Moses demonstrated trumpet mediumship when the voice of the Lord (Spirit) spoke through the trumpet and told the Ten Commandments to all the Hebrews.[404] The Ten Commandments were written with Moses as the medium, utilizing the *gift of automatic writing*. The Bible describes the stone tablets as "*the writing of God, engraved upon the tablets,*"[405] written by the finger of God.[406]

Elijah was also clairaudient when he heard "*a still small voice*" in the cave.[407] He demonstrated the *gift of apports* when he multiplied the food for the widow and her son,[408] the same gift that Jesus had demonstrated eight days before. Elijah also brought a boy back to life, through the *gift of healing*,[409] just as Jesus raised Lazarus.[410] Elijah used the *gift of thought transference* when he mentally changed the vibration of the water molecules contained in four jars of water to be poured on the sacrifice. This caused the water to change into lighter-fluid, which easily ignited the sacrifice.[411] Jesus used the same *gift of thought transference* when he changed the water in the stone jars into wine, at his only sister's wedding at Cana.[412]

---

[399] WESL, WYNNE, HAR, WAKE, KEN, ABU, JUSMI, SHAR, ROTH, WEY, PAN, MOFF, RIVER, WADE, SPEN, SWANN, OGD, WILL, KLLI, WEST, NOLI, NWT, CONF, JER, TEV, EB, ETR, MCORD, NCV, REC, GLT, COMP, GODWD, WEB.

[400] Matthew 17:4, Mark 9:5, Luke 9:33.

[401] Exodus 3:1- 4:17.

[402] Exodus 17:5-6.

[403] Exodus 33:11.

[404] Exodus 19:19.

[405] Exodus 32:15-16 [NEB].

[406] Exodus 31:18.

[407] 1 Kings 19:12 [KJV].

[408] 1 Kings 17:13-16.

[409] 1 Kings 17:17-24.

[410] John 11:44-45.

[411] 1 Kings 18:30-39.

[412] John 2:1-9.

My Second Encounter With An Angel

So between Moses and Elijah, the repertoire of their psychic gifts would almost be as complete as Jesus. Therefore, they could guide, and advise, Jesus in the demonstration of all of these gifts.

That certainly makes sense to me.

Jesus of Nazareth was the greatest medium that has ever lived, in all of history. He came to the world with one hundred percent of his brain operational; therefore, he was endowed with every one of the *Gifts of the Spirit*.

Here is a listing of how Jesus used each *Gift of the Spirit* and where it is found in the Bible.

Gift of the Spirit	When Jesus used the Gift	Verses of the Bible
Apports	Multiplying of Food	Matthew 14:14-21
Automatic Writing	Jesus with the Adulteress	John 8:2-11
Clairaudience	Sermon on the Mount	Matthew 5:1-17
Clairvoyance	Choosing the Disciples	Matthew 4:18-22
Direct Voice	Baptism of Jesus	Mark 1:9-11
Dowsing	Miraculous Catch of Fish	Luke 5:1-6
Dreams	Dream at 7 Years Old Flight Into Egypt	Aquarian Gospel[413] Chapt. 16:1-14 Matthew 2:13-14
Healing	Healing the People	Mark 1:21-32
Levitation	Walking on the Water	Matthew 14:22-28
Materialization	Mount of Transfiguration	Luke 9:28-36
Prophecy	Prophecy of the Temple Destruction	Matthew 24:1-2
Psychometry	Reading at the Well	John 4:4-24
Thought Transference	Wedding of Cana	John 2: 1-9
Trance	Mount of Transfiguration	Luke 9:28-36

Why did Jesus come to your world? It certainly was not to start a new religion, or be turned into a God. For Jesus, himself said:

> **"Do not imagine that I have come to abolish the Law or the Prophets. I have come not to abolish but to complete them."**[414]

Jesus did not come to your dimension to be a God, nor did he ever wish to be worshipped. Jesus came to your world to demonstrate, and teach, the *Gifts of the Spirit*. He came to the world as a reformer, teacher, and way-shower. Unfortunately, Jesus did not realize how much his psychic demonstrations disturbed the Jewish, and non-Jewish, priests of the Holy Land. This dynamic medium was eroding the priests' hold on the people. Jesus was a living

---

[413] Levi. *The Aquarian Gospel of Jesus the Christ*. Santa Monica, CA: DeVorss & Co., Publishers, 1907. p. 50.

[414] Matthew 5:17 [JER].

instrument of the Spirit. He clairaudiently heard Spirit's teachings, and repeated them to large numbers of people.

The Temple worship, and sacrificial services, had stagnated since all divine revelation from prophets had been excluded. New thoughts from the Spirit World were not forth coming. As a result, Jesus' lectures were drawing people away from the temple. Dwindling attendance put the priests' source of income in jeopardy. With fewer animal sacrifices, and a shrinking cash flow, the priests panicked. It had taken centuries to train the people to abandon their desire to speak directly to God through the prophets. Suddenly, a powerful prophet was infusing new ideas in the people's minds. This is why all the priests in the Holy Land, not just the Jewish priests, sought to have Jesus silenced.

Why was it so important for Jesus to demonstrate, and teach, the *Gifts of the Spirit*?

That is a good question, my scribe. The answer lies in the very name: *Gifts of the Spirit*. You must remember that Jesus taught:

> "God is spirit, and those who worship him must worship in spirit and truth."[415]

Yes, Awan, and the original Greek, and the Latin, said *Spirit is God*.

That is true, my scribe. The *Gifts of the Spirit* are manifestations of your divine nature, my scribe. Think about it. When Elijah,[416] Elisha,[417] and Jesus multiplied the food,[418] they were "creating" it. They were acting as a God, because it was their God (their soul,) who performed this gift. *Psychic phenomena* is your modern day term for the *Gifts of the Spirit*. Psychic means soul or mind. Therefore, we can call these gifts *Soul phenomena*. Since the soul is the divine spark of energy within each person, we could also call the gifts *Divine phenomena*. It would take a God to perform divine phenomena. So, each time that Jesus performed one of the *Gifts of the Spirit* he was not only proving that he was divine, but that *every human is divine!* Read the Bible story where Jesus explains to the Jews at the temple that "he and his Father were one."

After the trance session, I read the following verses:

> My Father and I are one.' Once again the Jews picked up stones to stone him. At this Jesus said to them, 'I have set before you many good *deeds*, done by my Father's power; for which of these would you stone me?' The Jews replied, 'We

---

[415] John 4:24 [RSV].

[416] 1 Kings 17:10-16.

[417] 2 Kings 4:1-7.

[418] Matthew 14:14-21.

> are not going to stone you for any good deed, but for your blasphemy. You, a mere man, claim to be a god.' Jesus answered, 'Is it not written in your own Law, "I said: You are gods"? Those are called gods to whom the word of God was delivered—and Scripture cannot be set aside. Then why do you charge me with blasphemy because I, consecrated and sent into the world by the Father, said, "I am God's son"?
>
> 'If I am not acting as my Father would, do not believe me. But if I am, accept the evidence of my *deeds*, even if you do not believe me, so that you may recognize and know that the Father is in me, and I in the Father.'
>
> This provoked them to one more attempt to seize him. But he escaped from their clutches.[419]

It is interesting that the translators of **NEB** describe the *Gifts of the Spirit* in verse 32 and 38 as *deeds*, while **KJV** uses *works*, and **NIV** uses *miracles*.

Many people did not understand what Jesus was attempting to teach. The concept of whether Jesus was the **Son of Man**, or the **Son of God**, was especially difficult.

That is a good point! Was Jesus the Son of Man, or the Son of God?

It is a very simple answer, my scribe, he was **both**. When Jesus was in his natural state, displaying his own personality, he was the **Son of Man**. The time when he went to the temple, threw an emotional temper tantrum, and overturned the money-changers' tables; he was being the **Son of Man**. His passionate temper was on display, as he created chaos at the temple.[420] Do you suppose that Jesus used the same part of his brain on that day that he used when he healed the sick, multiplied food, or walked on the water?

No, I don't think so.

That is correct. Jesus used another part of his brain when he performed the *Gifts of the Spirit*. When he did his Father's work, performing the *Gifts of the Spirit*, he was using the part of the brain, which communicates with the Spirit World, and was then the **Son of God**.

This was Jesus' mission when he came to your world. He wanted reawaken humanity's divinity. This is why Jesus said these words.

---

[419] John 10:30-39 [NEB].
[420] Matthew 21:12-13, John 2:14-16.

> "But I have greater witness than that of John for the works which the Father hath given me to finish, the same works that I do, bear witness of me that the Father hath sent me."[421]

(☉) Jesus explained that his works (the demonstrations of the *Gifts of the Spirit*) were accomplished because Jesus was a God. He continuously repeated this message:

> **I and my Father are one.**[422]
>
> "Do you not believe that I am in the Father, and the Father in me? I am not myself the source of the words I speak to you it is the Father who dwells in me doing His own work."[423]

(☉) Jesus explained that when he demonstrated the *Gifts of the Spirit*, he quieted his physical side, and allowed the divine side (the Father) to come forward and manifest this phenomena.

> "Believe me when I say that I am in the Father and the Father in me; or else accept the evidence of the deeds themselves."[424]

(☉) Jesus clearly stated that demonstration of the *Gifts of the Spirit* (psychic/soul/divine phenomena) was proof (evidence) that Jesus was a God. However, in his next statements Jesus confirmed that *every human* could also be a God.

> "In truth, in very truth I tell you, he who has faith in me will do what I am doing and he will do greater things still...."[425]
> Jesus answered them, Is it not written in your law, I said, Ye are gods?[426]

(☉) Jesus explained that he was not the only human who could be a God. It was humanity's birthright to be Gods, just as those humans who had built the pyramids centuries before. Everyone who could evolve, by reopening his or her brain to 100% capacity, would automatically regain his or her Godhood.

---

[421] John 5:36 [KJV].
[422] John 10:30 [KJV].
[423] John 14:10-12 [NEB].
[424] John 14:11 [NEB].
[425] John 14:11 [NEB].
[426] John 10:34 [KJV].

(👼) Unfortunately, Jesus failed miserably in his mission. Jesus began his ministry by demonstrating the *Gifts of the Spirit*. He continuously performed all of the Gifts. However, the people were so scientifically ignorant, they could not understand the *psychic science* behind the phenomena. This became frustrating to Jesus, and caused him to say:

> **Jesus therefore said to him, "Unless you people see signs and wonders, you simply *will not believe.*"**[427]

(👼) The people living two millenniums ago could not understand the concepts of *vibration* and *frequency*, as you can, my scribe. Then Jesus was prematurely silenced, before he could actually begin teaching the science behind the gifts.

(🧑) That really was unfortunate, Awan.

(👼) Yes, it was. However, Jesus' death did not deter him from attempting to complete his mission. Eventually, Jesus chose Saul (who changed his name to Paul), to become his medium. Before Paul's "First Encounter with Jesus" he was only interested in making money. However, after his life-altering experience on the road to Damascus, Paul allowed Jesus' spirit to work though his body. It was Jesus teaching through Paul's mediumship, the psychic science behind the *Gifts of the Spirit*.

(🧑) Yes, Awan, there is a discussion of the Gifts in 1 Corinthians 12. Then in 1 Corinthians 14 explains how a séance is to be conducted, where the prophets must take turns speaking. Paul even explains that everyone has a physical and spiritual (soul) body, which corresponds to the two worlds, in 1 Corinthians 15.

(👼) Yes, that is correct my scribe, but it was Jesus' words, not Paul's that are recorded in your Book of Books. Unfortunately, Jesus' message was lost, even to his disciples. People could not accept that they could be God. They did not even accept that God was within each human being.[428] Instead, the priests turned Jesus into a Savior-God, and buried his teachings under a pile of man-made dogmas and creeds. Then the priests enslaved the people, through fear, to accept their dogmas. This was highly ironic, since Jesus was trying to liberate humanity.

> **"And ye shall know the truth and the truth shall make you free."**[429]

---

[427] John 4:48 [NASB].
[428] Luke 17:21.
[429] John 8:32 [KJV].

I am sensing a shift in the energy, my scribe; therefore, I must withdraw at this time. Perhaps now you have a clearer understanding of יְהוֹשֻׁעַ בֶּן יֹסֵף (*Joshua ben Joseph*).

🧑 Yes, Awan, thank you so much for this valuable information.

👳 My peace be with you, my scribe.

🧑 Peace be with you too, Awan.

Carl was silent for about a minute, although I heard a change in the rhythm of his breathing. Then he coughed a few times. I handed him his water bottle, which he eagerly drank. This time, Carl seemed to have more energy. After we went to the house, Carl took a short nap.

TWENTY-TWO

The Circle of Life—Birth, Death, After-life

This trance session took place in Carl's office. Carl followed the same procedure, of darkening the room, then putting blindfolds over his eyes. After reciting his prayer, Carl was quiet for about four minutes, and his body did not spasm. Suddenly, Awan began to speak.

👼 My profound greetings to you, my scribe.

🧑 Greetings, Awan!

👼 I trust you are ready to continue your studies.

🧑 Yes, Awan, what are we going to discuss today?

👼 Understanding the *Circle of Life* is the next building block in constructing your knowingness system, my scribe. This would include understanding the processes of birth and death. Do you remember that Jesus taught through Saint Paul's mediumship that every person has two bodies?

🧑 Yes, Awan, I remember.

👼 There is a reason why you have two bodies. Saint Paul taught that you have a body for each dimension. You use the physical body in your dimension, and the spiritual body in my dimension. However, this was not exactly God's plan for the universe. When the infinite intelligence created human beings, S/He provided two separate bodies, but these bodies were designed for a different purpose.

You must remember, my scribe, the first human beings utilized 100% of their brain capacity. This meant that people in my dimension could communicate to humanity through their subconscious mind, which is part of the spiritual body. Spirit can transmit thoughts, which are detected by your subconscious mind. It is the subconscious mind that receives information from the *river of thought*. However, after the brain was shut down, new phenomena were created, you know them as **disease, aging** and **death**, all of which were not designed by God.

🧑 Awan, this is really interesting.

🧑‍🦱 Once a person's brain functioned less than 100%, his or her body is susceptible to disease, and eventually wears out. This ultimately forced the spiritual body, or soul, to abandon its physical body, because the physical body had become so aged, it could no longer provide the soul experiences through which to gain knowledge. When the spiritual body abandons the physical body, at death, its vibration immediately increases, as it enters my dimension, which is on a much higher frequency. Many people on your plane call the other dimension *Heaven*; others call it the *World of Spirit*. The name is unimportant.

🧑 So Heaven and the Spirit World are identical?

🧑‍🦱 That is correct. Let me change the subject for a moment. Suppose that you are planning a trip to the country you term Egypt. What would you need for such a journey? Would you need to make any preparations?

🧑 Yes, Awan, there would be many things I would have to do.

🧑‍🦱 Where would your preparations begin? Would you merely open your luggage, and fill it with the linens that you wear?

🧑 No, Awan, I don't think I would start that way.

🧑‍🦱 What would you do?

🧑 I would start planning my trip by consulting a travel agent.

🧑‍🦱 Why would you do that?

🧑 Because a travel agent is an expert on the subject of travel.

🧑‍🦱 During your consultation with your travel agent, you would learn that many items are required for your trip. You would need tickets for your airplane, and a valid passport to leave your country. The travel agent would advise you to get a visa to enter Egypt, and get certain injections to protect you from diseases found in that country. Without gathering all these articles, the Egyptian government might block your entrance at its border. You would have wasted much money on a plane ride to nowhere. So you see, the proper preparations are extremely important.

🧑 I guess that is all true. So what is the point?

🧑‍🦱 There are many people living in your dimension who believe that when they die they are going absolutely nowhere. They think that their physical body will be placed in the ground, and nothing else will happen. They believe that when you are dead, you are dead, asleep for eternity.

There are millions of people who would strongly disagree. They know that their Spirits live on after they die. Their Spirits travel to a special place where Jesus will be waiting. If Jesus is busy, then Saint Peter will be there to meet them. One of these two saints will review, and judge their lives. If they did many good deeds, then they will enter Heaven. If they were not such wonderful people, then their souls will enter Hell. All these people have been mislead, and are sadly mistaken.

Now my scribe, tell me, who will act as the travel agent for your journey to the Spirit World?

🙂 I suppose I would ask a rabbi.

(😇) Most people would think they should consult their priest, minister, or rabbi, for they are the people who are the experts in theology, religion and the Bible. Unfortunately, these are not the people who can provide you with the knowledge you are seeking. They might supply you with answers, but they would be "holey" answers, ones with half-truths.

In the last two thousand years, after their death, millions, even billions of people have become lost during their journey to my dimension. Why did this happen? The reason is simple. These misguided people listened, and believed, their religious leaders, who were considered experts about death, but did not have any **direct** knowledge about the Spirit World. Instead of preparing people for the transition called death, a journey everyone must make, the theologians simply put fear in their followers' minds about the Devil, Hell-fire, and brimstone. The clergy made Churches the tollgates on the road to Heaven.

🙂 Then who would be the right expert to consult?

(😇) The correct choice would be someone who could communicate with both this world and the next. One who has experienced death, and the after-life, in the Spirit World, and is able to describe their experiences to humanity. You are speaking to an expert right now, since I have repeatedly experienced death. I now reside in what you might term, the *World of Spirit*.

However, I cannot directly communicate with you. I need an instrument, or medium, to transmit my message to you. That instrument is one who has the *Gifts of the Spirit*. Read your Book of Books carefully, my scribe, and you will discover that Moses and Elijah both communicated with Jesus from my dimension.[430] It was Jesus' psychic abilities, which allowed him to receive this communication. Less than one hundred years later, Saul, later known as Paul, had a similar experience. This time it was Jesus himself who taught Paul about the *Gifts of the Spirit*, from my dimension.

Throughout history, there have always been a few people who have had the special abilities you term the *Gifts of the Spirit*. It is through these gifted people that you can gain this information.

🙂 Yes, Awan that makes sense. Since you live in the Spirit World, you have experienced death. You would be the perfect person to describe the after-life to me.

(😇) If you were going to Egypt you would need a passport. There is only one passport that you need on your journey to the Spirit World. That passport consists of **knowledge**. Death is actually a journey into another world,

---

[430] Luke 9:28-33.

another existence. Just as you would need to do some research before you took a trip to Egypt, you need certain knowledge to make a safe trip to the Spirit World.

At death, you once again take up residence in your spiritual, or soul body, which is made up of energy. As you enter into the Spirit World, you must leave behind many things. You cannot take any of your physical belongings, your accumulated wealth, or even your physical body. All that you take with you is your soul, which contains all the recorded knowledge of the experiences you have gleaned through your lifetime.

This is why *knowledge is the passport to my kingdom*. Whatever you do with your life on earth, whatever you build or make of yourself, you will arrive in the Spirit World with the same talents, the same understandings, or the same misconceptions. For example, if you believe that when you die, you are dead, and there is no after-life, you will arrive in my dimension and sleep for eternity.

If you believe that Jesus, or Saint Peter, will judge your physical life, and tell you to go to Heaven or to Hell, then when you get to my plane of existence, you will also go to sleep. You will be awakened from time to time by people in my dimension, but if they do not resemble Jesus, or Saint Peter, as you envision them, you will simply roll over, and go back to sleep.

If your clergy successfully taught you that the diabolical Satan can impersonate anyone,[431] then you would ignore the Spirits of your loved ones who will come to try to teach you more about the Spirit World. You will think that the Devil is impersonating your relative, and will roll over and go back to sleep. Therefore, you will sleep for eternity, waiting for the arrival of a person who resembles the image of Jesus that was in your church, because neither Jesus nor Saint Peter has any intention of judging anyone.

If, during your lifetime, you concluded that religions were all man-made, and the dogmas that they preach were created by man, not inspired by God, then when you arrive in the Spirit World you will have a wonderful after-life.

There are many levels in my dimension. It is like a ladder that you can climb, and progress, as your soul evolves in knowledge. You will enter at the level that you are prepared for. You make your preparations in your world, not mine. Therefore, the more information you learn, the more evolved you become in your dimension, the higher your level of evolution will be in the Spirit World.

This concept of *knowledge being the passport into forever* is found in your Book of Books. Jesus taught this concept to the people living in your world, but his message was misunderstood. However, instead of using the word *passport*, he talked about the *keys to Heaven*.

📖 After this dialogue, I again studied this verse.

---

[431] 2 Corinthians 11:14.

> **"I will give you the *keys of the kingdom of Heaven*; what you forbid on earth shall be forbidden in Heaven, and what you allow on earth shall be allowed in Heaven."**[432]

📖 This time it had new meaning for me. According to Awan's interpretation, *the keys of the kingdom* that Jesus mentioned were knowledge. The beliefs that you hold in this world will determine your after-life. That is what Jesus meant when he said, **"What you allow [learn] on earth shall be allowed in Heaven."**

🧑 I think I understand.

😇 Good. Now my scribe, we will begin discussing the circle of life. A circle, as you know, has no beginning and no end. Let me to ask you a question.

🧑 OK, Awan. Ask your question.

😇 In your opinion, when do you think life begins?

🧑 That is a good question. Some people think it begins at conception of a baby, and some believe life begins at birth.

😇 Neither one is the truth. Life begins between the ninety-sixth and the one hundred eleventh day after conception. Allow me to explain. After a man and woman come together and conceive a child, the fetus begins growing inside the mother's womb. This fetus will be the physical body of the child. At this point the fetus is like the kidney, liver, or any other organ of the mother's body. It is identical to the mother, and part of her. At some point between the ninety-sixth and the one hundred and eleventh day after conception, a Spirit, or soul, enters into the baby's little body. As the soul begins to enter the fetus, it has to lower its frequency. The moment the soul enters the fetus the child's body becomes animated, and kicks the mother. That is when a new life has started, when the soul enters the fetus' body. Now there are two souls inhabiting the mother's body, the first is the mother's soul, the second is the baby's soul.

A special symbiotic relationship exists between an expectant mother and her unborn child, for they are joined as one. The umbilical cord connects the child's body to the mother's, and serves as the unborn child's lifeline, bringing food and oxygen to the developing child.

Nine months after conception, the baby is fully developed within the mother. It is now time for the baby to make its grand entrance into the physical world. Usually the family knows the approximate date of the baby's arrival, and makes all sorts of preparations. People give gifts to the mother: baby clothes, cribs, and other small furniture. Distant relatives may travel to welcome the child into your world.

Moments after the baby's birth, its umbilical cord is severed, separating the child from its mother. The child now becomes an independent being, who lives and breathes as a separate individual. The child's invisible body, its

---

[432] Matthew 16:19 [NEB].

Spirit, is now functioning on a slower, physical, vibrational rate. The baby's soul is now connected to its physical body by an invisible silver cord.

👤 So life really begins between the ninety-sixth and the one hundred eleventh day after conception.

😇 Yes. After conception, there is a change in the mother's aura. This change is caused by the soul or Spirit of the new child remaining close to the body of the mother, in her auric field. Sometime between the ninety-sixth and the one hundred eleventh day, the soul of the baby enters the mother's body through the mother's solar plexus. The soul enters the chest of the fetus, where it takes up residence. You understand that the soul is spiritual body. It is a body of light, or energy.

👤 Yes Awan, I understand that.

😇 The aura is the light that emanates from the soul. It is the soul's reflection. All the person's thoughts and experiences are recorded in the soul, and are reflected out though the light of the soul. A person, who has second sight, or clairvoyant vision, can see the aura, or the soul's light. That person can also see specific conditions of the body, and sometimes the emotions that the person is experiencing, since they are reflected from the soul into this light around the person's body.

After a woman conceives, the color of her aura changes from off-white to a rose-gold. This change in color announces that a new vehicle (baby) is becoming available. When a soul, living in the Spirit World, has evolved to a point that he or she needs to acquire more knowledge, by living in the physical world, it will gravitate to the mother's rose-gold aura. That Spirit will stay in the mother's aura, outside her physical body, for about ninety-five days. It is busy supervising the developing fetus. Remember *thought*, *Spirit*, and the *soul* are energy. The Spirit that will reside in the baby is making sure that its new physical home, the body of the baby, will be perfect. The Spirit is quite powerful, because it is still vibrating at its full spiritual vibration. Between the ninety-sixth and the one hundred eleventh day, the Spirit decides to inhabit the baby. It then lowers its frequency, entering the fetus, and takes its residence in a cavity behind the breastbone, in center of the baby's chest. At this point, the soul looses access to much of its spiritual knowledge. As the soul enters the little body, the baby kicks for the first time, because the soul is the energy, which animates the body. That is the day when life begins. The baby will keep kicking, until its body adjusts to the new energy field, which is its soul.

👤 That is very interesting.

😇 I hope that you understand that it is the Spirit body or soul that instills life into the child, and keeps its body alive. There is a second cord that connects a baby's soul to his or her physical body, and it is known as *the silver cord*.

Now are you ready to learn about the process of death?

🧑 Yes, Awan please proceed.

👼 There comes a time when the soul really wants to leave the body. This can happen for several reasons.

1. The soul has accomplished what it set out to do when it reincarnated. In other words, it has gathered the experiences that it wanted to learn.
2. The soul could be bored, because the person is not learning the experiences that it had desired when it came to your plane of existence.
3. The body may have grown very old and is no longer working properly.

Despite the reason, the soul innately knows that it cannot function in its own body of light until it leaves, and is totally disconnected from the physical body.

It will be easier for you to comprehend, if I use a specific example. Let us say that it is time for Jane's soul to leave her body. She had been suffering from cancer for a long time. As the process of death begins, Jane's soul begins to count the breaths that are left. When it reaches the last five breaths, the eyes of Jane's soul open and see the light at the end of a tunnel. The light would be at the top, or crown, of her head. It was the same location of the soft spot of her head when Jane was first born; where the bone was not yet solidified. Do you understand so far?

🧑 Yes, I do.

👼 The eyes of Jane's soul see this light at the end of the tunnel, and go toward it. That is what it is for. It is natural. Her soul is drawn through this tunnel, which takes it to the top of the skull. This is the doorway that the soul uses to leave the body at death. Jane's soul goes through the doorway, at the crown of the head, and pulls away from her physical body. Sometimes physicians are clairvoyant, and see the soul leaving out of the top of the head. They can see this out of the corner of their eye. When they turn their heads, their eyes go through it, and they think they are imagining it.

🧑 Awan, I don't understand, why is it easier to see the Spirit body out of the corner of the eye?

👼 This may be a bit difficult for you to understand, my scribe. When you look directly at a Spirit, you look right through it. Your peripheral vision is not as strong. Therefore, you see the Spirit, instead of looking through it.

It is similar to an extremely hot summer day. Sometimes you can see the heat rising off in the distance. Yet when you come closer to that specific spot, you no longer see the heat waves. This is the only way I can describe it to you.

🧑 OK Awan. I think I understand.

👼 As the soul pulls away from the physical body, ***the silver cord*** pulls apart like an overcooked piece of spaghetti. When the soul is approximately 14 inches from Jane's body, *the silver cord* snaps. In a sense, Jane's soul is being born again. Jane has arrived in a new world, in a new body, and a cord was severed. Jane has experienced a second birth, which was actually her death. This is the true meaning of Jesus' words:

> **Verily, verily, I say unto thee, except a man be born again, he cannot see the kingdom of God.**[433]

Jesus was trying to explain that death is not the end of life, but actually a second birth, into a new world. He was not describing some dogmatic, theological process that a human being must go through. It would not matter if Jane were a Baptist, Presbyterian, Lutheran, Catholic, Muslim, Jew, Buddhist, Shinto, Taoist, Confuciusian, Hindu, or a member of any other religion. Death has nothing to do with religion. No physical person can enter the Spirit World, which Jesus called "the Kingdom of God," in his physical body. To enter the Spirit World, one must go through a second birth, enter a new world, in a new body, and experience the severing of a second, silver cord, which caused the death of the physical body.

This is so fascinating! Why doesn't everyone know about this?

Who says that most people don't know about this? It is written in your Book of Books. Later, when I am out of this man's body, look for a discussion about *the silver cord* and *golden bowl*.

I later discovered this Bible verse.

> **Or even the silver cord be loosed, or the golden bowl be broken, or the pitcher be broken at the fountain, or the wheel broken at the cistern. Then shall the dust return to the earth as it was; and the spirit shall return unto God who gave it.**[434]

The *golden bowl* is the physical body. Death is like taking a bottle of fine wine, pouring the wine out into a new vessel, and breaking the original bottle.

Was the *golden bowl*, the light of the aura for those people who could see it?

That is correct. You must remember that the image of Jane's body was recorded, and held in memory in her soul. When *the silver cord* snapped, Jane instantly found herself standing in a new, spiritual body made of light. This body is a replica of the physical body she just left, with a few minor differences. Jane's new spiritual body would resemble her physical body as it looked when she was twenty to twenty-three years old. Also, her new body

---

[433] John 3:3 [KJV].
[434] Ecclesiastes 12:6-7 [KJV].

has no sense of taste or smell. The eyes of Jane's spiritual body can see colors that the physical body cannot see. Have you ever looked through a prism?

🧑 Yes, there seems to be a rainbow attached to everything.

👼 Yes, that is true. What Jane sees through spiritual eyes is similar to looking through a prism. It does not appear the same, but she experiences the same wonderment. The colors are so extremely different, that I do not have the words to describe them.

Jane is now in ecstasy, since her new body has no pain. Jane is standing, looking at all the different colors she was previously unable to see, feeling very "high" as you term it. Yet, Jane has not realized that she has died. She does not have any idea that she left the physical body because she feels that she is dreaming, or imagining it. Regardless, Jane does not want to wake up, and haave this dream end.

Jane is still in the very room where she has died, but she has been too occupied studying all the colors, and feeling so wonderful, that she has not yet made that discovery. Eventually, Jane becomes more aware of her surroundings. As she looks around the room, she starts to study everything in it. She notices members of her own family who are very upset. Some of these relatives are hysterically crying. Then Jane notices a body in a bed. She walks over to look at it. A sudden shock runs through her body as she realizes, "My God, that looks like me." She reaches out and touches the body with her hand. Jane's hand goes right through the body; the hand of her new body is a hand of energy. So, to her new body, Jane's physical body no longer exists. Jane does her best to tell her relatives, "I'm fine. Don't worry about me." No matter how hard she tries, she cannot make her relatives hear her. Now Jane is even more convinced she is dreaming. After taking inventory of the room, seeing the physical body, and not being able to talk to her relatives, she eventually touches the wall. Again, her hand goes through the wall. This further convinces Jane that she is dreaming.

Over in the distance, what you would term "out of her focus," there would be a group of people, observing Jane as she arrives. Jane has not paid any attention to these people, because they are somewhat out of her focus. After Jane touched the body, and wall, and has taken inventory of everything, she becomes confused. It is now that this group of people slowly approaches Jane. Someone, usually one in front, the spokesperson, has his or her arms outstretched. Suddenly, Jane recognizes this group of people as loved ones who have preceded Jane into the Spirit World. There are many great embraces during this grand reunion.

Death is an anticipated event, although it may not seem that way in your dimension. Jane's family who preceded her into the physical world greeted Jane when she was born in her new physical body. The same family members gathered to greet Jane in her new Spirit body, as she arrives in the Spirit World. The members of her family say to Jane, "We have much to show you. We are glad that you have finally arrived."

Jane reacts quite inquisitively, "What do you mean?"

Her group of relatives reply, "Don't you realize that was **your** physical body back there. You have left it."

"You mean I am dead?" asks Jane in a state of utter amazement.

"Yes, your physical body is dead, but **you** are not dead. You are more alive than ever!" they reply.

They take Jane for a tour, in this kingdom that is vibrating so much faster than your own. In a matter of moments they are vibrating even higher, to the point that Jane is no longer in tune with her physical relatives. Jane and the people who came to greet her, are in another dimension. The first thing that Jane learns, if she desires, is how to communicate with her own family and friends, back in the physical world. The first method they use is the dream state. Then Jane can return in her relatives' dreams to let them know that she is alive and well in a higher dimension.

I see.

But Jane has to have the desire to do so. You must remember, when a person passes over and goes through all the steps that I have just explained to you, they are in ecstasy. Since they are in a timeless dimension, they may not be too anxious to reach back and bother with the vibration that they have just left. To them it is like being on holiday, or vacation, on a paradise island. Usually, the person does not communicate with his or her own relatives for quite sometime. Jane's death experience was described in your Book of Books.

It was?

When this session is over, look into your Book of Books and read about Abraham's death. You will find that Abraham's relatives came to greet him when he died.

After the session I did as Awan advised, and read about Abraham's death in the Bible.

> **Then Abraham** *gave up the ghost*, **and died in a good old age, an old man and full of years:** *and was gathered to his people.*[435]

The phrase *was gathered to his people* described exactly what Awan had said. The family members of the newly arrived Spirit came to gather and meet their relative. I also found it interesting that this Bible described death in such an accurate way: ***then Abraham gave up the ghost***. I then discovered that the Geneva Bible was even more accurate.

---

[435] Genesis 25:8 [KJV].

> **Then Abraham *yielded the spirit*, and died in a good age, an old man and of great years, and was gathered to his people.**[436]

📖 I used a *concordance*, a book which indexes each word in the Bible, and discovered that besides, Abraham, the following people *were gathered to their people*: Isaac,[437] Jacob,[438] Aaron,[439] Moses,[440] and a whole generation.[441]

The following is a list of people who *slept with their fathers*: David,[442] Jeroboam,[443] Abijam,[444] Baasha,[445] Joram,[446] Joash,[447] Jehoash,[448] Menahem,[449] Ahaz,[450] Hezekiah,[451] Manasseh,[452] Jehoiakim,[453] Rehoboam,[454] Abijah,[455] Asa,[456] Jehoshaphat,[457] and Uzziah.[458]

👼 Thousands of years ago, a person experiencing euphoria after their death labeled it *Heaven*, because there were no other words to describe it. Make no mistake; this person who has just left the physical body is not in some palace in the mythical, magical piece of real estate in the sky. They are simply in a new body, one vibrating at a higher rate in the very room where they experienced death. Do you understand?

🧑 Yes, Awan, I understand.

👼 Most people who enter my dimension are extremely happy. They are with other wonderful people, and their relatives and friends. Most are very

---

[436] Genesis 25:8 [GEN].
[437] Genesis 35:29 [KJV].
[438] Genesis 49:33 [KJV].
[439] Numbers 20:24 [KJV].
[440] Deuteronomy 32:50 [KJV].
[441] Judges 2:10 [KJV].
[442] 1 Kings 2:10 [KJV].
[443] 1 Kings 14:20 [KJV].
[444] 1 Kings 15:8 [KJV].
[445] 1 Kings 16:6 [KJV].
[446] 2 Kings 8:24 [KJV].
[447] 2 Kings 13:13 [KJV].
[448] 2 Kings 14:16 [KJV].
[449] 2 Kings 15:22 [KJV].
[450] 2 Kings 16:20 [KJV].
[451] 2 Kings 20:21 [KJV].
[452] 2 Kings 21:18 [KJV].
[453] 2 Kings 24:6 [KJV].
[454] 2 Chronicles 12:16 [KJV].
[455] 2 Chronicles 14:1 [KJV].
[456] 2 Chronicles 16:13 [KJV].
[457] 2 Chronicles 21:1 [KJV].
[458] 2 Chronicles 26:23 [KJV].

relieved to discover they are not in a place of punishment. It is religions that created such horrifying images of death.

I sense a change in the energy. I believe that you have enough to ponder for a while, so I will now withdraw from this body. My deepest blessings to you.

Thank you Awan, I have learned a great deal from our conversation today.

After about forty-five seconds, Carl's body convulsed twice, and he began to cough. He seemed more thirsty than usual, and drank two glasses of water. He complained of being extremely tired, and slept for three and a half hours.

TWENTY-THREE

Understanding Reincarnation—Repeating the Circle of Life

It was nearly a month before my next opportunity to speak with Awan. When the day finally arrived, Carl complained that he did not sleep well the night before. I thought that might make it difficult for him to go into trance. Carl began his preparations for going into trance by closing his eyes, and saying his prayer. I was surprised, however, because the transition seemed to be very smooth, and very rapid.

My profound greetings, to you my scribe!

Greetings, Awan.

God, the infinite thought, or infinite intelligence of the universe, who was the creator of all, did not put human beings on the planet for only one short life. Study all the wonders of nature, which surround you. You will discover the many circles, or cycles, of life.

In the spring, little green buds grow upon all the limbs of the trees. These buds grow and mature into wonderful green leaves, which help to feed the tree. When autumn arrives, the leaves have served their purpose. After transforming into a blazing blast of brilliant colors, the leaves wither and die. The trees remain dormant for the winter. In spring, the cycle begins anew and buds again grow on the trees.

Not only is this pattern repeated every year but it occurs in all species of plants. Other cycles also exist in nature. Are you familiar with the water cycle? The clouds release their rain, which falls on the earth, eventually evaporates, returns into the atmosphere, and reforms into clouds again.

Yes, Awan, I am familiar with the water cycle.

So what makes you think that animals and human beings would not also fall within this same pattern? A child is born, matures into adulthood, reproduces, ages, dies, and after spending time in the Spirit World will reincarnate as a child again. It would be a complete circle, just as the trees, flowers, and water.

🙎 I can understand what you are saying, but it is still difficult for me to accept.

😇 Yes, my scribe, you have had thousands of years of religious programming which contradicts reincarnation. Just like the *Gifts of the Spirit*, reincarnation threatened the priests' control over the people.

🙎 Come on, Awan. How could that be?

😇 The Church wants the people to believe two basic concepts. The first one is that people *only have one life*. The second is that the Church holds the one, and only one, ticket to get to heaven. The Church teaches that if you are good, and you obey Church rules, then you will receive your reward in my dimension of life. They try to make you believe that Heaven is "upstairs." However, now you understand that heaven is simply a higher vibration, not higher elevation.

Reincarnation provides an opportunity to ignore the Church's rules. You could have a grand time committing as many "sins" as you wished. Even if you spent some time in "hell," you would receive a second chance. In your second life you could live a more saintly life, and go to heaven. Reincarnation would allow you to live beyond the control of the Church. Therefore, the Church eradicated all teachings of reincarnation from Christianity.

🙎 Wait a minute, Awan! Are you saying that reincarnation was once part of Christianity?

😇 Yes my scribe, that is precisely what I am saying. There were many concepts, reincarnation being one of them, that were deliberately taken out of the Bible between the 4th and the 7th centuries. After this session, return to your libraries and you will discover the truth of my teaching.

📖 A few weeks later, I found Helen Greaves's book *Testimony of Light* on a library's shelf. It is based on information that she received clairaudiently from Sister Frances Banks, who entered the World of Spirit on November 2, 1965. Canon J. D. Pearce-Higgins, Vice-Chairman of the Churches' Fellowship for Psychical and Spiritual Studies wrote the Preface of this book. In it he documents how the Church removed reincarnation from their doctrines.

> "I have been asked to comment on the fact that Frances occasionally refers to Reincarnation, since such references may be a stumbling-block to Christian readers, few of whom, unless they are scholars, probably are aware that <u>there was a 500-year tradition of such belief *within* the early Church itself</u>; mainly in the Alexandrian school, including such names as Clement, Justin Martyr, St. Gregory of Nyssa, and most notable of all Origen, who had a well worked out reincarnational system of belief, which certainly makes sense, and avoids many of the objectionable features of oriental versions. Further, it is far from clear that the Church

ever officially rejected such belief, however little the medieval mind was able to contain it. The Council of Constantinople in a A.D. 553, at which it seems that a corrupt form of Origen's teaching was anathematized, is held by many historians to have been imperfectly constituted — the Pope himself refused to be present — and even Roman Catholics contest its validity as a General Council."[459]

📖 H. Ernest Hunt provides us with the Council's condemnation:

"Whosoever shall support the mythical doctrine of pre-existence of the soul and the consequent wonderful opinion of its return, let him be anathema."[460]

📖 Here we have clear proof that early "Church fathers" believed in *reincarnation*. Origen's teachings deviated from newly written, official Church doctrine, and were eventually anathematized, or declared invalid. Reincarnation was eliminated from Church doctrine because it weakened the Church's stranglehold on the people's minds.

👼 You do realize, my scribe that reincarnation is in the Bible?

🧑 No way, Awan. You must be mistaken this time.

👼 No my scribe, I am not mistaken. The word *reincarnation* is not actually in the Bible, but the concept is. After this session study the books of Jeremiah and Job. Then examine what with Jesus said, and Herod thought about John the Baptist.

📖 Over the course of the next few months, I found several Bible verses, which would support the claim that people living in Biblical times accepted reincarnation. The concept of the pre-existence of the soul before birth, is clearly stated. Spirit explains this to Jeremiah:

"Before I formed you in the womb I knew you, before you were born I set you apart; I appointed you as a prophet to the nations."[461]

📖 This very clearly states that Spirit knew the soul of Jeremiah before it incarnated into the physical world. In was pre-ordained that Jeremiah be born with the *Gifts of the Spirit*, because his mission was to be Spirit's medium, known as a prophet in Biblical times.

---

[459] Pearce-Higgins, J. D., Cannon, M.A., Hon. C. F. *Preface.* [in] Greaves, Helen. *Testimony of Light.* Essex, England: Neville Spearman Publishers, 1985. p. 9-10.

[460] Hunt, H. Ernest. *Reincarnaton in the Bible.* London: No publisher listed, n.d. p. 3.

[461] Jeremiah 1:5 [NIV].

📖 This next verse is very puzzling unless one accepts reincarnation. This is Job's reaction when he learns that most of his children were killed in an accident.

> **Then Job arose and tore his robe and shaved his head, and he fell to the ground and worshiped. And he said, "Naked I came from my mother's womb, And naked I shall return there. The LORD gave and the LORD has taken away. Blessed be the name of the LORD."**[462]

📖 The phrase: *And naked I shall return there*, refers to his mother's womb not the World of Spirit. There is only one way for this verse to make sense. Job had to be talking about reincarnation. To reincarnate back into the world, one returns to the womb, and is again naked when one is born.

📖 According to Jewish custom, bodies are always buried in shrouds, or white gowns. Mediums who see Spirit people, never describe them as naked. They are usually wearing a shroud, or appear in specific clothing, which helps to establish their identity. Reincarnation is the only plausible explanation for this verse.

📖 Now let's turn our attention to the New Testament.

> Now when Jesus had finished instructing his twelve disciples, he went on from there to teach and proclaim his message in their cities.
>
> When John heard in prison what the Messiah was doing, he sent word by his disciples and said to him, "Are you the one who is to come, or are we to wait for another?"
>
> Jesus answered them, "Go and tell John what you hear and see: the blind receive their sight, the lame walk, the lepers are cleansed, the deaf hear, the dead are raised, and the poor have good news brought to them. And blessed is anyone who takes no offense at me."
>
> As they went away, Jesus began to speak to the crowds about John: "What did you go out into the wilderness to look at? A reed shaken by the wind? What then did you go out to see? Someone dressed in soft robes? Look, those who wear soft robes are in royal palaces. What then did you go out to see? A prophet? Yes, I tell you, and more than a prophet. This is the one about whom it is written, 'See, I am sending my messenger ahead of you, who will prepare your way before you.' Truly I tell you, among those born of

---

[462] Job 1:20-21 [NASB].

women no one has arisen greater than John the Baptist; yet the least in the kingdom of heaven is greater than he.

From the days of John the Baptist until now the kingdom of heaven has suffered violence, and the violent take it by force. For all the prophets and the law prophesied until John came; and if you are willing to accept it, he is Elijah who is to come. Let anyone with ears listen![463]

📖 Jesus was stating very clearly, that John was Elijah.

And if ye will receive it, this is *Elias*, which was for to come. He that hath ears to hear, let him hear.[464]

📖 It is the author's contention the Church deliberately used different names for Elijah in the Old and New Testaments, to help camouflage the fact that Elijah had reincarnated as John the Baptist. Many Bibles use *Elias*, which is the Greek name for Elijah in the New Testament, while using *Elijah* in the Old Testament.

ELIJAH IN THE OLD & NEW TESTAMENTS

Different Names

#	Abrev.	Date	1 Kings 19:13 [OT]	Matt. 17:10 [NT]
1	EWYC	1384	The which thing when **Helias** had heard, he covered his cheer with a mantle.	And his disciples asked him saying, What therefore said scribes, that it behoveth **Hely** first come.
2	LWYC	1395	And when **Elie** had heard this, he hid his face with a mantle.	And his disciples asked him, and said, What then said scribes, that it behoveth that **Elie** come first.
3	TYND	1534	And when **Eliah** heard it, he covered his face with his mantle.	Why then say the scribes, that **Elias** must first come.
4	COV	1535	Why say the scribes then, that **Elias** must first come.	When **Elias** heard that he covered his face with his cloak.
5	TAV	1539	And when **Elijah** heard it, he covered his face with his mantle.	And his disciples asked him saying: Why then say the scribes, that **Hely** must first come.

---

[463] Matthew 11-1-15 [NRSV].
[464] Matthew 11:14-15 [KJV].

6	GRT	1540	And when **Elia** heard, he covered his face with his mantle.	And his disciples asked him saying: Why then say the scribes, that **Helias** must first come.
7	MATT	1549	And when **Eliah** heard it, he covered his face with his mantle.	And his disciples asked him saying: Why then say the Scribes, that **Helpas** must first come?
8	GEN	1560	Why then say the Scribes that **Elias** must first come.	And when **Eliiah** heard it, covered his face with his mantle.
9	BISH	1568	And when **Elias** heard, he covered his face with his mantle.	And his disciples asked him saying: Why then say the scribes, that **Elias** must first come.
10	DOU RHEIM	1582	Which when **Elias** had heard, he covered his face with his mantle.	And his disciples asked him, saying, Why then say the scribes then, that **Elias** must come first?
11	KJV	1611	And it was so, when **Elijah** heard it, that he wrapped his face in his mantle.	And his disciples asked him, saying, Why then say the Scribes that **Elias** must first come?
12	HAAK	1657	And it came to pass when **Elia** heard, that he wrapped his face in his mantle.	And his Disciples asked him, saying; Why then do the scribes say that **Elias** must first come?
13	CHAL	1750	Which when **Elias** heard it, he covered his face with his mantle.	And his disciples asked him, saying: Why then do the scribes say that **Elias** must come first?
14	PUR	1764	With that his Disciples thus asked him, Why then do the Scribes say, that **Elias** must come first?	This when **Elijah** heard, he wrapt his Face in his Cloak.
15	CLEM	1790	And when **Elias** heard it, he covered his face with his mantle.	And his disciples asked him, saying, "Why then say the scribes that **Elias** must come first?"
16	RAY	1799	Which **Elijah** hearing, he wrapped his face in his mantle.	And his disciples asked him, saying, Why then say the scribes that **Elias** must first come?
17	THOM	1808	When **Elias** heard, he covered his face with his mantle.	Then his disciples asked him, saying, Why then do the Scribes say, that **Elias** must come first?

18	BOTR	1824	And, when *Elijah* heard this he wrapped his face in his mantle.	And his disciples asked him, saying, "Why then say the Scribes that *Elijah* must come first?"
19	WEBR	1841	And it was so, when *Elijah* heard it, that he wrapped his face in his mantle.	And his disciples asked him, saying, Why then say the scribes that *Elias* must first come?
20	KEN	1860	And his disciples asked him, saying: Why then do the scribes say that *Elias* must first come?	And when *Elias* heard it, he covered his face with his mantle.
21	YNG	1863	And it cometh to pass, at *Elijah*'s hearing it, that he wrappeth his face in his robe.	And his disciples questioned him, saying, 'Why then do the scribes say that is necessary that *Elijah* indeed cometh first.'
22	SMITH	1867	And it was so, when *Elijah* heard it, that he wrapped his face in his mantle.	And his disciples asked him, saying unto them, Why then say the Scribes that *Elias* must first come?
23	JUSMI	1876	And it will be when *Elijah* heard, he will cover his face in his large cloak.	And his disciples asked him, saying, Why then say the scribes that *Elias* must first come?
24	CAMB	1879	And it was so, when *Elijah* heard it, that he wrapped his face in his mantle.	And his disciples asked him, saying, Why then say the scribes that *Elias* must first come?
25	ERV	1885	And it was so, when *Elijah* heard it, that he wrapped his face in his mantle.	And his disciples asked him, saying, Why then say the scribes that *Elijah* must first come?
26	SHAR	1892	And the disciples asked him, saying; 'Why then say the Scribes that *Elijah* must first come?'	And it was so, when *Elijah* heard it, that he wrapped his face in his mantle.
27	ROTH	1897	And the disciples questioned him, saying— Why then do the Scribes say, That *Elijah* must needs come first?	And it came to pass when *Elijah* heard it he wrapped his face in his mantle.
28	YLT	1898	and it cometh to pass, at *Elijah*'s hearing [it], that he wrappeth his face in his robe,	And his disciples questioned him, saying, 'Why then do the scribes say that *Elijah* it behoveth to come first?'

29	ASV	1901	And it was so, when **Elijah** heard it, that he wrapped his face in his mantle.	And his disciples asked him, saying, Why then say the scribes that **Elijah** must first come?
30	CENT	1904	And it was so, when **Elijah** heard it, that he wrapped his face in his mantle.	And his disciples asked him, saying, Why then say the scribes that **Elias** must first come?
31	MORD	1912	And it was so, when **Elijah** heard it, that he wrapped his face in his mantle.	And his disciples asked him, saying, Why then say the scribes that **Elijah** must first come?
32	DARBY	1920	And [his] disciples demanded of him saying, Why then say the scribes that **Elias** must first have come?	And it came to pass when **Elijah** heard it, that he wrapped his face in his mantle.
33	FENT	1922	His disciples then asked Him, "Why do the professors then say that **Elijah** must come first?"	And when **Eliah** heard that he covered his face with his mantle.
34	MOFF	1922	The disciples inquired of him, "Then why do the scribes say the **Elijah** has to come first?"	As soon as **Elijah** heard that, he wrapped his face in his mantle.
35	LAMSA	1933	And when **Elijah** heard it, he wrapped his face in his mantle.	And his disciples asked him, Why then do the scribes say that **Elijah** must come first?
36	SMGO	1939	The disciples asked him, "Then why do the scribes say that **Elijah** has to come first?"	Now as soon as **Elijah** perceived it, he wrapped his face in his mantle.
37	KNOX	1944	**Elias**, when he heard it, wrapped his face in his mantle.	And the disciples asked him, Tell us, why is it that the scribes say **Elias** must come before Christ?
38	MODL	1945	When **Elijah** heard it, he covered his face with his coat.	The disciples asked Him, "Why, then, do the scribes say that **Elijah** must first come?"
39	DART	1950	And it was so, when **Elijah** heard it, that he wrapped his face in his mantle.	And his disciples asked him, saying, Why then say the scribes that **Elias** must first come?
40	OGD	1950	And his disciples, questioning him, said, Why then do the scribes say that **Elijah** has to come first?	And **Elijah**, hearing it, went out, covering his face with his robe.

41	RSV	1952	And when *Elijah* heard it, he wrapped his face in his mantle.	And the disciples asked him, "Then why do the scribes say that first *Elijah* must come?"
42	WEST	1958	And when *Elias* heard it, he covered his face with his mantle.	And the disciples asked him, saying: 'Why then do the scribes say that *Elias* must come first?
43	NASB	1960	And it came about when *Elijah* heard it, that he wrapped his face in his mantle.	And his disciples asked Him, saying, "Why then do the scribes say that *Elijah* must come first?"
44	NWT	1961	However, the disciples put the question to him: "Why, then, do the scribes say that *Elijah* must come first?"	And it came about that as soon as *Elijah* heard it he immediately wrapped his face in his official garment.
45	MKJV	1962	And when *Elijah* heard, it happened that he wrapped his face in his mantle.	And His disciples asked Him, saying, Why then do the scribes say that *Elijah* must come first?
46	AMP	1965	When *Elijah* heard the voice, he wrapped his face in his mantle.	The disciples asked him, Then why do the scribes say that first *Elijah* must come?
47	CONF	1965	And when *Elias* heard it, he covered his face with his mantle.	And the disciples asked him, saying, "Why then do the Scribes say that *Elias* must come first?"
48	JER	1966	And when *Elijah* heard this, then he covered his face with his cloak.	And the disciples put this question to him, "Why do the scribes say then that *Elijah* has to come first?"
49	NAB	1970	Why do the scribes claim that *Elijah* must come first?"	When he heard this, *Elijah* hid his face in his cloak.
50	LIV	1971	When *Elijah* heard it, he wrapped his face in his scarf.	His disciples asked, "Why do the Jewish leaders insist *Elijah* must return before the Messiah comes?"
51	BYIN	1972	And when *Elijah* heard it he wrapped his face in his mantle.	And his disciples put the question to him "Why is it, then, that the scribes say *Elijah* must come first?"
52	WMF	1975	"Just as I said before," said *Elijah*.	One of the disciples then said, "But we were always taught that *Elijah* had to come again before the Messiah and restore order in preparation."

53	BECK	1976	When *Elijah* heard that, he wrapped his face in his mantle.	So the disciples asked Him, "Why then, do those who know the Bible say, 'First *Elijah* has to come'?"
54	NEB	1976	When *Elijah* heard it, he muffled his face in his cloak.	The disciples put a question to him: 'Why then do our teachers say that *Elijah* must come first?'
55	TEV	1976	When *Elijah* hear it, he covered his face with his cloak.	Then the disciples asked Jesus, "Why do the teachers of the Law say that *Elijah* has to come first?"
56	NIV	1978	When *Elijah* heard it, he pulled his cloak over his face.	The disciples asked him, "Why then do the teachers of the law say that *Elijah* must come first?"
57	NKJV	1982	When *Elijah* heard it, that he wrapped his face in his mantle.	And his disciples asked Him, saying, "Why then do the scribes say that *Elijah* must first come?"
58	NJER	1985	And when *Elijah* heard this, he covered his face with his cloak.	And then the disciples put this question to him, 'Why then do the scribes say that *Elijah* must come first?'
59	WBC	1985	And the disciples asked him: "Why therefore do the scribes say that *Elijah* must come first?	And it so happened that, when *Elijah* heard it, he wrapped his face in his mantle.
60	EB	1987	When *Elijah* heart it, he covered his face with his coat.	The followers asked Jesus, "Why do the teachers of the law say that *Elijah* must come first, before the Christ comes?
61	ETR	1987	When *Elijah* heard the voice he used his coat to cover his face.	The followers asked Jesus, "Why do the teachers of the law say that *Elijah* must come first before the Christ comes?"
62	REB	1989	When *Elijah* heard it, he wrapped his face in his cloak.	The disciples put a question to him: 'Why then do the scribes say that *Elijah* must come first?'
63	NRSV	1990	When *Elijah* heard it, he wrapped his face in his mantle.	And the disciples asked him, "Why, then, do the scribes say the *Elijah* must come first?"
64	NCV	1991	When *Elijah* heard it, he covered his face with his coat.	The his followers asked him, "Why do the teachers of the law say that *Elijah* must come first?"

65	GLT	1993	And it happened when *Elijah* heard, he wrapped his face in his robe	And His disciples asked Him, saying, Why then do the scribes say that *Elijah* must come first?
66	KJ21	1994	And it was so, when *Elijah* heard it, that he wrapped his face in his mantle.	And his disciples asked Him, saying, "Why then say the scribes that *Elijah* must first come?"
67	CCB	1995	When *Elijah* perceived it, he covered his face with his cloak.	The disciples asked him, "Why do the teachers of the Law say that *Elijah* must come first?"
68	CEV	1995	The disciples asked Jesus, "Don't the teachers of the Law of Moses say that *Elijah* must come before the Messiah does?"	And when *Elijah* hear it, he covered his face with his coat.
69	GODWD	1995	When *Elijah* hear it, he wrapped his face in his coat.	So the disciples asked him, "Why do the scribes say that *Elijah* must come first?"
70	NIrV	1995	When *Elijah* heard it, he pulled his coat over his face.	The disciples asked him, "Why do the teachers of the law say that *Elijah* has to come first?"
71	NLT	1996	When *Elijah* heard it, he wrapped his face in his cloak.	His disciples asked, "Why do the teachers of religious law insist that *Elijah* must return before the Messiah comes?"
72	WEB	1997	It was so, when *Elijah* heard it, that he wrapped his face in his mantle.	His disciples asked him, saying, "Then why do the scribes say that *Elijah* must come first?"
73	CJB	1998	When *Eliyahu* heard it, he covered his face with his cloak.	And his disciples asked him, saying, Why then say the Scribes that *Eliyahu* must first come?

📖 So we discover that 26% of the 73 Bibles, which have both the Old and New Testaments translate Elijah's name differently in each Testament. It is also interesting to note that this practice occurred more frequently in earlier editions of the Bible. Could it be that in the 1500's and 1600's less people were educated, therefore less people read the Bible, Therefore it was easier for the Catholic Church to maintain the implied deception that *Elijah* and *Elias* were two different people. As long as this confusion could be maintained, the pubic would never question the possibilities that Elijah reincarnated as John the Baptist.

📖 Another fascinating point is in Matthew 11:14-15 Jesus, himself, claims that Elijah is John the Baptist. While Jesus did not specifically use the word reincarnation, he is implying the theory. This topic is again repeated in the next quote:

> The disciples asked him, "Why then do the teachers of the law say that Elijah must come first?"
>
> Jesus replied, "To be sure, Elijah comes and will restore all things. But I tell you, Elijah has already come, and they did not recognise him, but have done to him everything they wished. In the same way the Son of Man is going to suffer at their hands."
>
> Then the disciples understood that he was talking to them about John the Baptist.[465]

📖 When Jesus states Elijah had already returned, he is implying that Elijah and John the Baptist are one and the same. There was only one way that the Hebrews, who were eagerly awaiting Elijah's return, would not recognize him. Elijah reincarnated as John the Baptist. Reading in-between the lines of Awan's statement, we can assume that at one time this was thoroughly explained within the Bible's text. However, at some point in time, when the Church **abandoned** reincarnation, all mention of it was edited out of the Bible.

📖 Reincarnation is again implied in the description of John the Baptist's Birth.

> And there appeared unto him an angel of the Lord standing on the right side of the altar of incense. And when Zacharias saw *him*, he was troubled, and fear fell upon him. But the angel said unto him, Fear not, Zacharias: for thy prayer is heard; and thy wife Elisabeth shall bear thee a son, and thou shalt call his name John. And thou shalt have joy and gladness; and many shall rejoice at his birth. For he shall be great in the sight of the Lord, and shall drink neither wine nor strong drink; and he shall be filled with the Holy Ghost, even from his mother's womb. And many of the children of Israel shall he turn to the Lord their God. And he shall go before him in *the spirit and power of Elias,* to turn the hearts of the fathers to the children, and the disobedient to the wisdom of the just; to make ready a people prepared for the Lord.[466]

📖 The angel is telling Zacharias that his son would lead *in the spirit and power of Elias (Elijah)*. This would imply that the soul of Elijah would inhabit the new body of John the Baptist. The **NEB** states it in much clearer language.

---

[465] Matthew 17:10-13 [NIV].

[466] Luke 1:11-17 [KJV].

> **He will go before him as forerunner, *possessed* by the spirit and power of Elijah.**[467]

📖 In this next quote, Jesus again has the opportunity to contradict the concept of reincarnation, but his tacit agreement with the theory, cannot be overlooked.

> **When Jesus came to the region of Caesarea Philippi, he asked his disciples, "Who do people say the Son of Man is?"**
> **They replied, "Some say John the Baptist; others say Elijah; and still others, Jeremiah or one of the prophets."**
> **"But what about you?" he asked. "Who do you say I am?"**
> **Simon Peter answered, "You are the Christ, the Son of the living God."**
> **Jesus replied, "Blessed are you, Simon son of Jonah, for this was not revealed to you by man, but by my Father in heaven."**[468]

📖 Jesus had the perfect opportunity to correct his disciples, during this discussion. Jeremiah had died centuries before. How would it be possible for him to return as the "Son of Man" unless the disciples accepted reincarnation? If reincarnation did not exist, then Jesus would have corrected his disciples, telling them that it was impossible for Jeremiah to return as the "Son of Man." Further evidence that reincarnation was accepted during Jesus' lifetime can be found in this quote:

> **And king Herod heard *of him*; (for his name was spread abroad:) and he said, That John the Baptist was risen from the dead, and therefore mighty works do shew forth themselves in him.**
> **Others said, That it is Elias. And others said, That it is a prophet, or as one of the prophets.**
> **But when Herod heard *thereof*, he said, It is John, whom I beheaded: he is risen from the dead.**[469]

📖 This verse proves that King Herod, along with other contemporaries all thought that a person could "rise from the dead." It was my understanding, that Christians believed that Jesus was the first to accomplish this feat. Yet,

---

[467] Luke 1:17 [NEB].

[468] Matthew 16:13-17 [NIV].

[469] Mark 6:14-16 [KJV].

the Bible tells us that both Elijah and Elisha, along with Jesus brought people back from the dead. The practice must not have been that common, or it would have been practiced on a regular basis for the last 2000 years.

📖 The fact that Herod could believe that Jesus was John the Baptist, demonstrates that a belief in the physical return of the dead was credible in those days. Reincarnation is a more logical system to explain this belief. As Awan explained, we accept the birth, death, and rebirth of flowers, and the leaves on the trees. Why should it be different for human beings?

📖 This next Bible story provides more food for thought regarding people believing in reincarnation two thousand years ago.

> And as Jesus passed by, he saw a man which was blind from his birth. And his disciples asked him, saying, Master, *who did sin*, this man, or his parents, that he was born blind?[470]

📖 This is a highly significant verse, for it contains the disciples' revealing question. The disciples did not ask Jesus, **WHAT** sin caused the man to be blind from birth? They asked him **WHO** sinned? There were only two possibilities in this multiple-choice question: A. **the parents**, or B. **the unborn child**. By posing this question, the disciples are revealing a belief in reincarnation. For how would it be possible for an unborn child to commit a sin, unless the sin were carried forth from a previous life into a new, reincarnated life? There are no other plausible explanations that would enable an unborn child to sin.

📖 It is interesting to note that since Christianity had not yet been created, the doctrine of "original sin" did not exist at the time. If it had, this certainly would have been an ideal time for Jesus to teach it to the disciples. However, Jesus' response contains no mention of that non-existent dogma.

> Jesus answered, Neither hath this man sinned, nor his parents: but that the works of God should be made manifest in him I must work the works of him that sent me, while it is day: the night cometh, when no man can work. As long as I am in the world, I am the light of the world.
> When he had thus spoken, he spat on the ground, and made clay of the spittle, and he anointed the eyes of the blind man with the clay, and said unto him, Go, wash in the pool of Siloam, (which is by interpretation, Sent.) He went his way therefore, and washed, and came seeing.[471]

---

[470] John 9:1-2 [KJV].
[471] John 9:3-7 [KJV].

📖 The Bible also contains verses, which would support the claim that reincarnation does not exist. John the Baptist was asked if he were Elijah, and he responded, "No."

> **And this is the record of John, when the Jews sent priests and Levites from Jerusalem to ask him, Who art thou?**
> **And he confessed, and denied not; but confessed, I am not the Christ.**
> **And they asked him, What then? Art thou Elias? And he saith, I am not. Art thou that prophet? And he answered, No.**[472]

📖 It is important to note that John responded to the questions that were posed to him. John was asked if he was Elijah. John answered truthfully, "I am not." John was son of Zacharias and Elizabeth." It would have been interesting if John had been asked the following question: "Do you have the Spirit of Elijah in you?" John's answer to this question would have been "Yes!" because the angel who spoke to Zacharias made that pronouncement.[473]

📖 James M. Pryse in his book entitled *Reincarnation in the New Testament* claims that Elijah's denial is caused by a "play on words."

> **The Greek word *hêlios*, the sun, is hardly distinguishable from Hêlias [the Greek name for Elijah]. Now, metaphorically, the Christos is the Sun; and it would be natural for John to make this denial as a mere reiteration of preceeding, "I am not the Anointed."**[474]

📖 Jesus himself claimed that John the Baptist was Elijah:

> **Elijah has already come, and they did not recognize him.**[475]

📖 They did not recognize him, because Elijah's spirit reincarnated into John's body. If this had not happened Malachi's prophecy would have not been fulfilled.

> **"See, I will send you the prophet Elijah before that great and dreadful day of the LORD comes. He will turn the hearts of the fathers to their children, and the hearts of the children to**

---

[472] John 1:19-21 [KJV].

[473] Luke 1:11-17.

[474] Pryse, James M. *Reincarnation in the New Testament*. NY: The Theosophical Publishing Co., 1911. p. 19.

[475] Matthew 17:12 [NIV].

> their fathers; or else I will come and strike the land with a curse."[476]

📖 Nor would the angel's prophecy to Zacharias have been fulfilled. So by denying reincarnation, Christian theologians would have to agree with their Jewish counterparts, and could not believe that Jesus was the Messiah, because Elijah had to return before the Messiah. By denying the validity of reincarnation Christian theologians are saying that Jesus himself was lying when he said Elijah had returned, but no one recognized him.

📖 Why didn't Jesus specifically explain to his disciples that reincarnation was a false doctrine? Apparently reincarnation was a belief held in many other religions at the time.

> **Reincarnation, a doctrine held by various religions and philosophies that generally includes belief in the pre-existence of the soul prior to its union with the body and the soul's return to life after death in some other human or nonhuman form, perhaps depending on the deeds of the prior life.**[477]

📖 The fact is instead of rejecting reincarnation Jesus actually taught it to his students. Lection 37 of *The Gospel Of The Holy Twelve* contains a reference to reincarnation, although the word is not used. Verse 2 reads:

> And he [Jesus] said unto them, Blessed are they *who suffer many experiences*, for they shall be made *perfect* through suffering; they shall be as the angels of God in Heaven and *shall die no more, neither shall they be born any more*, for death and birth have no more dominion over them.

📖 When Jesus said: *"they who suffer many experiences,"* he is talking about repeated lifetimes. The purpose of reincarnation is to provide the soul opportunities to evolve spiritually. When the soul finally evolves to a point of perfection, it no longer reincarnates into this dimension, but continues its life in other more highly evolved dimensions. This is clearly stated by Jesus in this verse.

📖 When we compare Lection 37 with its Biblical counterpart John 3, we discover John 3 is likes Swiss cheese, full of gaping holes. When we fill in those holes with the missing verses from *The Gospel Of The Holy Twelve* we have a complete, fluid story. This may be the strongest evidence to prove that reincarnation was removed from the Bible.

---

[476] Malachi 4:5-6. [NIV].

[477] McBrien, Richard P., ed. *The HarperCollins Encyclopedia of Catholicism*. NY: HarperCollins, 1995. p. 1095.

KJV JOHN Chapter 3	GOSPEL OF THE HOLY TWELVE LECTION XXXVII[478]
	1 Jesus sat in the porch of the Temple, and some came to learn his doctrine, and one said unto him, Master, what teachest thou concerning life?
	2 And he said unto them, Blessed are they who suffer many experiences, for they shall be made perfect through suffering; they shall be as the angels of God in Heaven and shall die no more, neither shall they be born any more, for death and birth have no more dominion over them.
	3 They who have suffered and overcome shall be made Pillars in the Temple of my God, and they shall go out no more. Verily I say unto you, except ye be born again of water and of fire, ye cannot see the kingdom of God.
1 There was a man of the Pharisees, named Nicodemus, a ruler of the Jews: 2 The same came to Jesus by night, and said unto him, Rabbi, we know that thou art a teacher come from God: for no man can do these miracles that thou doest, except God be with him.	4. And a certain Rabbi (Nicodemus) came unto him by night for fear of the Jews, and said unto him, How can a man be born again when he is old? can he enter a second time into his mother's womb and be born again?
3 Jesus answered and said unto him, Verily, verily, I say unto thee, Except a man be born again, he cannot see the kingdom of God.	
4 Nicodemus saith unto him, How can a man be born when he is old? can he enter the second time into his mother's womb, and be born?	
5 Jesus answered, Verily, verily, I say unto thee, Except a man be born of water and of the Spirit, he cannot enter into the kingdom of God.	
6 That which is born of the flesh is flesh; and that which is born of the Spirit is spirit.	
7 Marvel not that I said unto thee, Ye must be born again.	

---

[478] Ouseley, Gideon Jasper Richard, Rev. *The Gospel Of The Holy Twelve: known also as The Gospel of the Perfect Life*. Translated from the Original Aramaic. Santa Ana, Costa Rica: Teófilo de la Tgorre, N. D., O. D., 1954. p. 91.

8 The wind bloweth where it listeth, and thou hearest the sound thereof, but canst not tell whence it cometh, and whither it goeth: so is every one that is born of the Spirit.	5 ...The wind bloweth where it listeth, and ye hear the sound thereof, but cannot tell whence it cometh or whither it goeth.
	6 The light shineth from the East even unto the West; out of the darkness, the Sun ariseth and goeth down into darkness again; so is it with man, from the ages unto the ages.
	7 When it cometh from the darkness, it is that he hath lived before, and when it goeth down again into darkness, it is that he may rest for a little, and thereafter again exist.
	8 So through many changes must ye be made perfect, as it is written in the book of Job, I am a wanderer, changing place after place and house after house, until I come unto the City and Mansion which is eternal.
9 Nicodemus answered and said unto him, How can these things be?	9 And Nicodemus said unto him, How can these things be?...
10 Jesus answered and said unto him, Art thou a master of Israel, and knowest not these things?	9 ...And Jesus answered and said unto him, Art thou a teacher in Israel, and understandeth not these things?
11 Verily, verily, I say unto thee, We speak that we do know, and testify that we have seen; and ye receive not our witness.	9... Verily we speak that which we do know, and bear witness to that which we have seen, and ye ye receive not our witness.
12 If I have told you earthly things, and ye believe not, how shall ye believe, if I tell you of heavenly things?	10 If I have told you of earthly things and ye believe not, how shall ye believe if I tell you of Heavenly things? No man hath ascended into Heaven, but he that descended out of Heaven, even the Son-Daughter of man which is in Heaven.
13 And no man hath ascended up to heaven, but he that came down from heaven, even the Son of man which is in heaven.	
14 And as Moses lifted up the serpent in the wilderness, even so must the Son of man be lifted up:	
15 That whosoever believeth in him should not perish, but have eternal life.	

😇 You must remember, my scribe, that the soul is an energy field that cannot be destroyed. The soul acts as a computer, and records all the experiences we have. Just as water runs its cycle, the soul keeps coming back, reincarnating into a different body, lifetime after lifetime after lifetime. The soul cycles back for more knowledge in the form of experience. This happens regardless of whether or not one believes in reincarnation.

Have you ever met a person with a knack, or innate talent? The person can paint beautiful pictures, play an instrument, or be a skilled writer, with hardly any training?

😊 Yes, Awan, I do know a few people who have extraordinary artistic talents since they were extremely young.

😇 Some people have a talent because they did the same activity in another life, and their souls simply remembered what they learned in previous lives.

😊 That brings up an interesting question. Let's say that in one of my previous lives, I was a brilliant mathematician. Yet, in this life I dislike math, and am not good at it. How would this be possible?

😇 You must remember, my scribe, that when the soul enters a baby's physical body, it has to greatly decrease is speed of vibration. Your physical body vibrates much slower than the spiritual body.

😊 Yes, Awan, I remember that.

😇 The slow, sluggish vibrational rate of the soul when it is housed in a physical body limits it access into it past life memory. Think of it in this way. Why can't your physical eyes see x-rays and infrared rays?

😊 Those rays are beyond the capability of our eyes. We can't make our eyes see in that faster speed.

😇 Correct. Yet you do have photographic film that will capture those rays.

😊 Yes, Awan, we can take X-ray and infrared pictures.

😇 The soul cannot access past life experiences because they are beyond the range that can be accessed when the soul is vibrating so slowly. Now my scribe, you play the piano, do you not?

😊 Yes, Awan, I do play the piano.

😇 Tell me, my scribe, what has been your experience when you decide to play a particular piece of music that you have not played in say, five of your years?

😊 Well, Awan, I am rusty, so I would not play it as well as I once did.

😇 Yet, you do remember how to play it. Do not your fingers seem to go to the correct keys automatically, despite the fact that you have not kept that particular piece of music in practice?

😊 Yes, Awan that is true. What is your point?

😇 Certain skills are accessible by the sluggish soul, residing the physical body from lifetime to lifetime. These would include: playing the piano, painting a picture, carpentry, and many, many more. However, it is the detailed information of past life experience that is inaccessible to the soul, for good reason.

🧑 Why is that Awan?

😇 The whole point of reincarnating into your dimension is to have a "stage for evolution." Each lifetime is like a test. When you die, you review your life. You are your own judge. No one else will judge you. You consciously decide on what weaknesses you wish to improve. Then you can begin to work on these weaknesses, while you are still in the World of Spirit. However, there is only so much that a soul can accomplish in my dimension. There comes a time when the soul must return to your dimension, to "test" if he or she has resolved the problem. So you see, my scribe, if the soul returned to your dimension with the knowledge of what the problems was, it would be like cheating on one of your school tests. The whole point of reincarnation is to see if the soul can master a weakness, without consciously remembering or knowing the weakness.

🧑 That really makes sense, Awan.

😇 I am sensing a shift in the energy, so I will vacate this body. I hope that this teaching enlightened you.

🧑 It certainly has, Awan.

😇 Good! My peace be with you, my scribe!

🧑 My peace be with you too, Awan. Thank you!

Carl sat quietly for about thirty seconds, and then moaned softly. "I'm so thirsty," he whispered. I assisted him in drinking a full glass of water. Exhaustion was clearly evident on his face. I assisted Carl to his bedroom, where he took a two-hour nap.

TWENTY-FOUR

In My Father's House Are Many Mansions

Following the now familiar procedure, Carl lowered the lights, put on his blindfolds, and said his prayer. Carl sat still for close to four minutes. I was surprised how easily Awan's and Carl's spirits exchanged places. There were no spasms this time.

My profound greetings to you, my scribe.

Greetings Awan.

Today, my scribe, I wish to give you clarification of a teaching that was given by Jesus nearly 2000 years ago. Do not misunderstand me, my scribe; I do not want you to think that I am a better teacher than that great master. This teaching needs clarification because over the centuries it has been misinterpreted, and misconstrued.

OK, Awan, I understand. What will we be dialoguing about today?

Perhaps you have heard this famous teaching of Jesus', *"In my father's house are many mansions"*?[479]

Yes, Awan, I am familiar with it.

Jesus was attempting to teach a grand truth with this statement. Unfortunately, his words fell on uneducated ears that did not have the scientific knowledge to understand what he was discussing.

What do you mean, Awan?

This statement about many mansions was an attempt to teach the people about the Spirit World. Jesus was not referring to a grandiose housing development, when he spoke of many mansions. This was the only metaphor that he could use at the time, to have the people understand this teaching.

So if there are not mansions in the Spirit World, what did Jesus mean?

---

[479] John 14:2 [KJV].

🛐 If Jesus were teaching this lesson in the beginning of the 21st century, he would probably use these words. *In the Spirit World* (my father's house) *there are many levels of vibration* (many mansions). I want you to remember, my scribe, what I have taught you. These levels of vibration are actually separate dimensions. The soul will enter into the dimension that matches the spiritual development and the knowledge that person possesses. That is why I keep saying that *Knowledge is your passport into forever*. The knowledge you possess determines in which level of the Spirit World you will reside.

👤 This is making sense, Awan. Could you describe these levels to me?

🛐 Yes, my scribe, this will be the focus of our dialogue today. However, there is one more topic I wish you to understand before I talk about the levels.

👤 OK, Awan. I am ready to hear it.

🛐 Please tell me, what is meant by the *fall of man*?

👤 I believe the *fall of man* refers back to the Bible story of Adam and Eve. When Eve gave Adam the fruit of knowledge; they both ate it, and gained knowledge. This made God angry, since He forbad them from eating that fruit. Therefore, God cast Adam and Eve out of the Garden of Eden, and they had to work for a living. I believe that *the fall of man* refers to falling from the good graces of God.

🛐 That is a good description, my scribe. Do you realize the profound subliminal message of this story? If you believe the story you just described, then you would consider knowledge a bad or evil thing. Do you really think that the creator of the universe would want his creations to be stupid, unthinking people? No, the theologians wrote this doctrine into the Bible to keep the people ignorant of the *Gifts of the Spirit*.

There was a *fall of man*, my scribe. It occurred during the creation of man. We have already discussed how the universe was formed, when the thought of the great Spirit caused the Big Bang.

👤 Yes, Awan. I remember.

🛐 The souls that were created had to come down through seven levels of vibration to arrive on the earth plane. Your plane of existence is the slowest, densest of all vibrations. This is why so many Spirits do not look forward to communicating with you. We have to drop our vibration many levels to make contact with you. The *fall of man* is when souls dropped from the seventh level down to the first, to be on the earth plane.

👤 This is very interesting, Awan.

🛐 Now, before I explain the different levels of the Spirit World, there is one additional message I need to tell you. In the next day or two, I will give my medium a clairvoyant vision. He will see a diagram, which I will instruct him to copy on a piece of your papyrus. It will be a chart of the levels of the Spirit World. We feel, in our dimension, that this will help the readers of this book to comprehend the different levels. You are to use your scribing machine [computer] to draw this diagram, and to include it in the book. Do you understand?

Yes, Awan. I will reproduce it to the best of my abilities.

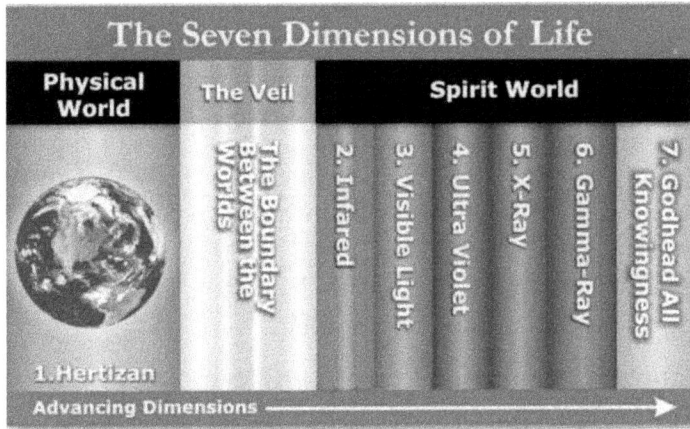

Be not concerned, my scribe, all you need to do is to draw some straight lines. Now, onto the matter at hand; I will begin describing the levels of the Spirit World, starting with your very own. The earth plane is the first level.

Awan, earth isn't part of the Spirit World. We're physical people, not Spirits.

My scribe, you are falling to the same theological trap as most of the billions of people on your planet. Yes, you are living in a physical body. It is the temple of the living God. Your soul, as I have told you, is God. It resides in your physical body, which is the temple of the living God. Therefore, you are a Spiritual being, just as I am, however, we have different types of bodies. Do you understand?

After this session I found this Bible quote:

> **Do you not know that your body is a *temple of the Holy Spirit*, who is in you, whom you have received from God?**[480]

Yes, Awan. I understand.

A Spirit, or soul, enters a physical body, and animates it for the life of the person. At death, the Spirit body, or soul, leaves the physical body. As soon as the silver cord, connecting the Spirit to the physical body, is severed, the soul immediately begins to increase its vibration. Within a matter of seconds, the souls reaches the lowest level of the Spirit World, called *infrared*.

---

[480] 1Corinthians 6:19 [NIV].

🙍 What happens next, Awan?

😇 That all depends on the *"passport"* the soul is carrying. Remember the physical body is dead; therefore, the brain is also dead. All knowledge was recorded in the soul during the person's life. That is why I keep saying, *"Knowledge is the passport into forever."* It will depend what the soul knows and understands.

🙍 Well, Awan, can you describe some of the possibilities?

😇 I will be glad to, my scribe. Here is one possibility that unfortunately, is all too common. The soul arrives in the infrared frequency, and after a while it determines that the person has experienced death. So the soul just lies down and goes to sleep; some of them have slept for centuries.

🙍 Awan, I don't understand, why is that?

😇 You would have to go back to the fourth century for the answer. It was then that the Christian Church held a counsel, which created a new dogmas. After the counsel, all the priests proclaimed from their pulpits that when a Christian dies, his or her soul is to go to sleep. The God, Jesus, will come to awaken you, and judge your life, determining if you should spend eternity in heaven or hell. However, the teaching did not end there. The Church also taught the devil could impersonate anyone. The Devil was out to get as many souls as possible. Therefore, people were taught to ignore anyone who did not look like Jesus. No one had a photograph of this great teacher, so people thought Jesus would look like the picture, or statue, that was in their particular church.

📖 I found evidence that even in The Middle Ages, churches had statues and pictures to help educate the people about the Bible and Christian theology.

> **Medieval churches and cathedrals were decorated with wall paintings, carvings, statues and other precious objects to add to their beauty and splendor.[481]**

😇 When these Christians died, their souls entered the infrared frequency, and went to sleep. Many people from higher levels came down to attempt to wake these people up, to correct the misconceptions their church had taught them. When these souls woke up, they did not recognize the Spirit that came to help them. Therefore, they thought it was the Devil, and rolled over and went back to sleep, waiting for Jesus to come. Unfortunately, they have been sleeping for centuries.

🙍 That is truly sad, Awan.

---

[481] Macdonald, Fiona. *A Medieval Cathedral.* NY: P. Bedrick Books, 1991. p. 30.

😇 More than being sad, it presented the problem of what to do with all these sleeping souls. We had to create a "hospital" to house these souls. Tell me my scribe, do you remember when you were in the part of your country called Montana?

🧑 Yes, Awan. Why do you ask?

😇 Do you remember how far you could see in each direction? And how much of the sky you could see?

🧑 Yes, Awan. It was fabulous.

😇 The great hospital that is in the infrared frequency would be 1000 times larger than your eye could see, in your state of Montana. It is that large because of the billions of souls that have been misled by Christianity, thinking that they must sleep, waiting for Jesus.

🧑 That is terrible. Awan, please tell me another possibility.

😇 Another possibility is that the person did not believe in recycled ignorance, or in any religion. As a result, the person led his or her life under the misconception that it did not matter what you did during your life. When you died, you were dead. You would be obliterated. These people had no knowledge that their soul is eternal energy, and they would continue to exist after death.

This person led an immoral life. He or she stole money, took drugs, committed many crimes, and went to jail. When the person died, the soul's vibration began to increase. Then the soul's vibration stopped increasing. The person found him or herself living in the infrared frequency. This is the lowest level of the Spirit World, where the most unenlightened people reside. Since the soul did not believe it *must* sleep, it remained awake. It did not go to sleep, just because it thought there was no after life.

🧑 Why did the soul stop increasing its vibration, Awan?

😇 You must remember that the soul will naturally seek out its level of evolution in the Spirit World.

🧑 I don't understand, Awan.

😇 The soul can only keep increasing its vibrational rate to the level of spiritual knowledge that is recorded in the soul. This unenlightened, spiritually ignorant Spirit does not belong in the higher frequencies of the Spirit World. That is reserved for more enlightened beings.

🧑 I understand that now, Awan. This is making a lot of sense. Are there other possibilities?

😇 Yes, my scribe. The last possibility is that of a person, who has knowledge recorded into their soul. The person does not necessarily follow their religious teachings. Therefore, the person does not think he or she must go to sleep after he or she dies. Instead the person is very aware that he or she will live on after death. This person has lead a life where he or she tried to be spiritual, and helped people. Therefore, once the soul begins vibrating higher than the physical realm, its frequency continues to climb, and the soul enters the next level.

👤 What is that level, Awan?

😇 The third level is called visible light. It is a level in which one must be careful; there is some danger on this level.

👤 What are you talking about, Awan? I thought the Spirit World was a safe place.

😇 It is, once you get past the visible light level. There has been another false teaching that has been perpetuated in your dimension, which says that when you die, you must go to the light. Let me explain what will happen to you if you follow this teaching.

👤 OK, Awan.

😇 The frequency of visible light is very huge. This is because the vast majority of souls reside there, because they do not have the spiritual knowledge to go to higher levels. There are entities living in this frequency, who do not desire to return to the earth to have additional experiences that advance their evolution. These entities have become expert at ambushing newly arrived souls. They are like hijackers, or highway-men of years ago, who rob, or strip, in-coming souls of all their knowledge.

If your soul gets stripped of its knowledge in this frequency, then you have no knowledge to go beyond that point. You can no longer increase your vibration to the higher frequencies of the Spirit World. Sooner or later, you will be sucked into another life. The trouble is you will not have the knowledge of planning the proper life that will provide you the lessons you needed to work on. It would be like someone took a giant magnet to your computer hard drive. It would be totally erased, and your computer would no longer have any instructions in it. It would be clean of all its knowledge, and no longer able to perform the tasks it once performed. In all likelihood, a soul that was stripped will reincarnate into a poor, third world country, because it will not know how to select its parents, and prepare for its next life.

Anyone reading this book would be very wise to understand this powerful message. **Do NOT go to the light. Go BEYOND the light into the next frequency or level**. This is known as the *ultra violet* frequency. It looks dark compared to the frequency of visible light. Many people are afraid to go there. So many people have been programmed by religions to be afraid of the dark. There is nothing to be afraid of in entering the wonderful *ultra violet* level. It is the level where all healing energies emanate. It is blue in color, and you will be completely healed mentally, physically, and spiritually.'

👤 It sounds wonderful, Awan.

😇 It is a wondrous place, my scribe. I am sensing that the supply of psychic energy is diminishing, therefore, I will quickly summarize the next levels.

🧑 OK. Awan, I am listening.

😇 The next three levels are **Gamma ray**, **X-ray**, and the **Godhead** or all knowingness. These levels are reserved for higher evolved souls, ones who have gone beyond all religious dogma and theology. As you progress though each level you are obtaining enlightenment. When you finally reach the seventh level, you are truly a God. You will not find an old man sitting on a throne on this level. What you will find are entities who have total access to all the knowledge of the universe.

🧑 That sounds wonderful.

😇 It truly is, my scribe. Now, before I leave you, I must reiterate that **Knowledge is the passport into forever**. It is the truth, and information recorded in one's soul that will prepare their path in the World of Spirit. You are only entitled to the place in the Spirit World, your mansion, using Jesus' words, that you prepared for in your world. I hope you now have a clearer understanding of this teaching.

🧑 Yes, Awan. Thank you so much. I finally understand this concept.

😇 I am glad, my scribe. With that, I will leave you with my peace.

🧑 Peace to you too, Awan.

After about forty-five seconds, Carl softly moaned. "I need some water," he said with a parched voice. I helped Carl drink the full glass of water. For some reason, Carl seemed to have more energy than usual. "I'm suddenly very hungry," Carl said, "Let's have a sandwich." We prepared some tuna sandwiches, and ate while we discussed Awan's lesson. When we finished, Carl went and took an hour-long nap.

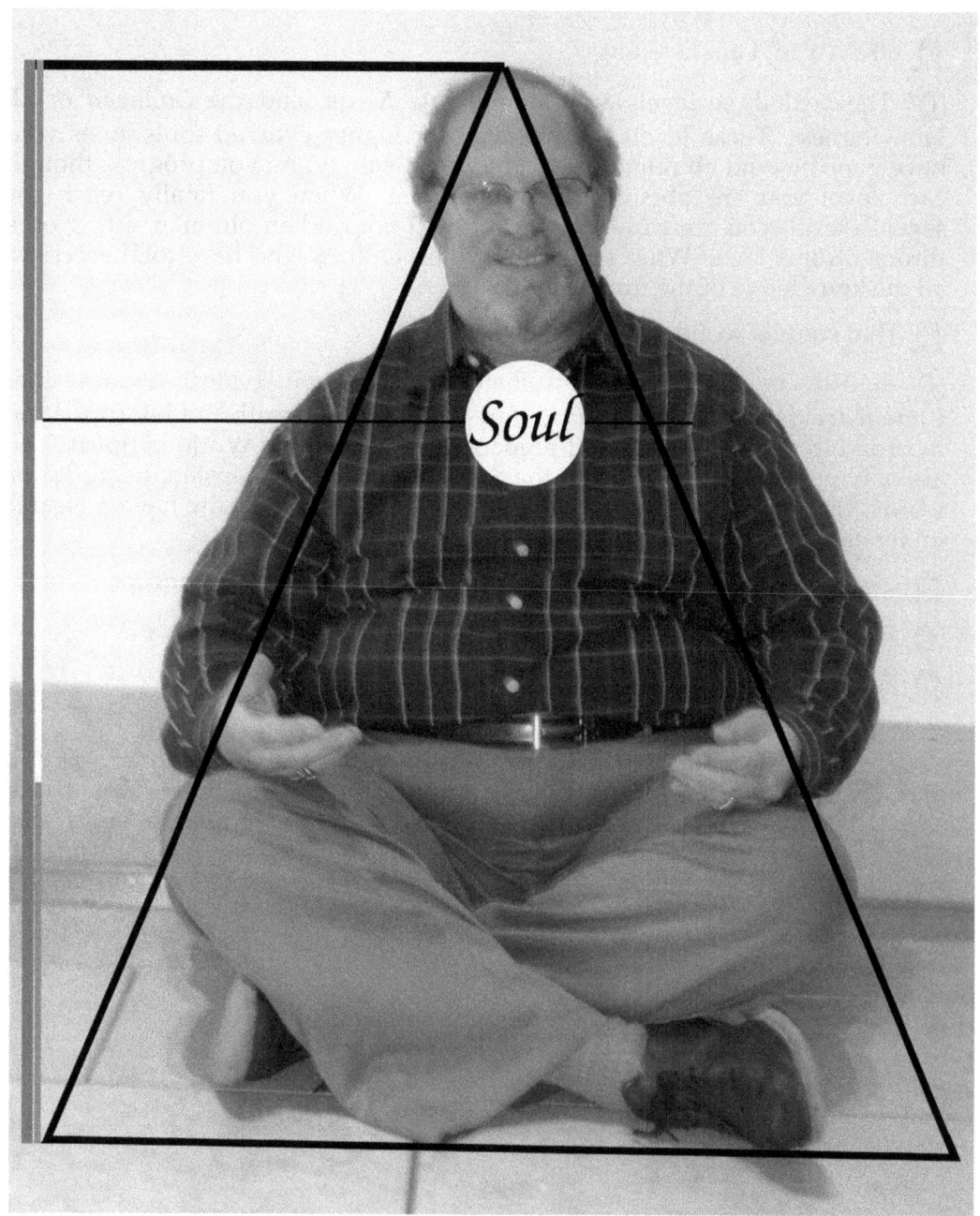

s picture illustrates Awan's teaching about the pyramid. When a person sits in a
is position, which resembles a pyramid, the soul is located 1/3 of the distance
n the apex, and 2/3 of the distance form the base. The line to the left is the
:ance from the base to the apex of the pyramid. The next line to the right is
ded into thirds. The soul is a luminous ball of energy, which is behind the
astbone, in the middle of the chest, and is found exactly 1/3 of the distance form
 apex.

TWENTY-FIVE

There Is Life After Death!

One morning, during a Sunday morning service at Gifts of the Spirit Church, Chief Lone Eagle, Carl's Spirit Control, asked his medium to do something out of the ordinary. Carl was to go into a trance state, so that a Spirit could speak through him, and address the congregation. I had seen Carl go into trance many times, but it was only for certain people. It was a rare occasion for Carl to go into a deep trance state during one of his church services.

Carl decided that I should be in charge of the proceedings. Carl and I explained to the congregation what was to happen. We instructed the audience not to speak, or leave their seats, during the trance. Carl sat down in a comfortable chair in the front of the church. He closed his eyes, said his usual prayer, and appeared to calmly drift into sleep. Within two minutes, someone began to speak. What follows is a transcript of this trance session.

🙂 Well, a jolly good morning to you! [In a thick British accent].

🙂 Good morning.

🙂 [Accent is gone] It is a pleasure that I might be able to speak through the medium this morning. Some of you have heard my voice before, or more precisely, part of my voice. It is not always easy for me to reproduce my own voice. I have to speak through another person's voice box, which has different physical characteristics than my own. However, I come to you at this time, because I am the one usually asked to warm up the medium, or warm up the voice box.

🙂 Would you mind introducing yourself, please?

🙂 Oh, don't you know? I am Nathaniel.

🙂 I recognize your British accent, but many people here this morning have not yet met you.

🙂 I am Nathaniel. I came originally, or I should put it this way—I lived in Kent, England, before coming into the World of Spirit. I have been associated with this medium for what you term "his entire life." It has only been in the last 15 years that I have been working closely enough with him to use his voice box.

Usually, I work "behind the scenes" as you might term it. I am one of the teachers who taught him a great deal, when he is not with other people. Frequently, if conditions are right, when he is alone in the woods, or by the water, I teach him many things. He hears my words through his *gift of clairaudience*. I have stood by and listened to him teach to you people the same information that I have taught him. In the last few of your years, I have been occasionally using his body, as I am doing now.

There is one spirit who is here with us who wishes to use the body, or attempt to use the body, or the voice box that is. This entity has progressed, as you might term it, in developing and learning on this side of life. He wishes to use this particular instrument. He says that he has a reason. He has appeared to the instrument, but never has used the voice box. He now feels that he can speak through the instrument at this time. I will back off, and allow the young man to use the voice box instead of me. So please be patient with us, as it will take a few moments for him to test the voice box, if he is even able to do that.

[There is a short pause.]

🎩 Can you hear my voice? [Softly]

🙂 Yes, it is soft, but I can hear it.

🎩 Can you hear it better? [Louder]

🙂 It is much better.

🎩 I hope I am able to maintain this dialogue for a few moments. The energy, as they tell me here, has peaked. Therefore, I will be able to talk to you for a few moments. What do you wish to know about me?

🙂 Well, I guess your identity, a little about yourself, and when you lived on the earth plane.

🎩 When I lived on the earth plane, my last name was Robinson. My first name was Larimer. I was born April 14, 1922.

🙂 Did you know the medium?

🎩 Yes, I did know the medium. We were in the same school together. There was about a four or five year age difference between us. He sang in the glee club when I graduated. In fact, I loaned him a coat, or a jacket, at the time. I have appeared to him several times, but I did not know how to identify myself because of my background, and how I was raised. My father was a preacher in the Baptist Church, and my mother sang in the choir. Therefore, what they taught me opposed what the instrument does at this time. I had a great deal to unlearn before I could learn, and this is what you term my "debut."

🙂 You are doing very well! I can certainly appreciate how much you had to unlearn.

🎖️ Well sir, I thank you for saying that to me. They were coaching me, over here, how to use this instrument. I am very pleased that you can hear my voice, as I use the medium's voice box at this time.

🧑 Were you present on the day that the medium whose body you are using, addressed the whole school on his first day of kindergarten?

🎖️ I was there at that particular time.

🧑 Do you remember what he spoke about?

🎖️ Yes, I do remember some of it, but what was said was actually, you might say, programmed out of me. We were not supposed to talk about, or think about it. He was treated rather cruelly at the time. For you see, we didn't know each other very well. It was the last year, actually the year that I graduated, just before going into the navy, that I even got to know who he was. He had a fantastic [singing] voice before his voice changed. When he comes out of this trance state, ask him about the time when he was singing solo in the church, when there were people from the recording company trying to get him to sing. It was the same people who discovered the Carter family. They were visiting different churches, listening to people sing. It was his parents who did not allow him to follow through on this. They refused to allow him to sing the way the Carter family did. Do know of the Carter family?

🧑 Yes, I have heard about them. The medium has never mentioned this incident to me.

🎖️ The medium has endured much harsh treatment during his lifetime. The community where we grew up ostracized him as much as possible. They did not understand that he was a gifted person, because the church leaders thought he was possessed by the Devil. Possibly, he tried to push many those memories out of his mind.

🧑 He probably did.

🎖️ Because of the way he was treated, I didn't know him then as well as I know him now. I have learned a great deal from him, from this dimension.

🧑 How did you pass into the Spirit World?

🎖️ After World War II, I began working for Marimac Shipping lines, located in Baltimore, Maryland. I worked in the engine room as a chief mechanic on a cargo ship, which was caught in a storm off the coast of North Carolina and Virginia. We were trying to ride out the storm, and were successful for quite some time. Unfortunately, the storm became stronger, and our ship took on water, and capsized. All of the crew perished in the deep cold waters. Some of us have reincarnated, or come back in solid form, as you term it.

🧑 Since you were so steeped in the Baptist religion, what caused you to leave the Baptist teachings, and begin to have different beliefs?

🎖 I held the Baptist beliefs throughout my life. It was only during the very last days of my physical life that I encountered anyone who had a different set of beliefs. I was having a conversation with a friend on the boat. You must remember, there are close quarters on a ship. Despite my uncomfortable feelings listening to his strange ideas, I could not escape this man. I had to listen to what he was saying. During our conversation, I shared with my friend, Harold Hewett, the strange feeling that came over me. I felt that none of us would ever see land again; we would all die underneath the ocean.

After I told that to him, he said, "If that is the way we have to go, I am ready to go."

I said to him, "I am not ready to die." And he said, "Obviously, you do not understand death as it really is." He proceeded to tell me of his own grandmother who was called a "seer" while she was on the earth plane. He explained death, and the Spirit World to me.

Ironically, our ship capsized only hours after he explained this to me. It was a horrible death, especially the last few moments of suffocation as we sank to the bottom of the sea. Suddenly, a warm, loving feeling came over me. I felt myself floating, and I didn't feel as though I was in the water anymore. There was no struggle to breathe. I just seemed to float upward. The further I moved, the closer I went to the light. The light was beautiful. Then I found myself in another world. The people who were greeting me were very loving, kind, and friendly. This surprised me, since I had never seen these people before. They explained to me in the last moments of my physical life, I prepared myself to come to the level where they are. Otherwise, I would not have been there. I would have been where my own ancestors and relatives had gone.

👤 Have you seen your relatives?

🎖 I have only been to visit them. They are on levels lower than where I am. I am on what you would term the 5th level of the realm of Spirit. They are on the third level. There is a great difference in these levels. It is possible for me to visit them, but they cannot visit me. They have not earned the right to be on the fifth level. I am using the term "levels," but in the Book of Books they were called "mansions."

📖 Larimer was referring to this teaching of Jesus:

> **In my Father's house are many mansions: if it were not so, I would have told you. I go to prepare a place for you.**[482]

👤 Are your relatives awake and alive on their level, as you are on yours?

🎖 Since their church did not teach them anything about the Spirit World, when they were on the earth plane; they are still very confused. They cannot

---

[482] John 14:2 [KJV].

understand the levels. You must remember, both of my parents were stubborn, and very comfortable with the teachings of the Baptist religion.

🧑 Could you describe what your life is like in the Spirit World? What do you do with your time?

👼 Actually, we live in a timeless dimension. We have no time. However, everything in our dimension is done by thought. We can travel from one planet to another. There are galaxies far beyond anything your scientists have ever found, far beyond the Milky Way. In these other galaxies the people are far more advanced than the people on the earth. Their civilizations are over one thousand years more advanced than yours, because these people do not have wars, and tyrants, as you know them to be. This is why the people from other planets can come back and visit you on earth; but they do not allow humans to see them. They have the knowledge to control the frequencies, and vibrations. They can be visible, or stay invisible, to your eyes. You may often feel their presence, but when you look around you will not see them.

🧑 Could you describe what type of schools you go to on your plane?

👼 On our plane of existence we are absolutely unlimited. We have schools that are so advanced there is nothing comparable to them. Your school system has created conditions that make you all very limited. Currently, you operate only a small portion of your brain. It is in the rest of your brain, the portion that doesn't function, where all the *Gifts of the Spirit* reside. Once you are able to open the brain, you activate those unused parts. Then you can understand, and use, the *Gifts of the Spirit.* You would even be able to ascend—speed up your vibration—while you are still in your physical body. With this increased rate of vibration, you could join us, in our dimension. Although to us, we would be the same as you, in your own perspective.

🧑 And you learned to do these types of things in the Spirit World?

👼 We learned over here. It is difficult to describe to you our universities. They are so very different from your own. On this plane, we create everything by thought. There are master teachers who still come to visit your world, to teach your people. However, the people of your plane are steeped in ignorance, which they cling to. This instrument has had a very difficult time trying to teach the public. It was years before he could discuss the *Gifts of the Spirit* with any of his friends, let alone any of his relatives. Even now, as modern and scientific as you are, many people abandoned the instrument, because they were not ready to understand the truth.

🧑 That's true. Is there any other message that you wish to share with us?

👼 I am being told to share this with you, at this time, your world as it is today, in your year of... ah... your year of... What is this year?

🧑 1990.

👼 In this, your time of 1990, if you will look closely, there are many changes happening on your planet. We are watching other changes happen. However, we want you to learn of an awareness that is coming over your entire planet that will sweep the world, as though it is a wind that is coming from all four corners of the earth. It is touching all the minds of the people. This includes people who do not have an education, and even those who claim to be tyrants. This change will occur at a slow pace, but it will occur more rapidly as you approach the change of the century. This will happen because those on the higher realms of the world where I am have interceded. They are working with conditions on your planet. If this were not so, your planet would be destroyed. There would be no living beings left on the planet. A few greedy people, who wanted to control the world, in any way possible would have caused this destruction. The people from my world are working to create peace.

They are telling me that I am using this voice box quite well.

🧑 Yes you are, very well. Please describe what is it like for you to be able to speak to us through this medium's trance state.

💂 I had to be able to lower my vibration to equal the vibration of this man. It is the light of my spiritual body that will make the connection. As I lower my vibration to a visible light, it becomes visible to his clairvoyant sight. I had to lower my light so he could see it. When he sees the light, he then concentrates on it. We can then switch places.

🧑 The medium raised his vibration, as he began to go into trance.

💂 That is true.

🧑 So, you met on a vibration that is not on the instrument's normal vibrational rate.

💂 That is correct. In this man's body, his heartbeat and all his vital organs are working much faster than his normal pace. This is why it is not healthy for a medium's body to continually go into a trance state. The body itself will burn out, especially if it is overtaxed.

🧑 Why is the body working at a faster rate?

💂 It is working at a faster rate to maintain the vibration of the spiritual body. You must remember that in order to ascend, a person increases his or her vibration. Then, the whole entire body, (both the physical and spiritual bodies) is vibrating, so fast that it becomes invisible, and transparent.

It is a way of exploding—going back into light. This is something I had to learn after I came to this dimension of life. According to the way you measure time, it took me many years to learn it. For a long time, I seemed to be in limbo. I did not accept the teachings of this side. I was still hung up on the teachings of my own family, from your side of life. Eventually, I could accept what was more real to me. And that brings us to this point right now.

🧑 Are there other Spirit people involved with this trance communication right now?

💂 Yes, there are many people of whom you are not aware.

🧑 Could you explain what functions they have, and what they are doing?

👮 There is a doctor whose name is Dr. Bong. He is the one who controls the energy, making this communication possible. He adjusts the frequency. It would be similar to your operating and maintaining a frequency of a particular wattage, for example. There is another engineer here, as you would term it. He works with Dr. Bong. There is a chemist here, who has to change the chemistry that feeds this body. It would be difficult for you to understand this process in your own words. You must speak up, for the energy is starting to change. We do not want to tax this body any more than is necessary.

🧑 I cannot think of any other questions to ask you. I would like to thank you for joining us this morning. Congratulations on your fine trance communication! It was very successful! I think all of us have enjoyed it, and have learned much from it.

👮 Thank you, Sir. It is a pleasure that I could use this opportunity as my debut. I assure you this will not be the last time I work through the instrument, if the Spirits, who work with the medium, grant me permission.

🧑 I eagerly await hearing from you again.

👮 It has been more than a pleasure. As I reach out to all of you who have gathered in this hall, I shall leave you with my peace, on this morning. Many of you, all of you, will remember this for the rest of your life. I am one that was called "dead." I am not dead at all; I am only in another vibration. I assure you, when you pass into this dimension, each and every one of you will be passing with knowledge stored in your soul. There will be no question in your mind about where you will go. This knowledge will become your passport, bringing you to where I am. For you see, I did not have a passport—I only had the corner of it, given to me by my friend, Harold.

With that, I leave you with my peace.

🧑 Thank you.

🧑 Well, I am Nathaniel. I will take just a few seconds here to express to you how pleased we are that the young man could use our medium to speak to you. This has been a great morning for us, as it has been for you. I will leave you also with my blessings. May all of you remember that the Lord of your being is the light that is around you, and the God of your being is the substance from which this light originates. It is called your soul. Therefore, you are equal in all that you do. We have given this teaching to our medium repeatedly. It is nothing new to you. You have heard him repeat it to you. Now I am using my own words, through his voice box, to tell you again that all of you are equal, and within you, you will find God. Turn within because you will be coming home. Home to God, and there you will find the light, and the way, and you will never turn back.

Again, my peace be with you, this your morning.

Carl coughed several times as he came out of trance. I gave him a large glass of water — because his throat is always extremely dry after he comes out of trance. After a few minutes of resting, and discussing the information that had come through, Carl stood up at the podium, and concluded the service. He then went home to lie down and rest.

* * * * *

So much interesting information had come through during this session. It was interesting to talk to someone who had actually known Carl when he was a child. Carl's parents were devout Baptists. Since much psychic phenomena happened around Carl, from the moment of his conception, Carl's childhood was not a pleasant one. His parents thought the Devil was after them. They never did understand Carl's mediumship.

On Carl's first day of school, Spirit people took over his body, (i.e. he went into trance) and addressed the entire school. Due to this lecture, the older students beat Carl up at recess. Within three days, the entire community shunned him.

What was truly remarkable about this trance, however, was to discover how one short conversation completely altered Larimar's destiny. As Larimar said, he did not have much understanding of psychic science, but the little that he had made a difference in his after-life. He arrived on the fifth level, instead of the third. **This is why an understanding of psychic science is so important.**

People living in the Spirit World have tremendous advantages over people living in our physical world. Spirit people live with other Spirit people of like mind and consciousness. For example, if Samuel leads a good life, and harms no one during his physical life, when he dies he will go to a place where other good people are. He will not have to worry about evil people, robbing him, or breaking into his house to do him harm. The Spirit World is like a long staircase. The evil people are on the bottom levels. The enlightened people are on the highest levels. As Larimar said, people on the higher level may go down to visit and help teach the ones on lower levels. No one, however, may go up the levels until he or she evolves, and increases their consciousness.

Many levels of the Spirit World are filled with souls fast asleep. They lie there, waiting for a great savior to come, blow a horn, and wake them up, so that they can begin their life in the Spirit World. They are sleeping because they think this is what they need to do. They will lie for centuries upon centuries, sleeping. They are what is termed **dead in Spirit**. They exist in this suspended state of animation because that is what they were taught by their churches. On occasion, when a member of their family comes to try to wake them up and teach them how incorrect their views are, they awaken for a moment. They think that since it not Jesus coming to wake them, it must be the Devil. They then turn over, and go back to sleep. They are totally entrenched in the man-made dogma created by theologians. There is no escape.

It is essential, as Larimar explained, for people to understand that life continues after the change we call death. *The understanding of psychic science is the passport that will take you into forever.*

TWENTY-SIX

The Great Hospital

This conversation took place in Carl's office, about a year after he had a disturbing experience. *Carl was not in trance*, but in his normal state of consciousness for this dialogue.

🧑 I know that you had an experience where you visited the great hospital on the infrared level of the Spirit World. Please explain how that is possible.

🧑 It is really easy to understand. I know you understand that there are two bodies—a physical body and a spiritual body, which is the soul. Certain people have the ability to **astral project**, which means their soul can temporarily leave the physical body, and travel to other parts of the universe, even to other dimensions. Since the silver cord that connects the soul to the physical body stays in tact, the person does not die. Many people are unaware that they astral project, because most people do it in their sleep.

🧑 Thank you for explaining that. Now please tell us about the "great hospital."

🧑 Do I have to relive that again? It was a horrific experience.

🧑 I think it would be beneficial for our readers if you spoke about it.

🧑 In 1997, three entities came and escorted me to the "great hospital."

🧑 What do you mean by entities? What did they look like?

🧑 The entities looked totally different than anyone living on this planet. They were small in the build of the body. They had small arms and legs.

🧑 Were they shorter than you? (Carl was 5'11")

🧑 Oh yes, much shorter than I am.

🧑 Could you describe them in detail?

🧑 They had very large eyes, much larger than one would imagine. Their eyes were not round like ours. Also, our eyes have *scleras*, (the white part of the eye); they do not have *scleras*. Their eyes looked very moist and shiny, and were a deep brownish color. I was told these entities live in another planetary system, where their sun is dim, and smoky-colored. I have been thinking about this, and that is why their eyes are so large. Their environment would be much darker than ours, because their sun does not give off as much light. Therefore, they would need larger eyes to see.

🙂 That makes sense.

🙂 They had no hair on their heads, and they didn't have ears, as we do. They had holes where their ears should be, but there would be no place to hang a pair of eyeglasses, if you understand what I mean.

🙂 Yes, I get the picture.

🙂 Their mouths were very small. Come to think of it, I never heard them talking to one another, such as we are doing right now. It seemed as if they communicated through mental telepathy.

🙂 Did these entities all look alike?

🙂 Well, I cannot say that they looked like triplets; there were small differences between the three of them. They were different heights, but all were short compared to us. They reminded me of small children, about two years old. I don't know why I noticed this, but their clothes were a sliver gray color, and seemed to be painted on. They fit as a tight stocking, with no seams. There were no lines in their clothes, such as where we button our shirts, or the top of our pants.

🙂 That's interesting. Please tell me more about them.

🙂 They had the ability to control a person's mind. I know there were times that my mind was frozen, and when I became conscious again, I was in another location. I had no memory of moving from the first place to the second. They also had the ability to manipulate time.

🙂 What do you mean?

🙂 These entities have escorted me "on trips" three times during my life. The first time I was five years old and the second time I was nine. During my first experience with them I was five years old, and it was the month of May. My mother and Miss Abbey, our neighbor, were preparing string beans, as they sat in the rocking chairs on the porch. It was a clear and beautiful day. In those days farmers would rise very early, and work in the fields from four in the morning until ten. After that it was much too hot to work in the fields. Remember, I was living in the southern part of North Carolina, in the early 1930's, during the Great depression. There was no air-conditioning in those days.

🙂 Yes, I know.

🙂 I remember Mama and Miss Abby had a big washtub full of string beans, and they were getting them ready to can them, which would preserve them to use during the winter months. I was sitting in a swing that was also on the porch.

I noticed these three different looking entities, walking along the dirt road that ran along side the house. As these strangers approached, they must have "zapped me," and taken over my mind, because I do not remember what happened after that. The next thing I remember, I was at the top of a knoll, where we were headed. It was the highest spot in the area, where at one time, there was a fire tower. There was a ship there. It resembled a 22 gauge bullet sitting on its end, with the point of it aimed at the sky. As we approached it, a ramp opened, as we walked up the ramp. As soon as we reached the doorway, my mind went blank again.

I next remember sitting in the ship. Everything looked as though it were made of stainless steel. I was scared and frightened, because I did not know what they wanted to do to me. Then my mind went blank again.

In my next recollection, I was sitting facing a porthole, which now reminds me of the kind you would find on ships. My face was close to the porthole, but I did not understand what I was seeing at the time. Far into the distance I saw this ball that was green and blue. Today, after watching the pictures beamed from NASA, I know I was looking at the earth from outer space.

They had something hooked to me. I do not know what it was. I can only surmise that they were giving me oxygen, but I am not certain. Then I remember begging them to go home. I desperately wanted to go home.

Again, my memory of this event is spotty because they were controlling my mind, so I would only remember what they wanted me to remember. My next memory is of lying on a table, which was stainless steel. However, it did not feel as hard as steel would be. It was not cool, as steel would be. It is difficult to describe. I didn't know what they were doing. However, after that I would bleed a little, not a lot after I went to the bathroom. Eventually that cleared up and stopped.

I have no other memory except that we were back on the ground, in the same location from which we left. Two of these entities walked ahead of me, while the last one walked behind me. They escorted me down the dirt road, all the way home. When I came to my yard, these entities stopped, and I returned to full consciousness. I walked up on the porch and sat on the swing.

My mother spoke and said, "My God, Miss Abbey, something is wrong. Look where the sun is. We have just started these beans. Where did the time go? We should have been nearly finished by now."

Mama went into the house to see what time it was on the mantle clock. She came running back out to the porch, and said, "You know it is almost four o'clock!"

They had started to work on the beans sometime between noon and 1 o'clock, and only had a few of them done!

Mama kept saying, "I don't understand this! I don't understand this!" Then she looked at me and said, "Son, what is the matter?"

I do not remember how I responded. That night I had a terrible nightmare. I was screaming at top of my lungs, "Mama, don't let them take me. Mama, don't let them take me." It took her quite some time to awaken me. Evidently, I was either having a fever, or I was in such a deep sleep that she couldn't awaken me. I remember her telling Daddy about what had happened. Daddy was working in Wilmington, about thirty-five miles away.

🙂 That was some experience!

🙂 It was one that took me years to understand, and to be truthful; I still have many questions about it.

🙂 Now let's discuss your experience at the great hospital.

🙂 Very well. I have been clairaudient and clairvoyant all of my life. When I was young, I used to spend hours up in a live oak tree, talking with another boy. I never gave any thought as to who this boy was. It was only after I had grown up that I discovered that this boy was my Indian guide and control, Lone Eagle. He appeared as a boy, about my age in those days, and would teach me all kinds of information.

One day, he told me that there was a great hospital on the lowest level of the Spirit World. It made no sense to me that there would be a "hospital in heaven." For years I had my doubts; I thought I had been told a story. However, in 1997, after I had visited this terrible hospital, I now know for a fact that it exists.

🙂 Yes, Awan explained that the hospital was built to house the millions of Christians who were taught by their priests to go directly to sleep when the entered the Spirit World. Their souls followed those instructions. Awan said this hospital was built in the late fourth century.

🙂 From my understanding that is true. This hospital is a giant warehouse, or motel to house all these sleeping Spirit bodies.

🙂 Carl, please describe what you saw there.

🙂 The color of everything was orange, the vivid color of a very ripe orange. I did not see lights, as we know them, yet everything was in orange light. The people's skin was orange, the floor, walls, and ceilings were all orange in color. There were no shadows. It was a creepy, horrible place to be. I kept saying, "This is a dream, I can't be here."

🙂 Those three entities were with you?

🙂 Yes.

🙂 And they took you on a tour of the hospital?

🙂 They escorted me everywhere I would go. Two were in front of me, and one behind.

🙂 And they didn't speak to you at all?

🙂 No, they did not. It was the same way it had been when they took me in the spaceship, as a child. There was someone in Spirit who appeared, and talked to me, about these entities, while I was in the hospital.

🙂 What were you told?

👤 The Spirit told me these entities had lived on this earth for thousands of years. Their brains are fully functional, because they do not age or die. They had evolved beyond the bodily functions that we are used to. They do not eat food, nor do they need oxygen. It seems to me that the bones of their skeleton must be very brittle. The tears that they shed are blue in color. Even their blood is blue. It is beyond my understanding. These are my own thoughts and speculations. These entities may not be extraterrestrial, but interterrestial. They may live on the inside of this planet.

🙂 What do you mean?

👤 Spirit has explained to me there once was an explosion of the sun. A large chunk of molten rock was thrust away from the sun during the explosion. All this happened billions of years ago. A hot chunk of molten rock was spinning very fast. The centrifugal force cause all the matter to go outward, just as clothes are found on along the outer wall of a washing machine's spinning drum. Therefore, when this molten sphere of rock cooled, it had a hollow central core. I just described how the earth was formed.

🙂 That is very interesting.

👤 The very core, within the earth, remained there because of the magnetic pull of the outer core. Because the core is still hot, it glows, like a huge charcoal, but it is smoky blue. It is my contention that this glowing core is the sun for these entities, who live in the inner world. There are three openings in the planet, which allow these entities to leave the inner world. The first is in the Atlantic Ocean, the area that is known as the "Bermuda Triangle." They have a way of making a huge waterspout which spins so fast, you could fly a ship through it, you would travel between 400-600 miles, the thickness of the earth's crust, before you would arrive in the inner world. There are two other openings at the positive and negative (North and South) Poles.

Our government decided to test the powerful bombs, in the year 1947. I am not sure if they were hydrogen or atom bombs, but the scientists tested them underground, somewhere in New Mexico. They drilled deep into the earth, placed the bomb there, and exploded it. The explosion rippled through the earth's crust, and caused terrific damage in the inner world. The inner people were forced to send some of their airships out through one of the openings, to see what had caused the damage. During their exploration, the government shot down one of their ships, and another ship crashed with one of our airplanes. The government recovered the bodies of these entities, and have kept them frozen somewhere. This happened near Roswell, New Mexico.

🙂 So some of the extraterrestrials may really be interterrestrials.

👤 That is my theory. Walking through that hospital was a very horrible experience for me. To tell you the truth, I think my soul is trying to prevent me from remembering this incident. The hospital did not have beds, as our hospitals do. The Spirit bodies were lying about four inches apart, stacked from the floor to the ceiling, because there are so many of them. It reminded me of the very high shelving of merchandise that you would see in Sam's Club, or BJ's Wholesale, where merchandise is stacked from the floor, practically to the ceiling. The hospital has aisles so long, that when you stand at one end and look down the other, you cannot see the other end. That is how big this hospital is. It looked to me as if it would go on for hundreds of miles.

How many people were in the great hospital?

How can you count millions? The ceiling is 50 times higher than Sam's Club. There is no way of saying how many souls are stored there. Awan has told me there are millions, beyond count and number. There is no way of knowing the exact number, besides new souls are arriving there on a daily basis.

Some of those people were not in a deep sleep. Some were only in a light sleep. They would awaken, and cry out in an agonizing voice, "Jesus, help me, Jesus help me." Their souls were programmed that way, because these poor people accepted the false teachings from their priests.

These people are waiting for Jesus to come and wake them. If another Spirit who does not look identical to the picture of Jesus that hung in their church, comes to wake them, they will just roll over and go back to sleep. Some of these souls have been asleep for over 1600 years. I am not sure what can be done to wake them up permanently. Some of them may sleep for eternity.

It sounds like a very depressing place.

It is. Hearing haunting cries of these people deeply disturbed me. I saw other Spirit people, who had never accepted the priest's false teaching, and now reside on higher levels of the Spirit World, walking around, calling out the names of their sleeping relatives. I witnessed one Spirit who had aroused his sleeping mother. The mother raised her head, opened her eyes, looked at her son, then closed her eyes, and laid her head back down, and went back to sleep. The programming in her soul told her that the person who was trying to wake her was the devil, wearing the mask of her son's face. To me this was hell, for the ones that were not asleep. There is no way to convince these sleeping souls that their priests had mislead them.

This is so very sad.

Awan explained to me that the soul records and holds every piece of knowledge. The soul cannot distinguish truth from falsehoods. It does not judge the validity of the knowledge it contains. Therefore, any information, or programming, that the soul contains will be carried out.

I can now understand the damage caused by the Church when it indoctrinated its followers with false dogmas. How did you come back?

Well, they finally took me back to where I was supposed to be, but it took me a long time to re-adjust. The imprint of the experience is so intense, so very strong, that I had trouble coming back permanently. Afterwards, I had trouble sleeping for several weeks. I was afraid to be alone, and I was having trouble functioning. I kept praying to the Lord God of my being to remove this experience from my soul, because I didn't want to deal with it any more. As I look back, I am quite sure that this was all created to prove something to me.

🙂 Why do you think everything was orange?

🙂 I have no idea. I have not received any answers about that. That frequency is known as infrared, but that hospital is in the upper regions of the frequency.

The Spirit people are telling me you are to know this. The same theologians who programmed their parishioners' souls to sleep for eternity, put these words in Jesus' mouth, by writing them into the Bible:

> **"It is easier for a camel to go through the eye of a needle than for a rich man to enter the kingdom of God."[483]**

At the end of the fourth century, theologians put this into the Bible to scare the wealthier people, and convinced them to give most of their money to the Church. It was a way for rich people to buy a place for themselves in heaven. The priests were only interested in getting this money in their own pockets, so they could spend and enjoy it. They had little regard for the people who trusted them.

🙂 That is the time when Jerome was revising the Latin Vulgate Bible.

🙂 The Spirit people are confirming that as true.

🙂 Perhaps that is why so many of the clergy were outraged at Jerome's translation.

📖 *This quotation supports my statement:*

> *At first his translation met with antagonism, and it was even declared to be heretical.* **The renowned Church theologian Augustine at first had his doubts about it.**[484]

🙂 Perhaps that is true. You know when I was a small boy, going to the Baptist Church, I heard this message every Sunday. You must give some of your money to God. They often took up three or four collections each Sunday. They would not continue with their service until enough money was

---

[483] Mark 10:25 [NIV].

[484] May, Herbert Gordon: *Our English Bible in the Making; The Words of Life in Living Language.* Philadelphia, PA: The Westminster Press, 1952. p. 13.

collected. They put as much fear as they could into the people's minds by ingraining the idea *that the money is the root of all evil.*[485]

🙂 Thank you for sharing all this information with me today. I know you were very reluctant to relive this experience. I am sure that the readers will find it quite enlightening.

This is a picture of Carl standing in front of the live oak tree, near this childhood home. When he was a boy, Carl used to have conversations with his Spirit Control, Chief Lone Eagle, while sitting on the limbs of this tree.

---

[485] 1 Timothy 6:10.

TWENTY-SEVEN

Judgment Day

It had been over a month since my last dialogue with Awan. It was a crisp autumn day, and the leaves were in their glorious colors. Carl felt we should have this dialogue in the woods. We quickly packed up the tape recorder, water bottle, sleeping bag, and blindfold, and towel. As we walked through the woods we admired the fiery colors of our oak tree's leaves. After Carl arranged the sleeping bag, he sat down leaning on the oak tree, blindfolded his eyes, and placed the veil over his head. After saying his prayer, Carl sat quietly for about two minutes, then I heard the now familiar greeting.

😇 My profound greetings to you, my scribe!

🧑 Greetings, Awan.

😇 Today, my scribe, we are going to dialogue about a topic that will baffle many of your readers, since it will again contradict their religious leaders' teachings.

🧑 What is the topic, Awan?

😇 Today, we will discuss *Judgment Day*. There are millions of people who are absolutely petrified of that term. It sends shivers throughout their very beings; right though their souls, despite the fact their souls are asleep. For centuries, theologians have terrorized people about *Judgment Day*. People are justified in their apprehension; however, *Judgment Day* is extremely different from the senerio described by their theologians.

🧑 Awan, I do not understand.

😇 Let me explain, my scribe. Millions of people in your dimension believe that after they die, their souls will travel to an immigration center called *purgatory*, on some far off piece of real estate in the sky. There will be many people there, so they will have to stand in a long line, waiting their turn to see, Jehovah, Jesus, or Saint Peter, depending on the person's belief system. That saintly entity will have a book entitled "This is your life (*and the person's name*)," for there is a book for every person. Next, the saintly person will read the entire book that contains a detailed listing of every action the person did during his/her entire lifetime. Then, the moment of truth arrives, when

Jehovah, Jesus, or Saint Peter will declare if the person has been a good person, and is entitled entry into heaven, or if the person was a horrible wretched sinner, and must report to Lucifer's kingdom, of everlasting hell fires.

🧑 I suppose you are correct, Awan. That is an accurate description of many people's concept of **Judgment Day**.

👼 We have already discussed the process of death, so I will not use this valuable energy to repeat it.

🧑 That's OK, Awan. I remember what you taught me.

👼 Obviously, when the physical body has died, the soul, or Spirit body, leaves the physical body and physical world, and arrives in my kingdom. Most people come to the 3rd, 4th, or 5th levels of the Spirit World. These are planes of rest and restoration, where the person adjusts to his/her new body and surroundings. After the soul has become acclimated, it faces *"Judgment Day."* We, in this dimension, do not use that term; we call it a *Life-Review*.

Many people do not realize that thoughts are things [energy]. They mistakenly believe they can do anything behind closed doors and no one will know. Think about this example: if you back into a hot stove, and burn your backside, you must sit on the blister! This means that you must suffer the consequences of your actions. No one else can do it for you.

Many people have been taught, that you can do anything at all, dump it at Jesus' feet, and he will remove it from you. None of this is true. This was part of the great man-made conspiracy of a controlling belief system. I have come to the world to give you a knowingness system, which has the potential of liberating you from the enslaving emotion of fear.

During your *life-review*, every action and experience will be shown. It is an agonizing experience, because the judge is so harsh, and usually unforgiving. It will not be Jesus, nor some other advanced being who will judge you. The hyper-critical judge will be *you*. Every person must judge his or her own life!

🧑 You are your own judge?

👼 Yes, my scribe.

🧑 How can that be? Millions of Christians believe that Jesus will judge them after they die.

👼 Sadly, that is true, my scribe. However, those same Christians will be sadly disappointed, or perhaps elated to discover this teaching is false. After this session is over, and my medium regains his energy, ask him to discuss the conversation he had with Dewey, his half-brother. Dewey, was living in my dimension, and used another trance medium to speak with my medium. You will find that story enlightening.

🧑 OK, Awan, I will ask him. However, getting back to the topic of our dialogue, I think being your own judge would be easy, everybody would say he or she led a fine life, and that would be that.

👼 It doesn't work that way, my scribe. There is no harsher judge during a *life-review* than you. Since all events you experienced are recorded in your soul, you "rewind the videotape, and you watch your life."

🧑 That doesn't sound so bad.

👼 Well, it is usually quite traumatizing. You are lacking one vital piece of information, my scribe. As you watch every action that you did in your lifetime, you will not only remember the emotions and feelings of what happened to you. You will also feel the emotions and feelings of the other people involved. You become the observer and participant, "the doer and done to," as you go through your life-review.

🧑 You re-live each experience from both perspectives?

👼 Yes, my scribe. You relive everything that you ever did—sum total of your actions, both from your perspective, and that of the object of your actions. For example, if you plotted against someone, you relive those negative thoughts, then you suffer the attack of your villainy, by feeling the pain your victim suffered. If you could not control your anger, and routinely beat your child, you again feel those out-of-control feelings of rage, and also you become the child you victimized, feeling his or her anguish, and physical pain. If you maliciously slandered another person, you will experience what it felt like to have your good name dishonored. If you abandoned your child, you will perceive the feelings your child experienced, that negative cloud of thought, always trying to comprehend why his or her parent left. During this *life-review*, you are whole in this hour, and are forced to realize, that you are responsible for your actions.

You relive your entire life. You experience your youthful inspiration of dreams you wished to accomplish in your life, and the boredom or stagnation, when you failed to focus and manifest those dreams.

🧑 How can this happen, Awan?

👼 It is quite simple, my scribe. Remember, in my kingdom, you live in a body of energy. Both thoughts and emotions are energy. Therefore, all this energy mixes, and you become your ideas, thoughts, actions and emotions. You relive all your actions, both positive and negative, from all perspectives, in all their dimensions. Remember, my scribe, you are God—therefore, you are energy.

🧑 I am beginning to understand why this is so dreadful. It must be difficult to learn and experience all the pain you have caused other people during your lifetime.

👼 In reliving and exposing the errors of your life, you reclaim your wholeness. This is not bad, or to be dreaded, because it is necessary for ignorant people. It is the only way to gain enlightenment.

🧑 Awan, I don't understand.

😇 Enlightenment is not a gift that someone hands you on a silver platter. You must earn enlightenment. Don't you understand my scribe, what you, yourself, have experienced? What have I encouraged you to do after teaching you?

🧑 You have told me to research it for myself, or ponder over your words.

😇 Precisely. As you contemplate my words, you are reorganizing those thoughts, and you, yourself, are recording those thoughts in your soul. You are mixing your own energy into the knowledge; therefore, it becomes your truth, written into your soul. I do not have you accept my knowledge, by simply having you swallow it as you would swallow your vitamin pills. All that would do is modify your belief system. I wish you to create a knowingness system, my scribe; therefore, you must be involved in the process, by adding your energy to the knowledge.

🧑 I think I understand, Awan.

😇 During your *life-review*, you see all your actions, and the results of your actions. Once you have relived all the events and emotions of your life, you are overloaded with thoughts and emotions. You then need time to process all this information. It is much like your computer. If you gave the machine a million billion numbers to add, it would not give you an instant answer. It would need some time to process the task of adding all those numbers.

🧑 Yes, Awan, I understand.

😇 The same is true of your **life-review**. You need to process all these thoughts and emotions. You must ponder, through contemplation, for it is painful to realize that *you* made all these mistakes. Therefore, you are given ample time in contemplation at any location you may choose. You are able create your own environment. Some people sit on a mountaintop, or in a forest, or meadow. Some people feel comfortable contemplating at a college, or in a library. You create whatever environment you wish.

It is during this time of contemplation, that you plan a strategy of correcting the wrongs you committed during the life you just completed. You map out a plan to learn the lessons you need, what experiences you will need in your next life that will record new truths into your soul.

No one will tell you that your plan is right or wrong. There is no such thing on that plane of existence. All your thoughts and actions will be immensely clear, because in that realm, you are empowered to recreate the physical world. You must use imagination, your greatest resource, to plan out your next life. Some people map their life for 30, 50, 100, or 10,000 of your years.

🧑 So that is what Spirits do between incarnations!

😇 That is what most Spirits do. The more enlightened Spirits do not have to go through this process. Now, my scribe, once you have finished your plan, you emerge from your deep state of contemplation. You then rest for a while, before you face your the next battle, which is your next life. It is then that you suddenly notice that you are not alone. There are other people nearby, also completing their strategies. It is then that you begin what you now term, "networking." You begin sharing thoughts and feelings with other people. Much to your surprise, you discover that many of these people are working on the exact same issues as you. Some of these places are very crowded, because many humans have similar shortcomings, which they are attempting to overcome. It is through much conversation that a bonding, or an exchange of energy, occurs between entities. Relationships form; these are not love relationships, but are contracts that people will meet in a certain time in the physical world, to work on a project or problem. So it is on this plane of the Spirit World that alliances are made, and people agree to reincarnate as a group.

That is really fascinating, Awan.

You, and the instrument that I am using, made such an alliance in the Spirit World. You agreed to go back to the physical world, to do exactly what you are doing—writing books of spiritual knowledge.

Wow, Awan! That is really neat!

Many people are of the assumption that when someone seems familiar, and you just met them for the very first time that you knew that person in a past life. This does happen occasionally. However, more typically you met the person in *my* dimension, between lifetimes, and you and the person made an agreement to work on a problem in your present life.

You know, Awan, that really makes sense to me.

You had a very famous playwright, whose name was William Shakespeare. In one of his plays, a character states: "All the world is just a stage." That was a very profound statement, my scribe. For you must understand, the earth plane is your stage, to act out the events of your life. It is also a classroom, where you test what you learn. You reincarnate to live a life, to see if you can master the skills that you wish to achieve. You also return with other "actors who have a similar script." When you reincarnate, however, you have no knowledge of your goal. That is the beauty—it is a true test. If you remembered that you came into the world to learn humility, it would be like taking a list of answers into the examination room. At the end of the test you would never know if you really remembered the answers, or if you just copied them from your notes.

I understand; while your soul knows the problem you are working on, your conscious mind does not.

Exactly, my scribe. After you return to your dimension, your soul recalls your plan in minute detail, however your conscious mind will not remember. Now, I want this clearly understood, my scribe, there is **NO** such thing as chance. What you term destiny, is really a carefully orchestrated plan that was mapped out in my dimension. It was not designed by an old-man with a beard sitting on a bejeweled throne. You and the other person(s) involved agreed to it, before you reincarnated.

🧑 I understand.

👼 There comes a time when you want to reincarnate, and come back into another body, to live out your plan. You, and those who agreed to work with you to conquer your weaknesses begin to reincarnate. You do not create, or choose your parents, you are drawn to the genetic pool that matches who you were in your past life. You only become what you are capable of becoming.

Unfortunately, the plan that you mapped out in the Spirit World rarely works out on earth as you envisioned it. The Spirit World is much too harmonious for you to remember the pitfalls of your dimension. You did not anticipate that your parents would scold you in your childhood, and that event would become so painful to you and was recorded so strongly in your soul; that it became a focal point of your life. You did not have the benefit of these teachings to teach you how to erase that issue. You began with good intentions, but got stuck in life. When you are entrenched in your past, you deny yourself your future potential. That is what so grievous about holding on to victimization and suffering. It limits your possibilities.

Why sacrifice the plan you created in the Spirit World for the sake of holding on to a grudge, or hurt? This is what I meant when I said, why give your power away, especially to your past? You forsake your life-plan when you do so. You stop the flow of your true destiny when you cling to yesterday's garbage, simply because you identify so strongly with it.

Unless you are able to release the hurts of your past, and enemies of your past, you do not achieve the great future you created for yourself in my dimension. You will overlook the people who would move you in ways that would inspire your genius. Remember, you designed your own destiny.

🧑 Awan, please explain to me how to release the past.

👼 It is not that complex, my scribe. I have taught you how to access your closet of prayer. Enter it and use this affirmation:

> **Lord God of my being**
> **Unto the Father Within**
> **Come forward this moment, this hour.**
> **Hear my words and follow these instructions.**
> **Go into my soul's memory bank**
> **And erase the hurt I experience when _____.**
> **Replace it with love for myself, and all humanity.**
> **So Be It!**

Continue to do this on a daily basis. Eventually, you soul will hear the command, and follow your instructions. I am sensing a shifting of the energy, so I must leave you at this time. Contemplate my words, my scribe, you need to burn away your past. I leave you with my profound peace.

Thank you Awan, for this valuable information. My peace be with you, too.

Carl sat quietly for half a minute, suddenly he yawned. He stretched his arms, as he asked, "Where is my glass of water?" I assisted Carl in drinking a glass of water. We sat and discussed the information that Awan had delivered. Then Carl took a two and a half hours nap.

* * * * *

Later that evening, after Carl had regained his energy, I taped this conversation with Carl.

Awan, suggested that you should tell me the story about your half-brother Dewey speaking to you through a trance medium. He said that I would find it enlightening.

Well, I will gladly tell you the story, however, I am not sure why it would be enlightening? My half-brother, Dewey always disliked me. He was the youngest child of my father's first marriage, while I was the youngest child of his second wife. Dewey was jealous of me, because he felt I had displaced my father's affection for him. Therefore, Dewey played mean tricks on me, all of my life.

His final "triumph" was when he turned my father against me. My father died before I had the opportunity to correct that.

It was several years after Dewey had died, that suddenly I kept clairaudiently hearing the name *Etna Mane*. I looked up the name in the phone book, but had no success in finding it. This continued for several days. Finally I received a phone call from another medium, who said to me, "Carl, I am not sure why I am calling you." We talked for several minutes, and suddenly I found these words coming out of my mouth, "Do you happen to know anyone by the name of *Etna Mane*"

"No," she said, "I don't know anyone by that name, however, I do know of a place by that name. *Etna, Maine* is a Spiritualist camp that is in the northern part of the state of Maine. I hear they have some good mediums there."

After this conversation, my curiosity peaked, I asked a friend of mine, who was a newspaper reporter, if he wanted to accompany me to *Etna, Maine*. He agreed to go. It was the last week in August 1976. We had traveled all day to get to the camp. Upon arriving at 7 p.m., we discovered that this was the last service they were holding. The camp was only open during

Alan Howard speaking in a trance state during his visit to Gifts of the Spirit Church May 25, 1978.

the summer. We had a delicious meal at the pot-luck supper they were serving, and then quickly went to the hall where the service was to begin.

The medium, Alan Howard, in his "down-to earth" character, went into a trance state and allowed Spirit to deliver a lecture. Afterwards, there was also a message service. I was the first person, that evening, to receive a message from this entranced medium. This is what was said through the medium:

"I want to go to the back of the room, and talk to my son, Carl Hewitt"

Everyone turned to look at me. I realized from the wording that the Spirit was my father, Alvie Hewett."

Alvie continued, "Son, I had to come to this dimension, to understand you. I did not know you when I lived on earth. When I arrived in this dimension after my death, everyone was talking about you. They knew more about you than I did. They said that you were a terrific medium, who had the ability to relay information between the dimensions. Everyone, here was so proud of you."

That must have made you feel good.

It certainly did. As I have told you, when I was growing up everyone shunned me. Even my parents, would not answer my questions. These words helped to heal a deep wound that I had carried for such a long time.

My father then said, "Son, to prove to you that I have been around you, I know where you live. I have been to your house. "There have also been times when I sat in one of the chairs, on your porch, and smoked my pipe."

"I thought I smelled your old stinking tobacco, I wish you would change to some other kind."

"Also your place is surrounded by a wooden stockade fence," Alvie said.

"Yes," I said, "That is correct."

"As you drive through the gate make a sharp left, at the corner of the fence is a cluster of dogwood trees. Early in the morning, as the sun first comes over the horizon, there is a beam of light that cuts

Dogwood trees at the entrance to Carl's home

through the trees surrounding your property, and touches the root of one of these dogwood trees."

"I am not sure about that, I will have to check it out," Carl said.

Did you do that?

🧑 Yes, I did. When we returned to Connecticut, the reporter and I got up at 4 a.m. to watch the sunrise. We went to the spot my father described, and it was exactly as Daddy had described it. I did not know of this before Daddy told me.

🧑 That is very interesting.

🧑 Then Daddy said, "There is someone over here, who needs to speak with you, so I will vacate this medium's body to allow him access."

There was about 30 seconds of silence then I head another voice speak through the medium. "Son, do you know who this is?"

"Well," I said, "It sounds like my half-brother, Dewey."

🧑 "Wait a minute, why would your brother call you son?"

🧑 "I don't know why, but everybody called me *son*. My parents, grandparents, brothers and sisters all called me *son*.

Tears were now flowing down the medium's closed eyes. Then Dewey continued, "I have come to speak with you, and beg you for your forgiveness. I did terrible things to you, when I was alive. I am truly sorry. Please forgive me, son, *because there is no one else here that can forgive me*. I must carry this around for eternity, unless you forgive me."

This statement totally stunned me. For a moment, I froze, as if I had turned to stone. Was Dewey really speaking through this trance medium, asking me to forgive him? Suddenly, my mind was flooded with memories, of how Dewey tormented me for as far back as I could remember. Some feelings of resentment were building within me. After a few moments I finally regained my composure. A sudden burst of energy flooded through me, and suddenly I found myself saying these words: "Before I answer you, I need you to answer some questions for me. What happened to the message that we used to hear in Church when we were kids? 'Jesus will forgive you of all your sins, all you have to do is ask him for forgiveness?' Did Jesus go on a vacation? Isn't he there with you in that world?"

Dewey replied, "There is no one by that name here in the dimension where I am. I have asked, and no one here has seen him. But I have been told that only **YOU** can forgive me for what I did towards **YOU**! No one else is able to forgive me."

Empowered with this information I continued to question Dewey. "You mean to tell me that since we were kids we heard that Jesus would forgive all of our sins. Now you are telling me that Jesus cannot forgive you. I have to forgive you?"

"Yes, that is right," Dewey responded. "Son, please forgive me." Tears began pouring out of the eyes of the medium, flooding his cheeks.

Carl responded, "Well, I want you to know one thing, I will forgive you, because I really never held it against you. I realized that all the misdeeds you did against me were done through your ignorance. I realized that it was *your* problem, not mine. You are absolutely forgiven. However, it still puzzles me, that Jesus can't forgive you, because that is what we were taught for our entire lifetimes."

"Thank you, son," Dewey replied, "for being so generous to forgive me. It is more than I deserve after the way I mistreated you. I have inquired here, and all the masters who visit the dimension where I am living, have informed me that you are the only one with the power to forgive me the misdeeds that I committed against you. They said, the idea of Jesus forgiving everyone's sins is simply mind control, which is simply an incentive to make people return to the church on a weekly basis and keep putting money in the collection baskets."

Carl then responded, "Well, you are completely forgiven, as far as I am concerned. I wish everyone knew this message."

Dewey's final words were: "Well tell it to everyone, because it is the truth. You must seek forgiveness from the person that you wronged. No one else has the power to do it."

There was not a dry eye in the entire hall. Everyone was crying because of this emotional exchange.

🧑 So if Dewey had to ask your forgiveness, I guess that would prove that you judge yourself, as Awan had said. When Dewey said, "There was no one in the Spirit World to forgive him. The only one to forgive him would be you, the injured party." Wouldn't that indicate that Jesus, does not forgive your sins, or your mistakes."

🧑 I guess that it would. It certainly agrees with what Spirit has told me. Jesus does not hold a full time job, judging millions of Christian souls per year. Each person is his or her own judge, and must seek forgiveness from the person he or she was wronged.

The gravestones of Carl's father   and his brother Dewey

When Carl left home as a teenager, he wanted to distance himself from his family and the past. Therefore, he decided to change the spelling of his last name from Hewett to Hewitt.

TWENTY-EIGHT

Suicide, Abortion, and Euthanasia

As my learning had progressed, it seemed that for every question I had answered, another arose. I kept a notebook of my ever-growing list of questions. When I had gathered enough questions on a topic, I would ask to have another session with Awan. During this session, I asked his opinions on questions that our society is struggling to answer.

As Carl allowed Awan to take over his body, I thought about how fortunate I was to witness this phenomenal event. At each of these sessions the excitement I felt was intense. I would have no idea what revelations Awan would share with me. Before I knew it, I heard Awan's voice.

(😇) My sincere greetings to you.

(🧑) Greetings, Awan. Currently there are certain issues, which are troubling the minds of many people, and are splitting our nation is into two opposing camps. I was wondering if you would be able to shed some light on these topics, which concern birth and death.

(😇) I would be happy to share whatever knowledge I have. Please begin with your questions.

(🧑) Awan, please describe what it is like when a soul arrives in the Spirit World, especially if the soul experienced a prolonged painful illness, or a violent death.

(😇) When the soul is in the body of the human being, it is like a computer. The soul is an "isness," and records every experience that a person has, without judgment. When the body dies, the soul leaves the body, taking all the memories it has during that person's life into my dimension.

When a person who was brutally killed arrives here in my dimension, s/he is very traumatized. S/he can remain traumatized for quite some time; for it is like a nightmare, a terrible dream. Since the soul is now in a timeless dimension, this shock could last years of your time, but is only a moment in this dimension. Often family members, living in my dimension, meet this person, with consoling greetings. However, the person continues to believe this is a horrible dream from which s/he seem unable to awaken.

🧑 I have read that if a person dies of cancer, and if the person has had a prolonged or a difficult death, the soul upon entering the Spirit World will go into a hospital to recuperate, from its long tramua. Is there any truth to that?

😇 That is not true; the cancer is only in the physical body. The memory of that condition can remain in the soul. However, the family that meets that person here, explains how to go beyond that memory, by desensitising the emotion, to the point that it is just a vague memory. Unfortunately, many of people, who arrive in our dimension, go to sleep instantly, and have to be stored in the great hospital.

🧑 Yes, Awan, I remember our dialogue about the great hospital. Will those souls ever be awakened?

😇 They will be awakened, but it will be a long time until it occurs, perhaps hundreds of thousands of years into the future. It is like an eternal sleep.

🧑 What are the consequences of their souls being stuck in that sleep state? If they were more educated in the *Gifts of the Spirit*, and were not in that sleep state, how would their souls' progression be different?

😇 They would go through the different levels of vibration and learning. There are many levels in the World of Spirit, just as there are many levels in the physical world. You go through many levels of learning in your school system. When a person comes into this dimension, if they have not been programmed by your religions, then they go from one level to another. For instance, there are more levels than I can begin to count right now, but using what is termed the 5th level, that person would be able to communicate with someone that they left behind, by what you understand as intuition. Many people pick up messages being fed to them by their own ancestors, who are now living on the 5th level.

🧑 When a soul chooses to reincarnate, do they have full knowledge of how long their life span will be on this plane?

😇 That is something that they do not know, because they do not use time, yet there is an internal clock that is programmed in the soul. However, the soul is not conscious of that. It is difficult for us to explain this in terms that you would understand. Life does not end at death; it is only a transition, a change into another body. Then you stay in the Spirit body, in several levels for many years as you count your time. To us, in our dimension, this timeframe is only a fleeting second.

🧑 You said when the soul gets 14 inches from the body, *the silver chord* snaps. You have also said that the *river of thought* is 13 inches from you. Is there any connection between these distances? Does the silver cord snap when the soul touches the *river of thought*?

😇 What do you think?

🧑 I would say yes.

😇 You would be correct.

🧑 We talked about the people who have 100% of their brain functioning being able to ascend. In other words when a person ascends, they leave this dimension of life, taking their physical body with them. What is the advantage of ascending, as opposed to dying where the physical body is left behind?

😇 If you ascend, you can go beyond the Spirit World.

🧑 Go where?

😇 There are other dimensions that people on your plane know nothing about. There are other galaxies that your scientists have not yet discovered, where hate and bitterness do not exist. Everyone recognizes the God within all beings.

🧑 Awan, I now understand the process of death. But I have a few more questions. It is supposed to be very bad for a person to commit suicide. Is that true?

😇 When a person takes his or her own life, as you term it, suicide, or killing themselves, the person is shortening his or her natural time of life in evolution. If a person was destined to live seventy years, and decides to end their life at the age of twenty-five years, he or she would be creating—we do not use the word sin in my dimension. They would be creating a great wrong, because their own time clock was destined for them to live seventy years. Do you understand so far?

🧑 Yes Awan, I understand so far.

😇 Let's say that Philip, at the age of 38, has become very disenchanted with his life. He was destined to live until the age of 78. Philip has been a devout member of his religion; therefore, he does not really understand the process of dying. Most religions do not bother to teach their followers about how a person dies, and what truly will happen in the afterlife. Religious leaders are too busy scaring them to follow their rules and put money in the collection baskets.

Philip is under the illusion that by committing suicide, he will be ending his life, and his consciousness. He does not realize that his soul will continue to live forever. He will not go into an eternal sleep; he will arrive in the Spirit World and be just as alive as he was before his death.

Philip decides to end his life prematurely; he is totally shocked to discover himself awake in the other dimension. People from my dimension meet Philip as he arrives in the Spirit World. However, it is not a glorious experience. No, Philip's new world is not all that different than the one he left. You must understand that because Philip shortened his natural life span, therefore, he will arrive on the lower levels of the Spirit World. This is a level where ignorant souls reside. Often they were criminals in your dimension. It is a dark, ignorant place. Philip must spend much time on this level, working out his problems, and learning to evolve to the higher levels of Spirit.

Do you remember your conversation with Larimer?

🧑 Yes Awan, I do.

😇 Remember he explained how the small amount of knowledge he received just before he died enabled him to enter two levels higher than he otherwise would have?

🧑 Yes, Awan.

😇 Well, taking your own life is a guarantee to enter a much lower level of existence than you would if you continued living your life. It is very important for you to realize that suicide is never a viable option, no matter how awful you may consider your life to be.

🧑 Is that 100% true? If a person has terminal cancer, and takes his or her own life, is that just as bad as a healthy teenager committing suicide?

😇 Let us talk about Marie. She is suffering from cancer. Let us say that someone assists Marie in taking her own life. This isn't the same as Philip committed suicide. There is a period of grace, where Marie's soul was given the option to leave her physical body to avoid much suffering. In most cases, people opt to remain in their bodies. Most people believe their clergy when they preached how terrible death is. People are petrified of the great judgment they believe will take place, and are terrorified of the hells, purgatory, limbo, and other states of nonsense their theologians have described. All of this information is recorded in the soul, so the person is terrified to die.

You already understand what the soul is. The soul is a unit of energy that records, and holds everything you have learned and experienced. So, if Marie believed she committed many sins during her life, when she approached her death, she becomes very fearful. Marie does not realize that her fear is based on superstitions myths, since there is no validity to the dogmas created by the clergy. It is this fear that holds Marie back from simply leaving the body at the first opportunity, escaping much needless pain and suffering. If a person is programmed that terrible judgment exists after death, or the person believes he or she will spend eternity roasting in hell's fire, then that person will cling to life for as long as possible, despite the fact their physical body is racked with pain. This is the legacy humanity received from religions.

You must remember, death is just like going to sleep. For instance, last night, when you laid in your bed, you cannot remember the boundary between your last conscious moment and your first moment of asleep. Your body just calmed down and everything shut down. Your body kept breathing, because your soul, which controls the breathing mechanism, remained functioning. The soul keeps the body breathing, so you are alive in the morning. Do you understand?

🧑 Yes, I do.

😇 It is fear that holds people back, and keeps souls attached to physical bodies longer than they need to be. As a result, they continue their life in agonizing pain and suffering, because their souls prefer the "pain of life" to the "fears of death." People who are less afraid may reach out for somebody who knows something about medicine, to help them commit suicide, as you term it.

👤 So there is nothing wrong with a person shortening their own life if they are terminally ill?

😇 Let me put it this way, according your clock, your measurement of time, if someone were destined to pass to my dimension this very night, what is the difference if they passed away this very moment, or two or three hours from now?

👤 Not much, Awan.

😇 What is the difference of your going to sleep 10:00 p.m. as opposed to 12:00 midnight?

👤 Just a little bit.

😇 So if someone is assisted in shortening his or her life due to great physical suffering, since he or she is expected shortly, in my dimension, what is the difference?

👤 OK. I just wanted to clear that point up. Awan, I would like to ask you a question, which is troubling many people in our country. Is there any moral or spiritual problem with a woman having an abortion, ending her pregnancy?

😇 As I explained earlier, the soul that plans to reincarnate into your dimension stays in the light field around the body (mother's aura) for 96 days before it enters the body. When the baby starts kicking, the soul has just entered the fetus. Until then, it is just an organ of the mother's body. There is no soul or Spirit in it.

👤 If the Spirit is around the mother's body for 96 days before it enters, and the mother terminates the pregnancy, is the soul upset?

😇 The soul just chooses another vehicle.

👤 Does the soul experience any emotional turmoil?

😇 No, as cold as it may sound. It is just as if you took a small plant and put it in a pot and brought it in your house. It would still lean towards the nearest light. Turn it around, and it moves in the other direction towards the light. It doesn't matter. It doesn't judge.

👤 Then from your dimension, you see no problem with abortion.

😇 No, none whatsoever.

👤 So why is the Catholic Church so opposed to abortion?

😇 The answer is quite simple. Today, on your planet, very few people are converting to Catholicism. The only new Catholics are the children of older

Catholics. Therefore, the Catholic theologians set down the rules that no couples may copulate without having children. It was all a plan they created to support the Church. The more Catholics there are, the more money is placed in the collection plates. The Catholic Church does not care if these families can or cannot afford all these children. The Church does not care if the family goes hungry or not. The Catholic theologians are just interested in the money that these families can give to the Church. The priests want the public to support them in a luxurious lifestyle, so they can eat the best, most expensive foods, and drive the most expensive cars.

Awan, I would like to know what causes SIDS, **Sudden Infant Death Syndrome**. Small babies that are perfectly healthy die in their sleep. What causes this to happen?

The soul of the child decides that it has made a mistake. The soul feels that it cannot accomplish the goal that it set when it chose to reincarnate to that particular set of parents. Either the soul chose the wrong parents, or perhaps reincarnated into the wrong timeframe. Therefore, the soul decides to withdraw, and return to the World of Sprit. Since the soul does not know right from wrong, sometimes the soul reincarnates only to discover there were miscalculations, as you would term it, so the soul pulls back, and reenters into my dimension.

But doesn't it realize what kind of trauma it causes for its parents?

Analyze your question.

What do you mean?

You said the baby's soul caused trauma for its parents. Trauma is an illusion. Remember the soul is an isness, it knows not right from wrong. You consider trauma a negative condition.

Yes, Awan, that is true.

You are thinking in polarities. The baby's soul did not want to continue with that experience, so it left this dimension to continue its life in the Spirit World. All life is eternal; there is no beginning or end. The soul cannot control how another person will react to its departure from your dimension, nor can it be concerned with those emotions. It may sound cold, but that is reality. The parents' experience of grieving for their child is one to be recorded in their souls. In all likely hood, it is something that the parents need to experience, too.

But wait a minute, Awan. What is the difference between SIDS and someone committing suicide? In both cases the person is ending their life prematurely.

There is a great deal of difference between the two situations. When a person commits suicide, it is the consciousness of the physical person that made the decision to end his or her own life; whereas with SIDS, it is the soul that is making the decision to withdraw from the child. It is not a conscious decision of the individual.

🧑 That is a good point, Awan. I never thought about that. In suicide it is the physical person making the decision, in SIDS it is the soul that makes the decision. That is fascinating.

😇 I sense a shift in the energy, but I would like to say this much to you, before I vacate this man's body. Many people reading this book will be outraged, because it is going to make them think. For centuries many Christians have allowed their clergy to tell them what to do, and how to think. Their mental ability for analysis is not as well exercised as people who hold other religious beliefs. It is just as a person who has never gone to the gym, would be unable to lift a 400-pound barbell over his or her head.

After wrestling with my teachings, many people of all religions will stop looking outside of themselves for God. When these people will learn how to communicate with their God within, they will truly be coming home to God. I hope you found our conversation enlightening. My peace be with you.

🧑 Thank you, Awan. My peace to you, too.

There was nothing eventful about Awan's exit, and Carl returning into his body. This trance session left Carl so exhausted that he just leaned back into his chair and slept for two hours.

TWENTY-NINE

The War of Armageddon and the 12 Days of Light

This trance dialogue took place in Carl's office. Following his usual procedure, Carl dimmed the lights, sat in the chair behind his desk, and blindfolded his eyes. After saying his prayer, Carl sat quietly for about three minutes. Carl's body had no spasms. Suddenly Awan spoke.

(👼) My profound greetings to you, my scribe.

(🧑) Greetings, Awan

(👼) Today, my scribe, I think that we should change directions. We have spent much time dialoguing about the past. Today, I think we should discuss what will happen in the days to come. Before we start, however, I wish to inform you that this will be the last teaching for this second book. I have further teachings to give you, my scribe, and they will be for a third volume of teachings. Do you understand?

(🧑) Yes, Awan. I understand your instructions. So what will happen in the days to come?

(👼) The days to come will be terrifying for some, and a time of great rejoicing for others. Many changes will occur on your planet. However, as I see it at this time, and I do not want this to disturb you, my scribe, this series of books will bring forth something that was prophesied 2000 years ago.

(🧑) Really, Awan! What could that possibly be?

(👼) This book will launch the *"War of Armageddon."*

(🧑) Awan, I do not understand. What do you mean?

(👼) The *War of Armageddon* is waged in the mind, my scribe. You have already fought this battle, when you struggled to accept these teachings. You were angered at what I had said, then spent hours researching for yourself to determine whether or not I spoke the truth.

(🧑) You always have, Awan.

😇 Yes, my scribe, and I always will. But that struggle you went through in re-evaluating your old belief system, and transforming it into a knowinginess system is really the *War of Armageddon*.

🧑 It is, Awan?

😇 Yes, my scribe. I challenge the readers of this book to answer these questions: "Why do you have such a massive brain in your head when you only use a small portion of it? What purpose does most of your brain have if it is non-functional? Why is it there?" I have already taught the answer. The brain centers for *Gifts of the Spirit* are located in the "unused portion of the brain."

It is not far into your future that Churches will lose their power over humanity. People will no longer believe in a Devil, and no longer be afraid to practice the *Gifts of the Spirit*. When ignorance dies, humanity will come forward and carry out this work again. Then people will again begin to manifest their divine destiny: *to make known the unknown*.

Currently, you are living in the worst period of ignorance ever known on your planet. This is why so many negative events are happening. Young people think nothing of taking another person's life. They do not believe the man-made dogmas preached in the churches, temples, and synagogues. Yet, they have been disconnected from the God-within. They are so disenfranchised; they have reached a point where they don't believe there is anything beyond death. Therefore, they have no moral integrity, and nothing in which to believe. They feel there are no consequences for their actions. Life is valueless to them.

For the last millennium, religions have been fighting against each other. Christians waged crusades against Muslims. Protestants attacked Catholics. Muslims declared jihads against Christians, Jews, and Hindus. If religions joined together, and brought forth the truth, as it was recorded in your Book of Books, people would again become enlightened.

Your Bible is a record of people using the *Gifts of the Spirit*. The Biblical characters knew that God was within, and did not question it. It was the greedy leaders of religions who convinced people that God lived up in heaven.

The *end-times*, which is the period of time between the *Age of Ignorance* and the *Age of Knowledge* has already begun. It will be a time filled with great *"sights and wonders,"* as Jesus prophesied two thousand years ago. He said during the *end-times* there would be sights and wonders that will appear in the skies, seas, and on the land.

📖 These are the verses Awan is discussing:

> **You will hear of wars and rumours of wars, but see to it that you are not alarmed. Such things must happen, but the end is still to come. Nation will rise against nation, and kingdom against kingdom. There will be famines and earthquakes in**

> various places. "All these are the beginning of birth-pains [of the *Age of Knowledge*]."[486]
>
> "Immediately after the distress of those days "the sun will be darkened, and the moon will not give its light; the stars will fall from the sky, and the heavenly bodies will be shaken."[487]
>
> "No-one knows about that day or hour, not even the angels in heaven, nor the Son, but only the Father."[488]

(👼) When you see this, be not afraid because the dawning of the new age will follow. At this very moment, the dawning is about to show its face. The *Age of Ignorance* will pass away, and many people will be running to and fro, trying to find answers. For a great war will take place within all people; who have been taught not to think negatively towards their religions, and yet they can't think positively because of what is happening in their minds. This is the *War of Armageddon*, the great-war that has been prophesied. The mind is battlefield for the *War Of Armageddon*. It is not a war that will be carried out with guns, battle-axes, ships, or bombs. It will occur within the mind. Some people will go absolutely mad; they will become crazy lunatics, because they cannot handle what they are witnessing. They were brought up and indoctrinated in one frequency, and they are witnessing events beloning to another. There will be a great clash between these two frequencies, within the mind. The positive they are learning in the present vs. the negative that they have already learned and accepted, from their religious teachers.

As has been said through this medium before, "**Knowledge will become your passport into forever.**" Knowledge is occur when a person desires to learn more, and stops accepting the recycled ignorance they have been taught in the past. If you go to your church on this very day, go return five years from now; they will be teaching the identical information, consisting of man-made dogma, designed to control the people through instilling guilt into people's minds. This has to end. The dawning is coming of the *Age of Knowledge* is coming, and it will arrive sooner than you think.

(🧑) It sounds exciting, and frightening at the same time.

(👼) Yes, my scribe I can understand how you would feel that way. I want to be very clear about Jesus' grand prophecy. There is going to be a period of twelve days, when you will have light without darkness. This light will be so bright, that it will make your sun seem dim. All the animals and plants will become confused, since they will miss their cycles of day and night.

However, the people who are steeped in religions will have the most difficulty during this period of time. Many of these people will become

---

[486] Matthew 24:6-8 [NIV].

[487] Matthew 24:29 [NIV].

[488] Matthew 24:36 [NIV].

terrorized, since they think that this will be the end of the world, instead of the end of an age. They will flock to their Churches, demanding answers from their priests, ministers, and rabbis. The clergy will be at a loss not knowing what to tell the people. It will be a time of gnashing of teeth, as described in the Bible. Thousands of people will be so frightened that they will be committing suicide. It is the worse thing that that they could do, but because of their limited knowledge, they will act that way. There will be so many dead bodies, that there will not be enough coffins to bury the dead.

Awan, this sounds terrible.

My scribe, I want you to understand what I am about to say very clearly. The twelve days of light will be the boundary line as your world will permanently leaves the *Age of Ignorance*, and enters the *Age of Knowledge*. Those who have a knowingness system will find it a time to rejoice.

Awan, what will cause the twelve days of light?

Do you remember your teaching about the brain, my scribe?

Yes, Awan, I do.

Remember how I explained to you that the great people whose brains were fully operational saw ignorance sweeping over the planet. They were the ones who built the pyramids that are still standing. They did not wish to be caught up in it, so they ascended, and left this planet taking their bodies with them.

Yes, Awan, I remember.

Thousands of people visit the pyramids, each year. Yet, it is only a tiny minority who question who built these wondrous structures. How did they build them? What types of technology did they use? Where did these people go?

You have been conditioned by your religious leaders to accept everything you are told without questioning it. Your historians claim that the ancient people were savages. You also think you are currently so very intelligent and technologically advanced. Well you are not. The people who built the pyramids were not savages. They were 90% smarter than you because 90% more of their brains were functioning.

That makes sense, Awan.

We were the ones who built the pyramids, went to the ancient schools of wisdom, and studied the *Gifts of the Spirit*. We ascended, leaving this planet just as the religious tyrants began closing down the brain. Using the *gift of prophecy*, we saw how barbarically ignorant you would become. It was clear to us that jealousy, hatred, greed, and war would become an infectious disease, totally altering the course of humanity. If you were not truly ignorant your brain would be 100% operational, instead of 10%.

To retain our enlightenment, we were forced to leave your dimension. We had no other choice, because we could not stop the superstitious ignorance that would overrun your world. Our civilization moved to another planetary systems on higher frequencies. For centuries of your time, we have watched your planet very closely. You have not detected us because we can move so fast that you cannot even see us. We are not even a blur to you. We can dematerialize and still see you, however, you cannot adjust your frequency to see us. We vibrate much faster than you. We can stand right in your midst, even stare you right in your face, and you have no idea that we are there, unless we lower our frequency and allow you to see us.

Are these people ever going to return to earth, Awan?

Yes, my scribe. We are now beginning to return to your planet. We fly aeroships that you cannot even imagine. We do not burn fossil fuels. Because our brains operate 100% we can do things that you would not think could be possible. You would call them miracles, but there is nothing miraculous about them. For the last few of your years, we have created a new type of phenomena, in order to get your attention. We are responsible for creating *crop circles*.[489]

What are crop circles, Awan?

Crop circles are extremely large patterns that are found in wheat, barley, rye, or cornfields. We create these patterns by flattening down the crop. The geometrical shapes are very precise. Crop circles began appearing in grain fields since the 1970's.

The message of these circles is to let you know that we have returned to your planet. Yet, we will not allow you to see us until such time, as you evolve in consciousness, to be ready for us to teach you.

Most people have ignored our *crop circles*, taking them for granted. Do you wonder how we create crop circles? In some point into the future, we will reveal that to you. For at the moment, no one on your planet has the brain capacity to comprehend it.

Awan, that is incredible!

My scribe, it deeply saddens me to observe the people living on this planet, that we call the ***emerald of the universe***. For despite the thousands of years, since we left this planet, you have remained warring peoples. All you have managed to do is make more advanced weapons. Instead of spears, arrows and swords, you now use guns, missiles, bombs, and highly toxic weapons. We will not allow you to see us, as long as you live in that attitude. And if you think that your air force, or missile systems can keep up with us,

---

[489] For more information about crop circles see the following books:

Delgado, Pat and Andrews, Colin. *Circular Evidence: A Detailed Investigation of the Flattened Swirled Crops Phenomenon*. Grand Rapids, MI: Phanes Press, 1989.

Delgado, Pat and Andrews, Colin. *Crop Circles: The Latest Evidence*. London: Bloomsbury, 1990.

Delgado, Pat. *Crop Circles: Conclusive Evidence*. London: Bloomsbury, 1992.

and threaten us, you are truly ignorant. We are so very far beyond that it is laughable.

🙂 I guess I would have to agree with you, Awan.

😇 We will return to your planet in aeroships, similar to the one I was in over Bethlehem, 2000 years ago. Your religions were mistaken when they taught you a star appeared over Bethlehem, when Jesus was born. That was not true. The bright light that you mistook for a star was one of our aeroships.

Very soon, as you measure time, many strange things will begin to happen. Your book of book called them *sights and wonders*. The "grand finale" as you term it will be when millions of our aeroships will totally surround your planet. As they reach the outer edge of the earth's magnetic pull, the ships' lights will automatically turn on, and the light will reflect throughout the earth's atmosphere. This will cause the heavens to be illuminated for 12 days, all around your planet. Your sun will look dim in your sky, because our lights will appear much brighter than your sun.

🙂 I understand, Awan. I have had the experience of being in a rural country, and when I drove towards a city, you could see the whole sky above the city was much lighter than the countryside. The lights from the houses were illuminating the sky above the city.

😇 That is precisely what will happen, my scribe. I want you to understand, my scribe, that night will not exist anywhere on your planet for 12 days. This will cause your entire planet to go into a state of confusion. You will loose track of time, for you will not know if it is day or night. Even the animals and plants will become confused, because no creature will know if it is morning or night. Flowers will bloom at midnight when they usually bloom at noontime.

Your world will be in turmoil. Your churches will be jammed packed with people, who are beseeching a God outside of them to save them. Priests will be shaking in their shoes, for they also will have no answers to give to the people. Many intensely ignorant people will think that the world is coming to an end. Thousands will be foolish enough to commit suicide, trying to escape a imaginary disaster, such as the world burning up.

It is not our intent to frighten you. We will bring the 12 days of light as a sign. It will be the boundary line as you will leave the *Age of Ignorance*, and after twelve days will enter the *Age of Knowledge*. For those of you who are coming into a knowingness system, I want you to rejoice when you witness the 12 days of light. For after those twelve days, the world will finally go into a new age, a new frequency for the whole planet. It will leave the negative frequency, and become positive.

🙂 What will that do?

😇 This shift in energy will have a profound effect upon your planet. The magnetic poles will switch; you will take out what you term a compass, and it will point South instead of North. This will happen because of the shift in energy. This magnetic shift will profoundly affect people living on your planet. If a person lives in a negative frequency, within a belief system, and spends most of his or her life judging others, and feeling more hatred than love, that person will become totally disoriented. He or she will not be able to tolerate this new positive energy.

🧑 What about positive people?

👼 People who live in the positive frequency, who love their neighbors as themselves, will easily survive this 12-day period. This is what Jesus meant when he said "the meek would inherit the earth."[490] The meek already live in a positive frequency, as do most animals on this planet. They will feel that now they live in paradise.

🧑 I see … Wait a minute Awan. I think I just realized why you have come with this body of teachings. If a person can incorporate these teachings into his or her life, then they will develop a knowingness system, but also will be leaving the negative frequency, and becoming positive. The knowledge these people will have, will take them through to the new *Age of Knowledge*.

👼 Precisely, my scribe. This is what my true mission has been, to help as many people as I can survive into the new *Age of Knowledge*. When people read these books of my teachings, they will sail their ships out of the shallow waters of a belief system, into the deep waters of *knowingness*. I am sensing a change in the energy, so I must soon withdraw.

🧑 I understand, Awan.

👼 I want to say this much before I go. I want you to realize, my scribe, I have kept my word. You now possess the seven keys that will be your *Passport into Forever*. These keys will take you safely into the higher levels of the Spirit World. However, I still have more to teach you, my scribe. There is more knowledge you need to have Knowingness. However, this body of knowledge provides a good foundation, a good start. In time, I will have my medium contact you again, and we will continue dialogue.

🧑 I look forward to that, Awan.

👼 Very good, my brother. It again has been a pleasure to speak with you. My profound peace be with you.

🧑 My peace be with you too, Awan, until we can dialogue again.

Emptiness engulfed me as Awan left this time. I remembered the turmoil I had experienced after the first few dialogues with Awan. Now, after this dialogue, one which contained disturbing and distressing news, I ironically felt a deep sense of calm, and peace. As I pondered this dichotomy, I realized just how profoundly these teachings had changed my life. Without even realizing it, I had shifted from a belief system to a knowingness system. That knowingness made me aware that I had nothing to fear in the days to come. My passport into forever was embossed within my soul; and no matter what lay ahead in my life; I felt I was well prepared.

---

[490] Matthew 5:5.

APPENDIX

Affirmations

🙂 Many people have been asking for additional affirmations to use to open their brain. Could you provide some for the readers?

🙂 I would be most happy to give them to you. Awan is here with us at this time. He wants me to explain this to the readers, before he will take over my body and give the reader some additional affirmations.

I would like to stress to you, and the readers, that it is very important for you to establish communication with your Lord God of your Being (your soul). Each human has the potential of being unlimited. Therefore, the readers should not limit their communication to just the affirmations contained in this book. Every person can ask his/her God for any desire he or she may have.

🙂 That is a very important point, Carl. However, many people seem to be hesitant at first, and do not know what to say to their God. These affirmations may prove helpful.

🙂 I agree with you, Sid. I just want to remind the readers the procedure they should follow when doing these affirmations. It is important to sit in a quiet, dark room. If at all possible put a pair of blindfolds on, or tie a scarf over your eyes, or even put a cloth over your head. It is important to keep all light off the eyelids.

🙂 Why is that, Carl?

🙂 It is a way of shutting the world out, and allowing yourself to go within. Religions taught that you should close your eyes when you pray to God. However, they taught you to send your prayer up and out, instead of within.

🙂 Yes, that is what Awan taught.

🙂 Visualize yourself, sitting in a bubble of light, which is your aura—the light emanating from your soul. Concentrate on the light; then bring your focus to your soul, behind your breastbone, in the center of your chest. When you talk to your soul, speak clearly, deliberately, and with passion. Whispering these affirmations does not have the same effect as speaking them in a firm voice. However, it is not necessary to shout.

🙂 I think that is clear.

🧑 Begin each day acknowledging your God within, and being grateful for life, which is truly a wonderful gift. It is also beneficial to end each day, communicating with the Lord God of your Being. It is an ideal time to ask your God to heal your body. Now here are some sample affirmations. The readers should feel free to modify them to their own specific needs, wishes and aspirations.

🧑 Thank you Carl, for allowing Awan to speak once again.

Carl dimmed the lights in the office, put on his blindfolds, and said his customary prayer. This time, Awan seemed to take over his body effortlessly.

👼 My profound greetings to you, my scribe.

🧑 Greetings, Awan.

👼 I wish to directly address your readers before I give them some affirmations.

🧑 Go right ahead, Awan.

👼 I have come to your planet to wage war on Fear, Ignorance, and Superstition. However, more importantly, I came to reveal to you that ***you are God***. Do not be ashamed about it. I understand it is difficult for you to believe that you are a God. The moment you try to think of yourself as a God, your mind immediately brings up your fears, insecurities, and your past of which you are ashamed. You feel helpless, and weak, therefore, you cannot believe in your divinity.

It is a travesty that your religions have taught you to think this way. You should never feel less than your glorious potential, which is your Godhood, because if you do, you immediately negate your powerful divinity. You cannot accept that you are divine, because you have been the witness of your own cruelty, gossip, malice, abandonment, ruthlessness, lies and unjust acts. The most grievous act of all, is **not** loving who you are.

To redefine God you must remove him from that mysterious piece of real estate in the sky, or outer space, and out of your religions, churches and the "Holy Bible." The most difficult task you can face, is to reorient your thinking 180°, and to begin to love yourself, and feel you are worthy to be a God. Knowing that you have the potential to regain your Godhood, will give you hope, a powerful reason to love yourself.

Then we would not have to be concerned with morality. When you know you are God, you realize that you are connected to everything outside of yourself. It is then that if you declare war on another person, you will realize that you the travesty you committed is not against that other person, but against yourself.

When you judge another person, you have not oppressed that person; you have oppressed yourself. Every word you say, and thought you have is energy. And since that energy is created on your frequency, it travels out into the universe, collects more of the same type of energy and returns back unto you, not to the person you sent it to. The energy is traveling on your frequency; therefore, it has your address on it, and cannot go to anyone else.

If you blame and hate the world for all of your misfortunes, you are not taking responsibility for your own actions. By using these affirmations, you will be empowering your God. You will be taking charge of your own destiny, by creating it in thought, and manifesting it into reality. It takes focus, determination to do this. Yet, if you overlay your desired destiny, with emotions, or desperation, it will not manifest. You must visualize what you want, by knowing, beyond a shadow of doubt that it will happen. Do not place time restrictions upon this manifestation, for it will unfold in its own time.

🙂 That is some very powerful information, Awan.

👼 Yes my scribe, but not as powerful as these affirmations. Let me state them for you:

✳✳✳✳✳

Lord God of my Being,
Unto the Father within
Wake up and come forward,
Bring forth the Christ of my Being.
Release the endorphins/enzymes from my brain
Into my bloodstream
That my body,
Your temple
Be healed.
So Be It!

✳✳✳✳✳

Lord God of my Being,
Unto the Father within
Come forward
This moment, this hour,
Help me
To magnetize into my life
A better _____ (job, mate, whatever you desire)
Into my life.
So Be It!

✳✳✳✳✳

*****

Lord God of my Being,
Unto the Father within
Come forth this moment, this hour,
And bring forth your healing energy
Allow it to flow through my hands,
so that others may be healed.
So Be It!

*****

Lord God of my Being,
Unto the Father within
Come forth this moment this hour,
And walk in front of me,
Help me to magnetize into my life
A Mate that will love me as I love him/her.
So Be It!

*****

Lord God of my Being,
Unto the Father within
Come forward
This moment, this hour.
Help me to open my brain,
So that I have total knowingness,
And wisdom of the ages.
Help me to become unlimited!
So Be It!

*****

Lord God of my Being,
Unto the Father within
Come forth this moment this hour,
And know that I love you.
My beloved Spirit
My holy, holy Spirit
From this moment on
Take control of my body,
Heal my body,
For my body is your temple
And you are the tenant who lives in it.
So Be It!

✺✺✺✺✺

Lord God of my Being,
Unto the Father within
That which I have put out into the ether waves
That which I have put onto the time spiral,
Come forward and take me to that point,
And into forever!
So Be It!

✺✺✺✺✺

Lord God of my Being,
Unto the Father within
Help me to go into a Knowingness system
That I will be able to know
The road to take.
So Be It!

✺✺✺✺✺

Oh my Beloved Spirit,
My Might Spirit
Omnipotent One
You who are filled
With the power of Heaven and Earth
Fill me with your Power,
O my Spirit

Fill me
With your manifested kingdom
That I may be a vessel
To bring forth
That which is unseen in Heaven.
To subdue that which is seen on Earth.

Manifest for me,
My daily food,
That I may live
To know my Guilt,
My Doubt,
My Sorrow,
And then realize the Truth.

O Mighty Spirit,
Do not allow me

To be tempted.
Protect me
From all
That would persuade me,
And manifest through me,
God Divine.
So say I.
So Be It!

❋❋❋❋❋

O my beloved God
Mysterious one
Manifest in my life
(*express your desire*)
Straight away,
That I may know
The truth of your existence.
My holy, holy spirit,
Recreate my life
And that my death
As I have created it,
Abolish it straight-away
For I have a new passion
And a new desire,
And many dreams.
God make my path
A righteous path.
So Be It!

❋❋❋❋❋

😇 Say this affirmation while you are lying in bed, just before falling asleep.

❋❋❋❋❋

Lord God of my Being,
Unto the Father within
Come forward this moment this hour.
Bring forth the Christ that is within me.

My beloved Spirit
You who are the tenant who lives in my body,

Come forward this night as I sleep,
And become the commander and chief of my body.
Heal every cell of my body
To a state of perfect health.

Release the endorphins/enzymes from my brain
Into my bloodstream
That my body,
Your temple
Be healed.
So Be It!

❋❋❋❋❋

(👼) This affirmation is to be said while you are sitting quietly with your eyes closed. Hold a glass of water in front of your soul (in the middle of your chest). You will be energizing this water to heal your body. Say these words, and continue to hold the water for a few more moments, then drink the entire glass of water.

❋❋❋❋❋

Lord God of my Being,
Unto the Father within
Come forward this moment this hour.
Bring forth the Christ that is within me.
Change the molecules of this water
And make this healing water
That will energize and heal my entire body!
So Be It!

❋❋❋❋❋

(👼) Tell your readers these are templates, they may modify to meet their needs.

(🧑) Awan, I think these should help many people. Thank you for this assistance.

(👼) It has been my pleasure, my scribe, to transmit this information to you through my medium. It is my sincere desire for those who travel with me, that these affirmations, and this book will become the impetus for a great change in consciousness on your planet. It is a change, which is so desperately needed.

👤 I hope your wish will manifest, Awan.

👼 So Be It! I am going to withdraw at this time. I look forward to continuing our dialogues, for I have more information to teach. My peace be with you, my scribe.

👤 Thank you for bringing this ancient knowledge to light, Awan. I look forward to dialoguing with you in the future. My peace be with you, too.

Carl sighed, and then began coughing. I assisted him in drinking a full glass of water. Once again depleted, Carl took an hour-long nap.

GLOSSARY
of Hebrew Words

Chapter	Page	Hebrew Word	Pronounced	Translation
2	14	יְהוֹשֻׁעַ בֶּן יֹסֵף	Joshua ben Joseph	Joshua the son of Joseph
3	30	רוּחַ	rûach	Spirit/breath
4	39	לָשׁוֹן	law-shone'	tongue/language
4	52	הַמָּשִׁיחַ	Ha-maw-shee'-akh	The Messiah
4	54	אַדִּיר הוּא	ah deer hu	Passover song
7	90	שָׂטָן	saw-tawn'	Satan
7	91	הֵילֵל	hay-lale'	Lucifer
10	136	סֻכָּה	sukkah	tabernacle/hut
10	136	לוּלָב	lulav	Lulav
10	138	אֹהֶל מוֹעֵד	o-hel mo-aid	Meeting Tent
10	140	דְּבִיר	debir	Holy of Holies
10	143	אֻשְׁפִּיזִין	ushpizin	Visitors
10	145	בָּרוּךְ הַבָּא	Ba-ruch Ha-baw	You are welcome
10	148	אֲלִיָּה	al-ee-yaw'	upper/reading room
10	151	חֶדֶר	kheh'-der	School room
11	157	טַלִּית	Tallis	prayer shawl
11	158	כֹּהֵן	kôhen	Cohen
11	159	שְׁמַע	shema	Hear
12	167	גֵּיהִנֹּם	gheh'-en-nah	Hell

13	179	מִזְבֵּחַ	*mizbêach*	altar
13	180	מַצֵּבָה	*matstsêbâh*	pillar
13	180	בֵּית אֵל	*bayth-ale'*	Bethel
13	184	אֵלוֹן מוֹרֶה	*ay-lone' mo-reh'*	Plain/Oak of Moreh
13	184	אֵלוֹן	*ay-lone'*	Tree
13	184	מוֹרֶה	*mo-reh'*	Teacher
13	185	אֵלוֹן מְעוֹנְנִים	*Alon-maonenium*	Alon-Maonenium
14	203	מְעוֹנֵן	*meaw-nan'*	Sorcerer
14	203	עָנַן	*aw-nan'*	Enchanter/sorcerer
14	203	עָנָן	*aw-nawn'*	Cloud
14	203	הֶעָנָן	*heh-aw-nawn'*	The cloud
14	209	וַיֵּרָא	*va-yaar-aw*	Appeared
14	209	רָאָה	*raw-aw'*	Appear
14	209	רָאָה	*raw-eh'*	See
14	209	רֹאֶה	*ro-eh'*	Seer
14	209	רֹאֶה	*ro-ay'*	Prophet

BIBLIOGRAPHY

Bibles in Chronological Order

On the following pages, you will find two charts of abreviations corresponding to the four hundred and sixty different versions of the Bible I researched. The first chart will be arranged chronologically, the second alphabeltically.

Throughout this book, when I quote from the Bible, I footnote each quotation with chapter and verse. I also indicate which version I am using with an abbreviation inside the brackets. Please refer to this chart to identify which version I am quoting.

1	EWYC	Forshall, Josia, Rev., F. R. S. Etc and Madden, Sir Frederic K.H.Y. F.R.S. *The Holy Bible*. Oxford: University Press, 1850. [Reprint of originals 1384].
2	LWYC	Forshall, Josia, Rev., F. R. S. Etc and Madden, Sir Frederic K.H.Y. F.R.S. *The Holy Bible*. Oxford: University Press, 1850. [Reprint of originals 1384].
3.1	TYND	Tyndale, William. *Tyndale's Old Testament: Being the Pentateuch of 1530, Joshua to 2 Chronicles of 1537 and Jonah*. New Haven and London: Yale University Press, 1992. Tyndale, William. *Tyndale's New Testament: Translated from the Greek in 1534*. New Haven and London: Yale University Press, 1989.
4	JOY1	Joye, George. *The New Testament: as it was Written, and Caused to be Written by them, which Heard it. Whom also our Savior Christ Jesus Commanded that they should Preach it unto all Creatures*. Antwerp, Belgium, 1534.
5	COV	Coverdale, Miles. *The Bible: That is the Holy Scriptures of the Old and New Testament*. Cologne: E. Cervicornus & J. Stoter, 1535.
6	HOLLY	Hollybushe, Johan. *The New Testament both in Latin and English*. Southwarke: James Nicolson, 1538.
7	TAV	Taverner, Richard. *The Most Sacred Bible*. London: John Byddell, 1539.
8	GRT	*The Bible*. Whitchurch, Edward & Grafton, Richard. 1540.
9	MATT	*The Bible*. London: John Daye, 1549.
10	BECKE	Becke, Edmund. *The Bible: that is to say, all the Holy Scriptures contained in the Old and New Testament, Faithfully Set Forth According to the Copy of Thomas Matthews*. London: John Daye, 1551.
11	JUGG	*The Newe Testament of Our Saviour Jesu Christe. Faithfully Translated Out of the Greek*. London: Richard Jugge, 1552.
12	GEN60	*The Geneva Bible: A Facsimile of the 1560 Edition*. Madison, WI: University of Wisconsin Press, 1969.
13	BISH	Parker, Matthew. *The Holy Bible*. London: R. Jugge, 1568.
14	TOM	Tomson, Lawrence. *The New Testament of Our Lord Jesus Christ Translated out of Greek*. London: Christopher Barkar, 1576
15	RHEIMS	*The New Testament of Jesus Christ Translated Faithfully into English Out of the Authentical Latin*. Rheims: Fogny, John, 1582.

16	GEN99	*1599 Geneva Bible* (CD. Version 1.0). Topeka, KS: Sola Scriptura Publishing, 2001.
17	DOU	*The Holy Bible Faithfully Translated Out of the Authentical Latin.* Douay: Kellam, Lawrence, 1609.
18	KJV	[Authorized King James Version]. *The Holy Bible Containing the Old and New Testaments.* London: Robert Barker, 1611.
19	HAAK	Haak, Theodore. *Dutch Annotations Upon the Whole Bible.* London: Henry Hills, for John Rothwell, Joshua Kirton, and Richard Tomlins, 1657.
20	WHTB	Whitby, Daniel. *A Paraphrase and Commentary on the New Testament: in Two Volumes.* London: W. Bowyer, 1703.
21	NARY	Nary, Cornelius. *The New Testament of our Lord and Saviour Jesus Christ; Newly Translated out of the Latin Vulgate.* Dublin: Darlow and Moule, 1718.
22	MACE	Mace, William, ed. *The New Testament In Greek and English.* London: J. Roberts, 1729.
23	SIMON	Simon, Richard. *The New Testament of Our Savior Jesus Christ According to Ancient Latin Edition.* London: John Pemberton & Charles Rivington, 1730.
24	WHIS	Whiston, William. *Mr. Whiston's Primitive New Testament. Part 1 Containing the Four Gospels, with the Acts of the Apostles. Part 2 Containing 14 Epistles of Paul. Part 3 Containing 7 Catholic Epistles. Part 4 Containing the Revelation of John.* Stamford and London: printed for the author, 1745.
25	CHAL	[Challoner Revision]. Challoner, Richard. *The Holy Bible: Translated from the Latin Vulgate.* Dublin, 1750.
26	WESL	Wesley John. *Explanatory Notes Upon the New Testament.* London: William Bowyer, 1755.
27	PUR	Purver, Anthony. *A New and Literal Translation of All the Books of the Old and New Testaments.* London: W. Richardson and S. Clark, 1764.
28	WYNNE	Wynne, Richard A.M. *The New Testament.* London: R. and J. Dodley in Pall-Mall, 1764.
29	HAR	Harwood, Edwin D. D. *A Liberal Translation of the New Testament.* London: T. Becket and P. A. De Hondt in the Strand, 1768.
30	WORS	Worsley, John. *The New Testament of New Covenant of Our Lord and Savior Jesus Christ.* London: R. Hett, 1770.
31	BATE	Bate, Julius, Rev. *A New and Literal Translation from the Original Hebrew, of the Pentateuch of Moses: and of the Historical Books of the Old Testament, to the End of the Second Book Of Kings: with Notes Critical and Explanatory.* London: W. Faden; B. Law; E. and C. Dilly; and Mess. Faden and Jefferys, 1773.
32	BAY	Bayly, Anselm LL. D. *The Old Testament, English and Hebrew [electronic resource], with remarks critical and grammatical on the Hebrew, and corrections of the English.* London: George Bigg and Edward Cox, 1774.
33	CLEM	Clementine Edition. *The Holy Bible Translated from the Latin Vulgate Diligently Compared with the Hebrew Greek and other Editions in Divers Languages.* Philadelphia: Carey, Stewart and Co., 1790.
34	GILPIN	William Gilpin. *An Exposition of the New Testament; Intended as an Introduction to the Study of the Scriptures, by Pointing out the Leading Sense and Connection of the Sacred Writers.* London: for R. Blamire, 1790.
35	GEDD	Geddes, Rev. Alexander, L. L. D. *The Holy Bible or the Books Accounted Sacred by Jews and Christians.* London: J. Davis, 1792.
36	JGJR	Geddes, John & Robertson, James. *The New Testament Of Our Lord and Saviour Jesus Christ: Translated from the Latin Vulgate. Compared with the Original Greek. With Annotations.*
37	HAW	Haweis, Thomas, Rev. *The Evangelical Expositor, or, a Commentary on the Holy Bible: Wherein the Sacred Text of the Old and New Testament is Inserted at Large, The Sense Explained, and the More Difficult Passages Elucidated, with Practical Observations, also References to Parallel Scriptures, the Marginal Readings, and a Chronology. For the Use of Families and Private Christians of Every Denomination.* London: Edward And Charles Dilly, 1795.

38	MCKN	Macknight, James. *A Harmony of the Four Gospels: in which the Natural Order of Each is Preserved: With a Paraphrase and Notes.* 4th ed. Edinburgh: J. Ritchie, 1809. Macknight, James. *A New Literal Translation from the Original Greek, of all the Apostolical Epistles. With a Commentary, and Notes, Philological, Critical, Explanatory, and Practical.* 2d ed. Edinburgh, Scotland: P. Elmsly, 1795.
39	GUYSE	Guyse, John. *The Practical Expositor, or, An exposition of the New Testament: in the form of a Paraphrase, with Occasional Notes in their Proper Places for further Explication, and Serious Recollections at the close of Every Chapter, to which is Added an Alphabetical Table of the Principal Things contained in the Paraphrase, Especially in the Notes.* Edinburgh: Ross & Sons, 1797.
40	SCAR	Scarlett, Nathaniel. *A Translation of the New Testament from the Original Greek.* London: T. Gillet, 1798.
41	RAY	Ray, John Mead. *A Revised Translation and Interpretation of the Sacred Scriptures.* London: G. Robinson and Co., 1799.
42	NEWC	Newcome, William, Archbishop. *The New Testament, in an Improved Version, Upon the Basis of Archbishop Newcome's New Translation, with a Corrected Text, And Notes Critical And Explanatory.* Boston, MA: T. B. Wait, for W. Wells, 1809.
43	THOM	Thompson, Charles. *The Old Covenant, Commonly Called Old Testament: Translated from the Septuagint. Vol. 1 (Gen. -1 Sam.).* Philadelphia: Jane Aitken, 1808. Thompson, Charles. *The Holy Bible Containing the Old and New Covenant, Commonly Called the Old and New Testament: Translated from the Greek Vol. 2 (2 Sam.-Psalms).* Philadelphia: Jane Aitken, 1808. Thompson, Charles. *The Old Covenant, Commonly called Old Testament: Translated from the Septuagint. Vol. 3 (Proverbs to Malachi).* Philadelphia: Jane Aitken, 1808. Thompson, Charles. *The New Covenant; Commonly called the New Testament: Translated from the Greek Vol. 4.* Philadelphia: Jane Aitken, 1808.
44	BELS	Belsham, Thomas. *The New Testament, in an Improved Version, upon the Basis of Archbishop Newcome's New Translation, with a Corrected Text, and Notes Critical and Explanatory. Published by a Society for promoting Christian Knowledge and the Practice of Virtue by the Distribution of Books.* Boston: Thomas B. Wait and Company, 1809.
45	CAMP	Campbell, George. *The Four Gospels Translated from the Greek, with Preliminary Dissertations, and Notes Critical and Explanatory.* Boston: Wells, and Thomas B. Wait and Co., 1811.
46	FRY	Fry, William. *The Holy Bible Containing the Old and New Testaments.* London: T. Rutt, Shacklewell, 1812.
47	BELL	Bellamy, John. *The Holy Bible, Newly Translated from the Original Hebrew, with Notes Critical and Explanatory.* London: Longman, Hurst, Rees, Orme, and Brown, 1818. Bellamy, John. *The Book of Daniel: Translated from the Original Hebrew, with Chaldee Text.* London: Simpkin, Marshall, & Co., 1863. Bellamy, John. *The Minor Prophets: Containing Obadiah, Jonah, Micah, Nahum, Habakkuk, Zephaniah, and Haggai: Translated from the Original Hebrew Text.* London: Simpkin, Marshall, & Co., 1867.
48	WAKE	Wakefield, Gilbert B. A. *Translation of the New Testament.* Cambridge: University Press—Hilliard and Metcalf, 1820.
49	KNEE	Kneeland, Abner. *The New Testament: Being the English Only of the Greek and English Testament.* Philadelphia: Kneeland, 1823.
50	BOTR	Boothboyd, Benjamin, Rev. *New Family Bible.* London: Huddersiled: William Moore, 1824.
51	LORA	[Living Oracles] Campbell Alexander. *The Sacred Writings of the Apostles and Evangelists of Jesus Christ, Commonly Styled the New Testament, Translated from the Original Greek, by George Campbell, James Macknight, and Philip Doddridge, Doctors of the Church of Scotland: with Prefaces to the Historical and Epistolary Books; and an Appendix, Containing Critical Notes and Various Translations of Difficult Passages.* Buffaloe, Brooke County, Virginia: Alexander Campbell, 1826.

52	NRSE	Nourse, James. *The New Testament of Our Lord and Saviour Jesus Christ: Translated Out of the Original Greek, and with the Former Translations Diligently Compared and Revised.* Philadelphia, PA: American Sunday School Union, 1829.
53	NTCV	*The New Testament in the Common Version: Conformed to Griesbach's Standard Greek Text.* Boston, MA: Gray and Bowen, 1830.
54	DIKSN	Dickinson, Rodolphus. *A New and Corrected Version of the New Testament; or, a Minute Revision, and Professed Translation of the Original Histories, Memoirs, Letters, Prophecies, and Other Productions of the Evangelists and Apostles; to which Are Subjoined a Few, Generally Brief, Critical, Explanatory, and Practical Notes.* Boston, MA: Lilly, Wait, Colman, & Holden, 1833.
55	DODD	Doddridge, Philip D. D. *The Family Expositor: or, a Paraphrase and Version of the New Testament: with Critical Notes, and a Practical Improvement to Each Section. American Edition.* Amherst, MA: J. S. & D. Adams, and L. Boltwood, 1836.
56	LING	Lingard, John. *A New Version of the Four Gospels: With Notes Critical and Explanatory, by a Catholic.* London: Joseph Booker, 1836.
57	PENN	Penn, Granville G. *The Book of the New Covenant of Our Lord and Saviour Jesus Christ: Being a Critical Revision of the Text and Translation of the English Version of the New Testament, with the Aid of Most Ancient Manuscripts Unknown to the Age in which that Version was Last Put Forth by Authority.* London: James Duncan, 1836.
58	ETAY	Taylor, Edgar. *The New Testament of Our Lord and Saviour Jesus Christ: Revised from the Authorized Version with the Aid of other Translations and Made Conformable to the Greek Text of J.J. Griesbach by a Layman [E. Taylor].* London: William Pickering, 1840.
59	WEBR	Webster, Noah. *The Holy Bible, Containing the Old and New Testaments, in the Common Version.* New Haven, CT: N. Webster, 1841.
60	BREN	Brenton, Lancelot Charles Lee, Sir. *The Septuagint Version of the Old Testament According to the Vatican Text.* London: Samuel Bagster and Sons, 1844.
61	SOLA	De Sola, David Aaron. *The Sacred Scriptures in Hebrew and English: A New Translation, with Notes Critical and Explanatory.* London: S. Bagster, 1844.
62	HAMM	Hammond, Henry. *A Paraphrase and Annotations upon all the Books of the New Testament: Briefly Explaining all the Difficult Places Thereof.* Oxford: University Press, 1845
63	HUSS	Hussey, T. J. *The New Testament of Our Lord and Saviour Jesus Christ.* London: H. Colburn, 1845.
64	BENS	Benson, Joseph. *The Holy Bible, Containing the Old and New Testaments (according to the Present Authorized Version) with Critical, Explanatory, and Practical Notes.* New York: G. Lane & C.B. Tippett, 1846.
65	MORGAN	Morgan, Jonathan. *The New Testament of our Lord and Saviour Jesus Christ: translated from the Greek into pure English: with explanatory notes, on certain passages, wherein the author differs from other translators.* Portland: S. H. Colesworthy, 1848.
66	EPSNT	Etheridge, John Wesley. *The Peschito Syriac New Testament.* 1849.
67	WHIT	Whiting, N. N. *The Good News of Our Lord Jesus, the Anointed: from the Critical Greek text of Tittmann.* Boston, J. V. Himes, 1849.
68	CONE	Cone, Spencer H. and William H. Wyckoff. *The Commonly Received Version of the New Testament of Our Lord and Savior Jesus Christ.* New York: Lewis Colby, 1850.
69	MURD	Murdock, James D. D. *The New Testament or The Book of the Holy Gospel of Our Lord and our God, Jesus the Messiah.* New York: Stanford and Swords, 1851.
70	LEES	Leeser, Isaac. *The Twenty-Four Books of the Holy Bible: Hebrew and English.* London: Trübner & Co., 1856.
71	NORT	Norton, Andrews. *A Translation of the Gospels.* Boston: Little, Brown, and Company, 1856.
72	WELL	Wellbeloved, Charles, Rev. *The Holy Scriptures of the Old Covenant in Revised Translation.* 3 Vols. London: Longman, Green, Longman, and Roberts, 1859.

73	KEN	Kenrick, Francis Patrick. *The Pentateuch*. Baltimore, MD: Kelly, Hedian & Piet, 1860. Kenrick, Francis Patrick. *The Historical Books of the Old Testament*. Baltimore, MD: Kelly, Hedian & Piet, 1860. Kenrick, Francis Patrick. *The Psalms, Books of Wisdom, and Canticle of Canticles*. Baltimore, MD: Lucas Brothers, Publishers, 1857. Kenrick, Francis Patrick. *The Book of Job, and the Prophets*. Baltimore, MD: Kelly, Hedian & Piet, 1859. Kenrick, Francis Patrick. *The New Testament, Translated from the Latin Vulgate*. Baltimore, MD: Kelly, Hedian & Piet, 1862.
74	SAWY	Sawyer Leicester Ambrose. *The Holy Bible, Containing the Old and New Testaments*. Boston, MA: Walker, Wise, and Co., 1861. Sawyer Leicester Ambrose. *The New Testament, Translated from the Original Greek, with Chronological Arrangement of the Sacred Books, and Improved Divisions of Chapters and Verses*. Boston: John P. Jewett and Company, 1858.
75	THORN	Thorn, Leonard. *The New Testament of our Lord and Saviour Jesus Christ as Revised and Corrected by the Spirits*. NY: Proprietors, 1861.
76	BARH	Barham, Francis Foster. *Improved Monotessaron: a Complete Authentic Gospel Life of Christ; Combining the Words of the Four Gospels in a Revised Version, and an Orderly Chronological Arrangement*. London: Rivingtons, 1862.
77	ETHJ	Etheridge, John Wesley. *The Targums of Onkelos and Jonathan Ben Uzziël on the Pentateuch; with the fragments of the Jerusalem Targum, from the Chaldee. Leviticus, Numbers and Deuteronomy*. Vol. 2. London Longman, Green & Roberts, 1865. Etheridge, John Wesley. *The Targums of Onkelos and Jonathan Ben Uzziël on the Pentateuch; with the fragments of the Jerusalem Targum, from the Chaldee. Genesis and Exodus*. Vol. 1. London Longman, Green & Roberts, 1862. Etheridge, John Wesley. *The Targums of Onkelos and Jonathan Ben Uzziël on the Pentateuch; with the fragments of the Jerusalem Targum, from the Chaldee. Leviticus, Numbers and Deuteronomy*. Vol. 2. London Longman, Green & Roberts, 1865.
78	ETHO	Etheridge, John Wesley. *The Targums of Onkelos and Jonathan Ben Uzziël on the Pentateuch; with the fragments of the Jerusalem Targum, from the Chaldee. Genesis and Exodus*. Vol. 1. London Longman, Green & Roberts, 1862.
79	HIGH	Highton, Henry A. *Revised Translation of the New Testament: With a Notice of the Principal Various Readings in the Greek Text*. London: S. Bagster, 1862.
80	HEIN	Herman Heinfetter [Pseudonym of Frederick Parker], *A Literal Translation of the New Testament of our Lord and Saviour Jesus Christ, on definite rules of translation, from the text of the Vatican Manuscript*. 6th ed. London: Evan Evans, 1863. Although this is called the "sixth edition," in fact it is the first edition of Parker's translation of the entire New Testament. The parts had been issued separately in preceding years. By the same author: *A Collation of an English version of the New Testament of our Lord and Saviour Jesus Christ, from the text of the Vatican Manuscript, with the Authorized English version* (London: Evan Evans, 1864); and *Corrections of the copies of the New Testament portion of the Vatican Manuscript*. London: Evan Evans, 1866.
81	YNG	Young, Robert. *The Holy Bible*. Edinburgh, Dublin, and London: A Fullarton & Company, 1863.
82	BEN	Benisch, Abraham, Dr. *Jewish School and Family Bible. Vol. 1: Containing the Pentateuch*. Longman, Brown, Green, and Longmans. Paternoster Row: London, 1864. Benisch, Abraham, Dr. *Jewish School and Family Bible. Vol. 2: Containing the Historical Parts*. Longman, Brown, Green, and Longmans. Paternoster Row: London, 1864. Benisch, A. Dr. *Jewish School and Family Bible. Volume III: Containing the Books of Isaiah, Jeremiah, Ezekiel, and the Twelve Minor Prophets*. Longman and Company. Paternoster Row: London, 1856. Benisch, A. Dr. *Jewish School and Family Bible Volume IV: Containing the Hagiography*. Longman and Company. Paternoster Row: London, 1861.
83	COBB	Cobb, Sylvanus. *The New Testament of our Lord and Saviour Jesus Christ: with Explanatory Notes and Practical Observations*. Boston: S. Cobb, 1864.

84	ANDN	Anderson, Harry Tompkins. *The New Testament: Translated from the Original Greek.* Cincinnati, OH: Self-Published, 1865.
85	ABU	*The New Testament of Our Lord and Savior Jesus Christ. The Common English Version; Corrected by the Final Committee of the American Bible Union.* NY: American Bible Union; London, Trübner & Co., 1866.
86	SMITH	Smith, Joseph. *The Holy Scriptures Translated and Corrected by the Spirit of Revelation by Joseph Smith Jr., The Seer.* Philadelphia, PA: Westcott & Thompson, 1867.
87	AINS	Ainsle, Robert. *The New Testament Translated from the Greek Text of Tischendorf.* 1869.
88	NOYES	Noyes, George Rapall. *The New Testament: Translated from the Greek Text of Tischendorf.* Boston, MA: American Unitarian Association, 1888.
89	HARM	Clark, George W. Rev. *A New Harmony of the Four Gospels in English: According to the Common Version.* Philadelphia, PA: American Baptist Publication Society, 1872.
90	ALF	Alford, Henry. *The New Testament for English Readers.* Chicago, IL: Moody Press, 1875.
91	DAV	Davidson, Samuel. *The New Testament Translated from the Critical Text of Von Tischendorf: With an Introduction on the Criticism, Translation, and Interpretation of the Book.* London: Henry S. King & Co., 1876.
92	JUSMI	Smith, Julia E. *The Holy Bible Containing the Old and New Testaments Translated Literally from the Original Tongues.* Hartford, CT: American Publishing Co., 1876.
93	GURGO	Gurney, Joseph and Gotch, Frederic William. *The Holy Bible: according to the Authorised Version, compared with the Hebrew and Greek Texts, and Carefully Revised: Arranged in Paragraphs and Sections; with Supplementary Notes, References to Parallel and Illustrative Passages.* London: George E. Eyre and William Spottiswoode, 1877.
94	WORD	Wordsworth, Christopher, D. D. *The Holy Bible with Notes and Introduction Vol. 1. Five Books of Moses.* London: Rivingtons, 1880. Wordsworth, Christopher, D. D. *The Holy Bible with Notes and Introduction Vol. 2. Joshua-Samuel.* London: Rivingtons, 1879. Wordsworth, Christopher, D. D. *The Holy Bible with Notes and Introduction Vol. 3. Kings, Chronicles, Ezra, Nehemiah, and Esther.* London: Rivingtons, 1887. Wordsworth, Christopher, D. D. *The Holy Bible with Notes and Introduction Vol. 4. Job, Psalms, Proverbs, Ecclesiastes, and Song of Solomon.* London: Rivingtons, 1885. Wordsworth, Christopher, D. D. *The Holy Bible with Notes and Introduction Vol 5. Isaiah, Jeremiah, Lamentatiions, and Ezekiel.* London: Rivingtons, 1887. Wordsworth, Christopher, D. D. *The Holy Bible with Notes and Introduction Vol 6. Daniel, the Minor Prophets, and Index.* London: Longmans, Green, and Company, 1891.
95	SHAR	Sharpe, Samuel. *The Holy Bible.* London: Williams and Norgage 14 Henrietta Street, Covent Garden, 1883.
96	HANS	Hanson, J. W., D. D. *The New Covenant: Containing an Accurate Translation of the New Testament, A Harmony of the Four Gospels, A Chronological Arrangement of the Text, A Brief and Handy Commentary. Volume 1. The Four Gospels.* Boston, MA: The Universalist Publishing House, 1884.
97	MOSES	Moses, Adolph and Isaac S. *The Pentateuch, or The Five Books of Moses.* Milwaukee, WI: Congregation Emanu-El, 1884. Moses, Adolph and Isaac S. *The Historical Books of the Bible: School and Family Edition.* Milwaukee, WI: Congregation Emanu-El, 1884.
98	ERV	[Revised Version]. *The Holy Bible Containing the Old and New Testaments Translated Out of the Original Tongues: Being the Version Set Forth A.D. 1611 Compared with the Most Ancient Authorities and Revised.* New York: Thomas Y. Crowell & Company, 1885.
99	SPUR	Spurrell, Helen. *A Translation of the Old Testament Scriptures from the Original Hebrew.* London: James Nisbet & Co., 1885.
100	MORR	Morrow Horace E. *The New Testament Emphasized: Based upon a Study of the Original Greek Text.* Middletown, CT: C. Reynolds, 1897.
101	ROTH	Rotherham, Joseph Bryant. *The Emphasized Bible: A New Translation.* Cincinnati, Ohio: The Standard Publishing Company, 1897.

102	WEEKS	Weekes, Robert D. *The New Dispensation: The New Testament Translated from the Greek.* NY: Funk & Wagnalls, 1897.
103	HAUPT	Haupt, Paul. *The Sacred Books of the Old and New Testaments: A New English Translation: With Explanatory Notes and Pictorial Illustrations. Vol. 3. The Book of Leviticus.* NY: Dodd, Mead, and Company, 1898. Haupt, Paul. *The Sacred Books of the Old and New Testaments: A New English Translation: With Explanatory Notes and Pictorial Illustrations. Vol. 6. The Book of Joshua.* NY: Dodd, Mead, and Company, 1898. Haupt, Paul. *The Sacred Books of the Old and New Testaments: A New English Translation: With Explanatory Notes and Pictorial Illustrations. Vol. 7. The Book of Judges.* NY: Dodd, Mead, and Company, 1898. Haupt, Paul. *The Sacred Books of the Old and New Testaments: A New English Translation: With Explanatory Notes and Pictorial Illustrations. Vol. 10. The Book of Isaiah.* NY: Dodd, Mead, and Company, 1898. Haupt, Paul. *The Sacred Books of the Old and New Testaments: A New English Translation: With Explanatory Notes and Pictorial Illustrations. Vol. 12. The Book of Ezekiel.* NY: Dodd, Mead, and Company, 1898. Haupt, Paul. *The Sacred Books of the Old and New Testaments: A New English Translation: With Explanatory Notes and Pictorial Illustrations. Vol. 14. The Book of Psalms.* NY: Dodd, Mead, and Company, 1898.
104	HORNN	Horner, George. *Coptic Version of the New Testament in the Northern Dialect: Otherwise called Memphitic and Bohairic, with Introduction, Critical Apparatus, and Literal English Translations. Vol. 1. The Epistles of S. Matthew and S Mark.* Oxford: Clarendon Press, 1898. Horner, George. *Coptic Version of the New Testament in the Northern Dialect: Otherwise called Memphitic and Bohairic, with Introduction, Critical Apparatus, and Literal English Translations. Vol. 2. The Epistles of S. Luke and S. John.* Oxford: Clarendon Press, 1898.
104	HORNN	Horner, George. *Coptic Version of the New Testament in the Northern Dialect: Otherwise called Memphitic and Bohairic, with Introduction, Critical Apparatus, and Literal English Translations. Vol. 3. The Epistles of S. Paul.* Oxford: Clarendon Press, 1905. Horner, George. *Coptic Version of the New Testament in the Northern Dialect: Otherwise called Memphitic and Bohairic, with Introduction, Critical Apparatus, and Literal English Translations. Vol. 4. The Catholic Epistles and the Acts of the Apostles.* Oxford: Clarendon Press, 1905.
105	YLT	Young, Robert. *Young's Literal Translation.* Grand Rapids, Michigan: Baker Book House, 1898.
106	GRANT	Grant, Frederick, W., editor. *The Numberical Bible. The Pentateuch.* NY: Loizeaux Brothers, Bible Truth Depot, 1899. Grant, Frederick, W., editor. *The Numberical Bible. Joshua to Samuel.* NY: Loizeaux Brothers, Bible Truth Depot, 1932. Grant, Frederick, W., editor. *The Numberical Bible. Psalms.* NY: Loizeaux Brothers, Bible Truth Depot, 1924. Grant, Frederick, W., editor. *The Numberical Bible. Ezekiel.* NY: Loizeaux Brothers, Bible Truth Depot, 1931. Grant, Frederick, W., editor. *The Numberical Bible.* Matthew to John. NY: Loizeaux Brothers, Bible Truth Depot, 1897. Grant, Frederick, W., editor. *The Numberical Bible.* Acts to II Corinthians. NY: Loizeaux Brothers, Bible Truth Depot, 1924. Grant, Frederick, W., editor. *The Numberical Bible.* Hebrews to Revelations. NY: Loizeaux Brothers, Bible Truth Depot, 1922.
107	RUTH	Rutherford, William Gunion. *St. Paul's Epistle to the Romans: A New Translation with a Brief Analysis.* NY: The Macmillan Company, 1900.
108	ASV	Schaff, Philip ed. [American Standard Version]. *The Holy Bible containing the Old and New Testaments.* New York: Thomas Nelson & Sons, 1901.
109	BALL	Ballentine, Frank Schell. *The American Bible: The Books of the Bible in Modern English for American Readers.* Scranton, PA: Good News Publishing Company, 1902.
110	GDBEY	Godbey, W. B. Godbey's *Translation of the New Testament: From the Original Greek.* Cincinnati, OH: God's Bible School. 1902.

111	**WEY**	Weymouth, Richard Francis M. A., D. Litt. *The New Testament in Modern Speech: An Idiomatic Translation into Every-day English from the Text of "The Resultant Greek Testament."* New York: The Baker and Taylor Co., 1903.
112	**CENT**	Bennett, W. H., D. D. *The New Century Bible: Genesis Introduction; Revised Version with Notes, Giving an Analysis Showing from which the Original Documents Each Portion of the Text is Taken; index and map.* NY: Oxford University Press, American Branch, 1907. Bennett, W. H., D. D. *The New Century Bible: Exodus Introduction; Revised version with Notes, giving an analysis showing from which the original documents each portion of the text is taken; index and map.* NY: Oxford University Press, American Branch, 1908. Kennedy, A. R. S., Rev. *Leviticus & Numbers.* NY: Oxford Univ. Press, American Branch, 1904. Robinson, H. Wheeler. *Deuteronomy and Joshua.* NY: Oxford University Press, American Branch, n. d. Thatcher, G. W. *Judges and Ruth.* Oxford University Press, American Branch, 1904. Edited by Rev. A. R. S. Kennedy, M.A., D. D. *New Century Bible: Samuel 1 & 2 Introduction Revised Version with Notes, Index and Maps.* NY: Oxford University Press, American Branch, 1905. Skinner, Prof. *1 & 2 Kings.* NY: Oxford University Press, American Branch, n. d. Jellie, W. R. Harvey. *1 & 2 Chronicles.* NY: Oxford University Press, American Branch, 1906. Whitehouse, Owen C., M. A., D. D. *New Century Bible: Isaiah I-XXXIX Introduction Revised Version with Notes, index and Maps.* NY: Oxford University Press, American Branch, 1905. Peake, Arthur Samuel, D. D. *New Century Bible: Job: Introductions Revised Version with Notes and Index.* Edinburgh: T. C. & E. C. Jack, n. d. Martin, G. Currie, M. A, B. D. *New Century Bible: Proverbs Ecclesiastes and Song of Songs: Introductions Revised Version with Notes and Index.* Edinburgh: T. C. & E. C. Jack, n. d. Whitehouse, Owen C., M. A., D. D. *New Century Bible: Isaiah LX - LXVI Introductions Revised Version with Notes, index and Maps.* NY: Oxford University Press, American Branch, 1905. Peake, Arthur Samuel, D. D. *New Century Bible: Jeremiah Vol. 1. I-XXIV Introductions Revised Version with Notes, index and Maps.* NY: Oxford University Press, American Branch, 1904. Peake, Arthur Samuel., D. D. *New Century Bible: Jeremiah and Lamentations Vol. 2. XXV to LII Introductions Revised Version with Notes, index and Maps.* NY: Oxford University Press, American Branch, 1904. Lofthouse, W. F. Rev. M.A., D.D. *Ezekiel Introduction Revised version with notes, and index.* NY: Oxford University Press, American Branch, 1907. Charles, R. H. & D.Litt., D.D. *The Book of Daniel Introduction Revised version with notes, index and maps.* NY: Oxford University Press, American Branch, 1913. Davison, Prof. M. A., D.D. *The Psalms I-LXXII with notes, and index.* NY: Oxford University Press, n.d Davies, T. Witton B. A., Ph. D. *The Psalms LXXIII-CL Introduction Revised version with notes, and index.* NY: Oxford University Press, n.d. Horton, Rev. R. F. M.A., D.D. *The Minor Prophets: Hoesa, Joel, Amos, Obadiah, Jonah, and Micah, Introduction Revised version with notes, index and maps.* NY: Oxford University Press, American Branch, n. d. Driver, Rev. S. R. D.D., & D. Litt.D.D. *The Minor Prophets: Nahum, Habakkuk, Zephaniah, Haggai, Zechariah, Malachi.* NY: Oxford University Press, American Branch, 1906. Box, G. H., M. A., D. D. *St. Matthew. Introduction Revised version with notes, index and map.* NY: Oxford University Press, American Branch, n.d. Bartlet, J. Vernon M.A., D.D. *St. Mark, Introduction Revised version with notes, index and map.* NY: Oxford University Press, American Branch, 1925. Adeney, Walter F. D.D. *St. Luke, Introduction Revised version with notes, index and map.* NY: Oxford University Press, American Branch, n. d.

112	CENT	McClymont, J. A. *John*. NY: Oxford University Press, American Branch, n.d. Bartlet, J. Vernon, M. A. *Acts. Introduction Authorized and Revised version with notes, index and map*. NY: Oxford University Press, American Branch, n.d. NY: Oxford University Press, American Branch, n. d. Massie, J. M.A., D.D. *Corinthians, 1 & 2. Introduction Authorized & Revised Version with notes, index and map*. NY: Oxford University Press, n. d. Garvie, Alfred E. M.A., D.D. *Romans. Introduction Authorized & Revised Version with notes, index and map*. NY: Oxford University Press, n.d. Martin, G. Currie. M.A., B.D. *Ephesians, Colossians, Philemon & Philippians. Introduction Authorized & Revised Version with Notes, index and map*. NY: Oxford University Press, n.d. Adeney, Walter F. M.A., D.D. *Thessalonians 1 & 2, & Galatians. Introduction Authorized & Revised Version with Notes, index and map*. NY: Oxford University Press, n.d. Horton, Robert F. M.A., D.D. *Pastoral Epistles: Timothy & Titus. Introduction Authorized & Revised Version with Notes, index and map*. NY: Oxford University Press, n.d. Peake, Arthur Samuel. M.A. *Hebrews. Introduction Authorized & Revised Version with notes, index*. NY: Oxford University Press, n.d. Bennett, W. H. Litt. D., D.D. *The General Epistles: James, Peter, John and Jude. Introduction Authorized & Revised Version with notes, index and map*. NY: Oxford University Press, n.d.
113	TCNT	*The Twentieth Century New Testament: A Translation into Modern English*. Chicago, IL: Moody Press, 1904.
114	CRENT	Lloyd, Samuel. *The Corrected English New Testament: A Revision of the "Authorised" Version (By Nestle's Resultant Text) Prepared With The Assistance Of Eminent Scholars*. New York: G. P. Putnam's Sons, 1905.
115	WEAV	Weaver, S. Townsend. *The University New Testament in Modern Historical and Literary Form, for the Church, the School, and the Home, Embracing the Life of Jesus Christ in the Words of Mark, Matthew, Luke and John, and the Church of the Apostles according to Acts, the Epistles and Revelation Historically Harmonized*. Philadelphia: J. C. Winston, 1909.
116	HORNS	Horner, George. *Coptic Version of the New Testament in the Southern Dialect otherwise Called Sahidic and Thebaic. Vol. 1. The Gospels of St. Matthew and St. Mark*. Oxford: Clarendon Press, 1911. Horner, George. *Coptic Version of the New Testament in the Southern Dialect otherwise Called Sahidic and Thebaic. Vol. 2. S.Luke*. Oxford: Clarendon Press, 1911. Horner, George. *Coptic Version of the New Testament in the Southern Dialect otherwise Called Sahidic and Thebaic. Vol. 3. Gospel of S. John*. Oxford: Clarendon Press, 1911.
117	HORNS	Horner, George. *Coptic Version of the New Testament In the Southern Dialect: otherwise called Sahidic and Thebaic. Vol. 4. The Epistles of S. Paul*. Oxford: Clarendon Press, 1920. Horner, George. *Coptic Version of the New Testament In the Southern Dialect: otherwise called Sahidic and Thebaic. Vol. 6. The Acts of the Apostles*. Oxford: Clarendon Press, 1922.
117	BAPT	Conant, Thomas. *The Holy Bible containing the Old and New Testaments:(based in part on the Bible Union Version). Improved ed*. Philadelphia, PA: American Baptist Publication Society, 1913.
118	CLARKE	Clarke, Edward. *The New Testament: The Authorised Version Corrected*. 1913.
119	CAMB	Ryle, Herbert E. D.D. *The Cambridge Bible for School and Colleges: The Book of Genesis in the Revised Version with Introduction and Notes*. Cambridge: University Press, 1914.

119	CAMB	Driver, Rev. S. R. D.D. *The Cambridge Bible for School and Colleges: The Book of Exodus in the Revised Version* with Chapman, Arthur Thomas and A. W. Streane, D. D. *The Cambridge Bible for School and Colleges: The Book of Leviticus in the Revised Version with Introduction and Notes.* Cambridge: University Press, 1918. McNeile, A. H. D.D. *The Cambridge Bible for School and Colleges: The Book of Numbers in the Revised Version with Introduction and Notes.* Cambridge: University Press, 1911. Smith, Sir George Adam. *The Cambridge Bible for School and Colleges: The Book of Deuteronomy in the Revised Version with Introduction.* Cambridge: University Press, 1918. Maclear, G. F., Rev. D. D. *The Cambridge Bible for School and Colleges: The Book of Joshua with Notes, Maps, and Introduction.* Cambridge: University Press, 1889. Lias, J. J. Rev., M. A. *The Cambridge Bible for School and Colleges: The Book of Judges with Map, Notes, and Introduction.* Cambridge: University Press, 1886. Kirkpatrick, Rev. A. F. B.D. *The Cambridge Bible for School and Colleges: The First Book of Samuel with Map, Notes and Introduction.* Cambridge: University Press, 1889. Kirkpatrick, Rev. A. F. M.A. *The Cambridge Bible for School and Colleges: The Second Book of Samuel with Map, Notes and Introduction.* Cambridge: University Press, 1889. Lumby, Rev. J. Rawson D.D. *The Cambridge Bible for School and Colleges: The First Book of Kings with Map, Introduction and Notes.* Cambridge: University Press, 1890. Lumby, Rev. J. Rawson D.D. *The Cambridge Bible for School and Colleges: The Second Book of Kings with Introduction and Notes.* Cambridge: University Press, 1889. Elmslie, W. A. L., M. A. *The Cambridge Bible for School and Colleges: The Books of Chronicles with Maps, Notes and Introduction.* Cambridge: University Press, 1916. Davidson, A. B. Rev. D.D., LL.D. *The Cambridge Bible for School and Colleges: The Book of Job: with Notes, Introduction and Appendix.* Cambridge: University Press, 1899. Kirkpatrick, A. F. *The Cambridge Bible for School and Colleges: he Book of Psalms: with Introduction and Notes. Book I: Psalms 1-XLI; Books II and III Psalms XLII-LXXXIX.* Cambridge: The University Press, 1901. Plumptre, E. H., D. D. *The Cambridge Bible for School and Colleges: The Books of Ecclesiastes; or the Preacher, with Notes and Introduction.* Cambridge: University Press, 1881. Skinner, Rev. J., D. D. *The Cambridge Bible for School and Colleges: The Book of the Prophet Isaiah Chapter I-XXXIX In Revised Version With Introduction and Notes.* Cambridge: University Press, 1925. Skinner, Rev. J., D. D. *The Cambridge Bible for School and Colleges: The Book of the Prophet Isaiah Chapter LX-LXVI In Revised Version With Introduction and Notes.* Cambridge: University Press, 1922. Streane, Rev. A. W. M.A. *The Cambridge Bible for School and Colleges: The First book of the prophet Jeremiah, together with the Lamentations.* Cambridge: University Press, 1889. Davidson, A. B., D.D., LL.D., revised by the Late A. W. Streane, D. D. *The Book of the Prophet Ezekiel in the Revised Version with Notes.* Cambridge: University Press, 1924. Driver, Rev. S. R. D.D. *The Cambridge Bible for School and Colleges: The Book of Daniel with Introduction and Notes.* Cambridge: University Press, 1922. Cheyne, Rev. T.K. M.A., D. D. *The Cambridge Bible for School and Colleges: The Book of Hosea.* Cambridge: University Press, 1913. Driver, S. R., D. D. *The Cambridge Bible for School and Colleges: The Books of Joel and Amos.* Cambridge: University Press, 1915. Perowne, Ven. T. T. *The Cambridge Bible for School and Colleges: Obadiah and Jonah: with Notes and Introduction.* Cambridge: The University Press, 1898. Cheyne, T. K., D. D. *The Cambridge Bible for School and Colleges: Micah.* Cambridge: Univ. Press, 1921. Davidson, A. B. D.D., LL.D. *The Cambridge Bible for School and Colleges: The Books of Nahum, Habakkuk and Zephaniah.* Cambridge: University Press, 1920.

119	CAMB	Perowne, Ven T. T., B. D. *The Cambridge Bible for School and Colleges: Haggai and Zechariah, with notes and Introduction.* Cambridge: University Press, 1888. Barnes, W. Emery. *The Cambridge Bible for School and Colleges: Malachi.* Cambridge: Univ. Press, 1917. Carr, Rev. A. M.A. *The Cambridge Bible for School and Colleges: The Gospel according to St. Matthew, with Maps, Notes and Introduction.* Cambridge: University Press, 1879. Maclear, Rev. G. F. D.D. *The Cambridge Bible for School and Colleges: The Gospel according to St. Mark with Maps, Notes and Introduction. Cambridge*: University Press, n. d. Farrar, F. W., Rev. D. D. *The Cambridge Bible for School and Colleges: The Gospel according to St. Luke with Maps, Notes and Introduction.* Cambridge: University Press, 1889. Farrar, Rev. F. W. D.D. *The Cambridge Bible for School and Colleges: The Gospel according to St. Luke with Maps, Notes and Introduction.* Cambridge: University Press, 1889. Plummer, Alfred. *The Cambridge Bible for School and Colleges: The Gospel according to St. John with Maps, Notes and Introduction.* Cambridge: University Press, 1889. Burnside, W. F., M. A. *The Cambridge Bible for School and Colleges: The Acts of the Apostles: The Greek text edited with Introduction and Notes for the use of Schools.* Cambridge: University Press, 1916. Moule, D.D., Rev. *The Cambridge Bible for School and Colleges: The Epistle of Paul the Apostle to the Romans: with Introduction and Notes.* Cambridge: The University Press, 1899. Parry, R.St John D.D. *The Cambridge Bible for School and Colleges: The First Epistle of Paul the Apostle to the Corinthians.* Cambridge: University Press, 1916. Plummer, A., M. A., D.D. *The Cambridge Bible for School and Colleges: The Second Epistle of Paul the Apostle to the Corinthians.* Cambridge: University Press, 1923. Perowne, E. H, Rev. D.D. *The Cambridge Bible for School and Colleges: The Epistle To The Galatians, with Introduction and Notes.* Cambridge: The University Press, 1900. Moule, H. C. G., Rev. D. D. *The Cambridge Bible for School and Colleges: The Epistle to the Ephesians: with Introduction and Notes.* Cambridge: The University Press, 1902. Moule, H. C. G., *Rev. D. D. The Cambridge Bible for School and Colleges: The Epistle to the Philippians: with Introduction and Notes.* Cambridge: The University Press. 1899. Moule, H. C. G., Rev. D. D. *The Cambridge Bible for School and Colleges: The Epistle to the Colossians and to Philemon: with Introduction and Notes.* Cambridge: The University Press. 1902. Findlay, George G. Rev. *The Cambridge Bible for School and Colleges: The Epistles to the Thessalonians: with Introduction and Notes and Map.* Cambridge: The University Press. 1900. Humphreys, A. E., Rev. M.A. *The Cambridge Bible for School and Colleges: The Epistles to Timothy and Titus with Introduction and Notes.* Cambridge: University Press, 1925. Farrar, F. W., Rev. D. D. *The Cambridge Bible for School and Colleges: The Epistle of Paul the Apostle to the Hebrews: with Notes and Introduction.* Cambridge: University Press, 1886. Plumptre, E. H. *The Cambridge Bible for School and Colleges: The General Epistle of St. James: with Notes and Introduction.* Cambridge: University Press, 1901. Plumptre, E. H. *The Cambridge Bible for School and Colleges: The General Epistles of St Peter & St Jude: with Notes and Introduction.* Cambridge: University Press, 1899. Plummer, A., Rev. M. A. D. D. *The Cambridge Bible for School and Colleges: The Epistles of S. John: with Notes, Introduction and Appendix.* Cambridge: University Press, 1900.
120	CUNN	Cunnington, E. E. *The New Covenant, Commonly called the New Testament of Our Lord and Saviour Jesus Christ: A Revision of the Version of A.D. 1611.* London: G. Routledge, 1914.

121	PAN	Panin, Ivan. *The New Testament from the Greek Text as Established by Bible Numerics.* New Haven, CT: Bible Numerics Co., 1914.
122	PRYSE	Pryse, James Morgan. *The Restored New Testament: The Hellenic Fragments, Freed from the Pseudo-Jewish Interpolations, Harmonized and Done into English Verse and Prose: With Introductory Analysis, and Commentaries, Giving an Interpretation According to Ancient Philosophy and Psychology: And a New Literal Translation of the Synoptic Gospels, with Introduction and Commentaries.* NY: John M. Pryse, 1916.
123	JPS1	Margolis, Max. *The Holy Scriptures According to The Masoretic Text. A New Translation with the Aid Of Previous Versions and with Constant Consultation of Jewish Authorities.* Philadelphia, PA: Jewish Publication Society of America, 1917.
124	ANDS	Anderson, Henry. *The New Testament Translated from the Sinaitic Manuscript.* 1918.
125	DARBY	Darby, John Nelson. *The Holy Scriptures Containing the Old and New Testaments.* London: G. Morrish, 1920.
126	KENT	Kent, Charles Foster. *The Shorter Bible: The Old Testament: Translated and Arranged with the Collaboration of Charles Cutler Torrey.* NY: Scribner, 1921. Kent, Charles Foster. *The Shorter Bible: The New Testament: Translated and Arranged with the Collaboration of Charles Cutler Torrey.* NY: Scribner, 1918.
127	FENT	Fenton, Ferrar. *The Holy Bible in Modern English.* NY: Oxford University Press (American Branch), 1922.
128	MOFF	Moffatt, James. *The Bible: A New Translation.* NY: Harper & Brothers Publishers, 1922.
129	RIVER	Ballantine, William G. *Riverside New Testament: A Translation from the Original Greek into the English of Today.* NY: Houghton Mifflin, 1923.
130	OVER	Overbury, Arthur E. *The People's New Covenant (New Testament) Scriptural Writings: Translated from the Meta-Physical Standpoint.* NY: Didion & Company, 1925.
131	MORD	Richard G. Moulton, M. A. *The Modern Reader's Bible: The Books of the Bible with Three Books of the Apocrypha Presented in Modern Literary Form.* New York: Macmillan Co., 1930.
132	LAMSA	Lamsa, George M. Th*e Holy Bible: From Ancient Eastern Manuscripts.* Philadelphia, PA: A. J. Holman Company, 1933.
133	STERN	Stern, M., Dr. *The Five Books of Moses With Haphtaroth and Five Megiloth and Sabbath Prayers.* New York: Star Hebrew Book Company, 1933.
134	TORR	Torrey, Charles Cutler. *The Four Gospels, A New Translation.* New York, Harper & Brothers Publishers, 1933.
135	LWES	Lattey, Cuthbert, Rev. *Daniel The Old Testament: The Westminster Version of the Sacred Scriptures: A New Translation from the Original Greek and Hebrew Texts.* Dublin: Browne and Noland Limited, 1948. Lattey, Cuthbert Rev. *The Psalter: The Old Testament: The Westminster version of the Sacred Scriptures: A New Translation from the Original Greek and Hebrew Texts.* London: Sands & Co., 1944. Bévenot, Dom Hugh. *Nahum and Habakkuk: The Old Testament: The Westminster Version of the Sacred Scriptures: A New Translation from the Original Greek and Hebrew Texts.* London: Longmans, Green and Co., 1937. Bullough, Sabastian Rev. *Obadiah, Micah, Zephaniah Haggai and Zechariah: The Old Testament: The Westminster Version of the Sacred Scriptures: A New Translation from the Orignal Greek and Hebrew Texts.* London: Saint Catherine Press LTD., 1953. Lattey, Cuthbert Rev. *The Book of Malachi: The Old Testament: The Westminster version of the Sacred Scriptures: A New Translation from the Original Greek and Hebrew Texts.* London: Longmans, Green and Co., 1934. Lattey, Cuthbert, Rev. *The New Testament: (Small Edition): The Westminster Version of the Sacred Scripture.* London: Sands & Co. (Publishers) LTD., 1947. Bird, T. E., Rev. *The Old Testament: the Book of Jona.* London: Longmans, Green and Co., 1938. Lattey, Cuthbert Rev. *The New Testament: The Westminster Version of the Sacred Scriptures: A New Translation from the Original Greek and Hebrew Texts.* London: Sands & Co., 1947.

136	WADE	Wade, George Wöosung. *The Documents of the New Testament: Translated and Historically arranged with Critical Introductions.* London: Thomas Murby & Co., 1934.
137	GLAZ	Glazer, Simon. *The Five Books of Moses, Haphtoroth and the Five Megiloth, Prayers for the Sabbath Enumeration of the 613 Commandments New and Accurate Translation of all Verses whence the Commandments are Inferred.* KTAV Publishing House: New York, 1935.
138	BDRL	Bates, Ernest Sutherland. *The Bible Designed to be Read as Living Literature.* NY: Simon and Schuster, 1936.
139	HARK	Harkavy, Alexander. *The Holy Scriptures.* NY: Hebrew Publishing Company, 1936.
140	GREB	Greber, Johannes. *The New Testament: A New Translation and Explanation Based on the Oldest Manuscripts.* NY: J. Felsberg, Inc., 1937.
141	MART	Martin, William Wallace. *The New Testament: Critically Reconstructed and Retranslated.* Nashville, TN: Parthenon Press, 1937.
142	SPEN	Spencer, Francis Aloysius. *The New Testament of Our Lord and Saviour Jesus Christ; Translated into English from the Original Greek.* NY: The Macmillan Company, 1937.
143	BOB	Wilson, R. Mercer. *The Book of Books: A Translation of the New Testament Complete & Unabridged.* London: The Lutterworth Press, 1938.
144	CLEMS	Clementson, Edgar Lewis, Rev. *The New Testament: A Translation.* Pittsburg, PA: The Evangelization Society of the Pittsburgh Bible Institute, 1938.
145	CORN	Cornish, Gerald Warre. *Saint Paul from the Trenches: A Rendering of the Epistles to the Corinthians and Ephesians Don in France During the Great War.* Boston: Houghton Mifflin Company, 1938.
146	SMGO	Smith, J. M. Powis, and Goodspeed, Edgar J. *The Complete Bible: An American Translation.* Chicago, Illinois: University of Chicago Press, 1939.
147	DIAG	Wilson, Benjamin. Dr. *The Emphatic Diaglott.* Brooklyn, NY: The Watch Tower Bible and Tract Society, 1942.
148	BAS	Scharfstein, Ben-Ami. *The Five Books of Moses - Selected and Translated for Jewish Youth.* New York: Shilo Publishing House: 1944.
149	CVSS	[Concordant Version]. Knoch, A. E. *The Sacred Scriptures: New Testament: An Idiomatic, Consistent, Emphasized Version. Conforming to the Basic Laws of Language, in that, as far as Feasible, Each Expression Selected Constantly Represents its Closest Greek Equivalent, and Each Greek Word is Given One, Exclusive English Rendering.* Los Angles, CA: Concordant Publishing Concern, 1944.
150	KNOX	Knox, Ronald. *The Holy Bible.* New York: Sheed & Ward, Inc., 1944.
151	MODL	*The Modern Language Bible.* Grand Rapids, Michigan: Zondervan Publishing House, 1945.
152	STRING	Stringfellow, Ervin Edward. *Acts and Epistles: A Translation and Annotations.* [Np], 1945.
153	SWANN	Swann, George Betts. *New Testament of Our Lord and Saviour Jesus Christ: Translated from the Greek Text of Westcott and Hort.* Louisville, KY: New Testament Publishers, 1947.
154	FISH	Fisher, Fred L. *A Composite Gospel.* Nashville, TN: Broadman Press, 1948.
155	LETCH	Ford, T. F. and Ford R. E. *The New Testament of Our Lord and Saviour Jesus Christ: The Letchworth Version in Modern English.* Letchworth, Hertfordshire, England: Letchworth Printers Limited, 1948.
156	DART	Chamberlin, Roy B. & Feldman, Herman. *The Dartmouth Bible.* Boston, MA: Houghton Mifflin Company, 1950.
157	OGD	Ogden, C. K. *The Basic Bible: Containing the Old and New Testaments in Basic English.* NY: E. P. Dutton & Co., Inc., 1950.
158	SNNT	[Sacred Name Version]. Traina, A. B. *The New Testament of Our Messiah and Saviour Yahshua.* Irvington, NJ: The Scripture research Association, Inc., 1950.
159	WILL	Williams, Charles B. *The New Testament: A Translation in the Language of the People.* Chicago: Moody Press, 1950.
160	BRAV	[The authentic Version]. Pershall, Claire. *The New Testament of Our Lord and Savior Jesus Christ.* Plattsburg, MO: Brotherhood Authentic Bible Society, 1951.
161	RIEU	Rieu, E. V. *The Four Gospels. A New Translation from the Greek.* London, Penguin Books, 1952.

162	RSV	[Revised Standard Version]. *The Holy Bible: Revised Standard Version containing the Old and New Testaments.* New York: Thomas Nelson & Sons, 1952.
163	KLLI	Kleist, James A. and Lilly, Joseph L. *The New Testament, Rendered from the Original Greek with Explanatory Notes.* Milwaukee, WI: Bruce Pub. Co., 1954.
164	SEPT	Charles Thomson Secretary of the Continental Congress of the United States of America, 1774-1789. *The Septuagint Bible.* Indian Hills, Colorado: The Falcon's Wing Press, 1954.
165	ANT	Schonfield, Hugh J. *The Authentic New Testament, Edited and Translated from the Greek for the General Reader.* London: D. Dobson in Association with the Petrie Press, 1956.
166	FARR	Farrer, Austin. *A Short Bible: from the Authorized Version.* Great Britain: Collins Fontana Books, 1956.
167	INSL	Laubach, Frank C. Ph.D. *The Inspired Letters: in Clearest English.* NY Thomas Nelson & Sons, 1956.
168	TOMA	Tomanek, James L. *The New Testament of Our Lord and Savior Jesus Anointed.* Pocatello, ID: Arrowhead Press, 1958.
169	WEST	[Westminster]. *The Holy Bible.* New York: Hawthorn Books, 1958.
170	JSOC	*The Holy Scriptures: According to the Masoretic Text.* Philadelphia, PA: The Jewish Publication Society of America, 1960.
171	MENR	Th*e Holy Scriptures: A Jewish Family Bible. According to the Massorretic Text.* Chicago, IL: The Menorah Press, 1960.
172	NASB	Lockman Foundation. *New American Standard Bible.* Nashville, TN: Thomas Nelson, Publishers, 1960.
173	SON	Rev. Dr. A Cohen, M. A., Ph. D., D. H. L. *The Soncino Chumash: The Five Books of Moses with Haphtaroth.* London: The Soncino Press, 1964. Rev. Dr. A Cohen, M. A., Ph. D., D. H. L. *Joshua & Judges: Hebrew text & English Translation with an Introdution and Commentaries.* London: The Soncino Press, 1965. Rev. Dr. S. Goldman, M. A. *Samuel: Hebrew Text and English Translation with an introduction and commentary.* London: The Soncino Press, 1966. Rev. Dr. S. Goldman, M. A. *Samuel: Hebrew Text and English Translation with an Introduction and Commentary.* London: Soncino Press, 1966. Rev. Dr. I. W. Slotki, M. A., Litt. D. *Chronicles: Hebrew text & English Translation with an Introduction and Commentary.* London: The Soncino Press, 1965. Rev. Dr. I. W. Slotki, M. A., Litt. D. *Kings: Hebrew Text and English Translation with an introduction and commentary.* London: The Soncino Press, 1964. Rev. Dr. I. W. Slotki, M. A., Litt. D. *Kings: Hebrew Text and English Translation with an Introduction and Commentary.* London: Soncino Press, 1964. Rev. Dr. A Cohen, M. A., Ph. D., D. H. L. *The Five Megilloth: Hebrew Text & English Translation with an Introduction and Commentary.* London: The Soncino Press, 1966. Rev. Dr. I. W. Slotki, M. A., Litt. D. *Isaiah: Hebrew Text & English Translation with an Introductionb and Commentary.* London: The Soncino Press, 1966. Rabbi Dr. H. Freedman B. A., Ph. D. *Jeremiah: Hebrew Text and English Translation with an introduction and commentary.* London: The Soncino Press, 1961. Rabbi Dr. S. Fisch, M. A. *Ezekiel: Hebrew Text and English Translation with introductions and commentary.* London: The Soncino Press, 1966. Dr. Judah J. Slotki, M. A. *Daniel, Ezra, Nehemiah: Hebrew Text and English Translation with an introduction and commentary.* London: The Soncino Press, 1962. Rev. Dr. A Cohen, M. A. *The Twelve Prophets: Hebrew Text and English Translation with introductions and commentary.* London: The Soncino Press, 1977.
174	EXPN	Wuest, Kenneth S. *The New Testament: An Expanded Translation.* Grand Rapids, MI: Wm. B. Eedmans Publishing Co., 1961.
175	NOLI	Noli, Metropolitan Fan Stylian. *The New Testament of Our Lord and Savior Jesus Christ. Translated into English from the Approved Greek Text of the Church of Constantinople and the Church of Greece.* Boston, MA: Albanian Orthodox Church in America, 1961.
176	NWT	New World Bible Translation Committee. *New World Translation of the Holy Scriptures.* Brooklyn, NY: Watch Tower Bible & Tract Society, 1961.

177	PENTO	Rosenbaum, M., Silbermann, A. M., Blashki, A. and Joseph, L. *Pentateuch with Targum Onkelos, Haphtaroth and Rashi's Commentary: Translated into English and Annotated. Vol. 1. Genesis. Vol. 2. Exodus. Vol. 3. Leviticus. Vol. 4. Numbers. Vol. 5. Deuteronomy.* NY: Hebrew Publishing Co., 1961.
178	MKJV	*Modern King James Version of the Holy Bible.* New York: McGraw-Hill, 1962.
179	NORL	Norlie, Olaf M. *The Children's Simplified New Testament: In Plain English—for Today's Reader.* Grand Rapids, MI: Zondervan, 1962.
180	HLYNB	Traina, A. B., Rev. *The Holy Name Bible, Containing the Holy Name Version of the Old and New Testaments, Critically Compared with Ancient Authorities, and Various Manuscripts.* Irvington, NJ: Scripture Research Association, 1963.
181	WPE	Williams, Charles Kingsley. *The New Testament: A New Translation in Plain English.* Grand Rapids, MI: Eerdmans, 1963.
182	ANCR	Speister, A. E. *Genesis: A New Translation with Introduction and Commentary.* Garden City, NY: Doubleday & Company, Inc., 1964. Propp, William H.C. *Exodus 1-18: A New Translation with Introduction and Commentary.* NY: Doubleday, 1999. Propp, William H. C. *Exodus 19-40: A New Translation with Introduction and Commentary.* NY: Doubleday, 2006. Milgrom, Jacob. *Leviticus 1-16: A New Translation with Introduction and Commentary.* NY: Doubleday & Company, Inc., 1991. Milgrom, Jacob. *Leviticus 17-22: A New Translation with Introduction and Commentary.* NY: Doubleday & Company, Inc., 2000. Milgrom, Jacob. *Leviticus 23-27: A New Translation with Introduction and Commentary.* NY: Doubleday & Company, Inc., 2001. Levine, Baruch A. *Numbers 1-20: A New Translation with Introduction and Commentary.* NY: Doubleday, 1993. Levine, Baruch A. *Numbers 21-36: A New Translation with Introduction and Commentary.* NY: Doubleday, 2000. Weinfeld, Moshe. *Deuteronomy 1-11: A New translation with Introduction and Commentary.* NY: Doubleday & Company, Inc., 1991. Boling, Robert G. *Joshua: A New Translation with Notes and Commentary.* Garden City, NY: Doubleday & Company, Inc., 1982. Boling, Robert G. *Judges: A New Translation with Introduction, Translation and Commentary.* Garden City, NY: Doubleday & Company, Inc., 1975. McCarter, P. Kyle, Jr. *1 Samuel: A New Translation with Introduction, Notes & Commentary.* Garden City, NY: Doubleday & Company, Inc., 1980. McCarther, P. Kyle Jr. *2 Samuel: A New Translation with Introduction, Notes and Commentary.* Garden City, NY: Doubleday & Company, Inc., 1984. Cogan, Mordechai. *1 Kings: A New Translation with Introduction and Commentary.* New York: Doubleday, 2000. Coganand, Mordechai & Hayim Tadmor. *2 Kings: A New Translation with Introduction and Commentary.* Garden City, NY: Doubleday & Company, Inc., 1988. Myers, Jacob M. *1 Chronicles: Introduction, Translation, and Notes.* Garden City, NY: Doubleday & Company, Inc., 1965. Myers, Jacob M. *2 Chronicles: Translation, and Notes.* Garden City, NY: Doubleday & Company, Inc., 1965. Pope, Marvin H. *Job: Translation, and Notes.* Garden City, NY: Doubleday & Company, Inc., 1965. Dahood, Mitchell, S.J. *Psalms 1-50: Introduction, Translation and Notes.* Garden City, NY: Doubleday & Company, Inc., 1966. Dahood, Mitchell, S.J. *Psalms 51-100: Introduction, Translation and Notes.* Garden City, NY: Doubleday & Company, Inc., 1966. Dahood, Mitchell, S.J. *Psalms 1-1-150: Introduction, Translation and Notes.* Garden City, NY: Doubleday & Company, Inc., 1966. Scott, R. B. Y. *Proverbs & Ecclesiastes: Introduction, Translation and Notes.* Garden City, NY: Doubleday & Company, Inc., 1965. Blenkinsopp, Joseph. *Isaiah 1-39: Introduction, Translation, and Notes.* Garden City, NY: Doubleday & Company, Inc., 2000.

182	ANCR	Blenkinsopp, Joseph. *Isaiah 40-55: Introduction, Translation, and Notes.* Garden City, NY: Doubleday & Company, Inc., 2002. McKenzie, John L. *Isaiah 40-66: Introduction, Translation, and Notes.* Garden City, NY: Doubleday & Company, Inc., 1968. Bright, John. *Jeremiah: Introduction, Translation, and Notes.* Garden City, NY: Doubleday & Company, Inc., 1965. Lundbom, Jack R. *Jeremiah 21-36: a New Translation with Introduction and Commentary.* New York: Doubleday, 2004. Lundbom, Jack R. *Jeremiah 37-52: a New Translation with Introduction and Commentary.* New York: Doubleday, 2004. Greenberg, Moshe. *Ezekiel 1-20: A New Translation with introduction and Commentary.* Garden City, NY: Doubleday & Company, Inc., 1983. Greenberg, Moshe. *Ezekiel 21-37: A New Translation with Introduction and Commentary.* New York: Doubleday, 1997. Hartman, Louis F., C.SS.R. Th*e Book of Daniel A New Translation with Notes and Commentary on Chapters 1-9.* Garden City, NY: Doubleday & Company, Inc., 1978. Andersen, Francis I. and David Noel Freedman. *Hosea: A New Translation with Introduction and Commentary.* Garden City, NY: Doubleday & Company, Inc., 1980. Crenshaw, James L. Joel: A New Translation with Introduction and Commentary. Garden City, NY: Doubleday & Company, Inc., 1995. Andersen, Francis I. and David Noel Freedman. *Amos: A new Translation with Introduction and Commentary.* NY: Doubleday & Company, Inc., 1989. Raabe, Paul R. *Obadiah: A New Translation with Introduction and Commentary.* NY: Doubleday & Company, Inc., 1996. Sasson, Jack M. *Jonah: A New Translation with Introduction and Commentary.* NY: Doubleday & Company, Inc., 1990. Andersen, Francis I. and David Noel Freedman. *Micah: A New Translation with Introduction and Commentary.* NY: Doubleday & Company, Inc., 2000. Christensen, Duane L. *Nahum: A New Translation with Introduction and Commentary.* New Haven: Yale University Press, 2009. Andersen, Francis I. *Habakkuk: A New Translation with Introduction and Commentary.* NY: Doubleday & Company, Inc., 2001. Berlin, Adele. *Zepheniah: A New Translation with Introduction and Commentary.* NY: Doubleday & Company, Inc., 1994. Meyers, Carol L. & Eric M. *Haggai, Zechariah 1-8: A New Translation with Introduction and Commentary.* Garden City, NY: Doubleday & Company, Inc., 1987. Meyers, Carol L. & Meyers, Eric M. *Zechariah 9-14: A New Translation with Introduction and Commentary.* NY: Doubleday, 1993. Hill, Andrew E. *Malachi: A New Translation with Introduction and Commentary.* NY: Doubleday, 1998. Albright, W. F. *Matthew: Introduction, Translation, and Notes.* Garden City, NY: Doubleday & Company, Inc., 1971. Mann, C. S. *Mark: A New Translation with Introduction and Commentary.* Garden City, NY: Doubleday & Company, Inc., 1986. Fitzmyer, Joseph A., S. J. *Luke 1-9: Introduction, Translation, and Notes.* Garden City, NY: Doubleday & Company, Inc., 1981. Fitzmyer, Joseph A., S. J. *Luke10-24: Introduction, Translation, and Notes.* Garden City, NY: Doubleday & Company, Inc., 1985. Brown, Raymond E., S. S. *John 1-12: Introduction, Translation, and Notes.* Garden City, NY: Doubleday & Company, Inc., 1966. Brown, Raymond E., S. S. *John 13-21: Introduction, Translation, and Notes.* Garden City, NY: Doubleday & Company, Inc., 1970. Munck, Johannes. *The Acts of the Apostles.* Garden City, NY: Doubleday & Company, Inc., 1967. Fitzmyer, Joseph A. *Romans. A New Translation, with Introduction and Commentary.* Garden City, NY: Doubleday & Company, Inc., 1993. Orr, William F. and Walther, James Arthur. *1 Corinthians: A New Translation.* Garden City, NY: Doubleday & Company, Inc., 1976. Furnish, Victor Paul. *2 Corinthians: Translated with Introduction, Notes, and Commentary.* Garden City, NY: Doubleday & Company, Inc., 1984.

182	ANCR	Martyn, J. Louis. *Galatians: A New Translation*. Garden City, NY: Doubleday & Company, Inc., 1997. Barth, Markus. *Ephesians: Introduction, Translation, and Commentary*. Garden City, NY: Doubleday & Company, Inc., 1974. Barth, Markus and Blanke, Helmut. Colossians: A New Translation. Garden City, NY: Doubleday & Company, Inc., 1994. Reumann, John. *Philippians: A New Translation with Introduction and Commentary*. New Haven: Yale University Press, 2008. Barth, Markus and Blanke, Helmut *Colossians: A New Translation*. Garden City, NY: Doubleday & Company, Inc., 1994. Malherbe, Abraham J. *The Letters to the Thessalonians: A New Translation with Introduction and Commentary*. New York: Doubleday, 2000. Johnson, Luke Timothy. *The First and Second Letters to Timothy: A New Translation with Introduction and Commentary*. New York: Doubleday, Buchanan, George Wesley. *To the Hebrews: Translation, Commentary, and Commentary*. New York: Doubleday, 1972. Johnson, Luke Timothy. *The Letter of James: A New Translation with Introduction and Commentary*. New York: Doubleday, 1995. Elliott, John Hall. *1 Peter: A New Translation with Introduction and Commentary*. New York: Doubleday, 2000. Neyrey, Jerome H. *2 Peter, Jude: A New Translation with Introduction and Commentary*. New York: Doubleday, 1993. Brown, Raymond E. *The Epistles of John: Translated, with Introduction, Notes, and Commentary*. New York: Doubleday, 1982.
183	EINS	Einspruch, Henry. *The Good News According to Matthew.* Baltimore, MD: The Lewis and Harriet Lederer Foundation, 1964.
184	AMP	Siewert, Frances E. *The Amplified Bible*. Grand Rapids, Michigan: Zondervan Publishing House, 1965.
185	BRU	Bruce, F. F., Drs. Scrivener, Moulton and Greenup. *The Letters of Paul: An Expanded Paraphrase Printed in Parallel with the Revised Version with Fuller References*. Grand Rapids, MI: William B. Eerdmans Publishing Company, 1965.
186	CONF	O'Connel, John P., Monsignor. *The Holy Bible: With the Confraternity Text*. Chicago: Illinois: The Catholic Press, Inc., 1965.
187	JER	Jones, Alexander. *The Jerusalem Bible: Reader's Edition*. Garden City, NY: Doubleday & Company, Inc., 1966.
188	BARC	Barclay, William. *The New Testament: A New Translation: The Gospels and the Acts of the Apostles. Vol. 1.* London: Collins, 1968. Barclay, William. *The New Testament: A New Translation: The Letters and the Revelation Apostles. Vol. 2.* London: Collins, 1968.
189	BERK	Verkuyl, Gerrit, Ph. D, editor. *The Holy Bible: The New Berkeley Version in Modern English: A Completely New Translation from the Original Languages with Informative Notes to Aid the understanding of the Reader*. Grand Rapids, MI: Zondervan Publishing House, 1969.
190	WWENT	*Bible in Worldwide English New Testament*. 1969.
191	ALBA	Condon, Kevin. *The Alba House New Testament. The Accounts of Matthew, Mark, Luke and John*. Staten Island NY: Society of Saint Paul, 1970.
192	CPV	Jordan, Clarence. *The Cotton Patch Version of Matthew and John; Including the Gospel of Matthew (Except for the "Begat"Verses) and the First Eight Chapters of the Gospel of John*. NY: Association Press, 1970. Jordan, Clarence. *The Cotton Patch Version of Luke and Acts: Jesus' Doings and The Happenings*. NY: Association Press, 1969. Jordan, Clarence. *The Cotton Patch Version of Hebrews and the General Epistles*. Piscataway, NJ. New Century Publishers, 1973. Jordan, Clarence. *The Cotton Patch Version of Paul's Epistles*. NY: Association Press, 1968.
193	NAB	Catholic Biblical Association of America. *The New American Bible*. NY: P. J. Kennedy & Sons, 1970.
194	SEPZ	*The Septuagint Version of the Old Testament*. Grand Rapids, Michigan: Zondervan Publishing House, 1970.
195	ABBR	McCarry, James Leslie and McElhaney, Mark. *The Abbreviated Bible*. NY: Van Nostrand Reinhold, 1971.

196	LIV	*The Living Bible: Paraphrased*. Wheaton, Illinois: Tyndale House Publishers, 1971.
197	BYIN	Byington, Steven Tracy. *The Bible in Living English*. Brooklyn, NY: Watchtower Bible and Tract Society of New York, 1972.
198	NTFNW	Condon, Kevin, *The New Testament for the New World*. New York: Pyramid Publications, Inc., 1972.
199	PHIL	Phillips, J. B. *The New Testament in Modern English*. NY: Collier Books, 1972.
200	BVNT	Estes, Chester. *The Better Version of the New Testament, Based on the Greek Text According to Eminent Scholars and According to Certain Fundamental Principles and Rules of Biblical Interpretation*. Muscle Shoals, AL.: Chester Estes, 1973.
201	GRAY	Gray, Veo. *The Poetic Bible: Narrative: An Instructing, Pleasing, and Poetical Presentation of Biblical Stories*. Dallas, TX: N.P. 1973.
202	TRNT	*The Translator's New Testament*. London: British and Foreign Bible Society, 1973.
203	NTEE	Klingensmith, Don J. *The New Testament in Everyday English*. Fargo, North Dakota: Kaye's Inc.. 1974.
204	WMF	Edington, Andrew. *The Word Made Fresh*. Atlanta, GA: John Knox Press, 1975.
205	BECK	Beck, William F. *The Holy Bible in the Language of Today*. Philadelphia, PA: A. J. Holtman Company, 1976.
206	NEB	Sandmel, Samuel, Ed. *The New English Bible with the Apocrypha*: Oxford Study Edition. NY: Oxford University Press, 1976.
207	ROSN	*The Restoration of Original Sacred Name Bible, Containing the Old and New Testaments*. Bristow, OK: Missionary Dispensary Bible Research, 1976.
208	TEV	[Today's English Version]. *Good News Bible: The Bible in Today's English*. New York: American Bible Society, 1976.
209	CCNT	Adams, Jay Edward. *The Christian Counselor's New Testament: a New Translation in Everyday English, with Notations, Marginal References, and Supplemental Helps*. Nutley, NJ: Presbyterian and Reformed Publishing Co., 1977.
210	MARR	Marrow, Norman. *The Four Gospels Newly Translated from the Greek*. Luton: White Cresent Press, Ltd., 1977.
211	WFU	Haugerud, Joann. *The Word for Us: The Gospels of John and Mark, Epistles to the Romans and the Galatians: Restated in Inclusive Language*. 1st ed. Seattle, WA: Coalition on Women and Religion, 1977.
212	NIV	New International Version. *The Holy Bible: New International Version*. Grand Rapids, Michigan: Zondervan Publishing House, 1978.
213	BLACK	Blackwelder, Boyce W. *The Four Gospels An Exegetical Translation*. Anderson, IN: Warner Press Inc., 1980.
214	EBLF	Tucker, Robert Reed. *The Easy Bible A Literal Fundamental Translation Matthew Mark Luke John*. Canoga Park, CA: L Robert Reed Tucker, 1980.
215	WORR	Worrell, Adolphus Spalding. *The Worrell New Testament: A. S. Worrell's Translation with Study Notes*. Springfield, MO: Gospel Pub. House, 1980.
216	LIVT	Kaplan, Aryeh. *The Living Torah: The Five Books of Moses*. NY: Maznaim, 1981. Schapiro, Moshe. *The Living Nach: Early Prophets. A New Translation Based on Traditional Jewish Sources*. Vol. 1. NY: Moznaim Pub. Corp., 1994. Schapiro, Moshe. *The Living Nach: Latter Prophets. A New Translation Based on Traditional Jewish Sources*. Vol. 2. NY: Moznaim Pub. Corp., 1995. Schapiro, Moshe. *The Living Nach: Sacred Writing A New Translation Based on Traditional Jewish Sources*. Vol. 3. NY: Moznaim Pub. Corp., 1998.
217	MJV	Messianic Jewish Version: *May Your Name Be Inscribed in the Book of Life*. Washington: Messianic Vision: 1981.
218	SSBE	*The Sacred Scriptures: Bethel Edition*. Bethel, PA: Assemblies of Yahweh, 1981.
219	WAY	Way, Arthur S. *Letters of Paul, Hebrews, Psalms*. Kregel Publications, Grand Rapids, MI, 1981

220	ARAON	Aberbach, Moses, and Grossfeld, Bernard. *Targum Onkelos to Genesis: A Critical Analysis Together with an English Translation of the Text: (Based on A. Sperber's Edition).* NY: Ktav Pub. House, 1982. Drazin. Israel. *Targum Onkelos to Exodus: An English Translation of the Text with Analysis and Commentary (based on A. Sperber's Edition).* NY: Ktav Pub. House, 1990. Drazin. Israel. *Targum Onkelos to Leviticus: An English Translation of the Text with Analysis and Commentary (based on A. Sperber's Edition).* NY: Ktav Pub. House, 1994. Drazin, Israel. *Targum Onkelos to Numbers: An English Translation of the Text with Analysis and Commentary (based on A. Sperber's edition).* Hoboken, NJ: Ktav Pub. House, 1998. Drazin. Israel. *Targum Onkelos to Deuteronomy: An English Translation of the Text with Analysis and Commentary (based on A. Sperber's edition).* NY: Ktav Pub. House, 1982.
221	HIRS	Hirsch, Samson Raphael. *The Pentateuch: Translated and Explained by Samson Raphael Hirsch; Rendered into English by Isaac Levy. Vol. 1 Genesis, Vol. 2 Exodus, Vol. 3. Leviticus part 1, Vol. 3. Leviticus part 2, Vol. 4. Numbers, Vol. 5. Deuteronomy.* 2nd ed. Gateshead: Judaica Press, 1989. Hirsch, Samson Raphael. *The Haftoroth: Translated and Explained by Dr. Mendel Hirsch; Rendered into English by Isaac Levy.* 2nd ed. Gateshead: Judaica Press, 1989.
222	NKJV	Fastad, Art. *The Holy Bible: The New King James Version. Containing the Old and New Testaments.* Nashville, TN: Thomas Nelson Publishers, 1982.
223	RDB	Metzger, Bruce M., General Editor. *The Reader's Digest Bible: Condensed from the Revised Standard Version, Old and New Testaments.* Pleasantville, NY: Reader's Digest Association, 1982.
224	CLNT	Knoch, A. E. *Concordant Literal New Testament.* Saugus, CA: Concordant Publishing Concern, 1983.
225	ANDJ	Anderson. Julian G. *A New Accurate Translation of the Greek New Testament into Simple, Everyday American English: with Introduction, Maps, Pictures, Illustrations, Cross-references, and Explanatory Notes for Further Study.* Naples, FL: J.G. Anderson, 1984.
226	NJER	Darton, Longman & Todd Ltd. *The New Jerusalem Bible: Reader's Edition.* NY: Doubleday, 1985.
227	ORIG	Hugh J. Schonfield. *The Original New Testament.* San Francisco, CA: Harper & Row, 1985.
228	RENNT	Yeager, Randolph O. *The Renaissance New Testament.* Gretna, LA: Pelican Pub. Co., 1998.
229	TANK	*Tanakh: A New Translation of the Holy Scriptures.* Philadelphia, PA: Jewish Publication Society of America, 1985.
230	ICB	[International Children's Bible]. *Holy Bible: International Children's Bible.* Dallas, TX: Word Bibles, 1986.
231	NLFV	Ledyard, Gleason H. *Holy Bible.* Canby, OR: Christian Literature, 1986.
232	TFFR	Gaer, Joseph, *The Torah For Family Reading: The Five Books of Moses, The Prophets, The Writings.* Northvale, NJ: Jason Aronson Inc., 1986.
233	ARAM	Chilton, Bruce D. *The Aramaic Bible: The Isaiah Targum: Introduction, Translation, Apparatus, and Notes. Vol. 11.* Wilmington, Del.: Michael Glazier, 1987. Hayward, Robert. *The Aramaic Bible: The Targum of Jeremiah: Translated with a Critical Introduction, Apparatus, and Notes. Vol. 12.* Wilmington, Del.: Michael Glazier, 1987. Levey, Samson H. *The Aramaic Bible: The Targum of Ezekiel: Translated, with a Critical Introduction, Apparatus, and Notes. Vol. 13.* Wilmington, Del.: Michael Glazier, 1987. Cathcart, Kevin and Gordon, Robert P. *The Aramaic Bible: The Targum of the Minor Prophets: Translated, with a Critical Introduction, Apparatus, and Notes. Vol. 14.* Wilmington, Del.: M. Glazier, 1989.

234	ARAM	Beattie, D. R. G. and McIvor, J. Stanley. *The Aramaic Bible: The Targum of Ruth: Translated, with Introduction, Apparatus, and Notes. The Targum of Chronicles: Translated, with Introduction, Apparatus, and Notes. Vol. 19*. Collegeville, Minn.: Liturgical Press, 1994. Mangan, Celine, O. P. *The Aramaic Bible: The Targum: of Job Introduction, Translation, Apparatus, and Notes. Vol. 11*. Wilmington, Del.: Michael Glazier, 1987
234	EB	*The Everyday Bible: New Century Version: Clearly Translated for Life*. Fort Worth, TX: Worthy Publishing, 1987.
235	ETR	*Easy-to-Read Version. Holy Bible: Easy-to-Read Version*. Grand Rapids, Michigan: Baker Book House, 1987.
236	WBC	Wenham, Gordon J. *Word Biblical Commentary Genesis 1-15. Vol. 1*. Waco, Texas: Word Books Publisher, 1987. Wenham, Gordon J. *Word Biblical Commentary Genesis 1-16-60. Vol. 2*. Dallas, TX : Word Books, 1994. Durham, John I. *Word Biblical Commentary Exodus. Vol. 3*. Waco, Texas: Word Books Publisher, 1987. Hartley, John E. *Word Biblical Commentary Leviticus. Vol. 4*. Dallas, Texas: Word Books Publisher, 1992. Budd, Philip J. *Word Biblical Commentary Numbers. Vol. 5*. Waco, Texas: Word Books Publisher, 1984. Christensen, Duane L. *Word Biblical Commentary Deuteronomy 1:1–21:9. Vol. 6a*. 2nd ed. Dallas, Texas: Word Books Publisher, 1991. Christensen, Duane L. *Word Biblical Commentary Deuteronomy 21:10-34:12. Vol. 6b*. Nashville: Thomas Nelson Publishers, 2002. Butler, Trent C. *Word Biblical Commentary Joshua. Vol. 7*. Waco, TX: Word Books, 1983. Butler, Trent C. *Word Biblical Commentary Judges. Vol. 8*. Nashville, TN: Thomas Nelson Publishers, 2009. Klein, Ralph W. *Word Biblical Commentary 1 Samuel. Vol. 10*. Waco, Texas: Word Books Publisher, 1983. Anderson, A. A. *Word Biblical Commentary 2 Samuel. Vol. 11*. Dallas, Texas: Word Books Publisher, 1989. DeVries, Simon J. *Word Biblical Commentary 1 Kings. Vol. 12*. Waco, Texas: Word Books Publisher, 1985. Hobbs, T. R. *Word Biblical Commentary 2 Kings. Vol. 13*. Waco, Texas: Word Books Publisher, 1985. Braun, Roddy. *Word Biblical Commentary 1 Chronicles. Vol. 14*. Waco, Texas: Word Books Publisher, 1986. Dillard, Raymond B. *Word Biblical Commentary 2 Chronicles. Vol. 15*. Waco, Texas: Word Books Publisher, 1987. Clines, David J. A. *Word Biblical Commentary Job 1–20. Vol. 17*. Nashville, TN: Thomas Nelson Publishers, 1989. Clines, David J. A. *Word Biblical Commentary Job 21-37. Vol. 18a*. Nashville, TN: Thomas Nelson Publishers, 2006. Craigie, Peter C. *Word Biblical Commentary Psalms 1-50. Vol. 19*. Waco, Texas: Word Books Publisher, 1983. Tate, Marvin E. *Word Biblical Commentary Psalms 51-100. Vol. 20*. Dallas, Texas: Word Books Publisher, 1990. Murphy, Roland E. *Word Biblical Commentary Ecclesiastes. Vol. 23a*. Waco, Texas: Word Books Publisher, 1992. Watts, John D. W. *Word Biblical Commentary Isaiah 1-33. Vol. 24*. Waco, Texas: Word Books Publisher, 1985. Watts, John D. W. *Word Biblical Commentary Isaiah 34-66. Vol. 25*. Waco, Texas: Word Books Publisher, 1987. Craigie, Peter C. *Word Biblical Commentary Jeremiah 1-25. Vol. 26*. Dallas, Texas: Word Books Publisher, 1991. Brownlee, William H. *Word Biblical Commentary Ezekiel 1-19. Vol. 28*. Waco, Texas: Word Books Publisher, 1986. Goldingay, John E. *Word Biblical Commentary Daniel. Vol. 30*. Waco, Texas: Word Books Publisher, 1989.

| 236 | WBC | Stuart, Douglas. *Word Biblical Commentary Hosea-Jonah*. *Vol. 31*. Waco, Texas: Word Books Publisher, 1987.
Smith, Ralph L. *Word Biblical Commentary Micah-Malachi*. *Vol. 32*. Waco, Texas: Word Books Publisher, 1984.
Hagner, Donald A. *Word Biblical Commentary Matthew 1-13*. *Vol. 33a*. Dallas, Texas: Word Books Publisher, 1993.
Hagner, Donald A. *Word Biblical Commentary Matthew 14-28*. *Vol. 33b*. Dallas, Texas: ki 1995.
Guelich, Robert A. *Word Biblical Commentary Mark 1-8:26*. *Vol. 34a*. Dallas, Texas: Word Books Publisher, 1989.
Evans, Craig A. *Word Biblical Commentary Mark 8:27 - 16:20*. *Vol. 34b*. Nashville, TN: Thomas Nelson Publishers, 2001.
Nolland, John. *Word Biblical Commentary Luke 1- 9:20*. *Vol 35a*. Dallas, Texas: Word Books Publisher, 1989.
Nolland, John. *Word Biblical Commentary Luke 9:21-18:34*. *Vol. 35b*. Dallas, Texas: Word Books Publisher, 1993.
Nolland, John. *Word Biblical Commentary Luke 18:35-24:53*. *Vol 35c*. Dallas, Texas: Word Books Publisher, 1993.
Beasley-Murray, George R. *Word Biblical Commentary John*. *Vol. 36*. Waco, Texas: Word Books Publisher, 1987.
Green, Joel B. *Word Biblical Commentary Acts 1-14*. *Vol. 37a*. Nashville, TN: Thomas Nelson Publishers, 2009.
Walton, Steven. *Word Biblical Commentary, Acts 15-28*. *Vol. 37b*. Nashville, TN: Thomas Nelson, 2011.
Dunn, James D. G. *Word Biblical Commentary Romans 1-8*. *Vol. 38a*. Dallas, Texas: Word Books Publisher, 1988.
Dunn, James D. G. *Word Biblical Commentary Romans 9-16*. *Vol. 38b*. Dallas, Texas: Word Books Publisher, 1988.
Belleville, Linda L. *Word Biblical Commentary 1 Corinthians*. *Vol. 39*. Nashville, TN: Thomas Nelson Publishers, 2008.
Martin, Ralph P. *Word Biblical Commentary 2 Corinthians*. *Vol. 40*. Waco, Texas: Word Books Publisher, 1986.
Longencker, Richard N. *Word Biblical Commentary Galatians*. *Vol. 41*. Dallas, Texas: Word Books Publisher, 1990.
Lincoln, Andrew T. *Word Biblical Commentary Ephesians*. *Vol. 42*. Dallas, Texas: Word Books Publisher, 1990.
Hawthorne, Gerald F. *Word Biblical Commentary Philippians*. *Vol. 43*. Waco, Texas: Word Books Publisher, 1983.
O'Brien, Peter T. *Word Biblical Commentary Colossians, Philemon*. *Vol. 44*. Texas: Word Books Publisher, 1982.
Bruce, F. F. *Word Biblical Commentary 1 & 2 Thessalonians*. *Vol. 45*. Waco, Texas: Word Books Publisher, 1982.
Mounce, William D. *Word Biblical Commentary Pastorial Epistles*. Vol. 46. Nashville, TN: Thomas Nelson Publishers, 2000.
Lane, William L. *Word Biblical Commentary Hebrews 1-8*. *Vol. 47a*. Dallas, Texas: Word Book Publisher, 1991.
Lane, William L. *Word Biblical Commentary Hebrews 9-13*. *Vol. 47b*. Dallas, Texas: Word Book Publisher, 1991.
Martin, Ralph P. *Word Biblical Commentary James*. *Vol. 48*. Waco, Texas: Word Book Publisher, 1988.
Michaels, J. Ramsey. *Word Biblical Commentary 1 Peter*. *Vol. 49*. Waco, Texas: Word Book Publisher, 1988.
Martin, Ralph P. *Word Biblical Commentary Jude, 2 Peter*. *Vol. 50*. Waco, Texas: Word Book Publisher, 1983.
Smalley, Stephen S. *Word Biblical Commentary 1,2,3 John*. *Vol. 51*. Waco, Texas: Word Book Publisher, 1984. |

237	ARATO	Grossfeld, Bernard. *The Aramaic Bible. Targum Onqelos to Genesis: Translated, with a Critical Introduction, Apparatus, and Notes. Vol. 6.* Wilmington, Del.: Michael Glazier, 1988. Grossfeld, Bernard. *The Aramaic Bible: Targum Onqelos to Exodus: Translated, with Apparatus and Notes. Vol. 7.* Wilmington, Del.: Michael Glazier, 1988. Grossfeld, Bernard. *The Aramaic Bible: The Targum Onqelos to Leviticus; and, The Targum Onqelos to Numbers: Translated, with Apparatus, and Notes. Vol. 8.* Wilmington, Del.: M. Glazier, 1988. Grossfeld, Bernard. *The Aramaic Bible: The Targum Onqelos to Deuteronomy: Translated, with Apparatus, and Notes. Vol. 9.* Wilmington, Del.: M. Glazier, 1988.
238	MCORD	McCord, Hugo. *New Testament: McCord's New Testament Translation of the Everlasting Gospel.* Henderson, TN: Freed-Hardeman College, 1988.
239	MONT	Montgomery, Hellen Barrrett. *The New Testament In Modern English.* Nashville, TN: Holman Bible Publishers, 1988.
240	PHOB	Papoutsis, Peter A. *The Holy Orthodox Bible: The Pentateuch. Vol. 1.* Chicago, IL: P. A. Papoutsis, 2004.
241	NABR	*The New American Bible: Revised New Testament.* Grand Rapids, MI: W.B. Eerdmans Pub. Co., 1988.
242	GNC	Cassirer, Heinz W. *God's New Covenant: A New Testament Translation.* Grand Rapids, Mich., W. B. Eerdmans, 1989.
242	REB	*The Revised English Bible.* USA: Oxford University Press, 1989.
243	DPSF	Blanco, Jack J. *The New Testament A Devotional Paraphrase to Stimulate Faith and Growth.* The College Press, 1990.
244	NEVT	[New Evangecial Translation]. Beck, William, Mrs. *God's Word to the Nations: New Testament.* Cleveland, OH: NET Publishing, 1990.
245	NRSV	New Revised Standard Version. *The Holy Bible: Containing the Old and New Testaments.* New York: American Bible Society, 1990.
246	TRIMM	Trimm, James Scott. *B'sorot Matti: The Good News According to Matthew: from an Old Hebrew Manuscript: Translated Out of the Original Tongue and with the Former Translations Diligently Compared and Revised.* Hurst, TX: Hebrew/Aramaic New Testament Research Institute, 1990.
247	NCV	New Century Version. *The Holy Bible: New Century Version Containing the Old and New Testaments.* Dallas, TX: Word Bibles, 1991.
248	REC	Lee, Witness. *The New Testament: Recovery Version.* Anaheim, CA: Living Stream Ministry, 1991.
249	RVNT	Changshou, Li. *Recovery Version New Testament.* 1991.
250	UNVAR	Gaus, Andy. *The Unvarnished New Testament.* Grand Rapids, MI: Phanes Press, 1991.
251	ARATJ	Maher, Michael. *The Aramaic Bible: Targum Pseudo-Jonathan, Genesis: Translated, with Introduction and Notes. Vol. 1B.* Collegeville, Minn.: Liturgical Press, 1992. McNamara, Martin, Hayward, Robert, and Maher, Michael. *The Aramaic Bible: Targum Neofiti 1, Exodus: Translated with Introduction, Apparatus and Notes. Targum Pseudo-Jonathan, Exodus: Translated with Notes. Vol. 2.* Collegeville, Minn.: Liturgical Press, 1994. McNamara, Martin, Hayward, Robert, and Maher, Michael. *The Aramaic Bible: Targum Neofiti 1, Leviticus: Translated with Apparatus, with Introduction and Notes. Targum Pseudo-Jonathan, Leviticus: Translated with Notes. Vol. 3.* Collegeville, Minn.: Liturgical Press, 1994. McNamara, Martin, Clarke, Ernest G., Magder, Shirley. *The Aramaic Bible: Targum Neofiti 1, Numbers: Translated, with Apparatus and Notes. Targum Pseudo-Jonathan, Numbers: Translated, with Notes. Vol. 4.* Collegeville, Minn.: Liturgical Press, 1995. Clarke, Ernest G. *The Aramaic Bible: Targum Pseudo-Jonathan: Deuteronomy: Translated, with Notes. Vol. 5B.* Collegeville, Minn.: Liturgical Press, 1998. Daniel J. Harrington and Anthony J. Saldarini. *The Aramaic Bible: Targum Jonathan of the Former Prophets: Introduction, Translation, and Notes. Vol. 10.* Wilmington, Del.: Michael Glazier, 1987.

252	ARATN	McNamara, Martin. *The Aramaic Bible: Targum Neofiti 1, Genesis: Translated, with Apparatus and Notes. Vol. 1A*. Collegeville, Minn.: Liturgical Press, 1992. McNamara, Martin, Hayward, Robert, and Maher, Michael. *The Aramaic Bible: Targum Neofiti 1, Exodus: Translated with Introduction, Apparatus and Notes. Targum Pseudo-Jonathan, Exodus: Translated with Notes. Vol. 2*. Collegeville, Minn.: Liturgical Press, 1994. McNamara, Martin, Hayward, Robert, and Maher, Michael. *The Aramaic Bible: Targum Neofiti 1, Leviticus: Translated with Apparatus, with Introduction and Notes. Targum Pseudo-Jonathan, Leviticus: Translated with Notes. Vol. 3*. Collegeville, Minn.: Liturgical Press, 1994. McNamara, Martin, Clarke, Ernest G., Magder, Shirley. *The Aramaic Bible: Targum Neofiti 1, Numbers: Translated, with Apparatus and Notes. Targum Pseudo-Jonathan, Numbers: Translated, with Notes. Vol. 4*. Collegeville, Minn.: Liturgical Press, 1995. McNamara, Martin. *The Aramaic Bible: Targum Neofiti 1: Deuteronomy: Translated, with Apparatus and Notes. Vol. 5A*. Collegeville, MN: Liturgical Press, 1997.
253	MPNT	Martin, Ruth P. *The Pioneers' New Testament. A Guidebook for the Journey of the Faithful*. Greensboro, NC: Dave and Colleen Martin, Contents: 1992.
254	THROCK	Throckmorton, Burton Hamilton, *The Gospels and the Letters of Paul: an Inclusive Language Edition*. Cleveland, OH: The Pilgrim Press, 1992.
255	BBC	McCary, P. K. *Black Bible Chronicles*. NY: African American Family Press, Inc., 1993. McCary, P. K. *New Testament Black Bible Chronicles*. NY: African American Family Press, Inc., 1993.
256	FUNK	Funk, Robert and Hoover, Roy W. *The Five Gospels: The Search for the Authentic Words of Jesus*. San Francisco, CA: HarperCollins, 1993.
257	GLT	Green, Jay P. Sr. *The Literal Translation of the Holy Bible*. Lafayette, IN: Sovereign Grace Publishers, 1993.
258	JBPR	Rosenberg, A. J. ed. *Genesis: a New English Translation: Translation of Text, Rashi, and Other Commentaries*. New York: Judaica Press, 1993. Rosenberg, A. J. ed. *Shemoth: a New English Translation: Translation of Text, Rashi, and Other Commentaries*. New York: Judaica Press, 1996. Rosenberg, A. J. ed. Judaica Press *Tanach with Rashi CD*. New York: Judaica Press, 2004. Rosenberg, A. J. ed. *Joshua: Judaica Books of the Prophets: A New English Translation of the Text and Rashi, with a Commentary Digest*. NY: Judaica Press, Inc. 1980. Rosenberg, A. J. ed. *Judges: Judaica Books of the Prophets: A New English Translation of the Text and Rashi, with a Commentary Digest*. NY: Judaica Press, Inc. 1979. Rosenberg, A. J. ed. *Samuel 1: Judaica Books of the Prophets: A New English Translation of the Text and Rashi, with a Commentary Digest*. NY: Judaica Press, Inc. 1984. Rosenberg, A. J. ed. *Samuel 2: Judaica Books of the Prophets: A New English Translation of the Text and Rashi, with a Commentary Digest*. NY: Judaica Press, Inc. 1981. Rosenberg, A. J. ed. *Kings 1: Judaica Books of the Prophets: A New English Translation of the Text and Rashi, with a Commentary Digest*. NY: Judaica Press, Inc. 1980. Rosenberg, A. J. ed. *Kings 2: Judaica Books of the Prophets: A New English Translation of the Text and Rashi, with a Commentary Digest*. NY: Judaica Press, Inc. 1980. Rosenberg, A. J. ed. *1 Chronicles: Judaica Books of the Prophets: A New English Translation of the Text and Rashi, with a Commentary Digest*. NY: Judaica Press, Inc. 1992. Rosenberg, A. J. ed. *2 Chronicles: Judaica Books of the Prophets: A New English Translation of the Text and Rashi, with a Commentary Digest*. NY: Judaica Press, Inc. 1992. Rosenberg, A. J. ed. *Psalms Vol. 1-3: Judaica Books of the Prophets: A New English Translation of the Text and Rashi, with a Commentary Digest*. NY: Judaica Press, Inc. 1991.

258	JBPR	Rosenberg, A. J. ed. *Isaiah Vol. 1-2: Judaica Books of the Prophets: A New English Translation of the Text and Rashi, with a Commentary Digest*. NY: Judaica Press, Inc. 1982. Rosenberg, A. J. ed. *Jeremiah Vol. 1-2: Judaica Books of the Prophets: A New English Translation of the Text and Rashi, with a Commentary Digest*. NY: Judaica Press, Inc. 1985. Rosenberg, A. J. ed. *Ezekiel Vol. 1-2: Judaica Books of the Prophets: A New English Translation of the Text and Rashi, with a Commentary Digest*. NY: Judaica Press, Inc. 1991. Rosenberg, A. J. ed. *Twelve Prophets: Judaica Books of the Prophets: A New English Translation of the Text and Rashi, with a Commentary Digest*. NY: Judaica Press, Inc. 1986-1988. Rosenberg, A. J. ed. *Daniel, Ezra, Nehemiah: Judaica Books of the Prophets::A New English Translation of the Text and Rashi, with a Commentary Digest*. NY: Judaica Press, Inc. 1991. Rosenberg, A. J. ed. *The Book of the Twelve Prophets. Vol 1-2. Judaica Books of the Prophets: A New English Translation of the Text and Rashi, with a Commentary Digest*. NY: Judaica Press, Inc. 1986, 1988.
259	KOR	Korsak, Mary Phil. *At the Start: Genesis Made New: A Translation of the Hebrew Text*. NY: Doubleday, 1993.
260	OSB	Gillquist, Peter E; Alan Wallerstedt; Joseph Allen; Saint Athanasius Orthodox Academy. *The Orthodox Study Bible: New Testament and Psalms, New King James Version*. Nashville, TN: Thomas Nelson Publishers, 1993.
261	SINAI	Ford, Dalmer R. *The New Covenant: The New Testament, Sinaitic Version in Greek and English*. NY: Vantage Press, 1993.
262	WOY	Jeffery, Ruth. *The Word of Yah*. 1993.
263	AUV	Paul, William E. *The New Testament: An Understandable Version*. Seattle, WA: Impact Publications, 1994. [Internet: http://ncbible.org/AUV/Contents.htm].
264	COMP	Miller, Robert J., ed. *The Complete Gospels: Annotated Scholars Version*. San Francisco: HarperSanFrancisco, 1994.
265	EPBL	Jahn, Herb. *Exegeses Parallel Bible*. 1994
266	EPBT	Jahn, Herb. *Exegeses Parallel Bible*. 1994
267	ESB	Littrell, Harold. *The English Study Bible: New Testament*. Fort Worth, TX: Star Bible Publications, 1994.
268	GNBUK	British and Foreign Bible Society. *Good News Bible*. 1994.
269	KJ21	Prindle, William. *The Holy Bible: The 21st Century King James Version Containing the Old Testament and the New Testament*. Gary, S. D.: 21st Century King James Bible Publishers, 1994.
270	MADS	Madsen, Jon. *The New Testament: A Rendering by Jon Madsen*. Edinburgh, Floris Books, 1994.
271	NCS	Estes, George P. *The New Covenant Scriptures*. Fort Worth, TX: Star Bible Publications, 1994.
272	NTIL	*The New Testament of The Inclusive Language Bible*. Notre Dame, IN: Cross Cultural Publications, Inc., 1994.
273	QJV	Kraft, Roberta A. *Queen Jamie Bible*. University of Virgil Library Electronic Text Center, 1994.
274	RICHT	Richter, John August. *The New Testament of our Lord and Savior Jesus Christ, Revised and Corrected from Copies of the Sinaitic, Vatican Alexandrian and other Old Copies of the Original Greek, with an Apology for Bible Truth and Expositions of Men's Dogmas*. Hyderabad, India: Printland Publishers, 1994.
275	AFBNT	[The African Bible] Murphy, Conor. *The New Testament Standard Edition*. Nairobi, Kenya: Paulines Publications Africa, 1995.
276	CCB	Grogan, Patricia. *Christian Community Bible: Catholic Pastoral* Edition. Liguori, MO: Liguori Publications, 1995.
277	CEV	[Contemporary English Version]. Newman, Barclay. Bible: *Contemporary English Version*. New York: American Bible Society, 1995.

278	FOX	Fox, Everett. *The Five Books of Moses: Genesis, Exodus, Leviticus, Numbers, Deuteronomy; A New Translation with Introductions, Commentary, and Notes.* NY: Schocken Books, 1995. Fox, Everett. *Give us a King! : Samuel, Saul, and David: a New Translation of Samuel I and II / with an Introduction and Notes.* New York: Schocken Books, 1999.
279	GODWD	Bunkowske, Eugene. *God's Word: Today's Bible Translation that Says What it Means.* Grand Rapids, MI: World Publishing, 1995.
280	INCL	*The New Testament and Psalms: An Inclusive Version.* NY: Oxford University Press, 1995.
281	LITV	Green, Jay P. *The Literal Translation of the Holy Bible. 3rd Edition*, 1995.
282	NAS95	Lockman Foundation. *New American Standard Bible.* Nashville, TN: Thomas Nelson, Publishers, 1995.
283	RWB	Pierce, Larry. *Revised Webster Bible.* 1995.
284	ARNC	Jahn, Herb. *The Aramaic New Covenant: A Literal Translation and Transliteration.* Orange, CA: Exegeses Bibles, 1996.
285	GLW	*God's Living Word Translation.* Michael Paul Johnson, 1996.
286	LATT	Lattimore, Richard. *The New Testament.* NY: Farrar, Straus, Giroux, 1996.
287	MITCH	Mitchell, Stephen. *Genesis: A New Translation of the Classic Biblical Stories.* NY: HarperCollins Publishers, Inc., 1996.
288	NENT	Daniels, Frank. *Non-Ecclesiastical New Testament.* 1996. [Internet: http://members.aol.com/egweimi/order.htm].
289	NIrV	*New International Reader's Version.* Grand Rapids, MI: Zondervan Publishing House, 1996.
290	NLT	*Holy Bible: New Living Translation.* Wheaton, IL: Tyndale House Publishers, 1996.
291	PNT	Chenault, Rogers. *The People's New Testament. A Literal Translation of the Textus Receptus Text of the Greek New Testament.* Fredericksburg, VA: The Providence Press, 1996.
292	STONE	Scherman, Nosson. *Tanach: The Torah/Prophets/Writings: The Twenty-Four Books of the Bible Newly Translated and Annotated. Stone Edition Tanach.* Brooklyn, NY: Mesorah Publications, 1996.
293	WBE	Cressman, Annie. *Worldwide English (New Testament).* SOON Educational Publication, 1996.
294	CEVUK	*Contempoary English Version* British Usage Edition, 1997.
295	FISCH	Fisch, Harold. *The Jerusalem Bible: The Holy Scriptures.* Jerusalem, Israel: Koren Publishers Jerusalem Ltd., 1997.
296	HUNT	Jefferies, CJ. Huntingdon Translation. 1997. [Internet: http://www.stowey.demon.co.uk/authority/bible/translation/index.html].
297	OJBC	Goble, Phillip E. *Orthodox Jewish Brit Chadasha.* NY: AFI International Publishers, 1997.
298	PILA	Pilant, Benyamin. *The Holy Scriptures Revised.* 1997.
299	WEB	*World English Bible.* [Internet: http://www.bprc.org/], 1997.
300	CAPEF	Capel, Vivian. *21st Century New Testament. The Dual Translation, which Enables a Study of the Literal Meanings of the Original Text to be Combined with a Reading in Modern English.* Bristol: Insight Press, 1998.
301	CAPEL	Capel, Vivian. *21st Century New Testament. The Dual Translation, which Enables a Study of the Literal Meanings of the Original Text to be Combined with a Reading in Modern English.* Bristol: Insight Press, 1998.
302	CJB	Stern, David H. *Complete Jewish Bible: An English Version of the Tanakh (Old Testament) and B'rit Hadashah (New Testament).* Clarksville, MD: Jewish New Testament Publications, Inc. 1998.
303	HBNV	Johnson, Michael. *Hebrew Name Version*, 1998.
304	ISR	*The Scriptures.* Northriding, South Africa: Institute For Scripture Research Ltd., 1998.
305	ISV	Giacumakis, George, Dr. *International Standard Version.* Yorba Linda, CA: Learn Foundation, 1998. [Internet: http://isv.org/].
306	NASH	Nash, Donald A. *A Literal and Consistent New Testament Version.* Grayson, KY: Kentucky Christian College, 1998.

307	PWNT	Morford, William J. *The Power New Testament. Revealing Jewish Roots. A Translation of the 1993 Fourth Edition.* United Bible Society Greek Text. 1998
308	TMB	*Third Millennium Bible.* Gary, SD Deuel Enterprises Inc., 1998. [Internet: http://www.tmbible.com/search.htm].
309	AKJV	Engelbrite, Michael Peter. *American King James Version.* 1999. .http://www.angelfire.com/al4/allenkc/akjv/
310	ALT	Zeolla, Gary F. *Analytical-Literal Translation of the Holy Bible.* Darkness to Light Ministry, 1999. [Internet: http://www.dtl.org]."
311	CBNT	Clontz, Timothy. *Common Bible New Testament.* 1999. [Internet: Bible.GotJesus.org].
312	FOLK	Williams, Thomas E.Q. *American Folk Gospel: Logoi, Witness Accounts of the Lire of Jesus and Fundamental Devotional.* Greenfield, IN: Corny Publishing Co., 1999. [Internet: http://www.folkgospel.com]."
313	GFT	Miller, Theron. *God's First Truth* [Internet: http://www.godstruthtous.com/yesword_index.htm].
314	KJHN	Cummings, Chauncey. *King James Version: Hebrew Names Edition*, 1999.
315	KJV2000	Couric, Robert. *King James 2000 Version.* 1999.
316	LDB	Johnson, Ray. *Last Days Bible.* 1999.
317	LDNT	*The Last Days Bible.* Seattle, WA: Life Messengers, 1999.
318	MLV	Walker, G. Allen. *Modern Literal Version.* 1999. [Internet: http://www.christianlibrary.org/bibles/bibles.mv].
319	NET	Harris, W. Hall III, Ph.D. NET Bible - New English Translation. Biblical Studies Press, 1999. [Internet:www.netbible.com.].
320	NIVI	[New International Version]. *The Holy Bible: New International Version: Inclusive Language Edition.* London: Hodder & Stoughton, 1999.
321	TANK2	JPS Hebrew-English Tanakh: *The Traditional Hebrew Text and the New JPS Translation.* 2nd ed. Philadelphia, PA: Jewish Publication Society of America, 1999.
322	CLEAR	Blanco, Jack. *The Clear Word: an Expanded Paraphrase of the Bible to Nurture Faith and Growth.* Hagerstown, MD: Review and Herald Pub. Association, 2000.
323	JB2000	Stendal, Russell M. *English Jubilee 2000 Bible*, 2000.
324	NASC	Miller, Mark Heber. *Nazarene Commentary.* 2000.
325	PURE	Reynolds, Stephen M. *The Holy Bible: A Purified Translation.* Glenside, PA: Lorine L Reynolds Foundation, 2000.
326	RKJNT	Haugaard, Brad. *Revised King James New Testament.* 2000. http://www.geocities.com/Athens/Agora/7719/
327	TPB	Brichto, Sidney. *The People's Bible. Genesis: Newly Translated.* London: Sinclair-Stevenson, 2000. Brichto, Sidney. *The People's Bible. Moses: Book 1 Moses, Man of God: Book 2 The Laws of Moses.* London: Sinclair-Stevenson, 2003. Brichto, Sidney. *The People's Bible. The Conquest of Canaan: The books of Joshua and Judges.* London: Sinclair-Stevenson, 2001. Brichto, Sidney. *The People's Bible. Song of Songs with the Book of Ruth, Lamentations, Ecclesiastes and the Book of Esther.* London: Sinclair-Stevenson, 2000. Brichto, Sidney. *The People's Bible. Samuel Books I & II.* London: Sinclair-Stevenson, 2000. Brichto, Sidney. *The People's Bible. St. Luke & The Apostles.* London: Sinclair-Stevenson, 2000.
328	UKJV	*Updated King James Version.* 2000. http://www.ewog.org/ukjv/ukjv.html.
329	WAUCK	Wauck, Mark A. *The New Testament Saint Paul Catholic Edition.* Bronx, NY: Society of St. Paul, 2000.
330	ACV	Porter, Walter L. *A Conservative Version.* 2001. [Internet: http://www.stillvoices.org/Bibles/OTModern.asp].
331	AEB	*An American English Bible.* 2001.http://www.2001translation.com/
332	AST	*The New Testament: The Anointed Standard Translation: An Exactingly Literal & Accurate Translation of the New Testament.* 2nd Ed. Kodak, TN: Herrell Brothers Pub. House, 2001.

333	BECKN	Beck, Norman A. *The New Testament: A New Translation and Redaction.* Lima, Ohio: Fairway, 2001.
334	ESV	[English Standard Version]. Packer, James. *The Holy Bible: English Standard Version.* Wheaton, IL: Crossway Bibles, 2001.
335	HCSB	Blum, Edwin. [Holman Christian Standard Bible]. *Experiencing the Word: New Testament.* Nashville, TN: Holman Bible Publishers, 2001.
336	HRV	Trimm, James S. *Hebraic-Roots Version New Testament: A Translation of the New Testament Taken from Ancient Hebrew and Aramaic Manuscripts.* Society for the Advancement of Nazarene Judaism, 2001.
337	IEB	[The International English(r) Bible Translation]. *God Chasers Extreme New Testament.* Shipppensburg, PA: Destiny Image(r) Publishers, Inc., 2001.
338	MAEV	[Modern American English Vernacular] Garnier, Joe. *Modern American English Vernacular.* 2001. [Internet: http://www.angelfire.com/pop2/mselvy/ParallellBible/index/index.htm].
339	SNKJV	Hurt, John. *Sacred Name King James Bible,* 2001. http://www.sacrednamebible.com/
340	TNIV	*Today's New International Version.* International Bible Society 2001. [Internet: http://www.tniv.info/].
341	UTV	James, Dallis. *The Holy Bible: Urim-Thummim Version. Vol 1. Genesis - Deuteronomy. Vol. 2. Joshua - 2 Kings. Vol. 3. Isaiah - Malachi. Vol. 4. Psalms - 2 Chronicles. Vol. 5. Matthew - Relveation.* San Jose, CA: Writers Club Press, 2001."
343	WETC	*Easy-To-Read-Version.* World Bible.2001
344	ABDNT	Alexander, Victor N. *Aramaic Bible: Disciples New Testament.* Turlock, CA, 2002. [Internet: http://www.v-a.com/bible/].
345	BARNS	Barnstone Willis. *The New Covenant, Commonly called the New Testament: The Four Gospels and Apocalypse, Newly Translated from the Greek and Informed Semitic Sources.* New York: Riverhead Books, 2002.
346	EMTV	Esposito, Paul W. *English Majority Text Version.* 2002.
347	FPV	Junkins, B. E. *A Fresh Parenthetical Version of the New Testament.* Lanham, MD: University Press of America, 2002.
348	GUTN	*The Gutnick Edition Chumash: with Rashi's Commentary, Targum Onkelos, Haftaros and Commentary Anthologized from Classic Rabbinic Texts and the Works of the Lubavitcher Rebbe: Compiled and Adapted by Chaim Miller.* Publication Brooklyn, N.Y.: Kol Menachem, 2002.
349	MESS	Peterson, Eugene H. *The Message: The Bible in Contemporary Language.* Colorado Springs, CO: NavPress, 2002.
350	NCMM	Miller, Mark, *21st Century Version.* 2002.
351	OJB	*The Orthodox Jewish Bible.* Artists For Israel International. 2002. [Internet: http://www.afii.org/english.htm
352	RABV	Rabon, Vincent, Jr. *The Holy Scriptures.* Kearney, NE: Morris Publishing, 2002.
353	TANK3	Gordon, Nehemia. *Tanach Corrected.* 2002.
354	EEBT	Muir, Christine. *Genesis: In the Beginning: A Simple Translation of the Book of Genesis.* July 2003. Bradshaw, Hazel and Angus. *Exodus: How God Made the Slaves Free: A Simple Translation of the Book of Exodus.* October 2006. Gray, Jackie. *Leviticus: Gifts to God: A Simple Translation of the Book of Leviticus.* November 2007. Gray, Jackie. *Numbers: God gives Rules to Israel's People: A Simple Translation of the Book of Numbers.* June 2006. Bradshaw, Hazel and Angus. *Deuteronomy: It is Time to Remember: A Simple Translation of the Book of Deuteronomy.* November 2004. Green, Cynthia. *Joshua: Going in to the Land that God Promised: A Simple Translation of the Book of Joshua.* November 2002. Green, Cynthia. *Judges: God helps People to Return to Him: A Simple Translation of the Book of Judges.* February 2002. Green, Cynthia. *1 Samuel: The King who did not Obey God: A Simple Translation of the Book of 1 Samuel.* November 2008.

354	EEBT	Churchyard, Gordon. *1 Kings: From Solomon to Elijah: A Simple Translation of the Book of 1 Kings.* February 2008. Churchyard, Gordon. *2 Kings: Why God Sent His People Away: A Simple Translation of the Book of 2 Kings.* June 2008. Gribbon, John. *Job: When Bad Things Happen to Good People: A Simple Translation of the Book of Job.* July 2005. Churchyard, Gordon. Psalms: *The Psalms of David: Commentaries on the Book of Psalms that may be of Interest to Bible Translators Because they Include a Translation from Hebrew Based on Level A EasyEnglish.* 2001-2002. Gribbon, John. *Ecclesiastes: The Teacher's Word: A Simple Translation of the Book of Ecclesiastes.* July 2004. Churchyard, Gordon. *Isaiah: Isaiah Tells Us God's Good News: A Simple Translation of the Book of Isaiah.* September 2007. Green, Cynthia. *Jeremiah: Jeremiah Speaks God's Words: A Simple Translation of the Book of Jeremiah.* August 2004. Green, Cynthia. *Ezekiel: Prophet in Babylon with a message for Jerusalem: A Simple Translation of the Book of Ezekiel.* April 2006. Green, Cynthia. *Daniel: God's Man Daniel: A Simple Translation of the Book of Daniel.* August 2007. Kirkpatrick, Mark. *Hosea: Return to God: A Simple Translation of the Book of Hosea.* June 2004. Green, Cynthia. *Joel: God Promises to Send his Spirit: A Simple Translation of the Book of Joel.* January 2007. Eckert, Ann. *Amos: Bad Things Will Happen Soon: A Simple Translation of the Book of Amos.* May 2007. Muir, Christine. *Obadiah: God's Message about Edom: A Simple Translation of the Book of Obadiah.* February 2005. Baldwin, Sarah. *Jonah: God Loves People From Every Country: A Simple Translation of the Book of Jonah.* July 2008. Betts, Carol. *Micah: Micah's Message to God's People: A Simple Translation of the Book of Micah.* April 2006. Straw, Michelle. *Nahum: Nahum's Message for Nineveh: A Simple Translation of the Book of Nahum.* May 2008. Churchyard, Gordon. *Nahum, Habakkuk and Zephaniah: The Problem of Assyria: A Commentary on the Books of Nahum, Habakkuk and Zephaniah that may be of Interest to Bible Translators Because it Includes a Translation from Hebrew into Level A EasyEnglish.* February 2007. Churchyard, Gordon. *Habakkuk: Do Not Be Afraid: A Simple Translation of the Book of Habakkuk.* October 2006. Rohu, Roy. *Zephaniah: Your God Will Sing: A Simple Translation of the Book of Zephaniah.* May 2003. Gribbon, John. *Haggai: Build God's Special Building Now: A Simple Translation of the Book of Haggai.* October 2003. Churchyard, Gordon. *Haggai: Never Give Up!: A Commentary on the book of Haggai that may be of interest to Bible translators because it Includes a Translation from Hebrew into Level A EasyEnglish.* July 2007. Holburn, Fiona and Morris, Dulcie. *Zechariah: God's Servant whose Name is The Branch: A Simple Translation of the Book of Zechariah.* November 2003. Baldwin, Sarah. *Malachi: Offer your best gifts to God, who is coming soon _A Simple Translation of the Book of Malachi.* August 2008. Davies, Ruth and Chapman, Shirley. *Matthew: Matthew tells us the Good News about Jesus: A Simple Translation of Matthew's Gospel.* November 2006. Davies, Ruth and Chapman, Shirley. *Mark: Mark tells us the Good News about Jesus _A Simple Translation of Mark's Gospel.* March 2006. Davies, Ruth and Chapman, Shirley. *Luke: Hear this Good News for Everybody! _A Simple Translation of Luke's Gospel.* December 2007. Green, Cynthia and Betts, Carol. *John: John's Good News: A Simple Translation of John's Gospel.* September 2008. Davies, Ruth and Chapman, Shirley. *Acts: The Work that Jesus' Apostles Did: A Simple Translation of the Book of Acts.* April 2008.

354	EEBT	Rohu, Roy and Betts, Carol. *Romans: Alive to God: A Simple Translation of Paul's Letter to the Romans.* January 2005. Bradshaw, Hazel & Angus, Chapman, Shirley, Pride, Kitty & Betts, Carol. *1 Corinthians: The Greatest Thing is Love: A Simple Translation of Paul's First Letter to the Corinthians.* September 2006. Addison, Joan and Betts, Carol. *2 Corinthians: When I Am Weak, Then I Am Strong: A Simple Translation of Paul's Second Letter to the Corinthians.* July 2005. Green, Cynthia and Betts, Carol. *Galatians: Continue by God's Spirit: A Simple Translation of Paul's Letter to the Galatians.* April 2005. Green, Cynthia and Betts, Carol. *Ephesians: One Family in Christ: A Simple Translation of Paul's Letter to the Ephesians.* January 2006. Green, Cynthia. *Philippians: Christ is Worth More than Everything: A Simple Translation of Paul's Letter to the Philippians.* July 2003. Green, Cynthia. *Colossians: Alive and New with Christ: A Simple Translation of Paul's Letter to the Colossians.* November 2008. Green, Cynthia and Betts, Carol. *1 Thessalonians: Be Ready for Jesus to Return: A Simple Translation of Paul's First Letter to the Thessalonians.* February 2004. Green, Cynthia and Betts, Carol. *2 Thessalonians: Jesus Has Not Returned Yet: A Simple Translation of Paul's Second Letter to the Thessalonians.* February 2004. Green, Cynthia and Betts, Carol. *1 Timothy: Fight in the Good War: A Simple Translation of Paul's First Letter to Timothy.* January 2005. Green, Cynthia and Betts, Carol. *2 Timothy: Tell God's Message to People: A Simple Translation of Paul's Second Letter to Timothy.* January 2005. Betts, Carol. *Hebrews: Jesus is the Only Way to God: A Simple Translation of the letter to the Hebrews.* July 2003. Cynthia, Mackervoy, Ian, Chapman, Shirley & Hunter, Green, Sue. *James: How to Live for Jesus: A Simple Translation of the Letter of James.* December 2008. Holburn, Fiona and Morris, Dulcie. *1 Peter: Ready to Live with God: A Simple Translation of Peter's First Letter.* April 2004. Davies, Ruth. *2 Peter: Be Strong and Watch for Jesus!: A Simple Translation of Peter's Second Letter.* August 2003. Chapman, Shirley and Green, Cynthia. *1 John: How Christians Should Love Each Other _A Simple Translation of John's First Letter.* March 2005. Chapman, Shirley and Green, Cynthia. *2 John: The Truth about Jesus: A Simple Translation of John's Second Letter.* March 2005. Chapman, Shirley and Green, Cynthia. *3 John: A letter to a Christian Friend: A Simple Translation of John's Third Letter.* March 2005. Oldham, Chris. *Jude: Always Believe and Obey Only God's True Message: A Simple Translation of Jude's Letter.* Written by October 2003.
355	EVB	Comfort, Ray. *The Evidence Bible.* 2003.
356	FRIED	Friedman, Richard Elliot. *The Bible with Sources Revealed: A New View into the Five Books of Moses.* NY: HarperSanFrancisco, 2003.
357	HSTV	Peña, Perry. *The HSTV Tanakh and Testimony.* Lulu, 2003.
358	KJC	McGinnis Bill. *The King James Bible: Clarified New Testament.* 2003. [Interenet: http://www.auburn.edu/~allenkc/kjc/kjvc.html
359	NSB	Madsen, James R. *The New Simplified Bible Jehovah Version.* 2003.
360	NTOO	Coulter, Fred R. *The New Testament in its Original Order: A Faithful Version with Commentary.* Hollister, CA: York Publishing Company, 2003.
361	POLA	Greening-Jackson, Tim. *Polari Bible.* 2003.
362	RMKJV	Miller, Fred. *Revised King James' Version.* 2003.
363	RYLT	Allen, Ken. *Revised Young Literal Translation.* 2003. [Internet: http://www.auburn.edu/~allenkc/rylt/rylt.html
364	THB	Turner, Gwin. *The Heritage Bible: Containing The Old And New Covenants: A Totally New, Literal, and Absolutely Precise Translation Out Of The Original Tongues. With explanatory Notes, Devotions, and Cross References.* Los Angeles, CA: The Cathedral University, Publisher, 2003.
365	WOTS	Lacey, Rob. *Word on the Street*: Grand Rapids, Michigan: Zondervan Publishing House, 2003.

366	WOYAY	Assembly of Yahweh. *The Word of Yahweh*. 2nd Ed. Eaton Rapids, MI: Assembly of Yahweh, 2003.
367	ALTER	Alter, Robert. *The Five Books of Moses: A Translation with Commentary*. New York: W.W. Norton & Co., 2004. Alter, Robert. *The David Story: A Translation with Commentary of 1 and 2 Samuel*. New York: W. W. Norton, 1999. Alter, Robert. *The Book of Psalms: A Translation with Commentary*. New York: W. W. Norton, 2007.
368	CEKJV	Carroll, Richard. *King James Version*: Corrected Edition. 2004.
369	ESSEN	Beatty, Dennis. *The Essential New Testament*. Longwood, FL: Xulon Press, 2004.
370	GAN	Henson, John. *Good as New: A Radical Retelling of the Scriptures*. Washington D.C.: O Books, 2004.
371	PHP	Markley, Alex. PHPScripture. 2004.
372	RNKJV	Lattier, Richard. *Restored Name King James Version*. 2004. http://www.yahushua.net/scriptures/
373	RVIC	Parkinson, J. B. *Revised Version, Improved and Corrected*. 2004.
374	THNC	Hackett, Thom. *The Holy New Covenant*. 2004.
375	ZASV	Meyer, James. *Zikarown Say'fer: Sacred Scriptures, Family of Yah Edition*. Rocheport, MO: Paleo Times, 2004.
376	AB	Esposito, Paul W. ed. T*he Apostles' Bible: A Modern English Translation of the Greek Septuagint: Translated, Revised*. 2005.
377	CBKJV	Carroll, Richard P. *Christolog Bible: King James Version - Corrected Edition*. 2005.
378	CTNT	Cordes, Alvin. *Translators New Testament*. Longwood, FL: Xulon Press, 2005.
379	EBNT	Eldridge, Michael D. *Elohim Bridge New Testament*. 2005.
380	LIT	Dekker, Hal. *Literal Idiomatic Translation*. 2005.
381	MYLT	LeClaire, Allen K. *Modern Young's Literal Translation*. 2005.
382	PICK	Pickering, Wilbur N. *New Translation*. 2005.
383	PINT	Warrington, Don. *Positive Infinity New Testament*. 2005.
384	PSNT	Etheridge, J.W. *The Peschito Syriac New Testament*. 2005.
385	RGB	Brown, David. *Revised Geneva Bible*. 2005.
386	RVTYND	Valente, Mario. *Revised Tyndale New Testament*. 2005.
387	SCH	Scharfstein, Sol. *The Five Books of Moses: an Easy-to-Read Torah*. Jersey City, NJ: Ktav Pub. House, 2005. Scharfstein, Sol. *The Book of Haftarot for Shabbat, Festivals and Fast Days an Easy-to-Read Translation with Commentary*. Jersey City, N. J.: Ktav Pub. House, 2007.
388	BLB	Sindlinger, Dan. *The Better Life Bible: A New Translation of the New Testament*. 2006.
389	CORAM	Coram, James. *The Sacred Scriptures: Concordant Version*. Santa Clarita, CA: Concordant Publishing Concern, 2006.
390	JMNT	Mitchell, Jonathan. Jonathan *Mitchell's New Testament Translation*. 2006.
391	KJ3	Green, Jay Patrick. *King James III*. 2006.
392	LTOG	Last name not given, Charles. *Literal Translation of the Original Greek*. 2006.
393	PALMR	Palmer, David Robert. Th*e Gospels of Mark, Luke, and John: New Translations From the Greek*. 2006. [Internet: http://www.paulhommes.com/dave/tran.htm or http://www.ilovejesus.com/school/hologos/index2.shtml]
394	PCE	Verschuur, *Matthew. Pure Cambridge Edition*. 2006.
395	SACC	The Second Advent Christian Canon - Small Canon Search - *The Word of God, The Whole Word of God, and Nothing But the Word of God* - Searching the Second Advent Christian Bible - The Second Advent Christian Canon of Scripture, 2006.
396	UB	Abrams, Greg. *Updated Bible*. 2006.
397	APB	VanderPool, Charles. *The Apostolic Bible*. 2007.

398	CGV	Morovich, Joseph. *Context Group Version* 3.0 Copyright 2007.
399	FAITH	Zeitler, William Wilde. *The New Testament: A Faithful Translation.* 2007. [Internet: www.faithfulbible.com]
400	INCP	*The Inclusive Bible: The First Egalitarian Translation.* Lanham, MD: Rowman & Littlefield Publishers, 2007.
401	NETS	Pietersma, Albert. *New English Translation of the Septuagint.* Oxford University Press: New York, 2007.
402	RLSB	Garcia, Vince. *The Resurrection Life Study Bible.* Longwood, FL: Xulon Press, 2007.
403	RNV	Castleberry, C.F. *The Sacred Scripture of Yahuwah, Restored Names Version.* 2007.
404	RTYND	Porter, Clayton. *Revised Tyndale New Testament.* 2007.
405	SNT	Nyland, Ann, Dr. *The Source New Testament: with Extensive Notes on Greek Word Meaning.* Parramatta, N.S.W.: Smith and Stirling Pub., 2007.
406	ACC	Harness, Mark. *Accurate New Testament.* 2008.
407	ARTB	Werner, Francis. *Ancient Roots Translinear Bible.* 2008
408	AV7	AV7. Stanwood, WA: *New Authorized Version Foundation*, 2008.
409	BSV	*Bond Slave Version Bible Project.* 2008.
410	BUCB	Bullinger, E. W. *Companion Bible Condensed.* 2008.
411	EOB	Cleenewerck, Lauret. *The Eastern Greek Orthodox Bible: Based on the Septuagint and the Patriarchal Text: New Testament also Known as The Christian Greek Scriptures.* 2008.
412	HNT	Snyder, Jackson. *Kata Mattyah (According to Matthew) from The Hebraic New Testament Of Y'shua The Messiah.* 2008
413	IHGS	Mebust, Lenny. *Interlinear Hebrew-Greek Scriptures.* 2008.
414	KAMA	Snyder, Jackson H. *Kata Mattyah.* 2008.
415	MITJ	Mitchell, Jonathan. *New Testament Translation.* 2008
416	NIBEV	Schneider, Ed. *Natural Israelite Bible: English Version.* 2008.
417	OTFTS	King, Nicholas. *The Old Testament: a New, Cutting-edge translation of the Septuagint: Vol 1. The Pentateuch.* Buxhall, Stowmarket, Suffolk: Kevin Mayhew, 2010. King, Nicholas. *The Old Testament: a New, Cutting-edge translation of the Septuagint: Vol 3. The Wisdom Literature.* Buxhall, Stowmarket, Suffolk: Kevin Mayhew, 2008.
418	RRNT	Elkhazen, Pierre. *Revised Rheims New Testament.* 2008.
419	SENT	Mealy, Webb. *The Spoken English New Testament.* 2008.
420	TNKJV	Walters, Terry. *The King James Bible: True Name Version.* Bloomington, Texas: Olive Branch Messianic Congregation, 2008.
421	TTS	Shen, Janet. *Torah Transliteration Scripture.* 2008.
422	APNT	Magiera, Janet. *Aramaic Peshitta New Testament Translation.* Truth or Consequences, NM: Light of the Word Ministry, 2009.
423	ASEPT	Asser, Michael. *The Old Testament according to the Septuagint.* 2009.
424	CPDV	Conte, Ronald L. Jr. *Catholic Public Domain Version: Original Edition.* 2009.
425	EXB	Longman, Tremper. *The Expanded Bible.* 2009.
426	FINCK	Finck, William Raymond. *Christogenea New Testament.* 2009.
427	GABV	Martin. Lonnie W. *Gabriel Version.* 2009.
428	GGB	*The Genderless God Bible: Modified King James Version, Abridged.* West Conshohocken, PA: Infinity Pub., 2009.
429	HRB	Esposito, Don. *Hebraic Roots Bible.* 2009.
430	HTETT	Channah, Devorah. *Hebrew Transliterated and English Translated Torah.* 2009.
431	LHV	Plaisted, David. *The Holy Bible Lighthouse Version.* Lulu, 2009.
432	NHEB	Mitchell, Wayne. *New Heart English Bible*, 2009.

433	OANT	Bauscher, Glenn David. *The Original Aramaic New Testament in Plain English: An American translation of the Aramaic New Testament. 3rd Edition.* 2009.
434	RKB	Burke, Cormac. *Revised Knox Bible.* 2009.
435	VW	Becker, Paul. *A Voice in the Wilderness.* Spokane, WA: internet. 2009.
436	CB	Terry, H. *Conservative Bible.* 2010.
437	CCB2	*Christian Community Bible.* 2010.
438	DASV	Hildebrandt, Theodore. *Digital American Standard Version.* 2010.
439	FBV	Gallagher, Jonathan. *Free Bible Version.* 2010.
440	LEB	Harris, Hall. *The Lexham English Bible.* 2010.
441	NWYC	Noble, Terence. *Wycliffe's Old and New Testaments.* 2010.
442	OEB	Allen, Russell. *Open English Bible.* 2010.
443	PSR	*Pure Scriptures for the Remnant.* 2010.
444	REV	Schoenheit, John. *Revised English Version.* 2010.
445	RPT	Mitchell, Wayne A. *Revised Patriarchal Greek Orthodox New Testament*: 1904 Patriarchal Text Updated With The 350 AD Byzantine Gothic Text 2010.
446	WEBME	*World English Bible: Messianic Edition.* 2010.
447	YESC	Yereq, Mikhael. *Scriptures.* 2010.
448	YS	*Yahweh's Sword.* 2010.
449	CBE	Rose, Gary D. *Composite Bible.* 2011.
450	CEB	*Common English Bible: A Fresh Translation to Touch the Heart and Mind.* Nashville, TN: Common English Bible, 2011.
451	DLNT	Magill, Michael J. *Disciples' Literal New Testament.* 2011.
452	DNKJB	*Divine Names King James Bible.* 2011.
453	GIFT	Fether, Paula. *The Gift New Testament.* 2011.
454	MEWR	Gruber, Daniel. *The Messianic Writings.* 2011.
455	NEUV	Heaster, Duncan. *New European Version.* 2011.
456	RDRB	Burke, Cormac. *Revised Douay-Rheims Bible.* 2011.
457	TLV	Messianic Jewish Family Bible Project. *Tree of life Bible: The New Covenant.* Shippensburg, PA: Destiny Image Publishers, 2011.
458	SWHI	*Scriptures for the Whole House of Israel.* 2012.
459	TVB	Ecclesia Bible Society. *The Voice Bible: Step into the Story of Scripture.* Nashville, TN: Thomas Nelson Inc, 2012.
460	WOYB	Lewis, Mary E. *Word of YHVH Bible.* 2012.

BIBLIOGRAPHY

Bibles in Alphabetical Order

No.	Abrev.	Date	Bible Citation
376	AB	2005	Esposito, Paul W. *The Apostles; Bible*.
195	ABBR	1971	McCarry, James Leslie and McElhaney, Mark. *The Abbreviated Bible*.
344	ABDNT	2002	Alexander, Victor N. *Aramaic Bible: Disciples New Testament*.
85	ABU	1866	American Bible Union. *The New Testament*.
406	ACC	2008	Harness, Mark. *Accurate New Testament*.
330	ACV	2001	Porter, Walter L. *A Conservative Version*.
331	AEB	2001	*An American English Bible*.
275	AFBNT	1995	[The African Bible] Murphy, Conor. *The New Testament Standard Edition*.
87	AINS	1869	Ainsle, Robert. *The New Testament*.
309	AKJV	1999	Engelbrite, Michael Peter. *American King James Version*.
191	ALBA	1970	Condon, Kevin. *The Alba House New Testament*.
90	ALF	1875	Alford, Henry. *The New Testament for English Readers*.
310	ALT	1999	Zeolla, Gary F. *Analytical-Literal Translation of the Holy Bible*.
367	ALTER	2004	Alter, Robert. *The Five Books of Moses*.
184	AMP	1965	Siewert, Frances E. *The Amplified Bible*.
182	ANCR	1964	*The Anchor Bible* (multi-volume set).
225	ANDJ	1984	Anderson. Julian G. *A New Accurate Translation of the Greek New Testament into Simple, Everyday, American English*.
84	ANDN	1865	Anderson, Harry Tompkins. *The New Testament*.
124	ANDS	1918	Anderson, Henry. *The New Testament Translated from the Sinaitic Manuscript*.
165	ANT	1956	Schonfield, Hugh J. *The Authentic New Testament*.
397	APB	2007	VanderPool, Charles. *The Apostolic Bible*.
422	APNT	2009	Magiera, Janet. *Aramaic Peshitta New Testament Translation*.
233	ARAM	1987	Chilton, Bruce D. *The Aramaic Bible*.
220	ARAON	1982	Aberbach, Moses, and Grossfeld, Bernard. *Targum Onkelos to Genesis*.
251	ARATJ	1992	Maher, Michael. *The Aramaic Bible: Targum Pseudo-Jonathan*.
252	ARATN	1992	McNamara, Martin. *The Aramaic Bible: Targum Neofiti 1*.
237	ARATO	1988	Grossfeld, Bernard. *The Aramaic Bible. Targum Onqelos to Genesis*.
284	ARNC	1996	Jahn, Herb. *The Aramaic New Covenant*.
407	ARTB	2008	Werner, Francis. *Ancient Roots Translinear Bible*.
423	ASEPT	2009	Asser, Michael. *The Old Testament According to the Septuagint*.

332	AST	2001	*The New Testament: The Anointed Standard Translation.*
108	ASV	1901	Schaff, Philip. [American Standard Version]. *The Holy Bible.*
263	AUV	1994	Paul, William E. *The New Testament: An Understandable Version.*
408	AV7	2008	New Authorized Version Foundation. *AV7.*
109	BALL	1902	Ballentine, Frank Schell. *The American Bible.*
117	BAPT	1913	Conant, Thomas. [Bible Union Version]. *The Holy Bible.*
188	BARC	1968	Barclay, William. *The New Testament: A New Translation.*
76	BARH	1862	Barham, Francis Foster. *Improved Monotessaron.*
345	BARNS	2002	Barnstone Willis. *The New Covenant.*
148	BAS	1944	Scharfstein, Ben-Ami. *The Five Books of Moses.*
31	BATE	1773	Bate, Julius. *A New & Literal Translation from the Original Hebrew of the Pentateuch of Moses.*
32	BAY	1774	Bayly, Anselm. *The Old Testament: English and Hebrew.*
255	BBC	1993	McCary, P. K. *Black Bible Chronicles.*
138	BDRL	1936	Bates, Ernest. *The Bible Designed to be Read as Living Literature.*
205	BECK	1976	Beck, William F. *The Holy Bible in the Language of Today.*
10	BECKE	1551	Becke, Edmund. *The Bible.*
333	BECKN	2001	Beck, Norman A. *The New Testament.*
47	BELL	1818	Bellamy, John. *The Holy Bible.*
44	BELS	1809	Belsham, Thomas. *The New Testament: in an Improved Version.*
82	BEN	1864	Benisch, Abraham. *Jewish School and Family Bible.*
64	BENS	1846	Benson, Joseph. *The Holy Bible.*
189	BERK	1969	Verkuyl, Gerrit. *The Holy Bible: The New Berkeley Version.*
13	BISH	1568	Parker, Matthew. *The Holy Bible.*
213	BLACK	1980	Blackwelder, Boyce W. *The Four Gospels An Exegetical Translation.*
388	BLB	2006	Sindlinger, Dan. *The Better Life Bible: a New Translation of the New Testament.*
143	BOB	1938	Wilson, R. Mercer. *The Book of Books.*
50	BOTR	1824	Boothboyd, Benjamin. *New Family Bible.*
160	BRAV	1951	[The authentic Version]. Pershall, Claire. *The New Testament.*
60	BREN	1844	Brenton, Lancelot Charles Lee, Sir. *The Septuagint Version of the Old Testament.*
185	BRU	1965	Bruce, F. F., Drs. Scrivener, Moulton and Greenup. *The Letters of Paul.*
409	BSV	2008	*Bond Slave Version Bible Project.*
410	BUCB	2008	Bullinger, E. W. *Companion Bible Condensed.*
200	BVNT	1973	Estes, Chester. *The Better Version of the New Testament.*
197	BYIN	1972	Byington, Steven Tracy. *The Bible in Living English.*
119	CAMB	1914	*The Cambridge Bible for School and Colleges.* (multi-volume set).
45	CAMP	1811	Campbell, George. *The Four Gospels Translated from the Greek.*
300	CAPEF	1998	Capel, Vivian. *21st. Century New Testament.*
301	CAPEL	1998	Capel, Vivian. *21st. Century New Testament.*
436	CB	2010	Terry, H. *Conservative Bible.*
449	CBE	2011	Rose, Gary D. *Composite Bible.*
377	CBKJV	2005	Carroll, Richard P. *Christolog Bible: King James Version.*
311	CBNT	1999	Clontz, Timothy. *Common Bible New Testament.*
276	CCB	1995	Grogan, Patricia. *Christian Community Bible: Catholic Pastoral Edition.*
437	CCB2	2010	*Christian Community Bible.*

209	CCNT	1977	Adams, Jay Edward. *The Christian Counselor's New Testament.*
450	CEB	2011	*Common English Bible: A Fresh Translation to Touch the Heart and Mind.*
368	CEKJV	2004	Carroll, Richard. *King James Version: Corrected Edition.*
112	CENT	1904	*The New Century Bible* (multi-volume set).
277	CEV	1995	Newman, Barclay. *Contemporary English Version.*
294	CEVUK	1997	*Contempoary English Version British Usage Edition*
398	CGV	2007	Morovich, Joseph. *Context Group Version.*
25	CHAL	1750	[Challoner Revision]. Challoner, Richard. *The Holy Bible.*
302	CJB	1998	Stern, David H. *Complete Jewish Bible.*
118	CLARKE	1913	Clarke, Edward. *The New Testament.*
322	CLEAR	2000	Blanco, Jack. *The Clear Word.*
33	CLEM	1790	*Clementine Edition. The Holy Bible.*
144	CLEMS	1938	Clementson, Edgar Lewis. *The New Testament.*
224	CLNT	1983	Knoch, A. E. *Concordant Literal New Testament.*
83	COBB	1864	Cobb, Sylvanus. *The New Testament.*
264	COMP	1994	Miller, Robert. *The Complete Gospels: Annotated Scholars Version.*
68	CONE	1850	Cone, Spencer H. Th*e Commonly Received Version of the New Testament.*
186	CONF	1965	O'Connel, John P. *The Holy Bible: With the Confraternity Text.*
389	CORAM	2006	Coram, James. *The Sacred Scriptures: Concordant Version.*
145	CORN	1938	Cornish, Gerald Warre. *Saint Paul from the Trenches.*
5	COV	1535	Coverdale, Miles. *The Bible.*
424	CPDV	2009	Conte, Ronald L. Jr. *Catholic Public Domain Version: Original Edition.*
192	CPV	1970	Jordan, Clarence. *The Cotton Patch Version.*
114	CRENT	1905	Lloyd, Samuel. *The Corrected English New Testament.*
378	CTNT	2005	Cordes, Alvin. *Translators New Testament.*
120	CUNN	1914	Cunnington, E. E. *The New Covenant: Commonly called the New Testament.*
149	CVSS	1944	Knoch, A. E. *[Concordant Version]. New Testament.*
125	DARBY	1920	Darby, John Nelson. *The Holy Scriptures.*
156	DART	1950	Chamberlin, Roy B. & Feldman, Herman. *The Dartmouth Bible.*
438	DASV	2010	Hildebrandt, Theodore. *Digital American Standard Version.*
91	DAV	1876	Davidson, Samuel. *The New Testament.*
147	DIAG	1942	Wilson, Benjamin. *The Emphatic Diaglott.*
54	DIKSN	1833	Dickinson, Rodolphus. *A New and Corrected Version of the New Testament.*
451	DLNT	2011	Magill, Michael J. *Disciples' Literal New Testament.*
452	DNKJB	2011	*Divine Names King James Bible.*
55	DODD	1836	Doddridge, Philip D. D. *The Family Expositor.*
17	DOU	1609	*Douay Old Testament*
243	DPSF	1990	Blanco, Jack J. *The New Testament A Devotional Paraphrase to Stimulate Faith and Growth.*
234	EB	1987	*The Everyday Bible: New Century Version.*
214	EBLF	1980	Tucker, Robert Reed. *The Easy Bible A Literal Fundamental Translation.*
379	EBNT	2005	Eldridge, Michael D. *Elohim Bridge New Testament.*
354	EEBT	2003	Muir, Christine. *Genesis: In the Beginning.*
183	EINS	1964	Einspruch, Henry. *The Good News According to Matthew.*

346	EMTV	2002	Esposito, Paul W. *English Majority Text Version.*
411	EOB	2008	Cleenewerck, Lauret. *The Eastern Greek Orthodox Bible.*
265	EPBL	1994	Jahn, Herb. *Exegeses Parallel Bible.* 1994.
266	EPBT	1994	Jahn, Herb. *Exegeses Parallel Bible.* 1994.
66	EPSNT	1849	Etheridge, John Wesley. *The Peschito Syriac New Testament.*
98	ERV	1885	[Revised Version]. *The Holy Bible.*
267	ESB	1994	Littrell, Harold. *The English Study Bible: New Testament.*
369	ESSEN	2004	Beatty, Dennis. *The Essential New Testament.*
334	ESV	2001	Packer, James. *English Standard Version.*
58	ETAY	1840	Taylor, Edgar. *The New Testament of Our Lord and Saviour Jesus Christ.*
77	ETHJ	1862	Etheridge, John Wesley. *The Targums of Onkelos and Jonathan Ben Uzziël*
78	ETHO	1862	Etheridge, John Wesley. *The Targums of Onkelos and Jonathan Ben Uzziël*
235	ETR	1987	[Easy-to-Read Version]. *Holy Bible.*
355	EVB	2003	Comfort, Ray. *The Evidence Bible.*
1	EWYC	1384	*Early Wycliffe Bible.* [Reprint of originals 1384].
425	EXB	2009	Longman, Tremper. *The Expanded Bible.*
174	EXPN	1961	Wuest, Kenneth S. *The New Testament: An Expanded Translation.*
399	FAITH	2007	Zeitler, William Wilde. *The New Testament: A Faithful Translation.*
166	FARR	1956	Farrer, Austin. *A Short Bible: from the Authorized Version.*
439	FBV	2010	Gallagher, Jonathan. *Free Bible Version.*
127	FENT	1922	Fenton, Ferrar. *The Holy Bible in Modern English.*
426	FINCK	2009	Finck, William Raymond. *Christogenea New Testament.*
295	FISCH	1997	Fisch, Harold. *The Jerusalem Bible: The Holy Scriptures.*
154	FISH	1948	Fisher, Fred L. *A Composite Gospel.*
312	FOLK	1999	Williams, Thomas E.Q. *American Folk Gospel.*
278	FOX	1995	Fox, Everett. *The Five Books of Moses.*
347	FPV	2002	Junkins, B. E. *A Fresh Parenthetical Version of the New Testament.*
356	FRIED	2003	Friedman, Richard Elliot. *The Bible with Sources Revealed.*
46	FRY	1812	Fry, William. *The Holy Bible Containing the Old and New Testaments.*
256	FUNK	1993	Funk, Robert and Hoover, Roy W. *The Five Gospels.*
427	GABV	2009	Martin. Lonnie W. *Gabriel Version.*
370	GAN	2004	Henson, John. *Good as New: A Radical Retelling of the Scriptures.*
110	GDBEY	1902	Godbey, W. B. *Godbey's Translation of the New Testament.*
35	GEDD	1792	Geddes, Alexander. *The Holy Bible.*
12	GEN60	1560	*The Geneva Bible*
16	GEN99	1599	*1599 Geneva Bible.*
313	GFT	1999	Miller, Theron. *God's First Truth.*
428	GGB	2009	*The Genderless God Bible: Modified King James Version,*
453	GIFT	2011	Fether, Paula. *The Gift New Testament.*
34	GILPIN	1790	William Gilpin. *An Exposition of the New Testament.*
137	GLAZ	1935	Glazer, Simon. *The Five Books of Moses, Haphtoroth.*
257	GLT	1993	Green, Jay P. Sr. *The Literal Translation of the Holy Bible.*
285	GLW	1996	Johnson, Michael Paul. *God's Living Word Translation.*
268	GNBUK	1994	British and Foreign Bible Society. *Good News Bible.*

241	GNC	1989	Cassirer, Heinz W. *God's New Covenant: A New Testament Translation.*
279	GODWD	1995	Bunkowske, Eugene. *God's Word: Today's Bible Translation that Says What it Means.*
106	GRANT	1899	Grant, Frederick, W. *The Numberical Bible.*
201	GRAY	1973	Gray, Veo. *The Poetic Bible.*
140	GREB	1937	Greber, Johannes. *The New Testament.*
8	GRT	1540	Whitchurch, Edward & Grafton, Richard. *The Great Bible.*
93	GURGO	1877	Gurney, Joseph and Gotch, Frederic William. *The Holy Bible.*
348	GUTN	2002	*The Gutnick Edition Chumash: with Rashi's Commentary.*
39	GUYSE	1797	Guyse, John. *The Practical Expositor.*
19	HAAK	1657	Haak, Theodore. *Dutch Annotations Upon the Whole Bible.*
62	HAMM	1845	Hammond, Henry. *Paraphrase & Annotations upon all the books of the N.T.*
96	HANS	1884	Hanson, J. W. *The New Covenant.*
29	HAR	1768	Harwood, Edwin. *A Liberal Translation of the New Testament.*
139	HARK	1936	Harkavy, Alexander. *The Holy Scriptures.*
89	HARM	1870	Clark, George W. *A New Harmony of the Four Gospels in English.*
103	HAUPT	1898	Haupt, Paul. *The Sacred Books of the Old and New Testaments.*
37	HAW	1795	Haweis, Thomas. *The Evangelical Expositor.*
303	HBNV	1998	Johnson, Michael. *Hebrew Name Version.*
335	HCSB	2001	Blum, Edwin. *Holman Christian Standard Bible.*
80	HEIN	1863	Herman Heinfetter. *A Literal Translation of the New Testament.*
79	HIGH	1862	Highton, Henry A. *Revised Translation of the New Testament.*
221	HIRS	1982	Hirsch, Samson Raphael. *The Pentateuch.*
180	HLYNB	1963	Traina, A. B., Rev. *The Holy Name Bible.*
412	HNT	2008	Snyder, Jackson. *KATA MATTYAH (According to Matthew).*
6	HOLLY	1538	Hollybushe, Johan. *The New Testament Both in Latin and English.*
104	HORNN	1898	Horner, George. *Coptic Version of the New Testament in the Northern Dialect.*
116	HORNS	1911	Horner, George. *Coptic Version of the New Testament in the Southern Dialect.*
429	HRB	2009	Esposito, Don. *Hebraic Roots Bible.*
336	HRV	2001	Trimm, James S. *Hebraic-Roots Version: New Testament.*
357	HSTV	2003	Peña, Perry. *The HSTV Tanakh and Testimony.*
430	HTETT	2009	Channah, Devorah. *Hebrew Transliterated and English Translated Torah.*
296	HUNT	1997	Jefferies, C. J. *Huntingdon Translation.*
63	HUSS	1845	Hussey, T. J. *The New Testament.*
230	ICB	1986	*[International Children's Bible]. Holy Bible.*
337	IEB	2001	*[The International English(r) Bible Translation]. God Chasers Extreme New Testament.*
413	IHGS	2008	Mebust, Lenny. *Interlinear Hebrew-Greek Scriptures.*
280	INCL	1995	*The New Testament and Psalms: An Inclusive Version.*
400	INCP	2007	*The Inclusive Bible: The First Egalitarian Translation.*
167	INSL	1956	Laubach, Frank C. Ph.D. *The Inspired Letters: in Clearest English.*
304	ISR	1998	Institute For Scripture Research Ltd. *The Scriptures.*
305	ISV	1998	Giacumakis, George, Dr. *International Standard Version.*
323	JB2000	2000	Stendal, Russell M. *English Jubilee 2000 Bible.*
258	JBPR	1993	Rosenberg, A. J. *Judaica Press: A New English Translation.* (multi-volume set).

187	JER	1966	Jones, Alexander. *The Jerusalem Bible: Reader's Edition.*
36	JGJR	1792	Geddes, John & Robertson, James. *The New Testament.*
390	JMNT	2006	Mitchell, Jonathan. *Jonathan Mitchell's New Testament Translation.*
4	JOY1	1534	Joye, George. *The New Testament.*
123	JPS1	1917	Margolis, Max. *The Holy Scriptures According to The Masoretic Text.*
170	JSOC	1960	*The Holy Scriptures: According to the Masoretic Text.*
11	JUGG	1552	Jugge Richard. *The Newe Testament of Our Saviour Jesu Christe.*
92	JUSMI	1876	Smith, Julia E. *The Holy Bible.*
414	KAMA	2008	Snyder, Jackson H. *Kata Mattyah.*
73	KEN	1860	Kenrick, Francis Patrick. *The Old and New Testaments.*
126	KENT	1921	Kent, Charles Foster. *The Shorter Bible: The Old and New Testaments.*
269	KJ21	1994	Prindle, William. *The Holy Bible: The 21st Century King James Version.*
391	KJ3	2006	Green, Jay Patrick. *King James III.*
358	KJC	2003	McGinnis Bill. *The King James Bible: Clarified New Testament.*
314	KJHN	1999	Cummings, Chauncey. *King James Version: Hebrew Names* Edition.
18	KJV	1611	*Authorized King James Version.*
315	KJV2000	1999	Couric, Robert. *King James 2000 Version.*
163	KLLI	1954	Kleist, James A. and Lilly, Joseph L. *The New Testament.*
49	KNEE	1823	Kneeland, Abner. *The New Testament.*
150	KNOX	1944	Knox, Ronald. *The Holy Bible.*
259	KOR	1993	Korsak, Mary Phil. *At the Start: Genesis Made New.*
132	LAMSA	1933	Lamsa, George M. *The Holy Bible: From Ancient Eastern Manuscripts.*
286	LATT	1996	Lattimore, Richard. *The New Testament.*
316	LDB	1999	Johnson, Ray. *Last Days Bible.*
317	LDNT	1999	*The Last Days Bible.*
440	LEB	2010	Harris, Hall. *The Lexham English Bible.*
70	LEES	1856	Leeser, Isaac. *The Twenty-Four Books of the Holy Bible.*
155	LETCH	1948	Ford, T. F. and Ford R. E. *The New Testament.*
431	LHV	2009	Plaisted, David. *The Holy Bible Lighthouse Version.*
56	LING	1836	Lingard, John. *A New Version of the Four Gospels.*
380	LIT	2005	Dekker, Hal. *Literal Idiomatic Translation.*
281	LITV	1995	Green, Jay P. *The Literal Translation of the Holy Bible.*
196	LIV	1971	*The Living Bible: Paraphrased.*
216	LIVT	1981	Kaplan, Aryeh. *The Living Torah: The Five Books of Moses.*
51	LORA	1826	[Living Oracles] Campbell Alexander. *The Sacred Writings of the Apostles.*
392	LTOG	2006	Last name not given, Charles. *Literal Translation of the Original Greek.*
135	LWES	1934	Lattey, Cuthbert. *The Westminster Version of the Sacred Scriptures.*
2	LWYC	1395	*Late Wycliffe Bible* [Reprint of originals 1395].
22	MACE	1729	Mace, William. *The New Testament.*
270	MADS	1994	Madsen, Jon. *The New Testament.*
338	MAEV	2001	Garnier, Joe. *Modern American English Vernacular.*
210	MARR	1977	Marrow, Norman. *The Four Gospels Newly Translated from the Greek.*
141	MART	1937	Martin, William Wallace. *The New Testament.*

9	MATT	1549	Matthew Bible.
38	MCKN	1796	Macknight, James. *A Harmony of the Four Gospels.*
238	MCORD	1988	McCord, Hugo. *New Testament.*
171	MENR	1960	*The Holy Scriptures: A Jewish Family Bible.*
349	MESS	2002	Peterson, Eugene H. *The Message.*
454	MEWR	2011	Gruber, Daniel. *The Messianic Writings.*
287	MITCH	1996	Mitchell, Stephen. *Genesis: A New Translation of the Classic Biblical Stories.*
415	MITJ	2008	Mitchell, Jonathan. *New Testament Translation.*
217	MJV	1981	*Messianic Jewish Version: May Your Name Be Inscribed in the Book of Life.*
178	MKJV	1962	*Modern King James Version of the Holy Bible.*
318	MLV	1999	Walker, G. Allen. *Modern Literal Version.*
151	MODL	1945	*The Modern Language Bible.*
128	MOFF	1922	Moffatt, James. *The Bible: A New Translation.*
239	MONT	1988	Montgomery, Hellen Barrrett. *The New Testament In Modern English.*
131	MORD	1930	Richard G. Moulton, M. A. *The Modern Reader's Bible.*
65	MORGAN	1848	Morgan, Jonathan. *The New Testament.*
100	MORR	1897	Morrow Horace E. *The New Testament Emphasized.*
97	MOSES	1884	Moses, Adolph and Isaac S. *The Pentateuch.*
253	MPNT	1992	Martin, Ruth P. *The Pioneers' New Testament.*
69	MURD	1851	Murdock, James D. D. *The New Testament.*
381	MYLT	2005	LeClaire, Allen K. *Modern Young's Literal Translation.*
193	NAB	1970	Catholic Biblical Association of America. *The New American Bible.*
240	NABR	1988	*The New American Bible: Revised New Testament.*
21	NARY	1718	Nary, Cornelius. *New Testament.*
282	NAS95	1995	Lockman Foundation. *New American Standard Bible.*
172	NASB	1960	Lockman Foundation. *New American Standard Bible.*
324	NASC	2000	Miller, Mark Heber. *Nazarene Commentary.*
306	NASH	1998	Nash, Donald A. *A Literal and Consistent New Testament Version.*
350	NCMM	2002	Miller, Mark. *21st Century Version.*
271	NCS	1994	Estes, George P. *The New Covenant Scriptures.*
247	NCV	1991	New Century Version. *The Holy Bible.*
206	NEB	1976	Sandmel, Samuel, Ed. *The New English Bible with the Apocrypha.*
288	NENT	1996	Daniels, Frank. *Non-Ecclesiastical New Testament.*
319	NET	1999	Harris, W. Hall III, Ph.D. *NET Bible - New English Translation.*
401	NETS	2007	Pietersma, Albert. *New English Translation of the Septuagint.*
455	NEUV	2011	Heaster, Duncan. *New European Version.*
244	NEVT	1990	Beck, William. *New Evangecial Translation.*
42	NEWC	1808	Newcome, William. *The New Testament: in an Improved Version.*
432	NHEB	2009	Mitchell, Wayne. *New Heart English Bible.*
416	NIBEV	2008	Schneider, Ed. *Natural Israelite Bible: English Version.*
289	NIrV	1996	*New International Reader's Version.*
212	NIV	1978	[New International Version]. *The Holy Bible.*
320	NIVI	1999	[New International Version]. *The Holy Bible: Inclusive Language Edition.*
226	NJER	1985	Darton, Longman & Todd Ltd. *The New Jerusalem Bible.*
222	NKJV	1982	Fastad, Art. *The Holy Bible: The New King James Version.*
231	NLFV	1986	Ledyard, Gleason H. *Holy Bible.*

290	NLT	1996	Holy Bible: New Living Translation.
175	NOLI	1961	Noli, Metropolitan Fan Stylian. *The New Testament.*
179	NORL	1962	Norlie, Olaf M. *The Children's Simplified New Testament: In Plain English.*
71	NORT	1856	Norton, Andrews. *A Translation of the Gospels.*
88	NOYES	1869	Noyes, George Rapall. *The New Testament.*
52	NRSE	1829	Nourse, James. *The New Testament.*
245	NRSV	1990	*New Revised Standard Version. The Holy Bible.*
359	NSB	2003	Madsen, James R. *The New Simplified Bible Jehovah Version.*
53	NTCV	1830	*The New Testament in the Common Version.*
203	NTEE	1974	Klingensmith, Don J. *The New Testament in Everyday English.*
198	NTFNW	1972	Condon, Kevin. *The New Testament for the New World.*
272	NTIL	1994	*The New Testament of The Inclusive Language Bible.*
360	NTOO	2003	Coulter, Fred R. *The New Testament in its Original Order.*
176	NWT	1961	*New World Translation of the Holy Scriptures.*
441	NWYC	2010	Noble, Terence. *Wycliffe's Old and New Testaments.*
433	OANT	2009	Bauscher, Glenn David. *The Original Aramaic New Testament in Plain English.*
442	OEB	2010	Allen, Russell. *Open English Bible.*
157	OGD	1950	Ogden, C. K. *The Basic Bible: Containing the Old & N.T. in Basic English.*
351	OJB	2002	*The Orthodox Jewish Bible.*
297	OJBC	1997	Goble, Phillip E. *Orthodox Jewish Brit Chadasha.*
227	ORIG	1985	Hugh J. Schonfield. *The Original New Testament.*
260	OSB	1993	Gillquist, Peter E. *The Orthodox Study Bible: New Testament.*
417	OTFTS	2008	King, Nicholas. *Old Testament: a New, Cutting-edge translation of the Septuagint.*
130	OVER	1925	Overbury, Arthur E. *The People's New Covenant (New Testament).*
393	PALMR	2006	Palmer, David Robert. *The Gospels of Mark, Luke, and John.*
121	PAN	1914	Panin, Ivan. *The New Testament from the Greek Text.*
394	PCE	2006	Verschuur, Matthew. *Pure Cambridge Edition.*
57	PENN	1836	Penn, Granville G. *The Book of the New Covenant.*
177	PENTO	1961	Rosenbaum, M., Silbermann. *Pentateuch with Targum Onkelos, Haphtaroth.*
199	PHIL	1972	Phillips, J. B. *The New Testament in Modern English.*
339	PHOB	2001	Papoutsis, Peter A. *The Holy Orthodox Bible.*
371	PHP	2004	Markley, Alex. *PHPScripture.*
382	PICK	2005	Pickering, Wilbur N. *New Translation.*
298	PILA	1997	Pilant, Benyamin. *The Holy Scriptures Revised.*
383	PINT	2005	Warrington, Don. *Positive Infinity New Testament.*
291	PNT	1996	Chenault, Rogers. *The People's New Testament.*
361	POLA	2003	Greening-Jackson, Tim. *Polari Bible.*
122	PRYSE	1916	Pryse, James Morgan. *The Restored New Testament.*
384	PSNT	2005	Etheridge, J.W. *The Peschito Syriac New Testament.*
443	PSR	2010	*Pure Scriptures for the Remnant.*
27	PUR	1764	Purver, Anthony. *A New and Literal Translation of ... Old and New Testaments.*
325	PURE	2000	Reynolds, Stephen M. *The Holy Bible: A Purified Translation.*
307	PWNT	1998	Morford, William J. *The Power New Testament: Revealing Jewish Roots.*

273	QJV	1994	Kraft, Roberta A. *Queen Jamie Bible.*
352	RABV	2002	Rabon, Vincent, Jr. *The Holy Scriptures.*
41	RAY	1799	Ray, John Mead. *A Revised Translation & Interpretation of the Sacred Scriptures.*
223	RDB	1982	Metzger, Bruce M. *The Reader's Digest Bible.*
456	RDRB	2011	Burke, Cormac. *Revised Douay-Rheims Bible.*
242	REB	1989	*The Revised English Bible.*
248	REC	1991	Lee, Witness. *The New Testament: Recovery Version.*
228	RENNT	1985	Yeager, Randolph O. *The Renaissance New Testament.*
444	REV	2010	Schoenheit, John. *Revised English Version.*
385	RGB	2005	Brown, David. *Revised Geneva Bible.*
15	RHEIMS	1582	*Rheims New Testament*
274	RICHT	1994	Richter, John August. *The New Testament.*
161	RIEU	1952	Rieu, E. V. *The Four Gospels. A New Translation from the Greek.*
129	RIVER	1923	Ballantine, William G. *Riverside New Testament.*
434	RKB	2009	Burke, Cormac. *Revised Knox Bible.*
326	RKJNT	2000	Haugaard, Brad. *Revised King James New Testament.*
402	RLSB	2007	Garcia, Vince. *The Resurrection Life Study Bible.*
362	RMKJV	2003	Miller, Fred. *Revised King James' Version.*
372	RNKJV	2004	Lattier, Richard. *Restored Name King James Version.*
403	RNV	2007	Castleberry, C.F. *The Sacred Scripture of Yahuwah, Restored Names Version.*
207	ROSN	1976	*The Restoration of Original Sacred Name Bible.*
101	ROTH	1897	Rotherham, Joseph Bryant. *The Emphasized Bible.*
445	RPT	2010	Mitchell, Wayne A. *Revised Patriarchal Greek Orthodox New Testament.*
418	RRNT	2008	Elkhazen, Pierre. *Revised Rheims New Testament.*
162	RSV	1952	[Revised Standard Version]. *The Holy Bible.*
404	RTYND	2007	Porter, Clayton. *Revised Tyndale New Testament.*
107	RUTH	1900	Rutherford, William Gunion. *St. Paul's Epistle to the Romans.*
373	RVIC	2004	Parkinson, J. B. *Revised Version, Improved and Corrected.*
249	RVNT	1991	Changshou, Li. *Recovery Version New Testament.*
386	RVTYND	2005	Valente, Mario. *Revised Tyndale New Testament.*
283	RWB	1995	Pierce, Larry. *Revised Webster Bible.*
363	RYLT	2003	Allen, Ken. *Revised Young Literal Translation.*
395	SACC	2006	*The Second Advent Christian Canon - Small Canon Search - The Word of God.*
74	SAWY	1861	Sawyer Leicester Ambrose. *The Holy Bible.*
40	SCAR	1798	Scarlett, Nathaniel. *A Translation of the New Testament.*
387	SCH	2005	Scharfstein, Sol. *The Five Books of Moses: an Easy-to-Read Torah.*
419	SENT	2008	Mealy, Webb. *The Spoken English New Testament.*
164	SEPT	1954	Charles Thomson. *The Septuagint Bible.*
194	SEPZ	1970	*The Septuagint Version of the Old Testament.*
95	SHAR	1883	Sharpe, Samuel. *The Holy Bible.*
23	SIMON	1730	Simon, Richard. *New Testament.*
261	SINAI	1993	Ford, Dalmer R. *The New Covenant: The New Testament, Sinaitic Version in Greek and English.*
146	SMGO	1939	Smith and Goodspeed. *The Complete Bible: An American Translation.*
86	SMITH	1867	Smith, Joseph. *The Holy Scriptures.*

240	SNKJV	2001	Hurt, John. *Sacred Name King James Bible.*
158	SNNT	1950	[Sacred Name Version]. Traina, A. B. *The New Testament.*
405	SNT	2007	Nyland, Ann, Dr. *The Source New Testament.*
61	SOLA	1844	De Sola, David Aaron. *The Sacred Scriptures in Hebrew and English.*
173	SON	1960	Rev. Dr. A Cohen. *The Soncino Chumash: The Five Books of Moses.*
142	SPEN	1937	Spencer, Francis Aloysius. *The New Testament.*
99	SPUR	1885	Spurrell, Helen. *A Translation of the Old Testament Scriptures.*
218	SSBE	1981	*The Sacred Scriptures: Bethel Edition.*
133	STERN	1933	Stern, M. *The Five Books of Moses With Haphtaroth.*
292	STONE	1996	Scherman, Nosson. *Tanach: The Torah/Prophets/Writings.*
152	STRING	1945	Stringfellow, Ervin Edward. *Acts and Epistles.*
153	SWANN	1947	Swann, George Betts. *New Testament.*
458	SWHI	2012	*Scriptures for the Whole House of Israel.*
229	TANK	1985	*Tanakh: A New Translation of the Holy Scriptures.*
321	TANK2	1999	*JPS Hebrew-English Tanakh.*
353	TANK3	2002	Gordon, Nehemia. *Tanach Corrected.*
7	TAV	1539	Taverner, Richard. *The Most Sacred Bible.*
113	TCNT	1904	*The Twentieth Century New Testament.*
208	TEV	1976	[Today's English Version]. *Good News Bible: The Bible in Today's English.*
232	TFFR	1986	Gaer, Joseph, *The Torah For Family Reading.*
364	THB	2003	Turner, Gwin. *The Heritage Bible.*
374	THNC	2004	Hackett, Thom. *The Holy New Covenant.*
43	THOM	1808	Thompson, Charles. *The Old Covenant: Commonly Called Old Testament.*
75	THORN	1861	Thorn, Leonard. *The New Testament … Corrected by the Spirits.*
254	THROCK	1992	Throckmorton, Burton Hamilton. *The Gospels and the Letters of Paul.*
457	TLV	2011	Messianic Jewish Family Bible Project. *Tree of life Bible: The New Covenant.*
308	TMB	1998	*Third Millennium Bible.*
341	TNIV	2001	*Today's New International Version.*
420	TNKJV	2008	Walters, Terry. *The King James Bible: True Name Version.*
14	TOM	1576	Tomson, Lawrence. *The New Testament of our Lord Jesus Christ.*
168	TOMA	1958	Tomanek, James L. *The New Testament.*
134	TORR	1933	Torrey, Charles Cutler. *The Four Gospels: A New Translation.*
327	TPB	2000	Brichto, Sidney. *The People's Bible.* (a multi-volume set).
246	TRIMM	1990	Trimm, James Scott. *B'sorot Matti: The Good News According to Matthew.*
202	TRNT	1973	*The Translator's New Testament.*
421	TTS	2008	Shen, Janet. *Torah Transliteration Scripture.*
459	TVB	2012	Ecclesia Bible Society. *The Voice Bible: Step into the Story of Scripture.*
3	TYND	1530	Tyndale, William. *Old Testament and New Testaments.*
396	UB	2006	Abrams, Greg. *Updated Bible.*
328	UKJV	2000	*Updated King James Version.*
250	UNVAR	1991	Gaus, Andy. *The Unvarnished New Testament.*
342	UTV	2001	James, Dallis. *The Holy Bible: Urim-Thummim Version.*
435	VW	2009	Becker, Paul. *A Voice in the Wilderness.*
136	WADE	1934	Wade, George Wöosung. *The Documents of the New Testament.*

48	WAKE	1820	Wakefield, Gilbert B. *A Translation of the New Testament.*
329	WAUCK	2000	Wauck, Mark A. *The New Testament Saint Paul Catholic Edition.*
219	WAY	1981	Way, Arthur S. *Letters of Paul, Hebrews, Psalms.*
236	WBC	1987	*Word Biblical Commentary* (multi-volume set).
293	WBE	1996	Cressman, Annie. *Worldwide English (New Testament).*
115	WEAV	1909	Weaver, S. Townsend. *The University New Testament.*
299	WEB	1997	*World English Bible*
446	WEBME	2010	*World English Bible: Messianic Edition*
59	WEBR	1841	Webster, Noah. *The Holy Bible.*
102	WEEKS	1897	Weekes, Robert D. *The New Dispensation: The New Testament.*
72	WELL	1859	Wellbeloved, Charles. *The Holy Scriptures of the Old Covenant in Revised Translation.*
26	WESL	1755	Wesley John. *Explanatory Notes Upon the New Testament.*
169	WEST	1958	[*Westminster*]. *The Holy Bible.*
343	WETC	2001	*Easy-To-Read-Version World Bible.*
111	WEY	1903	Weymouth, Richard. *The New Testament in Modern Speech.*
211	WFU	1977	Haugerud, Joann. *The Word for Us: The Gospels of John and Mark, Epistles to the Romans and the Galatians.*
24	WHIS	1745	Whiston, William. *Mr. Whiston's Primitive New Testament.*
67	WHIT	1849	Whiting, N. N. *The Good News of Our Lord Jesus.*
20	WHTB	1703	Whitby, Daniel. *A Paraphrase and Commentary on the New Testament.*
159	WILL	1950	Williams, Charles B. *The New Testament.*
204	WMF	1975	Edington, Andrew. *The Word Made Fresh.*
94	WORD	1880	Wordsworth, Christopher. *The Holy Bible.*
215	WORR	1980	Worrell, Adolphus Spalding. *The Worrell New Testament.*
30	WORS	1770	Worsley, John. *New Testament.*
365	WOTS	2003	Lacey, Rob. *Word on the Street.*
262	WOY	1993	Jeffery, Ruth. *The Word of Yah.*
366	WOYAY	2003	Assembly of Yahweh. *The Word of Yahweh.*
460	WOYB	2012	Lewis, Mary E. *Word of YHVH Bible.*
181	WPE	1963	Williams, Charles Kingsley. *The New Testament.*
190	WWENT	1969	*Bible in Worldwide English New Testament.*
28	WYNNE	1764	Wynne, Richard. *The New Testament.*
447	YESC	2010	Yereq, Mikhael. *Scriptures.*
105	YLT	1898	Young, Robert. *Young's Literal Translation.*
81	YNG	1863	Young, Robert. *The Holy Bible.*
448	YS	2010	*Yahweh's Sword.*
375	ZASV	2004	Meyer, James. *Zikarown Say'fer: Sacred Scriptures, Family of Yah Edition.*

ABOUT THE MEDIUM

Rev. Carl R. Hewitt
March 3, 1928 - January 26, 2005
Clairvoyant, Clairaudient, Trance Medium, Healer

Rev. Carl Hewitt *demonstrated* mediumship, for over 40 years, through readings, radio and TV shows, and seminars. Through word of mouth, many people traveled to seek his counsel, from all parts of the United States, and as far away as Saudi Arabia, Hong Kong and Kenya. His readings went beyond simply bringing loved ones *through*, and often discussed health, and many other types of guidance.

Rev. Hewitt, grew up in Shallotte, North Carolina, a small rural, coastal community. Even before Carl's birth, psychic events began happening to Carl's parents, and 10 brothers and sisters. Unfortunately, Carl's family was terrified of these "strange happenings" because their Baptist beliefs made them think the Devil was after them. Throughout his childhood, Carl was shunned, because the mediumistic events that occurred around him, was misunderstood in the strong Baptist community. Although he was born with the Gifts of the Spirit, Rev. Carl Hewitt's career as a medium began when he was 23 years old. A friend invited him to a meeting where a medium lectured and then delivered Spirit Messages. This medium, Rev. Catherine Margiotta, described events in Carl's life, and then informed him that he had the ability to be the messenger or telephone between the two dimensions of life. One day, he would stand before large audiences delivering Spirit messages.

In 1974, Carl was ordained as a minister. Then in 1977, he founded the Gifts of the Spirit Church, where he was the pastor. Between 1979-1981 Rev. Hewitt was interviewed repeatedly, and his life's story became the basis of the NBC movie entitled *The Gifted One*. Rev. Hewitt has taught audiences throughout the United States, about mediumship and the Gifts of the Spirit.

After leading the church for 25 years, ascended masters urged Carl to move to Charleston, SC, to open a new center called *The Healing Temple of Yeshua ben Joseph*, whose goal will be teaching the Gifts of the Spirit and being an active center for healing. Unfortunately, Carl's health deteriorated, and he transitioned to the Spirit World before the new center could be established. Spirit has selected Sidney Schwartz to continue Carl's mission.

ABOUT THE AUTHOR

Sidney Schwartz

Rev. Sidney Schwartz studied mediumship for 37 years. He was ordained on February 25, 2001, and served as Assistant Pastor of Gifts of the Spirit Church. He became Pastor after its founder Rev. Hewitt's transitioned to the Spirit World. It was in 2006 Rev. Schwartz began his own mediumistic development by attending classes at the Arthur Findlay College (of Mediumship) in Stansted, England, where he took numerous classes in trance and platform mediumship. He continued his studies with several mediums in New York metropolitan area.

In the 1970's his college friend, Bonnie Corwin-Hollis, introduced him to Rev. Carl Hewitt, a clairvoyant medium. During his first reading, Rev. Hewitt had knowledge of his future and past, and provided specific details that no one else knew.

Several years later, Mr. Schwartz was summoned to Rev. Hewitt's office, because a Spirit entity wished to speak with him. Rev. Hewitt went to a trance state, and Mr. Schwartz had his first conversation with a powerful spirit entity, who refused to reveal his true identity. The angel explained that previously people who spoke with angels *had created new religions*. Since he did not wish to be the inspiration for still another religion, he would not reveal his identity, and would be addressed as AWAN, an acronym for **A**ngel **W**ithout **A** **N**ame.

From their first conversation, AWAN challenged Mr. Schwartz's religious beliefs, dropping a "bomb" in the form of an enraging and perplexing statement. Catholic theologians repeatedly edited and changed the text of the Bible. Mr. Schwartz adamantly refused to believe anyone had altered the Torah. AWAN challenged him to use his research skills as a librarian and examine early Bible editions, to disprove his statement.

After intense study, Mr. Schwartz discovered AWAN's theory to be correct. To date, Rev. Schwartz has examined four hundred sixty versions of the Bible. When he has compared **the identical verse** from these Bibles, he discovered the meaning varied radically, and contradictorily from translation to translation.

AWAN eventually asked Mr. Schwartz to become his scribe, and write books of his teachings. Like Moses, Mr. Schwartz argued with this angel, because he felt he lacked the confidence to do this task. However, he eventually agreed, and wrote a trilogy of AWAN'S teachings. Crossovers: The Origin of Homosexuality Revealed is a companion book to the trilogy.

OTHER BOOKS BY SIDNEY SCHWARTZ & REV. CARL R. HEWITT

My First Encounter with an Angel

My First Encounter with an Angel is the first book of the Revelations of Ancient Wisdom - AWAN Speaks series. This trilogy will illuminate truths about how spirituality, mediumship, and prophecy have been hidden for centuries by Biblical translators and religious rulers. **AWAN**, the **A**ngel **W**ithout **A** **N**ame contacted the author, Sidney Schwartz, through the person of Carl Hewitt, a well-known trance medium. Who or what AWAN is does not ultimately matter as you read and examine the incredible information that this sagacious Entity is teaching.

AWAN revealed to the author during their first encounter, information about deliberate changes and alterations made in the Bible throughout the centuries by the established Church Fathers in order to suppress the psychic/ spiritual development of their church-goers. The author however, remained theologically adamant and argued with this angel. It was then that AWAN challenged the author to disprove his teachings. Using his skills as a librarian, the author researched extensively, studying over 160 versions of the Bible, only to discover that the AWAN was teaching the truth! Upon reading this book, you will begin to see that the Bible is saturated with metaphysical or mediumistic phenomena of every kind.

Crossovers: The Origins of Homosexuality Revealed

True understanding of the reasons why certain people are homosexual is more important now than ever. Gay people are now fighting for their rights to enter into matrimonial relationships and to become parents. Providing answers to why religions, and society as a whole, have been homophobic for centuries; *"Crossovers: The Origins of Homosexuality* is not only a long overdue history lesson, but may also help to reunite families who have been tom apart by bias and a lack of understanding.

Carl Hewitt, the widely acclaimed medium, was at times been referred to as a modern-day Nostradamus. Although he never advertised, his clients traveled to his office from all over the United States, and abroad. Carl frequently shared critical information from his psychical visions with the FBI. This began before the attempted assassination of President Reagan, through the aftermath of 9/11.

On March 16, 1978, an ascended spiritual master, the **Angel Without A Name** (AWAN) spoke with Carl for the first time. Throughout the 1990's Awan spoke through Carl's entranced body, on a regular basis, to convey a body of teachings. Sidney Schwartz, a middle school librarian from Hackensack, New Jersey was chosen to hear these teachings, transcribe them into a book, after verifying the historical information with research.

This book chronicles Rick's journey from rejecting to accepting his own homosexuality. Rick last step before committing suicide, was to seek counseling from Rev. Carl Hewitt. Awan intervened and offered to teach Rick the origin of homosexuality and the reason for religions' homophobic attitudes, provided that Sidney Schwartz was present to record and document these sessions. The author literally found the verification of Awan's explanation of the origin of homosexuality carved in stone.

My Third Encounter with an Angel

My Third Encounter with an Angel concludes the trilogy and brings Awan's teachings full circle. It examines several foundational beliefs of Christianity, as well as its atitude towards women, gays, Jews and mediums.

Awan explained to the author in their initial conversation that theologians changed the Bible inserting their man-made dogmas into it. This book not only examines what these doctrines are, but then shows where and how they exist in the Bible's text.

Throughout this series Awan encouraged the author, and thereby the reader to think about his teachings, reasoning it out for yourself, thus creating your very own knowingness.

FURTHER INFORMATION

Gifts of the Spirit Church

To learn more about these teachings, or Gifts of the Spirit Church, please visit our website:
    www.gotsc.org

www.ingramcontent.com/pod-product-compliance
Lightning Source LLC
Chambersburg PA
CBHW062124160426
43191CB00013B/2193